Barcelona Publishers

GUIDELINES FOR MUSIC THERAPY PRACTICE IN DEVELOPMENTAL HEALTH

EDITED BY

MICHELLE HINTZ

Guidelines for Music Therapy Practice
in
Developmental Health

Edited by Michelle R. Hintz

Print ISBN: 978-1-937440-44-2
E-ISBN: 978-1-937440-45-9

To obtain chapters separately in epub or Mobi formats, please visit:
www.barcelonapublishers.com

Distributed throughout the world by:
Barcelona Publishers
4 White Brook Road
Gilsum NH 03448
Tel: 603-357-0236 Fax: 603-357-2073
Website: www.barcelonapublishers.com
SAN 298-6299

Copy-editor: Jack Burnett

Dedication

This book is dedicated to three people who are my inspiration:

To my son, Samuel Reitman, who inspires me on a daily basis with his intellect, curiosity, and thoughtful personality;

To my daughter, Lauren Reitman, who reminds me to be more spontaneous, assertive, and find the humor in life;

And

To my late grandfather, Gordon Seffker, who reminded me often of the importance of living for today by finding a balance between work and family.

Acknowledgments

I gratefully acknowledge the invaluable assistance and support of Dr. Ken Bruscia for his guidance, support, and belief in my abilities to be part of such a worthwhile endeavor.

I also wish to thank the other editors in this project, Dr. Joke Bradt, Dr. Lillian Eyre, and Dr. Joy Allen. I am indebted to them for their collaboration, thoughtful dialogue, and companionship throughout this long project.

I also extend my appreciation to music therapy students Kendri Scarborough, Hannah Wilson, and Amy Wetter whose time and efforts enabled me to access literature and resources needed to write my own chapters.

Finally, I wish to express my gratitude to my family and friends, especially John Bankenbusch for his encouragement, sense of humor, and the early morning wake-up calls that got me up hours earlier than I would have liked. I also thank my children, Samuel and Lauren Reitman, for their understanding and patience with me during this especially difficult year of transition for us.

Table of Contents

Contributors

Christine Barton, MM, MT-BC is an award-winning composer and performer. In addition to her private practice, *Central Canal Creative Arts Therapies*, she is a music consultant to *Advanced Bionics, LLC* and provides music therapy services to the children of *St. Joseph Institute for the Deaf, Indianapolis*. Chris primarily serves D/HH children and their families, as well as those with ASD. She is the composer and performer of the songs on the *Tune Ups* CD, recipient of the 2009 Most Valuable Product (MVP) award by readers of TherapyTimes.com. Chris completed the post graduate "Certificate in Auditory Learning in Young Children" from the University of North Carolina - Chapel Hill in 2011. She is a consultant to the Project ASPIRE team, headed by cochlear implant surgeon, Dana Suskind, at the University of Chicago.

Paige A. Robbins Elwafi, MMT, MT-BC, is a music therapist working in the Cincinnati and Louisville areas. She is a graduate of Ohio University and Temple University in Philadelphia. Paige has worked with a number of clinical populations including individuals with autism, developmental disabilities, mental illness, oncology, and visual impairment. She has worked in the United States as well as abroad in the Middle East. Paige has a passion for multicultural issues in music therapy and studying how culture affects the lives of both clients and therapists.

Michelle R. Hintz, PsyD, MT-BC is a Licensed Psychologist and Board-Certified Music Therapist specializing in the treatment of autism and developmental disabilities, and behavioral disorders. She has also been a practicing, board-certified music therapist for 23 years and holds Bachelor's & Master's degrees in music therapy as well as a Master's degree in Clinical Psychology. She founded the *Cadenza Center for Psychotherapy and the Arts, Inc.* in 2000, an integrative psychology and creative arts center. Dr. Hintz has extensive training in behavior modification, developmental psychology, and numerous applications of music therapy. Dr. Hintz is the proud mother of two children, Samuel and Lauren.

Kathleen M. Howland, PhD, CCC-SLP, MT-BC is Professor of Music Therapy at Berklee College of Music in Boston. She is a licensed speech and language pathologist with extensive experience in music therapy for developmental problems in communication. She is also a performing musician, and has a special interest in music and cognition.

Douglas Keith, PhD, MT-BC, studied music therapy at the University of Georgia, the University of Applied Sciences in Heidelberg, Germany, and Temple University. As a clinician, he has worked with adults with psychiatric disorders, children with developmental disabilities, senior adults with dementia, and adults with HIV/AIDS. His dissertation examined ways that people make meaning of improvised music. Subsequent research has examined technology in music therapy education, music listening for premature infants, and the effects of music on breast milk production by mothers of premature infants. Douglas is currently Associate Professor of Music Therapy at Georgia College in Milledgeville, Georgia.

Patricia McCarrick, PhD, MT-BC, studied music therapy at Temple University where she is an Adjunct Faculty member training undergraduate and graduate music education majors to teach children with special needs. She has over 30 years clinical experience at the Bucks County Intermediate Unit, working with children and adolescents with emotional and behavioral disorders in residential and school settings. She currently provides music therapy services to children ages 3-21 with autism, multiple disabilities, and visual and hearing impairments, and supervises music therapy interns and practicum students. Patty is married to Steven Dix and loving mother to Brian, Kaitlyn, and Sean and is honored to be included among such respected researchers and clinicians in this unique publication.

Donna W. Polen, LCAT, MT-BC, is Coordinator for Music Therapy at Finger Lakes DDSO in Newark, NY, where she has trained close to 80 interns. Donna's clinical experience is concentrated on individuals with intellectual and developmental disabilities, dual diagnosis, and traumatic brain injury. Donna co-authored a chapter in *Inside Music Therapy: Client Experiences* and is a co-author of *Clinical Training Guide for the Student Music Therapist*, both from Barcelona Publishers. Donna presents extensively on her clinical work and occupational regulations, and has served AMTA in many roles including as Council Coordinator and as a member of the Education and Training Advisory Board. Donna teaches advanced clinical piano improvisation in the SUNY Fredonia Master's program and serves as Adjunct Clinic Supervisor in the Nazareth College music therapy clinic.

Elizabeth K. Schwartz, LCAT, MT-BC has practiced music therapy in New York for over 25 years. She specializes in early intervention and preschool treatment and provides staff development in local public schools. Beth is an Adjunct Instructor at Molloy College as well as a site supervisor. Beth is the author of *Music, Therapy, and Early Childhood: A Developmental Approach* and *You and Me Makes...We: A Growing Together Songbook*. She is a frequent presenter and contributor to early childhood and music therapy publications. In 2012, Beth co-founded the *Center for Early Childhood Music Therapy, LLC* known as Raising Harmony® which provides training and resources on early childhood music therapy and development. Raising Harmony® is home to Sprouting Melodies™ , a national parent/child music program.

Jennifer M. Sokira, MMT, LCAT, MT-BC is the founder and director of *Connecticut Music Therapy Services, LLC.* She works extensively with children and adults with developmental disabilities, autism, learning disabilities, physical disabilities, Rett Syndrome, and other neurological disorders in school, community and home settings, as well as with individuals in inpatient hospice. She has written about and presented on her clinical work and on various topics concerning music therapy private practice and business. A graduate of Duquesne University and of Temple University, she also serves in various positions in local, regional and national music therapy organizations.

Barbara L. Wheeler, PhD, MT-BC, retired as Professor of Music Therapy and University Professor from the University of Louisville and is Professor Emerita from Montclair State University. She presents and teaches in the U.S. and internationally and is currently affiliated with Molloy College and the State University of New York – New Paltz. Her clinical work has been with a variety of clientele, most recently as Neurologic Music Therapist at several facilities. Barbara edited *Music Therapy Research,* 2nd Edition, is coauthor of *Clinical Training Guide for the Student Music Therapist,* and has written other articles and chapters. She is a past president of the American Music Therapy Association.

Preface

An Evolving Perspective

Kenneth E. Bruscia

Music therapy has grown dramatically in the last 20 years—in theory, practice, and research. New training programs have been founded in many countries, and global networks have been formed through federations, conferences, journals, and online media. The technological revolution has made it possible for professionals and students around the world to communicate their thoughts and discoveries about music therapy in the flash of one simple click. New generations of music therapists have begun to explore the endless horizons of music therapy in different cultures, while the more experienced generations have had the time and resources to reflect upon what has been evolving in the field. Theory, practice, and research can no longer be defined or delimited in terms of a single culture, treatment philosophy, method, training program, or individual.

The traditional modus operandi of music therapists has always been to find or develop the most appropriate methodological approach to meet the unique health needs and resources of each individual client, population, and treatment milieu. This aim has not changed. What has changed, however, is the growing awareness that understanding what these needs and resources are is not as simple as we had previously imagined. Once the strait jackets of a particular theoretical orientation or a single method are removed, and once cultural and individual differences are fully acknowledged, most of the older guideposts disappear, and therapists today are faced with the daunting task of apprehending each client's resources and needs within the full richness and complexity of his or her own unique world.

The primary mission of this series is to provide new, diverse, and more up-to-date guideposts for clinical practice. This mission is based on the belief that music therapy students and professionals have an ethical responsibility to be knowledgeable of *all* approaches to clinical practice that have been found effective for clients within different contexts.

The implications are threefold. First, this series advances the notion that no potentially effective practice should be excluded from the study of music therapy for reasons of personal, organizational, or institutional bias. Gone are the days that music therapists can assert that *only* their own approaches belong within the definitional boundaries of music therapy. Gone are the days when music therapists can assert that music therapy is only improvisational, or that music therapy is only behavioral, or that improvisational or behavioral approaches can be used with every clientele in all contexts. This narrow-mindedness is no longer acceptable. Music therapy is not just what you do, or just what I do—it is what we all do within the boundaries of ethical practice—and within the context of a discipline that also includes theory and research. Moreover, ethical practice can no longer exclude what others do with significant clinical effect.

Second, this series underlines the premise that music therapy is first and foremost a discipline of practice. As such, the practice of music therapy cannot be based solely on theory and research, it must also be informed by what practitioners have learned over the years about what works and what does not work in actual clinical settings. Very often these clinical details and anecdotes cannot be subjected to the rigors of research, yet they have significant practical value. Thus, notwithstanding the contributions of theory and research, clinical practice must be based on the accumulated insights of practitioners who have the experience, expertise, and ethical values needed to serve as our models. In short, music therapy is not merely evidence based or theoretically informed, it is even more essentially clinically based.

Third, this series reinforces the notion that like in other scholarly health care disciplines, music therapists must begin to write about their own clinical work within the context of what others have done in the same area of practice. In the early days, music therapists developed their own ways of working with a particular clientele or method independently of one another, and without the benefit of a world-wide communication network—there were no journals, books, or websites that could provide the wealth of practical information available today. This had a rather bizarre outcome that to some extent still continues today. Not being aware of what had already been done in the field, music therapists often considered and presented themselves as pioneers—touting that their own particular method of working as if it were entirely new—when in fact other music therapists had already been doing the same thing for quite some time. This sometimes made attending a conference a deja-vu experience, where it seemed as if we were proudly re-inventing the wheel and then giving the wheel our own new brand. Mary from Podunk would give a presentation announcing that she had discovered how to use the cello in therapy, when unknown to her, Juliette Alvin had already been doing it for years. Then to further complicate the matter, therapists in Podunk would call it Mary's method, and people in England would call it Alvin's method, even if the methods were practically identical. Of course, this was not the case for the many true pioneers of music therapy who actually invented or created a specific approach or model. But the problem remains: how can one distinguish between ignorant vanity and a truly new contribution to the field? Today there is no excuse for not knowing what others have done, and even less justification for not being interested. All we have to do is a computer search of the rapidly developing literature, and we can find others who are working in the same area of practice. And then our responsibility is quite simple: we have to contextualize what we have discovered about clinical practice in terms of the current state of knowledge in the field. Just like researchers who are expected to review the literature on their research question, modern practitioners are expected to know what they are doing within the context of their discipline.

The specific objectives of the series is to provide practical guidelines for implementing receptive, improvisational, re-creative, and compositional methods of music therapy with major client populations, supported by a comprehensive and critical review of existing literature. These methods are thoroughly defined and discussed in every chapter of the series. The major client populations were identified and categorized by diagnosis and age. As a result, four main areas of practice were identified: developmental health, mental health, pediatric care, and adult medical care. Primary diagnosis was used to distinguish between populations with mental health versus medical needs, and age was used to distinguish between the needs of children, adolescents, and adults.

Authors were carefully selected according to two criteria. First, they had to have extensive clinical experience in the area of practice about which they were writing; and second, they had to acknowledge and recognize significant clinical work done by others in the same area. Their charge then was not to merely write about what they did and believed, but to present a comprehensive picture of a particular area of practice to which they themselves had contributed significantly. Obviously, some areas of practice are more developed than others and in some instances the authors could only rely upon their own experiences. Music therapy is practiced in so many areas that this unevenness in development is to be expected for some time, and also is bound to be evident in the present series.

Given the aims and issues addressed so far in this Preface, it should come as no surprise that unlike many edited books in music therapy that support the "pioneer" syndrome, every chapter in every volume of this series follows the same outline. Authors were not free to determine what would and would not be covered in their respective chapters. A uniform outline was fashioned to ensure not only that the same basic topics would be addressed for each area of practice, but also to ensure that all relevant literature on each area was included. The basic outline is as follows:

1) Diagnostic Information
2) Needs and Resources
3) Assessment and Referral
4) Multi-cultural Issues
5) Overview of Music Therapy Methods
6) Guidelines for Receptive Music Therapy
    a. Method A:
        i. Overview: Definition, indications, goals, contraindications
        ii. Preparation of Session and Environment
        iii. What to Observe
        iv. Procedures for Conducting Session
        v. Possible Adaptations
    b. Method B:
    c. Etc..
7) Guidelines for Improvisational Music Therapy
8) Guidelines for Re-creative Music Therapy
9) Guidelines for Compositional Music Therapy
10) Working with Caregivers
11) Research Evidence
    a. Receptive Music Therapy
    b. Improvisational Music Therapy
    c. Compositional Music Therapy
    d. Re-creative Music Therapy
12) Summary and Conclusions
13) References
14) Resources (Optional)

One of the consequences of following the same outline is that there are bound to be repetitions in the information presented. The editors and authors have done their best to reduce *unnecessary* redundancies, while recognizing that some redundancies are important to keep. For example, many redundancies *between* chapters were left because each chapter will be made available separately in electronic formats, apart from the other chapters. Thus, each chapter had to be a complete presentation in itself, without requiring the reader to consult another chapter that the reader may not have.

Redundancies *within* chapters are another matter. These kinds of repetitions can be quite revealing. Several clinical questions are pertinent. For example, why is it that with a particular population, contraindications or "what to observe" are the same across certain methods but not others, or why are they the same for one population but not others? In some cases, a redundancy can reveal something about the population—that regardless of method, there are certain fundamental considerations that must be made when working with them. In other cases, a redundancy can reveal something about methods and how, though very different, may make the same demands on the client. And lastly, some redundancies can reveal blind-spots in the practitioner, that is when the music therapist can only see certain aspects of the client or clinical situation, regardless of the many complexities or variations present. For this reason, readers are urged to interrogate each redundancy. What does it reveal about the client, method, or therapist?

Another consequence of following the same outline is the opposite problem—disagreements. The authors in these four volumes were sometimes definite about using specific terminology and definitions for music therapy phenomena, even if doing so created disagreements and inconsistencies with other authors or the editors. Sometimes there was good reason, other times there was not. Sometimes it was the "Mary-Podunk" problem of wanting to name and thereby own a particular method or procedure that the author believed that she or he developed; other times it reflected deep theoretical divisions in the field itself; and other times it merely revealed aspects of music therapy that still need further conceptual clarity.

It is important to be aware of these disagreements and inconsistencies, not only to better comprehend what the authors have written, but also to understand the theoretical and practical issues confronting present-day music therapy. Three important differences of opinion became obvious in the planning, writing, and editing of these four volumes—differences that could not always be resolved within the context of the editorial process.

First, there are inconsistencies in how basic terms such as model, approach, method, protocol, procedure, and technique are used and defined. What one calls a model, others call an approach, and what one calls method, others call a technique. In this series, the basic premise was that there are four main "methods" of music therapy: listening (or receptive) experiences, improvisational experiences, re-creative experiences, and compositional experiences, each with their own set of procedural variations. This premise was not shared by all authors.

Second, there are disagreements in how to differentiate these methods. When does improvising become listening, and when does composing a song become improvising? Isn't listening a part of all musical activity, and doesn't listening require activity? So then why and how do we differentiate between receptive and active? An even more important dilemma for music therapy is: Should a method be defined by what the client "experiences" or by what the therapist "does?" If the therapist improvises for the client, is the method improvisational or receptive? Again this dilemma remains unresolved in these volumes.

Finally, there are considerable controversies over what practices a particular "model" (or method, or approach) does and does not include. For example, there is substantive confusion over what practices are legitimately considered part of the "Bonny Method of Guided Imagery and Music (BMGIM)," and which are not, and whether this "method" should be called BMGIM or simply "Guided Imagery and Music" (GIM). Then there is the onslaught of terms for the various "whatevers" that also involve music and imagery. Can anyone explain the procedural differences between the terms "Guided Imagery", "Directed Music Imagery," "Music and Imagery," "Music-imaging," and "Music-assisted imagery?" And do these names actually reflect those procedural differences? This is an example of an area of practice that begs for greater conceptual clarity.

These are not idle or "so what?" questions. How can we communicate about practice if we ignore differences between a model and a method, and if we invent idiosyncratic names for every method and technique? How can we train music therapists in the "discipline" of music therapy if there is no shared vocabulary or common language? How can we develop sensible "protocols" of practice to test through research if we do not understand the basic properties of the music experience that we hope to study, and if we are unclear in specifying what the client experiences and what the therapist does? And, how can we ever imagine an organized body of theory if practitioners and researchers do not use language intentionally and consistently?

It is hoped that this first attempt to present procedural, populational guidelines for practice will highlight the myriad implications of how we talk and write about music therapy. We need to be more aware of our discourses, not only from a philosophical or theoretical perspective (as in feminist and sociocultural streams of thought), but also from a practical point of view. Hopefully, the language problems encountered in this series will lead to a discourse analysis that will spawn more serious efforts to clarify and unify our diverse vocabularies about practice.

One final issue needs to be addressed. This series was envisioned as a teaching tool. Its purpose is to inform students as well as professionals about areas of practice that may not have been studied or experienced previously. The hidden yet obvious assumption is that the way to learn how to practice music therapy is by studying it in reference to each client population rather than by method. This relates directly to the redundancy problem. If the reader scans across "receptive" methods used across different client populations, many redundancies will be found, and the same kinds of repetitions will be found in re-creative, improvisational, and compositional methods. This poses an important pedagogical question: Would it be more economical and effective to first learn how to design music experiences (or use different methods of music therapy), and then learn how to implement or adapt them for different clients? Or is it more economical and effective to first learn about the characteristics and needs of each population, and then learn to design methods within that specific context? Put another way, is it easier and more effective to generalize or extrapolate from method to clients or from clients to method? Should we be training specialists in working with each population, or generalists who master the methods of music therapy? The vote is still out on this because unfortunately these pedagogical issues have not been recognized or discussed widely in the field.

Notwithstanding the decided emphasis given to clinical practice in this series, theory and research are still very much needed in music therapy—and in music therapy education as well. It is hoped that these volumes will stimulate the field to address the myriad research questions and theoretical issues raised by an organized and comprehensive presentation of what we know in practice. Further, it is hoped that this presentation will soon become outdated, and that revised, new, and increasingly more effective methods of practice will be conceived and tested.

GUIDELINES FOR MUSIC THERAPY PRACTICE IN DEVELOPMENTAL HEALTH

Chapter 1

Introduction

Michelle R. Hintz

Aims

The use of music in therapy has been expanding in depth and breadth for nearly 70 years, and there is growing evidence of the clinical benefits of music therapy. Across the life span, music therapists are employing a wide range of methods based upon treatment philosophies and emerging research. Within the area of developmental health, the goals for this particular book in the series are to identify client populations for whom music therapy interventions are being used, the methods most commonly employed, and the goals addressed for each. Music therapy methods are organized by four intervention types: receptive, creative, re-creative, and improvisational. The intent is to provide the reader with practical guidelines for implementing the most commonly used music therapy methods in the United States to address developmental needs that are supported both by research and by clinical practice. The series aims to inform music therapy practice by providing information about both research perspectives and clinical applications.

Areas of Practice

This volume focuses on the use of music therapy methods within an area of practice defined as "developmental health," which is understood as the physical and mental health, well-being, coping, and competence of human beings (Keating & Miller, 1999). While difficult to define, the populations identified in this volume all encompass a common thread—the need for additional supports and interventions to promote learning and skill acquisition in early life. Often, learning comes in the form of play and exploration at birth and continues through early childhood to set a lifelong path for physical and social well-being. Experiences incorporating music are often a part of early childhood and are a part of primary educational experiences.

The decisions regarding which clinical populations to include in this volume did not come easily. How clinicians define the scope of their work with populations, setting, level of need, and impact of the condition on overall development were all considered. As a commonality, the populations identified within the scope of developmental health encompass conditions and clinical diagnoses that are most frequently treated by music therapists that occur and are attributed to problems in early life (e.g., physical, cognitive, behavioral, social, and academic development). Etiology is primarily considered to be attributable to intrapersonal conditions (e.g., health-related, organic, neurological) rather than imposed by environmental or situational circumstances. The music therapist's role in treatment, then, is based upon clinical needs, taking into consideration the assumed underlying dysfunction and associated methods for remediation.

Attempts to delineate client populations by goals addressed, service location, and level of practice all were ineffective. It was also too simplistic to define developmental health as including all clinical conditions that occur in early childhood. In fact, there are many reasons why an individual's development would be thwarted, and often one cannot easily extricate developmental issues from other medical conditions, life events or traumas, and mental health conditions.

The majority of the goals addressed by music therapists working with developmental health populations are aimed at addressing cognitive, behavioral, social, or academic functioning. However, delineation using clinical goals also proved to be ineffective since there are numerous overlaps in clinical aims for children and adolescents within both the mental health and the pediatric volume. Even within the pediatric volume, the goals are oriented toward more medical or rehabilitative goals, yet often address broader areas of functioning.

On the surface, the location of music therapy services appears to differentiate the populations identified in this volume from those in the pediatric or mental health volume, but this is not entirely accurate either. While the majority of work that music therapists do for populations identified in this volume is done within an educational or community setting, some client populations within the mental health volume also are served within the same environments. In addition, some chapters within the mental health volume address music therapy practice for at-risk children, victims of abuse or neglect, and substance abuse. Certainly, all of these situations impact an individual's development. Ultimately, the decision concerning which clinical populations to include in this volume came from a lengthy discussion between the publisher and other editors, taking into consideration a combination of clinical objectives, population characteristics, and role of the music therapist, as well as the general perception of where those clients best fit given the other clinical populations included in a given volume.

The Role and Significance of Music Therapy

There is a long history of music therapy for individuals with developmental issues. As far back as the 1960s, early music therapy pioneers such as Clive Robbins, Juliette Alvin, and others were documenting the fascinating and wonderful capacities of music to reach children with the most severe disabilities. Early articles are filled with subjective and qualitative accounts of music interventions, as well as therapists' understanding of underlying theoretical foundations and perceptions of the meaning in the work they did. There was an emphasis on the role of music and the relationship between the client and the therapist to effect change. Creativity, qualitative analysis, and perception of the meaning made within the context of the experience were highlighted. That was music therapy in its infancy.

Between the 1970s and 1990s, music therapy literature saw an explosion of case studies, descriptions of treatment programs, surveys about music therapy practice, and theoretical articles outlining commonalities between music therapy practice and psychological, behavioral, and medical practice. The focus of literature was outcome-oriented, meaning that writers discussed results rather than identifying any specific methods, musical qualities, or aspects of the therapeutic relationship that were responsible. Fast-forward to the 2000s, and one will find a strong emphasis on statistical analysis and attempts to standardize music therapy assessments. There were efforts to isolate aspects of music therapy methods, greater specificity of client populations, a focus on qualitative research, and comparisons of music therapy efficacy in comparison with other, more "established" treatment methods.

Research on current music therapy practices in the United States for individuals with developmental issues addresses a wide range of issues from attempts to describe underlying cognitive, neurological, and perceptual processes to the effects of isolated musical experiences on specific clinical populations. Music therapists are borrowing from and building upon clinical foundations in related fields to inform practice, guide research, and create new methodologies that incorporate technology. New assessment procedures and the development of treatment programs (rather than methods) are expanding the scope of music therapy practice for developmental populations. In addition, there is greater awareness of a possibility for deeper levels of working with these populations, as well as the potential for having a more central or primary role in a client's overall treatment.

Which goals music therapists address is likely related to the fact that most music therapists working with the developmental health populations provide treatment within academic and community settings. By aligning themselves with other professionals working with a child (for example), music therapists are often serving in consultative roles or are providing supportive or augmentative levels of intervention. This does not mean, however, that music therapy does not have the potential to address more psychological, spiritual, or humanistic needs. It simply means that the function of music therapy intervention with these populations is aimed primarily at more basic needs.

Approaches to Music Therapy

The vast majority of music therapy methods employed within this volume are based upon behavioral and cognitive behavioral orientations. It is important to keep in mind that behavior therapy does not involve one specific method, but instead encompasses a wide range of techniques that can be used in treatment. Broadly speaking, the music therapy methods discussed in this volume focus on either behaviors solely or on a combination of thoughts and feelings. Music therapists work, then, to support learning, influence changes in behavior, and facilitate development of cognitive, perceptual, or social areas of functioning.

For centuries, music has been used to aid in learning because of its ability to effectively embed information to promote recall. Through music, we learn about ourselves, our culture and that of others, science and math, creativity, jobs, the environment, celebration, and emotions. The music we sing provides vocabulary enrichment, teaches tenses and plurals, uses poetic language, fosters phonemic awareness, allows visualization, and encourages good pronunciation. Music inherently organizes by providing a temporal sequence and structure through the use of beat, rhythm, and melody. Early engagement in music helps very young children to understand concepts like high and low, fast and slow, and start and stop. Counting out the beats in music and keeping a steady beat reinforces the role of numbers and helps children to understand early math concepts. In addition, reading music notes from left to right reinforces their learning to read words from left to right in a book.

The positive effects of music instruction on academic performance are robust. Studies have found that children who can maintain a steady beat have a greater fluency in their reading. For example, SAT takers with a background involving musical instruction score significantly higher in both the verbal and mathematics portions of the test than do students without musical training (Vaughn & Winner, 2000).

Levels of Practice

Most authors in this volume identified music therapy methods as being at the augmentative level of treatment. This level of treatment is primarily described as helping clients participate in, learn, or benefit from educational or instructional programs. It is designed to promote learning, support development of adaptive skills such as those needed in daily living, and facilitate practice in social and communicative domains of functioning.

Within an augmentative level of treatment, the music therapist may work in collaboration with other professionals, work on similar treatment goals, and provide additional resources and information about an individual's functioning. Music therapists capitalize on the intrinsic qualities of music to structure and organize information, facilitate repeated exposure and practice, and motivate individuals as they address clinical objectives to improve behaviors and support academic skill acquisition.

Readers are encouraged to keep in mind that each method is presented from a specific perspective, yet individual client needs and the unique role that music therapy plays within the client's overall treatment program do vary. In addition, the music therapist's training, musical skill, and treatment philosophy can influence not only the clinical intent of individual methods, but also the overall course of treatment. For this reason, the levels of music therapy practice listed for each method are intended to be used solely as a guideline.

Organization of the Book

Given the educational nature of this volume and the intended audience, the chapters are organized in the same way and provide the same kinds of information by using a consistent format among chapters across the series. Consistency between chapters, therefore, is intended to make the series easier to read, study, and reference, while also enabling comparison of methods and goals between populations.

The content covered in each chapter in this volume follows the same format as those in the other three volumes in the series. Background information about the population is provided, including diagnostic criteria, definitions, and subcategories (if any), followed by a discussion of the population's clinical needs and resources. The intent of the background information is to provide the reader with a context for understanding the population's unique personal, social, cognitive, behavioral, and musical characteristics. Because the *Diagnostic and Statistical Manual of Mental Disorders, Fourth Edition (DSM-IV)* identifies clinical conditions based upon deficiencies, weaknesses, and needs, there is often very little discussion of characteristics of strengths or abilities. Authors were instructed to include information about musical characteristics of the populations; however, oftentimes very little was known or researched.

Each chapter also includes a discussion of the role of music therapy with caregivers as well as the unique role and objectives for different categories of music therapy methods. In an effort to avoid redundancy, commonalities between individual music therapy interventions within a method section were included. Authors were instructed to summarize the research on music therapy with each population, the methods most commonly used, efficacy, and general findings. From the review of literature and research, authors then chose the most common music therapy methods for inclusion in their chapter. Therefore, the methods included in each chapter are not intended to be exhaustive; rather, they represent the most commonly used methods for a population. Each method described in this series includes the same information: a brief overview and description of the method, indications and contraindications, preparations needed to implement the method, procedures for conducting the experience, and adaptations (if any).

Those who read several chapters in the series will find some overlap not only in the clinical needs of different populations, but also in the methods employed. The reader is encouraged to review how the same general method (e.g., music listening) can be used with different populations. More specifically, the same method may be implemented differently for one population vs. another, may require different music, or may address different clinical objectives. In addition, the adaptations listed for some methods are additional suggestions provided by authors to encourage a broader understanding of the flexibility of methods, as many methods can be used for both individual and group sessions.

Concluding Remarks

The clinical practice of music therapy is too broad and complex to be simply defined. Even within the scope of developmental music therapy populations, the effective practice of music therapy is contingent upon several factors, beginning with relevant education and training. Music therapy educators must first effectively instruct students about the vast needs of diverse clinical populations and provide a rationale for the use of music in therapy. Second, they must be knowledgeable about music therapy research and effects on human behavior for each clinical population. Finally, educators must teach state-of-the-art music therapy practices within the context of emerging theoretical and research-oriented foundations. However, providing music therapy students with intellectual knowledge is just part of the training process. Even experienced music therapists, like those in any profession, need to continually engage in continuing education.

Flexibility, creativity, and curiosity are all essential characteristics of an effective music therapist. Excellent musicianship is assumed. Effective music therapy practice, therefore, is contingent upon a music therapist's ability to address the unique needs and resources of a client within the milieu or system by using the most appropriate method. Truly effective music therapy clinicians are able to integrate knowledge with experience in order to apply the methods discussed in this volume.

As editor of this volume, I was struck by two things: the strong reliance on re-creative methods across populations and the supportive role that music therapy has as part of a multidisciplinary team. Most music therapy methods discussed in this volume are intended to address functional skill development, improve behavior to support learning, or enhance development of adaptive skills in social and communicative functioning. For these reasons, and for the mere fact that children learn best when they are actively engaged in multisensory experiences, many of the music therapy methods incorporate the use of live music. Certainly, the musicality and musicianship of the music therapist are important in general; however, the overwhelming use of re-creative methods with these populations necessitates a high level of musical skill.

Music therapists are encouraged to think beyond the supportive role and augmentative level of practice that music therapists currently seem to provide for developmental health populations. Client populations within this volume all have emotional and psychological needs, including needs related to self-esteem, belonging, self-expression, and connection with others. Music therapists risk underestimating their ability to treat the "whole" client as well as potentially undervaluing music therapy practice as a primary treatment method if they focus solely on functional skill development or behavior objectives. Undoubtedly, there are often positive impacts of music therapy interventions and the relationship with the therapist beyond the identified clinical goals. All of these aspects of the music therapy client can be addressed while supporting the more covert behavioral objectives.

Further, no chapter is intended to be an exhaustive collection of possible music therapy methods for a given population; readers are encouraged to explore other methods contained within the series (both within and outside of this volume) that may be appropriate. By finding commonalities within other populations in areas of clinical need, musical strengths, or goals and objectives for a method, it is quite possible that music therapy students, educators, and experienced music therapists will find creative ways to enhance their treatment, expand their repertoire of techniques, and deepen their understanding of how to prescriptively use music in therapy.

References

Keating, D., & Miller, F. K. (1999). Individual pathways in competence and coping: From regulatory systems to habits of mind. In D. Keating & C. Hertzman (Eds.), *Developmental health and the wealth of nations: Social, biological, and educational dynamics* (pp. 220–233). New York, NY: Guilford.

Vaughn, K., & Winner, E. (2000). SAT scores of students who study the arts: What we can and cannot conclude about the association. *Journal of Aesthetic Education, 34*(4), 77–89.

Chapter 2

Early Intervention

Elizabeth K. Schwartz

Overview

The guiding principle of music therapy in early intervention is a focus on the young child's healthy growth and development. The primary concern is to help the child evolve into becoming the "self." Therapy is viewed as needed when certain conditions that the child is born with or acquires or is exposed to delay or disrupt the typical course of development. The extent of the condition will determine whether the child's development will be delayed or whether the impact of the condition will result in a developmental disability. Therapy can be the catalyst for intervening before the condition's influence creates a significant delay. Therapy can also minimize the depth and breadth of the disability and allow for optimal developmental growth.

Determining which music therapy methods are effective and valuable for the young child is directly connected to appreciating the unique characteristics of early intervention. The term "early intervention" has a number of meanings that relate to understanding and practicing music therapy with young children. The use of the term *early intervention* can be to delineate treatment for clients in a targeted age range; used to distinguish an approach and philosophy toward therapy and treatment; and used in reference to a defined, government-supported treatment program for young children. This chapter will examine all of these meanings of early intervention—age, approach, and programming—and the impact of each on current methods of music therapy practice.

Early Intervention as an Age Range

The definition of early childhood, and therefore of the age range for early intervention, varies depending on society and tradition. The National Association for the Education of Young Children (NAEYC), the world's largest organization concerned with the issues of early childhood, refers to early childhood as being children from birth to age eight (2009). The United Nations International Children's Emergency Fund (www.unicef.org) also considers early childhood to be birth up to age eight. Other organizations, such as *Zero to Three* (www.zerotothree.org), generally look at children from birth to age five. For the purpose of this chapter, music therapy in early intervention will examine practice with children from birth to age five, with a particular emphasis on birth to age three, since in the United States, a delineation in services is usually made between children of school age (five years and up) and preschool children (under five years). The concentration will be on developmental issues for children within this targeted range.

It is a commonly accepted notion that the span from birth to five encompasses the greatest amount of overall change in human growth. Within those five years, children generally pass through a number of different phases; each of which has unique characteristics. Creating or adapting methods of music therapy in early intervention requires specific knowledge of all these developmental domains and phases—physical, cognitive, social, emotional, and musical—as a child grows from birth and includes an understanding of how the brain and sensory systems mature.

Early Intervention as an Approach

The term "early intervention" also describes a therapeutic framework for practice. The underlying premise of the early intervention approach is to "... prevent or arrest problems early in a child's life ..." (Fish, 2002). The United States Office of Special Education and Rehabilitation Services states:

> "Early intervention" means getting started as early as possible to address the individual needs of a child with disabilities. This is done to enhance the infant or toddler's development, to minimize the potential for developmental delay, and to enhance the family's capacity to meet the child's needs. http://www2.ed.gov/ bout/offices/list/users/products/openingdoors/ei.html)

Music therapy practice within the early intervention framework is most often pro-active and seeks to intervene with the child's environment and interactions in a manner that interrupts developmental damage from the disability. Some music therapists working in early intervention view the work as prevention rather than remediation (Abad & Edwards, 2004; Jonsdottir, 2002). Methods of music therapy in early childhood will reflect a high level of musical and therapeutic involvement from the therapist as well as from grown-ups in the child's life.

Early Intervention as a Program

Early Intervention is also used to label a program in the United States federal education law Individuals with Disabilities Education Act (IDEA). (In this chapter, reference to Early Intervention as a governmental program will always be capitalized.) In the United States, IDEA ensures that children with disabilities will be provided with educational supports such as special education or therapeutic-related services. Supportive services provided may include family training, counseling, and home visits; special instruction; speech-language pathology services; audiology services; occupational therapy; physical therapy; psychological services; medical services (only for diagnostic or evaluation purposes); health services needed to enable your child to benefit from the other services; social work services; assistive technology devices and services; transportation; nutrition services; and service coordination services. While music therapy is not specifically listed in the law, adding music therapy as a related or supportive service under both Part B and Part C of IDEA has been endorsed through federal regulation as well as through Department of Education letters of clarification. In most early childhood programs for children with special needs that employ a music therapist, music therapy services are provided as part of a comprehensive package of educational and therapeutic services to all children. Music therapy may or may not be outlined on a child's Individual Education Plan (IEP) or Individual Family Service Plan (IFSP). (Up-to-date information on music therapy and IDEA regulations can be found at www.musictherapy.org.)

The impact of this regulatory and funding program on music therapy assessment, goals, and methods is significant since young children with disabilities or those at risk for disability often gain access to music therapy through the Early Intervention Program (IDEA Part C) and the Preschool Program (IDEA Part B). Methods chosen by music therapists working within the Early Intervention system are required to address goals or outcomes identified by IDEA law and regulations within the areas of physical development (including vision, hearing, and health status); cognitive development; communication development; social or emotional development; and adaptive development [34 CFR §303.344(a)].

The model in which music therapy is provided is also prescribed by IDEA. Within Early Intervention, music therapy and other services "... to the maximum extent appropriate, are provided in natural environments, including the home, and community settings in which children without disabilities participate" [IDEA I C (632) (4) (G)]. These natural settings might include the child's home, a day care center, a local library, or other community location.

The Early Intervention program also requires a focus on the child as part of a family. IDEA provides for "... supports and services necessary to enhance the family's capacity to meet the developmental needs of the infant or toddler" [IDEA I C (636) (A) (2)]. This requirement means that the music therapist must design methods of treatment for the child as well as the family and for the child as part of the family. These interventions figure prominently both in the early childhood music therapy literature in the United States and in practice reports from other countries (Abad & Edwards, 2004; Oldfield, 2008; Oldfield, Bunce & Adams, 2003; Shoemark, 1996). Music therapists across the country have adapted their clinical methods to work within this natural environment model (among others: de l'Etoile, 2001; Humpal, 1991; Kern, 2001, 2006; Pasiali et al., 2004; Schwartz, 2009; Walworth, 2009b) and thus have established a unique model of music therapy provision.

Diagnostic Information

The path to recognizing a young child's developmental disability is as individual as the child. For some, diagnosis of physical, medical or orthopedic abnormalities can be made in utero through medical or genetic testing or may be detected by trained personnel soon after birth. Determining other difficulties can be more elusive. A number of conditions, such as autism, may not manifest sufficient symptoms for diagnosis until the child is 18 months or older. Sometimes a disability is acquired later through accident or illness.

Confounding the process of diagnosis in early intervention is the dynamic and individual nature of development. Children change and grow continuously. Their physical nature, behaviors, cognitive, social and emotional responses transform throughout early childhood. Identification of some disorders relies primarily on observation of behavior and can be especially difficult to separate from variances in individual development. This might delay a definitive early diagnosis. Professionals may subscribe to a "wait and see" approach and defer diagnosis to give sufficient time for developmental variables. Some families may be slow to understand or recognize that their child is not meeting typical developmental milestones. This diagnostic ambiguity in early intervention is reflected in special education law and practice. IDEA defines a child with a disability ages three through nine as "experiencing developmental delays ... in one or more of the following areas: physical development; cognitive development; communication development; social or emotional development; or adaptive development" [IDEA Title I/A /602 /3/B (i)]. In practice under IDEA, young children are legally referred to as an *infant or toddler with a disability* or a *preschooler with a disability*. Parents are not required to seek or obtain a specific diagnosis in order to receive services under IDEA.

In early intervention treatment, exact diagnoses are generally less important in assessment and planning than are the specific symptoms and their effect on the child's developmental process. This chapter will therefore be more concerned with the unique characteristics and needs of young children as they relate to therapy processes and methods.

Needs and Resources

The range of needs for little children is broad. So many events can align to make for developmental difficulties. It is best, then, to view the needs of the child in early intervention music therapy from a wide-ranging context. As stated earlier, the purpose of early therapy is to help the child grow and develop into the "self." What stops a child from realizing full growth toward self—the child's needs—will be examined from two different holistic perspectives: the *Human Motivation Theory* of Abraham Maslow (1943) and the musical development ideas proposed by some in the music therapy and music education community (Briggs, 1991; Gordon, 2003; Schwartz, 2008).

For a very young child, the most primary needs are the most basic—food, shelter, safety and security. These correspond to the ideas of Abraham Maslow (1943), described as the physiological needs and the safety needs. As those needs are met, Maslow suggests the need for love (affection and belonging), followed by the need for esteem, which, for the young child, can be qualified as the need for strength, achievement, independence, and freedom.

Physiological and Safety Needs

A young child who cannot eat or whose body functions cannot regulate may be in immediate and significant danger. The physical damage caused by lack of nutrition or health can cause development in other areas to cease, thus producing a delay or disability. There are several reasons why feeding may be an issue, including genetic abnormalities (such as Down Syndrome), sensory intolerances, poor regulation of automatic responses, etc. Some conditions require a tracheotomy tube or other device, which may make it difficult to breathe, eat, and swallow. Issues with motivation, energy, and stamina may also contribute to feeding issues.

Other physiological needs may arise and continue to impact many young children with developmental concerns, including requirements for environmental stimulation, touch, safety, and comfort. Methods developed for hospitalized infants could be appropriate for these children (Cevasco, 2008; Gooding, 2010; Shoemark, 2006; Stanley, 2003). Gooding (2010), reporting on the work of these music therapists and others, suggests a number of research-based music therapy methods to address physiological needs in young children. Prominent in this work was the use of recordings of the mother's voice (de l'Etoile, 2006) and combining music with physical stimulation (sucking a pacifier) or the use of touch (rhythmic stroking or rocking) (Standley, 2003). De l'Etoile (2006) and Shoemark (2006) describe infant-directed singing as a universal caregiving behavior that can be used as a clinical intervention and identifies the functions as "drawing and maintaining attention to caregiver; providing a vehicle for the grown-up to convey emotional information to the child; increasing ability for the child to regulate their affective state; and enabling the mother and child to coordinate emotional states and create social bonds" (pp. 24–25). The qualities of infant-directed singing include use of higher pitch; slower tempo; more sustained vowel sound with greater gliding between pitch; more "loving" timbre; and singing to convey positive emotions (p. 22). Shoemark and Grocke (2010) describe a method called "contingent singing," which is described as infant-directed singing to nurture, contain, and soothe the infant.

The safety needs of very young child are best understood from a developmental perspective. There are many circumstances in which young children's sense of safety and security is compromised. Some are as apparent as the need to be out of harm's way. Others are less apparent, such as the child's perceived threat from novel experiences in the environment. When all experiences are new, the child has no pattern of awareness or anticipation with which to formulate a response. This may cause the child to reject the experience. Children with extreme cognitive impairments may require additional time to process new information and stabilize responses. For some children, the environment itself is unpredictable and unstable. The child may be exposed to events and circumstances that do not allow for creation of firm paradigms of experience wherein they will be cared for and protected, and where the world is safe and predictable. Children who experience neglect, abuse, or abandonment; live in areas of war or strife; or experience chronic pain or discomfort from illness would be affected in the same way.

For a number of young children, regulation of responses to the environment is a constant challenge. Their sensory system might be easily overloaded, overresponsive, or underresponsive, making them unable to form and execute consistent responses. This lack of regulation impacts the child's sense of safety and security. Children with autism, Attention-Deficit/Hyperactivity Disorder, brain abnormalities, seizure, or severe processing issues might fit this pattern of need. This inability of the child to regulate to internal or external events and modulate responses could be considered a fundamental contributor to developmental difficulties. Overt signs of dysregulation will vary, depending on individual differences and developmental level. Some children might exhibit a flight response and turn away, engage in self-stimulatory behaviors, or run away. Others might cope through the fight response and become agitated or aggressive.

Music therapy interventions in the literature to address needs of safety and security, whether from internal or external stressors, focus considerably on attunement and attachment. Bowlby (1969) defines attachment as a deep and enduring emotional bond that connects one person to another. Oldfield (2006) explains attunement in music therapy as the process of child and parent sharing experiences of timing, rhythm, pulse, melody, and pitch in order to create the opportunity for attachment. Methods and interventions create immediate response to the child's signals and use the elements of music to support affect regulation. These methods then create the opportunity for synchronization of response both to the music provided and to the music-maker, allowing for attunement and attachment.

Throughout the literature on music therapy, there is emphasis on the use of the human voice and particularly the voice of the parent. Bargiel (2004) examined the impact of parental singing, particularly lullabies and play songs, in regulation of affect and the impact on attachment. Attachment is predicated on the supposition that infants transmit signals (facial affect, vocalization, movement) and that parents are biologically predisposed to respond (p. 1). The interventions relied heavily on parents' singing to the infant and the music therapist's modeling of musical attachment behavior. Bargiel proposes clinical interventions for both lullaby and play song singing as methods for helping the child to regulate and for parent/child attachment. Drawing on music development research, Bargiel describes a lullaby as having a sonorous quality, repetition, and simplicity of structure. A play song is livelier and might contain body percussion and a greater use of consonants (p. 5). The play song provides the opportunity of "... stimulating the young child" (p. 6).

Drake (2008) outlines a music therapy program designed to rework attachment patterns for vulnerable young children and their parents. She speaks of music therapy as a "... vital process of attuning to one another, for both child and parent, through shared experiences of timing, rhythm, pulse, melody, and pitch ..." (p. 41). Some of the interventions used include singing playful songs; imitation and reflection of the child's prespeech vocalizations; and modeling by the therapist for the parent (pp. 42–44).

The Need for Love, Affection, and Belonging

Children with impairments in communication, social interaction, cognition, and regulation are at risk for not developing the skills necessary to be a full and equal partner in relationships of love, affection, and belonging. The inability of young children to participate in reciprocity, emotional engagement, and social exchange may severely limit their developmental progress and overall growth. Love and belonging is dependent on a mutual communication system; an ability to respond to and initiate social overtures; and a capability for self-expression. It is also dependent on the child's behavior, ability to regulate reactions, and use of common language. A child's needs expand beyond reflexive attunement and two-way attachment to include finding their place in a community or society. Belonging also means accepting shared societal meanings, traditions, rituals, and laws as part of the "self."

Music therapists have created unique ways of providing music therapy for young children with social needs. Kern (2001, 2004, 2006, 2007) wrote about creating opportunites for social interaction on the playground using music for young children with special needs. Methods include designing and creating outdoor instruments and music play spaces in which typical children and children with needs interact through music-making. Her research showed that the musical adaptations combined with staff training and staff involvement in the music playground did produce increases in socialization.

Mosca et al. (2004) reported on using music groups to facilitate children's relationships, foster creative expression, and support disadvantaged children (pp. 1–2). Music therapy methods used included improvisation; rhythm and movement; music and relaxation; and composing songs. Morris (2010) describes a collaborative program for young children called the *Friendship Club* in which the music therapist and a social worker used musical and verbal processing to create social connections. Interventions include improvised songs, song composition, song recording, and listening. Pictures of the children engaged in social activities are used to showcase and reinforce group progress. In *Musical Bridges: Intergenerational Music Programs* (1996), Shaw and Manthey created a music therapy–based program combining preschool children and elderly clients using music, art, and movement activities. The supposition was that each age group has much to offer the other in terms of love, affection, and belonging.

Music-making with peers within groups, dyads, or triads is another therapeutic model used prominently in the literature and in practice. Humpal (1991) promotes a model of using music to facilitate interaction between typical children and children with special needs in an integrated preschool program. She focuses on the deficits children with special needs display with specific social behavior and with peer-to-peer social interactions (p. 162). Interventions include pairing children on musical tasks; choosing partners; use of songs and musical games; staff facilitation of social overtures; creative movement; and dancing. In 2006, Humpal and Tweedle wrote of combining music and play experiences for young children in a technique they call *Guided Group Play,* which built upon theories of play proposed by Parten (1932) and Linder (1990). In this strategy, the authors recommend gathering the children together in a common play space and using exploration and improvisation through music.

The Need for Esteem

It might be difficult to equate young children with the need for esteem if that quality is seen from an adult perspective. For the young child, esteem can be viewed as the need for strength, achievement, independence, and freedom. These qualities often require specific sets of skills that a young child in early intervention might not yet possess due to cognitive deficits, communication and language delays, and processing difficulties.

Many music therapists design treatment objectives to remediate deficits through skill-building, which can address any number of domains, including cognitive, motor, processing, communication, emotional, behavioral, musical, affective, or social. Standley and Hughes (1996) document a comprehensive list of developmentally appropriate learning objectives targeted within a music therapy session for an inclusive class of four-year-olds in an educational setting. They divided the areas of need addressed into communication; social/personal/emotional; cognitive concepts, including music skills; and motor skills. Interventions used in the studied sessions include singing and listening to familiar songs; fill-in-the-blank songs; identifying songs through listening; melodic and lyric imitation; listening and discussing content of song lyrics; music matched to picture books; structured movement; structured instrument play; and music-based direction-following.

Kaplan (2006) outlines a three-level hierarchical approach to skill-building in young preschool children. Level I describes children who are new to the preschool setting and need basic experience in social/behavioral and communication skills. Children engage in mutual instrument play and movement; pitch pattern imitation; and making musical choices of instrument. Level II aims to increase social/emotional skills, such as turn-taking and play skills, and communication skills (making comments or asking questions). Level II methods include song-singing; start-and-stop musical play; playing together on an instrument; taking turns; and using verbal requests. Level III needs include greater cooperation; answering "wh" questions; visual attending skills; and acquiring cognitive concepts. Level III interventions include using printed notation along with songs; playing solo; using fill-in-the-blank songs; choosing partners; and asking musical questions. Methods are meant to support the child in gaining success in academic curriculum material.

Geist et al. (2012) explored the connection between music and mathematics in early childhood education. Although the study was with typical children, the researchers found a connection between using chants and traditional songs in the classroom and the early learning of patterns, a necessary prerequisite to higher math skills. Kern et al. (2007) focused on self-care tasks within the classroom for a three-year-old child with autism. Interventions included training staff to sing specifically composed songs embedded within classroom routine to encourage independence in self-care.

Geist et al. (2008) examined a collaborative approach between music therapy and speech therapy to assist children with severe communication disorders. The goals were to increase the use of social greetings and to increase engagement in educational story time. Approaches used include created songs, instrument play, use of songbooks, and use of augmentative communication (ACC) devices to substitute for spoken or sung words or language. An increasing number of music therapists (Gadberry, 2011; Wellman, 2010) are using augmentative and alternative (AT) communication devices as a method within early childhood music therapy. Schwartz (2010 AMTA conference presentation) proposes three models for using ACC/AT devices within music therapy: to allow the child to create or participate in music therapy interventions, to function as a supportive tool in order to enhance music therapy experience, or to use music therapy interventions to support the child in skill acquisition using ACC/AT devices. In 2001, McGuire examined the use of music on the then popular children's program *Barney and Friends*. He argues that television can be a powerful communicator and may serve as the only source for musical information for children without access to music professionals (p. 141).

Referral and Assessment

Given the nature of music therapy in early intervention, it is not surprising that most referrals for service come from a parent, family member, teacher, or other therapist. Many times music therapy is sought out because the child is responsive to music in their environment. Sometimes a parent will report that the child "lights up" when music is used. Sometimes music seems to provide significant motivation for the child.

Music therapy assessment in early intervention is complicated by the broad range of developmental needs as well as by the overlay of individual developmental differences. Humpal and Colwell (2006) suggest that assessment in early childhood serves to determine eligibility for services; to gather information on levels of functioning; and to determine treatment goals (pp. 40–41). In the majority of literature reviewed, assessment was done through behavioral observation within the music-making session, with focus on the priority area of need such as parent/child interactivity (Oldfield, 2007); peer-to-peer social interaction (Kern & Wolery, 2001); use of communication and language (Geist et al., 2008); or cognitive functioning (Standley & Hughes, 1997). There does not appear to be a consistent procedure in the literature for accessing music therapy in early childhood. Music therapy methods have been employed in established early childhood music education programs such as *Kindermusik* (Pasiali et al., 2004) and *Music Together* (Hamlett & Mackenzie, 2005). Schwartz (2009) reported that IDEA Part C Early Intervention programs may fund parent/child developmental groups for children under three.

A number of early childhood music therapists have created assessment tools specific to their area of practice, theoretical orientation, or model of music therapy. Bargiel (2004) uses theories of attachment to assess the parent and infant. Assessment items include the parent's and infant's ability to establish and sustain an attachment bond; level of visual contact; presence and adaptation of singing and language; and indications of pleasure (p. 6). Gross et al. (2010) used two scales created by Nordoff/Robbins: the child-therapist relationship in music activity (CTR) and the musical communication ability (MCA) (p. 4). Magee et al. (2011) suggest that treatment for children with acquired brain injury needs to include assessment reflecting specific understanding of brain development at the time of injury. Nicholson et al. (2008) used non–music-based assessment checklists to determine parent/child interaction and child behavior (p. 229) in the Australian *Sing and Grow* parent/child program. In 1999, Liberatore and Layman published *The Cleveland Music Therapy Assessment of Infants and Toddlers,* a comprehensive guide to assessment and treatment planning for young children with developmental delay. Rainey Perry (2003) used a therapist-created assessment, *The Communication Profile that* incorporated elements of Bruscia's Taxonomy of Improvisation Techniques (p. 232). Walworth (2009a) reported therapist-created coding items looking at parent/child behaviors in a group music setting. Items included gestures, toy play, and vocalizations. Schwartz (2008) created a sequenced checklist of musical responses across the developmental range of young children age birth to five. The *Music Indicators of Early Childhood Development,* or MIECD, are used to indicate developmental levels purely through musical responses and are tied to the author's five levels of musical development (Schwartz, 2011).

In a 2002 article examining the methods used by experienced music therapy clinicians, Drieschner and Pioch (2002) concluded that "the goal of therapy and the target group together count for 25%–50% of the difference between therapeutic methods ..." (p. 15). Through assessment, the music therapist gains understanding of the target group—early childhood—and the developmental goals in early intervention music therapy. Assessment then becomes a critical link in selecting appropriate methods in music therapy for early intervention.

Guidelines for Music Therapy Methods in Early Intervention

Methods of music therapy in early childhood are designed to take advantage of the child's resources of time, resiliency, and trajectory toward growth. Most children exhibit amazing resiliency in the face of challenges. This may be due in part to the way the young brain absorbs and integrates information. LaGasse (2011), in a review of current research in music and early childhood development, points to the concept of brain plasticity: "Cortical plasticity is the ability of the brain to change, to be flexible or 'plastic,' in response to the environment" (p. 28). Scientists are just beginning to deeply understand the ability of the young brain to adapt and adjust. Clinical anecdotes from music therapy case studies frequently describe how young children with significant impairments are able to feel success and rise above challenges that might seem insurmountable to a grown-up. The methods currently used in early intervention practice reflect movement and dynamic progression rather than reflection and maintenance as might be seen in other areas of practice.

Methods in early childhood music therapy vary according to the overall developmental stage of the individual child and consider the child's musical developmental phase or level, but all methods address underlying deficits through skill-building. Several key elements reported throughout the literature include the importance of the repetition; use of the voice; reliance on flexible structures; and need to incorporate a grown-up in a child's musical life throughout the therapy process.

In the United States, laws and regulations such as the Individuals with Disabilities Education Act (IDEA) stipulate that a child with developmental needs receive assistance and support, including therapy. The quality of these services is ensured through regulation and evaluation. Early intervention music therapists should ensure that the methods of treatment they choose comply with these current standards of practice as well as developmentally appropriate practices (DAP), which are defined by the National Association for the Education of Young Children as

> "... a framework of principles and guidelines for best practice in the care and education of young children, birth through age 8. It is grounded both in the research on how young children develop and learn and in what is known about

> education effectiveness. The principles and guidelines outline practice that promotes young children's optimal learning and development." (NAEYC, 2009)

Designing, creating, and implementing methods in early childhood music therapy should take into consideration principles and guidelines from DAP. Particular guidelines in DAP that impact methods in music therapy are the emphasis on interactive play-based learning; planned environments for learning facilitation; inclusionary practices; and community-building (Copple & Bredekamp, 2009).

Many music therapists in early intervention have responded to developmentally appropriate practices by working within a collaborative/consultation method. Collaboration can be a powerful tool when planning methods for early intervention music therapy. Register (2004) studied methods to teach child-care personnel how to use music in the classroom. She found that providing a model of implementation may increase the amount of time music is used by the classroom teacher. De l'Etoile (2001) studied in-service training programs for child-care providers and found children were more visually, vocally, and physically engaged during music activities in classrooms where staff were trained in implementing music activities. Schwartz (2008) suggests that training personnel on successful music strategies gives children the opportunity to make music throughout their day and provides the framework for them to "generalize the positive outcomes from music-making into daily routines" (p. 145).

Identifying Developmental Needs through Music

Earlier in this chapter, models and methods of music therapy were examined as they relate to a young child's needs when viewed from an overarching system such as Maslow's Hierarchy of Needs. Music therapy has begun to generate its own music-based structures for understanding the needs of the developing young child. These structures allow music therapy practitioners to make a direct connection between the child's needs as seen through music responses and the creation and implementation of developmentally appropriate music therapy methods.

Young children have a unique progression in music development. Musical engagement, response, and behavior in therapy are viewed with respect for the child's musical developmental level. Gooding and Standley (2011) suggest that skill development is evidenced by changes in individuals' "musically relevant abilities, and that these changes occur in cumulative layers and patterns" (p. 32).

Briggs (1991), writing on the work developed by Bruscia (1985), proposed an integrated model of musical development that related specific music behaviors to theories of development from other disciplines. Her model examined developmental stages proposed in psychoanalytic, cognitive, and learning theories and related musical development to these constructs. Comparison of the child's musical responses with their chronological age could be used to indicate developmental delay and identify the child's developmental needs. Music therapy methods designed to address those developmental needs are created relating to specific musical behaviors. The levels she proposed are tied to chronological ages as well as theoretical stages in early childhood development:

Reflex Phase of Musical Development—0 to 9 months
Intention Phase of Musical Development—9 to 18 months
Control Phase of Musical Development—18 to 36 months
Integration Phase of Musical Development—36 to 72 months

In another view, Luce (2004) suggests that music therapists look to music learning theory, particularly the work of Edwin Gordon, when determining needs and creating interventions. Gordon (2003) described music learning in early childhood from birth to age five as "preparatory audiation" and defined a sequence of musical behaviors including absorption, random response, purposeful response, shedding egocentricity, breaking the code, introspection, and coordination. Although Gordon's theory comes from typical early musical development, Luce urged its use to connect to determining developmental needs and therefore music activities. "A music learning theory model can provide clinicians with an important understanding of musical development and a distinctively musical vocabulary in which to frame musical experiences that occur within the therapeutic process" (p. 26).

In 2008, Schwartz extrapolated from the phase model of Briggs (1991) to create a framework of early childhood music therapy practice based on five levels of musical development. The framework attempts to provide an overall structure of music development that can be used for assessment, treatment planning, and evaluation. Schwartz synthesized the five levels of musical development as follows:

> *Awareness* is reflexive and instinctual and represents "an awakening of the senses, of physical and sensual being. It is the beginning of thoughts and feelings" (p. 49).
>
> Within the level of *Trust,* "the young child reaches out and finds a response that helps to form a perception of the world as a place that has meaning, reliability, and safety. *Trust* also means looking inward and finding constancy and stability." (p. 59)
>
> The child gaining *Independence* "can have experiences separate from another person. He or she can create the opportunity for experience in response to his or her own internal motivation" (p. 69).
>
> As children move into the level of *Control,* "they can use their cognitive abilities and communication skills to make choices. These choices become integrated into the "self" (p. 79).
>
> *Responsibility* "implies the recognition of the interdependency of the self with the external world while preserving the capacity to maintain the "self" (p. 91).

Schwartz's framework provides guidance for understanding overall development as well as developmental difficulties through music. The child's individual needs are seen as both moving vertically through the developmental levels and expanding experiences horizontally within each level. Determining music therapy methods as well as creating and designing music therapy interventions for developmental growth is based on naturally occurring musical behaviors within each level.

OVERVIEW OF METHODS AND PROCEDURES

The following music therapy methods and procedures are used most commonly in early intervention:

Receptive Music Therapy

- Child-Directed Singing: Based on what the child is doing or experiencing, the therapist spontaneously sings as a means of communicating with or to the child.
- Music Listening: Children listen to recorded music as a background for stabilizing the stimulus environment.

Improvisational Music Therapy

- Vocal Improvisation: Children make up vocal sounds or songs spontaneously either alone or with peers, and with the therapist's presence or active support.
- Instrumental Improvisation: Children spontaneously make up music on an instrument either alone or with peers, and with the therapist's presence or active support.

Re-creative Music Therapy

- Singing Songs: Children sing precomposed songs and react to them.
- Instrumental Songs: Children play precomposed instrumental parts to a song.
- Structured Movement Songs: Children perform movements as indicated by the song lyrics.

Compositional Music Therapy

- Song Lyric Substitution: Children think of and suggest words to fill in or replace lyrics of a song they know.

Guidelines for Receptive Music Therapy

In receptive methods of music therapy, the purpose is to meet the child's needs through music that stimulates the child's fundamental sensory, processing, or cognitive systems. The therapist designs experiences in which the child's active music-making is not required. The critical role of the adult in providing what a child needs for growth is reflected in the importance of child-directed singing and adult-formulated listening experiences. The child's responses to receptive methods can be internal brain changes, sensory stimulation, movement modifications, or transformation in regulatory states. Many music therapists propose that these responses indicate less observable cognitive or emotional adjustments, leading to development of the "self."

In the literature, receptive music therapy methods in early intervention are used for two distinct yet connected purposes—engagement (e.g., Bargiel, 2004) and regulation (e.g., de l'Etoile, 2006). Many reports of clinical practice intertwined these two purposes when devising receptive methods. Cevasco (2008), in a study of maternal singing and full-term and preterm infants, found that the mothers of full-term infants used receptive music methods to both regulate (calm) and engage (bond).

Receptive music therapy interventions can be designed to attract, foster, and sustain children's engagement. The term "engagement" here is used broadly to indicate the areas of experience in which a young child can engage socially, emotionally, cognitively, sensorially, and motorically, as well as musically. Children need to actively connect with others and their environment as well as engage with internal feelings and thoughts.

Young children tend to be most engaged musically with unaccompanied singing (Ilari & Sundara, 2009) and many music therapists use only their voice in treatment. Lyrics that fit the melodic rhythm can be used, along with vocables or improvised language. Songs and melodies that are narrow in range and have rhythmic regularity tend to calm and soothe. For children in younger developmental levels, the fundamentals of infant-directed singing should be included—higher pitch, slower tempo, more gliding between tones, and a timbre that conveys positive emotion. Young children are particularly in tune with familiar voices, so the singing of a parent or other known adult might be most effective (de l'Etoile, 2006).

Children of all developmental levels who become dysregulated due to overstimulation, trauma, or stress might require therapeutic intervention to assist in regaining homeostasis. Some indications of dysregulation include increases in physical agitation, attempts to escape or turn away from the music, or self-stimulatory behaviors. For children in a dysregulated state, the lyrics are considerably less important than the musical material. Clinical experience and research has shown that repetition allows songs and melodies to be processed more easily, and its use might be best when working toward regulation through receptive methods. When a grown-up sings to a child for regulation and attunement, the musical material and vocal timbre of the adult can convey an emotional message of acceptance and calm. Accompaniment on guitar or piano, if used, might reflect rhythmic regularity and be prevalently consonant rather than dissonant.

Despite the stated purpose of using receptive music therapy methods in early intervention, the shifting nature of early development means that this method might not remain pure throughout treatment or even throughout a single session. The child might begin to respond in a more active musical manner.

Child-Directed Singing

Overview. Child-directed singing is based on typical early childhood experiences in which the grown-up uses their voice in song to communicate with and to the child. In this method, the child is an active listener and the therapist focuses on creating a specific music environment for the child to absorb rather than to promote an expressive behavior. Child-directed singing as a receptive music therapy method is described in relationship-based therapy (Bargiel) but also heavily used in a more developmental focus (Pasiali) and educational focus (Kaplan). The music components of child-directed singing, such as melody, rhythm, or lyrics, contain meaning and purpose that is specific to the child. The grown-up deliberately directs the sound and sensory experience toward the child and adjusts the music to reflect changes in the child's affect, regulation, positioning, attention, or engagement. The child's response to the singing is instinctive and natural and could include affect, physical, vocal, or motor adjustments.

The therapeutic possibilities of the child-directed singing method are endless. Therapists can use their creativity and knowledge of play to design interventions that can address many different goals and types of developmental needs. Child-directed singing has proven effective in addressing areas of initiating or increasing engagement and can be used with social engagement (Kern, 2006), emotional engagement (Bargiel, 2004), cognitive engagement (Pasiali et al.,, 2004), or motoric and sensory engagement (Shoemark, 2006). If the goal is social engagement, the therapist uses exaggerated facial affect along with the music to provide additional visual cues. The therapist may pair the music with the target of engagement. If the goal is for the child to engage with a feeling or an idea, the music can include specific lyrics that describe or explain. Melodic material and harmonic content can create an atmosphere that paints an auditory picture for the child of the feeling or idea. Physical cues can be added to the singing if accepted and welcomed by the child. Pictures, books, or props can support the music through visual or sensory reinforcement. The therapist can repeat or improvise within the singing to elicit longer periods of engagement.

Child-directed singing has been used very effectively in helping young children successfully engage with social behaviors, transitions, and classroom and self-care routines (Kern, Wakeford & Aldridge, 2007; Pasiali, 2004). A specific objective might be for the child to engage in toy play in response to a familiar child-directed song. Or the child will show facial engagement and attention toward a familiar adult during child-directed singing. Motoric or sensory goals might include a decrease in physical manifestations of stress such as flailing or agitation, slowing of heart rate and breathing, change in attunement toward grown-up, or increase in focus toward the music.

If the child begins to disengage, the therapist can change melodic or rhythmic content until attention is regained. Once the child is re-engaged, the therapist can choose to change treatment methods and goals or to change the object of engagement. Sometimes children in medical distress might become disengaged and dysregulated due to pain or urgent health concerns. The therapist can assess to see if the music or the presence of the therapist is contributing to the dysregulation and might choose to discontinue or change treatment methods. The level of therapy is augmentative or intensive.

Preparation. Check the environment and remove any items that might contribute to dysregulation, such as toys that make loud sounds, bright light, or offensive smells. Assess the child for specific triggers of dysregulation and remove them if possible. The therapist will need to be in fairly close physical and auditory proximity to the child. Keep movement, gestures, and extraneous talking to a minimum.

What to observe. The child's physical gestures, movements, and proximity to therapist can indicate whether and how they are responding to the intervention. The physiological state, including heart rate, pulse, breathing pattern, skin coloration, and automatic movements, such as tremors, will be one indication of internal status. Listen to the child's use of vocalization or verbalization to gauge if they are synchronizing with the music presented. As an indication of regulation and attunement, the child's facial affect will relax, and they might turn their facial presence toward therapist.

The therapist will be alert to the child's signals of engagement, such as eye contact, facial affect changes, motor movements, postural shifts, picking up the object, showing the object to the therapist, acting out an idea, moving to the music, following song lyric directions, or initiating communication with the therapist. Indications that the child-directed singing might not be engaging the child could be for the child to move or turn away from the therapist, communicate aversion through gestures or words, or become dysregulated.

Procedures. The therapist moves into proximity with the child and either begins singing immediately or creates a moment of silence and stillness before beginning. Eye contact and facial presence toward the child should be responsive to the child's signals of acceptance or rejection of the music. Use of touch, through stroking or rocking, might enhance the listening experience of the child. An intermediary object such as a soft blanket or touch toy can also be used.

The therapist should be comfortable with the musical material in a key and tempo range that suits the child's needs. Use of timbre and dynamics should be planned with musical developmental levels in mind. The therapist ought to be careful not to overload the child with multiple areas of attention such as singing and body percussion at the same time, until the child is ready to shift attentional focus easily. This is a developmental skill, so the therapist must be aware of the child's functioning level before added multiple points of engagement. An effective strategy within this method might be to add sufficient processing time for the child by slowing the tempo of the music or leaving spaces.

Music used in child-directed singing can be precomposed, therapist-created, or improvised. The qualities of the particular song or vocalization should be selected to match the targeted goal while referencing musical development. The therapist sings with qualities of the music, such as timbre or pitch structure, that have been shown to attract the child. The traits of play songs—brilliant vocal tone, rhythmic with a clipped sound, greater stress on consonants—are compatible with those of child-directed songs for engagement. Strategies might include tempo fluctuations, use of glissando or crescendo, silence, matching movements or pulse of the child, musical surprises, melodic variations, and use of consonance and dissonance. Lullabies may promote regulation and attachment. Qualities of lullabies include a smooth timbre, narrow melodic range, and repetition. Use of a meter such as 3/4 might promote rocking or swaying.

Adding movement, props, or visuals when indicated can enhance the musical experience. Visual referencing as well as pointing are important competencies in developmental growth. The therapist can model looking at or pointing to a person or object. It is best, when using this strategy, for the therapist to look toward the object as they point rather than at the child. Signs of affection such as hugs are also a way to celebrate musical attachment as well as engagement.

Adaptations. One significant adaptation in child-directed singing is for the therapist to teach or train the child's parent or other significant grown-up in the method. The therapist then adapts the goal from being child-centered to being relationship-centered. A grown-up who has a close relationship with the child (including family members and the music therapist) is generally most able to assist a child toward regulating through singing to the child. Facilitating the intervention gives parents the chance to engage with their child in a positive way or to engage alongside their child in activities or ideas that have meaning for the family.

If the grown-up is not familiar to the child, such as a new music therapist, effort should be made to emulate the singing quality, musical material, and rhythmic energy of the familiar adult. Singing can be adapted by using humming or other musical vocal sounds. If the therapist chooses to combine touch with child-directed singing, it is best to first assess the child's ability to regulate to physical contact. Consultation with an occupational therapist knowledgeable in sensory integration might be helpful.

There are limited reports in the literature of receptive music methods using child-directed instrument play without the addition of the voice. This method could be adapted using the same guidelines as child-directed singing. Some therapists have used kazoos to mimic the human voice (Oldfield, 2006). Other therapists have substituted instruments that have a humanlike quality to them, such as the violin or clarinet. It would be important to note that previously cited research demonstrates the importance of the human voice as a musical tool in early intervention.

John and his mother entered the music room together physically but were worlds apart emotionally. John writhed and squirmed as his mother tried to carry him. His shrieks and screams could be heard throughout the building. The music therapist quietly closed the door behind the pair and indicated to Mom to put John down on a fluffy cushion. John continued to wail as the music therapist and Mom sat cross-legged on the floor close to him, but not too near. As the music therapist began to hum, John's mother courageously started to sing her favorite hymn. She and the therapist didn't look at or touch John right away, but kept singing calmly with a steady meter, low tessitura, and a rising and falling melodic contour. Mom loved this song, and her pleasure in its sound was reflected in the warm timbre of her voice. The mother and therapist had planned this intervention prior to coming to music, but it still amazed them both how quickly John stopped moving his body, took a deep breath, and swung his posture toward them both. His face relaxed, and there was a hint of a smile. Mom reached out and squeezed John's hand gently in time to the music.

Sarah sat quietly in a blue chair pulled up to the piano. She did not move, did not talk or sing. She stared straight ahead at no apparent object. The music therapist put her fingers on the piano with an open fifth interval and played it several times in a predictable pattern. Sarah did not look at the therapist. The music therapist then began a simple melodic chant in time with the simple harmonic accompaniment. "My head, my hands, my knees, my feet; that all makes up me, me, me." The therapist repeated the chant again and again, each time increasing the dynamic and tempo of her singing. By the sixth time, Sarah had shifted her posture slightly to be more in line with the therapist. The therapist smiled and began the chant again, with greater intensity and excitement. As she almost reached the end phrase, she suddenly stopped and changed the melody to the B section of the song: "And sometimes my nose ... and sometimes ... my toes." The interval on the piano also shifted to a second, making a dissonant sound to accompany the sudden change. Sarah now turned fully toward the therapist, watching her mouth with great anticipation. Sarah's eyes became bright each time the dissonance was repeated. When the therapist returned to the beginning of the song, Sarah showed full attention and her eyes tracked down as the therapist patted her own chest three times while singing "me, me, me."

Music Listening

Overview. The receptive method of music listening in early intervention uses recordings to provide the music experience for the child. The recording could be selected from premade sources or produced by the therapist using specifically composed and performed music. In therapy, music recordings might be appropriate when live music is not practical, such as for carryover in the home environment, when a child is in transition, or if there is concern about contamination or overstimulation from the presence of a therapist or other adult, as when the child has a compromised immune system. Nicholson et al., (2008), Shoemark (2006), and Walworth (2009a, 2009b), among others, report making recordings of music used in therapy sessions to send home for families to support connections and allow for generalization. Listening to music recordings is an effective method for regulation and attunement (Gooding, 2010). Recordings may also be valuable for children who learn or absorb best with repeated exposure. Sometimes geographic distances make recordings the only practical way for a child to have access to selected therapeutic music in their environment. Recordings, and the new technology with which to play them, may also provide the child with an opportunity to control when and how to listen to the music.

Recorded music would not be the first method of choice for children whose primary need is for attachment and reciprocity because recordings do not allow for immediate adjustment to the responses of the child, a quality that is necessary for person-to-person interaction. Children whose response to music is rigid and reliant on sameness are also not good candidates for using recordings as a therapeutic method. The unwavering replication of recorded music can feed into inflexibility.

Use of recordings in receptive music therapy methods can target areas of engagement and regulation. Goals might be similar to those for child-directed singing: change in physical actions or physiological state, increase in attention to the music, and greater attunement to the musical material presented, such as tempo, meter, articulation, and melodic contour. For other children, the goal might include a change of focus from internal preoccupation to responding to the directions or intent of the lyrics of the song. Another goal might be for the child to increase coping skills through independent selection of recorded music to self-soothe or self-regulate. The level of therapy is augmentative or intensive.

Preparation. Equipment to play back recordings for young children must be sturdy, safe, and childproof while still providing high-quality sound. Music selections should be immediately available to limit the wait time for the child if silence is not therapeutically planned. The volume should be carefully monitored to match the needs of the child and of the environment and not allow harmful decibel or frequency levels. The therapist may choose from familiar or unfamiliar recordings, although familiarity with the music is reported to be used more frequently for regulation. The music can be songs or instrumental pieces. Particular timbres (voice or instrumental), texture (amount of musical material), rhythmic structure, harmonic content, and use of language should all be considered when selecting the best music to fit the needs of the child. Headphones, earbuds, or personal sound systems can all be used, although dysregulated children will often have strong reactions to equipment touching them or being too close. The auditory environment should be assessed in order to determine how much access to the music the child will have with each different type of sound system. If the child is controlling the recording, the therapist should train the child or an assisting adult in the use of the playback equipment.

What to observe. Look for physical, physiological, affect, and attention changes that indicate an adjustment to a different regulatory state. As the child responds positively to the recorded music by demonstrating greater regulation, the music therapist might want to use the attention and attunement created by this state to introduce other music therapy methods. Be alert to increases in dysregulation that would be a contraindication to continuing the use of recorded music, including an intense absorption in the visual or auditory aspects of the recording or recording equipment (the buttons, or the disc spinning).

Procedures. Decide the length and amount of musical material to be used, and whether it will be repetitions of the same material through looping or a sequence of songs. The music therapist may choose to include some child-directed singing or speech along with the recording. In order to support regulation, it is effective if talking or verbal prompts are kept to a minimum. The therapist needs to carefully consider if the child is ready for multiple sources of input before added either singing or speech. Expected outcomes from the method should be clear so that the therapist knows when to end or stop the recordings. If the outcomes are reached, the therapist can then move on to other methods and perhaps other goals or end the session, leaving the child in a regulated state and ready for a different experience. With newer technology, the therapist can quickly respond to the child's changes and switch songs or musical material to adapt to the new state.

If the recordings are to be used to develop coping strategies and the child is in charge of the equipment, the therapist can make sure that the music available is in sync with the treatment plan. The child should clearly understand the purpose of the recordings and know how to recognize changes that will indicate that they have been able to undergo a shift in regulatory states.

Adaptations. Music recordings provide an opportunity for the child or family to have greater access to music therapy experiences. The therapist can train the parent or other caregivers to use recorded music, making sure there is a clear understanding of how the music can affect the child and what responses to expect. The therapist could put together a playlist of songs or musical material from which the parent can choose. Educate the parent about the specific use of the music recording and urge them to not use the recording for purposes other than the one for which it was designed.

When engaging an older child in independent use of the recordings, pictures, stories, or therapist-created books can be used to provide a visual reminder of the how the child is expected to respond to the music. Pictures can also be used to teach the child how to operate the equipment.

The classroom of three-year-old children with significant delays was frequently the scene of chaos and upset. The adults assigned to the room were stressed by the amount of physical care that the children needed first thing in the morning—feeding, changing diapers, positioning them in their chairs. As they went about their work, the adults began to talk and complain among themselves. The children responded with increasing tension in their bodies, which made the necessary care all the harder. Soon one child began to vocalize in distress, triggering the other children to cry and the adults to speak even louder. In the middle of this, the music therapist entered and carefully placed the music system on a nearby table. The teacher in charge of the classroom indicated through gesture that the adults should stop talking. The recorded music began with a lively, consonant piece with simple instrumental texture, but no lyrics. As the songs played on the tempo slowed, the meter moved to triple and the melodic contour became narrower. The adults started to sway along with the sounds. As they went about their business, they began to slow their movements and look with a smile toward the children. The entire auditory environment of the room changed from frenetic to calm. When the music therapist detected synchrony of movement, sound, and emotion, she turned off the recording and invited the staff to sing together on a familiar greeting song.

Guidelines for Improvisational Music Therapy

Young children in every developmental phase or level can benefit from in-the-moment, interactive sound play with a grown-up. The very nature of initiating and sustaining attention and interaction for the young child is improvisatory, meaning that it is spontaneous, responsive in the moment, and instinctive. Since much of what a young child does is innate, the musical sounds that a child makes are generally instinctual. They see or feel or hear, and then they act. An accepted quality of improvisation is that it is not fully planned prior to being expressed. Young children are developmentally not ready for the higher-level cognitive skills necessary for planning, problem-solving, and sequential action. Improvisation, then, can be seen as a childlike response. The music therapist can create flexible musical interactions with a child by adapting or creating pitch and interval interplay, give-and-take of melodic phrases, rhythmic and meter variability, timbre exploration, and structural changes.

Goals in improvisatory music therapy methods for early intervention may include engagement, reciprocity, communication, self-expression, emotional release, social connection, and physical discharge. Playful improvisation supports the child's exploration and spontaneous expression and allows for practice in interacting with the world. The therapist's role during improvisation might vary according to the needs of the child and the goals of the therapy. The music therapist may provide support for the child's vocal or instrumental exploration and risk-taking. The therapist may take a role as an equal partner or follow the child. Words within vocal exploration can increase the layers of meaning of the experience while adding functional, useful communication. Strategies and techniques might include repeating a simple melodic motif, interjecting contrasting sounds or tones, matching pitches or melodic phrases, suggesting creative timbre changes, increasing vocal rhythmic intensity through tempo fluctuations, and added words, phrases, or nonsense syllables.

Group improvisation is an effective method for increasing awareness of group members, creating a motivating auditory environment for the children and stimulating group cohesion (Skewes & Thompson, 1998). Goals might be to increase communicative vocalization in a social setting (Gross et al., 2010), to increase use of social and/or expressive language, to develop peer-to-peer awareness (Mosca et al., 2004), to expand or increase reciprocal exchanges with peers (Kim et al., 2009), to initiate communication within a group, to use novel communicative language, to participate in call-and-response, or to take turns within a group setting (Kim et al., 2008).

It is important for the therapist to remember that improvisation does not mean a lack of structure. Young children thrive on repetition and need structure in order to begin to put meaning to experience. When using improvisation in early childhood, it is the therapist's responsibility to take the child's responses and create meaning through the use of flexibility within structure and variation within repetition. Studying specific developmental responses across phases or levels of early childhood is critical in order to know what music is at each point in a child's early life. Schwartz (2008) organizes indications of musical involvement into 10 sequenced steps: sensing, exploring, shaping, responding, communicating, interacting, collaborating, internalizing, refinement, and mastery (Chapter 13).

Bruscia (1987) delineated clinical techniques for improvisatory music therapy that provide an excellent guide for the early childhood music therapist. In the literature reviewed, the following techniques were most apparent: empathy (imitating, synchronizing, incorporating, pacing, reflecting, and exaggerating), structuring (rhythmic grounding, tonal centering, and shaping), intimacy (sharing instruments, giving, and bonding), elicitation (repeating, modeling, making spaces, interjecting, extending, and completing), redirection (introducing change, differentiating, modulating, intensifying, calming, and intervening), procedural (shifting, pausing, receding, experimenting, and conducting), referential (pairing, symbolizing in a developmental manner), and emotional exploration (holding, doubling, integrating, and sequencing).

Vocal Improvisation

Overview. Methods using improvisation have much in common with play. Improvisational, playful use of the voice does not limit the child/therapist interaction to one-dimensional emotional meaning such as happy. Rather, vocal play can encourage examination of many meanings—excitement, frustration, worry, contentment, anger, or joy. Vocal improvisation can be used in individual as well as group therapy in both informal and structured settings. The therapist can use voice to initiate the vocal play or use an instrument to introduce pitched sounds. Use of facial affect along with an open body posture is important, as is physical proximity to the child.

Vocal exploration and improvisation begins at the very earliest stages of life and can be an essential method throughout all of early childhood music therapy treatment. Vocalization is intrinsic for most children. Indeed, for the very young child, vocal improvisation in response to an adult's music is a more natural reaction than singing songs. Young children naturally engage in musical babble and in singing spontaneous song fragments. These responses are generally inwardly directed and loose in structure. Through vocal improvisation, the music therapist is using a method that is developmentally appropriate and therefore especially effective for children with developmental challenges (Shoemark, 2008).

For the child, vocal improvisation provides an immediate and concrete response and recognition to their produced sounds. The therapist supports the child through vocal improvisatory techniques such as synchronizing or reflecting, Vocal improvisation can be pitch-, rhythm-, dynamic-, timbre-, or lyric-based.

Free and spontaneous group vocalization in early intervention music therapy is often an outgrowth of structured song singing or child/directed singing. The young child's vocal responses can be tentative and sporadic, especially in a group setting. Sometimes this is an outcome of the disability, such as processing difficulties, but more often it is a natural manifestation of developmental level. It is typical for children to move in and out of attentional states when in a group. The very young child might also concentrate more on watching, listening, and absorbing the music in a group situation, so sometimes vocal offerings are delayed and might seem to be disconnected from the original song. The music therapist can then use changes in melody, pitch, or melodic rhythm to redirect the children's attention toward the music. While still connected to a musical structure, the vocalization becomes improvisatory and spontaneous. When children begin to respond vocally, the therapist can encourage further responses through pitch, interval, melodic, or rhythmic imitation of the sounds.

Not all young children will benefit from group vocal improvisation without prior experience in singing in a group. Some children might not be ready for the unexpected nature of group improvisation and will require additional cues from the therapist to learn how to prepare themselves for unanticipated sounds coming from multiple sources. The level of therapy may be augmentative, intensive, or primary.

Preparation. While the child's and adult's responses in this method are improvisatory, the therapist needs be extremely well prepared prior to beginning the session. First, the therapist should examine their own understanding of the boundaries of music. Can screaming happily in a child's crib be a musical response? If there is only the briefest of rhythmic synchrony, is that music? Next, the music therapist must learn how to play and how to be playful using the voice as the object of play. Humpal and Tweedle (2006) devotes an entire chapter to play-based techniques in music therapy.)

The therapist will generally initiate or facilitate vocal improvisation in early childhood. Beginning with a familiar song structure might help the child to become comfortable with sharing vocalizations. Chants also work well, and the natural progression from speech to singing is often appealing to children. The choice of pitch structure, tempo, rhythmic motifs, or use of harmony will depend on the goals of the session. A circle format is conducive to group vocal improvisation. When the children and grown-ups are seated or standing in a circle, the sound mixes in the center and is available to all the group members. While in the circle, the children can clearly see everyone seated around them. Observing the mouth movements, facial affect, and attending posture of a peer as well as hearing them sing can motivate a child to participate. In child and therapist vocal improvisation, the dyad might benefit from a more informal space arrangement which incorporates movement.

What to observe. Listening carefully when using vocal improvisation is paramount. It is often difficult to hear young children's vocalizations due to low volume, short duration of sounds, and use of nonspecific or scattered pitches. Children's natural pitch is often higher than that of an adult. Some children are particularly sensitive to certain pitches or will only respond to sounds within a certain pitch range. If the child is responding in an engaged manner, their vocalizations might be similar in pitch, duration of sound, timbre, rhythmic patterns, or melodic contour to that of the grown-up. An indication of reciprocity could be a vocal give-and-take, with spaces between sounds or direct imitation. Sometimes a child will repeat intervals or melodic fragments. While this could be improvisatory, it could also be the child's primary way of singing a familiar song. Listening closely to these repeated bits can provide a clue to the inner music that the child is trying to communicate. The therapist should listen for words or word attempts within spontaneous vocal expressions. Pitch matching is a very early developmental skill, so listening for pitch content from the children is important (Trehub, 2003). Listen also for interval use, repeated rhythmic patterns, and melodic contour. Within a group, each child should be assessed for whether vocalizations are within the context of key, meter, tempo, and tessitura of the musical material. Use of consonants, vowels, and sequences of sounds can also give some indication of developmental musical level. Engagement in the group improvisation is important and can be observed through facial presence, postural attention, amount of vocal participation, and facial affect.

Procedures. Vocal improvisation can begin with a sound from either the child or the therapist. The sound can have clear musical components such as pitch or duration or can be a word, a cry, or an exclamation. The therapist then creates a sound that is responsive or related. As the child begins to participate vocally or to attend to the music, the therapist can structure the vocal play through tempo variations, adding measures of musical material, or allowing short periods of silence. Improvisational musical material such as melody or rhythm patterns that is close to a familiar song might allow the children to feel more comfortable and perhaps more willing to share in the singing. In order to elicit a greater range of vocalizations, the therapist might introduce dissonance, tempo, or dynamic changes or interesting musical surprises such as sudden stops, glissando, or crescendo.

Adding functional or social language to vocal improvisation is useful in addressing language and communication goals. Even if the musical language is not attached to meaning, the children will have the opportunity within a motivating experience to practice using words and phrases.

In addition to imitating sounds the children produce, the therapist can use visual referencing or pointing to cue children to attend to a peer or the therapist. As one child sings a vocal response, the therapist can imitate the pitch or timbre of the child and then look toward another group member while repeating the sound or phrase. The therapist can facilitate passing this sound around the group in a kind of vocal ping-pong.

There might be times in group vocal improvisation when every member of the group is joining in the singing. The therapist can heighten the joy of the experience through exaggerated facial affect and big gestures. When the group is fully engaged in this experience, the therapist can choose to use the improvisation to move to a precomposed song or a more structured experience or to embed language or learning concepts.

Since young children's use of melody and pitch is still unformed, the total sound when vocalizing with a group of children might be harmonically chaotic. The therapist will need to choose how or whether to create a harmonic base. This can be done with a thicker sound through use of chords on the piano or guitar or with a more sparse sound using only simple intervals. The open fifth is a good choice for a grounding interval for children and can accommodate major and minor keys as well as modes. It also allows the therapist to direct the improvisation more freely within harmonic flow. If there are other grown-ups in the group, the therapist might want to consider whether or not to add vocal harmony. Sung harmony might add warmth to the auditory environment, or it might overwhelm or confuse the children.

Adaptations. Vocal improvisation can include humming and whistling or other inventive sounds such as popping lips or wiggling the tongue. Children often enjoy this humor. The use of body percussion or harmonic content on marimba, piano, guitar, or bells can increase motivation to explore a greater variety of sounds.

Vocal improvisation and musical gestures make a good pairing. Gestures such as clapping or patting knees can add rhythmic drive and vitality to group vocalizations. Gestures also provide a response choice for children who are not ready for vocalizing. Simple sensory props such as scarves or a light parachute can also enhance the experience.

It was obvious that Mark was alert to all the musical possibilities in the music therapy room. He pointed eagerly toward the bells and the drum, and tugged on the therapist's shirt to lead her in the direction of play. The therapist began to grunt in time to Mark's tugging. They tugged and grunted across the room. Just as they neared the drum, the therapist playfully skittered away with a long glissando on "whee." Mark made a small sound as if to laugh and ran back to the therapist and began tugging again. The therapist grunted with greater rhythmic regularity as she pulled back more from Mark's tugging. Mark made a guttural sound as he pulled back that surprised both of them. The therapist grunted in response with the same timbre of sound. Mark made another sound, and then another. The therapist adjusted her rhythm and frequency of sounds to match Mark's sounds. Soon, they both were grunting and vocally gliding in an improvised vocal dance across the room. Mark seemed to have forgotten all about the instruments as he gleefully joined in singing his new song.

All the grown-ups and children were gathered together facing each other in a tight circle. The song they were singing was the same one they sang every week as a way to gather into a musical group. There were song lyrics of greeting, but more important were the strong melodic pulse and synchronous gestures. As the song ended, one child was either carried away with the musical moment or delayed in singing the final sound. "Hey," she sang all by herself. Everyone looked toward her. "Hey" sang back the therapist in the same general pitch range and intensity. A mom from across the circle sang "hey," happily joining in the musical play. Soon all the children and grown-ups were adding their own sounds to the improvised chorus. The music therapist kept the momentum going through a steady pat on the knees and an occasional interjection of "Hey" when the vocalizations began to thin out. Finally, she raised her arms high, showing the adults that they should all join in with one big and final "Hey." Grown-ups and children alike moved their arms up and sang along together on a final jubilant chorus of "Hey!"

Instrumental Improvisation

Overview. Instrumental improvisation is a process wherein the instrument becomes the object on which the child and therapist or peer initiate a musical relationship. The improvisation can be started by either the therapist or the child and use any object that can make a musical sound. Instruments for early intervention described in the literature include drums, bells, small percussion, keyboards, musical toys, pitched percussion, and specially created equipment. The therapist accepts and responds to the child's sounds, creating a musical structure through melody or rhythm,

Instrumental improvisation can provide the child a chance to experience synchrony, reciprocity, self-expression, and engagement, creating opportunity for attunement and interaction. Instrumental improvisation can also provide a chance for the child to gain self-organization and self-regulation. The therapist guides the improvisation so the child learns to initiate interaction, express feelings, or listen to others. For children with little or no verbal or functional language, improvisation can encourage reciprocity, a building block of communication. Specific objectives might be to increase the number and duration of reciprocal musical exchanges, to explore novel sounds, to create expressive timbres, to imitate rhythmic or melodic patterns, to play in synchrony with another, or to tell a story through instrument use. Group instrument play can be with adults or peers or adults and peers. Instrumental improvisation in a group may be important for children who need to learn and practice social skills, are motivated to observe and model their peers' actions, or need alternate ways to communicate or express themselves. Group instrumental improvisation can also provide an opportunity for the child to initiate interaction, engage in peer-to-peer synchronization or reciprocity, practice self-organization and self-regulation, and experience group cohesion. Suggested goals might be to adjust tempo, meter, or dynamics to match the music of peers; imitate peers' rhythmic or melodic patterns; take turns; initiate musical ideas; or engage in reciprocal musical exchanges with peers.

Children who have extreme auditory, visual, or social difficulties might benefit more from individual child/adult instrumental improvisation than from a group setting. The level of therapy may be augmentative or intensive.

Preparation. All instruments should be thoroughly clean and checked to make sure that they are childproof and child-safe. Children at certain developmental levels will mouth instruments, so check to be sure that instruments contain no toxins. All young children need to explore, so the therapist should examine the equipment and eliminate anything with sharp edges or removable small parts. Children also jump and climb and throw, so instruments must be sturdy and nearly unbreakable. Larger, higher-quality instruments will allow the child to experience better sound and be independent in their explorations without fear of damage.

A wide assortment of instruments should be tried, including percussive sounds such as drums, maracas, eggs, triangles, and cymbals, and pitched sounds such as marimba, xylophone, resonator bells, and horns. Small guitars and toy pianos with good tone can be fun and motivating. Early childhood music sources also carry interesting instruments such as child-size accordions, zithers, and steel drums. Kern and Snell (2007) suggest designs for making and using outdoor instruments. Young children are also motivated by playing a full-size piano alongside the grown-up or strumming along on a guitar.

To allow for the greatest success in playing, the therapist can adapt instruments and mallets that adjust for the child's height, range of motion, grasp, and visual needs; ability to motor plan; and hearing sensitivity. One-handed instruments such as a maraca present a different challenge and experience for the child than a two-handed instrument such as resonator bells. Some children like to or need to sit, while others like to or need to stand. Prepare the room for both events.

The therapist chooses the number of instruments available for the child and decides how to arrange them in the music space depending on the goals of the intervention and the most suitable sound for the child.

When choosing instruments for a group, the therapist needs to be concerned with the auditory environment that is created in group instrument play. Some instruments are loud, some are soft. Depending on instrument choice, one instrument might overwhelm or totally overtake the sound and the improvisation then becomes less musical and perhaps less fulfilling for the group members. It might also make it difficult for the therapist's music to be heard and therefore make it more difficult to facilitate group goals. The therapist can prepare for this through instrument choice or placement.

What to observe. As with vocalization, the therapist should be very familiar with developmental music responses. For children who are very young developmentally, an appropriate response to an instrument might be to lick it or put it in their mouth. Another child might be interested in flicking the jingles on a tambourine. Knowledge of musical responses would indicate if the child's action is developmental or a symptom of the disability. Instruments can present a challenge to children who are not able to engage with objects in a functional manner, such as the child who is fixated on spinning the cymbal instead of playing. While this type of behavior might indicate that instrument play is contraindicated, the method of improvisational instrument play can be designed to musically draw a child toward the music in order to create awareness, interest, engagement, and interaction (Nordoff & Robbins, 2007).

Understanding the dynamics of groups as they relate to young children is critical. The therapist must think about the social, emotional, communication, and cognitive motivation that the improvisation provides for the group as well as for each member. As with adults, children will assume group roles. However, the role the child's music plays in the group might be an indication of disability rather than personality. A child who is unable to inhibit motor movement might play very loud and fast and not be able to attune to a peer's play. The drive to play in this manner might be organic or neurologically driven and may be very different from the internal view a child has of himself. Conversely, a young child with significant physical challenges might only be able to play in a quiet, limited manner, while inside she might have a "rock and roll" sensibility. The music therapist needs to be an objective observer of musical responses and use knowledge of the child's individual needs as well as developmental musical responses in order to discover the meaning behind the manner of a young child's play in an improvisation.

Procedures. The therapist chooses the instruments for optimal therapeutic benefit. Depending on the goal or objective, the instruments might be out and ready to play, or put away where the child would either request to use them (through gestures, words, or printed materials) or independently get them and set the music area for play. Clinical choices the therapist must consider are: Do the child and therapist play on the same instrument or different instruments? Playing on the same instrument can increase intimacy, allow for exploration of boundaries, or help the therapist be close enough to the child for hand-over-hand assistance. Will the therapist model instrument play or teach the child how to play? Both exploration and imitation are learning opportunities for young children. Should the child use a mallet (which is a tool) or use the palm of their hand to play the drum or tambourine? Mallets require grasp and stamina and put distance between the child and the feel of the drumhead. When the child uses their hand on a drum, the sensory input is quite different. Once again, the therapist should practice using all the therapeutic instruments with a detailed and open view of how children at all developmental levels will use them and benefit from their use.

After instrument choice and arrangement, the therapist either initiates play or waits for the child to play. As with vocal improvisation, young children feel more comfortable with repetition and familiarity. The therapist could use a familiar song or chant (re-creative method) to introduce and encourage the beginning of improvisatory play. Children in an instrumental improvisation group might be more engaged and responsive with a foundation provided by a familiar song or musical activity. The therapist can then begin musical play or cue (through word or gesture) for one of the group members to start. In addition to playing and musical support, the therapist can also guide the group through use of facial presence, facial affect, words, or gestures. Instrumental improvisations can focus on one musical element such as rhythm patterns or multiple elements, for instance, dynamics and tempo. A steady rhythm pattern played by the therapist or a group member can provide a foundation for others to experiment with or explore musically. Likewise, a predictable harmonic progression or repeated melody can ground the play and formulate a structure. Bruscia's clinical techniques for improvisation discussed above can provide a practice template.

Listening carefully to the children's sounds and being observant of indications of engagement or withdrawal will help the therapist know when to bring the improvisation to a close. Depending on the goals of the therapy and the developmental level of the child, the therapist may then choose to review the improvisation verbally or move on to another method.

It is important to be aware that young children are often more comfortable imitating than creating. While the therapist might be looking for original musical material, developmentally the child might not be able to formulate a novel response. Seize on any new sounds, motifs, or rhythms and incorporate them in the improvisation. Celebrate each group member's contribution, even if it is a copy of a peer's response.

Adaptations. Instrument improvisation and vocal improvisation methods fit well together. Developmentally, young children are most responsive to the voice, and including vocal play along with instruments can support engagement. Many early childhood music therapists also combine re-creative methods and improvisational play. Familiar songs help add organization to the session and refocus the child if the improvisatory play becomes dysregulated or disorganized. Within the set piece, the therapist can take a "time out" for a few measures of improvisatory play. Using singing along with instrument improvisation also allows the child to hear and use words that might describe the play.

The therapist can also function as a facilitator when the child and a parent or other familiar adult engage in improvisational play. The role of the therapist is to gently guide the grown-up in therapeutic techniques that can enhance the child/adult interaction and relationship. Some children will be ready and eager to be a musical leader. The therapist can support the child by becoming a member of the group and using facial and postural presence toward the "leader" to indicate to the other children to change their focus toward their peer.

Tommy and the music therapist are standing together on a brightly colored mat, with a large floor drum between them. Both are holding mallets high above the surface of the drum. The music therapist waits in anticipation, an eager look on her face. Tommy's mallets come crashing down on the drumhead. He looks toward the therapist, also waiting in anticipation of her play. Back and forth, the two exchange beats. Then the mallet skips off the side of the drum by accident, and creates a rhythmic pattern. The therapist imitates this unexpected sound. Tommy laughs and plays the same pattern. This becomes the new "conversation." But there is one more change in store. Soon, the therapist's patterns overlap with Tommy's and before long they are playing together in synchrony. The tempo gets faster and faster, both beating at the same time. Suddenly the excitement is overwhelming, and Tommy lifts the mallets once again high above the drumhead. Time to start again!

All the children from the four-year-olds' classroom are on the floor seated on or near a very large bass drum. The grown-ups from the classroom are directly behind the children, forming a ring of support. All have hands on or near the drum as the therapist begins a steady beat. Some children begin to play. Some children draw back. Some children put their faces very close to the vibrating surface. The adults continue to lightly tap the drum in a slow tempo. The therapist invites everyone to join in through a familiar sung chant and through her open posture and warm facial affect. The grown-ups encourage all the children to "feel the beat" through singing and gentle touch. The music therapist moves her hands across the drum, using slight articulation of play as she names each of the children through song. The beat goes on, and each attempt at play by the children is supported through rhythmic or timbre matching. One rough-and-tumble young boy starts to beat harder than the other children. His partner across the drum looks up and plays the drum really hard. The two drummers make eye contact and the widening of their eyes shows that there is a sudden and new recognition of another person outside themselves in the music-making.

Musical Movement Improvisation

Overview. Many movements of developmentally young children are spontaneous and unplanned, so it is the therapist who adds improvisational meaning to the child's activity. This is done through many of the same improvisational techniques discussed for instrument play. The child or the therapist initiates a specific movement or movement pattern with or without accompanying music. The therapist then uses the rhythm or contour of the movement to create a meaningful, reciprocal framework. Children who need to develop engagement and reciprocity would benefit from musical movement improvisation. The therapist uses the music to mirror, reflect, repeat, and create context for instinctual movements. Goals might be to initiate or sustain movement in response to music, increase the duration of movements to match the music provided, adjust the tempo or quality of movement to match the music provided, and/or display affect changes to indicate pleasure in movement.

Children who are further along developmentally can use musical movement as way to express themselves, to create, or to organize their thoughts and feelings. These children might learn or model a new movement repertoire in order to match the complexity of their emotions or thinking. The music can support this exploration through use of matching tempo, movement contour, and rhythmic intensity. Goals might include for the client to increase the variety of musical movement repertoire; use musical movement to express a cognitive, emotional, or social idea; use movement to demonstrate problem-solving skills; or display imagination through musical movement.

The music therapist should consult with a movement or physical professional to determine movement restrictions for the child. Some movement patterns should never be used with young children, especially picking a child up by the arms. Excessive spinning is generally contraindicated, although many young children find it gratifying. The level of therapy may be augmentative, intensive, or primary.

Preparation. The music space needs to be carefully set up when using improvisational musical movement so that young children can have freedom to move without concern for injury or danger. A movement area can be delineated using mats or instruments or adult helpers. The therapist should make sure that everything in the environment is childproof and child-safe. If working in a group, make sure that there is enough room for each child to have their own space.

What to observe. Movement patterns, like music responses, can be an observable indication of developmental problems. Developmental movement milestones would be important for the therapist to know. Consulting with a movement therapist or physical therapist might be beneficial. Look for constricted movement, jerkiness, lack of stamina when moving, difficulty or inability to lift arms or legs, loss of balance, lack of congruence with facial affect and movement intensity, and lopsided use of body.

Improvisational movement can add a new dimension of experience for the young child. The freedom to move as communication or expression is an idea that many young children are not able to comprehend, since movement is primarily instinctual. However, the ability to move in a way that is free and joyful can be exhilarating for a child. The therapist looks for affect changes, affirming language or increased attention during musical movement as an indication of the motivation and excitement.

Procedures. The music for improvisational movement can be precomposed or improvised, depending on the goal of therapy. Recorded music can be used, and the therapist can then use musical gestures to engage and motivate the child with the music serving as a support. Improvisation techniques mentioned above are applicable. The therapist might need to model or teach the child new movement patterns to add to their repertoire.

The flow of the session should be similar to what the therapist would use in a music-only session and include opportunities for intensity as well as calm. These states can be created through varying musical material.

Adaptations. New scientific discoveries have found certain brain properties (mirror neurons) that allow a child to experience action and movement on a neurological level even if they are not actually doing the action or movement. Very young children watching movement might be forming similar neural pathways as the child moving. Watching others move can then be an important movement adaptation for the young child who has delayed movement due to orthopedic or physical disability. The therapist can also modify movement to match the ability level of the child, even if it is only an eye blink, a toe tap, or a head sway.

How many times did the teacher call Jack's name during story time? Way too many for both the teacher and for Jack! The story was about making friends, but Jack's attention was too divided to hear, much less understand, any of it. As story time finished, the class moved to the music therapy room. Without speaking, the music therapist began to play a syncopated rhythm on a pair of tone blocks. Jack immediately moved toward her, and his body movements matched the music of the tone blocks in meter, tempo, intensity, and patterns. Jack's classmates eagerly joined in and formed a circle around the music therapist and Jack. The music therapist motioned one child at a time to join Jack in the middle of the circle. Jack grinned at each friend and adjusted his movements to match that of his new buddy. The music therapist shaped the music so that at the end of each duet, the children all joined in singing a song about friendship using the same language from the classroom book.

Guidelines for Re-creative Music Therapy

The collection of music resources in early childhood is extensive. Songs for children and songs sung by children have existed throughout history. Many of them have been passed down from generation to generation and contain cultural and traditional meaning. Humpal (1998) compiled a list of song repertoires of young children as perceived by music therapists as well as music educators and other early childhood professionals. On the top of the list were songs such as "Old MacDonald Had a Farm" and "Twinkle, Twinkle Little Star." There was a significant concurrence from those surveyed on which songs are most widely known to young children. Schwartz (2012) writes on the common musical qualities of popular songs for young children and describes them as repetition, rhyme, relationship, and ratio (p. 7).

The song format is particularly fitting in early childhood and composes a significant portion of re-creative music therapy discussed in the literature. A song, whether vocal or instrumental, has melodic, rhythmic, harmonic, and structural definition that allows the child to repeat, replicate, and internalize the musical material. Since young children learn with repeated experiences, the song as a therapeutic intervention can be critical in a child's developmental growth. Children make music independently, with the therapist or other grown-up, or in a group. Settings for therapy are formal and informal and include institutional, home, or community locations.

In early intervention music therapy literature, precomposed songs used fell into four categories: popular children's songs, traditional and cultural songs, adaptations of children's and traditional songs, and therapist-composed songs. Each category has benefits in early intervention. Popular children's songs are easily accessed by parents and other adults through recordings, making for easy carryover in the home or classroom. The children are exposed to the songs outside of music therapy and so can sing them in more generalized social situations. Traditional or cultural songs provide the therapist with a musical language that the child might have already formulated through early exposure. This musical language could be particular to cultural melodic construction, rhythmic patterns, meter use, harmonic progressions, and lyrics. Singing these songs could assist a child in connecting or relating to their home or community. Adapting familiar children's music takes advantage of the engagement the child has with the music due to exposure or repetition. The therapist then changes or modifies the melodic rhythm, tempo, meter, intent, and, most importantly, language in order to address specific developmental goals. Therapist-created songs are composed with specific and deliberate attention to musical elements in order to engage or motivate the child. The language used in therapist-created songs is often targeted to very specific therapeutic objectives.

The methods discussed below use all the types of song interventions discussed above. The music therapist should carefully consider all possible repertoire when planning for treatment in early intervention. However, it is important that the precomposed songs are not just borrowed from current adult music, but are appropriate for the child at their level of musical development.

Singing Songs

Overview. Independently singing a song means that a child is able to conserve and reproduce an object that has meaning and a level of communicative intent. For a child to sing a song, they must be able to process musical and linguistic information and process and plan how to express that information. They are moved through shared meaning, a desire to interact, or internal motivation to produce parts or the whole of an organized entity. The song, then, becomes an observable extension of the "self." Goals might include initiating favored familiar songs to engage or communicate; sustaining attention and focus through singing entire (or partial) song structures; developing use of language and grammar through melodic intonation and melodic rhythm; developing communicative vocal inflection; physical, emotional, or sensory stimulation; or expressing feelings, thoughts, or concepts through familiar, favored songs

Singing songs in a group appears to be an integrated part of human culture (Levitin, 2008). In the music therapy literature, group singing of learned songs was very prevalent in early childhood treatment (among others: Barrickman, 1989; Braithwaite & Sigafoos, 1998; Geist et al., 2012). Group singing in therapy provides many of the same benefits as group singing in society: peer awareness, group cohesion, a sense of belonging, and a connection to culture or tradition. Group singing also provides the individual with support for their individual efforts and motivation to engage. Singing in a group can mean the child and therapist singing together, two or more peers singing together, child and parent or other grown-up singing together, or larger groups of children or children and adults singing together. Children who benefit from this method include those who need to increase social engagement, reciprocity, social behavioral skills, communication, concept retention, and functional language. Goals might include matching tempo, dynamics, and timbre to the group music; remembering and reproducing learned songs; pairing learned songs with actions or concepts; adjusting singing quality to match the musical, emotional, or social sound of the song; increasing duration and accuracy of learned song material; and demonstrating engagement with the song material and with the action of group participation through song. The method of singing songs in a group meshes well with the legal and regulatory emphasis in early intervention on providing therapeutic services in community-based settings or in the least restrictive environment.

Some young children unerringly reproduce learned songs, including pitch, rhythm and language. This ability is not developmentally based and might be an indication of rigidity and inflexibility such as is seen in the autism spectrum disorders. The rigidity includes an insistence on pitch sameness; an inability to adjust structure, tempo, or dynamics; a focus on melodic rhythm rather than the underlying beat; and an intolerance for mutual or group singing. Use of the improvisational model would better address the goals of interaction and communication that these types of children require. The level of therapy: may be auxiliary, augmentative, or intensive.

Preparation. The song used in the re-creative method can be therapist-chosen or child-selected with consideration of therapeutic intent. The therapist supports the child through mutual singing, harmonic accompaniment, rhythmic grounding, use of recordings, or actively listening to the child. The song can be introduced by the therapist through a musical introduction or through a spoken invitation. The environment of expectation can also be created through musical cues so the child can independently initiate the song. Young children frequently use songs or song fragments while playing with other toys or instruments. The therapist can encourage this initiation of independent singing by supplying favored objects of the child such as dolls, toy cars, or symbolic play sets.

Close proximity or the circle arrangement is very conducive to therapeutic participation. Children can hear and see their peers and/or adults and model their responses or gain motivation from the therapist or others. Selection of songs to sing should be considered from musical, developmental, and therapeutic aims. When working in early childhood, the selection of singing key is very important. Children tend to sing in a higher pitch range, while many grown-ups are more comfortable with lower keys. Since young children need models of engagement, selecting lower keys to ensure that the grown-ups sing along can be an important strategy. With familiar, recorded songs, it might be best to use the same key that the children have previously heard. Therapist-created songs will need to be introduced and repeated to provide an opportunity for the child to become aware of, process, and participate in the novel material.

The therapist can choose to use voice alone; harmonic content on piano, guitar, or other pitched instruments; or a rhythmic foundation through body percussion or instruments. Many music therapists who compose for early intervention begin with a musical response that the child has offered within the therapy session. These responses could be interval use, a rhythmic pattern, a particular pattern, or a word phrase. The therapist then uses this musical material to create a song or instrumental piece that is a reflection, in the therapist's view, of the child. When the composition is used with the child in therapy, the therapist's strategy is to find a common ground of engagement predicated on the child's instinctual musical production.

What to observe. Singing learned songs is a developmental skill. Therapists should be knowledgeable about when and how interval use, melody, rhythmic imitation, meter, and lyric use begin within each developmental level. Young children are rarely able to maintain key structure throughout an entire simple song. Therapists should listen for and support identifying intervals (perhaps use of the minor third or ascending fifth found in many children's songs), melodic rhythm patterns (such as "round and round" from the familiar "Wheels on the Bus" song), repeated words, or approximate melodic contour. While the child's song might not sound fully formed to the untrained ear (such as with musical babble), the music therapist can "put together" the pieces and recognize the child's intent to be a song singer.

There is a great deal of musical information to observe in group singing. The therapist will need to listen for use of pitch, rhythm, and melody from each group member and the group as a whole. Visually observing the child's facial and oral/ motor actions gives an indication of the level of word and language use. Postural attention toward or away from the group can indicate engagement; however, some children have difficulty with processing multiple sensory stimulation and might need to limit their focus on only singing or listening or looking. Therapist facilitation in integrating these actions might be needed for individual group members.

Procedures. Songs can be introduced by the therapist through modeling or elicited from the child through musical cuing, verbal invitation, or active listening. The child will need to hear a song multiple times before being able to sing it alone. The therapist can sing along with the child to begin with and then use the technique of receding to make room for the child to sing alone. If a child is singing songs while engaged in other play such as with toys or instruments, it is often best for the therapist to support this independent singing through encouraging facial affect and active listening.

In early intervention, most children respond to and engage with music more quickly than with spoken language, so it is an effective technique to begin song singing with no verbal introduction. Musical cues could be melodic (singing bits of the song), rhythmic (setting up meter and pattern through body percussion or instruments), or through harmonic progressions. The musical cues allow the children to anticipate a learned song and motor-plan responses through time. Each child will bring differing vocal and musical qualities to group singing, and placement of the children can be a good strategy for using peer modeling or peer motivation.

Young children are just beginning to develop a lexicon of vocal responses, so they might respond to group singing through shouting, screaming, whispering, or shutting down. The child with developmental challenges will need repeated practice with all these vocal responses as well as with pitch and melody in order to have full access to all the vocal possibilities.

Young children generally do not maintain key structure, melodic rhythm, or meter throughout a song. In early intervention, the therapist supports the child by maintaining a consistent melodic, harmonic, and rhythmic organization but does so in a manner that is flexible in overall structure and tempo. This allows the child to enter into the music-making in their own way while still experiencing a musical whole. A strategy used by many music therapists is to leave space at the end of a phrase for the child to vocalize or "fill in the blank." The objective might be for duration of sound, use of related pitch or inflection, or production of the words or phrase of a familiar lyric.

Songs have a defined beginning and ending. When a song is over, the child or therapist can choose to do it again, repeat the experience with created changes, or move to a new song or method.

Adaptations. While the term "singing" has been used, the act of song musicking can be broadened to include whistling, humming, or chanting. For the young child, the line between speech and song is often blurred, so a combination of all of the above might occur.

Some children are limited in their ability to vocalize due to physical abnormalities, stamina, or motor planning. These children can make use of augmentative or alternative communication devices to "sing" where their voices cannot. Consultation or collaboration with a specialist in this area will help the therapist provide the best opportunity for success for the child.

Song singing can be easily combined with other music therapy methods and can be the jumping-off point for improvising vocally or engaging in instrument or movement play. In early childhood, the method of singing songs together should be flexible rather than rigid to allow for the child to have full, creative expression.

Singing familiar songs as a group is a therapeutic method that can be shared by the children in other settings such as in a classroom, at home with parents or siblings, or in a community setting. Song singing can be a comfortable musical expression for many grown-ups, and the music therapist can provide guidance and resources on developmentally and therapeutically effective songs for carryover in home, social, and educational situations. The therapist may provide recordings of song for receptive music listening.

Medical concerns had kept Susan from participating in any type of developmental therapy until she was four years old. A poorly developed vocal mechanism had been repaired, so Susan finally had the ability, but not the know-how, to speak. But in music, her eyes would light up and her body motions would substitute for her lack of voice. In the first few weeks of music therapy, the therapist introduced a song for Susan using the blues progression and song lyrics that described things that Susan did during the day. Soon, Susan began to fill in vowel sounds on the words at the end of each phrase. She would mouth the consonants and keep time by tapping her toes. As the weeks went by, the therapist sang less and less and Susan sang more and more. One day, it happened. The therapist began to play the arpeggiated 7th chord that was the introduction to this now favorite song. Susan began to sing and didn't stop until the whole song was finished.

The playground at the day care center was a busy place, with children on the swings, climbing up the stairs of the playhouse, or sliding down the slide. One boy, though, ran back and forth and back and forth along the fence line. The adults let him be and the other children hardly noticed him at all. Suddenly, the music therapist drove up and carried her bag of tambourines into the play space. She set them on the ground and began to sing in a strong voice, "Sit down and join my circle." The melody was simple and lively; the meter and pulse, strong and steady. As she sang, she held up the tambourines, inviting the children to come and join in. The boy at the fence stopped running and turned to look toward the music. The therapist walked calmly over to him, singing and playing all the way. The words and the melody were familiar. The boy took the therapist's hand and let her lead him to the tambourines and to the music place. The children, one by one, came over and took a tambourine to play. Since the music was so familiar, they were all able to sing along. The grown-ups began to join in. The boy sat down next to another child and took a tambourine. He began to sing, "Sit down and join MY circle."

Instrumental Songs

Overview. As with vocal songs, instrumental songs provide a child with a predictable template in which they can understand, process, and provide a musical response. The therapist engages individuals in a musical experience that incorporates the use of instruments, repetition, and structure that allows for familiarity and opportunity for practice. It also may give a supporting framework in which the child can feel comfortable trying new things with a clear picture of the expectations for response. The child who might benefit most from this method would need assistance in organizing information; preparation and planning for response; motivation to initiate, sustain, or complete an action; or assurance of a secure foundation in which participation will be accepted.

Particular goals for this method are numerous and can be justified for every early childhood developmental level. Some may include starting and stopping play along with selected music; adjusting tempo, meter, dynamics, timbre, or intensity of play to selected music; imitating rhythmic or melodic patterns; engaging in reciprocal pattern play; mutual or joint play; playing in synchrony; responding to a music cue with learned rhythmic or melodic pattern; grading quality of play to match tempo or dynamics; increasing duration of play; independent completion of a musical task; and/or initiation of a musical structure.

The indications for group instrumental songs are similar to those for singing songs in a group. The addition of instruments can add musical complexity and variety as well as opportunity for a wider range of music-based communication. Group instrumental songs can serve children who have a developmental need to increase socialization and reciprocity, generalization of specific skills in a group setting, listening skills, direction-following, anticipation and motor-planning of defined responses, and environmental awareness. Particular goals might be to play learned patterns in a musical structure; to anticipate musical events; to play in synchrony; to adjust tempo, meter, dynamics, or timbre of play to match selected music; to take turns or to wait; to imitate; or to demonstrate satisfaction or pleasure in a group activity.

This method is contraindicated for children who have extreme auditory, visual, or social difficulties and might benefit more from individual child/adult instrumental songs than group songs. The level of therapy may be auxiliary, augmentative, or intensive.

Preparation. Re-creative instrument songs require specific instruments, so the therapist should examine needs and goals of the child prior to selecting the particular song intervention. It is best to set up the instruments in the environment to maximize the opportunity for success, including consideration of safety, placement, ease of use, and quality of sound. Instruments, mallets, and other equipment can be modified or adapted to fit the needs of the individual child.

The therapist should also consider the auditory environment when using group instrumental songs. No instrument should be able to overwhelm the musical structure or intimidate members of the group. Instruments should be selected or positioned so that each group member can have visual as well as auditory cues. Peer-to-peer attention and modeling is an important component.

What to observe. The developmental level of the child will determine the type and quality of their instrumental play. The music therapist in early intervention should be intimately familiar with developmental musical responses throughout the levels. General responses to observe would be how the child interacts with the particular instrument, how responsive their play is to the selected music, how the child communicates with the therapist during instrumental song play, and affect, physical, or communicative indications of pleasure or satisfaction in the experience.

Group instrumental play requires the therapist to be observant of group dynamics. As in group instrumental improvisation, the child's playing might be an indication of physical, neurological, or cognitive difficulties rather than personal intent. Group instrument songs are a great place for each child as a member of a group to practice self-organization, self-regulation, group reciprocity, and group responsibility. General areas of observation should include how the child interacts with their instrument, how the child responds to the demands of the selected music, how the child attends to and reacts to the music of their peers, how the child integrates the expectations of the therapist into their play, and how the child demonstrates affective or emotional connection to the group activity .

Procedures. When first introducing a song, the instruments can be presented to the child to play at the identified moment in the music. The therapist could also cover the instrument with their hand until the specific time for play. Other strategies might include setting instruments in the order in which they are to be played, using gestures or pointing to cue the child when to play, using visual symbols such as picture cards to cue responses, using song lyrics to explain directions, and modeling the actions for the child. Some children will require hand-over-hand assistance to play or produce the expected responses; however, the therapist fades this level of prompt as the child gains skill.

The therapist can set up and direct instrumental songs or encourage the children to get and set up their own instruments. Repetition of instrument songs will help a child to anticipate, learn, and produce expected responses. Strategies for success could include adjusting the tempo of the song across time or within the song to allow for individual responses; using gestures or pointing cues to show a child when and how to play; using song lyrics, verbal, visual, or picture cues to help children know when and how to play; keeping the duration of the songs short; pairing adults with children to assist in play; pairing peers to assist in play; or using hand-over-hand assistance to cue.

Instrumental songs in early intervention most often focus on learning, remembering, and reproducing simple rhythmic or melodic patterns. Some use sequencing of instruments either by one child or by several children. Instruments are generally easy to understand and use simple cause-and effect thinking, such as one mallet strike, one sound. Pitch changes are usually supported through spatial placement, as in a marimba or the piano. Instruments needing blowing to sound, such as the Nordoff/Robbins reed horns, are commonly set up to make only one pitched sound. The therapist can use rhythmic, harmonic, or melodic accompaniment to incorporate the instrument sounds into a meaningful musical composition.

Adaptations. Instrumental songs are a good lead-in to instrument improvisation. These two methods can and should flow easily back and forth in early intervention practice.

Technology is available to provide instrument experiences (sound and visuals) that mimic real instruments. Substituting virtual instruments for real ones might be indicated if a child has significant physical limitations. Some young children are particularly drawn to technology, and use of virtual instruments might create a level of engagement in song play that could lead to engagement with real instruments. New devices have been created that are not substitutes, but are unique and distinctive instruments. These new instruments present a wealth of opportunities for young children who will be part of the generation that integrates personal technology into every facet of life. Music therapists should continue to educate themselves in these advances and use their creativity and flexibility to incorporate them into music therapy interventions.

Group instrumental songs are also an excellent method to share with family members and other adults in a child's life. The children can replicate the group experience in different settings to help generalize their skills. Many music therapists have used group instrumental activities to support cognitive skills or academic curriculum in early intervention music therapy (among others: Geist et al., 2012; Register, 2001). Consulting or collaborating with these education professionals can benefit the overall development of the child.

Rachel loved being with the music therapist and loved being in music. She loved it so much that she only wanted to play her one favorite song in just the way she had always played it. One week, the therapist moved the drum over just slightly and put a large cymbal down right near it. Rachel began to sing and play her favorite song, but at the end, the music therapist suddenly stopped the music and looked at Rachel. The therapist turned back to the piano and played a full dominant chord with her left hand. With her right hand, the therapist picked up the cymbal and "offered" it for Rachel to play as the end sound instead of the drum. Rachel played once as the therapist sounded the tonic chord. The next week, the cymbal was there, but also a set of hanging wind chimes. The therapist played Rachel's now familiar song with the drum and cymbal, but instead of stopping, she added eight new bars of music in a very different mode and feel. She helped Rachel play the wind chimes along with this new music. When Rachel came to music the following week, she went to the corner of the music room and set up the drum and the cymbal and the wind chimes. Then she looked at the music therapist and said, "I'm ready now."

James and Tony and Raymond all came to music together. All three boys enjoyed playing the instruments. All three boys did not like waiting their turn to play the instruments. In their classroom, the boys were unable to be in the same toy center, since they grabbed from each other and hit when they did not get what they wanted. The classroom staff was skeptical of how music could help them with their social behavior. The music therapist joined the boys in small chairs set in a circle. She began to pat her knees in a very precise and steady rhythm. Then she began to sing a song about taking turns. The words and melody and rhythm were very matter-of-fact. Soon she added a tambourine beat while the boys tapped along on their knees. As the boys began to sing along, the therapist held out the tambourine in front of each boy in turn, remaining in front of them only long enough for a single beat of the rhythm. As they sang it through again and again, the boys caught on to beating the instrument in sequence. Before long, the therapist simply held the tambourine in the center of the circle and the boys beat in order, with only the music to guide them. The next week, she gave each boy his own instrument, but continued to sing the same, familiar turn-taking song. Without question, the boys each played one time on the beat in order around the circle.

Structured Movement Songs

Overview. Structured movement songs are ubiquitous in early childhood music. Music and movement is intertwined so tightly in early childhood music that it is difficult to separate the two (Metz, 1989). All children can benefit from structured movement songs. Early intervention movement songs provide an opportunity for multiple types of expression for young children. Young children particularly like to move along with an adult. Bouncing, jumping, swaying, and bumping with a grown-up while singing is a great movement activity that encourages awareness, engagement, and reciprocity. Movement, supported by music, can be a powerful combination for the child who is challenged developmentally. Structuring movement through music does not mean limiting responses, but allows for modeling, repetition, practice, auditory reinforcement of action, and opportunity for self-organization and self-regulation. The goals are almost too many to count but could incorporate starting and stopping movement with selected music; adjusting tempo, intensity, or rhythmic feel of movement along with the selected music; exploring various movement actions along with the music; following directions for movement; moving with a peer partner; imitating movements of peer or adult; suggesting movements for incorporation into the song; using language to describe movement; anticipating movement expected by the song; and demonstrating satisfaction or pleasure in being involved in the music movement experience.

Consult with family or staff to make sure the child has no movement restrictions. A new concern has been increasing in early intervention over very young children with asthma or breathing concerns. Monitor children's facial affect, breathing, and skin tone carefully to intervene or stop the movement intervention if there is a risk of breathing complications. The level of therapy may be auxiliary, augmentative, or intensive.

Preparation. Structured movement songs can be in large as well as small environments. Check to make sure that all required movements can be done safely, while allowing individual room. Children can lie or sit on the floor or be in a chair or on other movement equipment such as playground equipment. There are many opportunities outside of a dedicated music space for therapeutic movement songs, including on the playground.

The therapist carefully selects songs and musical material that support and enhance the desired movement or sequence of movements. Explore all the different types of movement as they connect to music. Duple meter is great for running; 6/8 is a jumping sound; 3/4 can be for rocking or swaying. 5/8 or 7/8 provide an opportunity for uneven duration of motions and can help to strengthen attention or muscle tone. Harmonic or melodic elements can create a mood or atmosphere that can help the children to put learned movement patterns into a larger world context.

What to observe. Movement patterns, like music, develop sequentially in early childhood. Consult with a movement therapist or physical therapist for help in knowing which movement activities are developmentally appropriate for the child. Many children will gain just by watching movement. The supporting music can help suggest movement vocabulary for the child. Be alert to issues of stamina in young children.

Procedures. Although movement is instinctual for young children, they will generally require modeling of movement or movement sequences within a structured format. The supporting music can be provided with rhythmic percussion, voice only, or harmonic progressions, or through recorded music. Exaggerated actions and affect often help a child to attempt new motions. As with other methods, the therapist might want to use a receding technique to encourage greater movement initiation and independence in the children. Greater focus on independence can sometimes lead to dysregulation. This is frequently a challenge for children, but structured movement songs are designed in part to assist a child with self-regulation and self-organization. If the child or group begins to become dysregulated, the most effective intervention is to use the music to change the musical movement signals. This can be done through slowing the tempo, changing meters, adjusting timbre, or beginning a new intervention. If the children tire, the therapist might also want to change the music or change the movement expectations.

Adaptations. As with instrumental play, children can feel and experience movement in many ways—through technology, sensory props such as scarves, or vocal or instrumental play. Movement experiences can translate wonderfully into instrumental song play. Running or jumping on the drum by playing eighth notes is almost as much fun as actually running.

Christopher and his mom spent a lot of their time together. Christopher needed help to do almost everything, and his mom was the one who had to provide all the help. While Mom seemed happy to do this, it was obvious that she rarely had the opportunity to just play and have fun with her son. When the other mothers were moving easily with their children in an improvised way, Christopher's mother just held his hand and watched. The following session, the music therapist asked Mom to put Christopher on her lap and to imitate the movement actions of a new song. As the therapist sang, she modeled how to wrap her arms around Christopher. Mom complied. Then the song called for Mom to sway back and forth with her son. Mom complied. Christopher smiled. The third phrase told Mom to bounce Christopher on her knee. Mom did, and Christopher giggled. At the very end, the therapist tumbled onto the floor with a silly, sung glissando. Mom and Christopher followed. Suddenly, Mom and son were face-to-face in a huge hug. The therapist said "Let's do it again!," and Christopher and his mom were the first ones to start singing and moving.

Guidelines for Compositional Music Therapy

Song or instrumental composition in therapy generally indicates a desire or thought process on the part of the client to create a musical product that can be replicated and reviewed or shared. Thinking about external structures such as a musical composition means that there must be a level of future intent, planning, and execution. This type of thinking is generally not found in children under five, especially those who are developmentally delayed. That is perhaps the reason why compositional music therapy as a method does not figure much, if at all, within the early intervention music therapy literature.

There are, though, several aspects of compositional music therapy that music therapists employ. However, the focus is therapist-generated rather than child-generated.

Song Lyric Substitution

Overview. For young children with developmental issues, thinking of and suggesting language to fill in or replace familiar song language can be challenging. However, this method can foster cognitive and processing skills and encourage creativity. The impetus for becoming involved in this intervention comes from the therapist's therapeutic and developmental goals. It is generally not motivated by a child's need or plan for a unique and personal musical outcome. Geist et al. (2008) used song language substitution to increase social greetings and support literacy. Song lyric substitution might also be designed to increase use of novel language, to provide an opportunity for expression, and to encourage problem-solving and creativity. The level of therapy may be auxiliary, augmentative, or intensive.

Preparation. In early intervention, the therapist will most often create or adapt a musical structure with enough flexibility for the child to contribute new song lyrics. Prior to beginning, the therapist determines the melodic, rhythmic, and structural format of the song. Lyrics allow for multiple responses so that every child's input can be incorporated. For children with limited speech, the therapist might have drawing materials or assistive technology available.

What to observe. Song lyric substitution relies on active participation from the child, including singing, speaking, or drawing the new lyrics. However, the therapist should be alert to behaviors that indicate that a child is thinking or processing a response and give time or space within the music for the child to independently answer.

Procedures. The therapist composes or adapts a song that has lyric content that is appropriate to the developmental level and needs of the child. Harmonic, melodic, or rhythmic elements should create a musical atmosphere that matches or enhances the concepts or themes chosen. For instance, to encourage lyric substitution about emotions, the therapist might change the mode of the melody to minor. The therapist will most often introduce the song either through words or by beginning to sing or play. The child will need to understand the expectation for adding lyrics. The therapist can do this through verbal directions or through using musical pauses and facial affect to indicate that they will wait for the child.
The words offered are then incorporated into the melody using similar melodic rhythm and melodic contour. The therapist can also suggest words or ideas and help make the cognitive, social, or emotional connection from the music to the child's new words and ideas. Language use can be reinforced by using melody and rhythm to support developmental syntax and grammar.

Adaptations. The goals for song lyric substitution can be bolstered by combining the music with other artistic expression such as movement, drawing, or painting. The therapist can collaborate or consult with educators or other arts therapists on developmentally appropriate methods. Many children are further engaged in song lyric substitution through making a recording of the new composition. The recording could be shared with family members or peers or in the community. Song lyric substitution might also be a way to ease a child into verbal processing of ideas or issues. Music therapists who are not trained or comfortable in verbal therapy can consult with other mental health professionals.

WORKING WITH CAREGIVERS

Discussion of the needs of children in early intervention requires consideration of the child as part of the larger circle of people surrounding the child. Young children are fundamentally dependent upon an adult for most, if not all, of their needs. Music therapists may work from the perspective of treating the child, the family, or the relationship between the child and the adults in their world. Jonsdottir (2002) aligns with the ideas of Daniel Stern (1995) in suggesting that when designing clinical treatment in early intervention, the client is not the child itself, but the relationship between the child and its caregivers (p. 7). Oldfield (2006, 2008) writes extensively about early childhood music therapy that revolves around the parent/child connection as it relates to the child's emotional and social needs. Creating music therapy methods requires that the therapist address the complexity of the child's place in the web of grown-ups that surrounds them. Sharing music therapy strategies with others help to ensure generalization, opportunity for practice, and retention of skills for the child. Geist et al. (2008), Humpal (1991), Kern and Aldridge (2006) and Kern and Snell (2007), among others, advocate for cotreatment, collaboration, and consultation as best practice in early intervention.

The child's family, and particularly the parent, is the cornerstone of external resources for many children in early intervention. Even parents who are struggling to accept and nurture their young child with special needs will often find a way to satisfy the basic physiological and safety needs of their child. Abad and Edwards (2004) concentrated on interventions that strengthen the parent/child relationship in at-risk families by extending the repertoire of parenting skills and increasing the opportunity for interactive play. Their program, *Sing and Grow,* works toward prevention rather than treatment. Methods include recorded songs for listening as well as interactive music therapy groups. Within the groups, familiar and composed children's songs and instrument play were used, and the therapist's strategies modeled "... face-to-face interactions, hand-over-hand facilitation, and coactive use of instruments ..." (p. 3). The process also uses close physical proximity, along with the parent singing to the child.

Music therapists have written extensively about providing music therapy interventions within the context of early childhood, community-based, parent/child groups (Abad & Oldfield, 2006; Schwartz, 2009, 2011; Standley et al., 2009; Walworth, 2009a, 2009b; Warren & Nugent, 2010). The goals and music therapy methods used are remarkably similar, with an emphasis on unaccompanied singing, use of traditional and familiar children's tunes, and incorporation of precomposed songs and improvised songs for singing and for instrument/movement experiences. In addition, the use of routine and structure both within sessions and across sessions was highlighted. Oldfield (2006) includes a period of adult-directed information followed by a greeting song, mutual instrument play, opportunity for child or adult to lead the group, action song, ending song, and a chance to review the session with the parents (pp. 100–102). Abad's and Edwards' *Sing and Grow* program (2004) follows a structure that includes a hello song, action and nursery songs, movement songs and games, instrumental play, quiet music, and a good-bye song. Warren and Nugent's program (2010), *Music Connections,* follows a schedule according to the needs of the child but includes well-known songs or songs composed for the child, instrumental play, use of sensory props, and relaxation techniques. In her program *My Grownup and Me*, Schwartz (2009, 2012) categorized music therapy methods by identifying the function of the music: toy play and socialization using embedded songs, transition songs to signal changes, gathering songs for bringing the group together, bonding songs to encourage dyad interaction, movement songs to encourage independence and expression, connections songs for mutual play, book songs to support early literacy, and good-bye songs.

Goals for the music therapy interventions are to increase positive parent/child interactions, to increase the child's developmental skills, to provide an opportunity for peer-to-peer modeling and interaction, and to provide a venue to disseminate information and demonstrate parenting techniques to families. The main intervention used in each group includes using toy play, movement, sensory experiences, play-acting, and book reading in addition to or in conjunction with music.

Research Evidence

The research literature in early intervention music therapy has primarily focused on providing general evidence of outcomes rather than comparing music therapy methods. Indeed, it is sometimes difficult to determine exactly which methods were used and how interventions were chosen in light of the individual needs and goals of the child. Often, multiple methods were put in place during study conditions. Theoretical orientation, organizational requirements, and the clinical expertise of the therapist appear to factor into the decision on which therapeutic method is chosen in many cases.

Synthesizing early intervention methods under the four categories—receptive, improvisational, re-creative, and compositional—points in the direction of seeing commonalities in practice across varied settings and theoretical underpinnings. For instance, improvisational methods were reported extensively in practice centered on family-focused interactive parent/child music therapy, but was also reported as a natural extension of play in early childhood music therapy across the board. Best practices in early childhood show that play is the way that children learn, so the improvisational method as a play-based equivalent is a natural fit.

In almost every description of early intervention music therapy, re-creative methods were incorporated as a significant element in treatment. Many clinicians compose songs specific to the individual child or group of children, and those songs comprise their primary clinical intervention. Young children require familiarity, repeated experiences, and opportunity for practice in order for development to happen. Re-creative music methods support these three elements of early growth and might suggest why music therapists from all orientations report its frequent use.

Re-creative Methods

The greatest amount of research has been conducted using re-creative music. This is perhaps due to the seemingly universal use of this method in early childhood music therapy. The re-creative method allows the music therapist to provide young children with familiarity, repetition, and practice. In research and clinical work, this method has been shown to be effective and helpful in reaching certain goals. Humpal (1991) sought to implement successful socialization of typical and nontypical preschool children through participation in group music activities, particularly singing, playing instruments, and movement. Basing her study on prior research, she showed that increases in duration of social play using a combination of re-creative and musical play (improvised) methods targeting social contact resulted in increased interaction among the children after music therapy interventions.

A 1998 study by Braithwaite and Sigafoos reported increased appropriate social communication responses for young children with developmental disabilities when embedding social opportunities in song. The song interventions used in this study were precomposed and sung by the therapist. The children responded with musical gestures, vocalization, or word attempts. Kern and others (2001, 2006) used innovative outdoor instruments and created songs to encourage social interaction, meaningful play, and engagement with peers on the playground. The work showed that the mere presence of instruments on the playground was not sufficient to address these goals and that it was the active presence of therapist-directed music along with the musical opportunities presented by the instruments that elicited the children to interact and engage. A study by Pasiali (2004) with slightly older children with autism supported the notion that young children with autism tended to follow directions better when the directions were embedded in song lyrics. Kern et al. (2007) in a similar case examination using embedded songs, states: "Results indicated that familiar and sung materials promote greater learning than unfamiliar songs or spoken words" (p. 49).

Register and Humpal (2007) studied and found support for created songs designed and used to help in making easier transitions for children and staff alike in inclusive preschool classrooms. Support for using re-created songs in early intervention also comes from the music and brain research. Trollinger (2010) writes, "Musically, the immersion approach of teaching songs works the same way: The more children hear the songs, the more they will imprint the melody and words in their memories" (p. 21). While the aim of this research was not therapeutic, the idea is one that can be translated to music therapy in early intervention—the more young children hear, sing, and play a song, the more they will integrate both music and words into their memory and incorporate it into their development.

Improvisational Methods

Improvisation methods also have a body of supporting research in music therapy. The concept of improvisation is closely aligned in the literature with musical play, which is viewed as a developmentally appropriate practice offering child-directed, child-centered singing, movement, and instrument play. Goals for choosing this method tended to be relationship-based and included engagement, attachment, and reciprocity. Gross et al. (2010) used instrument and vocal improvisation to study the effects of music therapy for young children with speech impairments. Their findings show that isolated aspects of speech development within music therapy were not as influenced by the music as were the larger communicative building blocks of spoken communication such as relationship-building and prosody. Kim et al. (2008, 2009) specifically looked at improvisational music therapy methods for young children with autism. The studies were particularly interested in joint attention and emotional, motivational, and interpersonal responsiveness of the children while engaged in instrument and vocal play. The landmark 2008 study indicated that improvisational music therapy was more effective than nonmusic toy play in facilitating joint attention and nonverbal communication in young children with autism. The 2009 study determined that young children with autism participating in improvisational music therapy demonstrated greater "joy," "emotional synchronicity," and initiation of engagement than when involved in toy play. In addition, the researchers found greater positive (compliant) responses from the children in music as opposed to toy play.

The researchers in these and additional studies with older children stress the importance of the improvisational method in providing the children with flexibility as well as stability in creating relationships. In reviewing current brain research and music, Flohr (2010) reported that the brain is more active during improvising music than during reproducing music. The improvisational method of music therapy gives early intervention clinicians the opportunity to engage the child in musical play. The play-based interventions allow for child-centered, child-directed reciprocity while being able to move freely back and forth between a comfortable, familiar musical outline and an engaging musical give-and-take.

Improvisational methods, re-creative methods, and child-directed singing blend and weave within most of the early childhood literature. The efficacy of providing these methods in early intervention music therapy is supported through several important outcome studies. Allgood (2005) looked at how parents of young children perceived family-centered music therapy groups for young children with autism. The groups used mixed methods of composed songs, repetitive format, and improvisation. In her naturalistic inquiry, she states that "[a]s a group, these people experienced transformation" (p. 98). Nicholson et al. (2008, 2010) looked at the *Sing and Grow* program and found a high degree of parent satisfaction with the program across multiple sites. There was a noted improvement in parenting behaviors and child outcomes. Walworth (2009a) showed positive effects of social behaviors for young children attending parent/child developmental music therapy groups. She states: "This study confirms that infants 6–24 months old attending only three group developmental music therapy sessions engaged in significantly more social toy play behaviors than infants matched for developmental age not attending music sessions" (p. 50). De l'Etoile (2001) looked at training child care personnel to carry over music therapy techniques and found that this type of music facilitation resulted in positive outcomes.

Wigram and Gold (2005) sum up the flow of improvisational and re-creative methods: "The structure and predictability found in music assist in reciprocal interaction, from which tolerance, flexibility, and social engagement to build relationships emerge, relying on a systematic approach to promote appropriate, meaningful interpersonal responses" (p. 535).

Summary and Conclusions

Music therapy in early intervention is a dynamic area of practice that has unique emphasis on the healthy development of the child and a focus toward prevention of delay or disability. The clinical practice also requires an acceptance of the critical importance of the child's family and a willingness to include the parents and extended family in therapy and treatment planning, provision and carryover. The nature of young children also requires the music therapist to thoroughly understand all facets of early development, including music, and to adjust for developmentally appropriate practice. This includes an emphasis on providing services in naturalistic or community settings and integration in typical activities alongside peers.

Music therapy methods in early intervention as seen in both research and practice tend to be used flexibly and in a blended, intertwined manner. The importance of re-creative methods supports the young child's need for repetition, familiarity, and practice. Improvisational methods mirror the play of young children and are important in providing for flexibility within stability. Receptive methods reflect the need of young children for adult assistance and nurturing.

Early childhood is a time of change, of anticipation, and of growth. Music and music therapy methods have the flexibility to adjust easily to change, provide the foundation to continually support the anticipation of forward momentum, and give the range of experiences that encourage the individual growth of each and every child.

References

Abad, V., & Edwards, J. (2004). Strengthening families: A role for music therapy in contributing to family centered care. *Australian Journal of Music Therapy, 15,* 3-17.

Allgood, N. (2005). Parents' perceptions of family-based group music therapy for children with autism spectrum disorder. *Music Therapy Perspectives, 23*(2), 92–99.

Allgood, N. (2006). Collaboration: Being a team player. In M. Humpal & C. Colwell (Eds.), *Effective clinical practice in music therapy: Early childhood and school age educational settings* (pp. 110–119). Silver Spring, MD: American Music Therapy Association.

Bargiel, M. (2004). Lullabies and play songs: Theoretical considerations for an early attachment music therapy intervention through parental singing for developmentally at-risk infants. *Voices: A World Forum for Music Therapy, 4*(1). Retrieved from https://normt.uib.no/index.php/voices/article/viewArticle/149/125

Barrickman, J. (1989). A developmental music therapy approach for preschool hospitalized children. *Music Therapy Perspectives, 7,* 10-16.

Bower, J., & Shoemark, H. (2009). Music therapy to promote interpersonal interactions in early paediatric neurorehabilitation. *Australian Journal of Music Therapy, 20,* 59–75.

Bowlby, J. (1969). *Attachment: Attachment and loss: Vol. 1.* New York, NY: Basic Books.

Braithwaite, M., & Sigafoos, J. (1998). Effects of social versus musical antecedents on communication responsiveness in five children with developmental disabilities. *Journal of Music Therapy, 35*(2), 88–104.
Briggs, C. A. (1991). A model for understanding musical development. *Music Therapy, 10*(1), 1–21.
Briggs, C. A., & Bruscia, K. (1985). *Developmental models for understanding musical behavior*. Paper presented at the Joint Conference on the Creative Arts Therapies, National Coalition of Arts Therapy Associations, New York.
Bruscia, K. E. (1987). *Improvisational models of music therapy*. Springfield, IL: Charles C. Thomas.
Bruscia, K. E. (1998). *Defining music therapy*. (2nd ed.). Gilsum, NH: Barcelona Publishers.
Cevasco, A. M. (2008). The effects of mothers' singing on full-term and preterm infants and maternal emotional responses. *Journal of Music Therapy, 45*(3), 273–306.
Copple, C., & Bredekamp, S. (Eds.). (2009). *Developmentally appropriate practice in early childhood programs*. Washington, DC: NAEYC.
DEC/NAEYC. (2009). *Joint Position Statement of the DEC and NAEYC*. Washington, DC: NAEYC.
de l'Etoile, S. K. (2001). An in-service training program in music for child-care personnel working with infants and toddlers. *Journal of Research in Music Education, 49*(6), 6–20.
de l'Etoile, S. K. (2006). Infant-directed singing: A theory for clinical intervention. *Music Therapy Perspectives, 24*(1), 22–29.
Drake, T. (2008). Back to basics: Community-based music therapy for vulnerable young children and their parents. In A. Oldfield & C. Flower (Eds.), *Music therapy with children and their families* (pp. 37–51). Philadelphia, PA: Jessica Kingsley.
Drieschner, K., & Pioch, A. (2002). Therapeutic methods of experienced music therapists as a function of the kind of clients and goals of therapy. *Music Therapy Today*, 1-17. Retrieved from http://www.wfmt.info/Musictherapyworld/startup/MTT2000-3.pdf
Fish, E. (2002). The benefits of early intervention. *Stronger Families Learning Exchange Bulletin, 2*, 8–11. www.aifs.gov.
Flohr, J. (2010). Best practices for young children's music education: Guidance from brain research. *General Music Today, 23*(2), 13–19.
Gadberry, A. L. (2011). Augmentative and alternative communication in music therapy for children with autism spectrum disorder. *Imagine: Early Childhood Music Therapy Newsletter, 2*(1), 40-43.
Geist, K., Geist, E., & Kuznik, K. (2012). The patterns of music: Learning mathematics through beat, rhythm and melody. *Young Children, 67*(1), 74–79.
Geist, K., McCarthy, J., Rodgers-Smith, A., & Porter, J. (2008). Integrating music therapy services and speech-language therapy services for children with severe communication impairments: A co-treatment model. *Journal of Instructional Psychology, 35*(4), 311-316.
Gooding, L. (2010). Using music therapy protocols in the treatment of premature infants: An introduction to current practices. *The Arts in Psychotherapy, 37*(3), 211–214.
Gooding, L., & Standley, J. (2011). Musical development and learning characteristics of students: A compilation of key points from the research literature organized by age. *Applications of Research in Music Education, 30*(1), 32–45.
Gordon, E. E. (2003). *A music learning theory for newborn and young children*. Chicago, IL: GIA Publications, Inc. (Originally published 1997).
Gross, W., Linden, U., & Ostermann, T. (2010). Effects of music therapy in the treatment of children with delayed speech development: Results of a pilot study. *Complementary and Alternative Medicine*, 39. http://www.biomedcentral.com/1472-6882/10/39.
Hamlett, K., & Mackenzie, J. (2005). The music together program: Addressing the needs of "well" families with young children. *Australian Journal of Music Therapy, 16*, 43-59.

Humpal, M. (1991). The effects of an integrated early childhood music program on social interaction among children with handicaps and their typical peers. *Journal of Music Therapy, 28*(3), 161–177.

Humpal, M. (1998). Song repertoire of young children. *Music Therapy Perspectives, 16,* 37–42.

Humpal,M. & Colwell, C. (Eds.) (2006). *Effective clinical practice in music therapy: Early childhood and school age educational settings.* Silver Spring, MD: American Music Therapy Association.

Humpal, M. E., & Tweedle, R. (2006). Learning through play: A method for reaching young children. In M. Humpal & C. Colwell (Eds.), *Effective clinical practice in music therapy: Early childhood and school age educational settings* (pp.153–173). Silver Spring, MD: American Music Therapy Association.

Ilari, B., & Sundara, M. (2009). Music listening preferences in early life: Infants' responses to accompanied versus unaccompanied singing. *Journal of Research in Music Education, 56*(4), 357–369.

Individuals with Disabilities Education Improvement Act of 2004, 34 CFR §300.34. (2004). PL 108–446, Title 20 United States Code, Section 1400 ed. seq.

Jonsdottir, V. (2002). Musicking in early intervention. *Voices: A World Forum for Music Therapy, 2*(2). Retrieved from https://normt.uib.no/index.php/voices/article/view/86/68

Kaplan, R. S. (2006). Step by step: A hierarchical approach to group music therapy intervention in preschool settings. In M. Humpal & C. Colwell (Eds.), *Effective clinical practice in music therapy: Early childhood and school age educational settings* (pp. 97–109). Silver Spring, MD: American Music Therapy Association.

Kenney, S. (2008). Birth to six: Music behaviors and how to nurture them. *General Music Today, 22,* 32-34. doi:10.1177/1048371308323033

Kern, P. (2004). Making friends in music: Including children with autism in an interactive play setting. *Music Therapy Today, 5*(4), 1–43.

Kern, P., & Aldridge, D. (2006). Using embedded music therapy interventions to support outdoor play of young children with autism in an inclusive community-based child care program. *Journal of Music Therapy, 43*(4), 270–294.

Kern, P., & Snell, A. M. (2007). *Volume 1 songbook: Songs & laughter on the playground.* Santa Barbara, CA: De La Vista.

Kern, P., Wakeford, L., & Aldridge, D. (2007). Improving the performance of a young child with autism during self-care tasks using embedded song interventions: A case study. *Music Therapy Perspectives, 25*(1), 43–51.

Kern, P., & Wolery, M. (2001). Participation of a preschooler with visual impairments on the playground: Effects of musical adaptations and staff development. *Journal of Music Therapy, 38*(2), 149–164.

Kern, P., Wolery, M., & Aldridge, D. (2007). Use of songs to promote independence in morning greeting routines for young children with autism. *Journal of Autism and Developmental Disorders, 37*(7), 1264–1271.

Kim, J., Wigram, T. & Gold, C. (2008). The effects of improvisational music therapy on joint attention behaviors of autistic children: A randomized controlled study. *Journal of Autism and Developmental Disorders, 38*(9), 1758–1766.

Kim, J., Wigram, T., & Gold, C. (2009). Emotional, motivational and interpersonal responsiveness of children with autism in improvisational music therapy. *Autism, 13*(4), 389-409.

LaGasse, B. (2011). Research snapshot 2011: Music and early childhood development. *Imagine: Early childhood music therapy newsletter, 2*(1), 28-30. Silver Spring, MD: American Music Therapy Association.

Levitin, D. J., (2008). *The world in six songs: How the musical brain created human nature.* New York, NY: Penguin Group.

Liberatore, A. M., & Layman, D. L. (1999). *The Cleveland music therapy assessment of infants and toddlers: A practical guide to assessing and developing intervention strategies.* Cleveland, OH: The Cleveland Music School Settlement.

Luce, D. W. (2004). Music learning theory and audiation: Implications for music therapy clinical practice. *Music Therapy Perspectives, 22*(1), 26–33.

Magee, W. L., Baker, F., Daveson, B., Kennelly, J., Leung, M., & Tamplin, J. (2011). Music therapy methods with children, adolescents, and adults with severe neurobehavioral disorders due to brain injury. *Music Therapy Perspectives, 29*(1), 5–13

Maslow, A. H. (1943). A theory of human motivation. *Psychological Review, 50*(4), 370–396.

McGuire, K. M. (2001). The use of music on Barney and Friends: Implications for music therapy practice and research. *Journal of Music Therapy, 38*(2), 114–148.

MENC. *The K–12 national standards, pre-K standards and what they mean to music educators.* Retrieved May, 2012, from www.menc.org/resources

Metz, E. (1989). Movement as a musical response among preschool children. *Journal of Research in Music Education, 37,* 48-60.

Morris, I. B. (2010). Music therapy and social work: Working together in friendship club. *Imagine: Early Childhood Music Therapy Newsletter, 1*(1), 56-57. Silver Spring, MD: American Music Therapy Association.

Mosca. L., DiFranco, G., & Moselli, B. (2004). Music therapy for three hundred three-year-old children. *Music Therapy Today, 6*(4), 1200–1205.

NAEYC. (2009). *Developmentally appropriate practice in early childhood programs serving children from birth through age 8. Retrieved from* www.naeyc.org

Nicholson, J. M., Berthelsen, D., Abad, V., Williams, K., & Bradley, J. (2008). Impact of music therapy to promote positive parenting and child development. *Journal of Health Psychology, 13*(2), 226-238.

Nicholson, J. M., Berthelsen, D., Abad, V., & Williams, K. (2010). National study of an early parenting intervention: Implementation differences on parent and child outcomes. *Society for Prevention Research, 11,* 360–370.

Nordoff, P., & Robbins, C. (2007). *Creative music therapy: A guide to fostering clinical musicianship.* Gilsum, NH: Barcelona Publishers.

Oldfield, A. (2006). *Interactive music therapy, a positive approach: Music therapy at a child development centre.* Philadelphia, PA: Jessica Kingsley.

Oldfield, A. (2007). *Interactive music therapy in child and family psychiatry: Clinical practice, research and teaching.* Philadelphia, PA: Jessica Kingsley.

Oldfield, A. (2008). Providing support and working in partnership: Music therapy with pre-school children and their parents at a child development centre. In A. Oldfield & C. Flower (Eds.), *Music therapy with children and their families* (pp. 19–36). Philadelphia, PA: Jessica Kingsley.

Oldfield, A., Bunce, L., & Adams, M. (2003). An investigation into short-term music therapy with mothers and young children. *British Journal of Music Therapy, 17*(1), 26–45.

Oldfield, A., & Flower, C. (Eds.). (2008). *Music therapy with children and their families.* Philadelphia, PA: Jessica Kingsley.

Pasiali, V., de l'Etoile, S. K., & Tandy, K. (2004). Kindermusik and music therapy. In A. Darrow (Ed.), *Introduction to approaches in music therapy* (pp. 35–49). Silver Spring, MD: The American Music Therapy Association.

Pasiali, V. (2004). The use of prescriptive therapeutic songs in a home-based environment to promote social skills acquisition by children with autism: Three case studies. *Music Therapy Perspectives, 22*(1), 11–20.

Patel, A. D. (2008). *Music, language, and the brain.* New York, NY: Oxford University.

Rainey Perry, M. M. (2003). Relating improvisational music therapy with severely and multiply disabled children to communication development. *Journal of Music Therapy, 40*(3), 227–246.

Register, D. (2001). The effects of an early intervention music curriculum on prereading/writing. *Journal of Music Therapy, 38*(3), 239–248.

Register, D. (2004). The effects of live music groups versus an educational children's television program on the emergent literacy of young children. *Journal of Music Therapy, 41*(1), 2–27.

Register, D., & Humpal, M. (2007). Using musical transitions in early childhood classrooms: Three case examples. *Music Therapy Perspectives, 25*(1), 25–31.

Ringwalt, S. (2008). Developmental screening and assessment instruments with an emphasis on social and emotional development for young children ages birth through five. *The National Early Childhood Technical Assistance Center.* Retrieved from www.nectac.org

Robb, S. (1999). Piaget, Erikson, and coping styles: Implications for music therapy and the hospitalized preschool child. *Music Therapy Perspectives, 1, 14–19.*

Robb, S. L. (2003). Music interventions and group participation skills of preschoolers with visual impairments: Raising questions about music, arousal, and attention. *Journal of Music Therapy, 40*(A), 266–282.

Schwaiblmair, F. (2005). Infant research and music therapy: The significance of musical characteristics in early mother-child interaction for music therapy. *Music Therapy Today, VI*(1), 48–59.

Schwartz, E. (2006). Eligibility and legal aspects. In M. Humpal & C. Colwell (Eds.), *Effective clinical practice in music therapy: Early childhood and school age educational settings* (pp. 27–36). Silver Spring, MD: American Music Therapy Association.

Schwartz, E. (2008). *Music, therapy, and early childhood: A developmental approach.* Gilsum, NH: Barcelona Publishers.

Schwartz, E. (2012). *You and me makes we: A growing together songbook.* Melrose, MA: The Center for Early Childhood Music Therapy.

Schwartz, E. K. (2009). In the beginning: Music therapy in early intervention groups. *Imagine: Early Childhood Music Therapy Newsletter, 15,* 13-14. Silver Spring, MD: American Music Therapy Association.

Schwartz, E. K. (2010, November). *Making technology our friend: Communication alternatives in early childhood music therapy settings.* Presentation at the American Music Therapy Association Conference.

Schwartz, E. K. (2011). Growing up in music: A Journey through early childhood music development in music therapy. In T. Meadows (Ed.), *Developments in music therapy practice: Case study perspectives* (pp. 70-85). Gilsum, NH: Barcelona Publishers.

Shaw, J., & Manthey, C. (1996). *Musical bridges: Intergenerational music programs.* St. Louis, MO: MMB Music.

Shoemark, H. (1996). Family-centered early intervention: Music therapy in the playgroup program. *Australian Journal of Music Therapy, 7,* 3-15.

Shoemark, H. (2006). Infant-directed singing as a vehicle for regulation rehearsal in the medically fragile full-term infant. *Australian Journal of Music Therapy, 17,* 54-63.

Shoemark, H. (2008). Mapping progress within an individual music therapy session with full-term hospitalized infants. *Music Therapy Perspectives, 26*(1), 38-45.

Shoemark, H., & Grocke, D. (2010). The markers of interplay between the music therapist and the high risk full term infant. *Journal of Music Therapy, 47*(4), 306–334.

Simpson, J. (2011). Individuals with disabilities education act (IDEA). Part C, final regulations. *Music Therapy Matters, 14*(3), 3.

Skewes, K., & Thompson, G. (1998). The use of musical interactions to develop social skills in early intervention. *Australian Journal of Music Therapy, 9,* 35-44.

Standley, J. M. (2003). *Music therapy with premature infants.* Silver Spring, MD: American Music Therapy Association.

Standley, J. M., & Hughes, J. E. (1996). Documenting developmentally appropriate objectives and benefits of a music therapy program for early intervention: A behavioral analysis. *Music Therapy Perspectives, 14,* 87–94.

Standley, J. M., Walworth, D., & Nguyen, J. (2009). Effect of parent/child group music activities on toddler development: A pilot study. *Music Therapy Perspectives, 27*(1), 11-15.

Stern, D. N. (1995). *The motherhood constellation: A unified view of parent infant psychotherapy.* New York, NY: Basic Books.

Sussman, J. (2009). The Effect of music on peer awareness in preschool age children with developmental disabilities. *Journal of Music Therapy, 46*(1), 53–68.

Trainor, L. J. (1996). Infant preferences for infant-directed versus non-infant-directed playsongs and lullabies. *Infant Behavior and Development, 19,* 83–92.

Trainor, L. J., Austin, C. M., & Desjardins, R. N. (2000). Is infant-directed speech prosody a result of the vocal expression of emotion? *Psychological Science, 11,* 188–195.

Trainor, L. J., Rock, A. M. L., & Addison, T. L. (1999). Distinctive messages in infant-directed lullabies and play songs. *Developmental Psychology, 35*(2), 527–534.

Trainor, L. J., & Zacharias, C. A. (1998). Infants prefer higher-pitched singing. *Infant Behavior and Development, 21*(4), 799–806.

Trehub, S., Bull, D., & Thorpe, L. A. (1984). Infants' perception of melodies: The role of melodic contour. *Child Development, 55,* 821–830.

Trehub, S. E. (2003). The developmental origins of musicality. *Nature Neuroscience, 6,* 669–673.

Trehub, S. E., & Trainor, L. J. (1998). Singing to infants: Lullabies and playsongs. *Advances in Infancy Research, 12,* 43–77.

Trollinger, V. L. (2010). The brain in singing and language. *General Music Today, 23*(2), 20-23.

Vogiatzoglou, A., Ockelford. A., Welch, G., & Himonides, E. (2011). Sounds of intent: Software to assess the musical development of children and young people with complex needs. *Music and Medicine, 3*(3), 189-195.

Walworth, D. D. (2009a). Effects of developmental music groups for parents and premature or typical infants under two years on parental responsiveness and infant social development. *Journal of Music Therapy, 46*(1), 32–52.

Walworth, D. D. (2009b). Bright start music: Connecting the dots for infants and tots: An infant/toddler developmental learning curriculum. *Imagine: Early Childhood Music Therapy Newsletter, 15,* 8.

Warren, P., & Nugent, N. (2010). The *Music Connections* programme: Parents' perceptions of their children's involvement in music therapy. *New Zealand Journal of Music Therapy, 2010*(8), 8–33.

Wellman, R. (2010). Augmentative communication and assistive technology in early childhood music therapy. *Imagine: Early Childhood Music Therapy Newsletter, 1*(1), 58-59.

Wheeler, B. L., & Stultz, S. (2008). Using typical infant development to inform music therapy and children with disabilities. *Early Childhood Education, 35,* 585–591.

Wigram, T., & Gold, C. (2005). Music therapy in the assessment and treatment of autistic spectrum disorder: Clinical application and research evidence. *Child: Care, health and development, 32*(5), 535–542.

Wilson, F. R., & Roehmann, F. L. (Eds.). (1990). *Music and child development.* St. Louis, MO: MMB Music.

Wolfe, D. E., & Noguchi, L. K. (2009). The use of music with young children to improve sustained attention during vigilance in the presence of auditory distractions. *Journal of Music Therapy, 46*(1), 69–82.

Chapter 3

Autism

Michelle R. Hintz

Overview

Autistic Spectrum Disorder (ASD) or autism is a lifelong neurological and developmental disorder of unknown etiology estimated to affect at least four out of every 10,000 children in the United States. According to the *Diagnostic and Statistical Manual, Fourth Edition* (*DSM-IV;* American Psychiatric Association, 1994), autism has an onset before age three and affects boys four times more often than girls. Its features include the presence of marked abnormal development and qualitative impairments in the areas of social interaction and communication, as well as a severely restricted repertoire of activities and interests (American Psychiatric Association, 1994). Because autism results from brain dysfunction, the typical rate and patterns of childhood development are interrupted.

Even though persons may share the same diagnosis of autism, ASD is considered a "spectrum" disorder, meaning that the severity of symptoms and affected behaviors can vary greatly from individual to individual. For example, those with the most profound impairment will meet criteria for Autistic Disorder, while those with some severe and pervasive impairment in the development of reciprocal social interaction or verbal/nonverbal communication skills, or when stereotyped behavior, interests, and activities are present, will be diagnosed with Pervasive Developmental Disorder–Not Otherwise Specified (PDD-NOS). Individuals who do not have a language delay but present with qualitative impairments in social interaction and restricted repetitive and stereotyped patterns of behavior are likely to be diagnosed with Asperger's Syndrome. (Note: Rett's Disorder is covered in a separate chapter in this volume, while Childhood Disintegrative Disorder is no longer a separate diagnosis under the *DSM-5*.)

Generally, children with disabilities require special education and related services designed to meet their unique learning needs as well as to prepare them for further education, employment, and independent living. Not surprisingly, the vast majority of individuals with ASD will require at least some special education services and therapies. The Individuals with Disabilities Education Act (IDEA) (2004) ensures that all students ages three through 21 are provided a Free Appropriate Public Education (FAPE). This means that those children with special needs are given equal access to their education and are entitled to receive educational supports such as special education or therapeutic-related services. Supportive services provided may include family training, counseling, and home visits; special instruction; speech/language pathology services; audiology services; occupational therapy; physical therapy; psychological services; medical services (only for diagnostic or evaluation purposes); health services needed to enable your child to benefit from the other services; social work services; assistive technology devices and services; transportation; nutrition services; and service coordination services. While music therapy is not specifically listed in the law, adding music therapy as a related or supportive service under both Part B and Part C of IDEA has been endorsed through federal regulation as well as through Department of Education letters of clarification.

Typical Interventions for Autism Spectrum Disorders

There are four main categories of treatment interventions used for autism. These include behavioral strategies (e.g., applied behavioral analysis, behavior modification, discrete trial training, etc.), traditional therapies (e.g., speech, occupational, and physical therapy), communication methods [e.g., Treatment and Education of Autistic and Related Communication Handicapped Children (TEACCH), Picture Exchange Communication System (PECS), and augmentative devices], biological/health related methods (e.g., gluten-free/casein-free diets, mercury detoxification, various pharmacotherapy, etc.), and alternative/complimentary methods (e.g., cranial-sacral therapy, massage, chiropractic care, Greenspan's floor time, art therapy, and music therapy). Each category of treatment has its unique perspective and underlying philosophy of the underlying issues in autism.

Behavioral Interventions

Applied behavior analysis (ABA) has created an extensive procedure for effective interventions to address a variety of behavior deficits and excesses. Comprehensive ABA programs have been successful in teaching a range of skills (Lovaas, 1987). Behavior modification techniques such as Discrete Trial Training (e.g., Lovaas, 1987) and Pivotal Response Training (PRT) (e.g., Koegel, Koegel, & Surratte, 1992; Pierce & Schreibman, 1995) have been effective in teaching ASD children. Discrete Trial Training (DTT) involves breaking down skills into individual components and teaching one skill at a time until mastered. Although DTT accounts for generalization by using new stimuli to teach the same skills, it lacks generalizability in the natural environment and does not encourage spontaneity (Whalen, 2001).

The Developmental, Individual Difference, Relationship-based (DIR®)/Floortime™ Model is a comprehensive framework used to conduct assessments and intervention programming for children with ASD. The DIR model attempts to create a comprehensive view of the child's social-emotional functioning and potential, biological processing differences, and emotional interactions with his or her caregiver (Greenspan & Weider, 2006a, 2006b). According to the DIR®/Floortime™ Model, children with ASD display difficulty in engaging in affective learning interactions as a result of individual differences in their nervous system (Greenspan, 1992). These neurological differences manifest as difficulties with motor-planning, sensory modulation, sequencing, and sensory processing challenges. Because learning takes place within the context of relationships with caregivers, therapists, and peers, all interactions and interventions are done within the context of those relationships with intent to maximize and foster affective and robust two-way purposeful interactions.

The Social Communication/Emotional Regulation/Transactional Support (SCERTS) Model is an educational model developed by Prizant, Wetherby, Rubin, and Laurant (2010). SCERTS uses practices from other approaches, including ABA (in the form of PRT), and TEACCH. The SCERTS Model differs most notably from the focus of "traditional" ABA because it promotes child-initiated communication in everyday activities. The SCERTS model is most concerned with helping children with autism to learn and spontaneously apply functional and relevant skills in a variety of settings and people.

Pivotal Response Training (PRT) involves getting a child's attention, providing a choice or stimuli and reinforcers, taking turns, reinforcing attempts, and providing contingent and natural reinforcement. PRT has the advantage of using naturalistic training procedures to enhance generalization by maintaining a child's motivation. PRT and DTT differ in that PRT emphasizes child motivation by providing choices, preferences, and reinforcers that are related to the task. Koegel, Koegel, Harrower, and Carter (1999) suggest that joint attention may be a key pivotal skill in early childhood development.

Traditional Therapies

Speech therapy is often a component in an overall therapy program for individuals with ASD since language deficits are one of the core aspects of autism. Speech therapists typically address issues with receptive and expressive language, pragmatic language, and supralinguistic skills. Treatment may be administered individually or in groups both at school and privately.

Occupational therapy may also be required because many children with ASD have sensory issues, hypotonia, or coordination difficulties. Although not listed in the *DSM IV* as one of the recognized deficits in autism, clinicians have found that many children with autism have significant motor-planning and coordination problems affecting their ability to perform fine-motor tasks such as writing. Occupational therapists are an essential part of the treatment team working on these deficits and primarily work on improving functional skills.

Physical therapy is less frequently prescribed, but sometimes necessary for individuals with ASD who also have difficulties with gross motor skills such as walking, riding bikes, skipping, kicking, throwing, and catching. These skills are important not only for physical development, but also for social engagement in sports, recess, and general play.

Communication Methods

There are a number of methods designed to address the communication needs of individuals with ASD. Among the most common is the Treatment and Education of Autistic and Related Communication Handicapped Children (TEACCH) method. TEACCH is a behavioral intervention approach that does not work on behaviors directly, but on their underlying reasons, such as lack of understanding of what the person is expected to do or what will happen to them next, and sensory under- or overstimulation. By addressing communication deficits, the child with ASD will be supported to express their needs and feelings by means other than challenging behavior.

The Picture Exchange Communication System (PECS) (Bondy & Frost, 1998) has also been used successfully to teach a variety of communication behaviors to children with developmental disabilities. The system uses a large collection of pictures laminated onto thick paper or cardboard to represent objects in the child's environment. Instruction focuses initially on the requesting function of communication, often using food or other highly motivating objects. Using behavioral shaping and fading techniques, the child is taught to use the picture in exchange for the desired object. The person holding the object then labels the item being requested and rewards the child by providing the object. As the child masters more sophisticated levels of interaction, he is taught to discriminate between objects using descriptors of size, color, shape, etc., and eventually places pictures together into "sentences" to be given to the adult. In response, the adult reads the picture sentence and provides an appropriate exchange. Later, the system teaches more social communication functions, such as initiating and commenting. Conventional gesturing and gaze alternation are not a specific focus of intervention. Likewise, verbal language on the part of the child is not a requirement for effectively using this system.

There are also several developmentally based interventions designed specifically for ASD children (Hwang & Hughes, 2000; Klinger & Dawson, 1992; Koegel et al., 1999; Landry & Loveland, 1988). Klinger and Dawson (1992) used interventions focused on facilitating social awareness by progressing through a sequence (e.g., eye contact, attention to adult, turn-taking, anticipation behaviors, spontaneous requesting, and nonverbal joint attention). By using ongoing interactions that involve interesting and novel activities, adults follow a child's lead. No specific prompts are used to teach; however, adults imitated the child's behavior in an effort to engage him in an interaction and thus elicit joint attention (Jones & Carr, 2004).

Biological/Health-Related Interventions

Several types of methods are included in this area, including the use of specialized diets and supplements, medical procedures, and medication. The gluten- and casein-free diet is a popular intervention for people with autism. Gluten is an elastic protein in wheat that gives cohesiveness to dough. Casein is a protein in milk, cheese, and other dairy products. Some parents and professionals assert that gluten-free and casein-free diets are successful in improving communication, social interaction, and sleep patterns, while reducing digestive problems and autistic behaviors. The use of hyperbaric oxygen therapy as well as other common supplements (e.g., melatonin, omega-3 fatty acids, and vitamin methyl B_{12}) is also common.

There are some who believe that ASD is the result of an autoimmune disorder or related to the presence of high levels of toxins such as mercury in an individual's body. A good number of parents believe that their children's ASD is the result of exposure to mercury (thiomersal) or other neurotoxins in the vaccines or within the environment. These parents report that their children were developing as expected until the child received required vaccines and immunizations around the age of 18 months. Others believe that ASD is the result of an underlying autoimmune disorder and attempt to medically intervene. Individuals with ASD are often known to have a range of other health problems, including digestive problems, sensory issues, sleep disturbances, chronic inflammation, and many others. For this reason, some individuals with ASD undergo chelation therapy to remove heavy metals from the body. Chelation therapy has a long history of use in clinical toxicology; however, the most common forms of heavy metal intoxication involve lead, arsenic, or mercury.

Pharmacological Interventions

Medications such as mood stabilizers (e.g., Lamictal, Depakote, Seroquel), SSRIs (e.g., Zoloft, Prozac, Paxil), antidepressants (e.g., Abilify, Wellbutrin, Lexapro), and psychostimulants (e.g., Ritalin, Concerta, Vyvanse, Focalin, Adderall) might be prescribed to address behavioral and emotional symptoms present in children with ASD. It should be noted that there is no medication to correct the repetitive behavior, communication, or social challenges that make up the core deficits of autism.

Alternative/Complementary Interventions

There are a myriad of other interventions that aim to address deficits common in children with ASD. Among them are animal-assisted therapy (e.g., dogs, dolphins, horses), sensory integration therapies, augmentative communication, social skills training, and creative arts therapies (including art therapy, dance/movement therapy, and music therapy).

The guiding principle of music therapy in ASD is a focus on the development of communication and social skills. The primary concern is to help the child meet developmental milestones in all areas of development and support their education. Determining which music therapy methods are effective and valuable for an individual with ASD is directly connected to understanding their unique clinical profile and determining how music can improve functioning in areas of behavior, interaction, and responsiveness to others and the environment, communication, cognition and perception, and emotional development. This chapter will examine the unique role that music therapy can play in the treatment of individuals with ASD and their families.

Diagnostic Information

Autism is defined and diagnosed solely on the basis of symptoms. Although parents often report developmental concerns prior to age three years, autism is not usually diagnosed until a child reaches age three or four years due to the variability in individual development, environment, and hesitancy in labeling a child with a pervasive disorder without ruling out other possible causes (e.g., hearing loss, seizures, mood disorders, language or learning disabilities, etc.). Formal diagnosis often comes from a medical professional such as a pediatrician, neurologist, or a psychologist.

There is no single behavior that serves as a definitive diagnostic indicator, since children with ASD present with a variety of symptoms across cognitive, emotional, and behavioral domains (also see Kabot, Masi, & Segal, 2003). Autism spectrum disorders also include Pervasive Developmental Disorder–Not Otherwise specified (PDD-NOS), which is sometimes referred to as high-functioning autism, and Asperger's Syndrome, in which affected individuals typically do not display the early language deficits inherent in autistic disorder.

With the publication of the new *Diagnostic and Statistical Manual—Fifth Edition (DSM-5)* in late 2013 (American Psychiatric Association), there are several modifications to the autism spectrum disorders. In an effort to more accurately and consistently diagnose children with autism, the new *DSM-5* will incorporate several diagnoses from *DSM-IV* (including Autistic Disorder, Asperger's Syndrome, Childhood Disintegrative Disorder and Pervasive Developmental Disorder–Not Otherwise Specified) into the diagnosis of Autism Spectrum Disorder. According to the proposed diagnostic criteria, individuals must demonstrate deficits in social-emotional reciprocity, nonverbal communication behaviors, and developing and maintaining relationships and have restricted, repetitive patterns of behavior, interests, or activities and hyper- or hyporeactivity to sensory input or unusual interest in sensory aspects of environment. These symptoms must limit and impair everyday functioning and be present in early childhood (although a specific age requirement is not listed).

As stated in the diagnostic criteria, the qualitative impairments observed in autism can be grouped into three categories: behavior, communication, and socialization. In the behavior category, children with ASD may display perseveration, demonstrate poor compliance, lack ability to generalize previously learned materials, have catastrophic reactions to trivial events, and exhibit severe interfering behaviors (e.g., aggression). Impairments in communication (which includes areas of social play) may include echolalia, delayed nonverbal and verbal communication, and poor abstraction and representational thought. In addition, individuals with ASD typically have difficulty in understanding the intention of others, have problems in sequencing, and lack pretend play. Socially, those with ASD may exhibit lack of eye contact and low motivation to interact with others, use people as tools, and lack imitation abilities.

Behavioral Impairments

It is well understood that individuals with ASD present with numerous behavioral challenges. Individuals with ASD may be more prone to temper tantrums and sudden changes in mood and affect, and may have behavioral responses that do not seem to fit with the situation. Many children demonstrate stereotypical repetitive movements (e.g., hand flapping, rocking, spinning), as well as preoccupation with parts of objects (e.g., turning wheels on toy cars) and obsessive behaviors (e.g., insistence on closing doors, repeatedly watching same parts of a video). In addition, many individuals with ASD strive for sameness and familiarity and resist novel experiences. For this reason, they avoid trying new foods and wearing different clothing, and become upset when there is a change in routine.

Many individuals with ASD also meet diagnostic criteria for Attention-Deficit/Hyperactivity Disorder (ADHD) because of their struggles with attention and concentration, working memory, impulsivity, and organization. These deficits make it difficult for the child with ASD to pay adequate attention during classroom instruction, modify their behaviors as needed, and plan ahead for longer assignments. Children with ASD also become easily overwhelmed with larger assignments and longer reading passages. Children with ASD often have sensory issues (especially with textures and sounds) that they attempt to compensate for by avoiding situations that might cause them discomfort. Environments with loud sounds or a lot of background noise, like a cafeteria, can be particularly difficult for them to handle. To compensate, they may cover their ears, scream, or attempt to avoid those situations entirely.

The development of play skills is also interrupted in a child with ASD (Meltzoff & Moore, 1994; Mundy & Sigman, 1989), and some children do not develop symbolic representation through play (Klinger & Dawson, 1992), which typically develops between 12 and 22 months of age and involves attributing animate characteristics to inanimate objects and using an object as if it were another object.

Motor imitation and vicarious learning are also interrupted for many individuals with ASD. DeMyer et al. (1972) reported that ASD children were impaired in both imitation of body movements and actions on objects relative to mental age matched subjects. Dawson and Adams (1984) found that ASD children had more severely impaired imitation skills than other sensorimotor abilities such as object permanence. Further, several research studies (Dawson, 1991; Rogers & Pennington, 1991; Meltzoff & Gopnik, 1993) have proposed that poor imitation may be a critical deficit in autism that interferes with development of abilities in reciprocity, joint attention, and understanding emotional states.

Communication Impairments

It is not surprising that ASD children have significant impairments in language development. In fact, just a few decades ago, approximately 50% of ASD children remained mute throughout their lives (Rutter, 1978), but with improvements in early diagnosis and intensive early intervention, a greater percentage of individuals are able to use some form of verbal language. However, for many individuals with ASD, language and nonverbal communication skills are either absent or significantly delayed (American Psychiatric Association, 2000).

Higher-order language processes are often impaired for those children at the "higher" end of the autism spectrum. They have difficulty with nonliteral language (e.g., figures of speech), idioms, inferencing skills (e.g., using background knowledge in order to arrive at the speaker's intended meaning), and pragmatic language skills. Pragmatic language skills include being able to recognize appropriate topics for conversation, selecting relevant information for directions or requests, adjusting the communication level to the situational factors (e.g., age, relationship, setting), and using language to express gratitude, sorrow, and other feelings.

Theory of mind (often abbreviated "ToM") is the ability to attribute mental states, including beliefs, intents, desires, pretending, and knowledge to oneself as well as to others. It is the ability to understand that others have beliefs, desires, and intentions that are different from one's own. Deficits in ToM are common in individuals with ASD and ADHD. Although ToM is a widely accepted theory of social development, it is unclear why children with ASD fail on ToM tasks and succeed on other social tasks (Whalen, 2001). Not all researchers agree that ToM underlies the social deficits in autism (Whalen, 2001). For example, ASD children who pass the false belief tests also tended to show insightful and interactive social behavior (Frith, Happé, & Siddons, 1994).

Social Impairments

The early works of Kanner (1943) and Rutter (1978) about autism emphasized developmental deviance and delay as one of the defining features of ASD. Infants with autism are often described as not seeking affection from others and stiffening when held or picked up. These infants may fail to acquire a social smile (Volkmar, Carter, Grossman, & Klin, 1997). Unlike typical children, some ASD children fail to seek comfort from their parents when they are hurt or frightened. Such behaviors as eye contact, facial expressions, affect, peer relationships, social reciprocity, awareness of others, and spontaneous social initiation are frequently impaired.

Of the identified deficit areas, social interaction is felt to be one of the most basic developmental impairments that impact other areas of functioning including language development and academic achievement. Within the domain of social interaction, joint attention skills have been the subject of considerable research during the last decade because joint attention has been suggested as a source for an autistic person's failure to make meaningful connections with others (Rogers & Pennington, 1991).

Social deficits are readily observed in children with ASD, as they typically fail to appropriately interact with peers. Low incidence of peer play and social interaction along with developmentally delayed contextual or inappropriate play tend to limit the development of peer relationships. By analyzing videotapes, Osterling and Dawson (1994) found that ASD children displayed significant deficits in joint attention behaviors as early as their first birthday. They found that behaviors such as looking at others, pointing, showing objects, and visually responding to their name were markedly lacking.

Joint attention is one of the only skill deficits to discriminate autism from other developmental disabilities, mental retardation, and other childhood disorders (Roeyers, Van Oost, & Bothuyne, 1998). Joint attention is described as two or more persons coordinating their attention toward objects or events of mutual interest. This process helps a child to learn about his environment and most often occurs during routine events such as bathing, feeding, traveling in a car, etc. It also encompasses the ability to coordinate attention between others with respect to events or objects, or to share an awareness of such with another person (Adamson & Chance, 1998; Bakeman & Adamson, 1984; Jones & Carr, 2004). Social cues such as gaze direction, pointing gestures, and postural cues indicate to another person the object or event that is currently under consideration.

Joint attention is the quintessential social milestone that develops toward the end of the first year after birth and is understood as the process whereby an infant and caregiver share an experience and recognize that the experience is being shared. Infants begin coordinating their attention by the age of six months and can follow a pointed finger by nine months of age. The earliest demonstration of joint attention occurs around eight months of age, when an infant follows a caregiver's gaze and looks in the same direction. Late in the first year of life, a child is able to consistently respond to adults' bids for attention and consistently turns his head to the speaker when his name is called by 10 months. Between 12 and 14 months, after development of the ability to follow the direction of an adult's gaze and point, children begin to check back with the adult by alternating their gaze from the object to the adult and back to the object (Tomasello, 1995). The usual consequence of initiating social interaction is that the adult often looks at the object or event and comments or labels it for the child (Bruner & Sherwood, 1983).

By the middle of a child's second year, joint attention skills are well coordinated and provide him with a means to interact with adults about the surrounding world and its events. At this time, between the ages of 18 and 24 months, a basic understanding that persons are intentional beings is acquired typically. A child actively shifts attention to match that of an adult's in learning new words. At this point, a child also begins to develop supported joint attention (SJA), meaning that a child's play with an object is altered by the actions of another person (Lewy & Dawson, 1992). For example, when a child is playing with an adult, the child may imitate a novel action modeled by the adult. Coordinated joint attention (CJA) also develops at this time. This is demonstrated when a child alternates his gaze between an object and another person while actively engaged with that object (Lewy & Dawson, 1992). The shifting demonstrates not only a child's appreciation of another's point of view, but also his attentional flexibility.

By age two years, a child also uses language and gestures to direct an adult's attention to aspects of the environment when gaze direction is insufficient (Mundy & Sigman, 1989). Protodeclarative pointing (i.e., pointing with intent to direct another person's attention toward something) also emerges. These behaviors rely on a child's ability to take the perspective of another person and attribute such characteristics as attention, interest, affect, intention, and prior experience in relation to the object or event at hand. The table below outlines the basic development of joint attention behaviors.

JOINT ATTENTION MILESTONES

Interaction	Age
Reciprocal smiling	2 months
Coordinating attention with another person	6 months
Gaze monitoring Initiating joint attention	8 months
Following a pointed finger	9 months
Showing objects Following another's eye gaze	10 months
Pointing to obtain an object Pointing to indicate to another an object of interest	12 months
Checking back with the adults by alternating gaze from the object to adult and back	14 months
Social referencing	16 months
Consistent responding to adults' bids for attention	18–24 months
Using language and gestures to direct an adult's attention	24 months

Joint attention is becoming an increasingly important behavior in autism research; it is one of the earliest emerging social behaviors, as deficits are noticeable even before the acquisition of language. Mundy and his colleagues reported that deficits in referential looking correctly diagnosed 94% of ASD children in a group of preschoolers that included both children with ASD and children with mental retardation. In fact, it has been demonstrated that observations of joint attention skills development alone is able to differentiate 80%–90% of samples of ASD children from children with other developmental delays (Mundy, 1995).

Wetherby and Prizant (2000) state that "language that follows an infants' attention focus is a kind of scaffolding for early language, which helps infants who are just getting started to discern the mother's communicative intentions and so to enter into a state of joint attention focus" (p. 35). According to Loveland and Landry (1986), joint attention is crucial for the development of functional speech. A deficit in joint attention affects a child's ability to use spontaneous language and may result in more echolalic and stereotyped speech. The deficit in functional communication is apparent when children are not able to develop higher social-communication skills such as giving information, asking questions, and directing others' attention (Wetherby & Prutting, 1984).

ASD children also have deficits in symbolic play (Wing, 1978). Field, Field, Sanders, and Nadel (2001) examined the effect on ASD children's social initiation and responsiveness when adults imitated their behaviors. The distal social behaviors shown included looking, vocalizing, smiling, and participating in reciprocal play. During the third session, these same children spent greater amounts of time demonstrating proximal social behaviors toward the adult than the children in the comparison group.

These behaviors included being close to, sitting next to, and touching the adult. The researchers conclude that adult imitative behavior may be an important component of early intervention treatment.

Needs and Resources

Individuals diagnosed with ASD have a wide range of needs that require intervention to address deficits in language and communication, cognitive and academic abilities, behavioral needs, social skills, and emotional functioning. However, each person with ASD has his own unique talents and strengths that can be capitalized upon.

Language and Communication

Successfully communicating with the child with ASD not only involves an understanding of how they communicate but also requires an understanding of why they communicate. In order to understand a child's communicative strengths and needs, they need to be observed closely. An individual with ASD may use some of the following to communicate with others: crying, taking the adult's hand to the object they desire, looking at the object they desire, reaching, using pictures, and echolalia.

Oftentimes, the child may appear not to hear what is said to them, fail to respond to their name, and/or be indifferent to any attempts of communication that are made. Other times, a child with ASD will use echolalia (the repetition of other people's words). Initially, when the child uses echolalia, it is likely that they are repeating words that they do not understand and are doing so with no communicative intent. However, echolalia is a good sign, as it shows that the child's communication is developing—in time, the child may begin to use the repeated words and phrases to communicate something significant. For example, the child may memorize the words that were said to them and use them later in a different situation.

Aside from the obvious communication deficits present in the individuals most severely impacted by ASD, individuals with high-functioning autism and Asperger's Syndrome struggle with the organization and flexibility that is required in a conversation. As part of the challenge of the lack of perspective-taking, there is the lack of awareness of the listener's needs. The individual with high-functioning autism and Asperger's Syndrome may have a focus on and interest in "odd topics" and not appreciate the lack of interest in them by others. On a more simplistic level, many individuals with high-functioning autism and Asperger's Syndrome struggle with initiating and sustaining a conversation. Part of this may be due to variations in motivation and interest. It may helpful to view children with ASD as being on a continuum in terms of their intentional communication. At one end of the continuum are children who communicate mainly to get the things they want, while at the other end are children who communicate to ask questions, comment on something, or be sociable.

Cognitive and Academic Abilities

Many individuals with ASD have uneven cognitive development, meaning that they may be very gifted in some aspects of functioning (such as perceptual reasoning), but have severely inadequate functioning in others (e.g., verbal comprehension). It used to be thought that the majority of individuals with ASD present with intellectual disabilities or even mental retardation. However, a good number of students may be above average or even gifted in certain areas, such as mathematics, broad reading skills, or computers. In addition, many individuals with ASD have slower processing speed and cognitive fluency skills, making it difficult for them to keep up academically with their peers.

Some children with ASD will also meet eligibility for a learning disorder and require intensive or remedial instruction in reading, writing, or mathematics. Most individuals with ASD require some academic accommodations and meet eligibility for an Individualized Education Plan (IEP). The IEP is tailored to each student's needs to help teachers and related service providers understand the student's disability and how the disability affects the learning process. It is designed to help children reach educational goals more easily than they otherwise would. Common accommodations include flexible scheduling (e.g., frequent breaks), small group instruction, extra time in standardized testing situations, and class notes given prior to lectures and presentation of new materials, among others.

Behavioral Needs

Most individuals with ASD present with some behavioral difficulties. Many of them will meet clinical criteria for Attention-Deficit/Hyperactivity Disorder (ADHD), which is characterized by a persistent pattern of hyperactivity and/or impulsivity that is inconsistent with peers of a comparable age and level of development. Symptoms must be present before the age of seven and present in two or more settings, such as home, school, work, etc., for at least six months. Symptoms need to be severe enough to interfere with appropriate family, academic, social, and occupational functioning (American Psychiatric Association, 2000).

Because many individuals with ASD will have distractibility, difficulty focusing and maintaining attention to task until completion, and poor organizational skills, they often have social difficulties as well. These individuals have difficulty listening and following directions in class, may appear restless, have excessive movements, or be disruptive to the classroom such as by exhibiting constant demands for attention, low frustration tolerance, emotional outbursts, temper tantrums, and oppositional behavior.

Social Needs

Social situations are often very difficult for individuals with ASD because there are so many social rules that people without ASD learn instinctively. Understanding the social norms and expectations for different situations is also difficult. How we are expected to behave at a fast food restaurant is different from how we are expected to behave in a fancier restaurant. Similarly, the type of language used when speaking with your friends is vastly different from that needed to address someone in authority. Individuals with ASD often have to be implicitly taught these rules in order to learn them. It can often be confusing and cause anxiety, as many social rules are unwritten and not spoken about. These unspoken rules apply to very basic things such as understanding personal space, starting conversations, making "small talk," recognizing nonverbal communication/body language, and choosing appropriate topics for conversation. Individuals with ASD may also misunderstand sarcasm and teasing, and are at risk for being taken advantage of by their peers.

Emotional Functioning

Individuals with ASD are at greater risk for comorbid mood disorders. It is quite common for children to develop symptoms of anxiety and/or obsessive-compulsive disorders that arise from symptoms associated with ASD. Because of cognitive rigidity, individuals with ASD are not as comfortable in novel situations, have difficulty with transitions, and may feel unsafe. Although fears are common throughout childhood, the fears children with ASD have may be unusual (e.g., of holiday decorations, things of a certain color) or may not be readily identifiable at all. Without proper intervention from a mental health clinician, these children are at risk for a decline in educational performance, school refusal or avoidance, and reluctance to participate in age-appropriate social activities. It is also common for anxiety to be somaticized as vague symptoms of being tired and having aches and pains.

Obsessive-Compulsive Disorder (OCD) is also common among individuals with ASD. It is characterized by recurrent obsessions or compulsions that are time-consuming and cause significant impairment in daily living. Obsessions are defined as persistent thoughts or impulses that are inappropriate and intrusive, causing distress and anxiety. Initially, these behaviors and thoughts may serve an adaptive function; however, they can quickly become rigid and interfering.

It is also not uncommon for individuals with milder forms of ASD to recognize that they are different from their peers. This can lead to depression, low self-esteem, and social isolation. These individuals are often able to perform well academically, but are frequently easy targets for bullying and are susceptible to peer pressure.

Referral and Assessment

Persons with autism present unusual and unique issues for assessment. Behavior problems and limited communication, just two of the common problems encountered in assessment, often require professionals to make a variety of special accommodations during evaluations. To make matters even more complex, persons with autism typically display unusual or uneven developmental profiles. In addition, ASD cannot be diagnosed with a single instrument or test. Instead, it requires careful evaluation of different domains of development and functioning in order to determine an individual's strengths and weaknesses.

Assessment of persons with autism and pervasive developmental disorders are completed by a myriad of professionals, including child psychologists and psychiatrists, speech and language pathologists, neurologists, and pediatricians, among many others. Assessments for autism fall into several broad categories. Some tools gather information through checklists, inventories, and interviews with parents, teachers, and professionals. Some tools attempt to describe the individual from a developmental perspective; others, from a behavioral perspective. Still other tools attempt to gather information about diagnostic criteria or intelligence, or a specific area of dysfunction such as sensorimotor skills, play skills, communication, vocabulary, and behavior.

Psychological, communicative, academic, and behavioral assessments are the most frequently obtained. Each discipline tends to view the disorder from its own unique perspective in an effort to provide specific information about the individual as well as attempt to place him/her into a broader categorical framework. Separately, each assessment may only capture a small part of the individual's full picture, but when part of an interdisciplinary battery, they may provide a more comprehensive clinical picture upon which a team of professionals can build its recommendations for treatment and intervention.

Music Therapy Referral and Assessment

Music therapists are frequently referred children for therapy by parents, teachers, or other therapists. Referrals for music therapy services within the school setting often come from a child's teacher, speech therapist, or IEP team. Within the community, private music therapy services are frequently sought by parents or other therapists as an additional augmentative treatment after other more traditional therapies have been put into a child's therapy schedule. The most cited goal that parents state is the desire for their child to talk and/or communicate.

The most often cited reason for the music therapy referral is the child's inherent interest in and love of music. Speech therapists frequently state that the child is more engaged when music is present and parents note that their child becomes excited and focused when hearing their favorite songs. During an intake interview with parents, music therapists often hear stories about how the child takes a particular interest in the musical parts of television programs and movies.

Music therapy assessment can identify limitations and weaknesses in children, as well as their strengths and potentials. Yet, only a few formal music therapy assessment processes are cited in the literature. Most music therapy assessments serve to determine eligibility for services, to gather information on levels of functioning, and to determine treatment goals. Most assessments are conducted through behavioral observation within the music-making session with assessing peer-to-peer social interaction (Kern, 2001), use of communication and language, or musical responses as indicators of developmental levels of functioning (Schwartz, 2008, 2011).

Coleman and Brunk developed the Special Education Music Therapy Assessment Process, or SEMTAP (Coleman & Brunk, 1999) to assess the functioning of children and adolescents who receive special education services. The purpose of the SEMTAP is to determine eligibility for music therapy services for children who have an Individualized Education Plan (IEP). The SEMTAP process allows for comparison of the client's responses with and without music. Another assessment tool, from Baxter et al. (2007), is the Individualized Music Therapy Assessment Profile (IMTAP), which assesses client functioning in several domains of functioning including gross and fine motor skills, sensory, communication, emotional, social, and musicality. Both the IMTAP and the SEMTAP are flexible tools for music therapists who work with clients with developmental disabilities such as ASD.

Wigram (2000) outlines a music therapy assessment process used to differentially diagnose ASD children from children with other disorders. His interpretation of musical material as well as behaviors and social engagement during the evaluation process includes both quantitative and qualitative data. The process during a music therapy assessment focuses on the way the child interacts—whether he is a leader or a follower, whether he is intentional or accidental, whether there is flexibility or rigidity, and how he attempts to control the environment. He states, "A music therapy framework allows children potential for revealing preverbal and alternate communication systems that they have developed which can, in turn, support or negate a diagnosis of autism" (p. 15).

Carpente (2009) created the Individual Music-Centered Assessment Profile for Neurodevelopmental Disorders (IMCAP-ND), a specific improvisational music therapy assessment to be used within the DIR®/Floortime™ Model. While not specifically designed to assess individuals with ASD, the IMCAP-ND is a criterion-based assessment that provides an in-depth musical understanding of each child's ability to musically attune, engage, relate, adapt, and communicate in musical play (Carpente, 2009). The IMCAP-ND targets six music domain areas related to the child's social-emotional responses, considering individual differences and how they impact the musical interactions. Music domain areas are evaluated by clinical observation and listening to the child's responses in play through any one or all of the four modes of musical expression (i.e., instrument play, voice, movement, gestures).

It is suggested that the music therapist have access to the student's diagnosis, treatment plan, prior evaluations, and IEP prior to or after completing assessment to effectively plan and design music therapy sessions. Through assessment, the music therapist gains understanding of the individual's unique clinical profile and strengths and weaknesses and prioritizes needs. From the data gathered in the assessment, the music therapist can select appropriate methods for treatment. Music therapy goals then ideally should address the child's needs as well as the concerns of the person making the referral.

Guidelines for Music Therapy Methods

There are several common guidelines that music therapists should consider when conducting experiences for individuals with ASD. While techniques for implementing music therapy vary from therapist to therapist, there are several common recommendations cited in the literature that apply to working with individuals with ASD. First, the music therapist needs to have a high level of clinical musicianship and also interpersonal skills (Carpente, 2009), in order to be sufficiently flexible and spontaneous. Music therapists should consider their client's unique individual and musical differences while engaging them in music. Jones and Carr (2004) suggest engaging the child in experiences of their choice during intervention as well as providing children with choice from a variety of novel and interesting objects (musical instruments and accompanying props) that have salient sensory consequences (making music, noise, moving, etc.).

As stated in the literature about pivotal skills detailed above, it is recommended that music therapists use natural consequences to help to motivate the child to engage in joint attention. The literature demonstrates that interspersal methods (e.g., alternating easier activities with more difficult ones) can be used to increase the rate of difficult skill acquisition while also motivating a child to sustain interest in a task (Dunlap, 1984; Koegel, Koegel, Harrower, & Carter, 1999).

In her study, Reitman (2005) suggested incorporating several strategies into music therapy treatment, including:

1) using short phrases when speaking or singing;
2) using simple, concrete vocabulary;
3) using repetition and review;
4) limiting directions to ensure the child's success;
5) imitating and validating the child's efforts to engage the therapist;
6) expanding on the child's communication, play, affect, and language;
7) using a visual schedule of musical activities being presented during the session;
8) providing a variety of materials;
9) providing a variety of musical experiences; and
10) facilitating interaction using present interest and motivation. (p. 58)

Carpente (2009) stated that it is important to understand "both the characteristics of ASD that may impede a child's ability to engage in musical play as well as the child's musical responses upon which musical goals are based" (p. 13). He suggests that music therapists keep in mind that the difficulties a child with ASD has in engaging in musical interactions may be due to underlying deficits with motor planning, visual processing, or sensory modulation.

Increasing object salience can also enhance motivation (Bruner, 1981; Butterworth, 1995). Researchers have suggested that presenting a variety of preferred items not only increases novelty but also helps to sustain attentional focus in persons with disabilities (Dunlap et al., 1995). The props and instruments used in music therapy treatment provide enhanced sensory stimulation by moving, making noise, etc. Reitman (2011) presented activities, songs, and experiences in slightly different ways to facilitate increased interest and novelty while promoting opportunity for generalization of skills. For example, although each session has a greeting and closing song, these songs may be presented on the omnichord, guitar, or keyboard. Other variations may include tempo and/or rhythmic accompaniment, as well as changes in key.

For very low-functioning individuals with ASD or those with severely impaired communication, Reitman (2011) suggested using a picture schedule using a 2" x 2" picture and word representation for each of the session's activities. The activity pictures can be affixed with Velcro to a piece of cardboard (also with Velcro) in a horizontal, left-to-right order. The child may turn over each picture when its corresponding activity is finished. At the same time, the music therapist may reinforce the child's behavior by providing appropriate verbal feedback (e.g., "Good. It's all done") and accompanying manual sign at times.

Overview of Methods and Procedures

Music therapists have documented their work with individuals with ASD for decades (Alvin & Warwick, 1992; Nordoff & Robbins, 1964, 1977; Stevens & Clark, 1969) in order to promote nonverbal expression and communication, socialization, self-awareness, sensory integration, and musical and interpersonal relatedness (Alvin & Warwick, 1992; Nordoff & Robbins, 1968). The following methods and procedures are used most commonly with clients with ASD.

Receptive Music Therapy

- Social Stories in Music Therapy: use of music to support learning of concepts, sequences, and basic information from short stories, often depicted with short sentences with accompanying pictures, sequences to teach clients expected behaviors during interactions, social experiences, or activities of daily living.
- Child-Directed Singing: Based upon what the child is doing or experiencing, the therapist spontaneously sings as a means of communicating with or to the child.

Improvisational Music Therapy

- Instrumental Improvisation: The therapist and client create spontaneous musical improvisations using instruments.
- Referential Improvisation: Clients participate in improvised music structured around a nonmusical theme or idea using musical concepts of rhythm, dynamics, and tonality.

Re-creative Music Therapy

- Song Singing: Clients sing precomposed songs with or without instrumental accompaniment.
- Instrumental Songs: consist of musical pieces with accompaniment and assigned instruments for clients to play parts.
- Adaptive Music Lessons: a form of individual music therapy in which the music lesson format (most commonly using voice, piano, or guitar) is used to accomplish therapeutic goals such as sequencing ability, self-awareness, and self-regulation.

Compositional Music Therapy

- Songwriting: occurs when changes are made to some or all of the lyrics and/or music of an existing song, or when a new song is written in its entirety.

Guidelines for Receptive Music Therapy

Receptive music therapy experiences are intended to engage the client in a musical experience designed to provide stimulation of sensory or cognitive processes. The child is not expected to produce an outward response, but there is intent for receptive methods to meet the client's needs for connectedness or engagement with others and regulation (de l'Etoile, 2006). Receptive music therapy interventions can be designed to attract, foster, and sustain children's engagement in any number of ways—socially, emotionally, cognitively, sensorially, and motorically, as well as musically.

As with strategies used for younger children or those with severe developmental delays, music therapists are more apt to engage individuals who are more severely impaired by ASD with simple, live accompaniment or unaccompanied singing using a higher pitch, slower tempo, more gliding between tones, and an interesting timbre. The use of familiar melodies and repetition allows clients opportunity to make associations with the music.

Social Stories in Music Therapy

Overview. Music therapists often put stories into songs both to enhance children's interest and provide a framework to convey concepts and ideas. Just as the use of mnemonics has long been known to enhance recall and memory abilities (such as the alphabet song, which helps children to remember all of the letters), the use of music to tell social stories can assist in the recall of rules for social engagement, social experiences, and expected behavior. By using musical elements of pitch, phrasing, and chord progression, targeted words or concepts can be highlighted and emphasized.

Social stories were originally developed by Carol Gray for children with ASD to communicate ways in which an autistic person can prepare for social interaction. A social story is an individualized short story that breaks down a challenging social situation into understandable steps by using pictures and short relevant phrases designed to help an individual with ASD understand the entirety of a situation. Social stories can be written about pragmatic themes (e.g., conversational turn-taking, making eye contact to learn new things), social situations such as responding to teasing and knowing what to do when lost, and language skills (e.g., building vocabulary, following directions). The stories combine auditory and visual information that can be repeated frequently. There are books available with prewritten social stories that a music therapist can use for ideas (Baker, 2003; Gray, 2010). A significant benefit of social stories is that they can be customized to the individual and their situation. No contraindications are known for using social stories in music therapy. Level of therapy: augmentative.

Preparation. The therapist identifies a targeted social situation such as asking a teacher for help and outlines the main parts of the situation. Using short descriptive sentences written in the first person (i.e., "I" rather than "you"), the main parts or steps in the situation are identified. It is suggested that the music therapist use words such as "usually" or "sometimes" within the social story song to allow for unknown variables should they occur (Gray, 1995). Pictures (hand-drawn, clip art, or photographs) are then created for each sentence and a visual is created for use in the session. There are several ways to create the social story, including making a cartoon strip, short picture book, or poster. Music therapists then create a melody for the text that emphasizes key words melodically, rhythmically, and/or with stress. An example of the text for a social story about needing a break is as follows:

> *Sometimes I need a break even when I'm having fun.*
> *When I need a break, sometimes I like to color pictures.*
> *Other times, I like to listen to soft music.*
> *Sometimes I need a break for only a few minutes,*
> *But sometimes I need a break for a little longer.*
> *I can go back and have more fun when I am ready!*

What to observe. During the music therapy session, the music therapist will observe the client's level of engagement while listening. She will also observe whether the client has an affective response to the experience while listening. After the session, the therapist will communicate with other staff or family members regarding the client's behaviors in the targeted situation. Certainly, improvement on the targeted behaviors indicates that the experience is successful, as would the client's ability to retell the social story or sing the verses.

Procedures. The musical social story may be either the entire focus of the music therapy session or a single component within the session. When possible, the musical social story should be presented several times across multiple sessions to promote familiarity and retention of the information.

The musical social story is usually presented within the context of preparing for an upcoming event or for recalling expected behaviors during common activities and experiences. The music therapist teaches the social story and its accompanying music in order to enhance familiarity and promote recall. Depending upon the functioning level of the client, the music therapist may sing the song with or without an accompaniment while referencing the accompanying visual. Reviewing relevant parts of the story prior to the song may improve client engagement. Pointing to the relevant pictures while singing may also reinforce comprehension of the intended message. Questioning the child after the social story may assist the music therapist in determining the child's level of comprehension and facilitate generalization of the social stories' message.

Child-Directed Singing

Overview. In child-directed singing, the client is an active listener while the therapist uses her voice in song to communicate with and to the child. The therapist focuses on creating a specific music environment for the child to absorb rather than to promote an expressive behavior. The music components of child-directed singing, such as melody, rhythm, or lyrics, contain meaning and purpose that is specific to the child and their present situation. Sounds are deliberately directed toward the child in an effort to reflect in-the-moment changes in the child's affect, movement, attention, or engagement.

Kern, Wakeford, and Aldridge (2007) and Pasiali (2004) effectively used child-directed singing in helping young children successfully engage with social behaviors, transitions, and classroom and self-care routines. Physical cues and actions or gestures can be added to the singing to reinforce the messages. Child-directed singing has proven effective in addressing areas of initiating or increasing engagement and can be used with social engagement. For example, the therapist's exaggerated facial expressions along with the music can serve to provide additional visual cues. The therapist can repeat or improvise within the singing to elicit longer periods of engagement.

If the child begins to disengage, the therapist can change melodic or rhythmic content until attention is regained. Once the child is re-engaged, the therapist can choose to change treatment methods and goals or to change the object of engagement. Sometimes children in medical distress might become disengaged and dysregulated due to pain or urgent health concerns. The therapist can assess to see if the music or the presence of the therapist is contributing to the dysregulation and might choose to discontinue or change treatment methods. No contraindications are known for child-directed singing. Level of therapy: augmentative.

Preparation. Check the environment and remove any items that might contribute to distraction or dysregulation. The room should have adequate space to allow for some movement while allowing the music therapist to maintain physical proximity and visual contact at all times. Only objects and materials that are okay for the child to handle and interact with should be accessible in the room, as this will aid the therapist in avoiding corrective prompts and redirection.

What to observe. The music therapist will observe for any indications of engagement, such as eye contact, facial affect changes, motor movements, postural shifts, picking up the object, moving to the music, following directions in the song lyrics, or initiating communication (in any manner) with the therapist. The child's physical gestures, movements, and proximity to therapist can indicate whether and how they are responding to the intervention. Turning or moving away from the therapist might be an indication either that the child is not engaged in the experience or that the child is, in fact, responding in an avoidant manner. The music therapist is attuned to the child's use of vocalization or verbalization, quality of movements, and engagement with objects in the environment to gauge if they are synchronizing with the music presented.

Procedures. Music used in child-directed singing can come from a number of sources. It can be precomposed, therapist-created, or improvised. The qualities of the particular song or vocalization should be selected to match the targeted goal while referencing the child's level of musical development.

The music therapist may choose to move into closer proximity to the child and either begin singing immediately or create a moment of silence and stillness before beginning. By orienting the music therapist's body to the child, making gentle eye contact, and exuding an open, inviting facial expression, the music therapist attempts to convey safety and willingness to engage with the child. Use of touch, through stroking or rocking, might enhance the listening experience of the child. An intermediary object such as a soft blanket or touch toy can also be used.

The music therapist's singing should incorporate musical qualities that have been shown to attract the child's interest. By incorporating preferred musical qualities while also adding elements of surprise (e.g., tempo fluctuations, use of glissando or crescendo, silence), the music therapist creates interest and anticipation. By vocally matching the movements or pulse of the child, the therapist may see the child begin to recognize his influence on the therapist's singing.

The therapist should choose appropriate meter, timbre, and dynamics to support the client at their level of musical development. The therapist ought to be careful not to overload the child with multiple stimuli (e.g., singing and using percussion, adding syncopation), which can cause anxiety and distress as the child struggles to shift attention.

Guidelines for Improvisational Music Therapy

Nordoff and Robbins (1964, 1968, 1971, 1977) found that music improvisation and musical composition could nurture, challenge, and support the "music child" so that the child could develop beyond their present condition and form new ways of experiencing themselves and the world. Their improvisational music therapy method (initially referred to as Creative Music Therapy), Nordoff-Robbins Music Therapy (NRMT), holds as its primary focus the interaction in the musical relationship between the child and therapists. Because the primary focus is on music, this is where both the musical and clinical processes lie (Aigen, 2005), and therefore the therapist's primary objective is to develop musical experiences to deepen the child's musical engagement and interaction.

The musical experiences improvised during sessions typically arise from the vocal and motor output provided by the child. The music therapist musically reflects and expands on this experience using musical instruments, voice, and expressive language to capture the affective essence of the behavior. The child plays a central role in the creation of the music and is an active creator. The child plays various instruments that require no formal training or experience, while the music therapist improvises music built around the child's music-making, emotional state, and/or movements. The purpose is to "musically engage, match, support, and enhance whatever the child is offering, musically or nonmusically, therein promoting relatedness, communication, socialization, and awareness within the music itself" (Carpente, 2009, p. 10).

During the process of mirroring, the music therapist musically captures the child's behaviors, energy, and affect. The child may recognize the therapist as a provider of the music, but eventually may accept the music therapist's presence and participation in their own experience. After acceptance is attained, the music therapist seeks to shape the child's responses by working melodic motifs into a melody and possibly adding lyrics. Finally, the music therapist assumes control of the session—requiring the child's attention in following musical and verbal cues to play and stop playing.

By joining the child in his experience, the music therapist strives for the child to recognize his influence on what is happening in his environment and on the music therapist's behavior. Once a child realizes this influence, he often pauses for a moment to check his thought. After affirming the thought, the child often erupts into a huge smile, initiates brief eye contact with the music therapist, and then resumes the behavior with increased vigor.

Goals in improvisatory music therapy methods may include engagement, reciprocity, communication, self-expression, emotional release, social connection, and physical discharge. The therapist's role during improvisation can vary from providing support for the child's vocal or instrumental exploration to risk-taking to building on themes.

It is important for the therapist to remember that improvisation does not mean a lack of structure. Younger children with ASD seek repetition and familiarity. They need structure in order to begin to put meaning to experience. Bruscia (1987) delineated clinical techniques for improvisational music therapy that provide an excellent guide for music therapists, including musical techniques for empathy, structuring, intimacy, elicitation, redirection, procedural, referential, and emotional exploration.

Instrumental Improvisation

Overview. Instrumental improvisation is a process wherein the music therapist and the client create music using instruments that become the vehicle on which they form a musical relationship. The improvisation can be started by either the therapist or the child, and any object that can make a musical sound can be used. The purpose is to promote relatedness, communication, socialization, and awareness within the music itself. This is accomplished by musically engaging, matching, supporting, and enhancing the child's expressions, musically or nonmusically (Carpente, 2009).

Instrumental improvisation can provide the child a chance to experience synchrony, reciprocity, self-expression, and engagement with another person. It can also provide opportunity for self-organization and self-regulation. Instrumental improvisation can encourage reciprocity and provide a foundation for meaningful communication for individuals with little or no verbal language. Children who have extreme auditory, visual, or social difficulties might benefit more from individual child/adult instrumental improvisation than being in a group setting. No contraindications are known for instrumental improvisation. Level of therapy: augmentative, intensive.

Preparation. A wide assortment of instruments that require no formal training or experience to play should be readily accessible to the child. Percussive instruments such as drums, maracas, eggs, triangles, cymbals, and melodic instruments (e.g., marimba, xylophone, resonator bells, and horns) are all appropriate. If needed, instruments and mallets should be adapted to accommodate for children with physical limitations (e.g., grasp, range of motion, strength) and to improve the likelihood of success should there be issues with motor planning or sound sensitivity. The music therapist then chooses the instruments for the child and arranges them in the music space depending on the goals of the intervention and the most suitable sound for the child. The child should have adequate space to move about the room and have easy access to all instrument possibilities.

What to observe. The music therapist should be very familiar with the client's developmental music responses. Instruments can present a challenge to children who tend to engage with objects in a nonfunctional matter (e.g., spinning the cymbal, dropping mallets, throwing maracas); however, improvisational instrument play can be implemented to musically draw a child toward the music in order to create awareness, interest, engagement, and interaction (Nordoff & Robbins, 2007).

The music therapist improvises music using her musicianship, creativity, intuition, and clinical knowledge of the child. The intent is to actively improvise music wherein children can experience themselves in a new way. Although the focus is on musical goals and the child's musical experiences, these goal areas can also address underlying cognitive, expressive, sensory, and social deficits.

Procedures. The therapist chooses the instruments depending upon the child's goal or objective. The therapist must consider whether she and the client will play the same or different instruments, allow for exploration or provide assistance, encourage individual expression or encourage imitation, etc. It is important to remember that both exploration and imitation are opportunities for learning and relating for children with ASD.

After instrument choice and arrangement, the therapist either initiates play or waits for the child to play. Use of a familiar song or chant (re-creative method) might be used to introduce and encourage the beginning of improvisatory play. The therapist can then begin musical play or cue (through word or gesture) for the child to start or to join in playing.

For clients needing more structure and grounding, providing a steady rhythm pattern as well as a predictable harmonic progression or repeated melody can provide a foundation for musical exploration. Listening carefully to the children's sounds and observing for engagement or withdrawal guides the music therapist in techniques to encourage or discourage playing. It is important to keep in mind that those individuals with more severe ASD symptoms are often more likely to imitate in short spurts rather than create longer improvisational motifs.

Adaptations. Instrumental improvisations are easily adaptable both to vocal improvisations and to group improvisations. The goals for group improvisation include developing awareness (Mosca, DiFranco, & Moselli, 2004), increasing use of social and/or expressive language, expanding or increasing reciprocal exchanges with peers (Gross, Linden, & Ostermann, 2010; Kim, Wigram, & Gold, 2008), and participating in call-and-response or turn-taking (Kim, Wigram, & Gold, 2008). Group instrumental improvisation can also provide an opportunity for the child to initiate interaction, engage in peer-to-peer synchronization or reciprocity; practice self-organization and self-regulation; and experience group cohesion. Suggested goals might be to adjust tempo, meter, or dynamics to match the music of peers; imitate peers' rhythmic or melodic patterns; take turns; initiate musical ideas; or engage in reciprocal musical exchanges with peers.

Referential Improvisation

Overview. Referential improvisations consist of improvised music structured around a nonmusical theme or idea sometimes called a "referent." They are indicated for those clients who have adequate receptive language skills and who demonstrate ability to use imaginative play skills. The goals differ from those of improvisations without a theme (nonreferential) because clients are asked to connect their thoughts to music and vice versa. No contraindications are known for referential improvisation. Level of therapy: augmentative.

Preparation. The client should be positioned in close proximity to the music therapist, with any instruments being used within reach. Because this experience is based upon an idea or theme, the music therapist will need to verbally set up and describe the theme, be able to provide cues and prompts as needed, and assist the client during the improvisation if needed. Whenever possible, make certain that the room is free of visual and auditory distractions (windows, loudspeaker announcements, noise from neighboring rooms, other instruments within visual or physical range that are not included in the improvisation experience, etc.) to ensure that the client's participation and success are optimized.

It is recommended that the client have access to a variety of musical instruments to allow for contrast among sounds. The themes that the music therapist chooses should relate directly to the client's clinical needs. For example, if a goal is to improve awareness of others' feelings, the therapist might consider themes that are relevant to the emotional and social domains. She might facilitate short improvisations on a variety of disparate feelings (e.g., happy/mad, sad/excited) by either encouraging the client to choose an instrument and create an expression or musically representing an emotion and asking the client to identify it and re-create it.

What to observe. During themed improvisations, music therapists observe clients' musical and nonmusical behaviors. They interpret their understanding of the theme (e.g., emotion such as anger, or event such as a party) by the appropriateness of the musical expressions and qualities of their playing. Engagement is typically easy to determine based upon their level of active participation and responsiveness during the improvisation itself.

For more abstract themes (e.g., feelings), the music therapist can interpret the client's musical improvisations by looking at their choice of instrument, creativity, length of improvisation, musical qualities used to communicate the theme (e.g., volume, tempo), and accompanying facial expressions and body language. Lack of congruity between the musical expression and facial expression/body language may be an indicator that the client needs additional training and awareness in how their expressions may lead to miscommunication and misunderstanding.

Procedures. Themed (referential) improvisations can be implemented individually or within a group. They can be the focus of an entire session or one experience among several. In most cases, themed improvisations start with a nonmusical idea, which is then expressed musically in some way. The referential improvisation may take the form of short individual improvisations, group improvisations of varying lengths, dyad or small group improvisations, or any combination of these, depending on the nonmusical idea chosen and the purpose of the experience. One common childhood group improvisation is to create a thunderstorm. Regardless of the theme for the improvisation, the music therapist must take time to properly explain and set up the musical experience before starting, as well as lead a discussion about the experience after it is done.

Adaptations. There are endless options for adapting a referential improvisation experience. Some options include all participants having the same instrument, using body percussion, using one melodic instrument while the remainder of group members use rhythm instruments, playing together vs. taking turns (e.g., call-and-response), and vocal improvisations.

Guidelines for Re-creative Music Therapy

Singing, dancing, and action songs are common childhood experiences. Throughout history, all cultures have used songs both for learning and for play. The majority of children's songs consist of simple melodies and use repetition, rhythm, and rhyme (Schwartz, 2012). Popular children's songs are widely known and are easily accessed by parents and other adults through television and videos as well as music CDs. This makes them easily accessible to children outside of the music therapy sessions, which allows for repeated exposure.

Not surprisingly, the majority of music therapy literature focuses on the use of re-creative methods with individuals with ASD. Precomposed songs include popular children's songs, traditional and cultural songs, adaptations of children's songs, and therapist-composed songs. Singing these songs provides a child with ASD opportunity for connecting or relating with others. Adaptations of familiar children's music provide opportunity for addressing clinical needs while taking advantage of the child's motivation and interest in preferred music. Therapist-created songs are composed with specific therapeutic objectives in mind.

It is important that the music therapist be familiar with current children's music groups and artists and theme songs of popular children's programs as well as their clients' favorite musical songs and styles. Oftentimes, even functionally nonverbal children with ASD will insert small musical motifs from their preferred programs and favorite songs into their sessions. Therefore, having an awareness of what music clients encounter will enhance rapport and engagement within the session, as the music therapist then is able to incorporate these melodies into the session.

Singing Songs

Overview. Singing songs is very prevalent in music therapy literature (Barrickman, 1989; Braithwaite & Sigafoos, 1998; Geist, 2012), most likely because of its prevalence across all cultures and societies. Singing songs can be therapist-directed or child-directed and implemented with or without instrumental accompaniment. Nearly all children enjoy singing songs, but it is the music therapist who determines the therapeutic intent. The beauty of singing songs is that the experience can serve multiple functions at the same time. For children with ASD, singing songs can serve a number of clinical needs, including providing opportunities for learning new information (e.g., academics, manners), practicing fundamental communication skills (e.g., call-and-response, filling in the blanks), challenging and practicing shifting attention, increasing motivation for engagement with others, and expanding repertoires of responding. However, underlying all other intents for singing songs is the child's need for increasing social motivation, engagement, and reciprocity. Singing songs inherently requires both a singer and a listener fluidly responding and adjusting in the moment. Sometimes the same individual is both the singing and the listener—much like in a verbal conversation.

Children with ASD benefit from singing songs because it provides them with structured, time-limited, and intrinsically motivating experiences that address underlying deficits in social engagement, reciprocity, social behavioral skills, communication, concept retention, and functional language. While the musical objectives for singing songs might include matching tempo, dynamics, and timbre or adjusting singing quality to match the musical, emotional, or social sound of the song, the underlying clinical value is much deeper.

For a child to sing a song, they must sufficiently motivated to process musical stimuli, but this does not necessarily mean that there is intent or a desire to interact and share the experience with others. In fact, many individuals with ASD engage in self-directed behaviors (including singing songs to themselves) as a means of stimulation. Therefore, the clinical use of singing songs requires a relationship between the music therapist, the client, and the song itself. There are no known contraindications for singing songs. Level of therapy: auxiliary/augmentative.

Preparation. The music therapist will set up the room to allow for the client to engage in singing songs. Sometimes, this requires no more than a place for the child to sit or stand while participating. When using a piano (for example), the music therapist should have ability to visually attend to the client should he move about the room during the experience. If there is use of microphones, amplifiers, or recording equipment, these should be set up in advance. Any sheet music needed should also be ready.

The music therapist needs to determine, as best as possible, how the songs will be presented, meaning sung a cappella, using piano or guitar, or accompanied with rhythmic accompaniment (e.g., percussion instruments). Any instruments that will be used should also be readily available. If the therapist plans to allow the client choices, all acceptable possibilities for songs and instruments should be available as well. Sometimes, creation of a list of song titles or pictures of acceptable instruments will assist the child with ASD in understanding available options and making choices.

What to observe. The music therapist will observe the client's verbal, vocal, and gestural responses while engaged in singing songs. Signs that the child is engaged in the experience include eye contact, positive facial expressions (regardless of whether directed toward the therapist), arousal behaviors (e.g., alert body posture, widening eyes), and continued singing or playing along. Singing songs can be implemented in both individual and group sessions.

Musically, the therapist will listen for the child's use of pitch, rhythm, and melody as well as the ability to entrain to the beat, tonal center, or tempo of the song. If action songs are used, the music therapist will observe the timing and quality of those actions as well as the child's ability to remain in sync with the song's lyrics. Affective responses such as becoming frustrated due to lack of coordination, poor timing, or general confusion can add clinical information about the client's weaknesses.

When facilitating singing songs within a group, the music therapist will have much more to observe. There will be both intra- and interpersonal responses to notice. In addition, there are responses to observe within the singing experience as well as responses before and after the experience.

Procedures. The music therapist can present the songs in any number of ways, depending upon the functioning level of the child and the therapeutic intent of the experience. Children who require more structure will likely respond best when songs are introduced by the music therapist or when their choices of songs are limited (at least initially). In these cases, the music therapist may need to be more directive and provide the child with expectations for their participation and responses desired. Songs can also be requested by the child, which can be either independently initiated or facilitated by the music therapist.

Songs can be introduced by the therapist through a musical introduction or through a spoken invitation. The environment of expectation can also be created through musical cues so that the child can independently initiate the song. Therapists listen for and support identifying intervals, familiar and repeated musical motifs, and melodic rhythm patterns. Lyrically, the use of repeated phrases or verbal utterances (even those without true words) might become material for the songs being sung. For individuals with ASD who present with echolalia, songs might provide an opportunity for interruption of this process or may be incorporated into the song to be an "appropriate" response.

Most children with ASD will not naturally sing along with another person. Oftentimes, the music therapist will sing the song while the child strums the guitar or plays along using a handheld instrument. Similarly, those without functional expressive language often do not produce long, held-out notes. Instead, their singing often consists of short, sporadic, staccato-like utterances. Initially, the music therapist can sing the song to the child and later make musical space for the child to add words at the end of phrases (e.g., filling in the blank). While singing, the music therapist visually engages the child through use of eye contact, smiling, and an encouraging expression. Exaggerated responses of positive emotions may reinforce the child with ASD when targeted responses are shown. The child will need to hear a song multiple times before being able to sing it alone.

One effective technique is to begin song singing with no verbal introduction, using musical cues to promote anticipation of a learned song. Musical cues can be melodic, rhythmic, or harmonic in nature. Regardless of how the song is presented, the music therapist supports the child by maintaining a consistent melodic, harmonic, and rhythmic organization but does so in a manner that is flexible in overall structure and tempo. This allows the child to enter into the music-making in their own way while still experiencing a musical whole. The objective might be for increasing duration of sound, use of related pitch or inflection, or production of the words or phrase of a familiar lyric.

Adaptations. There are a myriad of ways that singing songs can be adapted. Singing does not need to be defined specifically as the act of giving melody to words; it can also be more widely defined as including any vocalizations or oral responses. In this way, humming, whistling, tongue clicking, grunting, etc., can all be included. For individuals without functional expressive language skills, the acceptance of any vocal utterance can become the foundation for more meaningful expressive communication.

It is also important to note that singing songs invariably occurs within the context of other musical experiences and is easily combined with other music therapy methods. Often, singing familiar, precomposed songs may lead naturally into an improvisational intervention designed to promote individual expression and relatedness with the therapists. Similarly, more structured, academically oriented musical experiences often incorporate the use of singing songs to support learning objectives while providing a secure structure and foundation for the experience itself.

Singing songs is also something that can easily be carried over into other settings outside of the music therapy session. Advancements in technology, applications for electronic media, and music-sharing software make it very easy for songs to travel with their "owner." For a child with ASD, it may very well be the act of sharing the song with another person outside of music therapy that has the most clinical value.

Instrumental Songs

Overview. Instrumental songs are musical experiences wherein a client plays along with an accompaniment or as specifically instructed. The music therapist engages individuals in a musical experience that incorporates repetition and structure to promote functional skills in initiating, responding, modulating, processing, and planning responses. In this method, the client's response within music is instrumental rather verbal or vocal. Some basic goals for instrumental songs include foundational skills for communication such as awareness of and responding to environmental cues (e.g., starting and stopping, modulating play to match musical qualities, imitating rhythmic or melodic patterns), early play skills (e.g., engaging in reciprocal pattern play, mutual or joint play, playing in synchrony, responding to a music cue with learned rhythmic or melodic pattern), and more sophisticated responses that promote independence and creativity.

Instrumental songs can be used within individual and group sessions. When used in group settings, the goals often include social skills development such as socialization and reciprocity, generalization of specific skills in a group setting, listening skills, direction-following, anticipation and motor planning of defined responses, and environmental awareness. This method may need to be modified in order to be used for children with severe auditory, visual, or social difficulties. However, other than the possibility of the inability to adapt instruments to accommodate physical or sensory limitations, there are no known contraindications to using instrumental songs in therapy. Level of therapy: auxiliary/augmentative.

Preparation. The music therapist will need to spend some time setting up the room and gathering appropriate instruments prior to implementing this method. Considerations of possible therapeutic needs for space, seating, and safety should all be made. The choice of song to be used for instrument-playing should be made prior to the session as well; however, the music therapist is advised to have a few backup selections should the original piece not be appropriate. Choices of songs are made by keeping in mind the client's need for structure and stability, rhythmic sophistication, sound tolerance, and musical style and instrument preferences. Since many children with ASD present with sensory sensitivities and avoidances, it is suggested that they be allowed to handle and try out any novel instruments prior to their use in the experience.

The therapist should also consider the client's clinical profile when using instrumental songs. In particular, the music therapist will consider the child's typical style of interacting with the therapist, ability to recognize musical structure, and ability to selectively attend. Songs that have multiple juxtaposing rhythms, thick harmonic structures, or sophisticated chord progressions might not be suitable for lower-functioning clients with ASD. Instead, the music therapist may choose songs that have accessible, familiar meter; repetitive rhythms; simpler instrumentation; and predictable structure.

What to observe. The music therapist will pay attention to how the client interacts with the instrument chosen or assigned. For example, it may be of interest for the music therapist to see how responsive the child is to the selected music, whether the experience is shared with the therapist (joint attention), affective responses, and the range of creativity shown while playing. When presented in a group setting, the music therapist will observe not only intrapersonal, but also interpersonal responses and interactions. How a child participates in a group instrument song is often an indication of self-organization, self-regulation, awareness of others, and relatedness to the group as a whole.

Procedures. The music therapist can set up and direct instrumental songs in any number of ways. They can be directive and take full leadership of the experience, or they can encourage the client to take some responsibility in setting up for the experience themselves (e.g., instrument choice, song choice, leadership role, etc.). When first introducing a song, the instruments can be presented to the child to play at the identified moment in the music. The therapist could also provide positional prompts or gestural cues to indicate when to play their instrument. Other strategies might include setting instruments in the order in which they are to be played, using gestures or pointing to cue the child when to play, using visual symbols such as picture cards to cue responses, and using song lyrics to explain directions.

Instrumental songs most often focus on learning, remembering, and reproducing simple rhythmic or melodic patterns. For the child with ASD, these experiences and skills serve to address key deficits in relatedness with others. While children with ASD thrive on repetition and familiarity, it is advised that these experiences be modified slightly once the general concepts and goals for the song have been mastered. This can be accomplished by assigning different instrumental parts, using similar task demands with different songs, adjusting one musical aspect of the song (e.g., tempo, key, etc.), or simply changing the order of the instruments played. All of these minor adjustments are valuable for the child with ASD to enable generalization of newly learned skills into novel situations. This also ensures that the child has made the appropriate associations to the experience rather than memorizing the task demands of that particular song.

Adaptations. The adaptations for using instrumental songs in music therapy are countless. Often, instrumental songs can become a warm-up experience that leads into an instrument improvisation. Similarly, it is quite common for music therapists to combine action or movement activities with instrument-playing. By incorporating movement paired with instrument-playing, the client gains practice in more sophisticated levels of responding and has opportunity for greater self-organization and self-regulation. By using virtual or electronic instruments rather than real instruments, the child with ASD is given opportunities for expanded creativity, novel sensory experience, and adaptive use of technology.

Adaptive Music Lessons

Overview. Adaptive music lessons are a form of individual music therapy wherein the intent of instruction is on clinical goals rather than development of musical skill. While adaptive music lessons could be conducted on any instrument, the most common are typically voice, piano, guitar, and drums. During the adaptive music lesson, the therapist interacts with the client in the process of making music on a selected instrument. The intent of the session is to address clinical goals to improve the client's functioning in areas of motor control and coordination, self-regulation and modulation, self-awareness, sequencing, working memory, and selective attention. Most often, the music therapist works with the client individually; however, it is not uncommon for clients to work in small groups (e.g., duets) in order to expand on previously mastered goals.

For higher functioning individuals with ASD, adaptive music lessons can address a broad variety of goals as stated above; however, the primary goals are likely to be related to development of leisure skills, improving frustration tolerance, enhancing social skills, and increasing self-esteem. Because individuals with ASD often have limited awareness of how others perceive them, the adaptive music lessons also provide practice in improving their understanding of how others view them, how their assessments of performance compare with those of others, and critical and abstract thinking skills. It should be noted that referrals for adaptive music lessons often come from parents of children with ASD rather than from the children themselves. For this reason, the music therapist will need to spend some time explaining the intent and purpose of the sessions to parents. No contraindications are known for adaptive music lessons. Level of therapy: auxiliary/augmentative.

Preparation. The decision to engage in an adaptive music lesson requires preparation prior to the first session. The music therapist will need to assess the client's basic functioning level, ability to follow directions and self-correct, level of engageability and motivation, and physical or emotional barriers that may influence the choice of instrument. For example, a child with poor auditory discrimination skills and limited attention span might not be a good candidate for adapted violin lessons. Lessons on piano are suggested for individuals with low frustration, short attention span, or limited self-awareness. It is the music therapist's responsibility to help clients and their families make realistic instrument choices, given the clinical needs and abilities as well as therapeutic goals.

Preparation for sessions needs to take into consideration the needs for physical space for the lesson and required equipment (e.g., music stand). The music therapist will have appropriate sheet music and CD player and/or recording device, as well as other materials needed to conduct the session (e.g., tuners, metronome, extra strings for guitar, etc.).

What to observe. The music therapist observes the client's quality of participation in the session, paying particular attention to frustration, ability to understand instructions, and physical limitations and coordination issues, as well as cognitive skills related to the process of learning music. Because the adapted music lesson involves more than simply playing the instrument, the music therapist must be able to communicate basic musical constructs to the child in a manner that supports their process. At some point, most clients will be expected to be able to play notes from a page of sheet music. Therefore, didactic instruction on musical notation, music theory, and music history may all enter the session. The music therapist will also pay particular attention to the level of effort and motivation the client demonstrates. The music therapist will be interested in finding out if the client practices their instrument between sessions and their expectations for their lessons as well as their progress in playing it.

Procedures. As in traditional music lessons, clients will spend at least some time with warm-ups, review of familiar materials, technical exercises, and learning new information. While adaptive music lessons are conducted much like other music lessons, music therapists adapt procedures and devise teaching strategies according to the needs of the student. Some simple teaching strategies may include the use of color-coded keys (e.g., on the piano), labeling notes with letters, using larger notation, or creating and improvising musical jingles to remember note names, key signatures, etc.

During the adaptive music lesson, the music therapist maintains an active and supportive role with the client by providing encouragement and gentle redirection, and eliciting responses on the performance. The music therapist attempts to assist the client in improving underlying cognitive weaknesses by pointing out commonalities among errors, indicating aspects of playing to attend to, and providing assistance in how to overcome common hurdles. The music therapist may accompany the child by playing the same thing or providing harmonic structures in order to practice playing along with others. At the end of the session, the music therapist will identify tasks to practice at home, theory worksheets to complete, etc.

Guidelines for Compositional Music Therapy

Within the context of compositional methods, the focus is on the use of therapist-generated musical experiences to address nonmusical goals. Songs and instrumental compositions in therapy generally arise out of an identified clinical issue and the music therapist's desire to support therapeutic aims in a more structured manner. Sometimes the composition arises out of the client-therapist's musical interaction or musical themes from the session. At other times, the composition can arise out of verbal discussions, such as those with a higher-functioning individual with ASD or Asperger's Syndrome.

When the music therapist creates compositional experiences for lower-functioning individuals with ASD, the resulting composition likely contains more basic information in a simplistic musical frame. Compositions may be created to address simple pre-academic skills such as rules for good classroom behavior (e.g., staying in seat, raising hands to speak), using manners (e.g., recognizing when to use "please" and "thank you"), or basic life skills (e.g., understanding roles of community helpers such as police and firefighters, recognizing safety signs), etc. For higher-functioning individuals with ASD, compositional themes of peer pressure, bullying, self-esteem, disappointment, competition, self-identity, problem-solving, and other psychological processes may be expressed.

Songwriting

Overview. Songwriting is simply the composing of original music and lyrics to express an idea or feeling. In individual music therapy, therapists use songwriting for clients with ASD to share information, problem-solve situations (including examining the nature of problems and providing solutions), express feelings, and provide for creative expression. Songwriting can be used to promote understanding of past experiences or to anticipate future ones. It can serve as a vehicle for remembering information, sequencing, or representing symbolic thinking.

Songwriting typically involves more sophisticated processes than found in receptive or re-creative music therapy interventions. For this reason, the music therapist works with the client on the lyrics for the song while taking more responsibility for composing the music. When writing songs for clients with ASD, the lyrics are just as important as the music. The lyrics can be created to support prosocial behaviors (e.g., apologizing, being assertive), address coping skills (e.g., perfectionism), or facilitate understanding of emotions (e.g., worry and anxiety).

Individual goals for songwriting with lower-functioning individuals with ASD often serve the purpose of developing vocabulary, expanding behavioral repertoire, promoting social understanding, and learning new information. For higher-functioning individuals with ASD, goals for songwriting align more with traditional psychotherapy goals: needs for self-esteem, expression of feelings, and creativity. Regardless of the functioning level of the client, songwriting may be used to provide personal reflection, encourage problem-solving, and promote emotional growth.

Songwriting can be facilitated in either an individual or group setting. Group songwriting can be used to develop problem-solving skills, increase group cooperation and participation, and improve tolerance and respect for others. Group songwriting helps develop shared responsibility and the ability to compromise and work cooperatively for a single purpose. Songwriting within a group setting may be particularly therapeutic for meeting the social needs of individuals with ASD.

Songwriting may be contraindicated for those who struggle with basic expressive language skills. However, the music therapist may find it appropriate to take more of a leadership role in the composition and modify the demands on the client in order to facilitate the experience. For example, individuals with poor verbal communication may be able to make choices from laminated pictures, fill in the blanks, or participate in the composition in some other way. Level of therapy: auxiliary/augmentative.

Preparation. Songwriting may occur spontaneously or have been previously discussed in therapy. Which comes first, the melody or the lyrics? Either may provide the inspiration for songwriting. The music therapist must be aware of the needs of the individual or group and the goals for therapy. Musical themes, melodic ideas, or rhythmic patterns may have evolved in musical improvisations and can be utilized in songwriting. The room must be adequate in size for the needs of the individual or group, with a piano or guitar to provide accompaniment. Instruments should be of the highest quality affordable with accurate acoustics. Paper and pen may be needed to transcribe or create lyrics, and staff paper or musical software is needed to notate music. A recording device is needed to record ideas and revisions. The final product may be videotaped, recorded, or performed.

The music therapist must be familiar with a variety of musical styles and accompaniments. The music therapist may facilitate the songwriting process or assist the client with the songwriting process by transcribing the melody and lyrics musically.

What to observe. The therapist must observe and assess the client's receptivity to expressing thoughts and feelings through songwriting. The therapist must observe the client's emotional state, affect, and willingness to cooperate. Be aware of any resistance or attempt at avoidance. Some students may not be ready to explore personal feelings or may lack awareness of feeling states at all. In a group setting, the therapist must evaluate group attitude and group dynamics to determine the ability to participate in songwriting activities. Group cooperation and participation must be encouraged to facilitate each person's involvement in songwriting. The therapist must facilitate group discussion at least initially.

Procedures. Songwriting may be approached in a variety of ways. Songwriting may be initiated by the individual or group or suggested by the therapist. A melodic motif or rhythmic pattern from an improvisational activity may be utilized in songwriting. A theme may be presented by the individual or group based on a present problem or past experience. The individual or a group member may base lyrics on an original poem or journal writing. Lyrics may be suggested by a personal or group experience or past memory.

Songwriting may occur spontaneously or be planned by the therapist. The therapist or individual or a group member may suggest a theme, which is utilized and developed. As the process unfolds, the lyrics may be written down to capture ideas to be developed and revised. The songwriting process may be recorded as it occurs and then transcribed to musical notation. The client may sing or suggest a melody, which can be further developed by the group and facilitated by the therapist. The song can later be videotaped, performed, or recorded by the individual or group.

Working with Caregivers

When working with children with ASD, consideration of the child as part of a larger system is essential. Therefore, music therapists are encouraged to recognize the essential role that parents and other family members play in children's development. Music therapists have a unique opportunity to support and collaborate with teachers and other therapists by listening and observing the interaction between the child and other colleagues while creating a musical environment that enhances the experiences of their interaction (Carpente, 2012). By sharing music therapy strategies with others, children are afforded help to ensure generalization and opportunity for practice and retention of skills.

Within a consultative role to the classroom teacher, the music therapist can serve as a resource for designing and implementing interventions to address the general classroom environment, transitioning, or supporting specific academic skills. Other therapists (e.g., speech/language pathologist, occupational therapist, behavior therapist, psychologist) may benefit from having a music therapist guide and inform them regarding simple strategies to deepen their musical experience with their clients by using music intentionally, but within their scope of practice.

Music therapists have written about providing music therapy interventions within the context of the family. The goals for family music therapy interventions are often to increase positive parent/child interactions, promote communication between family members, provide an opportunity for generalization of skills, and demonstrate techniques to family members (Allgood, 2005). The main interventions used in family sessions include using movement, sensory experiences, improvisation and instrument-playing, and singing songs.

Research Evidence

During the last 40 years, research in music therapy and autism has been broadly focused. As early as the 1960s and 1970s, research and anecdotal accounts of the effectiveness of music therapy interventions for persons with autism could be found in the literature (e.g., Alvin, 1965; Stevens & Clark, 1969). Given the wide interests of researchers on this topic, the literature has been categorized in two ways, according to intended outcome, and where possible according to methodology.

Music therapists' work with ASD children typically focuses on four main deficit areas: (a) language development, (b) social and emotional development, (c) cognitive concept development (pre- and academic skills), and (d) sensorimotor development. There are two main methods of approaching therapy when music therapists work with children with ASD—those primarily employing improvisational techniques and those using more structured/directed techniques.

Because music is transcultural and considered overwhelmingly pleasurable by the majority of persons, the use of music in therapy is often viewed as a motivating and mediating object. Yet it is the significance of time, rhythm, and temporal processing that is important in influencing communication and learning in children, and especially children with autism. Trevarthen (2000) states that:

> Psychosocial or interpersonal techniques that meet the child where they are, picking up on his or her interests, purposes, and sensitivities, can help physiological regulation, emotions, and learning. The efficacy of music therapy and other forms of nonverbal communication in modifying autonomic state, engaging attention, and improving development of skills validates such a strategy. (p. 42)

Music Therapy and Motivation

Music captures and helps maintain attention (Paul, 1982; Watson, 1979). It is highly motivating and engaging. It can be used as a motivator and as a natural reinforcer for desired responses. Nelson, Anderson, and Gonzales (1984) state that music focuses attention to on-task behaviors and that this focus can be reinforcing to ASD children. They report further that the positive affective responses often occurring when ASD children participate in music activities can strengthen their attention and augment a child's participation in other activities that assist them in attaining goals in other social and language areas. In other words, there seems to be a transfer effect possible once a child demonstrates a level of attention and skill during music therapy activities.

According to Oppenheim (1974), most ASD children enjoy music and can carry a tune at a very young age. In addition, they usually not only have a good sense of rhythm, but also enjoy the process of trying. Children with autism often enjoy singing by themselves, but the process of singing with others is difficult and takes much time. DeMyer (1979) found that 90% of ASD children in her study demonstrated a positive response to music, while only six percent of children in her study rejected music. Children with autism tend to prefer only one or two types of music—more specifically, music that is simple and repetitive in nature. Normal children had better movement to rhythm than did children with autism. A year later, Kolko, Anderson, and Campbell (1980) found that most ASD children are more likely to attend to an auditory stimulus than a visual stimulus when the auditory stimulus is musical.

Braithwaite and Sigafoos (1998) compared social vs. musical antecedents on appropriate communication responses in a group of five children with developmental disabilities. Their assumption was that being able to identify antecedent factors that increase a child's responsiveness might enable therapists to create effective interventions and opportunities for communication. Their findings were somewhat inconclusive; however, they suggest that musical antecedents may facilitate communication responses in some children with developmental delays. The researchers point out that motivational and attention factors may have played a significant role in generating greater responses from some of the participants.

Music therapists are well qualified to analyze the objective characteristics of music and are best able to make optimum therapeutic matches between specific activities and the developmental needs of their clients. Nelson, Anderson, and Gonzales (1984) describe ways to incorporate music activities according to a child with autism's neuropsychological characteristics. In their article, the authors describe the uses of music to develop skills in the areas of responsiveness to therapy, responsivity to sensory stimuli, attentional processes, transfer of learning and adapting to change, temporal perception, rhythmic movement and praxia, language and symbolic functions, communication and socialization, and meaning and affect. Music may provide a useful context for facilitating the development of curiosity and exploratory interest. In theory, concepts learned through music experiences may transfer to other stimuli.

Music Therapy for Language and Communication

By definition, ASD children show delays in acquisition of language that range from complete absence of communication to deficits in use of language for conversation (Tager-Flusberg, 2001). A child's ability to function in society is largely dependent upon his/her ability to acquire functional speech and language (Davis, Gfeller, & Thaut, 1999). If a child with autism does not begin to use functional speech and language by the age of five, speech and language delays will continue to be evident throughout their development. Common problems for ASD children include echolalia, perseverative language, improper use of language in context, and limited use of vocabulary. Delays can occur in pre- and linguistic language (meaning the production of sound) and in both expressive and receptive areas.

In attempts to facilitate speech acquisition, researchers have found that pairing manual (or gestural) systems of communication with speech is successful for children with mental retardation, autism, and language deficits (Layton, 1988; Yoder & Layton, 1988). In terms of language development, many children with mental retardation and autism exhibit difficulties in cognitive functions, including memory. In 1975, Ricks and Wing studied the role of music with ASD children and their ability to accurately recall sound patterns. They found that other stimuli were significantly more likely to be remembered if they were paired with a melodic pattern. Nelson, Anderson, and Gonzales (1984) accounted for this trend by concluding that it is easier to transfer learning from musical situations to other, more difficult situations.

Music Therapy for Social Development

Music therapy is an effective way for ASD children to work on their problems related to creativity and initiation (Goldstein, 1964; Hollander & Juhrs, 1974; Mahlberg, 1973; Saperston, 1973, 1982; Schmidt & Edwards, 1976; Stevens & Clark, 1969). In 1976, Purvis and Samet described how incorporating music therapy in developmental therapy is designed to promote social and emotional growth. Music is "proved to be a highly effective tool for fostering social-emotional development in autistic and troubled children" (p. 3). The authors provide a list of specific guidelines for different types of music activities that could be used in developmental therapy.

Receptive Methods

Empirical efficacy studies have shown that music therapy is effective in increasing socialization and communication (Edgerton, 1994; Hollander & Juhrs, 1974), decreasing perseverative behaviors (Hollander & Juhrs, 1974); developing musical and nonmusical communication (Edgerton, 1994), improving parent/child relationships (Allgood, 2005), and facilitating peer interactions (Kern, 2004).

Improvisational Methods

Several studies have explored the use of improvised music with ASD children (Alvin & Warwick, 1992; Carpente, 2011; Edgerton, 1994; Nordoff & Robbins, 1964, 1968, 1971, 1977; Saperston, 1973).

Learning processes of children with autism are always negatively affected by perceptual problems such as lack of concentration, fluctuating attention, limited eye contact, and preoccupation with ritualistic behaviors. Yet, ASD children are able to perceive and process musical stimuli despite their various other perceptual deficits (Appelbaum, Egel, Koegel, & Imhoff, 1979; DeLong, 1978; Tanguay, 1976). Although attention is usually a weak skill in handicapped children, most children seem to memorize music and songs without effort. In her book, Alvin (1965) elucidated reasons for using music as a treatment modality: "When a child shows a reaction of pleasure to music, whether a physical, a sensuous, an intellectual, or an emotional one, we can conclude that the child is sensitive to music in some way, and that music can be of value in his education" (p. 14).

Benenzon (1981) views the main benefit of music therapy as its ability to provide a context to facilitate exchange and reciprocity. Volkmar et al. (1997) state that "vocal expressions are observed from the first days of life, and long before an infant can respond differentially to the verbal content of speech, he or she can respond with great accuracy to tone and pitch of the voice" (p. 177). Additionally, children in music therapy conditions have been found to produce higher levels of spontaneous speech and verbal responding.

Music can create a feeling of security and act as a bridge between the familiar and the unknown. According to Alvin (1965), "the emotional desire to express himself in music may help and even hasten the perceptual maturation of the child" (p. 27). Recent studies have found that music therapy can increase general levels of responsiveness and engagement in children with disabilities (Hairston, 1990; Edgerton, 1994; Toolan & Coleman, 1994). Toolan and Coleman (1994) found that music therapy enhances engagement in persons with learning disabilities.

In Edgerton's study (1994), an improvisational format was used based on the work of Nordoff and Robbins's (1977) Creative Music Therapy approach to determine the effects on a number of communicative behaviors from the first music therapy session to the last (10th) session. She measured the communicative behaviors using the Checklist of Communicative Responses/Acts Score Sheet (CRASS) that was specifically created for the study. This checklist contains a total of 107 items, with 91 in a musical category and 16 in a nonmusical category. She categorized 69 items as communicative responses and 38 items as communicative acts. Not only did Edgerton find a positive trend during her intervention when compared to the reversal phases, but also she found significant score differences ($p < .01$) on subjects' scores on the CRASS from the first to last session. Edgerton measured such behaviors as matching a fast basic beat, imitating the rhythm of a melodic motif, taking turns in a rhythmic "give and take," etc. Communicative acts were defined as behaviors that the child initiated in an attempt to influence the experimenter's expression. Results from the study indicate that improvisational music therapy is effective in eliciting and increasing communicative behaviors in ASD children within the musical setting as found in other previous studies (Alvin & Warwick, 1992; Hollander & Juhrs, 1974; Nordoff & Robbins, 1964, 1968, 1971, 1977; Saperston, 1973).

Edgerton's work (1994) found that ASD children tended to beat/vocalize in a steady tempo and match the therapist's tempo. By using synchrony of the improvised music to the children's repetitive movements and vocalizations, there seemed to be an increase in their sense of awareness and control over their environment as well as the fundamental building blocks for a means of communication. She concluded that tempo may initially be one communicative modality wherein autistic children can experience immediate success because of their rhythmic behaviors.

Re-creative Methods

Music therapy provides a nonverbal means to communicate. Seybold (1971) examined whether a structured music therapy intervention would encourage spontaneous speech in eight boys identified with speech delay. Four of the boys participated in song-based music activities, while the other four boys participated in a control condition that involved verbal imitation and labeling. The children in the music therapy condition produced more frequent spontaneous speech, suggesting that music may help stimulate communication. While specific statistical procedures and results are not discussed in this article, he found that the four children in the music therapy condition produced higher levels of spontaneous speech. In their study, Harding and Ballard (1982) used songs and singing to reinforce spontaneous speech. They found that this intervention also produced an increase in spontaneous speech.

Music therapy can play an integral role in the assessment of nonverbal children or children with communication disorders simply because of the nonverbal nature of the medium being used. The nature of music-making between two people relies on timing, turn-taking, sharing, and creating. These are all necessary components of effective communication. Therefore, music therapy may play a crucial role in the development of rudimentary communication skills often lacking in children with autism.

Thaut (1984) outlines a music therapy treatment model for working with autistic children. His model addresses four relevant treatment areas: language development, socioemotional development, cognitive development, and perceptual motor disturbances. Within each treatment area, Thaut outlines music therapy techniques appropriate for basic, intermediate, and complex levels of ability. A child who meets the description for the most basic levels in these areas may be one who has limited awareness of his environment, rarely demonstrates efforts to communicate, often physically rejects or ignores others' attempts at social contact, engages in stereotyped movements and activities, and has very limited perceptual and motor development. Thaut describes the work of a music therapist for this type of child as basically attempting to foster a desire to communicate by expanding his awareness of music and his own actions. Once he is motivated, therapy aims to expand his perceptual awareness by pairing rhythmic/melodic and kinesthetic activities.

Research has shown that music therapy with ASD children can increase appropriate communication responses. Hairston (1990) evaluated the responses of four ASD children and four children with severe to profound mental retardation (mean age of 8 years 10 months) to art therapy and music therapy. Subjects were rated using the Developmental Therapy Objectives Rating Form to assess four areas of development (i.e., behavior, communication, socialization, and pre-academics) and the Systematic-Who-to-Whom-Analysis Notation (from W. Swan, 1971) to obtain behavioral ratings in five categories (i.e., work, nonunderstandable verbalization/inappropriate work, contact received, observed teacher, and play). Music therapy experiences were designed using short demonstrations with concrete examples and explicit directions, began with a minimal number of music materials, provided for success and promoted pleasure-producing responses, and were conducted so as to encourage the children to participate. Also, the music therapy experience did not extend beyond the "peak" of motivation.

Reitman's study (2011) found that music therapy interventions were effective in increasing joint attention behaviors in children with severe ASD [as measured by the Childhood Autism Rating Scale (CARS) (Schopler, Reichler, & Renner, 1988)] both within treatment and as reported by parents outside of treatment. Participants received eight 30-minute individual music therapy sessions, twice weekly. Sessions consisted of five categories of musical experiences using live and recorded music: greeting song, seated imitation activity, instrument-playing, gross motor musical movement/imitation activity, and closing/good-bye song. Video analysis of initial and final music therapy sessions showed that approximately 70% of participants had noticeable increases in joint attention behaviors. The range of improvement was between 36% and 200%. Results indicate that the addition of music therapy intervention to a child's treatment program can have positive outcomes and may be an effective method for increasing joint attention skills in some children with autism.

Summary and Conclusions

The incidence of autism is increasing at an alarming rate. Yet, there is no known cause for this debilitating, lifelong neurological disorder. The needs of persons with ASD are almost as varied as the goals addressed in music therapy practice. Research on the effectiveness of music therapy interventions has been ongoing for the past 40 years. The most commonly used music therapy methods for persons with ASD were improvisational methods and re-creative methods. However, the specific approaches employed within these methods range from incorporation of academic strategies, behavior therapy, and speech/language interventions to strategies designed to support psychological, emotional, and social functioning.

Clearly, there is growing evidence for the efficacy of music therapy interventions in addressing core deficit areas in persons with ASD. The music therapy methods described in this chapter all have in common that they provide opportunity for engaging a child's affective being, his creative self, and the chance to create something of value and meaning. Music therapy interventions strive to support and encourage interaction and responding to and engaging with another person. They provide a unique opportunity for self-expression, choices, and enjoyment in the life of a child who is frequently faced with therapists who demand specific responses to stimuli. With continuation of this promising work, music therapy stands to become a legitimate and effective treatment intervention for individuals with autism.

REFERENCES

Adamson, L. B., & Chance, S. E. (1998). Coordinating attention to people, objects, and language. In A. M. Wetherby, S. F. Warren, & J. Reichle (Eds.), *Communication and language intervention series: Vol. 7. Transitions in prelinguistic communication*, 15–37. Baltimore, MD: Brookes.

Allgood, N. (2005). Parents' perceptions of family-based group music therapy for children with autism spectrum disorder. *Music Therapy Perspectives, 23*(2), 92–99.

Alvin, J. (1965). *Music for the handicapped child.* London, England: Oxford University Press.

Alvin, J., & Warwick, A. (1992). *Music therapy for the autistic child* (2nd ed.). London, England: Oxford Press.

American Psychiatric Association (APA). (2000). *Diagnostic and statistical manual of mental disorders—Text revision* (4th ed.). (DSM-IV-TR). Arlington, VA: Author.

Appelbaum, E., Egel, A., Koegel, R., & Imhoff, B. (1979). Measuring musical abilities of autistic children. *Journal of Autism and Developmental Disorders, 9,* 279–285.

Bakeman, R., & Adamson, L. (1984). Coordinating attention to people and objects in mother-infant and peer-infant interaction. *Child Development, 55,* 1278–1289.

Baker, J. (2003). *The social skills picture book teaching play, emotion and communication to children with autism.* Arlington, TX: Future Horizons.

Barrickman, J. (1989). A developmental music therapy approach for preschool hospitalized children. *Music Therapy Perspectives, 7,* 10-16.

Baxter, H., Berghofer, J., MacEwan, L., Nelson, J., Peters, K., & Roberts, P. (2007). *The individualized music therapy assessment profile.* Philadelphia, PA: Jessica Kingsley.

Benenzon, R. O. (1981). *Music therapy manual.* Springfield, IL: Charles C. Thomas.

Bondy, A. S., & Frost, L. A. (1998). The picture exchange communication system. *Seminars in Speech and Language, 19,* 373–389.

Braithwaite, M., & Sigafoos, J. (1998). Effects of social versus music antecedents on communication responsiveness in five children with developmental disabilities. *Journal of Music Therapy, 35*(2), 88–104.

Bruner, J. (1981). The social context of language acquisition. *Language and Communication, 1,* 155–178.

Bruner, J., & Sherwood, V. (1983). Thought, language, and interaction in infancy. In J. D. Call, E. Galenson, & R. L. Tyson (Eds.), *Frontiers of infant psychiatry (pp.* 38–55). New York, NY: Basic Books.

Bruscia, K. E. (1987). *Improvisational models of music therapy.* Springfield, IL: Charles C. Thomas.

Bruscia, K. E. (1998). *Defining music therapy* (2nd ed.). Gilsum, NH: Barcelona Publishers.

Butterworth, G. (1995). Origins of mind in perception and action. In C. Moore & P. J. Dunham (Eds.), *Joint attention: Its origins and role in development (pp.* 29–40). Hillsdale, NJ: Erlbaum.

Carpente, J. (2009). *Contributions of Nordoff-Robbins music therapy within the developmental, individual-difference, relationship-based (DIR®)/Floortime™ addressing core features of autism framework to the treatment of children with autism: Four case studies*. Doctoral dissertation, Temple University. Ann Arbor, MI: ProQuest/UMI.

Coleman, K., & Brunk, B. (1999). *Special education music therapy assessment process*. Grapevine, TX: Prelude Music Therapy.

Davis, W. B., Gfeller, K. E., & Thaut, M. H. (1999). *An introduction to music therapy: Theory and practice* (2nd ed.). Boston, MA: McGraw-Hill College.

Dawson, G. (1991). A psychobiological perspective on the early socio-emotional development of children with autism. In D. Cicchetti & S. Toth (Eds.), *Rochester symposium on developmental psychopathology, Vol. 3* (pp. 207-234). Rochester, NY: University of Rochester Press.

Dawson, G., & Adams, A. (1984). Imitation and social responsiveness in autistic children. *Journal of Abnormal Child Psychology,* 209–225.

de l'Etoile, S. K. (2006). Infant-directed singing: A theory for clinical intervention. *Music Therapy Perspectives, 24*(1), 22–29.

DeLong, G. R. (1978). A neuropsychological interpretation of infantile autism In M. Rutter & E. Schopler (Eds.), *Autism: A reappraisal of concepts and treatment.* New York, NY: Plenum Press.

DeMyer, M. K. (1979). *Parents and children in autism.* Washington, DC: V. H. Winston.

DeMyer, M. K., Alpern, G. D., Barton, S., DeMyer, W. E., Churchill, D. W., Hingtgen, J. H., Bryson, C.Q., Pontius, W., & Kimberlin, C. (1972). Imitation in autistic, early schizophrenic, and nonpsychotic subnormal children. *Journal of Autism and Childhood Schizophrenia, 2,* 264–287.

Dunlap, G. (1984). The influence of task variation and maintenance tasks on the learning and affect of autistic children. *Journal of Experimental Child Psychology, 37(1),* 41–64.

Dunlap, G., Foster-Johnson, L., Clarke, S., Kern, L., & Childs, K. E. (1995). Modifying activities to produce functional outcomes: Effects on the problem behaviors of students with disabilities. *Journal of the Association for Persons with Severe Handicaps, 20,* 248–258.

Edgerton, C. L. (1994). The effect of improvisational music therapy on the communicative behaviors of autistic children. *Journal of Music Therapy, 31,* 31–62.

Field, T., Field, T., Sanders, C., & Nadel, J. (2001). Children with autism display more social behaviors after repeated imitation sessions. *Autism, 5,* 317–323.

Frith, U., Happé, F., & Siddons, F. (1994). Autism and theory of mind in everyday life. *Social Development, 3,* 108–124.

Goldstein, C. (1964). Music and creative arts therapy for an autistic child. *Journal of Music Therapy, 1,* 135–138.

Gray, C. (2010). *The new social story book, revised and expanded 10th anniversary edition.* Arlington, TX: Future Horizons.

Greenspan, S. I. (1992). *Infancy and early childhood: The practice of clinical assessment and intervention with emotional and developmental challenges.* Madison, CT: International Universities Press.

Greenspan, S. I., & Weider, S. (2006a). *Engaging autism: Using the Floortime approach to help children relate, communicate, and think.* New York, NY: Da Capo Lifelong Books.

Greenspan, S. I., & Weider, S. (2006b). *Infant and early childhood mental health: A comprehensive developmental approach to assessment and intervention.* Washington, DC: American Psychiatric Association.

Gross, W., Linden, U., & Ostermann, T. (2010). Effects of music therapy in the treatment of children with delayed speech development—results of a pilot study. *Complementary and Alternative Medicine, 10,* 39 http://www.biomedcentral.com/1472-6882/10/39.

Hairston, M. (1990). Analyses of responses of mentally retarded autistic and mentally retarded non-autistic children to art therapy and music therapy. *Journal of Music Therapy, 27,* 137–150.

Harding, C., & Ballard, K. D. (1982). The effectiveness of music as a stimulus and as a contingent reward in promoting the spontaneous speech of three physically handicapped preschoolers. *Journal of Music Therapy, 19*(2), 86–101.

Hollander, F. M., & Juhrs, P. D. (1974). Orff-Schulwerk: An effective treatment tool with autistic children. *Journal of Music Therapy, 11,* 1–12.

Hwang, B., & Hughes, C. (2000). Increasing early social-communicative skills of preverbal preschool children with autism through social interactive training. *Journal of the Association for Persons with Severe Handicaps, 25,* 18–28.

Jones, E. A., & Carr, E. G. (2004). Joint attention in children with autism: Theory and intervention. *Focus on Autism and Other Developmental Disabilities, 19,* 13–26.

Kabot, S., Masi, W., & Segal, M. (2003). Advances in the diagnosis and treatment of autism spectrum disorders. *Professional Psychology: Research and Practice, 34,* 26–33.

Kanner, L. (1943). Autistic disturbances of affective contact. *Nervous Child, 2,* 227–250.

Kern, P. (2004). Making friends in music: Including children with autism in an interactive play setting. *Music Therapy Today, 5*(4), 1–43.

Kern, P., Wakeford, L., & Aldridge, D. (2007). Improving the performance of a young child with autism during self-care tasks using embedded song interventions: A case study. *Music Therapy Perspectives, 25*(1), 43–51.

Kim, J., Wigram, T., & Gold, C. (2008). The effects of improvisational music therapy on joint attention behaviors of autistic children: A randomized controlled study. *Journal of Autism and Developmental Disorders, 38,* 1758–1766.

Kim, J., Wigram, T., & Gold, C. (2009). Emotional, motivational and interpersonal responsiveness of children with autism in improvisational music therapy. *Autism, 13*(4), 389-409.

Klinger, L. G., & Dawson, G. (1992). Facilitating early social and communicative development in children with autism. In S. F. Warren & J. Reichle (Eds.), *Communication and language intervention series: Vol. 1. Causes and effects in communication and language intervention* (pp. 157–186). Baltimore, MD: Brookes.

Koegel, R. L., Koegel, L. K., & Surratt, A. V. (1992). Language intervention and disruptive behavior in preschool children with autism. *Journal of Developmental Disorders, 22,* 141–153.

Koegel, L. K., Koegel, R. L., Harrower, J. K., & Carter, C. M. (1999). Pivotal response intervention: I. Overview of approach. *Journal of the Association of Persons with Severe Handicaps, 24(3),* 174–185.

Kolko, D. J., Anderson, L., & Campbell, M. (1980). Sensory preference and overselective responding in autistic children. *Journal of Autism and Developmental Disorders, 10,* 259–271.

Landry, S. H., & Loveland, K. A. (1988). Communication behaviors in autism and developmental language delay. *Journal of Child Psychology and Psychiatry, 29*(5), 621–634.

Layton, T. (1988). Language training with autistic children using four different modes of presentation. *Journal of Communication Disorders, 21,* 333–350.

Leekam, S. R., Hunnisett, E., & Moore, C. (1998). Targets and cues: Gaze-following in children with autism. *Journal of Child Psychology and Psychiatry, 39,* 951–962.

Lewy, A., & Dawson, G. (1992). Social stimulation and joint attention in young autistic children. *Journal of Abnormal Child Psychology, 20*(6), 555–566.

Lovaas, O. I. (1987). Behavioral treatment and normal educational and intellectual functioning in young autistic children. *Journal of Consulting and Clinical Psychology, 55,* 3–9.

Loveland, K., & Landry, S. (1986). Joint attention and language in autism and developmental language delay. *Journal of Autism and Developmental Disorders, 16,* 335–349.

Mahlberg, M. (1973). Music therapy in the treatment of an autistic child. *Journal of Music Therapy, 10,* 189–193.

Meltzoff, A., & Gopnik, A. (1993). The role of imitation in understanding persons and developing a theory of mind. In S. Baron-Cohen, H. Tager-Flusberg, & D. Cohen (Eds.), *Understanding the minds of others: Perspectives from autism* (pp. 335–366). New York, NY: Oxford University Press.

Meltzoff, A. N., & Moore, M. (1994). Imitation, memory and the representation of persons. *Infant Behavior and Development, 17,* 83–99.

Mosca, L., DiFranco, G., & Moselli, B. (2004). Music therapy for three hundred three-year-old children. *Music Therapy Today, 6*(4), 1200–1205.

Mundy, P. (1995). Joint attention and social-emotional approach behavior in children with autism. *Development and Psychopathology, 7,* 63–82.

Mundy, P., & Sigman, M. (1989). The theoretical implications of joint attention deficits in autism. *Development and Psychopathology, 1*(3), 173–183.

Nelson, D. L., Anderson, V. G., & Gonzales, A. D. (1984). Music activities as therapy for children with autism and other pervasive developmental disorders. *Journal of Music Therapy, 21,* 100–116.

Nordoff, P., & Robbins, C. (1964). Music therapy and personality change in autistic children. *Journal of the American Institute of Homeopathy, 57,* 305–310.

Nordoff, P., & Robbins, C. (1968). Improvised music as therapy for autistic children. In E. T. Gaston (Ed.), *Music in therapy* (pp. 191–193). New York, NY: MacMillan Publishers.

Nordoff, P., & Robbins, C. (1971). *Music therapy in special education.* New York, NY: John Day.

Nordoff, P., & Robbins, C. (1977). *Creative music therapy.* New York, NY: John Day.

Nordoff, P., & Robbins, C. (2007). *Creative music therapy: A guide to fostering clinical musicianship.* Gilsum, NH: Barcelona Publishers.

Oppenheim, R. (1974). *Effective teaching methods for autistic children.* Springfield, IL: Charles C. Thomas.

Osterling, J., & Dawson, G. (1994). Early recognition of children with autism: A study of first birthday home videotapes. *Journal of Autism and Developmental Disorders, 24*(3), 247–257.

Pasiali, V. (2004). The use of prescriptive therapeutic songs in a home-based environment to promote social skills acquisition by children with autism: Three case studies. *Music Therapy Perspectives,* 22(1), 11–20.

Paul, D. W. (1982). *Music therapy for handicapped children: Emotionally disturbed.* Washington, DC: National Association for Music Therapy.

Pierce, K., & Schreibman, L. (1995). Increasing complex social behaviors in children with autism: Effects of peer-implemented pivotal response training. *Journal of Applied Behavior Analysis, 28*(3), 285–295.

Prizant, B. M., Wetherby, A. M., Rubin, E., & Laurent, A, C. (2010). The SCERTS Model. In K. Siri & T. Lyons (Eds.), *Cutting-edge therapies for autism: 2010–2011* (pp. 314-320). New York, NY: Skyhorse.

Purvis, J., & Samet, S. (1976). *Music in developmental therapy.* Baltimore: University Park Press.

Reitman, M. R. (2005). *The effectiveness of music therapy interventions on joint attention in children diagnosed with autism: A pilot study.* (Doctoral dissertation). Retrieved from ProQuest Dissertations and Theses. (AAT 3195248)

Reitman, M. R., Lim, N. K., & Long, L. A. (2011). *Effects of music therapy on joint attention in children with autism: A pilot study.* Saarbrücken, Germany: VDM Verlag Dr. Müller.

Roeyers, H., Van Oost, P., & Bothuyne, S. (1998). Immediate imitation and joint attention in young children with autism. *Development and Psychopathology, 10,* 441–450.

Rogers, S. J., & Pennington, B. F. (1991). A theoretical approach to the deficits in infantile autism. *Development and Psychopathology, 3,* 137–162.

Rutter, M. (1978). Diagnosis and definition. In M. Rutter & E. Schopler (Eds.), *Autism: A reappraisal of concepts and treatment* (pp. 1-25). New York, NY: Plenum.

Saperston, B. (1973). The use of music in establishing communication with an autistic mentally retarded child. *Journal of Music Therapy, 10,* 184–188.

Saperston, B. (1982). Case study: Timmy. In D. W. Paul (Ed.), *Music therapy for handicapped children: Emotionally disturbed* (pp. 42–57). Washington, DC: Office of Special Education.

Schmidt, D., & Edwards, J. (1976). Reinforcement of autistic children's responses to music. *Psychological Reports, 39,* 571–577.

Schwartz, E. (2008). *Music, therapy, and early childhood: A developmental approach.* Gilsum, NH: Barcelona Publishers.

Schwartz, E. (2012). *You and me makes we: A growing together songbook.* Melrose, MA: The Center for Early Childhood Music Therapy.

Schwartz, E. K. (2011). Growing up in music: A journey through early childhood music development in music therapy. In A. N. Meadows (Ed.), *Developments in music therapy practice: Case study perspectives* (pp. 70-85). Gilsum, NH: Barcelona Publishers.

Seybold, C. D. (1971). The value and use of music activities in the treatment of speech delayed children. *Journal of Music Therapy, 8*(3), 102–110.

Stevens, E., & Clark, F. (1969). Music therapy in the treatment of autistic children. *Journal of Music Therapy, 6,* 98–104.

Tager-Flushberg, H. (2001). Understanding the language and communicative impairments in autism. In L. M. Glidden (Ed.), *International review of research in mental retardation* (pp. 185–205). San Diego, CA: Academic Press.

Tanguay, P. (1976). Clinical and electrophysiological research. In E. R. Ritvo (Ed.), *Autism: Diagnosis, current research and management* (pp. 75-84). New York, NY: Spectrum Publishers.

Thaut, M. H. (1984). A music therapy treatment model for autistic children. *Music Therapy Perspectives, 1,* 7–13.

Tomasello, M. (1995). Joint attention as social cognition. In C. Moore & P. Dunham (Eds.), *Joint attention its origins and role in development* (pp. 103–130). Hillsdale, NJ: Lawrence Erlbaum.

Toolan, P. G., & Coleman, S. Y. (1994). Music therapy, a description of process: Engagement and avoidance in five people with learning disabilities. *Journal of Intellectual Disability Research, 38,* 433–444.

Trevarthen, C. (2000). Autism as a neurodevelopmental disorder affecting communication and learning in early childhood: Prenatal origins, post-natal course, and effective educational support. *Prostaglandins, Leukotrienes, and Essential Fatty Acids, 63,* 41–46.

Volkmar, F., Carter, A., Grossman, J., & Klin, A. (1997). *Social development in autism.* In D. Cohen & F. R. Volkmar (Eds.), *Handbook of autism and developmental disorders* (2nd ed.). (pp. 173–194). Hoboken, NJ: John Wiley & Sons.

Watson, D. (1979). Music as reinforcement in increasing spontaneous speech among autistic children. *Missouri Journal of Research in Music Education, 4,* 8–20.

Wetherby, A. M., & Prizant, B. M. (2000). *Autism and spectrum disorders: A transactional developmental perspective.* Baltimore, MD: Paul H. Brookes.

Wetherby, A. M., & Prutting, C. A. (1984). Profiles of communication and cognitive-social abilities in autistic children. *Journal of Speech and Hearing Research, 27,* 364–377.

Whalen, C. (2001). *Joint attention training for children with autism and the collateral effects on language, play, imitation, and social behaviors.* Unpublished doctoral dissertation, University of California, San Diego.

Wing, L. (1978). Social, behavioral and cognitive characteristics: An epidemiological approach. In M. Rutter & E. Schopler (Eds.), *Autism: A reappraisal of concepts and treatment* (pp. 27-45). New York, NY: Plenum Press.

Yoder, P. J., & Layton, T. L. (1988). Speech following sign language training in autistic children with minimal verbal language. *Journal of Autism and Developmental Disorders, 18,* 217–229.

Chapter 4

Rett Syndrome

Jennifer M. Sokira

Diagnostic Information

Rett Syndrome (RS) is the second most commonly occurring developmental disability in women (Ellaway & Christdoulou, 2001), and it affects 1 out of 10,000 children (Rett Syndrome, 2012). Because this neurodevelopmental disorder is linked with the X chromosome gene methl-CpG-binding protein 2 (MeCP2), females, who have two X chromosomes, are able to survive with one normal X chromosome and one affected chromosome, whereas males with the MeCP2 mutation on their one X chromosome very rarely survive (Rett Syndrome, 2012).

A clinical diagnosis of Rett Syndrome is determined by symptoms since not all types of Rett Syndrome are linked with the MeCP2 mutation. Diagnostic criteria for Rett Syndrome include decelerating head growth, loss of purposeful hand skills, loss of speech, stereotypical hand movements (e.g., hand washing, wringing, or tapping), gait difficulty, and posture difficulty. Supportive criteria include hyperventilation or breath holding, air swallowing, teeth grinding, scoliosis or kyphosis, and laughing and/or screaming spells. Due to some of its shared symptoms, Rett Syndrome may be misdiagnosed as cerebral palsy or Autism Spectrum Disorder (Rett Syndrome, 2012).

While the onset age of Rett Syndrome varies, children experience seemingly normal development for the first 6 to 18 months, followed by the appearance of difficulties with crawling, low muscle tone, feeding problems, and loss of eye contact. Development of symptoms ensues in a variety of areas. Physical symptoms include "floppy" arms and legs, loss of purposeful hand movements, and development of repetitive hand movements, as well as gait difficulties and toe walking, breathing problems during wakefulness, scoliosis, sleep problems, seizures, gastrointestinal and circulatory problems, and excess saliva. Other symptoms include language development issues, learning difficulties, feeding issues, breathing difficulties, and loss of social interaction, (Rett Syndrome, n.d.; Rett Syndrome Fact Sheet, 2012).

Although a significant regression of skills is present early in life, Rett Syndrome is not degenerative, and progress and maintenance of skills can be achieved throughout the life of a person with Rett Syndrome (Cass et al., 2003). The progression of Rett Syndrome is classified into four interrelated stages, summarized in Table 1 (Hagberg, 1997, 2002; Hagberg & Witt-Engerström, 1986). Stage I, "Early Onset Stagnation," includes initial developmental delays. Stage II, "Developmental Regression," results in loss of motor and communication skills. Stage III, "Pseudostationary Period," is considered a "wake-up" stage, in which clients demonstrate maintained ambulation and some recovery of communication skills. Stage IV, "Late Motor Deterioration," begins when ambulation ceases or when individuals develop complete wheelchair dependency.

Several variants of classical Rett Syndrome exist, including Forme Fruste Rett Syndrome, Congenital Onset Rett Syndrome, and Preserved/Regained Speech RS (Hagberg, 2002), each with minor variation in course and symptoms. Life expectancy in Rett Syndrome is approximately 40 years of age, with reports of individuals living into their 60s or later (Hagberg, 2002; Jacobsen, Vitken, & Von Tetzchner, 2001). At the time of this writing, research in mouse models of Rett Syndrome is being conducted, showing that some symptoms of Rett Syndrome can be reversed in mice. This provides hope among families and caregivers of individuals with Rett Syndrome that a cure may be possible in the future. In a broader sense, because MeCP2 mutations have also be linked to other more common disorders, including autism, research advances in Rett Syndrome are of great interest to families of individuals with special needs, the therapist, and the educational, medical, and scientific communities at large (Rett Syndrome Research Trust, n.d.).

Table 1. Progression of Rett Syndrome

Stage	Age	Duration	Characteristics
I. Early Onset Stagnation	5 months– 1.5 years	Weeks or months	• Delayed developmental progress • Dissociated development • Changes may not be initially noticed • Loss of eye contact • Delays in sitting and crawling
II. Developmental Regression	1–4 years	Weeks– 1 year	• Rapid or gradual onset • Loss of previously acquired fine and gross motor and communication skills • Development of repetitive hand movements • Slowed head growth
III. Pseudostationary Period	Completion of Stage II	Years–decades	• Slow neuromotor regression • Some communication skills regained • Maintenance of ambulation in some individuals
IV. Late Motor Deterioration, 2 subgroups: Previous walkers, now nonambulant Never Ambulant	When ambulation ceases	Decades	• Decreased mobility • Scoliosis development • Improved emotional contact

Adapted from Hagberg, 1997, 2002; Hagberg & Witt-Engerström, 1986; Rett Syndrome Fact Sheet, 2012.

Needs and Resources

Individuals with Rett Syndrome have multiple limitations which interfere with development of communication, emotional expression, and motor and sensory function making it difficult to look at the clinical needs of each symptom of Rett Syndrome in isolation. The severe physical regressions experienced by individuals with Rett Syndrome result in multiple difficulties in other areas, including difficulty with ambulation, hyperventilation, and seizure activity. Fine motor difficulties and loss of verbal communication result in the need to have assistive technology for communication as well to perform self-care tasks. The areas of need within each client with Rett Syndrome are highly interrelated, for example, loss of verbal language and loss of meaningful hand use impact use of assistive technology, which impact communication, self-care and ability to assess cognitive skills (Budden, 2006).

Motor, Self-Care, and Sensory Needs

As motor skills regress in clients with Rett Syndrome, the impact of these regressions is seen in all domains. With the decrease and or loss of ambulation, clients rely upon caregivers for mobility assistance. Some clients with Rett Syndrome are able to ambulate independently but may demonstrate toe walking or an unsteady or stiff gait while others require use of a wheelchair (Rett Syndrome, 2012). Purposeful hand use is another major factor in overall motor development. Since purposeful hand use declines early in the progression of Rett Syndrome, crawling is limited or adapted by young clients. The development of repetitive hand behaviors also limits fine motor coordination, which then impacts the client's ability to grasp and gesture functionally. It is common to observe individuals with Rett Syndrome engaging in hand clasping and wringing at midline, repetitive "plucking" at midline, and hand mouthing, among other variations. Autonomic differences in Rett syndrome can cause gastrointestinal problems and feeding problem, but poor sensory-motor integration and other physical symptoms like apnea, hyperventilation, air swallowing, irregular breathing, and sleep disturbances impact daily life (Budden, 2006). It is clear that these physical needs indicate that clients are dependent on caregivers for feeding, movement, and ambulation and self-care needs (Rett Syndrome Fact Sheet, 2012).

Communication, Cognitive, and Emotional Needs

As part of the progression of Rett Syndrome, clients lose initially learned or gained speech and rely on nontraditional communicative means. These include vocalization, gestures, facial expressions, and eye gaze (Sandberg, Ehlers, Hagberg, & Gillberg, 2000). Because many enjoy or show interest in music (Perry, 1991; Wesecky, 1986; Yasuhara & Sugiyama, 2001), it may be considered a form of communication for these clients and allow opportunities for verbal and nonverbal communicative interactions (Elefant, 2001; Elefant & Wigram, 2005; Elefant & Lotan, 2004; Wigram, 1991).

The limitations of traditional communication skills thus greatly impact the potential for professionals to evaluate the cognitive abilities of clients with Rett Syndrome. Although clients with Rett Syndrome are reported to have strong receptive skills (Budden, 2006), there have been reports of minimal intentional communication (Budden, Meek, & Henighan, 1990; Sandberg, Ehlers, Hagberg, & Gillberg, 2000; Woodyatt & Ozanne, 1992a, 1992b, 1993, 1994). These authors cite the challenges of standardized forms of measurement and tests in use with individuals with limited communication and physical skills. Conversely, studies of the use of assistive technology with this population have provided evidence of communicative intent, choice-making, and ability for meaningful participation (Hetzroni, Rubin, & Konkol, 2002; Koppenhaver, Erickson, Harris, McLellan, Skotko, & Newton, 2001; Koppenhaver, Erickson, & Skotko, 2001; Sigafoos et al., 2009; Skotko, Koppenhaver, & Erickson, 2004; Van Acker & Grant, 1995; Watson, Umansky, Marcy, & Repacholi, 1996). Notably, music therapy studies (Elefant, 2001, Elefant & Wigram, 2005) demonstrated communicative intentionality of clients with Rett Syndrome, specifically with picture symbol and song choice. Notwithstanding, it is clear that each client must be approached as an individual, and that each client requires an individualized approach to understanding the client's communication and cognition, which may require caregiver interpretation, based upon the therapeutic relationship.

Resources and Strengths

Clients with Rett Syndrome have been found to have strong nonverbal communication skills, particularly in the area of "eye pointing" and in other nonverbal communication areas such as gestures, facial expression, and eye contact (Sandberg, et al., 2000). They are reported to have stronger receptive communication than expressive, and are able to learn and demonstrate new skills (Budden, 2006). It is commonly expressed that individuals with Rett Syndrome greatly enjoy and are highly motivated by music (Hagberg, 2002; Perry, 1991), even to the extent that they may utilize their hands functionally (Go & Mitani, 2009). In the present author's clinical experience, clients with Rett Syndrome show positive affect, vocalize, may vocalize in tune, demonstrate motivation to play instruments functionally, and increase motivation or duration of ambulation within music therapy. Because of the positive responses of clients with Rett Syndrome to musically adapted experiences, music therapists have been sought as direct service providers and consultants to girls with Rett Syndrome and their caregivers in both home and school settings. Because of the client therapist relationship that is built through music therapy, as well as the natural preference for music held by many clients with Rett Syndrome, music therapy experience has been found to be positive for all involved.

Referral and Assessment

Individuals with Rett Syndrome may be referred to music therapy from a variety of sources. Referrals may come from members of the public school interdisciplinary team, including the special educator, physical therapist, occupational therapist, school psychologist, or speech-language pathologist. In a public school setting, music therapy services may be provided to an individual with Rett Syndrome as part of a group, individually, or consultatively, based upon the team's determination regarding the least restrictive environment necessary for the student to make reasonable progress on their Individualized Education Plan (IEP). Music therapy may also be provided to a student with Rett Syndrome as educational enrichment (Coleman & Brunk, 1999).

An individual with Rett Syndrome may also be referred to music therapy by a parent desiring private, individualized services, or by a physician or other therapist working on a client's behalf. Because individuals with Rett Syndrome are often drawn to music and display strong, positive emotions in response to hearing or participating in music experiences, caregivers may report that they would like to use music therapy to "capitalize" upon this positive response and motivation.

Music therapy assessment for persons with Rett Syndrome should be individualized based upon both the setting in which music therapy is taking place and upon their particular needs and musical preferences, giving strong credence to the role of music in the client's culture and environment (Lotan, 2006; Wigram & Lawrence, 2005). Based upon the overall clinical profile of individuals with Rett Syndrome, the following areas of need should be assessed with regard to musical responses and appropriate music therapy interventions: expressive and receptive communication, fine and gross motor skills, cognitive and academic ability. These may be assessed through the methods described below, including improvisation, re-creative, receptive, and composition. Several music therapy studies (Wigram, 1991; Wigram & Lawrence, 2005) describe the use of music therapy in assessing children with Rett Syndrome overall, describing how this information contributes to the other modalities who are also assessing the client (Cass et al., 2003).

Considerations for the assessment of expressive and receptive communication skills include the client's ability to answer yes/no questions and make choices using two or more symbols (high- or low-tech) and whether the client can express themselves vocally, and, if so, whether using either words or both words and sounds. Additionally, the music therapist should consider the musical quality of the client's vocal expressions, the types of nonverbal communication strategies employed by the client, and the methods used by caregivers and school staff to interpret her nonverbal communications.

The music therapist should consider the range of emotions which can be observed with the client, their preferred types of music, and their emotional response to different types of music. The music therapist should also consider the client's response to new and known staff and students. Assessment of fine and gross motor skills should include the music therapist's consideration of the client's types of repetitive hand movements and any functional hand use, how these hand behaviors affect/inhibit her communicative expressions, and the effect of music on the client's hand behaviors. Consideration should also be given to the effect of the client's hand behaviors, how they affect her self-help/self-care skills, the client's ability to ambulate independently or with assistance, and the impact of music on the client's ambulation.

Assessment of cognitive and academic abilities should consider in which types of grade-level–appropriate academic experiences the client is participating and what types of adaptations are made to allow for the student to participate in grade-level/inclusive education. Also, it is important for the music therapist to consider the impact of the student's physical and communicative abilities upon the therapist's ability to assess academic and cognitive performance; the current use, if any, of the special education team and caregivers utilizing music; and whether music assists this client in participating/tolerating nonpreferred academic work.

It is very important for the music therapist to note that many of these assessment areas may have significant overlap. For example, evaluation of receptive communication skills is determined through responses such as completing a one-step task which may require use of assistive technology, yet fine motor skills may be delayed or severely impacted. In other words, the individual with Rett Syndrome may not be able to provide a consistent response for reasons other than deficits in receptive communication. For example, while she may be able to indicate a choice once with her hand, she may become overstimulated, hyperventilate, or have a seizure and not able to confirm the choice by touch a second time.

When assessing a student with Rett Syndrome in music therapy, it is recommended that multiple opportunities over time be provided to establish consistent responses. For example, eye gaze may be used in lieu of a client touching a picture symbol if in fact they are having difficulty indicating a choice with their hands. Multiple options for responding should be utilized in order to ensure that the client's intent is indeed being communicated. While this requires additional time during the therapy session, it is also essential to allow for full respect for the client's communication in light of their, at times, delayed response.

While no standardized music therapy assessment tools or forms exist which are specifically for clients with Rett Syndrome, the SEMTAP Assessment tool (Coleman & Brunk,1999) and MT-SEAS (Bradfield, Carlenius, Gold, & White, 2008) may be appropriate, as they were developed to establish appropriateness for Related Service Music Therapy in public schools. Further, the Individual Music Therapy Assessment Process (IMTAP) (Baxter, Berghofer, MacEwan, Nelson, Peters, & Roberts, 2007) may be used with this population to evaluate music therapy needs and potential goals in a variety of domains.

The music therapist should collaborate with other professionals working with the student with Rett Syndrome during the assessment and treatment process. Some music therapists may want to establish a clinical relationship and independent impression of the student prior to reading extensive reports about the student's level of functioning. This allows them to develop an impression of the client independent of the expectations that may accompany a more detailed record, and therefore a clinical impression independent of any difficulties and challenges presented by the client to other team members over time. Other music therapists may elect to do the opposite. Regardless, prior to the first clinical meeting, information such as about diagnosis, safety concerns, allergies, positioning, and seizure disorders should be obtained. Reports and evaluations from occupational therapists, physical therapists, speech-language pathologists, special educators, family members, and others should also be considered when establishing a music therapy treatment plan. The following guidelines outline music therapy interventions which may be appropriate in assisting individuals with Rett Syndrome in addressing the above mentioned areas of need.

GUIDELINES FOR MUSIC THERAPY

When providing music therapy with clients with Rett Syndrome, general considerations should be made regarding needed adaptations to physical space and instruments. There are also important considerations for the client's safe participation in music therapy, including physical space, instrument selection, fine motor ability, and physical safety.

The therapy space should be prepared to ensure access to musical materials as well as for the safety of the client and therapist. The music therapist should consider the client's ability to ambulate and the incorporation of movement within the therapy room. For a client with Rett Syndrome who is able to ambulate and addressing gait or walking goals within the music therapy session, the music therapist should ensure that open space is available and tripping/falling hazards are removed. With the guidance of a physical therapist, a gait belt may be incorporated for additional safety, and two adults may be needed to support music and movement experiences: one to stand behind the client and/or to guide the client in their movement and another to stand in front of the client, providing accompaniment, instruments, motivation, and directions. Physical space considerations are equally important for clients who can ambulate and for those who utilize wheelchairs, with regard to the positioning of instruments and of assistive technology for independent access by the client if at all possible.

Adapted instruments, based upon each individual's hand abilities, should be incorporated to allow maximal independent use of instruments. Mallets may be adapted to add weight, thicken grasp, textured grasp, or attach directly to the client's to hand for drumming and mallet instrument-playing. Drums may be attached to clients' wheelchairs, positioned in range of dominant hand movement, or manipulated by the therapist in space to provide flexible positioning in relation to therapeutic need. Auxiliary percussion like egg shakers, maracas, bells, and cabasa may be attached to a wheelchair, attached to hands, or suspended on a bar to provide an additional structure, again allowing flexible positioning in relation to the client's range of dominant hand movement. It should also be noted that instruments may also be adapted to be activated by the client's feet (kicking or toe tapping) or by the client's rocking movements. Electronic music technology may be utilized to capitalize on smaller purposeful movements like eye and finger movements. Instrumental improvisation experiences should also take into consideration response time needed and sensory processing needs as appropriate.

Because of their repetitive hand movements, it has been shown that clients with Rett Syndrome may be able to utilize their hands more functionally when one hand is splinted or when the hands are separated. It is important for the music therapist to understand that hands should not be separated/forced apart without training from the appropriate professional to avoid potential of injury to a client who has muscle tone differences. Similarly, arm splints should not be incorporated without training from the appropriate professional, for example, occupational therapist, physical therapist, or physician.

From a physical perspective, it is crucial that music therapy interventions not worsen physical symptoms of Rett Syndrome. For example, if an intervention becomes overwhelming for a client, breathing difficulties like breath holding or hyperventilation could occur, and the music therapist should then adapt the music therapy intervention to allow the client to recover or adjust the intervention to ensure that the client can participate safely. The music therapist should be prepared to be flexible in all interventions, with a clear understanding of the client's physical needs prior to the start of the session.

Overview of Methods and Procedures

The following methods and procedures are used most commonly with individuals with Rett Syndrome.

Receptive Music Therapy

- Active Music Listening: Clients listen to preselected music to address sensory needs, address attention and concentration, and improve social skills.
- Vibroacoustic Therapy: use of preselected frequencies played through specially designed recliners or pads to create sympathetic somatic resonance.

Improvisational Music Therapy

- Instrumental Improvisation: Client and therapist create spontaneous music using musical instruments with intent to communicate emotions and provide opportunity for creative expression.

Re-creative Music Therapy

- Vocal Re-creation: Clients sing precomposed songs with or without instrumental accompaniment.

Compositional Music Therapy

- Adapted Composition and Songwriting:

Guidelines for Receptive Music Therapy

Receptive music therapy may be used with clients with Rett Syndrome to address a variety of goals areas, including listening skills, choice-making, relaxation, and stimulation, in which the client responds by listening to live or recorded music (Bruscia, 1998). The assumption that clients with Rett Syndrome do in fact possess communicative intent and the ability to learn, despite their physical limitations and our ability to measure their abilities, is becoming more widely considered. In her research, Elefant studied choice-making intentionality for this purpose, and her results suggested that in fact her participants made intelligent, consistent, confirmed choices and demonstrated the ability to learn and retain learning over time (Elefant, 2001; Elefant & Wigram, 2005). The intervention that she described used a procedure requiring the client with RS to select a song using choices represented with visual symbols. After making a confirmed choice, the client with RS then enjoyed listening to the selected song. Indeed, the motivator of the listening opportunity may have influenced the consistency and response time of the client's selection, demonstrating that receptive listening to client-preferred music is an important intervention for consideration in music therapy.

Active Music Listening

Overview. In the method of Active Music Listening, the client utilizes listening experiences, facilitated by the music therapist, for a variety of needs. Like other interventions, active music listening is indicated based upon client need and available resources, and since receptive interventions have the potential to provide flexibility in expectations of performance by clients with Rett Syndrome, they may be particularly effective in meeting their needs. Goals may include sensory stimulation, following direction, answering yes/no questions, academic learning, and improved social skills.

Active Music Listening may take place on various levels of music therapy; however, it is most likely to occur on the auxiliary and augmentative levels, as it may combine with and enhance the work done collaboratively with other areas. Active Music Listening may be contraindicated if a client with Rett Syndrome becomes overstimulated given particular songs, tempi, etc., and therefore the music therapist should have prior knowledge of the potential for hyperventilation and/or breath holding as outlined above.

Preparation. When preparing the therapeutic environment for a session which includes active music listening, consideration should be given to the quality of sound equipment or instruments being used, ensuring that they are individualized as appropriate to the client's needs. Similarly, any supportive materials, such as written lyrics, accompanying assistive technology, etc., may be appropriate.

What to observe. When conducting Active Music Listening interventions, the music therapist should be prepared to observe the client's physical, emotional, musical, and communicative responses and document them according to the clinical goals at hand.

Procedures. The following procedures may be utilized when conducting an active music listening intervention:

1) Greeting
2) Music or Song choice: The therapist guides the client in selecting a song based upon the goal of the session or intervention
3) Listening Experience: The client participates in listening to music within one of several contexts:
    - Directive listening. Within Active Music Listening, Directive Listening incorporates the use of song discussion and lyric analysis. This intervention subtype incorporates simple questions posed by the therapist to the client and may be used to elicit or practice yes/no responses or allow the client to select a correct answer or express an option. It should be ensured that the client is confirming any unclear response using multiple modes of communication.
    - Academic song listening. This intervention subtype incorporates the use of "learning songs" to preteach, teach, or reinforce concepts which pertain to a client with Rett Syndrome's learning curriculum. These songs may be precomposed for the client, and they may be recorded for use by the client outside of their music therapy session.
    - Social Experience/Integration. The intervention subtype of Social Experience Integration incorporates uses of music in the social realm, often occurring in inclusionary philosophies (inclusion and community music therapy references here). While a client with Rett Syndrome may struggle with learning a band or orchestra instrument or singing in a choir, the client's presence with his or her age-appropriate peers is nonetheless a valuable learning opportunity and reinforcement of the client with Rett Syndrome's equal importance in the school

community. The client may serve a managerial role, participate in adapted experiences using assistive technology, or work with a "peer buddy" in order to benefit from this type of community intervention.

4) Evaluation/Good-bye song

Adaptations. This type of intervention may be used as the only intervention during a session, or it may be combined with other interventions. The music therapist may provide this type of experience outside the context of a typical MT session, e.g., in the classroom as needed. Another adaptation of this method is Receptive Music Listening, which takes place at the augmentative level of music therapy as it can prepare the client to be optimally functioning or assist them in shifting their sensory experience for "optimal" classroom attention or participation, addressing physical relaxation, sensory stimulation, and aided motor responses. Like other music therapy interventions with clients with Rett Syndrome, Receptive Music Listening may be contraindicated if the client becomes overstimulated when given particular songs, tempi, etc. Therefore, the music therapist should have prior knowledge of the medical interpretations of the client's physiological responses and be prepared to flexibly make adaptations as the music therapy session progresses.

One variation on this is Receptive Relaxation or Stimulation, in which the client is provided the opportunity to listen to preferred music in order to promote physical or emotional relaxation or stimulation and which may take place casually as a "break" from areas or times of stress, as indicated by the client's emotions or as a planned time. The client should have input into the music selections either in general or specifically, and the client-therapist relationship is still utilized in order to interpret the client's responses and to intuit the progress and the amount of time the intervention is used. The client can be seated in a chair, in a wheelchair, or in adapted seating or may lie down or recline using adapted equipment such as a Somatron vibroacoustic chair or beanbag.

During Receptive Routine Support, clients may be moved by or with a music therapist and/or a cotherapist, such as an occupational or physical therapist, utilizing the structure, rhythm, melody, or tempo of the music. At the augmentative level, this type of intervention has been described by Elefant and Lotan (2004) as a way in which clients with Rett Syndrome may be motivated to participate more fully in nonpreferred therapy interventions, due to their enjoyment of music.

Vibroacoustic Therapy

Overview. During Vibroacoustic Therapy (VAS) (Skille, 1989), the client lies on a specially designed bed or multiple transducer bed pad or sits in a VAT recliner. Preselected frequencies are played through speakers. Sound waves then vibrate the body with sympathetic resonance. VAS is useful for people with a wide range of needs, including those who need to reduce pain or stress, those who need to relax, and those with sensory issues. With school-age children, VAS is used primarily at an augmentative level since it is intended to minimize physical or medical problems. The goals may include increasing sensory stimulation, reducing stress, decreasing muscle tone, and increasing range of motion.

Preparation. VAS is most often done individually. Clients should be in a comfortable position and able to get to (perhaps be moved to or placed upon) the chair or mat that is used for delivering the sounds and vibrations. The therapist and client should be able to see each other and make physical contact. The room should have as few distractions as possible and preferably light that can be reduced to ensure that the client can focus on the music and the therapist.

What to observe. The therapist needs to observe the client's responses, particularly as they relate to the child's specific goals. Any unexpected increase in tension, for instance, should be noted and adjustments made in the music when possible. In addition, all responses should be noted and taken into account in planning for future sessions.

Procedures. Therapist should select the music in advance and take the client's preferences into account in the selection. Care should be taken to ensure that the volume of the music is appropriate for the client. The client should be oriented to what will occur through instructions by the therapist and should be seated or lying in proper position for the duration of the session.

Adaptations. Vibroacoustic devices may be made by the therapist with the assistance of technicians. Others are made commercially, including Somatron® products such as mats, mattresses, and chairs.

Guidelines for Improvisational Music Therapy

When working with a client with Rett Syndrome, improvisational music therapy techniques may be incorporated in order to address the client's clinical goals. Various methodologies of improvisation may be used as appropriate to the client's needs and responses and clinical settings. In improvisation experiences, the client, aided, creates music extemporaneously (Bruscia, 1998). Instrumental improvisation may be a stand-alone intervention during a session, or it may be one of several interventions.

Instrumental Improvisation

Overview. Instrumental improvisation is an experience wherein the therapist and client create immediate and spontaneous music using musical instruments for the intent of communicating emotions, facilitating symbolic communication, and providing opportunity for creative expression. It may be utilized to meet a variety of clinical goals in areas including communication, self-expression, emotional expression, fine motor coordination, and purposeful hand use.

Because of the aforementioned sensory processing delays and need for response time experienced by clients with Rett Syndrome, instrumental improvisational experiences can provide a natural setting for accommodating such needs (Wigram & Elefant, 2009). For example, a client who has a hard time creating an instrumental sound can be musically supported by the music therapist during an instrumental improvisation experience, and the processing time or delay that results from Rett Syndrome can then be musically incorporated into the improvisation. Typical instruments used include drums, mallet instruments, guitar, autoharp, xylophone, piano, and other percussion. Choice of instrument is determined by client preference, client physical needs, and clinical goal.

Instrumental improvisation may address goals at multiple levels of therapy. For example, at the auxiliary level, music therapists may use instrumental improvisation to address issues with motivation to participate within other therapeutic modalities and have other positive although nontherapeutic experiences. Instrumental improvisation could assist at the auxiliary level of practice by addressing goals to improve leisure skills such as participating in a recreational music-making group. At the augmentative level of practice, instrumental improvisation is used to aid and enhance the client's overall treatment plan, possibly cotreating and collaborating with other professionals. An excellent example of work at this level (Elefant & Lotan, 2004) describes the successful use of music therapy and physical therapy collaboration in assisting with helping a girl with Rett Syndrome participate more fully and achieve therapeutic goals in the physical therapy setting. At the intensive level of practice, instrumental improvisation is used to address the most significant areas of need, including improved hand use and expressive communication. Music therapists may be called to work at this level due to the client's resistance to other forms or therapy and/or due to the client's motivation by music. Improvisational experiences with clients with Rett Syndrome are most likely to fall on the intensive level, and work at this level differs from the collaborative nature of the augmentative level in that the music therapist and music have a more individualized role for the client; while goals may still be in common with other disciplines, the music therapist is incorporating improvisation in a way that is not central to the work or success of the other disciplines.

There are several contraindications to using instrumental improvisational experiences with clients with Rett Syndrome. First, it is important to understand the client's responses to loud sounds. Also, in the present author's clinical experience, some clients with Rett Syndrome may experience high levels of frustration or hyperventilation when given high demands for hand use. Therefore, a client's affective and behavioral responses should be carefully monitored to avoid this negative and potentially harmful situation if hyperventilation is not stopped. Instruments which are adapted for use in improvisation should be checked for sharp edges and points, as mallets could pose hazards to the eyes of both client and therapist and instruments may become inadvertent projectiles. Additionally, care should be given with regard to hand splinting or separation as described above.

Preparation. The therapist will need to have appropriately adapted mallets and other instruments available when preparing for a session during which instrumental improvisation will be used. Additionally, depending upon the client's seating arrangements, a table or tray placed at midline may assist the client in accessing the instruments independently or with assistance. Positioning of the client in relation to the instruments and therapist is also crucial, as eye contact may be used communicatively by clients with Rett Syndrome. The therapist using a guitar may seat her-/himself directly in front of the client; at the piano, the client may be positioned facing the therapist, with the therapist angling her or his body in the direction of the client. Based upon whether the intervention is preplanned and whether accompaniment is used, several scenarios are possible. At the piano, the client may be positioned at either the treble or bass side of the therapist in order for the therapist to be able to provide physical assistance to the client's nondominant hand. When guitar is used, again, the therapist should position her-/himself in such a manner as to allow the client the best access to strum the strings. When preparing for a group music therapy session during which a client with Rett Syndrome will be participating, in addition to the considerations listed above, it is crucial that multiple accessible instruments continue to be available to the client.

What to observe. During instrumental improvisation experiences, the music therapist observes the client's motivation to utilize instruments, for example, whether the client is independently reaching to access an instrument, whether the client reaches for similar instruments from session to session, and the length of time the client sustains the instrumental improvisation. The therapist should also observe the level of assistance required by the client to improvise with an instrument successfully. What is their emotional response to the sounds that they are creating? Similarly, it is important for the therapist to observe the client's reactions to the music which is being produced by the therapist or others in the session, with regard to the client's emotional, physical, and musical responses. Audio and video recording may be of great assistance in analyzing these responses. The music therapist also observes the client's behavior, as well as their facial expressions, eye gaze, and other nonverbal gestures, including hand and body movements. These observations assist the therapist in determining the intent of the client's communication. The present author proposed that the client's communicative intent may be understood through both the therapist's clinical knowledge and in-the-moment observations of the client with Rett Syndrome during music therapy experiences, concluding that interpretations of these communications guided clinical decisions within the music therapy session (Sokira, 2007).

Procedures. Procedures for conducting an instrumental improvisation intervention may vary greatly according to the clinical setting and personality of the client, as well as the clinical goals within the treatment plan. Use of structure and predictability should be considered, allowing the client with

Rett Syndrome to be able to predict the general expectations of the session. First, the client and therapist are seated together in close proximity as described above. Then, the therapist begins the improvisation, indicating nonverbally, verbally, or through sung directions for the client to play. The music therapist may take musical cues from the client's tempi, vocalizations, or movements to guide the improvisation. Based on the clinical goals, the improvisational experiences using instruments may include opportunities for the client to respond musically to structure provided by one or more components of the therapist's accompanying music (on voice, piano, drum, guitar, etc.) or the music of other group members or caregiver participants. The converse may also take place, with the client's music guiding the music of the therapist and others. As the music continues, the therapist takes cues from the client and responds musically in the moment, vocally or instrumentally reflecting the client's music and affirming their participation. Through the improvised music, the therapist intends to create opportunities for the client to address their goals, and then improvises to respond to the participation of the client.

Adaptations. Vocal improvisation is an adaption of this method. Indications for using "solo" vocal improvisation without instruments may include the client becoming overstimulated with the use of guitar, piano, or other instrument. It may also be indicated when the music therapist needs to use his or her hands to physically assist the client, and therefore it is not practical for the therapist to be sitting at the piano or holding a guitar or other accompaniment instrument for clinical reasons. While several communicative and motor goals may be addressed, like instrumental improvisation, vocal improvisation may also be utilized at multiple levels of music therapy, described above. Unaccompanied vocal improvisation may be contraindicated in cases where a hearing impairment is a secondary diagnosis. Vocal improvisation may be used specifically to encourage the client with Rett Syndrome to utilize her voice or vocalizations in an expressive or purposeful manner. This can impact the area of social/emotional skills in that encouraged vocalizations can be helpful also to peers in developing an understanding that the girl with Rett Syndrome has "something to say." In the area of gross motor skills, vocal improvisation might be used to spontaneously create melodies and songs which accompany a specific movement of the arms, legs, or body. These improvisations may be saved for future use, turned into songs, etc. In a humanistic framework, in cases in which the client is motivated by the music therapist and therapeutic relationship, this can be a good opportunity for the client to try less familiar and/or nonpreferred experiences within the context of a musical experience.

Guidelines for Re-creative Music Therapy

When working with clients with Rett Syndrome, re-creative music therapy interventions may be employed to address a variety of goals, including social and emotional expression, communication, and motor skill development. For clients with Rett Syndrome, it is often reported that preferred music exists; therefore, engaging the client in vocal or instrumental tasks that involve reproducing music in some way (Bruscia, 1998) may be highly motivating (Elefant & Wigram, 2005).

Vocal Re-creation

Overview. In vocal re-creation, the client and therapist sing precomposed songs, re-creating the songs either in full or in part. Re-creative music therapy interventions might be indicated by several factors, particularly the client's clinical goals, need for structured experiences, and need for familiar/comfortable songs for sensory and emotional purposes. Clinical goals in using this type of intervention may include needs in the area of communication and emotional expression. Like other interventions mentioned here, re-creative interventions using the voice may be utilized on multiple levels. At the auxiliary level, they may encourage use of the voice in nontherapeutic settings. At the augmentative level, they may enhance the work of the client in the area of special education or speech language pathology. At the intensive and primary levels, re-creative interventions using the voice will address more primary needs such as expression of the client's personality, preferences, and emotions, and actualization of the self. If a client does not vocalize or demonstrates a great deal of difficulty or overstimulation when using the voice, this may preclude the use of re-creative interventions using the voice. Re-creative interventions using the voice may also be contraindicated should a client demonstrate a great deal of emotional or physical difficulty or demonstrate overstimulation in response to demands for using instruments.

Preparation. When preparing the MT environment for a session that may utilize re-creative interventions using the voice, consideration should be made with regard to the positioning of the student and therapist. In some cases, particular attention should be paid to the client's ability to see the therapist's face. It may be appropriate for recording equipment to be provided, and the therapist should ensure that access is available to sheet music for any preplanned songs. Finally, any preparation needed to ensure that the client's assistive technology devices contain the appropriate words and choices should be made.

What to observe. When observing a client participating in a re-creative intervention using the voice, the music therapist should be prepared to observe the client's vocal efforts and breathing, listening carefully to ensure that all musical efforts are taken into consideration.

Procedures. Music therapists often follow a structure such as the following when implementing a vocal re-creation experience.

1) Introduction/Greeting Song
2) Vocal experience: The music therapist may encourage the client to "sing along" with a preferred precomposed song, vocalizing within their capacity.
    - Singing with Known Songs: This intervention includes a music therapist presenting a song with a client with Rett Syndrome with the goal of re- creating through singing the full song, or section of the song. The client's responses may vary greatly, depending on the client's capacity to vocalize, ranging from joining in on melodies, phrases, and words to vocalizing nonverbally but melodically, humming along to the melody or harmony of the song. The therapist may support the client by singing full phrases/lyrics, providing accompaniment on piano or guitar, and adjusting the tempo and dynamics to the client's responsiveness. One example of this in the MT literature is the use of a "Body Parts Song" in which the music therapist, alongside a physical therapist, utilized a theme song to reinforce "body scheme" and for "framing and improving body awareness" (Elefant & Lotan, 2004).
    - Phrase Completion in Known Songs: This intervention involves a music therapist providing structured opportunities for a client with Rett Syndrome to complete a sung phrase using a vocalization, word, or sound. The client's desire to have the preferred song continue may also provide a context in which she will become motivated to respond in a different or more timely way.
3) Singing in a Group: Vocal work within a group setting, such as a music class, music therapy group, or formal choir or chorus may be appropriate, as the client with Rett Syndrome may be motivated to participate vocally with her classmates or fellow group members. In music therapy, procedures will vary based upon the nature and size of the group. Pairing the client with Rett Syndrome with a peer ("buddy system") who can assist them may be appropriate. Similarly, visual prompts via symbols, lyrics and assistive

technology may allow the client to access and meet expectations on a more independent basis. While it is clear that working in a typical/inclusionary ensemble may not be appropriate in all cases, a client with Rett Syndrome who is working on social skills and is content to participate in vocal experiences with peers is a strong candidate for this type of intervention. Adaptive thinking on the part of the music educator and collaboration with the music therapist and special education team would be appropriate in assisting this type of intervention to be maximally successful.

4) Good-bye song

Adaptations. One or more vocal re-creative experiences may be incorporated within a session, along with other interventions. Adaptations for using vocal re-creative interventions include using assistive technology to supplement the client's voice, using recording technology to play back or enhance the client's vocal efforts, and creating client-appropriate vocal-production expectations.

Another adaptation of vocal re-creation is re-creative interventions using instruments. Like re-creative interventions using the voice, re-creative music therapy interventions using instruments can be indicated by the client's clinical goals, need for structured experiences, and need for familiar/comfortable songs for sensory and emotional purposes. As with vocal re-creation experiences, clinical goals in using this adaptation may address communication, emotional, and motor goals at multiple levels of music therapy. Considerations for preparation are similar to those described above for instrumental improvisation experiences; however, a more musically structured, precomposed song is used, and it is noted that preparation is required to ensure that the client's assistive technology devices contain the appropriate words and choices as needed.

Similar procedures are then used, including Introduction/Hello Song, followed by Instrument Playing. This could include Song Re-production with Adapted Instrument Playing, in which the client and therapist work together to re-produce a known/familiar song. The therapist may sing and play an accompaniment instrument while the client plays another appropriate adapted instrument, either melodic or percussive in nature. The client may play a steady rhythm or may play intermittently. The clinical rationale for the client's participation in this type of intervention may be the duration during which they demonstrate grasp, the frequency of their playing of the instrument at or across midline, the frequency of their independently creating a sound, etc.

This could also incorporate Structured Use of Instruments to Complete Phrases, in which the therapist creates silence/spaces within a song during which the client is expected to activate an instrument/create a musical response. The therapist's musical accompaniment may be adapted to allow for response time, e.g., longer pauses, or it may continue at a regular rhythm depending on the particular clinical goal being addressed. Like Phrase Completion in Known Songs (vocal) described above, emphasis on preferred and familiar instruments may be of particular importance.

Finally, Playing Instruments in a Group allows for the client to work as one of several group members playing instruments in an ensemble. The ensemble may vary in size as well as in the ability of the peers. Instrumentation varies based on the group members, with particular considerations for the participant/client with Rett Syndrome's physical ability to grasp and activate instruments as well as her or his preferences for sounds.

Guidelines for Compositional Music Therapy

When working with clients with Rett Syndrome, a music therapist may elect to utilize compositional music therapy techniques and interventions in assisting them to address their clinical goals at various levels. Within this category of intervention, the therapist may assist with various aspects of the composition, musically and technically, and the finished product may include a recording, written composition, or musical piece (Bruscia, 1998).

Various musical considerations include creation of theme, lyrics, rhythm, tempo, melody, harmony, and instrumentation, and emphasis on one or more of these various aspects will differ depending on the client's goals and the clinical situation. Therefore, the therapist should be prepared to support one or all of these musical areas.

Theme: The theme of a piece may be developed by the client, therapist or both together. The theme material can vary to include leisure-related topics, expression of emotions, academic/cognitive topics, question/answer songs, songs which narrate or structure daily life experiences, and others. The client's preferences can be indicated through multiple means of communication and can include the incorporation of assistive technology.

Lyrics: Lyrics may be created through various means. A client's words or sounds can be incorporated and extrapolated to create phrases. Assistive technology may be used to provide choices to the client or allow her to spell out or speak her desires. The therapist may elaborate on the client's words or phrases, make selections, and confirm the client's choices, again using high- and/or low-"tech" means.

Rhythm, tempo, and dynamics: The rhythm and tempo of a client's songwriting experience may be indicated to the therapist by the client through verbal, vocal, assistive technology, or musical means.

Melody, harmony, and instrumentation: The melodic line of a song or composition may be indicated through musical means—for example, the client, with or without the assistance of the therapist, may play a melody on a keyboard instrument and the therapist may assist by matching this melody with lyrics. The melody and harmony of a songwriting composition may also be developed through trial-and-error/question-and-answer between the therapist and client, in which the therapist plays a short phrase and requests that the client confirm whether they like it or would like something different. Third, the melody, harmony, and instrumentation may be developed by the client through the use of various composing/songwriting applications within assistive technology that provide choices.

Adapted Composition and Songwriting

Overview. Adapted composition is a variation on the process of "Songwriting with Technology Adaptations" described by Federico & Niedenthal (2011). A similar process for composition has been used by the present author in her clinical practice with clients with Rett Syndrome, although it has not previously been described in the literature. It may be indicated by a client who is working to clinically address needs in the areas of self-expression, choice-making, and cognitive and academic skills. At the auxiliary and augmentative levels of therapy, a client who is motivated to participate in songwriting may be able to feature her or his intellectual abilities if the songwriting experience includes academic concepts with which the client can demonstrate her knowledge. For example, a client could participate in adapted composition about an academic concept like counting and then demonstrate counting knowledge by performing the song with her music therapist. In addition, a client may engage in songwriting to create meaningful songs that can be used to structure experiences throughout her or his life, to accompany experiences in therapies, education, and self-care. At the intensive and primary levels of music therapy, songwriting experiences may serve as an outlet of meaningful, deeper communication about a client's life, feelings, and experiences, elicited through the therapeutic and musical relationships developed between client and therapist at this level.

Clients with Rett Syndrome who participate in adapted composition should be able to make choices from a field of two, and to confirm these choices using vocalization, hand use, and/or eye gaze.

Adapted composition may be frustrating and therefore contraindicated if the client with Rett Syndrome is young, is learning to communicate, or displays heightened levels of frustration given the presentation of the therapeutic interventions.

Preparation. When preparing a session in which adapted composition will be used with a client with Rett Syndrome, consideration of the client's individual communication needs and musical preferences is crucial. The therapist should ensure that all needed communication aids are available prior to the session beginning. Availability of audio or video recording and editing equipment, along with staff paper/pencil for notation, is also crucial.

What to observe. The music therapist should be prepared to observe the client's choices, emotional responses, and physical movements to interpret the client's intent in answering questions and contributing musical choices and materials.

Procedures. The following procedures, informed by Federico and Niedenthal (2011), for adapted composition may be utilized with individuals with Rett Syndrome.

1) Greeting Song: The therapist welcomes the client(s) into the session.
2) Musical Choices: After introducing the composition experience, the therapist provides the client with musical choices, providing appropriate means for the client to respond. Musical choices can include theme, lyrics, rhythm, tempo, dynamics, melody, harmony, and instrumentation, as outlined above.
    - Composition: As a result of the client's musical choices, the composition may follow one of several directions:
    - Original Songwriting: In Original Songwriting experiences, a client is provided the opportunity to compose a completely original song "from scratch" through assistance from the therapist. The client and therapist make decisions together about each musical aspect of the song, and then the piece is performed and recorded by the client, therapist, both, or others. This process may happen over one or (likely) more sessions.
    - Song Rewriting: In Song Rewriting, a known or preferred precomposed song is changed to suit the clinical purposes of a session. At the augmentative level, this may include the changing of lyrics to create a song to structure an appropriate music experience or to create a musical structure for a nonmusical experience.
    - Original Composition: As in Original Songwriting, Original Composition includes opportunities for the client to compose an original musical piece from scratch. The client and therapist work together to make decisions about the musical aspects of the piece, and then it is recorded and performed by the client, therapist, both or others. Again, this process may happen over one or more sessions.
    - Therapist-Composed Songs: At times, a specific song or type of song may be needed for a client to best access a therapeutic, educational, or life experience. Given the time-oriented nature of songwriting and composition with clients with Rett Syndrome, a therapist may select to compose a song for a client to use in music therapy and in other therapeutic settings in consultation with family and team members.
    - Group Songwriting and Composition: A client with Rett Syndrome may benefit from participating in Group Songwriting and Composition Experiences by creating music alongside of peers. Several positive therapeutic outcomes may

arise from this type of opportunity, including the development of social skills, group membership, and turn-taking.

3) Recording and Notation
4) Good-bye Song/Session Closure

Adaptations. Adapted composition may be used in one session, or may extend over several. It may be used as the only intervention during a session, or it may be used in combination with other interventions.

Working with Caregivers

Because of the extensive needs of clients with Rett Syndrome in all domains, the music therapist may be called upon to support both the client's family and caregivers. When working with clients with Rett Syndrome in home-based settings, the music therapist should be prepared to communicate about music therapy interventions to family members, as well as include family members and caregivers in the music therapy session as appropriate. Because clients with Rett Syndrome utilize music for motivation and communication, music therapy interventions may allow family members to see new aspects of their child or sibling with Rett Syndrome in a new way, revealing skills, communications, and potentials that are not revealed in therapeutic work with other modalities. Working in collaboration or in consultation with family members also may provide the music therapist with the opportunity to create musical experiences that can be carried over or practiced with the client during in-between music therapy sessions. As a consultant, the music therapist may serve as a resource for family members in incorporating music into their family's routine or as a clearinghouse for music recommendations for the client. Additionally, while working within the scope of their competence and training, the music therapist may also provide valuable support to family members in developing positive coping strategies with regard to the grief and loss associated with changed expectations following a Rett Syndrome diagnosis. Furthermore, the music therapist may be able to assist family members in developing strategies for coping with stress related to caregiving for the client.

Research Evidence

Receptive Music Therapy

In addition to Elefant's work with children with Rett Syndrome using song choices to help demonstrate communication intent, the music therapy/Rett Syndrome literature also supports the use of receptive listening to therapist instrument-playing (namely ocean drum) for sensory benefit and relaxation (Elefant & Lotan, 2004) as well as in making song choices, again motivated by the receptive experience to occur after the choice has been made.

Wigram (1997) described the use of vibroacoustic therapy with several individuals with Rett Syndrome, noting that after one initial session, several clients demonstrated decreased hand wringing, increased visible relaxation of muscle tone, reduced movement, and slowed breathing. In their study of vibroacoustic therapy in Rett Syndrome, Bergström-Isacsson, Julu, and Witt-Engerström (2007) found that, while clients with Rett Syndrome demonstrated calming and alerting responses with measurable effect from receptive listening to music, these responses were not outwardly observable within the clients' behavioral emotional responses. The authors noted that different music was effective for different clients using vibroacoustic therapy. This highlights that what one observes may not be consistent with the inner experience of the client with Rett Syndrome; therefore, it is important to ask questions and wait for responses, following cues, as well as use all information available from other therapists and caregivers regarding overstimulation and other negative physiological states.

Improvisational Music Therapy

The use of improvisational music therapy with children with Rett Syndrome has been described in the music therapy literature, with anecdotal descriptions of effectiveness of this method with outcomes of communication, visual focus, and nonverbal communication. However, specific methods were not studied in detail to develop evidence of effectiveness with therapeutic outcomes with this client population.

An example of improvisational music therapy with a client with Rett Syndrome was outlined by Hill (1997), as she described the use of vocal improvisation to encourage a client's development of meaningful communication. Hill also discussed the use of instrumental improvisation on the triangle and its use in developing outcomes of visual focus and nonverbal communication. Wigram, in his case study of Helen, a client with Rett Syndrome, used improvisation in the assessment and music therapy treatment process (1991). This included piano and guitar accompaniment to his client's strumming, "improvised duets" in which he and his client with RS improvised together, and improvised vocalizations from the client. Since clients with Rett Syndrome are reported to have positive clinical outcomes as a result of participating in improvisation experiences, and because the music therapy method of improvisation has not yet been fully studied, future research in this area is recommended in order to ascertain best practices and possible therapeutic outcomes.

Re-creative Music Therapy

The use of re-creative music therapy interventions to work on multiple goals has been more broadly studied and discussed within the music therapy literature. Wigram (1991) describes the use of instrument-playing in which the client plays with hand-over-hand assistance as well as independently in order to work on physical goals. Similarly, Wigram and Lawrence (2005) describe an assessment session during which piano-playing, instrument-playing, and vocalization are used to evaluate both the physical and the communication skills of the client. Instrument-playing and singing interventions have been discussed in relation to addressing grasp, physical coordination, and communication (Hadsell & Coleman, 1988; Wylie, 1996; Yasura & Sugiyama, 2001), demonstrating positive outcomes in case studies.

Elefant and Lotan (2004) discussed the use of a re-created song about the topic of body parts to meet various physical and body awareness goals. They also discuss the incorporation of drum- and guitar-playing in their music therapy/physical therapy collaboration. Elefant and Wigram (2005) studied the ability of clients with Rett Syndrome to demonstrate learning through making choices of preferred and motivating songs. This study in particular highlights not only that clients with Rett Syndrome can indeed learn and maintain knowledge, but also the importance of the use of music as a motivational factor in learning. While evidence exists in support of the use of re-creative music therapy methods with clients with Rett Syndrome, continued research into its impact on therapeutic outcomes for these clients is warranted.

Compositional Music Therapy

While the use of therapist-composed songs has been mentioned in the literature for use within re-creative music therapy methods with clients with Rett Syndrome, there are no specific mentions of the use of compositional music therapy techniques within the MT and Rett Syndrome literature. The ability of individuals with Rett Syndrome to show preference and make intentional song choices has been established (Elefant, 2002; Elefant & Wigram, 2005); therefore, it is the present author's clinical experience and belief that the use of compositional music therapy experiences with clients with Rett Syndrome is both possible and clinically effective to work on goals of choice-making, communication, and self-expression. The use of consistent choice-making procedures as outlined by Elefant (2002) can be adapted to allow clients to provide responses which contribute to all aspects of composition as described. Furthermore, the use of assistive technology, as described by Magee et al. (2011), is applicable to music therapy composition with clients with Rett Syndrome. While the compositional procedures outlined by Federico and Niedenthal (2011) for work with children with cerebral palsy provide a starting point, research to expand procedures and outcomes of compositional methods of music therapy with clients with Rett Syndrome is needed.

Summary and Conclusions

In conclusion, a range of receptive, improvisational, re-creative, and compositional music therapy experiences has been reported from music therapy with clients with Rett Syndrome. Receptive, improvisational, and re-creative methods have been researched, while compositional methods are only beginning to be discussed for this client population. While the current research in the music therapy literature is limited with regard to interventions, anecdotal reports continue to support the effectiveness of MT in addressing the complex clinical needs of these clients' communication, motor, sensory, cognitive, and emotional needs. Since music has been reported to be an effective tool to achieve therapeutic growth, further study is warranted to codify methods and outcomes in order to provide the best possible music therapy experiences for clients with Rett Syndrome.

References

Bergström-Isacsson, M., Julu, P. O. O., & Witt-Engerström, I. (2007). Autonomic responses to music and vibroacoustic therapy in Rett syndrome: A controlled within-subject study. *Nordic Journal of Music Therapy, 16*(1), 42–59.

Baxter, H., Berghofer, J, MacEwan, L., Nelson, J., Peters, K., & Roberts, P. (2007). *The individualized music therapy assessment profile.* Philadelphia, PA: Jessica Kingsley.

Bradfield, C., Carlenius, J., Gold, C., & White, M. (2008). MT-SEAS: *Music therapy special education assessment scale.* Grapevine, TX: Prelude Music Therapy.

Bruscia, K. (1998). *Defining music therapy.* Gilsum, NH: Barcelona Publishers.

Budden, S. (2006). *Rett syndrome.* Retrieved from http://www.novita.org.au/library/ftpdownloads/PowerPoint/rett_syndrome_files/outline/index.html

Budden, S., Meek, M., & Henighan, C. (1990). Communication and oral-motor function in Rett Syndrome. *Developmental Medicine & Child Neurology, 32*(1), 51–55.

Cass, H., Reilly, S., Owen, L., Wisbeach, A., Weekes, L., Slonims, V., Wigram, T., & Charman, T. (2003). Findings from a multidisciplinary clinical case series of girls with Rett syndrome. *Developmental Medicine and Child Neurology, 45*(5), 325–337.

Coleman, K., & Brunk, B. (1999). *Special education music therapy assessment process.* Grapevine, TX: Prelude Music Therapy.

Elefant, C. (2001). Speechless yet communicative: Revealing the person behind the disability if Rett syndrome through clinical research on sons in music therapy. In D. Aldridge, G. Franco, E. Ruud, & T. Wigram (Eds.), *Music therapy in Europe* (pp. 13–128). Rome, Italy: ISMEZ.

Elefant, C., & Lotan, M. (2004). Rett syndrome: Dual intervention—music and physical therapy. *Nordic Journal of Music Therapy, 13*(2), 172–182.

Elefant, C., & Wigram, T. (2005). Learning ability in children with Rett syndrome. *Brain and Development, 27*(S1), S97–S101.

Ellaway, C., & Christodoulou, J. (2001). Rett syndrome: Clinical characteristics and recent genetic advances. *Disability and Rehabilitation, 23,* 98–106.

Federico, G., & Niedenthal, R. (2011). Music therapy & cerebral palsy. Songwriting with technology adaptations. *Proceedings of XIII World Congress of Music Therapy,* Seoul, Korea.

Go, T., & Mitani, A. (2009). A qualitative motion analysis study of voluntary hand movement induced by music in patients with Rett syndrome. *Neuropsychiatric Disease and Treatment, 5,* 499–503.

Hadsell, N. A., & Coleman, K. A. (1988). Rett syndrome: A challenge for music therapists. *Music Therapy Perspectives, 5,* 52–56.

Hagberg, B. (1997). Condensed points for diagnostic criteria and stages in Rett syndrome. *European Child and Adolescent Psychiatry, 6*(S1), 2–4.

Hagberg, B. (2002). Clinical manifestations and stages of Rett syndrome. *Mental Retardation and Developmental Disabilities Research Reviews, 8*(2), 61–65.

Hagberg, B., & Witt-Engerström, I. (1986). Rett syndrome: A suggested staging system for describing impairment profile with increasing age towards adolescence. *American Journal of Medical Genetics, 24,* 47–59.

Hetzroni, O., Rubin, C., & Konkol, O. (2002). The use of assistive technology for symbol identification by children with Rett syndrome. *Journal of Intellectual and Developmental Disability, 27*(1), 57–71.

Hill, S. (1997). The relevance and value of music therapy for children with Rett syndrome. *British Journal of Special Education, 24*(3), 124–128.

Jacobson, K., Vitken, A., & Von Tetzchner, S. (2001). Rett syndrome and aging: A case study. *Disability and Rehabilitation, 23*(3/4), 160–167.

Koppenhaver, D., Erickson, K., Harris, B., McLellan, J., Skotko, B., & Newton, R. (2001). Storybook-based communication intervention for girls with Rett syndrome and their mothers. *Disability and Rehabilitation, 23*(3/4), 149–159.

Koppenhaver, D., Erickson, K., & Skotko, B. (2001). Supporting communication of girls with Rett syndrome and their mothers in storybook reading. *International Journal of Disability, Development and Education, 48*(4), 395–411.

Lotan, M. (2006). Rett syndrome: Guidelines for individual intervention. *The Scientific World Journal, 6,* 1504–1516.

Magee, W. L., Bertolami, M., Kubicek, L., LaJoie, M., Martino, L., Sankowski, A., & Zigo, J. B. (2011). Using music technology in music therapy with populations across the life span in medical and educational programs. *Music and Medicine, 3*(3), 146–153.

Perry, A. (1991). Rett syndrome: A comprehensive review of the literature. *American Journal on Mental Retardation, 96,* 275–290.

Rett Syndrome. (2012). In *ADAM medical encyclopedia*. Retrieved from http://www.ncbi.nlm.nih.gov/pubmedhealth/PMH0002503/

Rett Syndrome Fact Sheet. (2012). Retrieved from http://www.ninds.nih.gov/disorders/rett/detail_rett.htm

Rett Syndrome Research Trust. (n.d.). Retrieved from http://www.rsrt.org/rett-and-mecp2-disorders/

Sandberg, A., Ehlers, S. Hagberg, B., & Gillberg, C. (2000). The Rett syndrome complex: Communicative function in relation to developmental and autistic features. *Autism: The International Journal of Research and Practice, 4*(3), 249–267.

Sigafoos, J., Green, V. A., Schlosser, R., O'Reilly, M. F., Lancioni, G. E., Rispoli, M., & Lang, R. (2009). Communication intervention in Rett syndrome: A systematic review. *Research in Autism Spectrum Disorders, 3*(2), 304–318.

Skille, O. (1989). Vibroacoustic therapy. *Music Therapy, 8*(1), 61–77.

Skotko, B., Koppenhaver, D., & Erickson, K. (2004). Parent reading behavioral and communication outcomes in girls with Rett syndrome. *Exceptional Children, 70*(2), 145–166.

Sokira, J. (2007). Interpreting the communicative behaviors of clients with Rett Syndrome in music therapy: A self-inquiry. *Qualitative Inquiries in Music Therapy, 3,* 103–131. Gilsum, NH: Barcelona Publishers.

Van Acker, R., & Grant, S. (1995). An effective computer-based requesting system for persons with Rett syndrome. *Journal of Childhood Communication Disorders, 16*(2), 31–38.

Watson, J., Umansky, R., Marcy, S., & Repacholi, B. (1996). Intention and preference of a 3-year-old with Rett syndrome. *Journal of Applied Developmental Psychology, 17*(1), 69–84.

Wesecky, A. (1986). Music therapy for children with Rett syndrome. *American Journal of Medical Genetics,* S1, 253–257.

Wigram, T. (1991). Music therapy for a girl with Rett's Syndrome: Balancing structure and freedom. In K. E. Bruscia (Ed.), *Case studies in music therapy* (pp. 39–53). Gilsum, NH: Barcelona Publishers.

Wigram, T. (1997). Vibroacoustic therapy in the treatment of Rett syndrome. In T. Wigram & C. Dileo (Eds.), *Music vibration and health* (149–156). Cherry Hill, NJ: Jeffrey Books.

Wigram, T., & Elefant, C. (2009). Therapeutic dialogues in music: Nurturing musicality of communication in children with autistic spectrum disorder and Rett syndrome. In S. Malloch, C. Trevarthen, S. Malloch, & C. Trevarthen (Eds.), *Communicative musicality: Exploring the basis of human companionship* (pp. 423–445). New York, NY: Oxford University Press.

Wigram, T., & Lawrence, M. (2005). Music therapy as a tool for assessing hand use and communicativeness in children with Rett syndrome. *Brain & Development, 27*(S1), S95–S96.

Woodyatt, G., & Ozanne, A. (1992a). Communication abilities and Rett syndrome. *Journal of Autism and Developmental Disorders, 22*(2), 155–173.

Woodyatt, G., & Ozanne, A. (1992b). Communication abilities in a case of Rett syndrome. *Journal of Intellectual Disability Research, 36*(1), 83–92.

Woodyatt, G., & Ozanne, A. (1993). A longitudinal study of cognitive skills and communication behaviors in children with Rett syndrome. *Journal of Intellectual Disability Research, 37*(4), 419–435.

Woodyatt, G., & Ozanne, A. (1994). Intentionality and communication in four children with Rett syndrome. *Australia and New Zealand Journal of Developmental Disabilities, 19*(3), 173–184.

Wylie, M. E. (1996). A case study to promote hand use in children with Rett syndrome. *Music Therapy Perspectives, 14*(2), 83–86.

Yasuhara, A., & Sugiyama, Y. (2001). Music therapy for children with Rett syndrome. *Brain and Development, 23*(S1), S82–S84.

Chapter 5

Developmental Speech and Language Disorders

Kathleen M. Howland

Diagnostic Information

The development of speech and language is an astounding process of skill acquisition in the life of a child. Learning words includes programming how they are pronounced, what they mean, and what grammatical roles they fulfill. This is accomplished through immersion and engagement with seemingly the greatest of ease. By two years of age, a child has grown from a single word vocabulary at one year to a 200–300 word vocabulary and is using these words in short, incomplete sentences to express their basic needs, wants, feelings, and opinions. Three years later, that child has a vocabulary of 2,100–2,200 words with 90% grammar acquisition (Owens, 2011). This is truly one of the great feats of child development. When this development is not progressing in a typical way, the ease of learning is replaced with hard work—drills, repetitions, explicit learning. A child has to learn language much like an adult learns a second language—with tremendous effort. This path can negatively impact a child's self-esteem and their literacy and academic abilities. Music therapy has the ability to contextualize the "hard work" with joy and playfulness. Music can take the boredom out of drills, give meaning to repetitions, and instruct learning explicitly through song. The disorders of pediatric speech and language will be defined in this chapter, and clinical approaches will be presented to facilitate the professional development of a music therapist treating this population and other therapists who wish to add music to their treatment activities.

Although we use the terms "speech and language" together, they reference very different skill sets. The key to understanding developmental speech and language disorders begins by defining the two terms.

"Language" is a symbolic system. A word is a symbol that represents something—an idea, an object, an action. In Helen Keller's autobiography, she describes the day that she made the connection between the reference (water) and the finger spelling (w-a-t-e-r) that symbolized it. Helen reconnected Annie Sullivan's finger spelling to the word she knew before she became deaf and blind. At that moment, she came to understand that the finger spelling Annie had been doing for so many months were for words that meant something. Up until that moment, Helen had not made the symbolic connection necessary for her language to develop and flourish. Helen writes, "I stood still, my whole attention fixed upon the motions of her fingers. Suddenly I felt a misty consciousness as of something forgotten—a thrill of returning thought; and somehow the mystery of language was revealed to me" (Keller & Sullivan, 1921, p. 23).

The term "speech" refers to a motor (movement) act, much like finger spelling and sign language are a motor acts. Speech is the coordination of respiration, phonation (at the level of the larynx), and articulation (at the level of the mouth) that conveys language. The centers in the brain that are primarily responsible for speech and language also reflect the distinctions of these two skills. The speech center is located in the frontal lobe of the brain along the inferior aspect of the motor strip from which movements are primarily generated. The language center is located in the temporal lobe, which is posterior (to the back) of the frontal lobe.

Babies are able to coordinate movements to approximate the gestures of sign language earlier than they are able to speak (Petitto, 2000; Petitto & Marentette, 1991). This is due to the motor complexity of speech production and the ease by which signs can be made. This ability to sign earlier than one is able to speak illustrates an important point: Receptive language (comprehension) is more advanced than expressive language. This is notable at age six, when children have an expressive vocabulary of 2,600 words but a receptive vocabulary of 20,000–24,000 words (Owens, 2011). This ability to understand more than one can say holds true for people with intellectual disabilities. This informs clinical work that maximizes comprehension.

Speech is an asymmetrical neural skill set. The majority of people are right-handed, and about 95% of those right-handers have left-hemispheric speech dominance (Rasmussen & Milner, 1977). The left hemisphere appears to be highly efficient in the neural activation of this skill. Whitmore, Hart, and Villems (1999) state that most left-handed children have no learning disability, but there does appear to be a prevalence of left-handedness in reports of children who have specific learning disabilities.

Language is a more complicated process and subsequently requires activation from many areas in the brain, namely the parietal, temporal, and frontal lobes (three of the five major lobes in the brain). Language has bihemispheric activation, and this offers improved recovery from brain injuries that is not always fully realized for speech. An example is the radical surgical removal of the left hemisphere of children who suffer from intractable seizures. Language reaches presurgical baselines within weeks of the surgery. Speech, however, remains a great challenge to these children, as it is not as effectively produced from the right hemisphere (Restak & Grubin, 2001).

Developmental speech and language disorders may be complicated by concomitant conditions such as autism, intellectual disability, attention deficit disorder, hearing deficits, and anatomical and physiological constraints such as cleft lip and/or palate (a congenital anomaly of the soft/hard palate and/or lip caused by malformation of the face during gestation).

Speech and language disorders may be a delay in skill acquisition that is treatable, or it may represent an underlying neurological or physical disorder. A disruption at any point along the track from intention to articulation can be problematic, resulting in various diagnoses of speech disorders, including stuttering, apraxia, dysarthria, articulation disorders, phonological disorders, and voice disorders. According to the American Speech-Language-Hearing Association (ASHA), the number of children with speech and language disabilities ages 3 to 21 years totaled over 6 million, with approximately one quarter of these individuals receiving services. This statistic reflects those who have a primary speech-language disorder and not those for whom it is a secondary condition (e.g., Down's Syndrome, cleft lip, autism, cerebral palsy).

Speech and/or language delays in early childhood can negatively impact literacy, school learning, development of self-esteem, and life success. Early identification and treatment are key to maximizing a child's potential for success.

Speech Disorders

Speech is a complicated task of coordinated and sequenced movement of respiration, phonation (vocal cord engagement), and articulation. Specialized neural pathways and centers in the brain result in the production of meaningful and interpretable sounds. Speech disorders can be neural (at the level of the brain) or peripheral (at the level of muscles). Speech disorders are described by the muscular weakness, paralysis, timing and/or coordination issues that result in distortions, substitutions, omissions, dysfluencies, or simplifications of sound productions.

It is very important for a therapist to understand a speech disorder in the context of normal development. Generally, three-year-olds should be able to be understood by unfamiliar listeners (e.g., non–family members). There are age-appropriate substitutions and distortions that typically developing children make as they learn to master the production of speech. Understanding normal development will help distinguish if the child is presenting with a disorder or not. For example, a five-year-old may substitute /w/ for /r/ and say "wabbit." This would be considered an age-appropriate substitution as the rhotic sound /r/ is difficult to articulate. One would expect that a child who is 8 to 9 years old can say the /r/ sound correctly in a variety of contexts: initial position "rose," medial position "around," final position "soccer," and in consonant blends "free" and "start." Scales for speech development can be found online and should be a part of a music therapist's resource notebook. Scales describe the production expectations of children from birth to 6 to 8 years of age. References for these scales can be found at the end of this chapter.

Stuttering. According to the Stuttering Foundation, approximately 1% of the population worldwide is affected by stuttering. In the United States, this number equates to approximately 3 million people, with males being affected four times more than females. While the causes are not know, genetic predispositions to stutter account for approximately 60% of those who stutter (Stuttering Foundation, 2012). A recent study of twins by Dworzynski, Remington, Rijsdijk, Howell, and Plomin (2007) reported that stuttering ratings by parents at ages 3 and 4 years were predictive of later stuttering. Concordance rates were consistently higher for identical (monozygotic) than for fraternal (dizygotic) twins, suggesting high inheritability.

Other factors that may contribute to stuttering include developmental problems or delays, issues with neural processing of speech and language (shown to be different for stutterers vs. nonstutterers), and family dynamics (e.g., fast talking, fast-paced family systems). In general, it would seem that a number of factors interact to create long-term stuttering.

There are several types of stuttering. The presenting features may include prolongations (e.g., pppppeople), repetitions (e.g., pi, pi, pi people), circumlocutions (person substitutes an intended word with another, using the word "folks" instead of people), blocks (no sound), and concomitant disorders (e.g., facial tics, tongue clicking). Success in treatment is based on the age of onset and genetic heredity. The younger a child is, the more likely his stuttering can be ameliorated. If there is a genetic predisposition for stuttering in the family, the likelihood of achieving fluency decreases.

Speech therapists generally use two approaches to treating stuttering. The first teaches an individual how to stutter more easily (Van Riper, 1973) using techniques such as:

- Cancellations: After a child stutters on a word, they are taught to repeat the word using gentle or easy stuttering. This includes easy onset of voicing and initial syllable plus gentle transitions between subsequent syllables.
- Pull-outs: This is the second tier of treatment in this treatment program. This stage teaches a child to make changes (per above) to the stuttering word while they are in the act of stuttering.
- Preparatory sets: Stutterers know which words they will be stuttering on as they approach them. This technique teaches preparation for easy onset and easy articulation of the word.

The other treatment philosophy is to work toward eliminating stuttering by systematically increasing fluent output in specific settings (e.g., the speech therapy office) and then generalizing to all settings of a child's life. Treatment scaffolds in complexity from single phrases to more complex phrases to conversational speech.

A would-be-helpful conversational partner may encourage a stutterer to "calm down" or "take a big breath and try again." These comments are meant to be supportive, but they can actually backfire and increase anxiety for the stutterer. Negative emotions that come from speech-related stress can impact a child's development of self-esteem. It is best to check your body language so that you are offering a relaxed and patient presentation to the stutterer. It is important to tell them that you value what they have to say and are comfortable and happy to wait until they are complete. Because of self-esteem, confidence, and anxiety issues, teens should definitely be considered partners in their treatment programs in order to optimally realize their potential for success.

Apraxia. This is a developmental disorder of speech named from the Greek word *praxis* which refers to "action." It is a disorder of action that is not related to ability. Key to understanding this disorder is assessing a child's difficulty in performing voluntary movements when compared with automatic ones. For example, a child can perform a speech-related movement (e.g., opening mouth to yawn) but cannot perform it on request. A child can repeat a word you say but is not able to generate it independently. Children with apraxia present with speech errors unrelated to weakness or coordination issues. The features of apraxia include groping, effortful speech, inconsistent errors, and difficulty being understood, especially during longer utterances. Apraxic children demonstrate speech capabilities similar to those of adults with Broca's aphasia.

Broca's aphasia is often described as telegraphic speech. When telegrams were in use, one had to pay for each word. Communications were abbreviated to save money. This was done by eliminating nonessential words (e.g., adjectives, adverbs, prepositions, articles). People with Broca's aphasia or children with apraxia have severely reduced speech output limited mainly to single words or short word combinations. Their output conveys meaning with little grammatical complexity. Children with apraxia and adults with Broca's aphasia both demonstrate groping, effortful speech with inconsistent errors. In both conditions, they typically are able to sing better than they talk. This provides music therapists with important opportunities to provide meaningful clinical services.

Speech-language pathologists differentially diagnose oral apraxia (difficulty with volitional control for nonspeech movements) and verbal apraxia (difficulty with volitional control for movements related to speech). Like stutterers, apraxic children are generally able to anticipate their errors and begin efforts to repair them before, during, and after the word. Output is thus observed as effortful and groping as described above.

Dysarthria. This is a term that describes a group of motor speech disorders caused by central (brain and spinal cord) or peripheral (cranial or spinal nerves) nervous system damage that control the muscles of the speech system. Dysarthria does not include disorders related to structural injury such as cleft lip or other facial injuries. These disorders can be congenital (Down's Syndrome, cerebral palsy) or acquired (brain injury, stroke). The overall effect is reduced speech intelligibility. The speech may sound slurred, mumbled, or too quiet. This occurs for a variety of reasons. The child may have limited or poor range of motion of the tongue (cannot move tongue up and down or side to side), lips (cannot pucker or smile broadly) and jaw (cannot open widely or close completely).

Dysarthria may be due to poor muscle tone in the tongue and lips, as is typical with people who have Down's Syndrome. The child with poor muscle tone may present with poor saliva control (drools). Poor speech intelligibility may also be due to poor breath control, which results in too quiet a voice. The term dysarthria can describe poor vocal quality that makes a child's voice sound stuffy, as if they have a cold. Children with poor muscle tone and range of motion for speech may also have chewing and swallowing difficulties (known as dysphagia). The nervous system damage that results in dysarthria is described by issues related to respiration, phonation, articulation, resonance, and prosody.

Disorders of respiration. These typically manifest as a quiet or breathy voice, frequent breaths during speech (may even breathe after one or two words or between syllables within a word), and fatigue. Breathing may be clavicular (expansion of ribs) and not diaphragmatic, which results in shallow, ineffective breaths for audible speech production. *Phonatory disorders* refer to dysfunction of the vocal folds in the larynx. This may manifest as a breathy or hoarse vocal quality. The child may have a reduced pitch range or poorly regulated loudness (too loud or too soft). Phonatory disorders may be the result of poor respiration which does not effectively set the vocal folds into effective movement. *Articulation disorders* are caused by the weak or poorly coordinated musculature of the lips, tongue, and jaw. The tongue has four paired extrinsic and four paired intrinsic muscles. Extrinsic muscles attach the tongue to other structures such as the jaw, and intrinsic muscles are contained within the tongue. The anatomy and physiology is complex, and thus any disruption in innervation of signals from the brain or damage of the tongue itself will result in distortions of speech. The lips are richly connected to muscles that allow them to move both for speech and for facial expressivity. *Resonance disorders* are due to a weak muscular coupling between the soft palate at the back of the mouth and the nasal cavity. People with resonance disorders often sound "stuffy" like they have a cold because this coupling is weak or poorly coordinated and all speech sounds are nasalized. In English, the coupling (known as the velopharyngeal sphincter) is open during nasalized sounds (/n/ in "and," /m/ in "man," and /ŋ/ as in "ring"). In addition to listening to the quality of speech productions, speech therapists will test for nasal air emission in people with dysarthria. When the velopharyngeal sphincter is open, air loss can be heard and measured at the nares (nostrils). This is very notable during the production of plosives, the class of speech sounds that require the column of air to be closed by an articulator (lips or tongue) and then suddenly released. Plosives in English include /p/ and /t/ as in "pat" and /b/ and /d/ as in "bed." While saying the word "pat" or "pack," a client may have audible release of breath through the nose.

Among the dysarthric disorders described above, the most impressive gains can be made at the level of articulation. In the past, speech therapists working with dysarthric patients would target specific speech sounds and prompt the patient through levels of production—the sound in isolation, at the syllable level, the word level, the phrase level, the sentence level, and then in conversational speech. The speech sounds would be practiced at the initial place in a word (put), medial (apple), and final place (tap), focusing on specific elements of motor production (e.g., firm lip closure). This work is challenging and fairly dull, and does not always generalize well to conversational speech. The Lee Silverman Voice Training (LSVT) program focuses on loud vocal productions from both a motor and sensory perspective. It is delivered in an intense treatment protocol of four one-hour sessions per week for a month, totaling 16 sessions, with Parkinson's patients who are dysarthric. The positive outcomes on articulation demonstrate improved consonant production (Dromey, Ramig, & Johnson, 1995), tongue strength and motility (Ward, Thoedoros, Murdoch, & Schlaug, 2000), and rate of speech (Ramig et al., 2005). By improving breath control and learning how to be loud, people with dysarthria related to Parkinson's disease improve their articulation without the pyramid of traditional training described above. This bottom-up approach (focus on respiration) has been demonstrated to be more effective than the top-down approach (working on speech sounds) with Parkinson's patients. An additional benefit in the work with Parkinson's patients is improvement in swallowing, even though this, like articulation, is not a targeted function (El Sharkawi et al., 2002).

This leads to an important point. A therapist should treat symptoms and not necessarily a disease. Although the neurology of Parkinson's disease differs from the etiology of many childhood dysarthrias, treatment can utilize the concepts of LSVT, which focus on vocal loudness to the betterment of many other key speech and nonspeech functions.

Articulation and Phonological Disorders

Children naturally make speech errors as they attempt to say words that they have in their minds but are not yet able to physically execute. There are developmentally appropriate phonological processes that children use to simplify speech productions. For example, while the intended word might be "banana," a child might be able to say only "nana," as they can't yet program the production of three syllables. Similarly, a child may say "gog" for "dog," as he can't manage the tongue movement from /d/ to /g/.

Phonological disorders are systematic patterns of speech errors. An example of a developmentally appropriate modification is the reduction of consonant clusters. For example, the “tr” in “try” is reduced to “tie,” and “truck” would be reduced to “tuck.” This reduction is appropriate until the age of four years. Another common pattern is called final consonant deletion. A child will say /pæ/ which could mean “pat,” “pass,” “pack,” “patch,” etc. Final consonant deletion can dramatically reduce a child’s speech intelligibility. Phonological disorders differ from articulation disorders in the complexity and systematic nature of the errors. The errors typically involve many phonemes (speech sounds) or patterns.

The International Phonetic Alphabet (IPA) is the notation system that SLPs use to document sound productions. The IPA symbols are different from orthographic symbols (the alphabet) that we use to read or write. For example, the orthographic “th” as in “this” is notated as /ð/ while the sound “th” as in “think” is noted as /θ/ in IPA. Orthographic notation does not phonetically represent the change in the production of these two sounds, namely the voicing of the former (put your fingers to the side of your Adam’s apple and feel the buzz of your vocal cords on “this” but not during “think”). Phonetics represent the spoken sound of a child who says /wæbɪt/ and uses “w” instead of the sound “r” for the word “rabbit.”

Of note: Dictionaries use a slightly different system of sound representation called pronunciation respelling. For example it will present <sh> for the pronunciation of “sure.” The IPA would use the symbol /ʃ/. Notation in IPA represents three qualities of the production of consonants: manner, place, and voice. Manner refers to classes of sounds as described below:

- *Plosives* have an exploding (hence “plosive”) quality to them when airflow is blocked by an articulator (lips or tongue) and then released. The sounds in this class include /p/ and /k/ as in “pack,” /b/ and /t/ as in “bat,” /k/ and /g/ as in “cog.”
- *Fricatives* have a hissing quality when airflow is constricted by an articulator. The sounds in this class include /ʃ/ as in “show” or /f/ as in “fall,” /s/ as in “some,” /z/ as in “zoo,” /ʒ/ as in “vision,” and /v/ as in “veil.”
- *Nasals* are sounds that are produced with nasal coupling. The sounds in this class include /m/ as in “mom,” /n/ as in “neat,” and /ŋ/ as in “ring.” If you put your fingers next to your nose when you say these words, you can feel the nasal resonance.
- *Affricates* are a combination of stops and fricatives. The sounds in this class include /tʃ/ as in “chair” and /dʒ/ as in “jazz.”
- *Rhotic* consonants are sounds that are difficult to classify, as they have no identifying motion. This class of sounds includes /r/ as in “race” and /l/ as in “laugh.” Rhotic consonants are also called “liquids” in phonetics.

Place refers to the placement of the articulators. For example, /m/ is a bilabial describing the involvement of both lips in making the sound. Other bilabial sounds are /p/ and /b/. Other placement references include labiodental, lingua-alveolar, lingual-palatal and glottal. *Labio* refers to lip, and *dental* refers to teeth to describe when the teeth are placed on the lip to produce /f/ or the sound /v/. *Lingua-* refers to the tongue, and *alveolar* references the ridges in the hard palate behind the front teeth. *Velar* refers to the back of the tongue and/or throat.

Voicing refers to whether the vocal folds are vibrating or not. For example, /f/ is voiceless and /v/ is voiced. You can feel the vibration by putting your fingers alongside your larynx (Adam’s apple). Examples of IPA classification of consonants would include the following:

/m/ is a voiced, bilabial, nasal
/k/ is an unvoiced, velar, plosive
/s/ is an unvoiced, alveolar, fricative

Vowels are described by the position of the tongue. The charting of vowels is called a vowel quadrangle. It maps the mouth's position by height (closed to open) and backness (front, near-front, central, near-back, and back). An example of this mapping is as follows:

> the sound /a/ as in "father" would be described as an open, near-front vowel
> the sound /i/ as in "key" would be described as a high, closed vowel

Music therapists are encouraged to learn to understand and use the IPA to document the nonverbal and verbal sounds of their clients. Many books are available to help develop this skill. Two books are listed below in the bibliography for reference (Nicolsi, Harrman, & Kresheck, 2003; Pullum & Ladusaw, 1996). Online references include descriptions plus recordings of the sounds and their symbols. In addition, music therapists should have references on developmental norms for speech sound acquisition, consonant charts, and vowel charts on hand in a resource notebook when treating this population. All client productions should be understood in the context of a child's age and what is expected at that time in addition to the speech sounds that should be emerging next.

Voice Disorders

Voice disorders can occur in children who talk a lot, talk too loudly, or scream excessively, especially during play. Children can get vocal nodules (tissue mass on the vocal folds) just as adults can. Presenting features include variances in volume (too high or too low), fundamental frequency (pitch too high or too low), and vocal output (breathy, hoarse). It is important that every child who presents with abnormal vocal quality be seen by an ear, nose, and throat physician (otolaryngologist) prior to initiation of treatment to rule out life-threatening conditions such as cancer, vocal fold paralysis, etc.

There are speech-language pathologists who specialize in voice disorders. Generally they can be found at major hospitals. Once a diagnosis has been established, a music therapist can work with a child on breath supply, pitch, loudness, and muscular tension. Introducing a child to dynamics with auditory and visual materials (e.g., sound-level meters) can support their self-regulation in productions that are too loud or too soft. Traditional vocal pedagogy can be helpful for decreasing extra-laryngeal muscle tension (through the jaw, neck, and shoulders). Muscle tension can tighten the vocal folds and create abnormal vocal fold physiology leading to injury.

Language Disorders

As noted above, language is the most fascinating human skill to watch a child develop. The normal development of language means that we translate a word into a concept, a sound (phonetic) map, meaning, and grammatical function. A language disorder is a serious issue because it is neurological and may be more challenging to develop than speech. A slow acquisition of words and meaning can be indicative of a language disorder or even an underlying cognitive disorder. The child may present with difficulty remembering words he has used before, particularly nouns. A child may not be using the plural "-s" on nouns. The speech therapist needs to determine if this is a phonological issue (speech issue) or a language issue (morphological issue).

Language disorders can be divided into two categories: expressive (vocabulary, grammar) and receptive (following directions, understanding another's speech). Language disorders include selective mutism (the unwillingness to speak despite ability) and expressive and receptive problems. If a child has receptive problems, he will certainly have expressive ones. Receptive disorders are much more challenging since language comprehension is key to all language and cognitive development. Receptive disorders may be due to intellectual impairment, auditory processing issues (they can hear but cannot decode the auditory signal appropriately at the neural level), a hearing deficit, or poor listening skills. Receptive disorders present with features of difficulty following directions (especially novel ones), difficulty following a conversation or written passage, and difficulty with figurative vs. literal language.

Expressive disorders may present with features such as limited vocabulary, limited use or lack of use of morphologic elements of language (e.g., walk, walk<u>s</u>, walk<u>ed</u>), and limited conversational skills. These disorders may be related to a developmental language delay or concomitantly related to an intellectual disability. If a child is able to follow commands (e.g., point to body parts, follow multistep directives), this may be key to distinguishing an expressive disorder from an underlying intellectual disability. Children may demonstrate the ability to express simple thoughts or opinions but may not have the age-appropriate vocabulary and grammar to elaborate.

Assessments for language disorders are done with standardized tests, interviews, and observations. The standardized tests used in speech-language pathology are age-specific (e.g., preschool, school-age, adolescence), and offer general or specific information on categories of language function. The following are the key terms of categories that speech therapists use to assess and treat children with language disorders.

- *Semantics*: words and word meanings, relates to vocabulary depth and breadth. An example of this is the lack of generalization children with autism will demonstrate about a word. For example, a dog may be their dog and no other dog. The meaning for "dog" is highly restrictive.
- *Syntax:* sentence construction, the arrangement of words into meaningful sequences, for example noun, verb, and object.
- *Morphology*: the modification of words that change its meaning. For example, the plural "-s," past tense "-ed," prefix "a-," prefix "anti-." Each prefix or suffix is called a morpheme.
- *Pragmatics:* the social use and appropriateness of language. Includes eye contact, conversational turn-taking, initiation and termination, appropriate register (e.g., formal register for formal conversations with an elder, informal register for friends)

Pragmatic Disorders

Pragmatics are nonverbal skills which are key to communicative success and often overlooked. Pragmatics skills involve the ability to initiate a conversation, maintain a topic through a number of exchanges, and terminate the topic appropriately. People who "hijack" a conversation by asserting their own agenda in a tangential way present with a pragmatic disorder. Eye contact is another pragmatic skill that is crucial to communicative success (e.g., knowing when a person is looking to enter a conversation, acknowledging another speaker's comments with visual attention). It has been assessed that the percentage of communication that consist of nonverbal communication (e.g., body language) is estimated to be 60%–70% (Mehrabian, 2007) or as high as 93% (Borg, 2010). Pragmatic disorders are one key to diagnosing autism.

Referral and Assessment

Prior to assessing a child's speech and language disorders, a speech-language pathologist will often request an audiological assessment. A hearing assessment is essential because a child who can't hear a sound cannot produce it and a child who can't hear speech cannot pick up the grammatical and semantic distinctions key to language learning. Although universal hearing screenings after birth ensure early detection of congenital hearing disorders, it does not guarantee adequate hearing later in childhood.

Acquired hearing deficits can be subtle but crucial to proper speech and language development. For example, a hearing disorder classified as mild is a hearing loss range of 26–40 decibels (the measure of sound loudness). This eliminates the following speech sounds: /f/, /s/, "th," /k/, /p/, /h/, /g/, /z/, /v/, and the possibility of others, depending on pitch range. The important thing to understand about hearing loss is that it is anything but mild. Even a person with a mild hearing loss would hear the word "anything" as "any I"—which is basically unintelligible.

Music therapy (MT) referrals for speech-language disorders can come from two primary sources: the parent(s) or a speech-language pathologist (SLP). In order to determine if a child is appropriate for music therapy, the MT should post a "checklist" of promising skills for either a parent or SLP to use prior to a formal assessment. The key to a successful referral is the identification of skill sets that are more advanced or more functional in a music context than in a nonmusic one. An excellent example of a referral checklist is the one posted at Roman Music Therapy Services' website (www.romanmusictherapy.com). Meredith Pizzi, MT-BC and founder and director of Roman Music Therapy, listed the following skills as appropriate for a referral:

- Child is particularly motivated to participate in music activities.
- You notice an increase in eye contact and attention when singing with a child.
- A child will turn to look when sung to, but not necessarily when spoken to.
- Child sings parts of or entire songs using pitch and melody but is not using the correct words.
- Child disengages with loud or unexpected sounds.
- Child will imitate movements or gestures in a song, but is not imitating in general.
- Child is not babbling or making many sounds, but is attentive to singing.
- Child demonstrates levels of engagement during music activities that are not typically seen at other times during the day.
- Child has limited spoken language abilities and initiates communication by singing familiar songs.
- Child will readily attempt and/or perform actions such as songs or with musical instruments despite significant challenges when faced with basic motor tasks.
- Child displays an extremely strong reaction, positive or negative, to sound.

Children who have trouble processing and integrating recorded music, sung music, or other sounds would also be an appropriate referral for music therapy to help address aural sensitivities that may disrupt learning.

A different but similar format for a referral can be found on the website of McKee Music Therapy (www.mckeemusictherapy.com). This too distinguishes musical and nonmusical behaviors in the key domains of cognition, communication, social/emotional behaviors, and sensory/motor function.

In order to facilitate getting referrals, it is recommended that a music therapist network with speech therapists in their areas. Networking can include observations of their work and invitations for them to observe your work. It can also include copresenting at state speech therapy conferences and possibly publishing case studies. When sharing a case, the music therapist should be impeccable in communications with the treating speech therapist. This will optimize the potential for client improvement and further the speech therapist's understanding of the process of music therapy.

Music therapy assessments evaluate a client's abilities in musical and nonmusical contexts. Those abilities are quantitatively and qualitatively described, compared to age norms, and prioritized for clinical treatment, as deemed appropriate. If the child is over the age of three, the assessment must consider state and federal laws that govern the role of music therapy in preschool and school services. Identifying music therapy as a required and necessary service for a child makes it possible for its inclusion in the Individualized Education Plan (IEP). Those recommendations are based on the child's ability to meet IEP objectives better in a musical context than in a nonmusical context. Services can be direct (1:1 or group services) and/or consultative (regular meetings with IEP team).

Many standardized tests in speech and language qualify purchasers regarding their credentials in order to maintain professional standards for testing. For example, Pearson is a major publisher of speech and language assessments, including the Preschool Language Scale (PLS), the Goldman-Fristoe Test of Articulation, the Boehm-3 Preschool Assessment, Clinical Evaluation of Language Fundamentals (CELF), and Comprehensive Assessment of Spoken Language (CASL). Their website states that there are four qualification levels that ensure that the user has the professional credentials, training, and expertise to properly administer the test (see: www.pearsonassessments.com). A music therapist's education and training might qualify for them to utilize various tests. Repetition of assessment tools negatively impacts the validity of scores and thus must be carefully considered when school-based and/or private speech-language pathologists are involved with the same child.

Review of speech-language pathology assessments, as available, will be informative for the music therapist and thus eliminate the need to repeat standardized testing. The music therapist should review the overall scores, the skill sets in which the child did poorly (e.g., grammatical endings), and specific test items (e.g., present progressive "-ing" endings on verbs, irregular plurals of nouns). The SLP's objectives from the assessment will serve as part of the basis of the music therapy assessment. All other school-based assessments should be carefully reviewed prior to the formal music assessment. Occupational therapy assessments may also provide helpful information about the child's cognition and processing skills. IEP goals will also serve as the foundation for the assessment and the planning of specific tasks and activities for the school-age child.

A music therapist should schedule an interview with the parents to identify their concerns and their observations. Using an intake questionnaire will facilitate this process and document important information (e.g., birth information, musical abilities and interests, sensory sensitivities, medications, developmental milestones to include speech/language, gross/fine motor, and social/emotional maturity). A core component of the intake interview is understanding the frequency and nature of communication breakdowns within the family setting. If the child has siblings, it will be important to determine their contributions to the child's communication issues. For example, an elder sibling will often talk for their younger sibling, which gives them fewer opportunities to practice their speech and language skills.

GUIDELINES FOR MUSIC THERAPY

Once the assessment has been completed and the objectives defined, the music therapist can create activities that offer predictability plus variability for the duration of the anticipated course of treatment. Fundamental to success in working on speech and language objectives with children is maintaining their attention to various tasks. Children's attention spans are relatively short, while their kinetic needs are high. They need time and space to move in order to sit and learn. In meeting all of these needs, music therapy is an ideal clinical intervention, especially with young children. A song can be used in a myriad of ways to provide predictability (e.g., repetition of lyrics, melodic and harmonic predictability) and variability (e.g., using a well-known song as a waltz, with a reggae beat, in an operatic voice). Sounds (both familiar and novel) can capture a child's attention both visually and auditorily. The music therapist can provide both nonverbal and verbal prompting to facilitate comprehension. Effective changes with our voice (from louder to softer, for example) are very helpful in capturing and sustaining a child's attention. Using improvisation allows us to meet them where they are and begin to shape their responses to meet clinical objectives. Movement is natural to music-making and can provide both a break from focused work and an additional opportunity for learning, per the pedagogy of Dalcroze (Findlay, 1999).

Preschool children who have speech and/or language difficulties may be using behavior as a communication. In fact, many speech therapists view behaviors as a communication intent gone awry rather than as a behavioral disorder. In a great number of cases, maladaptive behavior is the result of an unsuccessful communication attempt. The older a child is without adequate speech and language capabilities, generally the more frequent and severe the behaviors are because of a lack of control of his environment through language and the subsequent frustration experienced. Collaborating with a speech-language pathologist and a behaviorist helps to identify any potential behavioral antecedents and distinguish a communication breakdown from a true behavior problem.

Children with language disorders have to be taught more explicitly than a typically developing child who learns by immersion and engagement. These children need to be taught in a similar way that we learn a second language (e.g., conjugating verbs, learning rules and exceptions to rules). This is a tedious way of learning that music therapists can contextualize in a reinforcing, dynamic, and playful clinical medium. It is important to offer a child with a speech and language disorder abundant opportunities to control his environment in the music setting. This can be done both musically and verbally. This alone can minimize negative behaviors that had previously been used by the child to assert control of their environment. Choices can include the sequence of activities, songs, instruments, lyrics, etc. Letting the child's vocalizations and movements inspire an improvisation is empowering.

Music therapists should be aware of the language they use for prompting and instructing. For example, "What do you want?" and "What do you want to sing?" are examples of questions that are too broad for people with speech and language limitations. In order to maximize a child's potential to engage with therapy, choices should be offered in limited-choice paradigms (two or three options). It may be helpful and necessary to pair the name of the song with visual representation for younger children. For example, the therapist sings the first line of a song and shows the child the photo or drawing that represents the song (Google Images is a wonderful resource for this). Because of a delay in response time, even making a decision poses challenges. Eye contact with the visual stimulus can be a method of decision-making for young children, especially those with autism.

When working with children who have language disorders, especially receptively, it is imperative that the therapist use explicit directives. For example, say "it's your turn to play," emphasizing "play," instead of just saying "it's your turn." These are subtle differences in giving directions but key to facilitating comprehension for those with receptive disorders. Use visual schedules with symbols and "first this/then that" boards to help children organize what they are doing now and what will follow. Use the visual symbol system that the SLP and/or classroom staff are using. They may include Meyer-Johnson symbols, real photographs, or representations of objects (e.g., a doll's plate to represent "eat"). Music therapists in training would benefit from recording themselves in a session to review their use of verbal and nonverbal cuing. The success of a response is built upon the success of the prompt.

Music can serve as cues to establish joint visual attention to an object. Joint attention is essential to learning language since it is the way two people look at the same thing at the same time. Parents naturally use pitch and rhythm in child-directed speech (motherese, parentese) to establish joint attention. The rise of pitch captures the attention of a child. The melodic accent of the name helps focus cognitive resources to perceiving the phonological, semantic, and syntactic qualities of the word. An example of child-directed speech is *"mi, mi, mi, sol"* as a melodic accompaniment to "look at the bird"). Music therapists can use pitch variation to good effect in establishing joint attention for language learning.

Provide ample opportunities for children to follow directions that are both routine and novel in music sessions. Ask for return demonstrations. This requires that the student repeat or interpret the directions you just gave them to check comprehension.

Overview of Methods and Procedures

The following methods and procedures are used most commonly with children with developmental speech and language disorders.

Receptive Music Therapy

- Auditory Perception Training: the use of live or recorded music for perceptual and discrimination development.
- Social Stories in Music Therapy: use of music to support learning of concepts, sequences, and basic information from short stories, often depicted with short sentences with accompanying pictures, sequences to teach clients expected behaviors during interactions, social experiences, or activities of daily living.

Improvisational Music Therapy

- Improvisation: Clients create spontaneous musical expressions alone or with others, using instruments or singing with support from the music therapist.

Re-creative Music Therapy

- Vocal Intonation Therapy: systematic use of music techniques to address voice disorders involving respiratory support and phonation.
- Musical Speech Stimulation: Music therapists use familiar songs to facilitate client's reflexive, timed, and spontaneous responses to provide missing words within the musical context.
- Melodic Intonation Therapy: Music therapists teach clients to use short, familiar phrases intoned on tones/melodies which are determined by the phrases' natural prosody.
- Oral Motor and Respiratory Exercises: Clients sing precomposed songs to improve muscular coordination and respiration needed for articulation and improve vocal quality.
- Rhythmic Speech Cuing: specific use of musical elements of rhythm to address motor skills related to speech production in clients when language comprehension is not an area of need.
- Therapeutic Singing: The therapist facilitates clients in a process of singing that is geared toward attentive listening to his/her own voice, which then becomes a means of growing self-awareness.

Compositional Music Therapy

- Musical Mnemonics Training: The music therapist creates lyrics and melody to facilitate learning of academics or other information relevant to the client's needs.
- Musical Executive Function Training: The therapist uses individual or group improvisation and composition exercises to practice executive function skills, including organization, problem-solving, reasoning, decision-making, and comprehension.

Guidelines for Receptive Music Therapy

Receptive music therapy activities use live and recorded music in listening tasks that can improve perceptual acuity of sound and the learning of action sequences as well as develop vocabulary. Listed below are a number of clinical activities that can support the habilitation and rehabilitation of childhood speech and language disorders.

Auditory Perception Training

Overview. Auditory Perception Training (APT) is a Neurologic Music Therapy technique that uses live or recorded music for perceptual and discrimination development as described below (Thaut, 2005). APT has other applications these descriptions. There are two levels to APT that can be used in receptive music therapy: auditory localization and auditory discrimination. Research shows that the ability to discriminate between sounds is the key to language learning and literacy (Forgeard et al., 2008). With very young children or children with intellectual deficits, the music therapist will initially assess a client's localization skills (the ability to turn one's head or eyes toward a sound source). This is basic to auditory processing and cognitive attention. Research indicates that newborns and one-month-old babies turn either their heads or their bodies toward a sound source 80% of the time (Muir & Field, 1979). Strait and Kraus (2011) suggest that auditory training may "aid in the prevention, habilitation, and remediation of individuals with a wide range of attention-based language, listening, and learning impairments" (p. 1).

Auditory discrimination tasks are important clinical activities for children with hearing disorders. This is especially true for those with cochlear implants who are reorienting to sound. For these children, music presents an easier set of sounds to discriminate than speech sounds that are more refined and faster-changing in the sound signal. That is primarily due to the wide range of pitches available in musical instruments and the rhythmic cuing that can be readily perceived through sound and vibration. For further information on this specialized population, refer to the writings of Kate Gfeller (2012) and Driscoll, Oleson, Jiang, and Gfeller (2009).

There is a commercially available game called "What's That Sound?" by Discovery Toys which presents 36 different sounds to be matched on a Bingo-like card. This is a good format for promoting auditory discrimination. Using a computer, a music therapist could easily reproduce the playing cards and record sounds of familiar and meaningful sounds to a child. However, not all of the sounds included in the commercially available game may be familiar to young children, necessitating customization.

Preparation. The therapist will collect and print colored pictures of their instruments and then record them being played. GarageBand is an excellent computer program for this. The stimuli should be played long enough to be auditorily processed by the child (about 5 seconds).

What to observe. The therapist will collect data on correct or incorrect responses using pictured or verbal responses. The therapist also evaluates motivation, interest, and attention to task while taking into consideration patterns of response errors and level of effort.

Procedures. The therapist presents the client with a recorded sound and their choice of accompanying pictures while requesting that the client provide a response. The child may need to make a request to hear the stimulus again as needed. When presenting pictures in pairs, begin by making the references as contrastive as possible (e.g., a drum and a piano sound). As they demonstrate competence in these discriminating pairs, use more similar pairings such as a bell and a tambourine.

Adaptations. The recorded instrument stimuli can be made more complex by having the familiar instrument played in an unfamiliar context (e.g., a trumpet playing a solo in a band). A music therapist can also adapt this task using the format of the book "Brown bear, brown bear, what do you hear?," using the child's name to replace "brown bear." The pictures can be organized onto "Bingo" boards in 2x2, 3x3, or 4x4 arrangements, depending on children's capacity to process complex visual stimuli. The music recordings can be played in pairs to be identified as "same" or "different." The ability to comprehend these terms is an important prerequisite skill. It may take numerous trials to train a child in this cognitive/linguistic distinction.

Altering the words of a known song and looking for a child to correct you is a good linguistic discrimination task. An example would be singing "Row your boat" with the substitution "life is but ice cream" or "life is but a scream." They should recognize the mistakes and look to inform you of it in some way (e.g., eye contact, verbal correction).

When targeting a specific phoneme (speech sound), the therapist can intone two words (the correct word and the incorrect word) using two or three tones (depending on the number of syllables). An example would be to present /krækɚ/ for "cracker" vs. /trækɚ/ for "tracker" and have the child identify which is correct for the reference "something to eat." This task can utilize a song that informs the child of the expectation. The lyrics would include cues to "listen, listen, tell me which one is right."

Social Stories in Music Therapy

Overview. Social stories were originally developed by Carol Gray to "describe a situation, skill, or concept in terms of relevant social cues, perspectives, and common responses" (www.thegraycenter.org). The stories combine auditory and visual information that can be repeated frequently. Social stories can be written about pragmatic concerns (e.g., conversational turn-taking, making eye contact to learn new things), social issues (e.g., bullying, being with a babysitter, thanking people), and receptive language (e.g., building vocabulary, following directions). These tools were initially developed for children on the autism spectrum but are very appropriate for use with children who have speech and language delays or who are very young and developing typically. There are books available with prewritten social stories that a music therapist can use for ideas (Baker, 2003; Gray, 2010). A significant benefit of social stories is that they can be customized to the individual and their situation.

Music therapists can put a story to song to enhance the interest of the child and provide a vehicle in which to organize the text with phrasing and rhythm. Music is a valuable asset to the social story program, as text presented in song has been demonstrated to be recalled better than text learned without melody (Wallace, 1994). Targeted words or concepts can be highlighted with a variety of musical elements to include rising pitch, pauses, and a rhythmic shift.

Brownwell (2002) reported case studies of four first- and second-grade children with autism who used social stories in two conditions: reading the story and singing the story. In one of the cases, the music condition was found to be significantly more effective in reducing the target behavior than the reading condition. In the other three cases, the targeted behaviors were reduced but not significantly so. This early but limited success warrants further clinical practice and research to determine efficacy for this intervention. Music therapists who use this protocol should strongly consider publishing their findings so that more can be known about the most effective musical elements and the most reliable behaviors to target.

Preparation. The therapist identifies the targeted behaviors in consultation with educational staff (teacher, behaviorist) and parents and then outlines the story with single sentences. Sentences are written using the child's perspective and using the first person singular "I" (e.g., "when I"). Use language that is appropriate to the child's comprehension level. Gray (1995) suggests that words like "will" and "always" should be avoided as the expectations are too high and rigid. Instead, use the words "usually" or "sometimes." Taking pictures of the child engaged in the activity (e.g., making eye contact with the therapist) and not engaged in the activity (e.g., looking away) are useful as children generally like to look at themselves. Stock pictures, icons, or hand-drawn drawings can also be used. Music therapists then create a melody for the text that emphasizes key words melodically, rhythmically, and/or with stress.

What to observe. The therapist will observe the modification of behaviors in the targeted situation and compare it to baseline data. The therapist will contact family members and school staff to collect information about the child's responses in natural contexts. The client's ability to retell the social story or sing the verses may be an indication of comprehension.

Procedures. The social story may be one of several experiences during a music therapy session or may be the entire session. The social story song should be a choice among other activities. The child's selection will be a positive indicator of his affinity for it and enhance the potential for learning the information. The social story is presented within the context of preparing the child for an upcoming event or for recalling expected behaviors during common activities and experiences. The therapist will teach the social story and its accompanying music in order to enhance familiarity and promote recall. Questioning the child after the social story may assist the music therapist in determining the child's level of comprehension and facilitate generalization of the social stories' message.

Adaptations. When the child is engaged in the targeted activity in a negative or inappropriate way, use a melodic prompt of the song to remind him of the expected behavior. Carol Gray has recently created "Storymovies," and the use of filming could also be adapted musically.

Guidelines for Improvisational Music Therapy

Improvisation

Overview. Improvisational experiences are defined as those in which a client creates music while singing or playing an instrument alone or with others (Bruscia, 1998). The therapist supports the child by offering instruction, ideas, reflections, extensions of their ideas, and/or accompaniment. It is a very versatile and key technique in music therapy. With children who have speech and language disorders, it is an opportunity to explore nonverbal aspects of communication, such as turn-taking. This is particularly important for those who have pragmatic disorders and are unaware of the nonverbal rules for conversing with another. The improvisation experience provides opportunities to develop cognitive and perceptual skills through sustained attention and listening. The freedom and empowerment that improvisation provides can be an important building block in clinical relatedness. The nonverbal aspects of improvisatory music-making can also provide a welcome relief to a child who struggles with their ability to verbally express themselves.

Preparation. The music therapist prepares the room by making appropriate musical instruments available from which the child may choose. A clustered arrangement of instruments might be set out on a large surface such as a table or counter within easy reach of the client. This arrangement allows the child to move easily from one instrument to another. If the child has focusing problems, it might be advantageous to have the instruments farther apart to encourage them to explore and play with one instrument for an extended period of time. A therapist might consider having some instruments that are rhythmic and some that are melodic, depending upon the speech and language goals. For example, language goals involving prosody of speech might better be served using melodic instruments such as xylophones or desk bells, while rhythmic instruments often serve to promote opportunity for development of timing or rate of responses, breath control, or phonological issues related to sound discrimination.

What to observe. The therapist will listen or watch for vocalizations and/or movements that can be responded to musically. Nordoff and Robbins (1977) write that when you find a child is responding to the music and this is influencing their sounds, you can introduce a clear, well-defined motif that can be repeated freely. The motif can be rhythmic, melodic, and/or harmonic. The musical stimulation can then be followed by a rest so that the child can perceive, anticipate, and respond to the musical structure. This is the essence of the improvisation experience. Music therapists are also encouraged to observe the timing of vocal/verbal responses during improvisations. By paying attention to the pitch quality, timbre, and volume, music therapists can identify areas where the improvisation supports the development of a targeted goal.

Procedures. Although improvisation allows for great clinical freedom, a music therapist should have treatment objectives in mind, such as increasing the number of exchanges, broadening the range of responses, expanding the length of response, etc. Turn-taking in music mirrors turn-taking in a conversation. For example, a rhythm call-and-response experience can have a target phrase added to the drumming to practice articulation or fluency. If a child has a restrictive vocabulary, the improvisational experience can target various adjectives, such as "energetic," "lethargic," etc.

The therapist should develop a series of musical improvisation experiences specific to the goals of the child. For example, if a client needs to improve production of initial consonants in words, such as /b/, the music therapist should create improvisational structures that cue and support the child in creating that sound. The process of choosing an instrument for the improvisation may become part of the session as the child and therapist try out different sound combinations and decide which ones fit the desired outcome.

The music therapist determines the amount of structure the child needs in order to be successful during the improvisation. At the most basic level, the therapist may use a metronome to provide a steady, temporal cue and encourage the child to produce the desired response. Over time, the amount of structure and number of cues can fade and the child may begin to take on more control of speech and language production.

Guidelines for Re-creative Music Therapy

Bruscia defines re-creative music therapy as one in which a client "learns or performs precomposed vocal or instrumental music or reproduces any kind of musical form presented as a model" (1998, pp. 117–118). Children who would benefit from re-creative experiences are those who need structure to facilitate the development of targeted skills. Re-creative music experiences can be used with children who have speech-language disorders to teach techniques to improve the use of their voice and to help those with speech impairments improve the time-ordered motor behaviors of articulation or fluency. The following music therapy methods have been reported in the music therapy literature or in clinical practice.

Vocal Intonation Therapy

Overview. Vocal Intonation Therapy (VIT) is a Neurologic Music Therapy technique that addresses voice disorders (Thaut, 2005). Voice disorders include issues of respiratory support and phonation (the engagement of the vocal cords). This technique is similar to the Lee Silverman Voice Treatment (LSVT) program described earlier. The key difference is the use of music to address sustained phonations and loud productions.

Music therapists can facilitate improvement of breath control by training diaphragmatic breathing—a technique that most musicians and singers use and are adept at using. This is very useful for children with cerebral palsy, spina bifida, and other conditions that create phonatory issues such as a voice that is too quiet or too breathy to be heard. Familiar music lyrics can facilitate respiratory objectives as the phrase lengths are known and a breath can be planned for accordingly. A therapist can physically prompt a client to breathe in preparation for the onset of the phrase and to maintain that breath across the phrase much like a conductor would cue an orchestra. Music is an ideal vehicle for parsing lyrics into manageable and then more challenging breath lengths. Working on speech can be more difficult for breath control, as there is less predictability to nonpropositional speech. Nonpropositional speech is spontaneous and created in the moment, generally in response to a thought or shared experience. The utterances could be short, one-word responses or a long stream of thought.

Preparation. The therapist prepares songs of increasing phrase length for respiration objectives. Choice of songs and melodic phrases are based upon the client's interest, musical preferences, and vocal range. Instruments used during treatment should be available, as well as musical notation. Clients may be seated or standing, depending upon their physical limitations and postural needs.

What to observe. The therapist should observe diaphragmatic breathing vs. clavicular (movement of the ribs), quality of voice (e.g., breathy, creaky, tremored, making "catching sounds"), and syllables sung on one breath. A full-length mirror may be useful in the client making these observations and self-correcting.

Procedures. The therapist should work on diaphragmatic breathing in isolation (breathing in and out) and then move on to sustained phonations (vocalizing as long as possible on one breath). Use pitches that are above, below, and at their typical speaking range to begin. Take data using a stopwatch to count the seconds of sustained phonations on various pitches. Stop counting when the voice deteriorates in quality. Call-and-response patterns are an excellent activity for working on increasing phrase lengths on one breath.

A sound-level meter is useful to track the range of amplitudes produced. The screen of the sound-level meter also provides a child with visual feedback. There are computer programs (e.g., Vaghmi Computerized Voice Therapy software) to consider if the music therapist is seeing a large number of clients with voice disorders. Listen for glottal fry—the sound of the voice collapsing without sufficient respiratory support. The sound is a bit like a creaking door. A voice that sounds like it's "catching" may have spasticity in the vocal fold movement. The NPR broadcaster Diane Rehm has a condition called "spastic dysphonia." Her voice demonstrates this "catching" quality. Loudness productions should be done as crescendos and decrescendos. Children will benefit from gestures for loudness (arms out wide) and softness (arms coming together).

Adaptations. With very young children, have them draw straight lines and hills (both tall and small) on large index cards. Provide a model, using your finger, of going up the hills (getting louder or higher in pitch depending on treatment objectives) and down the hills (getting softer or lower in pitch). Straight lines are for sustained phonations. Have the child trace the lines with their fingers or a toy car and vocalize per the model. Reinforce that it has to be done on one breath. Add cards to increase the length of the exercise as appropriate. Encourage a slower finger to extend the phonation.

Another technique with very young children is to use Silly Putty. Use the putty to make balls and stretch it to make lines. Under one breath, they need to utter short and sustained vocalizations representing the balls and lines. Based on the exercises in isolation, music therapists select lyrics of songs with equal length. Decrease the tempo, add additional lyrics (e.g., adjectives), and/or vary loudness to make the task more challenging for respiratory control. Cue breathing with gestures as a conductor would and diminish cues as appropriate.

Intoning and singing can be very useful techniques with the aprosodic speech (aka robotic or flat speech) that some children with autism use. Exercises that increase vocal range, model stress in word productions, and demonstrate rising pitch for questions can be taught in music to generalize to speech.

Musical Speech Stimulation

Overview. Musical speech stimulation (MUSTIM) is a Neurologic Music Therapy protocol that was initially designed to elicit nonpropositional speech in people with aphasia (Thaut, 2005). Although the aphasia population is different from that with developmental speech-language disorders, the protocol can be adapted because the goals of stimulating speech through overlearned, familiar songs are the same for children. Thaut (2005) states that music's effectiveness in this protocol is most likely due to the following three elements: overlearned lyrics to familiar songs, anticipation of target words facilitated by rhythm, and arousal of reflexive speech.

Preparation. Choose songs that are familiar and known by the child. These can include "Twinkle, Twinkle" and the "ABC" song.

What to observe. The music therapist observes whether the child is able to provide the targeted response within the expected time frame. Motivation, effort, and frustration are all monitored during the procedure as well.

Procedures. The therapist presents a familiar song, leaving space for the child to provide reflexive, timed, spontaneous responses. Most often, the therapist can leave off the last word in a phrase, as noted below:

Twinkle, twinkle little star
How I wonder what you are
Up above the world so high
Like a diamond in the sky
Twinkle, twinkle little star
How I wonder what you are

In the beginning, a therapist may cue the expected production by slowing the tempo of the song prior to the word the child is to provide, taking a breath prior to the targeted word or using a strummed cue on a guitar to enhance attention and musically prompt the response. Repetitions of the song and the cues may be helpful in the beginning. A parent providing a model can also be very supportive for a child. From nonpropositional singing, the therapist would build to propositional singing by offering forced choices (pictured or verbal), open choices in a known and familiar context (e.g., at breakfast, I ate _______), and then wide open choices (e.g., my favorite song is _______). The emphasis should continue to utilize high-frequency, familiar words.

Melodic Intonation Therapy

Overview. A promising technique to utilize with apraxic children is Melodic Intonation Therapy (MIT). This treatment approach was first reported by Albert, Sparks and Helms (1973), Sparks, Helms and Albert (1974), and Sparks and Holland (1976). The similarities of symptoms between childhood apraxia and Broca's aphasia implicate the use of Melodic Intonation Therapy with developing disorders. There are some studies that support this hypothesis, namely by Keith and Aronson (1975), Beathard and Krout (2008), and Helfrich-Miller (1994). The protocol was developed following observations of patients who had a specific type of stroke that resulted in Broca's or expressive aphasia. These clients could sing when they couldn't speak. U.S. Congresswoman Gabrielle Giffords has Broca's aphasia and has benefited from MIT during rehabilitation from a brain injury following a violent gun attack at an Arizona shopping mall. Films of her rehabilitation demonstrate the significant difficulties she had in generating speech (e.g., naming objects), expressing her feelings (saying "boo-hoo" when she was frustrated), and uttering more than one or two words at a time. This contrasts with the fluency with which she could sing along with her therapist.

While speech-language pathologists are generally introduced to MIT in their language disorders class, only a small percentage of clinicians appear to utilize the protocol despite widespread acceptance for its theoretical foundations. This may be due to a number of reasons, including that speech-language pathologists, like the general population, can be reticent to sing, the notation system is not transparent, and there is a lack of available sound or video files to serve as a model.

A new surge of interest in the protocol has advanced our understanding of its efficacy. Gottfried Schlaug and his colleagues at Beth Israel Hospital in Boston have been researching this treatment program with Broca's aphasics using neuroimaging. In 2008, Schlaug et al. reported that two aphasics showed significant improvements of propositional speech (automatic, reflexive speech) for unpracticed words and phrases compared to a control condition. Subsequent reports continue to positively support the use of MIT with expressive aphasics. Schlaug, Norton, Marchina, Zipse, and Wan (2010) report that recruitment of right hemispheric structures and engagement of interhemispheric connections are a positive result of MIT training. His research lab has now expanded to adapting MIT for use with nonverbal children on the autism spectrum (Wan & Schlaug, 2010; Wan et al., 2011).

Preparation. The therapist will rely on the assessment to identify assessment key phrases that the child would benefit from mastering. It is important to ask the family as well as educational staff about communication breakdowns and what phrases would be important and relevant to develop to minimize them. Using the natural contour of the targeted phrase, identify intonational stress in the phrase. The therapist will sing the higher pitch on stressed syllables. For example, "I am <u>hun</u>gry" would be sung as mi-mi-sol-mi.

What to observe. The therapist observes the child's ability to wait for and attend to the vocal model, their ability to imitate the model (assessed as a percentage of correct vs. incorrect syllables), and their ability to answer a question with the targeted phrase at the end of a drill set, such as "What would you say if you wanted to eat?"

Procedures. The fundamental steps to MIT, as taught at the Center for Biomedical Research in Music at Colorado State University, are as follows:

1) Prompt the child to listen (using a hand up for "stop" or a finger to the mouth like "hush") and hum the melody while tapping the child's hand (as tolerated). A drum can be used in substitution with or without mallets.
2) Prompt the child to listen while you repeat the toning, adding the words.
3) Prompt the child to join you and repeat the intoned phrase. Lots of repetitions are key here.
4) Fade your voice as appropriate while repeating the phrase. The therapist can continue to mouth the phrase entirely or just an initial sound of a word or the phrase itself. Ideally, the child would be independent.
5) Repeat step #2 (provide vocal model with child listening and watching).
6) Put the sentence in a functional context as noted above: "What would you say if you wanted to eat?" Avoid the words targeted in the phrase so that generalization can be properly assessed.

What is essential in using MIT is the use of nonverbal cues to listen, to wait, and to sing together (pointing finger at child and then at you while nodding), and to reinforce the child with smiles. These nonverbal cues decrease the linguistic burden on the child and provide them with important visual models that facilitate motor programming. Another important element of the protocol is sitting opposite the child, which engages the mirror neuron system. This system in the brain helps us learn to do something by watching somebody else do it (Rizzolatti & Craighero, 2004).

Adaptations. Schlaug's team has adapted the elements of Melodic Intonation Therapy for use with nonverbal children on the autism spectrum (Wan et al., 2011). This work is yielding promising results. The protocol has been renamed "auditory-motor mapping training." It aims to train associations between sounds and the motor actions necessary to produce them. Two tuned drums are used to intone the pitches of the target words and phrases. An intensive 40-session training with nonverbal children (ages 5 to 9) with autism resulted in significant improvements in their ability to articulate words and phrases with carryover to words that were not practiced (Wan et al., 2011, 2010).

Another adaptation for Melodic Intonation Therapy is to utilize both duration and stress in the protocol for children who are apraxic (Helfrich, 1984; Krauss & Galloway, 1982) and/or are dysarthric. An example of this application is training in the articulation of multisyllabic words. If you alter the syllabic duration by lengthening the syllables, slowing down the rate, and/or accenting the target, you can provide the neural system the extra time it needs to successfully command the motor sequence. For example, a child might articulate the word "ambulance" as "amblance," collapsing the syllable structure of the word to accommodate their production limitations. The therapist can elongate "am" and stress "bu." The pattern could be represented as "ammBU-lance" (mi-sol-mi). The constant voicing throughout the production can facilitate fluency of the word as a whole. High-frequency functional words and phrases should be the initial treatment targets.

Oral Motor and Respiratory Exercises

Overview. Oral motor and respiratory exercises (OMREX) are a protocol of Neurologic Music Therapy that addresses articulatory control through oral motor exercises (Thaut, 2005). Oral motor exercises are nonspeech exercises of the jaw, tongue, cheeks, palate, and lips that are prescribed for motor speech and swallowing disorders. Examples of exercises for the tongue include elevations (raising the tongue to the roof of the mouth, making clicking sounds), protrusions (sticking the tongue forward), retractions (bunch the tongue toward the back of the mouth), and lateralizations (movement left to right). Lip exercises include puckers, retractions (smiles), whistling, and "fish faces" (pucker lips and suck in cheeks). These exercises can be done in alternation: lip retraction–rounding (smiling to pucker), tongue lateralization (side to side). Thaut (2005) notes that respiratory exercises under OMREX can overlap with the respiratory exercises noted above under Vocal Intonation Therapy. The difference is the objective being addressed—respiration for vocal quality vs. respiration for articulation.

It is important to note that the efficacy of oral motor exercises is in debate within the field of speech-language pathology. A systematic review of 15 studies by McCauley, Strand, Lof, Schooling and Frymark (2009) reported that there was insufficient evidence to either support or refute the use of OMEs in the treatment of speech disorders. If the collaborating speech therapist is recommending OMEs, the music therapist can embed these exercises into songs. Horns and whistles can be added that can strengthen oral motor musculature (lip rounding and closure). Specialized horns have been constructed with a "blowing hierarchy" that graduates the difficulty of resistance (see Talk Tool Original Horn Kit at www.dysphagiaplus.com).

Preparation. The therapist can write songs that address the recommended oral motor objectives. The treatment plan is written to develop articulation competencies in a hierarchical fashion. Initially, the approach is to have the child articulate the targeted sound in isolation, in CV (consonant vowel), and CVC (consonant-vowel-consonant) combinations. The targeted phoneme (e.g., /k/) would be drilled in the initial (<u>c</u>ake), medial (pa<u>ck</u>ing), and final (ma<u>k</u>e) positions. From there, the scaffolding would move to articulate the targeted sounds and words at the phrase, sentence, and conversational levels. A speech therapist will work on multiple speech sounds at various levels. Children with articulation disorders have to speak with effort and intentionality. This contrasts with the typically developing child who effortlessly and fluently articulates speech sounds at developmentally appropriate stages. Music is a wonderful resource to make the drills more fun and engaging. As described above, the music therapist can use the musical elements of rhythm, duration, and stress to support motor planning and execution.

What to observe. The therapist should observe motor coordination (less groping), motor sequencing and correct articulation (calculate syllable errors per total syllables of targeted phrase) in various contexts. Range of motion and strength of oral motor musculature can be challenging to measure. Consult with the speech therapist to determine how best to collect data on these parameters. Adopt their practices so that progress in the music setting can be compared to nonmusic settings.

Procedures. The music therapist will have the child follow sung directions to drill the various targeted motor patterns. Using mirrors and modeling the intended movement can help the child correctly make the motion. A mirror larger than a hand mirror is recommended. Gestures can also help a child stretch to achieve the most range of motion. For example, if a child is working on tongue lateralization (movement from side to side), the motion can be extended by gesturing to the side of their face or even to their shoulder.

Rhythmic Speech Cuing

Overview. Rhythmic speech cuing (RSC) is a Neurologic Music Therapy treatment protocol that uses auditory rhythm as a rate-control technique (Thaut, 2005). Rhythm is a clinical tool to facilitate initiation and organization of motor sequencing. It can be used to regulate speech rates in those who are dysfluent (stutterers, clutterers), dysarthric, or apraxic. The rhythm can be provided either with a metronome or embedded in music.

There are two categories for rhythmic cuing: metric and patterned. In the former, the beat is set to match the tempo of the syllables. This metric cuing makes the speech sound somewhat robotic but fluent. Patterned cuing will sound more speechlike, as the beat patterns are more like the natural rhythm of speech. The beats are not isochronous (evenly spaced) like a metronome. They are instead asymmetrical. In order to understand how this would sound, read the previous two paragraphs aloud and note the rhythmicity of your speech by tapping your hand. Then reread the text to a steady beat.

Preparation. The therapist needs to determine the level of RSC that is appropriate for the child. It may be necessary to begin treatment with a hypothesis of what may be most effective approach and test that hypothesis with a number of trials. There are some general guidelines that Thaut (2005) notes that will inform your treatment planning. First, dysarthric speakers can frequently improve their intelligibility by slowing down the cuing rate. Second, metronomic cues may be more challenging for some people, particularly those with right-hemisphere brain lesions, due to their signal complexity.

Use picture description activities or questions about specific activities (hobbies, toys) or provide a conversational topic to elicit speech in a natural context with and without the rhythmic cuing. Eliciting speech samples is best done during play with characters (animals, dolls). It is helpful when eliciting speech samples to have shared references to best determine what the child is attempting to say. Picture description activities and hands-on activities are best for this.

What to observe. It is ideal to record speech productions with and without the rhythmic cuing for more thorough data analysis after the session. For children who are dysfluent, therapists will note the number and characteristics of dysfluencies. For those who are dysarthric, therapists will estimate the percentage of intelligible words overall. With people who are apraxic, therapists will note the average length of utterance, intelligibility, and phonetic inventory (especially noting emerging sounds).

Procedures. The music therapist uses a steady beat and initially matches a syllable to each beat. As the client becomes more fluid, the beat can be matched to the rhythm of the words or phrases to sound more natural or speechlike. Call-and-response music-making is an effective activity for this protocol. The music therapist can use basic patterns with variations to create challenges for the child using a variety of instruments such as drums, keyboards, and xylophones. The call-and-response format can continue to follow the hierarchy toward the phrase and sentence level. Hand-tapping can be incorporated to facilitate vocal productions. Following treatment, therapists are encouraged to take a speech sample and identify how the rhythmic cuing has generalized to natural speech.

Adaptations. Sometimes children will tap their hand or their foot to facilitate their speech efforts. This compensatory strategy is a useful tool for the child to use outside of therapy. The articulation of certain phonemes will not lend themselves to increased duration, notably the class of affricates, e.g., /tʃ/ as in "church." For these phonemes, the music therapist will want to match the music to the natural characteristics of the sound.

For very young children working on multisyllabic words, use an object to represent each syllable (e.g., alphabet blocks, sand blocks). Provide a model and then have the child touch the objects. This author has generally not found it helpful to use beaters with these very young children, as attention is moved from speech or singing to the act of coordinating the beater. The objects are there to represent rhythm and help the timing of production of syllables or words.

Therapeutic Singing

Overview. Wan, Rüber, Honmann and Schlaug (2010) assert that singing is a promising tool in improving characteristics of neurologic disorders. Singing is efficacious in treating speech-motor difficulties such as apraxia because the continuous voicing maintains a connectedness between syllables and words. Singing also slows the rate of syllables (speech has faster changes in articulation than singing) and increases awareness of individual phonemes. Articulatory disorders may benefit from singing because of the sound-motor mapping that is practiced and enhanced in therapeutic singing. The Neurologic Music Therapy protocol of Therapeutic Singing (TS) is a versatile and useful technique in which to practice other therapeutic techniques such as Oral Motor and Respiratory Exercises, Vocal Intonation Therapy, and Melodic Intonation Therapy (Thaut, 2005). TS provides the child with opportunity to integrate and apply exercises in the natural and motivational context of singing.

Singers have been shown to have more dense arcuate fasciculi than nonsingers or instrumentalists (Halwani, Loui, Ruber, & Schlaug, 2011). The arcuate fasciculus is a white matter tract that connects the temporal and frontal regions of the brain and functions in sound perception and production for both speech and music. The results from the study demonstrate the anatomical changes that occur from the specialized training of singers. It is a reasonable hypothesis that children with speech disorders may benefit from therapeutic singing, specifically for the neural changes that can improve motor productions for speech. Since it is a fun, engaging, and natural activity, the likelihood of home practice for the child and family is much more probable.

Wan et al. (2010) noted that singing has been identified as having important therapeutic potential for people who stutter. Healey, Mallard, and Adams (1976) investigated the reduction of stuttering in reading or singing lyrics of well-known songs with familiar or unfamiliar texts. Overall dysfluencies were reduced in the singing conditions, particularly in those songs with familiar texts. The increased phonation duration, intonation, and familiarity may have contributed to these positive effects. These effects on dysfluencies have been reported by other researchers as well (Andrews, Howie, Dozsa, & Guitar, 1982; Colcord & Adams, 1979; Davidow, Bothe, Andreatta, & Ye, 2009).

Preparation. Select songs that meet the child's preferences and therapeutic needs for articulation, breath control, fluency, etc. Focus on the musical demands for articulation (rapidity of syllables) and breath control (phrase length per breath). Establish good visual positioning with the child (e.g., facing the child) in order to promote optimal unison singing through modeling. This is particularly effective with children who are apraxic. Prepare any accompaniment instruments used for the singing experiences. Decrease support as appropriate.

What to observe. The therapist should assess singing success with chosen songs, levels of prompting needed, ability to match pitch, and ability to sing with decreased modeling. Hand-tapping or external auditory cuing will likely improve vocal output and should be considered in treatment (Pilon,

McIntosh, & Thaut, 1998). If a child is resistive to hand-over-hand tapping in the beginning, use percussion instruments. Be alert to the child's level of frustration, level of effort, ability to self-correct, and self-awareness.

Procedures. Therapeutic singing can be a part of a music therapy session or the focus of the entire session. When used alongside other music therapy interventions within a session, the music therapist should choose music that the child prefers and begin with an easier song. It is recommended that a child alternate between Therapeutic Singing and other challenging activities. This is essential for children who have an easier time singing than speaking since they can get "relief" from the efforts to speak by singing. This brings joy and freedom into the session while providing the client with neurally engaging activities that may ultimately make speaking easier. Recordings of the song accompaniment can be created by the music therapist for use at home. The more time that a child is engaged in Therapeutic Singing, the greater probability there is of making changes in the white matter tracking as noted above.

Adaptations. Establishing choirs for children with and without disabilities is a unique setting in which to promote cognition through lyric recall, language development through the introduction of new vocabulary, self-expression through a learned repertoire, expressivity through dynamics, and cooperative engagement with others. Solos within the choir setting allow for mastery of a single part while making a unique contribution to the whole.

Children should have recordings of the songs made with and without the therapist singing for home practice. It would be helpful to adopt the practices of early childhood music programs that provide two recordings for families to use—one for the car and one for the home. Optimal gains can be expected from such intense practice.

Guidelines for Compositional Music Therapy

In compositional music therapy experiences, the music therapist supports the client in writing lyrics, melodies, or instrumental pieces in order to create a musical product (Bruscia, 1998). With children who have language disorders, the opportunity to create song lyrics is a powerful tool to rehearse and expand vocabulary. It is also very powerful as a mnemonic vehicle for memorizing information or sequenced activities. The music therapist should structure songwriting experiences to meet the cognitive and linguistic abilities of the child.

Musical Mnemonics Training

Overview. Musical Mnemonics Training (MMT) is a very useful Neurologic Music Therapy technique that has been used by teachers and in children's television programming. In MMT, the music therapist creates lyrics and melodies to facilitate acquisition of new material such as categories, sequences, and other information that is relevant to the client's goals. MMT builds rote memory for embedded information by providing rhythmic and melodic cues to facilitate recall while providing repeated practice within the short time the song or chant is being performed.

An excellent example of Musical Mnemonics Training that many people would be familiar with is *Schoolhouse Rock!,* an animated educational program that embedded information about grammar, mathematics, history, etc., into songs. When asked, many people can still recall the words of "Conjunction Junction" or "The Shot Heard 'Round the World." Music is an effective carrier of information because it organizes a narrative into chunks and then sequences it in time (Thaut, 2005). If you are not able to recall the words in a phrase, you generally know how many syllables are left because of the musical structure. The music primes and prompts the linguistic recall. This is very helpful for children with language disorders.

In an elegant study of the effect of melody on the recall of text, Wallace (1994) showed that melodic repetition was of the utmost importance in promoting better recall of text information. For example, *Schoolhouse Rock!* does an excellent job of creating songs that support information learning through repetition. If you listen to "Three Is a Magic Number," for example, you will hear that the multiplication table for three is sung ascending twice, descending once, ascending once more, and then backward for a total of five repetitions in three minutes.

A poor example of a music mnemonic is the Gilbert and Sullivan song "The Elements." This song sets the Periodic Table of Elements to song at an extraordinarily rapid tempo with high articulatory demand, much like speakers who say as many words as possible at the end of an advertisement. One could describe the singing as cluttering (the term used for people whose speech is so rapid that it decreases intelligibility). In this song, there is barely time to breathe. These are features of composing that are ineffective for the purposes of clinical work.

Gfeller (1983) reported that a novel melody can enhance memory if the child is given enough exposure to it. Claussen and Thaut (1997) reported the use of familiar melodies in an investigation that trained the experimental group for one day on multiplication tables. The practicing music therapist should consider time frames for learning (short- or long-term objectives) when choosing novel or familiar melodies in compositions for mnemonics.

Preparation. Generally, most of a music therapist's efforts in MMT will be devoted to setting a text to music that effectively matches the rhythm and contour of the text, provides repetition, and balances simplicity and complexity so that the song will not be too dull or too elaborate. Compositions should avoid musically demanding elements such as large melodic intervals or complex rhythms. It is important to note that jingle writers use unexpected melodic leaps, especially at the end of a phrase, to increase the likelihood of listener recall. The chorus should have the most salient information in it, as it is the part of a song that is repeated. Repetition of the most important information is crucial to its success. The text may be simple enough to help a child learn to say his name and address clearly or it may be more complex, to teach an entire academic lesson. A child may be involved in the composition process to the degree that their speech and language impairments allow.

What to observe. The therapist should identify how long it takes the child to learn the song from beginning to end. Data should reflect the number of times the child has listened to the song in the clinic and at home until they have learned the information embedded in the lyrics. Information regarding carryover to the classroom or nonmusic settings should be considered for data collection.

Procedures. Teach the song by isolating a word or phrase for the child to learn and listen for in the music. Have the child learn the song in parts; typically, the chorus first, followed by individual verses. The music therapist may have the child complete the ends of phrases as they learn the lyrics. Recordings of the song can be made for the child to practice at home.

Musical Executive Function Training

Overview. Musical Executive Function Training (MEFT) is a Neurologic Music Therapy technique that addresses metacognitive and metalinguistic skill development through compositional activities. In MEFT, the music therapist creates individual or group improvisation and composition exercises to facilitate practice of executive functioning skills such as organization, problem-solving, reasoning, decision-making, and comprehension. According to Dawson and Guere (2010), executive function refers to "high-level cognitive processes required to plan and direct activities, including task initiation and follow-through, working memory, sustained attention, performance monitoring, inhibition of impulses, and goal-directed behavior" (p. vii). The opportunity to brainstorm ideas for lyrics and musical structure, problem-solve, take turns, negotiate with cocreators, and sustain attention to the activity is an ideal and motivating experience for a child. Executive functions are mediated by language. In order to respond to a teacher's assignment or a parent's request, a child has to process their directives in working memory and then construct a response. The language mediation is the "self-talk" that guides our actions (e.g., asking for clarifications) by inhibiting other actions (e.g., looking out the window or "spacing out"). It is the self-talk that prompts a child to remember to bring home their assignments and later to work on them. Children with language deficits need to be taught both linguistic and metalinguistic (self-talk) strategies (Singer & Bashir, 1999).

Preparation. It is important to know a child's strengths and weaknesses in executive functioning as assessed by speech-language pathologists or by neuropsychologists. A music therapist should know how these strengths and weaknesses are exhibiting themselves in linguistic tasks. If the child is old enough, they can be a good interview source, as well as parents, teachers, and other therapists on the team. The music therapist should find a topic that is compelling and favored by the child for consideration as a composition. When working with executive functions, it is ideal for children to be engaged in a longer-term project rather than a short-term (e.g., one-day) activity. Longer-term projects require more planning (e.g., brainstorming, composing, recording, distribution, performing) and thus more problem-solving and sustained attention.

What to observe. A therapist should video or audio record sessions to collect both qualitative and quantitative data regarding targeted executive functions. A therapist should be explicit with students regarding expectations and the employment of specific strategies. The therapist should model the metalinguistic (self-talk) strategies that the child needs to adopt in order to increase success. When modeling self-talk, the therapist verbalize their decision-making processes, their observations, and their rationale for choices. Independence in the use of these strategies in sessions is important evidence of progress. Generalization of the use of these strategies to the classroom or at home is further evidence of success. If a child is old enough, they can be encouraged to evaluate their own performance and progress.

Procedures. The process of MEFT is dependent on the executive functions of the child and their age. Skills may vary greatly. One child may need standby assistance to initiate a process or they may require forced choices because of limits in their ability to divergently think (brainstorm). In general, the more a child can struggle, problem-solve, reengage, and reflect on this process, the greater the benefits will be for the development of their executive functioning.

Adaptations. It is useful to consider extending the artistry of composing to a theatrical setting using costuming, set design, and dialogue. Engaging visual art to accompany the song (e.g., CD cover) provides additional experiences to engage executive functioning (e.g., planning, sequencing, execution).

Research Evidence

A literature review of music therapy treatment with pediatric speech and language disorders revealed few articles. Most articles that relate to pediatric disorders are population-specific (e.g., autism, Down's Syndrome). Part of the paucity of research could be due to the controversies regarding diagnostic categories; this is notable in apraxia (Morgan & Voxel, 2008). A disorder such as dysarthria can have many etiologies that confound establishing homogenous groupings for research. For example, dysarthria can result from Down's Syndrome, cerebral palsy, brain injury, etc. Recruiting children for formal research studies can be challenging in terms of numbers, homogeneity of diagnosis, and clarity of diagnostic features.

The paucity of evidence-based research in pediatric speech and language disorders is not unique to music therapy. A search of reviews done by the National Center for Evidenced-Based Systematic Reviews, an independent agency which conducts reviews to inform evidence-based practice guidelines, revealed few studies. Even those disorders that have reviews (apraxia, dysarthria, pragmatics) report a lack of studies on which to base efficacious practices, a lack of definition for diagnostic classifications, poorly controlled studies, and limited numbers of subjects (Gerber et al., 2011; Morgan & Votel, 2008).

Music therapists interested working with this population of children should be aware of the research published both for adults as well as children in order to understand the characteristics of the diagnosis, the neurological foundations of the diagnosis, and promising clinical approaches. By focusing on commonalities of symptoms between childhood symptoms and other adult conditions (such as Parkinson's disease), music therapists may find effective methods to adapt for working with children with speech and language disorders.

The most productive neuroscience laboratory for the study of music with speech and language disorders is that of Dr. Gottfried Schlaug and his colleagues at the Beth Israel Deaconess Hospital in Boston. His website (www.musicianbrain.com) lists all of the publications of the work they have accomplished. A music therapist interested in treating speech and language disorders is recommended to follow this lab closely by reading their publications and attending conferences where they are speaking.

Working with Caregivers

The work that music therapists do requires extensive music training, yet several techniques may be taught to parents and teachers to utilize musical activities to the best of their abilities. As young children are particularly drawn to music, parents should be encouraged to sing to them and with them on a regular basis using either known tunes (with or without lyric substitution) or novel tunes that they can improvise. It's important to reinforce to parents that it doesn't matter how well they sing. Classroom teachers and speech-language pathologists may be able to make use of the techniques that we develop in treatment at various levels (to prompt a child, to provide reinforcement, etc.).

Collaborating with speech-language pathologists is a wonderful opportunity for music therapists, as they frequently are working on the same objectives. It provides opportunities for professional development in the specifics of linguistics and treatment approaches. In a 2008 survey by McCarthy, Geist, Zojwala, and Schock, nearly three-fourths of respondents reported having worked with speech-language pathologists at some point in various roles and in various settings. Sharing knowledge was noted as a top benefit of collaborating with SLPs. An excellent example of collaboration is reported by Geist, McCarthy, Rodgers-Smith, and Porter (2008). The intervention process included assessments and team meetings with the parents to target priority communication goals and interventions. The treatment moved from individual music therapy sessions to small group music sessions and then to the classroom, where the teacher would implement the music activities during group time. In the reported case study, the speech-language pathologist acted as a consultant to both the music therapist and the classroom teacher. The music therapist also served as a consultant to the classroom teacher.

Summary and Conclusions

The typical development of speech and language is a magical experience to watch unfold in a child. When it does not develop in a typical way, it compromises a child's readiness for school, the development of a positive self-esteem, the freedom of self-expression, and success for life. Music therapy interventions are an ideal set of techniques to treat these disorders. Activities embedded in music afford children compelling and relevant experiences to improve both speech and language. This chapter has outlined the major disorders of speech and language in the developing child, the terminology of our speech-language therapy colleagues, and a variety of music therapy interventions for clinicians to use and evolve. Additional research is needed, both qualitative and quantitative, on the efficacy of music therapy interventions in the treatment of speech and language disorders. It is this author's hope that this chapter will define and inspire the need for further clinical research in this important area of child development.

References

Albert, M. L., Sparks, R. W., & Helms, N. A. (1973). Melodic intonation for aphasia. *Archives of Neurology, 29*(2), 130–131.

Andrews, G., Howie, P. M., Dozsa, M., & Guitar, B. E. (1982). Stuttering: Speech pattern characteristics under fluency-inducing conditions. *Journal of Speech and Hearing Research, 25,* 208–216.

Baker, J. (2003). *The social skills picture book teaching play, emotion and communication to children with autism.* Arlington, TX: Future Horizons.

Beathard, B., & Krout, R. E. (2008). A music therapy clinical case study of a girl with childhood apraxia of speech: Finding Lily's voice. *The Arts in Psychotherapy,* 2, 107–116.

Borg, J. (2010). *Body language: 7 easy lessons to master the silent language.* Upper Saddle River, NJ: FT Press.

Brownell, M. D. (2002). Musically adapted social stories to modify behaviors in students with autism: Four case studies. *Journal of Music Therapy, 39*(2), 117-144.

Bruscia, K. (1998). *Defining music therapy.* Gilsum, NH: Barcelona Publishers.

Claussen, D. W., & Thaut, M. H. (1997). Music as a mnemonic device for children with learning disabilities. *Canadian Journal of Music Therapy, 5,* 55-66.

Colcord, R. D., & Adams, M. R. (1979). Voicing duration and vocal SPL changes associated with stuttering reduction during singing. *Journal of Speech and Hearing Research, 22*(3), 468–479.

Davidow, J. H., Bothe, A. K., Andreatta, R. D., & Ye, J. (2009). Measurement of phonated intervals during fluency-inducing conditions. *Journal of Speech and Language Hearing Research, 52,* 188–205.

Dawson, P., & Guere, R. (2010). *Executive skills in children and adolescents: A practical guide to assessment and intervention.* New York, NY: Guilford Press.

Dromey, C., Ramig, L. O., & Johnson, A. B. (1995). Phonatory and articulatory changes associated with increased vocal intensity in Parkinson disease: A case study. *Journal of Speech and Hearing Research, 38*(4), 751–763.

Dworzynski, K., Remington, A., Rijsdijk, F., Howell, P., & Plomin, R. (2007). Genetic etiology in cases of recovered and persistent stuttering in an unselected, longitudinal sample of young twins. *American Journal of Speech-Language Pathology, 16,* 169–178.

El Sharkawi, A., Ramig, L., Logemann, J. A., et al. (2002). Swallowing and voice effects of Lee Silverman voice treatment: A pilot study. *Journal of Neurology, Neurosurgery and Psychiatry, 72*(1), 31–36.

Forgeard, M., Schlaug, G., Norton, A., Rosam, C., Iyengar, U., & Winner, E. (2008). The relationship between music and phonological processes in normal-reading children and children with dyslexia. *Music Perception, 24*(4), 383–390.

Geist, K., McCarthy, J., Rogers-Smith, A., & Porter, J. (2008). Integrating music therapy services and speech-language therapy services for children with severe communication impairments: A co-treatment model. *Journal of Instructional Psychology, 35*(4), 311-316.

Gerber, S., Brice, A, Capone, N., Fujiki, M. & Timler, G. (2011). Language use in social interactions of school-age children with language impairments: An evidence-based systematic review of treatment. *Language, speech and hearing services in schools, 43,* 235-249. doi:10.1044/0161-1461(2011/10-0047)

Gfeller, K. (1983). Musical mnemonics as an aid to retention with normal and learning disabled students. *Journal of Music Therapy, 20*(4), 179–189.

Gfeller, K., Jiang, D., Knutson, J. F., Oleson, J. J., Olszewski, C., Turner, C., Drisoll, V. & Gantz, B. J. (2012). The effects of musical and linguistic components in recognition of real-world musical excerpts by cochlear implant recipients and normal-hearing adults. *Journal of Music Therapy, 49*(1), 68-101.

Gray, C. (1995). *Social stories: Improving responses of students with autism with accurate social information.* Rockville, MD: Aspen Publishers.

Gray, C. (2010). *The new social story book, revised and expanded 10th anniversary edition.* Arlington, TX: Future Horizons.

Halwani, G. F., Loui, P., Ruber, T., & Schlaug, G. (2011). Effects of practice and experience on the arcuate fasciculus: Comparing singers, instrumentalists, and nonmusicians. *Frontiers in Psychology, 2,* 156. *doi*:10.3389/fpsyg.2011.00156

Healey, E. C., Mallard III, A. R., & Adams, M. R. (1976). Factors contributing to the reduction of stuttering during singing. *Journal of Speech and Hearing Research, 19,* 475–480.

Helfrich-Miller, K.R. (1984). Melodic intonation therapy with developmentally apraxic children. *Seminars in Speech and Language, 5,* 119-125.

Helfrich-Miller, K. R. (1994). A clinical perspective: Melodic intonation therapy for developmental apraxia. *Clinics in Communication Disorders, 4*(3), 175–182.

Keith, R. L., & Aronson, A. E. (1975). Singing as therapy for apraxia of speech and aphasia: Report of a case. *Brain and Language, 2,* 483–488.

Keller, H., & Sullivan, A. (1921). *The story of my life.* New York. NY: Doubleday, Page & Co.

Krauss, T., & Galloway, H. (1982). Melodic intonation with language delayed apraxic children. *Journal of Music Therapy, 19,* 102–113.

McCarthy, J., Geist, K., Zojwala, R., & Schock, M. Z. (2008). A survey of music therapists' work with speech-language pathologists and experiences with augmentative and alternative communication. *Journal of Music Therapy, 45*(4), 405–426.

McCauley R. J., Strand E., Lof, G. L., Schooling T., & Frymark, T. (2009). Evidence-based systematic review: Effects of nonspeech oral motor exercises on speech. *American Journal of Speech-Language Pathology, 18,* 343–360.

Mehrabian, A. (2007). *Nonverbal communication.* New Brunswick, NJ: Aldine Transaction.

Morgan, A. T. & Vogel, A. P. (2008). *Intervention for childhood apraxia of speech.* Cochrane Database of Systematic Reviews, Jul 16;(3):CD006278. doi: 10.1002/14651858.CD006278.pub2

Muir, D. & Field, J. (1979). Newborn infants orients to sounds. *Child Development, 50*(2), 431-436.

Nicolis, L., Harryman, E., & Kresheck, J. (2003). *Terminology of communication disorders: Speech-language-hearing.* Baltimore, MD: Lippincott Williams & Wilkins.

Nordoff, P., & Robbins, C. (1977). *Creative music therapy.* New York, NY: John Day.

Owens, R.E. (2011). *Language development: An introduction.* Boston, MA: Pearson Education.

Petitto, L. A. (2000). The acquisition of natural signed languages: Lessons in the nature of human language and its biological foundations. In C. Chamberlain, J. P. Morford, & R. I. Mayberry (Eds.), *Language acquisition by eye* (pp. 41–50). Mawwah, NJ: Lawrence Erlbaum Associates.

Petitto, L. A., & Marentette, P. (1991). Babbling in the manual mode: Evidence for the ontogeny of language. *Science, 251,* 1483–1496.

Pilon, M. A., McIntosh, K. W., & Thaut, M. H. (1998). Auditory vs. visual speech timing cues as external rate control to enhance verbal intelligibility in mixed spastic-ataxic dysarthric speakers: A pilot study. *Brain Injury, 12,* 793–803.

Pullum, G. K., & Ladusaw, W. A. (1996). *Phonetic symbol guide.* Chicago, IL: University of Chicago Press.

Ramig L. O., Fox C., & Sapir, S. (2004). Parkinson's disease: speech and voice disorders and their treatment with the Lee Silverman voice treatment. *Seminars in Speech Language, 25*(2), 169-80.

Ramig, L., Countryman, S., Thompson, L. L., Horii, Y. (1995). Comparison of two forms of intensive speech treatment for Parkinson disease. *Journal of Speech and Hearing Research, 38*(6), 1232-1251.

Rasmussen, T., & Milner, B. (1977). The role of early left-brain injury in determining lateralization of cerebral speech functions. *Annals of the New York Academy of Sciences, 229,* 355–369.

Restak, R., & Grubin, D. (2001). *The secret life of the brain.* Washington, DC: Joseph Henry Press.

Rizzolatti, G., & Craighero, L. (2004). The mirror-neuron system. *Annual Review of Neuroscience, 27,* 169–192.

Schlaug, G., Norton, A., Marchina, S., Zipse, L., & Wan, C. Y. (2010). From singing to speaking: Facilitating recovery from nonfluent aphasia. *Future Neurology, 5*(5), 657–665.

Singer, B. D., & Bashir, A. S. (1999). What are executive functions and self-regulation and what do they have to do with language-learning disorders? *Language, Speech and Hearing Services in Schools, 30,* 265–273.

Sparks, R. W., Helm, N., & Albert, M. (1974). Aphasia rehabilitation resulting from melodic intonation therapy. *Cortex, 10,* 303–316.

Sparks, R. W., & Holland, A. (1976). Method: Melodic intonation therapy for aphasia. *Journal of Speech and Hearing Disorders, 41,* 287–297.

Strait, D. L., & Kraus, N. (2011). Can you hear me now? Music training shapes functional brain networks for selective auditory attention and hearing speech in noise. *Frontiers in Psychology, 2*(113), 1–10.

Thaut, M. (2005). Neurologic music therapy in speech and language rehabilitation. In *Rhythm, music and the brain: Scientific foundations and clinical applications* (pp. 165–178). New York, NY: Routledge.

Van Riper, C. (1973). *The treatment of stuttering*. Englewood Cliffs, NJ: Prentice Hall.

Wallace, W. T. (1994). Memory for music: Effect of melody on recall of text. *Journal of Experimental Psychology: Learning, Memory and Cognition, 20*(6,) 1471–1485.

Wan, C. Y., Bazen, L., Baars, R., Libenson, A., Zipse, L., Zuk, J., Norton, A., & Schlaug, G. (2011). Auditory-motor mapping training as an intervention to facilitate speech output in non-verbal children with autism: A proof of concept study. *PLoS ONE, 6*(9). e25505. doi:10.1371/journal.pone.0025505

Wan, C. Y., & Schlaug, G. (2010). Neural pathways for language in autism: The potential for music-based treatments. *Future Neurology, 5*(6), 797–805.

Wan, C. Y., Rüber, T., Hohmann, A., & Schlaug, G. (2010). The therapeutic effects of singing in neurological disorders. *Music Perception: An Interdisciplinary Journal, 27*(4), 287–295.

Ward, E. C., Thoedoros, D. G., Murdoch, B. E., & Silburn, P. (2000). Changes in maximum capacity tongue function following the Lee Silverman voice treatment program. *Journal of Medical Speech-Language Pathology, 8*(4), 331–335.

Whitmore, K., Hart, H., & Willems, G. (1999). *Neurodevelopmental approach to specific language disorders.* Cambridge, UK: Cambridge University Press.

Resources for Music Therapy Assessments of Speech and Language Disorders in Children

Brunt, B., & Coleman, K. (2000). Development of a special education music therapy assessment process. *Music Therapy Perspectives, 18*(1), 59–68.

Coleman, K., & Brunk, B. (2003). *Special education music therapy assessment process* (SEMTAP). Grapevine, TX: Prelude Music Therapy.

Davis, W., Gfeller, K., & Thaut, M. (1992). *An introduction to music therapy: Theory and practice.* Boston, MA: McGraw-Hill College.

Gantt, L. (2000). Assessments in the creative arts therapies: Learning for each other. *Music Therapy Perspectives, 18*(1), 41–46.

Gfeller, K., & Baumann, A. (1988). Assessment procedures for music therapy with hearing impaired children. *Journal of Music Therapy, 25*(4), 192–205.

Grant, R. (1995). Music therapy assessment for developmentally disabled clients. In T. Wigram, B. Saperston, & R. West (Eds.), *The art & science of music therapy: A handbook*. London, England: Harwood Academic.

Gregory, D. (2000a). Test instruments used by Journal of Music Therapy authors from 1984–1997. *Journal of Music Therapy, 37*(2), 79–94.

Gregory, D. (2000b). Information sharing: Technological assistance in client assessment: Implications for music therapy. *Music Therapy Perspectives, 18*(1), 69–71.

Griggs-Drane, E., & Wheeler, J. (1997). The use of functional assessment procedures and individualized schedules in the treatment of autism: Recommendations for music therapists. *Music Therapy Perspectives, 15*(2), 87–93.

James, M. (1986). Utilization of motor skill assessments in clinical practice. *Music Therapy Perspectives, 3*, 9–12.

Sabbatella, P. (2004). Assessment and clinical evaluation in music therapy: An overview from literature and clinical practice. *Music Therapy Today, V*(1), 1-32. Retrieved from http://musictherapyworld.net

Wigram, T. (1995a). A model of assessment and differential diagnosis of handicap in children through the medium of music therapy. In T. Wigram, B. Saperston, & R. West (Eds.), *The art and science of music therapy: A handbook*. London, England: Harwood Academic.

Wigram, T. (2000b). A method of music therapy assessment for the diagnosis of autism and communication disorders in children. *Music Therapy Perspectives, 18*(1), 13–30.

Wilson, B., & Smith, D. (2000). Music therapy assessment in school settings: A preliminary investigation. *Journal of Music Therapy, 37*(2), 95–117.

Online Resources

American Speech and Hearing Association (www.asha.org)

National Center for Evidence-Based Practice in Communication Disorders

Center for Biomedical Research in Music (www.colostate.edu/depts/cbrm)
Neurologic Music Therapy training center, research laboratory and clinic

The Gray Center for Social Learning and Understanding (www.thegraycenter.org)
Information and resources on social stories

Music and Neuroimaging Laboratory (www.musicianbrain.com)
Dr. Gottfried Schlaug, Director

National Institute on Deafness and Other Communication Disorders (www.nidcd.nih.gov/health/voice)

Secret Life of the Brain film series by PBS. An accompanying book by Richard Restak and David Grubin (2001)

Stuttering Foundation of America (www.stutteringhelp.org)

Vaghmi Computerized Voice Therapy Software (voiceandspeechsystems.com)

Speech and language developmental milestone references: See
http://www.nidcd.nih.gov/staticresources/health/voice/speechlanguagedevelopmentalmilestonesenglishfs.pdf
http://nichcy.org/disability/milestones
http://www.cdc.gov/ncbddd/actearly/milestones/index.html
http://www.speech-therapy-information-and-resources.com/grammar.html
http://www.speech-language-therapy.com/index (excellent information)

Phonologic development

http://www.speech-therapy-information-and-resources.com/speech-sound-development-chart.html

http://d102.org/blogs/trippspeech/phonological-processes/elimination-of-phonological-proccesses-chart/

Phonetics

http://www.speech-therapy-information-and-resources.com/phonetics.html

Chapter 6

Attentional Deficits in School Children

Michelle R. Hintz

Overview

The prevalence of persons diagnosed with Attention-Deficit/Hyperactivity Disorder (ADHD) and other disruptive behavioral disorders is on the rise. According to the Centers for Disease Control and Prevention, approximately 11% of school-age children have now received a diagnosis of ADHD, with boys being diagnosed three times as often as girls. In the *Diagnostic and Statistical Manual of Mental Disorders, 4th Edition–Text Revision (DMS-IV-TR)* (American Psychiatric Association, 2000), this category of childhood disorder includes three subtypes of ADHD (predominantly inattentive type, predominantly hyperactive-impulsive type, and combined type), Oppositional Defiant Disorder, and Disruptive Behavior Disorder.

Attentional deficits characterize a number of childhood conditions and diagnoses. There is a significant amount of comorbidity between ADHD and conduct disorders, oppositional-defiant disorders, mood disorders, speech and language disorders, mental retardation, and learning disabilities. Up to 30% of children with ADHD also have a learning disability, and nearly half of students with ADHD will be required to repeat a grade in elementary or middle school. These children tend to fail at a rate 250% higher than their peers without ADHD (Lavoie, 2007). For purposes of this chapter, reference to ADHD and/or ADHD symptoms is intended to encompass all possible clinical diagnoses that present with this cluster of symptoms.

Diagnostic Information

ADHD is considered a developmental disorder of behavioral inhibition that interferes with self-regulation and organization of behavior (Barkley, 1996). Individuals with ADHD have significant deficits in behavioral inhibition and the executive functions needed for effective self-regulation. The diagnostic features of ADHD include a persistent pattern of inattention with or without hyperactivity and impulsivity that significantly interferes with development of appropriate social, academic, and occupational functioning. These symptoms must be present before the age of seven years and must be more frequent and more severe than those of typically developing children at comparable ages. Yet, ADHD is difficult to diagnose in children younger than four to five years of age. Girls are more likely to present with problems related to mood, affect, emotion, and inattention, while boys present with more activity, aggression, and antisocial behaviors typically thought of in ADHD. According to McGee, Williams, and Silva (1987), the occurrence of ADHD in boys and girls may be equal if controls are used for the differences in how the disorder is expressed.

Studies have suggested that ADHD is not a unitary syndrome, but rather a cluster of loosely associated symptoms affecting alertness, arousal, selective/focused attention, distractibility, sustained attention, and span of apprehension (Ross & Pelham, 1981). In addition, there must be evidence that there is interference in functioning in at least two environments (e.g., home, school, work). Children must have at least six symptoms from either (or both) the inattention group of criteria and the hyperactivity and impulsivity criteria, while older adolescents and adults (over age 17 years) must present with five. While the criteria have not changed from *DSM-IV,* examples have been included to illustrate the types of behavior that children, older adolescents, and adults with ADHD might exhibit. The descriptions will help clinicians better identify typical ADHD symptoms at each stage of patients' lives. Based on criteria of the *DSM-IV*, the three types of ADHD are identified as (1) ADHD, Combined Type— if both criteria 1A and 1B have been met for the past six months; (2) ADHD, Predominantly Inattentive Type—if criterion 1A has been met but criterion 1B has not been met for the past six months; and (3) ADHD, Predominantly Hyperactive-Impulsive Type—if criterion 1B has been met but criterion 1A has not been met for the past six months. The criteria below are taken from the *DSM-IV-TR* (2000, p. 92).

A. Either (1) or (2):

1) Six or more of the following symptoms of inattention have been present for at least six months to a point that is disruptive and inappropriate for developmental level:

Inattention

- Often does not give close attention to details or makes careless mistakes in schoolwork, work, or other activities.
- Often has trouble keeping attention on tasks or play activities.
- Often does not seem to listen when spoken to directly.
- Often does not follow instructions and fails to finish schoolwork, chores, or duties in the workplace (not due to oppositional behavior or failure to understand instructions).
- Often has trouble organizing activities.
- Often avoids, dislikes, or doesn't want to do things that take a lot of mental effort for a long period of time.
- Often loses things needed for tasks and activities.
- Often is easily distracted.
- Often is forgetful in daily activities.

2) Six or more of the following symptoms of hyperactivity-impulsivity have been present for at least six months to an extent that is disruptive and inappropriate for developmental level:

Hyperactivity

- Often fidgets with hands or feet or squirms in seat.
- Often gets up from seat when remaining in seat is expected.
- Often runs about or climbs when and where it is not appropriate.
- Often has trouble playing or enjoying leisure activities quietly.
- Often is "on the go" or often acts as if "driven by a motor."
- Often talks excessively.

Impulsivity

- Often blurts out answers before questions have been finished.
- Often has trouble waiting one's turn.
- Often interrupts or intrudes on others.

B. Some symptoms that cause impairment were present before age seven.

C. Some impairment from the symptoms is present in two or more settings (e.g., at school/work and at home).

D. There must be clear evidence of significant impairment in social, school, or work functioning.

E. The symptoms do not happen only during the course of a Pervasive Developmental Disorder, Schizophrenia, or other Psychotic Disorder. The symptoms are not better accounted for by another mental disorder (e.g., Mood Disorder, Anxiety Disorder, Dissociative Disorder, or a Personality Disorder).

A few modifications to the diagnostic criteria are forthcoming in the *DSM-5,* namely that several of the individual's ADHD symptoms must be present prior to age 12 years (vs. seven years as the age of onset in the *DSM-IV*). In addition, the *DSM-5* includes no exclusion criteria for people with autism spectrum disorder, since symptoms of both disorders co-occur. In order to receive the diagnosis, children must still have at least six symptoms from either (or both) the inattention group of criteria and the hyperactivity and impulsivity criteria, while older adolescents and adults (over age 17 years) must present with five.

As toddlers and preschoolers, children with ADHD often present differently than typically developing peers. They are unable to sit still, follow even simple directions, and control impulses, and are frequently "on the go" and "get into everything." These children have difficulty engaging in sedentary activities (e.g., puzzles, listening to stories), are known to climb on furniture, and are very fidgety. Parents are constantly repeating directions, saying "no" to the same things, and redirecting them to do what they are supposed to do. Preschoolers with ADHD may appear to become angry for no reason, hit or bite others, throw objects when upset, and have frequent tantrums when denied their way. In addition to a very high level of energy, they may also have a high threshold for pain or no sense of danger.

School-age children with ADHD often have trouble sitting still at meals, kick their feet while sitting, disrupt and interrupt others, and make noise during quiet activities and independent work. Impulsivity manifests as difficulty with delaying gratification, blurting out answers before questions have been completed, starting work before reading directions, frequently interrupting, and grabbing objects from others. Often children with ADHD can seem not to hear others when they are spoken to or may appear as if their minds are elsewhere (e.g., daydreaming).

Brighter children with ADHD (especially girls and those with less hyperactivity) may be able to compensate for their symptoms until middle school. But, students begin to struggle once there are greater demands on being organized and efficient due to switching classes and having more teachers during the day. Around the time of adolescence, ADHD may also be associated with other problems, including low self-esteem, depression, and even eating disorders. Because it's not always easy for a parent to differentiate between common adolescent swings in mood and behavior and those related to ADHD or other causes, experts recommend seeking professional help for any adolescent who experiences unexplained changes in school performance, mood, energy level, or socialization.

Persons with ADHD present with behavioral and cognitive processing difficulties that often contribute to social, emotional, and academic struggles. As one would imagine, these symptoms worsen when the individual needs to engage in nonpreferred activities that require sustained attention or mental effort or during repetitive tasks. The child will also have significant difficulty with tasks that require organization, planning, inhibition, self-monitoring, and sustained effort. Contrary to popular belief, individuals with ADHD may have minimal or no symptoms when engaging in preferred activities (e.g., video games), when receiving frequent rewards for appropriate behavior, when they are under close supervision, in new or novel situations, and when engaged in interesting activities. Symptoms may also appear to be absent in one-to-one situations such as a therapy session. In contrast, symptoms are likely to be more prevalent during group situations.

Behavioral Impairments

One major behavioral symptom of ADHD is increased motor activity; however, there is no consistent or predictable expression of this activity. Some children with ADHD are able to stay in their seat but are constantly moving, shuffling their feet, tapping a pencil, etc. Other children are more accident-prone, since there is an aspect of clumsiness as they move through space that results in frequent tripping, underestimating the time needed to stop or adjust their movement to avoid bumping into others, and minor injury. Researchers have found that individuals with ADHD have deficiencies in motor coordination and sequencing abilities (Barkley, 1997; Mariani & Barkley, 1997).

Depending upon the age and developmental level of the child with ADHD, individuals may demonstrate low frustration tolerance, temper tantrums, poor sense of responsibility, oppositional behavior, stubbornness, fidgeting, and interrupting others, and/or engage in potentially dangerous activities without consideration of possible consequences.

Deficits in behavioral inhibition then impact four cognitive processes called executive functions (which emerge later in development): working memory, self-regulation of affect/motivation/arousal, internalization of speech, and reconstitution. Barkley (1996) argues that these four executive functioning deficits are secondary to the deficits in behavioral inhibition. Therefore, if individuals improve their inhibition, the other executive functions should likewise improve. He proposed that behavioral inhibition emerges first in development and that this influences motor control. Behavioral inhibition is understood to be related to the capacity to inhibit responses that receive immediate gratification and the creation of self-directed behaviors that enable the individual to return to goal-directed actions until a successful outcome can be achieved.

Cognitive Processing Difficulties

Researchers have found that individuals with ADHD have deficiencies in other associated abilities, such as working memory and mental computation (Barkley, 1997; Mariani & Barkley, 1997; Zentall & Smith, 1993), impulsivity, sustained attention, physiological underarousal (Spreen, Risser, & Edgell, 1995), and self-regulation of emotional arousal (Barkley, 1997; Cole, Zahn-Waxler, & Smith, 1994). Individuals with ADHD are also reported to have IQ scores several points lower, on average, than typical peers of the same age.

Working memory is defined as the process of temporarily storing and managing information required to carry out complex cognitive tasks. It is involved in the selection, initiation, and termination of information-processing functions such as encoding, storing, and retrieving data. These processes are essential in learning, reasoning, and comprehension. Self-regulation is defined as the capacity to monitor our own behaviors and alter them as needed to accomplish a goal. Internalization of speech is basically understood to be the "self-talk" we do when we are reading silently, engaging in a task, or contemplating options. Internalization of speech serves to help keep us on task, sequence events, or comment on observations. The term "reconstitution" refers to the mental processes that assist us in planning and problem-solving to overcome obstacles so that we can achieve a desired goal. Children with difficulty in reconstitution processes often have struggles to rapidly, accurately, and efficiently form complete thoughts and ideas. They also struggle to generate multiple plans of action or options to accomplish a desired outcome.

The process of attention and its role in information processing has been discussed for decades. During continuous performance tests (CPT), children with ADHD tend to detect fewer signals than typical peers (Kasper et al., 1971), make more errors of omission (fewer correct detections) and of commission (more incorrect responses), are less able to inhibit premature or repetitive responding, and demonstrate poor impulse control (Fischer, Barkley, Edelbrock, & Smallish, 1990).

Social Difficulties

ADHD is described in the *DSM-IV* as a disruptive behavior disorder because of the significant difficulties it creates in social conduct and general social adjustment. These children are often more intense, intrusive, emotional, and disorganized. They are frequently considered to be bossy, stubborn, needy, impatient, and impulsive. Parents often describe their children as being more talkative, more in need of assistance, less able to play or work independently, and more negative or defiant.

Success in social situations requires children to complete three basic tasks consistently: listen, follow direction, and wait their turn (Lavoie, 2007). If a child is able to accomplish these simple procedures, he will likely enjoy social success. However, for the child with ADHD, these "simple" skills are greatly compromised. "Simple" is not always "easy." Their relationships with peers are negatively impacted. Often, they often have fewer friends and are less liked because they have difficulty working cooperatively. They are also frequently viewed as troublemakers.

Emotional Difficulties

An individual with ADHD is also more likely to have associated emotional or mood difficulties. They are seen as being more susceptible to overreacting, having a broader range of affect, and being more easily disappointed, and view even minor setbacks as huge ordeals. They may become dysphoric, irritable, and/or anxious, which, in turn, can lead to poor self-esteem. From the child with ADHD's perspective, he feels he is continually blamed, reprimanded, and censured for behavior that is beyond his control. He may begin to feel angry, resentful, and frustrated. As a result, he may begin to develop negative associations about school and teachers and lose motivation to learn. In middle school, children with ADHD become increasingly aware of the discrepancy between their potential and their performance. Many of them know that they are bright and intelligent, yet there is little or no evidence of this from teachers or on their report card.

Academic Struggles

As expected, children with ADHD can have significant academic struggles. An estimated 30% of children with ADHD also have learning disabilities (Barkley, 1996). Even though they are often very capable (even brilliant), these students perform below their abilities due to disorganization, careless work, failure to give close attention to details, incomplete or missing assignments, and lost papers. They have a strong dislike for activities that require them to slow down and be careful. They may be the first student to finish a test, yet they make careless errors, miss items, and fail to apply multistep processes to obtain correct answers (e.g., in mathematics).

For the child with ADHD, performance and motivation are influenced by three factors: the level of interest in the activity, the difficulty of the activity, and the duration of the task. The key to motivating the child with attentional problems is to modify and adjust the learning environment (Lavoie, 2007). Often, teachers will invest significant time and effort in attempting to change the child when the expectations of the traditional classroom conflict with the limitations of the child.

Needs and Resources

There are a myriad of needs for an individual with ADHD, ranging from basic behavioral needs to emotional and social needs, each with requiring some sort of intervention. The best treatment outcomes arise from a multimodal treatment approach that incorporates medications, behavioral therapy, and/or education. Numerous studies indicate that a multimodal treatment was particularly effective for improving social skills in children in highly stressful environments. It also was effective for those with anxiety and depression in addition to ADHD. In general, children who received multimodal treatment needed lower doses of medications as compared to children receiving only medication (Barkley, 1996).

Behavioral Interventions

Behavioral therapy interventions are primarily designed to help a child decrease problematic behaviors, such as improving organization or fostering emotional control. Educating parents about the disorder and its management is another important part of ADHD treatment. For parents, this may include learning parenting skills to help their child manage behavior. Common strategies taught to parents include giving positive feedback for desirable behaviors, ignoring undesirable behaviors, and giving time-outs when the child's behavior is out of control.

Cognitive-behavioral therapy has also been widely used. Cognitive-behavioral therapy combines behavioral techniques with cognitive strategies to directly address problems of impulse control, problem-solving, and self-regulation. Children with ADHD also have deficits in time perception awareness and motor timing. Some evidence has also indicated that cognitive-behavioral techniques may produce desired changes in sustained attention, impulse control, hyperactivity, and self-concept (Fiore, Becker, & Nero, 1993; Smith, Taylor, Warner Rogers, Newman, & Rubia, 2002).

Behavioral management therapy involves working with a therapist and teacher in order to set clear goals and establish rewards and consequences for behavior. Positive reinforcement encourages a child's good behavior (like getting more computer time for finishing homework). Bad behavior, on the other hand, might result in time out or losing computer privileges. Self-management and regulation strategies are also effectively used with children who have ADHD. Several studies have examined the effectiveness of self-management techniques with ADHD children. This type of intervention focuses on teaching the child how to systematically rate their own behavior according to the rating of their teachers. The goal of self-management interventions is to help the child more accurately measure their behavior against the standard set by their teacher.

Several studies found that teaching children self-management skills with reinforcement led to decreases in disruptive behavior (Carr, & Punzo, 1993; Prater, Hogan, & Miller, 1992; Webber, Scheuermann, McCall, & Coleman, 1993). Hinshaw and Melnick (1992) suggested that reinforcement and rehearsal-based behavioral interventions can be combined with self-management techniques to supplement and extend the gains induced by behavioral procedures alone. They argue that, when combined with pharmacologic and behavioral approaches, self-management procedures should be considered for addressing the social and behavioral problems of children with ADHD.

DuPaul, Guevremont, and Barkley (1992) examined the efficacy of response-cost contingencies alone and in combination with directed-rehearsal procedures for managing classroom behavior and academic productivity. They found that the response-cost contingencies led to marked improvements in task-related attention and reduction in other ADHD symptoms. Response-cost effects on academic productivity were also seen. These researchers suggested that response-cost procedures promote greater attention to independent seatwork and have the potential to affect other important areas of classroom functioning such as behavioral control during teacher lectures.

Pharmacological Interventions

Pharmacological treatment for behavior and learning problems has been used since the 1930s. Initially, stimulant medications were prescribed for children with a wide variety of behavioral difficulties, but by the 1950s, stimulants were more widely used for hyperactivity. During the 1970s, as many as 2% of the elementary school population in the U.S. was receiving stimulant medication for hyperactivity. To this day, stimulants are the preferred treatment (Spreen, Risser, & Edgell, 1995).

Commonly prescribed ADHD medications include stimulants such as methylphenidate (including Ritalin, Metadate, Concerta, Daytrana, Focalin) or amphetamines (including Dexedrine, Dextrostat, Adderall, Vyvanse). One drug, atomoxetine (Strattera), is not a stimulant. Side effects of these medications may include reduced appetite, sleep problems, feeling jittery, stomach upset, and acne. These side effects may start at the beginning of treatment and often get better after a short period of time.

Alternative/Complementary Interventions

In a meta-analysis of neurofeedback in treatment of ADHD, Arns, deRidder, Strehl, Breteler, and Coenen (2009) concluded that there was high efficacy for neurofeedback in the areas of inattention and impulsivity, but only moderate efficacy on measures of hyperactivity. Neurofeedback (NFB) in the treatment for ADHD is based on findings that people with ADHD have excess theta waves and fewer-than-average beta waves when measured on an EEG. NFB treatment involves teaching the patient how to increase their arousal levels by increasing beta waves and decreasing theta waves. NFB illustrates brain activity using real-time displays of electroencephalography or functional magnetic resonance imaging (fMRI), with a goal of helping an individual improve control of central nervous system activity. Sensors are placed on the scalp to measure activity and measurements are displayed using video displays or sound.

Referral and Assessment

The vast majority of children with ADHD receive other forms of treatment, with medication, psychological services, and occupational therapy being the most common. Referrals for music therapy often come from parents rather than other providers or teachers. Within the community, private music therapy services are frequently sought by parents or other therapists as an additional augmentative treatment after other more traditional therapies have been put into a child's therapy schedule. As such, the music therapist's role in the treatment of children with ADHD tends to be as part of a multidisciplinary team, but this is dependent upon the setting, referral source, and clinical needs. Music therapy assessment can identify limitations and weaknesses in children, as well as their strengths and potentials. Yet, only a few formal music therapy assessment processes are cited in the literature.

> When music therapists develop an assessment tool that not only measures music-related functioning, but uses musical tasks and experiences as well as

> requiring a music therapist for its administration, music therapy will have an independent identity among health care professionals. (Hintz, 2000, p. 36)

Most music therapy assessments serve to determine eligibility for services; to gather information on levels of functioning; and to determine treatment goals. Most assessments are conducted through behavioral observation within the music-making session, by assessing peer-to-peer social interaction, use of communication and language, or musical responses as indicators of developmental levels of functioning (Schwartz, 2008, 2011).

Brunk and Coleman developed the *Special Education Music Therapy Assessment Process (SEMTAP)* (1999) to assess the functioning of children and adolescents who receive special education services. The purpose of the *SEMTAP* is to determine eligibility for music therapy services for children who have an Individualized Education Plan (IEP). The *SEMTAP* process allows for comparison of a client's responses with and without music.

Another assessment tool, from Baxter et al. (2007), is the *Individualized Music Therapy Assessment Profile (IMTAP),* which assesses client functioning in several domains of functioning for individuals with a wide range of functioning and diagnoses, including physical disabilities, communication disorders, autism, emotional disturbances, social impairments, and learning disabilities, among others. The *IMTAP* allows music therapists to use their own repertoire of methods and experiences to conduct the assessment. It is intended to be used as a tool for treatment planning and goal development, providing a baseline of overall functioning for treatment, and as a communication tool for parents and other therapists. In addition, the IMTAP attempts to identify effective strategies for each client.

Carpente (2009) created the Individual Music-Centered Assessment Profile for Neurodevelopmental Disorders (IMCAP-ND), a specific improvisational music therapy assessment to be used within the DIR®/Floortime™ model. While not specifically designed to assess individuals with ADHD, the IMCAP-ND is a criterion-based assessment that provides an in-depth musical understanding of each child's ability to musically attune, engage, relate, adapt, and communicate in musical play (Carpente, 2009). The IMCAP-ND targets six music domain areas related to the child's social-emotional responses, considering individual differences and how they impact the musical interactions. Music domain areas are evaluated by clinical observation and listening to the child's responses in play through any one or all of the four modes of musical expression (instrument play, voice, movement, gestures).

It is suggested that the music therapist have access to the student's treatment plan, prior evaluations, and IEP prior to or after completing assessment to effectively plan and design music therapy sessions. Through assessment, the music therapist gains understanding of the individual's unique clinical profile and strengths and weaknesses, and prioritizes needs. From the data gathered in the assessment, the music therapist can select appropriate methods for treatment. Music therapy goals then ideally should address the child's needs as well as the concerns of the person making the referral.

Guidelines for Music Therapy Methods

There are several common guidelines that music therapists should consider when conducting experiences for individuals with ADHD. While techniques for implementing music therapy vary from therapist to therapist, there are only a handful of articles specifically addressing interventions for individuals with ADHD or attentional deficits. However, it goes without saying that music therapists need a high level of clinical musicianship and also interpersonal skills in order to be sufficiently flexible and spontaneous when working with this population. Music therapists should consider their client's unique individual and musical differences while engaging them in music. Jones and Carr (2004) suggest engaging the child in experiences of their choice during intervention, as well as providing children with a choice from among a variety of novel and interesting objects (musical instruments and accompanying props) that have salient sensory consequences (making music, noise, moving, etc.).

There are numerous nonmusical suggestions for working with children with ADHD that are applicable to music therapists working with individuals with ADHD. It is advised that music therapists be knowledgeable about basic behavioral techniques and concepts of operant conditioning. Music therapists need to understand concepts such as types of reinforcement (stimuli that increase behavior), types of punishment (stimuli that decrease behavior), escape, avoidance, and simple schedules of reinforcement (e.g., continuous reinforcement, fixed and variable ratio, fixed and variable interval). In music therapy treatment, the effect of reinforcement on behavior may be measured as an increase in the frequency of its expression (e.g., demonstrating the behavior more frequently), duration (e.g., demonstrating the behavior longer periods of time), magnitude (e.g., demonstrating the behavior with greater force or intensity), or decrease in latency (e.g., demonstrating the behavior more quickly following the onset of an environmental event).

Additional suggestions for music therapists to use when interacting with clients with ADHD include:

- Increasing motivation
- Providing a structured, predictable environment
- Giving simple, single-step instructions with visual input
- Offering positive reinforcement, praise, and encouragement
- Allowing for breaks as needed
- Having clear rules, limits, and expectations
- Allowing use of movement and activity when needed
- Assisting the child on starting tasks
- Gaining the child's attention before giving a direction
- Asking the child to repeat instructions back to you

Previous research indicates that some specific musical elements may play a role in a music therapist's choice of intervention. For example, several sources cite music's role in increasing memory functions and auditory perception in learning (Morton, Kershner, & Siegel, 1990; Roskam, 1979; Shehan, 1981; Wolfe & Horn, 1993), teaching social skills (Abikoff, Courtney, Szeibel, & Koplewicz, 1996), increasing attention span (Cripe, 1986), serving as a contingent reinforcer (Reid, Hill, Rawers, & Montegar, 1975; Wilson, 1976), reducing hyperactivity (Scott, 1970), and increasing academic task performance (Abikoff, Courtney, Szeibel, & Koplewicz, 1996). Regardless of the music therapy methods used in treatment, music therapists most often addressed behavioral goals, followed by psychosocial goals, and then cognitive goals (Jackson, 2003).

Overview of Methods and Procedures

The following methods and procedures are used most commonly with clients with attentional deficits.

Receptive Music Therapy

- Contingent Music: the playing of music dependent upon the absence of a undesired behavior or in the presence of a desired behavior.
- EEG-Guided Music Therapy: the use of EEG-mediated musical and visual neurofeedback with a goal of influencing self-control over brain wave activity.

Improvisational Music Therapy

- Instrumental Improvisation: The therapist and client create spontaneous musical improvisations using instruments.

Re-creative Music Therapy

- Musical Play: includes a wide variety of musical interventions, including action songs, playing instruments with songs, instrumental songs (not improvisation), and musical games.
- Adaptive Music Lessons: a form of individual music therapy in which the music lesson format (most commonly using voice, piano, or guitar) is used to accomplish therapeutic goals such as sequencing ability, self-awareness, and self-regulation.

Compositional Music Therapy

- Musical Social Stories: use of music to support the learning of concepts, sequences, and basic information from short stories, often depicted with short sentences with accompanying pictures in sequences to teach clients expected behaviors during interactions, social experiences, or activities of daily living.

GUIDELINES FOR RECEPTIVE MUSIC THERAPY

Receptive music therapy interventions are intended to engage the client in a musical experience designed to provide stimulation of sensory or cognitive processes. Yet, there is a wide range of applications of receptive music therapy experiences as well as purposes. Receptive music therapy interventions can be designed to attract, foster, and sustain children's engagement in any number of ways—socially, emotionally, cognitively, sensorially, and motorically, as well as musically. The use of familiar melodies and repetition allows clients opportunity to make associations with the music. Strategies such as vibroacoustic music therapy (VAS), guided imagery and music, contingent music, auditory stimulation, and bio-guided music therapy all have different clinical objectives. While these methods are receptive in nature, they also combine behavioral music therapy techniques, meaning that they are intended to change observable behavior in some way.

According to Miller (2011b), bio-guided approaches differ from other music therapy approaches in that the client's physiological data is presented in real time either through music or visual means as part of the therapy session. The use of music as a reward or cue is taken to another level in that it serves to create or improvise music based upon physiologically driven tones. When used in this manner, Miller argues, music has the "potential to simultaneously be a stimulus, cue, response, reward, and creative improvisational product" (p. 3).

Contingent Music

Overview. Contingent music is defined as the playing of music dependent upon the absence of a undesired behavior or in the presence of a desired behavior. There are many applications of playing music to increase wanted behaviors and decrease unwanted behaviors. The premise for the effectiveness of contingent music is based upon the concepts of behavioral modification strategies, especially operant conditioning, wherein desired behaviors are either positively or negatively reinforced. There are no known contraindications for this method. Level of therapy: augmentative.

Preparation. In advance of applying contingent music, the music therapist needs to assess both the environment and the clients. Use of preferred music or musical styles is suggested due to increased motivation and saliency. Once this is determined, the music therapist needs to prepare the music—either via speakers or using live music. If using recorded music, the music therapist should have music selections organized into a playlist (e.g., downloaded onto an iPod, recorded onto a CD) and ready to be played and stopped easily using a handheld remote control (if possible). If live music is used, the instruments should be tuned and ready to be played. The target behavior and how the music will be administered must be decided prior to implementing contingent music in order to provide consistency of feedback and to strengthen associative qualities of music with that target behavior. Considerations for how the music is presented include determining the duration of the music. For example, will the music be played for the duration of the targeted behavior (e.g., while children are walking in line), or will it be played only when all children are lined up at the door? The music therapist must also determine when the music will be stopped. For example, will the music stop if the child is not on task during an independent academic task or will it be stopped once the child is engaged in disruptive or hyperactive behavior (e.g., getting out of his seat, calling out in class)?

What to observe. The music therapist will monitor the targeted behavior and will fine-tune the contingent use of music to produce the best results. Qualitative data about the child's affective experience to the music (e.g., is it still motivating) can be assessed through observation of the child's facial expression as well as verbalizations. The music used in the procedure should be changed and/or modified as needed to ensure saliency. Observation of the targeted behavior without music must also be made in order to evaluate for generalization of the behavior into nonmusical conditions and across settings.

Procedures. The music therapist determines the child's preferred music, asking for a selection(s) that he would like to hear. Recordings of that music are prepared and readied for play. With remote in hand, the music therapist informs the child of when the music will be played (e.g., "as long as you stay sitting in your seat") and when it will be stopped (e.g., "when you get out of your seat"). Once the child understands the conditions for the music to be played, the music therapist begins the procedure. Contingent music can be administered according to natural time frames in the child's day, such as during math class, while at recess, or during dinner. However, in order for there to be demonstrated improvement on the targeted behavior, the child must have sufficient opportunities for repeated practice. In some studies, contingent music was used for a period of several weeks; other studies reported on 30 to 40 trials (e.g., car rides).

The music therapist must determine the threshold for mastery. Typically, behaviors are considered mastered when they occur in an average of 80% of trials or four out of five opportunities. Once mastery has been reached, the music therapist will change to an intermittent application of the music treatment, meaning that music will only sometimes be presented during the targeted behavior. During this phase of treatment, the music therapist is still monitoring the target behavior to ensure that mastery is maintained.

Adaptations. Contingent music can be applied in individual situations as well as used in groups. It can be administered in any number of environments, including school, home, therapy office, playground, etc.

EEG-Guided Music Therapy

Overview. The theoretical basis for the bio-guided approaches such as music-assisted relaxation, vibroacoustic therapy, and music and medicine procedures are based upon physiological responses to music (Wigram, Pedersen, & Ole Bonde, 2002). Miller (2011b) suggests that a bio-guided approach "expands beyond the use of music as cue or as a reward, to the point where physiologically driven tones in real time contribute to the creation of improvisational music" (p. 3).

Electroencephalography (EEG) and functional magnetic resonance imaging (fMRI) are the recording of electrical activity in the brain as measured through sensors placed on the scalp. EEGs are often used to assess brain activity across four common wavelengths: beta, alpha, theta, and delta. Beta waves are the most rapid of the four brain wave patterns and are associated with normal waking consciousness, concentration, arousal, alertness, and cognition. When beta waves are at their highest, they are associated with anxiety, disharmony, and unease. Alpha waves are slower and are associated with a state of deep relaxation that is often found during the period between sleeping and waking. Theta waves are even slower than alpha waves and are thought to be associated with increased memory and creativity and "integrative experiences" such as having an insight (e.g., "Ah-ha!" moments). Delta waves are the slowest and are present during dreamless sleep.

Beta waves are produced when we are fully engaged in an activity and are associated with concentration and arousal. However, even when children with ADHD are fully engaged and interested in an activity, their brain wave function remains at a lower level than that of children without ADHD. In other words, they to not reach beta wave levels. EEG-guided music therapy is the clinical application of EEG neurofeedback using musical and visual feedback, with a goal of influencing self-control over in-the-moment brain wave activity. It is one method of bio-guided music therapy that combines neurofeedback to enhance mental focus and calm excessive movements. The music chosen can be used to facilitate learning attentional skills. This method could be construed as within the scope of bio-medical music therapy (Taylor, 1997) and being related conceptually in some ways to Neurologic Music Therapy (Thaut, 2008).

EEG-guided music therapy may be contraindicated for clients who demonstrate extreme difficulty with impulse control to maintain a proper EEG hookup. Their erratic and unexpected hyperactivity can cause malfunction in the readings. Level of therapy: augmentative.

Note: Music therapists will need additional training and experience beyond traditional music therapy education in order to properly implement these methods.

Preparation. The music therapist must have the necessary equipment and programs to facilitate reading EEGs and playing music (e.g., CD players, stereo systems), and screens for video/visual feedback (e.g., computer monitor, TV screen). The room must be free from distractions and have comfortable seating arranged so that the music therapist and client are able to see the monitor and have access to the other equipment. All equipment to come into physical contact with the client (e.g., sensors) should be cleaned and ready to be applied. Any required pastes or gels should also be available, as well as paper towels or cloths for wiping afterward.

Before implementing the music therapy intervention, the client's musical preferences must be determined to assist with selection of background music. Once this is accomplished, the music therapist can then identify the physiologically triggered musical components (e.g., pentatonic scale in an accompanying key for the music selected). Clients can bring their own music, or music selections can be chosen by the music therapist. Once the music selection is made and the musical components are identified, the music therapist sets up the biofeedback program, adjusting the visual display and audio settings to meet client preferences, preparing for recording, and saving the file with the client's identifying information, date, and any other notes. The client is then hooked up to the EEG equipment; ear clips are applied to the client's ears, and lead sensors are applied to the selected location on the client's scalp, using EEG paste. The music therapist explains the procedure as well as how to understand the audio and visual feedback measures.

What to observe. The music therapist monitors the client's affective response toward the procedure in general, overall energy, and mood. Observations of the level of motivation, willingness to engage in the procedure, and attitude are made. The client's psychomotor activity and attention are subjectively assessed to determine if readiness to be hooked up to the equipment. During the procedure, the music therapist will monitor physiological measurements such as electrodermal activity (galvanic skin response), breathing, and heart rate. The music therapist should pay special attention to monitor for signs of fatigue and avoidance as the session progresses.

Procedures. During a typical 30- to 45-minute session, the child is seated in front of a computer monitor with wires leading from different points on his head. The child is taught how to use the neurofeedback equipment and the goals of the procedure. The music therapist starts up the music-mediated program on the child's screen and monitors the brain waves on another screen. The music therapist begins playing the child's preferred music while the child uses the visual and musical feedback to modify brain wave activity. In most cases, the music therapist is looking for an increase in beta wave activity.

When this process is used for improving attention and concentration, slow-wave EEG activity is assigned to a musical scale in a key that matches the background music selections (Miller, 2011a). Real-time data may be presented in key, scale, and tempo for flexibility in musical interaction with the music therapist or group. The tones themselves are initially assigned to a scale and a synthesized instrument patch for increased musicality (over older nonmelodic biofeedback systems) and superimposed over a base musical background that the subject selects from a menu of several musical genres.

Physiological data obtained during the intervention provide both the client and music therapist with information that guides the therapeutic process. Data presented in real time can be represented in a particular key, scale, or tempo that can be determined by the music therapist or client or collaboratively determined. Music therapists typically work individually with clients two or three times per week, with each session lasting approximately 35–45 minutes over the course of several weeks or months, depending upon treatment progress (Miller, 2011a).

Adaptations. There are a number of exciting bio-guided music therapy processes that use physiological responses and computer-generated musical or rhythmic feedback, and more are being developed. One of them is Interactive Metronome (IM). Interactive Metronome training involves listening to a computerized rhythmic beat that the person then tries to mimic with hand or foot tapping. The person using Interactive Metronome training is provided feedback that indicates how well they match the beat of the metronome.

Supporters of Interactive Metronome training believe that the behavioral problems associated with ADHD stem from a motor planning and timing deficit. In their study, Shaffer et al. (2001) compared results from the group that received the interactive metronome training, the group that received no training, and the group that received video-game training. They concluded that the group of boys with ADHD who received Interactive Metronome training had a significant improvement in attention span, motor control, and selected academic skills. Shaffer and his colleagues believe that over time, the individual using Interactive Metronome training can learn to focus for extended periods of time, to filter out distractions, and to monitor their physical and mental actions as they occur.

Guidelines for Improvisational Music Therapy

The musical experiences improvised during sessions typically arise from the vocal and motor output provided by the child. The child plays a central role in the creation of the music and is an active creator. The child plays various instruments that require no formal training or experience, while the music therapist improvises music (e.g., reflecting and expanding the child's music-making, emotional state, and/or movements).

Some researchers describe music improvisation as a "right brain" activity that is related to feeling, creative expression, and artistic talent, while typical "left brain" activities are associated with cognitive analysis, linear and sequential tasking, and numeric calculation. It is the intent of the music therapist to create a musical environment that is responsive to the dynamics of physiological measures and aimed at clinical goals (Miller, 2011a).

Goals in improvisatory music therapy methods with individuals with ADHD may include improving impaired timing, decreasing impulsivity, enhancing self-organization, improving body awareness, and increasing self-control. Creating music with others requires considerable attention and self-control. Accuracy in the timing of motor responses (such as playing a drum during an improvisation) depends upon an individual's ability to plan and organize a response. It requires estimation of time and anticipation of future events. These skills are directly related to working memory, a cognitive process often impaired in individuals with ADHD. The therapist's role during improvisational methods for ADHD is to provide the necessary structure, reinforcement, and organization to support clinical objectives.

Instrumental Improvisation

Overview. Instrumental improvisation is a process wherein the music therapist and the client create music using instruments which become the vehicle on which they form a musical relationship. The improvisation can be started by either the therapist or child, and any object that can make a musical sound can be used. The purpose is to promote relatedness, communication, socialization, and awareness within the music itself. This is accomplished by musically engaging, matching, supporting, and enhancing the child's expressions, musically or nonmusically (Carpente, 2009).

Instrumental improvisation can provide the child with ADHD a chance to experience synchrony, reciprocity, self-expression, and engagement with another person. It can also provide opportunity for self-organization and self-regulation. Instrumental improvisation can encourage reciprocity and provide a foundation for meaningful communication for individuals with little or no verbal language. Oftentimes, individuals with ADHD can be demanding, overpowering, and inflexible when relating with others. However, improvisational experiences provide the child with ADHD practice in deferring immediate rewards for later or greater gain, opportunity for positive peer interaction, and training in flexibility and patience with others.

Children who have extreme auditory, visual, or social difficulties might benefit more from individual child/adult instrumental improvisation than from being in a group setting. No contraindications are known for instrumental improvisation. Level of therapy: augmentative.

Preparation. A wide assortment of instruments that require no formal training or experience to play should be readily accessible to the child. This in and of itself challenges and tests the child's impulse control. Percussive instruments such as drums, maracas, eggs, triangles, cymbals, and melodic instruments (e.g., marimba, xylophone, resonator bells, and horns) are all appropriate. If needed, instruments and mallets should be adapted to accommodate for children with physical limitations (e.g., grasp, range of motion, strength) and to improve the likelihood of success should there be issues with motor planning or sound sensitivity. The music therapist then chooses the instruments for the child and arranges them in the music space, depending on the goals of the intervention and the most suitable sound for the child. The child should have adequate space to move about the room and have easy access to all instrument possibilities.

Because individuals with ADHD are often very egocentric (self-focused), music therapists are encouraged to either audio or video record improvisations for viewing after the experience. These recordings will provide an opportunity for the music therapist and the child to evaluate their playing in relation to others. Did they lead more than they followed? Did they overpower the rest of the group? Did they demonstrate cooperation and patience? In addition, recordings can be compared across multiple sessions to evaluate for progress in areas related to self-organization, impulsivity, or cooperation with others.

What to observe. The music therapist should be very familiar with the client's developmental music responses. Those children who have more energy may need to use a more durable but less loud instrument. Percussion instruments, especially hand drums, can present a challenge to children with ADHD as there is a natural inclination to beat it loudly. The music therapist improvises music using her musicianship, creativity, intuition, and clinical knowledge of the child. The intent is to actively improvise music such that children can experience themselves in a new way.

The music therapist will observe the child's choice of instrument, how it is used, range of musical expression, and overall rhythmic/harmonic/melodic structure. There is also observation of the child's incorporation of others' themes, adjustments to variations in tempo and dynamics, and relatedness between the child's music and others' music. Although the focus is on nonmusical goals such as working cooperatively with peers and following directions, these goals actually address underlying cognitive deficits in self-organization, working memory, selective attention, and impulsivity.

Procedures. The therapist chooses the instruments depending upon the child's goal or objective. The therapist must consider whether they will play the same or different instruments, allow for exploration or provide assistance, encourage individual expression or encourage imitation, etc. It is important to remember that both exploration and imitation are opportunities for learning and relating for children with ADHD. After instrument choice and arrangement, the therapist either initiates play or waits for the child to play. Use of a familiar song or chant (re-creative method) might be used to introduce and encourage the beginning of improvisatory play. The therapist can then begin musical play or cue (through word or gesture) for the child to start or to join in playing.

Many children with ADHD will have underlying deficits with timing and therefore have disorganized rhythms and weak ability to replicate beats. For these clients, providing a steady pulse or simple four-beat rhythm pattern can provide a foundation for musical exploration. Similarly, these children also benefit from predictable harmonic I-IV-V7-I progressions or A-B-A structures.

Adaptations. Instrumental improvisations are easily adaptable both to vocal improvisations and to group improvisations. The goals for group improvisation include decreasing motor impulsivity; engaging in peer-to-peer synchronization or reciprocity; practicing self-organization and self-regulation; and experiencing group cohesion. Suggested goals might be to adjust tempo, meter, or dynamics to match the music of peers; imitate peers' rhythmic or melodic patterns; take turns; initiate musical ideas; or engage in reciprocal musical exchanges with peers and call-and-response methods.

Guidelines for Re-creative Music Therapy

Singing, dancing, and action songs are common childhood experiences. Re-creative methods are commonly used with persons with ADHD. Experiences like musical play and group singing often pair music and information while music and movement experiences address auditory perception skills and memory. Not surprisingly, the majority of music therapy literature focuses on the use of re-creative methods for individuals with ADHD to address specific underlying symptoms.

It is important that the music therapist be familiar with current popular children's music groups and artists and theme songs to popular children's programs, as well as their clients' favorite musical songs and styles. Adaptations of familiar children's music provide opportunity for addressing clinical needs while taking advantage of the child's motivation and interest in his preferred music. Therapist-created songs are composed with specific therapeutic objectives in mind.

Musical Play

Overview. Research has shown that music and movement activate both brain hemispheres (Hannaford, 1995; Morton, Kershner, & Siegel, 1990). Musical play experiences include a wide variety of interventions, including action songs, playing instruments with songs, instrumental songs (not improvisation), and musical games. Most musical play experiences are highly structured activities that actively engage the client in playing along with a song or moving in time to music. The music therapist engages individuals in a musical experience that incorporates repetition and structure to promote functional skills in initiating, responding, modulating, processing, and planning responses. In these methods, the client's response within music can be instrumental, verbal, vocal, or behaviorally oriented (e.g., movement). Some basic goals for musical play methods include foundational skills for communication, such as awareness of and responding to environmental cues (e.g., starting and stopping, modulating play to match musical qualities, imitating rhythmic or melodic patterns), early play skills (e.g., engaging in reciprocal pattern play; mutual or joint play; playing in synchrony; responding to a music cue with learned rhythmic or melodic pattern), and more sophisticated responses that promote independence and creativity.

Musical play experiences can be used within both individual and group sessions. When used in group settings, the goals often include social skills development such as listening skills; direction-following; anticipation and motor planning of defined responses; and self-organization (e.g., impulse control). These methods may need to be modified in order to be used for children with severe behavioral or social difficulties. However, other than the possibility of the inability to adapt instruments to accommodate physical or sensory limitations, there are no known contraindications to using musical play experiences in therapy. Level of therapy: augmentative.

Preparation. The music therapist will need to spend some time setting up the room and gathering appropriate instruments prior to implementing this method, especially when more than one musical play experience will be used in the session. Considerations of possible therapeutic needs for space, seating, and safety should all be made. The choice of songs to be used should be made prior to the session as well. Choice of songs are made by keeping in mind the client's need for structure and stability, rhythmic sophistication, sound tolerance, and musical style and instrument preferences. Since many children with ADHD struggle with impulsivity and hyperactivity, care should be taken to ensure that the musical experiences do not overexcite or overarouse the child. In addition, they may have difficulty waiting to play the instruments, so it suggested that they be allowed to handle and try out any novel instruments prior to their use in the experience.

The therapist should also consider the client's clinical profile when using musical play activities. In particular, the music therapist will consider the child's typical style of interacting with the therapist and peers, ability to work cooperatively and delay gratification, and general psychomotor tendencies. Children who are more hyperactive will not likely benefit from a movement activity that allows freedom to move around the room. Instead, providing structure and facilitating musical experiences while seated is more likely to be successful. Songs that have multiple juxtaposing rhythms, thick harmonic structures, or sophisticated chord progressions might not be suitable for some clients with ADHD, since many children lack perceptual organization and can become overwhelmed or confused. In addition, they lack motor coordination to organize their responses and can become frustrated if rhythms are too difficult. Instead, the music therapist may choose songs that have accessible, familiar meter, repetitive rhythms, simpler instrumentation, and predictable structure.

What to observe. The music therapist will pay attention to how the client interacts with the instrument chosen or assigned. For example, it may be of interest for the music therapist to see how responsive the child is to the selected music, whether the experience is cooperative in nature, or if playing is self-focused. Affective responses and range of creativity shown while playing are also important. When presented in a group setting, the music therapist will observe not only intrapersonal, but also interpersonal responses and interactions. How a child participates in a group instrument song is often an indication of self-organization, self-regulation, awareness of others, and relatedness to the group as a whole.

Procedures. The music therapist can set up and direct musical play experiences in any number of ways. Initially, music therapists will need to be highly directive and take full leadership of the experience. When first introducing a song, game, or music and movement experience, the equipment can be placed in front of the child (but within easy reach) to minimize impulses to play while holding it. Instrumental songs most often focus on learning, remembering, and reproducing simple rhythmic or melodic patterns. For the child with ADHD, these experiences and skills serve to address key deficits in meta-cognition, working memory, and self-awareness. While children with ADHD perform best under highly structured conditions, it is advised that these experiences be modified slightly once the general concepts and goals for the song have been mastered. This can be accomplished by decreasing the amount of structure and control within the experience, providing clients an opportunity to lead or direct the activity, or modifying rules for play. The interest and motivation of children with ADHD can be maintained during their favorite activities by assigning different instruments, adjusting one musical aspect of the song (e.g., tempo, key, etc.), or simply changing the order of the instruments played.

Some examples of musical play activities include musical versions of Simon Says. A simple three-chord song can be written by the music therapist and sung while accompanying on the guitar. In this experience, the chorus of the song reinforces the rules ("Only do what Simon says"), while the verses convey the action ("Simon says, Touch your head, Simon says, Touch your toes, Simon says, Stomp your feet ... Everybody, touch your ... nose"). The rhyming lyric structure of doing three actions but not the fourth can be repeated until children master the concept, while the musical elements of the predictable V7 chord builds anticipation, which lends to automatic (impulsive) responding. The game can be modified to be more challenging by increasing the song's tempo, giving the child the opportunity to lead the activity, or modifying the action structure (e.g., repeating "Simon says" commands twice rather than three times).

Other musical play experiences include assigning children to play instruments at designated times (e.g., when they hear a word) during a song or story, doing seated rhythmic imitation using egg shakers to instrumental music, musical chairs, musical hot potato games (using directives to repeat a rhythm on the instrument passed around the circle), rhythm stick activities, and more.

Adaptations. The adaptations for using musical play in music therapy are countless. Often, these activities can become a warm-up experience that leads into others. Similarly, it is quite common for music therapists to combine action or movement activities with instrument-playing and singing. By incorporating movement paired with instrument-playing, the client gains practice in more sophisticated levels of responding and has opportunity for greater self-organization and self-regulation. By using virtual or electronic instruments rather than real instruments, the child with ADHD is given opportunities for expanded creativity, novel sensory experience, and adaptive use of technology.

Adaptive Music Lessons

Overview. Adaptive music lessons are a form of individual music therapy wherein the intent of instruction is on clinical goals rather than development of musical skill. While adaptive music lessons could be conducted on any instrument, the most common are typically voice, piano, guitar, and drums. During the adaptive music lesson, the therapist interacts with the client in the process of making music on a selected instrument. The intent of the session is to address clinical goals to improve the client's functioning in areas of motor control and coordination, self-regulation and modulation, self-awareness, sequencing, working memory, and selective attention. Most often the music therapist works with the client individually; however, it is not uncommon for clients to work in small groups (e.g., duets) in order to expand on previously mastered goals.

For individuals with ADHD, adaptive music lessons can address a broad variety of goals as stated above; however, the primary goals are likely to be related to addressing underlying deficits in motor planning, internal timing and organization, working memory, and self-awareness. Because individuals with ADHD tend to be self-focused, adaptive music lessons also provide practice in considering others and adjusting their behavior. It should be noted that referrals for adaptive music lessons often come from parents of children with ADHD at the request of the child themselves. For this reason, the music therapist will need to spend some time explaining the intent and purpose of the sessions to parents. No contraindications are known for adaptive music lessons. Level of therapy: augmentative.

Preparation. The decision to engage in an adaptive music lesson requires preparations prior to the first session. The music therapist will need to assess the client's basic functioning level, ability to follow directions and self-correct, level of engageability and motivation, and physical or emotional barriers that may influence the choice of instrument. For example, a child with poor auditory discrimination skills and limited attention span might not be a good candidate for adapted violin lessons. Lessons on piano are suggested for individuals with low frustration, short attention span, or limited self-awareness. It is the music therapist's responsibility to help clients and their families make realistic instrument choices given the clinical needs and abilities as well as therapeutic goals.

Preparation for sessions needs to take into consideration the needs for physical space for the lesson and required equipment (e.g., music stand). The music therapist will have appropriate sheet music and CD player and/or recording device, as well as other materials needed to conduct the session (e.g., tuners, metronome, extra strings for guitar, etc.). It will be particularly important for the child with ADHD to have as few distractions in the room as possible. Therefore, do not conduct the lesson next to a window, near a fan, or near a cluttered table. If at all possible, the music and instrument should be the only things in his line of sight.

What to observe. The music therapist observes the client's quality of participation in the session, paying particular attention to frustration, ability to understand instructions, physical limitations, and coordination issues, as well as cognitive skills related to the process of learning music. Because the adapted music lesson involves more than simply playing the instrument, the music therapist must be able to communicate basic musical constructs to the child in a manner that supports their process. At some point, most clients will be expected to be able to play notes from a page of sheet music. Therefore, didactic instruction on musical notation, music theory, and music history may all enter the session. The music therapist will also pay particular attention to the level of effort and motivation the client demonstrates. The music therapist will be interested in finding out if the client practices their instrument between sessions and their expectations for their lessons as well as their progress in playing it.

Procedures. As with traditional music lessons, clients will spend at least some time with warm-ups, review of familiar materials, technical exercises, and learning new information. While adaptive music lessons are conducted much like other music lessons, music therapists adapt procedures and devise teaching strategies according to the needs of the student. Some simple teaching strategies may include the use of color-coded keys (e.g., on the piano), labeling notes with letters, using larger notation, or creating and improvising musical jingles to remember note names, key signatures, etc.

During the adaptive music lesson, the music therapist maintains an active and supportive role with the client by providing encouragement and gentle redirection, and eliciting responses on the performance. The music therapist attempts to assist the client in improving underlying cognitive weaknesses by pointing out commonalities between errors, indicating aspects of playing to attend to, and providing assistance in how to overcome common hurdles. The music therapist may accompany the child by playing the same thing or providing harmonic structures in order to practice playing along with others.

At the end of the session, the music therapist will identify tasks to practice at home, theory worksheets to complete, etc.

GUIDELINES FOR COMPOSITIONAL MUSIC THERAPY

Compositional methods focus on the use of either therapist-generated or client-generated musical experiences to address nonmusical goals. Songs and instrumental compositions in therapy generally arise out of an identified clinical issue and/or the music therapist's desire to support therapeutic aims in a more structured manner. Sometimes the composition arises out of the client-therapist musical interaction or musical themes from the session. At other times, the composition can arise out of a verbal discussion of interpersonal struggles or emotional difficulties.

When the music therapist creates compositional experiences for or with individuals with attentional deficits, the resulting composition likely contains lyrics that provide information on improving behavior, attention, and working memory. Compositions may be created to address rules for good classroom behavior (e.g., staying in seat, raising hands to speak), using manners (e.g., recognizing when to use "please" and "thank you"), or basic life skills (e.g., understanding roles of community helpers such as police and firefighters, recognizing safety signs), etc. For higher-functioning individuals with ADHD, compositional themes of peer pressure, bullying, self-esteem, disappointment, competition, self-identity, problem-solving, and other psychological processes may be expressed.

Musical Social Stories

Overview. Music therapists often put stories into songs to both enhance children's interest as well as provide a framework to convey concepts and ideas. Just as the use of mnemonics has long been known to enhance recall and memory abilities (such as the alphabet song, which helps children remember all of the letters), the use of music to tell social stories can assist in the recall of rules for social engagement, social experiences, and expected behavior. By using musical elements of pitch, phrasing, and chord progression, targeted words or concepts can be highlighted and emphasized.

Social stories were originally developed by Carol Gray for children to address challenging behaviors and expected social behaviors. A social story is an individualized short story that breaks down a challenging social situation into understandable steps by using pictures and short relevant phrases designed to help an individual with ADHD improve self-awareness and increase self-regulation. Social stories can be written about potentially angering social situations, such as responding to teasing,

The stories combine auditory and visual information that can be repeated frequently. There are books available with prewritten social stories that a music therapist can use for ideas (Baker, 2003; Gray, 2010). A significant benefit of social stories is that they can be customized to the individual and their situation. No contraindications are known for using social stories in music therapy. Level of therapy: augmentative.

Preparation. The therapist identifies a targeted social situation such as asking a teacher for help and outlines the main parts of the situation. Musical themes, melodic ideas, or rhythmic patterns may have evolved within the context of other music therapy interventions and can be utilized in creating a musical social story.

The room must be adequate in size for the needs of the individual or group, with a piano or guitar to provide accompaniment. Instruments should be of the highest quality affordable, with accurate acoustics. Paper and pen may be needed to transcribe or create lyrics, and staff paper or musical software is needed to notate music. A recording device is needed to record ideas and revisions. The final product may be videotaped, recorded, or performed. The music therapist will also need to have materials available for creation of the visuals to accompany the story's lyrics. This process can be done any number of ways, from asking clients to make their own pictures to the therapist providing choices of preselected photographs, clip art, or other pictures. The music therapist must be familiar with a variety of musical styles and accompaniments. The music therapist may facilitate the songwriting process or assist the client with the songwriting process by transcribing the melody and lyrics musically.

Using short descriptive sentences written in the first person (i.e., "I" rather than "you"), the main parts or steps in the situation are identified. It is suggested that the music therapist use words such as "usually" or "sometimes" within the social story song to allow for unknown variables should they occur (Gray, 1995). Pictures (hand-drawn, clip art, or photographs) are then created for each sentence, and a visual is created for use in the session. There are several ways to create the social story, including making a cartoon strip, short picture book, or poster. The music therapist then creates a melody for the text that emphasizes key words melodically, rhythmically, and/or with stress. Music should be composed in the child's preferred style (e.g., rock, rap, blues) and use elements of rhythm, melody, and harmonic structure to support the accompanying lyrics. An example of the text for a social story about handling frustration appropriately is as follows:

Sometimes people bother me.
They say mean things or hurt my feelings.
But even when I am angry or frustrated,
I can be in control of my actions.
Being in control makes me feel proud of myself.
When I make good choices, everyone is happier.

What to observe. During the music therapy session, the music therapist will observe the client's level of engagement while writing the social story. She will also observe if the client has an affective response to the experience while listening. After the session, the therapist will communicate with other staff or family members regarding the client's behaviors in the targeted situation. Certainly, improvement in the targeted behaviors indicates that the experience is successful, as would the client's ability to retell the social story or sing the verses.

Procedures. The musical social story may be either the entire focus of the music therapy session (such as when composing the social story) or a single component within the session (such as when singing it in later sessions). When possible, the musical social story should be presented several times across multiple sessions to promote familiarity and retention of the information.

The musical social story is usually presented within the context of preparing for frustrating situations, using adaptive and coping skills, and addressing disruptive, aggressive, or impulsive behaviors. Musical social stories can also be used to address common social issues for children with ADHD, such as being easily annoyed, bothering others, cooperating, sharing and waiting, conflict resolution, and problem-solving with peers. The music therapist works collaboratively with the student to create the lyrics, accompanying pictures, or graphics (clip art or cartoon/comic strip formats work well) and write the music. Once all parts of the musical social story are completed, the music therapist works with the child to perform it. Depending upon the functioning level of the client, the music therapist may sing the song with or without an accompaniment while referencing the accompanying visual. Reviewing relevant parts of the story prior to the song may improve client engagement. Comprehension can be supported by pointing to the relevant pictures while singing. Children can play along with the musical social story, using handheld percussion instruments, shared drum, or melodic instruments set up in the proper key. Questioning the child after the social story may assist the music therapist in determining the child's level of comprehension and facilitate generalization of the social stories' message.

Adaptations. Musical social stories can easily be adapted for use in groups using similar procedures of songwriting. In fact, songwriting is one of the essential components in creating musical social stories. Once a musical social story has been rehearsed enough to be memorized, it actually becomes a song that can be sung with others unfamiliar with it to share information, problem-solve situations (including examining the nature of problems and providing solutions), and express feelings, and for creative expression. Songwriting can be used to promote understanding of past experiences or to anticipate future ones. It can serve as a vehicle for remembering information, sequencing, or representing symbolic thinking.

WORKING WITH CAREGIVERS

When working with children with ADHD, consideration of the child as part of a larger system is essential. Therefore, music therapists are encouraged to recognize the essential role that parents and other family members play in children's development. Music therapists have a unique opportunity to support and collaborate with teachers and other therapists by listening to and observing the interaction between the child and other colleagues while creating a musical environment that enhances the experiences of their interaction (Carpente, 2012). By sharing music therapy strategies with others, children are afforded help to ensure generalization and opportunity for practice and retention of skills.

Within an a consultative role to the classroom teacher, the music therapist can serve as a resource for designing and implementing interventions to address the general classroom environment, transitioning, or support of specific academic skills. For other therapists (e.g., speech/language pathologist, occupational therapist, behavior therapist, psychologist), a music therapist may guide and inform them regarding simple strategies to deepen their musical experience with their clients by using music intentionally, but within their scope of practice.

Music therapists have written about providing music therapy interventions within the context of the family. The goals for family music therapy interventions are often to increase positive parent/child interactions; to promote communication between family members; to provide an opportunity for generalization of skills; and to demonstrate techniques to family members (Allgood, 2005). The main interventions used in family sessions include using movement, sensory experiences, improvisation and instrument-playing, and singing songs.

RESEARCH EVIDENCE

Receptive Methods

Several studies have examined the therapeutic effects of various receptive methods of music therapy using operant learning paradigms. Many of these studies arise out of findings that (a) the rhythmicity and intense repetitive beats of music can increase arousal in the cerebrum, (b) strong beats such as those found in rock music can override environmental distractions and result in improved attending behaviors, and (c) strong repetitive beats tend to lead to lessened muscle tension and motor activity. There is also a general understanding that music, an assumed distractor, can actually facilitate and enhance performance in individuals with ADHD rather than interfere with it.

A study by Zimny and Weidenfeller (1962) used galvanic skin responses (GSR) to measure physiological excitement. They found that stimulative music increased excitement, while sedative music decreased excitement in elementary school–age children. Reardon and Bell (1970) found that stimulating music (rock and roll) reduced activity levels in severely intellectually impaired boys. Mowsesian and Heyer's study (1973) concluded that listening to rock music did not distract children during arithmetic and spelling achievement tests. They argue that music may make taking tests and studying less boring and less stressful.

Furman (1978) found that more beta waves were produced during musical stimulation, while alpha waves were decreased in number. Wilson (1976) found that children showed increases in desirable classroom behavior and decreases in undesirable behavior when using contingent rock music as a reward in a special education setting. He concluded that the findings imply that the subjects increased their arousal and orienting responses.

Cripe (1986) examined the effects of contingent rock music on hyperactivity and attention span in children with ADHD. Music conditions were administered via headphones without options for volume control. During 20-minute sessions, clients either engaged in free play or were instructed to work on mazes and coloring pictures. Results were clinically significant and indicated that subjects engaged in more off-task behaviors during the nonmusic conditions of the study vs. the music conditions. Although the sample size was small, Cripe argues that music therapy may be an effective and appropriate adjunct therapy for individuals with ADHD.

Morton, Kershner, and Siegel (1990) examined the effects of memory and attention on nondisabled children using a selective listening task. This task, verbal dichotic listening, requires a subject to discriminatively listen for information stated in one ear while ignoring information simultaneously presented in the other ear. Performance on this task was measured in two conditions: following exposure to music listening and following exposure to silence. Results indicated that subjects exposed to music prior to the dichotic listening task demonstrated increased memory (remembering more information) as well as reduced distractibility (intrusions of information presented in the nontargeted ear). They conclude that "music may increase bilateral cerebral arousal levels, possibly through the mediating role of the right hemisphere" (p. 195).

Abikoff et al. (1996) compared the effects of "extra-task stimulation" on arithmetic task performance in boys with ADHD and typical peers (those without ADHD). Subjects' performance was evaluated across three conditions: high stimulation (preferred music), low stimulation (voice recording of an evening business report), and no stimulation (silence). The music was individually chosen for the subjects to ensure saliency. Abikoff and his colleagues found that the children without ADHD performed similarly under all three conditions, while those children with ADHD performed significantly better under the music condition than the other two conditions.

Improvisational Methods

There are very few music therapy articles that specifically address the efficacy of improvisational methods for individuals with ADHD. However, it bears mentioning that a good number of studies incorporate more than one method (including improvisation). Therefore, several articles within the re-creative methods section (below) might also fit into this category. Rickson (2006) examined the impact of instructional and improvisational music therapy approaches on the levels of motor impulsivity in adolescent boys with ADHD. While no strong conclusions could be made, there were qualitative indicators that subjects displayed a reduction in restless and impulsive behaviors in the classroom.

Re-creative Methods

There are numerous research articles on the use of re-creative methods to address deficits and skills generally lacking in individuals diagnosed with ADHD. There is general agreement that rehearsal of rhythmic tasks are likely to lead to improvement in internal organization and impulse control (Gaston, 1968; Gibbons, 1983; Thaut, 1992), body awareness (Wigram, Pederson, & Bond, 2002), and motor coordination (Gibbons, 1983; Moore & Mathenius, 1987; Thaut, 1985). Several case studies found positive outcomes in internal organization using creative or eclectic music therapy approaches (Aigen, 1997; Haines, 1989; Lefebvre, 1991; Robbins & Robbins, 1991).

Some music therapy research set out to identify the musical skills and deficits of individuals with ADHD. The research generally agrees that individuals with ADHD demonstrate poor impulse control, which has been associated with disordered beating, inability to organize rhythms, and inability to sustain a steady beat (Hong, Hussey, & Heng, 1998; Moore & Mathenius, 1987).

Compositional Methods

A few studies have examined the use of social stories in music therapy to address problem behaviors. Brownell (2002) examined the effectiveness of sung social stories versus read social stories on challenging behaviors in students with autism. Results indicated that both conditions reduced problem behaviors, but sung social stories were more effective. Pasiali (2004) evaluated the effectiveness of sung social stories on challenging behaviors within a home setting. While the use of sung social stories reduced the targeted challenging behaviors, inconsistent findings were noted when looking at visual analysis of the behaviors. De Mers, Tincani, Van Norman, and Higgins (2009) examined the effects of musical social stories on challenging behaviors of young children in a special education setting. Negative behaviors such as hitting and screaming were targeted.

Summary and Conclusions

There is growing interest in the use of music therapy methods to address meta-cognitive and behavioral difficulties found in individuals with ADHD and other disorders with attentional deficits. Clearly, with nearly 10% of the school-age population in the U.S. being identified as having attentional difficulties, effective noninvasive treatments are desirable. According to Jackson (2003), music therapists identified that they used several methods of music therapy interventions with children with ADHD. The most commonly cited methods included music and movement, instrumental improvisation, musical play, and group singing. Results of her survey seemed to indicate that there was no single methodology or intervention used more frequently than another. In fact, according to the literature, it appears that a combination of re-creative (active) and receptive methods are used most often.

The applications of music therapy interventions for children with ADHD are numerous, and research findings influence clinical care for these clients in a number of settings. For example, encouraging medical professionals to use individual listening (through headphones or ear buds) on their own personal devices can decrease disruptive, avoidant, and anxious behaviors during stressful situations such as being in doctors' offices, hospitals, classrooms, and waiting rooms in general. Since many children intuitively use music listening while studying, parents can be informed about the positive influence of listening rather than continuing to believe that this decreases the effectiveness of studying.

Given the neurological and musical deficits identified in the literature, there is the potential for music therapists to have both a diagnostic and treatment role for these individuals. However, more research is needed regarding the specific effects of music on individuals with ADHD (Jackson, 2003). More research is also needed on examining how the effects of music therapy can be generalized to other settings for individuals with ADHD.

References

Abikoff, H., Courtney, M.E., Szeibel, P.J., & Koplewicz, H.S. (1996). The effects of auditory stimulation on the arithmetic performance of children with ADHD and nondisabled children. *Journal of Learning Disabilities, 29*(3), 238–246.

Aigen, K. (1997). *Here we are in music: One year with an adolescent creative music therapy group* (Vol. 2). Gilsum, NH: Barcelona Publishers.

Allgood, N. (2005). Parents' perceptions of family-based group music therapy for children with autism
American Psychiatric Association (APA). (2000). *Diagnostic and statistical manual of mental disorders—Text revision* (4th ed.). (DSM-IV-TR). Arlington, VA: Author.
Arns, M., de Ritter, S., Strehl, U., Breteler, M., & Coenen, A. (2009). Efficacy of neurofeedback treatment in ADHD: The effects on inattention, impulsivity, and hyperactivity: A meta-analysis. *Clinical EEG and Neuroscience, 40*(3), 180–189.
Barkley, R. A. (1996). Attention-deficit/hyperactivity disorder. In E. J. Mash & R. A. Barkley (Eds.), *Child psychopathology* (pp. 63–112). New York, NY: Guilford Press.
Barkley, R. A. (1997). Behavioral inhibition, sustained attention, and executive functions: Constructing a unifying theory of ADHD. *Psychological Bulletin, 121,* 65–94.
Baxter, H. T., Berghofer, J. A., MacEwan, L., Nelson, J., Peters, K., & Robers, P. (2007). *The individualized music therapy assessment profile: IMTAP*. Philadelphia, PA: Jessica Kingsley.
Brownell, M. D. (2002). Musically adapted social stories to modify behaviors in students with autism: Four case studies. *Journal of Music Therapy, 34,* 117–144.
Bruscia, K. (1987). *Improvisational models of music therapy*. Springfield, IL: Charles C. Thomas.
Carpente, J. (2009). *Contributions of Nordoff-Robbins music therapy within the developmental, individual-difference, relationship-based (DIR®)/Floortime™ addressing core features of autism framework to the treatment of children with autism: Four case studies*. Doctoral dissertation, Temple University. Ann Arbor, MI: ProQuest/UMI.
Carr, S. C., & Punzo, R. P. (1993). The effects of self-monitoring of academic accuracy and productivity on the performance of students with behavioral disorders. *Behavioral Disorders, 18,* 241–250.
Cole, P. M., Zahn-Waxler, C., & Smith D. (1994). Expressive control during a disappointment: Variations related to preschoolers' behavior problems. *Developmental Psychology, 30,* 835–846.
Coleman, K., & Brunk, B. (1999). Special education music therapy assessment process. Grapevine, TX: Prelude Music Therapy.
Cripe, F. F. (1986). Rock music as therapy for children with attention deficit disorder: An exploratory study. *Journal of Music Therapy, 23*(1), 30–37.
Davis, W. B., Gfeller, K. E., & Thaut, M. H. (1999). *An introduction to music therapy: Theory and practice,* (2nd ed.). Boston, MA: McGraw-Hill College.
de Mers, C. L., Tincani, M., Van Norman, R. K., & Higgins, K. (2009). Effects of music therapy on young children's challenging behaviors: A case study. *Music Therapy Perspectives, 27,* 88–96.
Fiore, T. A., Becker, E. A., & Nero, R. C. (1993). Educational interventions for students with attention deficit disorder. *Exceptional Children, 60,* 163–173.
Fischer, M., Barkley, R. A., Edelbrock, C. S., & Smallish, L. (1990). The adolescent outcome of hyperactive children diagnosed by research criteria: II. Academic, attentional, and neuropsychological status. *Journal of Consulting and Clinical Psychology, 58,* 580.
Furman, C. (1978). The effect of musical stimulation on the brainwave production of children. *Journal of Music Therapy, 15,* 108–117.
Gaston, E. T. (1968). *Music in therapy*. New York, NY: McMillan.
Gibbons, A. C. (1983). Rhythm responses in emotionally disturbed children with differing needs for external structure. *Music Therapy, 3*(1), 94–102.
Haines, J. H. (1989). The effects of music therapy on the self-esteem of emotionally disturbed adolescents. *Music Therapy, 8*(1), 78–91.
Hannaford, C. (1995). *Smart moves: Why learning is not all in your head*. Arlington, VA: Great Ocean.
Hinshaw, S. P., & Melnick, S. (1992). Self-management therapies and attention-deficit hyperactivity disorder: Reinforced self-evaluation and anger control interventions. *Behavior Modification, 16,* 253–273.

Hintz, M. R. (2000). Geriatric music therapy clinical assessment: Assessment of music skills and related behaviors. *Music Therapy Perspectives, 18*(1), 31–40.

Hong, M., Hussey, D. L., & Heng, M. (1998). Music therapy with children with severe emotional disturbances in a residential treatment setting. *Music Therapy Perspectives, 16,* 61–66.

Jackson, N. A. (2003). A survey of music therapy methods and their role in the treatment of early elementary school children with ADHD. *Journal of Music Therapy, 40*(4), 302–323.

Kasper, J. C., Millichap, J. C., Backus, D. C., Child, D., & Schulman, J. (1971). A study of the relationship between neurological evidence of brain damage in children with hyperactivity and distractibility. *Journal of Consulting and Clinical Psychology, 36,* 329-337.

Lavoie, R. (2007). *The motivation breakthrough: 6 secrets to turning on a tuned-out child.* New York, NY: Simon & Schuster.

Lefebvre, C. (1991). All her yesterdays: An adolescent's search for better today through music. In K. Bruscia (Ed.), *Case studies in music therapy* (pp. 219–230). Gilsum, NH: Barcelona Publishers.

Mariani, M., & Barkley, R. A. (1997). Neuropsychological and academic functioning in preschool boys with attention deficit hyperactivity disorder. *Developmental Neuropsychology, 13*(1), 111–129.

McGee, R., Williams, S., & Silva, P. A. (1987). A comparison of girls and boys with teacher-identified problems of attention. *Journal of the American Academy of Child and Adolescent Psychiatry, 26,* 711.

Miller, E. (2013). Theoretical considerations of bio-guided music therapy. *Voices: A World Forum for Music Therapy, North America,* October 11, 2011. Retrieved from https://normt.uib.no/index.php/voices/article/view/598/472.

Miller, E. B. (2011a). *Bio-guided music therapy: A practitioner's guide to the clinical integration of music and biofeedback.* Philadelphia, PA: Jessica Kingsley.

Miller, E. B. (2011b). Theoretical considerations of bio-guided music therapy. *Voices: A World Forum for Music Therapy, 11*(3). Retrieved from https://normt.uib.no/index.php/voices/article/view/598

Moore, R., & Mathenius, L. (1987). The effects of modeling, reinforcement, and tempo on imitative rhythmic responses of moderately retarded adolescents. *Journal of Music Therapy, 24,* 160–169.

Morton, L. L., Kershner, J. R., & Siegel, L. S. (1990). The potential for therapeutic applications of music on problems related to memory and attention. *Journal of Music Therapy, 27*(4), 195–208.

Mowsesian, R., & Heyer, M. The effect of music as a distraction on test-taking performance. *Measurement and Evaluation in Guidance, 6,* 104–109.

Nigg, J. (2009). Cognitive impairments found with attention-deficit/hyperactivity disorder. *Psychiatric Times, 28*(6). Retrieved from http://www.psychiatrictimes.com/adhd/content/article/10168/1389777?pageNumber=1

Pasiali, V. (2004). The use of prescriptive therapeutic songs in a home-based environment to promote social skills acquisition by children with autism: Three case studies. *Music Therapy Perspectives, 22,* 11–20.

Prater, M. A., Hogan, S., & Miller, S. R. (1992). Using self-monitoring to improve on-task behavior and academic skills of an adolescent with mild handicap across special and regular education settings. *Education and Treatment of Children, 15,* 43–55.

Reardon, D., & Bell, G. Effects of sedative and stimulative music on activity levels of severely retarded boys. *American Journal of Mental Deficiency, 75,* 156–159.

Reid, D. H., Hill, B. K., Rawers, R. J., & Montegar, C. A. (1975). The use of contingent music in teaching social skills to a nonverbal, hyperactive boy. *Journal of Music Therapy, 12*(1), 2–18.

Rickson, D. J. (2006). Instructional and improvisational models of music therapy with adolescents who have attention deficit hyperactivity disorder (ADHD): A comparison of the effects on motor planning. *Journal of Music Therapy, 43*(1), 39–62.

Robbins, C., & Robbins, C. (1991). Creative music therapy in bringing order, change and communication to the life of a brain-injured adolescent. In K. Bruscia (Ed.), *Case studies in music therapy* (pp. 231–251). Gilsum, NH: Barcelona Publishers.

Roskam, K. (1979). Music therapy as an aid for increasing auditory awareness and improving reading skill. *Journal of Music Therapy, 16,* 31–42.

Ross, A. O., & Pelham, W. E. (1981). Childhood psychopathology. *Annual Review of Psychology, 32,* 243.

Scartelli, J. P. (1989). *Music and self-management methods: A physiological model.* St. Louis, MO: MMB Music.

Schwartz, E. (2008). *Music, therapy, and early childhood: A developmental approach.* Gilsum, NH: Barcelona Publishers.

Schwartz, E. K. (2011). Growing up in music: A journey through early childhood music development in music therapy. In A. Meadows (Ed.), *Developments in music therapy practice: Case study perspectives* (pp. 70–85). Gilsum, NH: Barcelona Publishers.

Scott, T. J. (1970). The use of music to reduce hyperactivity in children. *American Journal of Orthopsychiatry, 40,* 677–680.

Shaffer, R. J., Jacokes, L. E., Cassily, J. F., Greenspan, S. I., Tuchman, R. F., & Stemmer, P. J., Jr. (2001). Effect of interactive metronome training on children with ADHD. *American Journal of Occupational Therapy, 55*(2),155–162.

Shehan, P. K. (1981). A comparison of mediation strategies in paired-associate learning for children with learning disabilities. *Journal of Music Therapy, 18,* 120–127.

Smith, A., Taylor, E., Warner Rogers, J., Newman, S., & Rubia, K. (2002). Evidence for a pure time perception deficit in children who have ADHD. *Journal of Child Psychology & Psychiatry, 43*(4), 529–542.

Spreen, O., Risser, A., & Edgell, D. (1995). Attention disorders and hyperactivity. *Developmental Neuropsychology* (pp. 363–382). New York, NY: Oxford University Press.

Taylor, D. (1997). *Biomedical foundations of music as therapy.* St. Louis, MO: MMB Music.

Thaut, M. (1985). The use of auditory rhythm and rhythmic speech to aid temporal muscular control in children with gross motor dysfunction. *Journal of Music Therapy, 22,* 108–128.

Thaut, M. (1992). Music therapy in the rehabilitation of stroke and traumatic brain-injured clients. In W. B. Davis, K. E. Gfeller, & M. H. Thaut (Eds.), *An introduction to music therapy theory and practice* (pp. 251–273). Dubuque, IA: Wm. C. Brown.

Thaut, M. H. (2008). *Rhythm, music, and the brain: Scientific foundations and clinical applications.* New York, NY: Taylor and Francis.

Toplak, M. E., Rucklidge, J. J., Hetherington, R., John, S. C. F., & Tannock, R. (2003). Time perception deficits in attention-deficit hyperactivity disorder and comorbid reading difficulties in children and adolescent samples. *Journal of Child Psychology & Psychiatry, 44*(6), 888–903.

Wigram, T., Pedersen, I. N., & Ole Bonde, L. (2002). *A comprehensive guide to music therapy: Theory, clinical practice, research and training.* Philadelphia, PA: Jessica Kingsley.

Wilson, C. (1976). The effect of intensity levels upon physiological and subjective affective response to rock music. *Journal of Music Therapy, 14,* 60–76.

Webber, J., Scheuermann, B., McCall, C., & Coleman, M. (1993). Research on self-monitoring as a behavior management technique in special education classrooms: A descriptive review. *Remedial and Special Education, 14,* 38–56.

Wolfe, D. E., & Horn, C. (1993). Use of melodies as structural prompts for learning and retention of sequential verbal information by preschool students. *Journal of Music Therapy, 30,* 100–118.

Zimny, G., & Weidenfeller, E. (1962). Effects of music upon GSR of children. *Child Development, 33,* 891–896.

Chapter 7

Learning Disabilities In School Children

Michelle R. Hintz

Overview

Learning disabilities are thought to arise from neurological differences in brain structure and function that, in turn, affect the brain's ability to store, process, or communicate information. It has only been approximately 25 years since systematic research began to investigate the underlying causes, developmental course, treatment conditions, and long-term outcomes of learning disabilities (Lyon, 1996). There is growing evidence to suggest that there are neurobiological causes for learning disabilities, including new evidence for genetic components (Cortiella, 2011).

According to the *Diagnostic and Statistical Manual of Mental Disorders, 4th Edition–Text Revised (DSM-IV-TR)* (APA, 2000), the prevalence of learning disorders is thought to range from 2% to 10%, depending upon the definition applied. Approximately 2.5 million public school students, nearly 5%, are identified as having a learning disorder. The incidence of learning disabilities is found to be higher for persons of lower socioeconomic status (e.g., those living in poverty) and persons of other/multirace populations (such as Hispanic, black, Native Americans), but was substantially lower among Asian/Pacific Islander students. There is also some data to suggest that children communicating in two languages and accommodating two cultures could contribute to some degree in the disproportionate number of Hispanic students classified as having learning disorders (U.S. Office of Special Education, 2002). Males are diagnosed with a specific learning disability nearly three times more often than females (Cortiella, 2011).

There are two relevant definitions of learning disabilities aside from the specific learning disorder definitions provided in the *DSM-IV-TR* (discussed later in this chapter). In 1990, the Individuals with Disabilities Education Act (IDEA) defined specific learning disability as:

> a disorder in one or more of the basic psychological processes involved in understanding or in using language, spoken or written, which disorder may manifest itself in the imperfect ability to listen, think, speak, read, write, spell, or do mathematical calculations. Such term includes such conditions as perceptual disabilities, brain injury, minimal brain dysfunction, dyslexia, and developmental aphasia. Such term does not include a learning problem that is primarily the result of visual, hearing, or motor disabilities, of mental retardation, of emotional disturbance, or of environmental, cultural, or economic disadvantage. [20 U.S.C. §1401(30)]

The National Joint Committee on Learning Disabilities (NJCLD) (1990) defines learning disabilities as follows:

> Learning disabilities is a general term that refers to a heterogeneous group of disorders manifested by significant difficulties in the acquisition and use of listening, speaking, reading, writing, reasoning, or mathematical skills. These disorders are intrinsic to the individual, presumed to be due to central nervous system dysfunction, and may occur across the life span. Problems in self-regulatory behaviors, social perception, and social interaction may exist with learning disabilities but do not, by themselves, constitute a learning disability. Although learning disabilities may occur concomitantly with other disabilities (e.g., sensory impairment, mental retardation, serious emotional disturbance) or with extrinsic influences (such as cultural differences, insufficient or inappropriate instruction), they are not the result of those conditions or influences.

In 2008, Congress passed the Americans with Disabilities Act (ADA) Amendments Act to improve persons' ability to meet criteria for disability by expanding definitions, lowering the threshold for determining impact of disability, and expanding the list of areas for consideration to include reading, thinking, and concentrating. Currently, children and youth with disabilities, ages three to 21 years old, receive special education services through the Individuals with Disabilities Education Act (IDEA). This law guarantees each child a free, appropriate public education tailored to meet individual needs. It also protects the right of the children and their parents/guardians to timely evaluations, access to all meetings and paperwork, and transition planning and related services (Cortiella, 2011).

Studies have shown that effective instruction and intervention approaches—such as "Response to Intervention" (RTI)—provide early help for children with learning disabilities (LD) and can, in some cases, ameliorate the need for special education. Historically, students with LD are more likely to repeat a grade and are involved in much higher rates of school disciplinary actions than those without disabilities. Fortunately, implementation of federal regulations as well as improvements in the identification and instruction of individuals with LD are having a positive impact. During the past decade, there has been a decline in the numbers of school-age children being identified as having an LD. This may be the result of multiple factors, including a better understanding of reading acquisition, efforts to provide intervention activities before a special education designation is made, and changes in the definitions of disability categories in special education law and regulations.

Based upon 2008 data, 64% of students with LD are graduating with a regular high school diploma as compared to 52% a decade earlier. In addition, the dropout rate for students with LD is estimated at 22% (down from 40% in 1999). Students with LD are also being mainstreamed much more than ever before. Data from 2000 estimated that over half of students with LD were placed in special education settings. Today, nearly 80% of individuals diagnosed with LD remain within a general education setting (Cortiella, 2011).

Diagnostic Information

For the past 20 years or more, learning disabilities fell into the three distinct and separate categories of reading, writing, and mathematics. According to the *DSM-IV-TR* (APA, 2000), learning disorders are diagnosed when an individual's achievement is substantially below expected levels (e.g., defined as a discrepancy of two or more standard deviations between measures of achievement and intellectual ability) based upon their age, schooling, and level of intelligence. The individual's level of achievement is based upon scores obtained on an individually administered, standardized test in the areas of reading, writing, and mathematics. It is believed that learning disabilities persist into adulthood.

Diagnosis of learning disabilities must be differentiated from normal variations in academic achievement as well as difficulties that can be attributable to lack of opportunity, poor teaching, cultural factors, impaired vision or hearing, or other sensory deficit. Individuals with learning disabilities frequently have underlying deficits in cognitive processing skills (e.g., visual perception, linguistic processing, attention, memory, fluency, and processing speed, among others). In addition, learning disabilities are frequently found in individuals with a variety of general medical conditions such as lead poisoning, fetal alcohol syndrome, fragile X syndrome, etc. Learning disabilities are frequently comorbid conditions for persons with pervasive developmental disorders, attentional difficulties (e.g., ADHD), and communication disorders. In addition, individuals with intellectual disabilities (formerly mental retardation) often present with learning difficulties. However, the level of achievement in reading, written expression, and mathematics must be significantly below expected levels for the individual's schooling and severity of intellectual disability.

In recent years, the psychiatric community has been rethinking learning disorders, taking into consideration the input of international experts, educators, and advocacy groups. The *Diagnostic and Statistical Manual of Mental Disorders, 5th Edition (DSM-5),* scheduled for publication in the spring of 2013 by the American Psychiatric Association, stands poised to change the way clinicians and educators conceptualize learning disabilities by making two significant changes. First, research has shown that areas of learning are highly interrelated and shouldn't be divided as though they were separate disorders. In fact, the *DSM-IV-TR* specifically mentions that "mathematics disorder and disorder of written expression most commonly occur in combination with reading disorder" (APA, 2000, p. 51). Therefore, the three separate learning disabilities will be categorized into a single, overarching diagnosis called "Specific Learning Disorder" that intends to incorporate multiple deficits impacting academic achievement.

The second major change is the removal of requirements for a pronounced gap between a person's intellectual ability (IQ) and their academic achievement scores. According to Tannock (2013), the research did not support the inclusion of specific cognitive impairments in the diagnostic criteria because relationships between such deficits and learning difficulties were not robust. Therefore, *DSM-5* criteria include a low-achievement indicator and require that academic problems must have persisted for at least six months despite efforts to provide intervention. This change is significant because it provides clinicians enough guidance to diagnose with specificity and accuracy while lessening the reliance on rigid specific scores or grades.

Because it will take some time before changes in conceptualization, diagnosis, and treatment of learning disabilities will take place, information about *DSM-IV-TR* learning disorders is presented below.

Reading Disorder: In order to meet diagnostic criteria for a reading disorder, individuals must demonstrate poor reading achievement, as measured on an individually administered standardized test. Measures of reading such as reading accuracy, speed, and/or comprehension must be substantially below expected levels for an individual's chronological age, measured intelligence, or age-appropriate education. These deficits must significantly interfere with academic achievement or with activities of daily living that require reading. Reading difficulties must also be in excess of those typically found in individuals with other comorbid conditions (e.g., sensory impairments, pervasive developmental disability). It is estimated that 30% of school-age children have difficulty with reading, but there is no single method for effective remediation. The effects of reading disorders reach well beyond the classroom.

Persons meeting clinical criteria for a reading disorder may have any number or combination of difficulties, including difficulty with phonological processing, struggles with oral or silent reading (e.g., distortions, substitutions, or omissions), poor visual perception abilities (e.g., visual discrimination, visuospatial orientation, form constancy, spatial relations, closure, and figure ground), visual tracking problems, focusing problems, or difficulty with visual acuity.

The term "dyslexia" is often used interchangeably with "reading disorder." However, dyslexia is just one of several reading components within this broader definition. Dyslexia is a specific learning disability that is neurological in origin and characterized by difficulties with accurate and/or fluent word recognition and by poor spelling and decoding abilities. These difficulties typically result from a deficit in the phonological component of language that is often unexpected in relation to other cognitive abilities and the provision of effective classroom instruction. Secondary consequences may include problems in reading comprehension and reduced reading experience that can impede growth of vocabulary and background knowledge.

According to the International Dyslexia Association's fact sheet (2012), people diagnosed with dyslexia also have other problems, such as learning to speak, learning letter names and sounds, memorizing number facts, organizing written and spoken language, spelling, correctly doing math computations, and reading with sufficient speed. People with dyslexia may find it difficult to express themselves clearly or to fully comprehend what others mean when they speak. Such language problems are often difficult to recognize, but they can obviously lead to major problems at school and socially.

Mathematics Disorder: The specific term for mathematics disorder is "dyscalculia." In order to meet diagnostic criteria for a mathematics disorder, individuals must demonstrate poor achievement in mathematics, as measured on an individually administered standardized test. These deficits must significantly interfere with academic achievement or with activities of daily living that require mathematics. There are several different skills that may underlie poor achievement in mathematics, including language-based difficulties (e.g., understanding or naming mathematical terms, operations, or concepts, and decoding written problems into mathematical symbols), sequencing difficulties (e.g., following rules for applying mathematical steps), memory difficulties (e.g., attending to details, applying the correct operation, learning math facts), and visual-perceptual abilities (e.g., reading numerical symbols or arithmetic signs, visual chunking, etc.).

Disorder of Written Expression: In order to meet diagnostic criteria for a disorder of written expression, individuals must demonstrate poor achievement in writing, as measured on an individually administered standardized test. These deficits must significantly interfere with academic achievement or with activities of daily living that require composition of written texts (e.g., organized paragraphs or grammatically correct sentences). The act of writing is a highly integrative ability that involves language as well as perceptual and motor processes.

Disorders of written expression can be divided into two distinct categories: those involving expression of thought and those involving the mechanics of producing written work. There are several different skills that may underlie poor achievement in written expression, including difficulties with grammar or punctuation errors, poor paragraph organization, spelling errors, and excessively poor handwriting (formally known as dysgraphia). Impaired handwriting can interfere with learning to spell words in writing and speed of writing text.

Children with dysgraphia (referring to a disorder of handwriting) often have difficulty planning sequential finger movements, which may result in only impaired handwriting, only impaired spelling (without reading problems), or both impaired handwriting and impaired spelling. Some children with dysgraphia may demonstrate reversals of the directions of letters along a vertical axis (such as writing /b/ for /d/), inversions (flipping letters along a horizontal axis so that the letter is upside down), or transpositions (sequence of letters in a word is out of order). It is believed that these errors are symptoms rather than causes of handwriting problems (Brooks, Berninger, Abbott, & Richards, 2011).

Generally, poor handwriting and spelling are not, by themselves, enough to warrant the diagnosis. Instead, they must significantly impact the individual's ability to produce acceptable written work. Except for spelling, standardized tests for written skills are less well developed than those measures used to assess reading or mathematics ability. Instead, evaluation often relies on comparison between samples of the individual's written schoolwork and expected performance for the individual's age and IQ. In addition, the ability to copy, take dictation, and write spontaneously are all prerequisite skills needed to establish the presence and extent of the disorder. As one can see, the deficits and symptoms of learning disabilities are intertwined.

Learning Disorder–Not Otherwise Specified: This category is used for diagnosis of disorders in learning that do not meet criteria for any specific learning disorder. It may include problems in all three areas that significantly interfere with academic achievement, even though the student's performances on standardized, individually administered tests do not meet the required level of significance

Nonverbal learning disabilities (NVLD) are specific disorders that are right-brain–based and cause difficulties with "visual-spatial, intuitive, organizational, evaluative, and holistic processing functions" (Cortiella, 2011, p. 6). Children with NVLD are theorized to have right hemisphere deficits that contribute to problems with visuospatial organizational skills, psychomotor coordination, tactile-perceptual skills (sensory integration), reasoning, concept formation, and scientific reasoning (Spreen, Risser, & Edgell, 1995). They present as being poorly coordinated in both fine- and gross-motor skills, struggle with handwriting, and have difficulty performing mathematical computations. Individuals with NVLD are also reported to have attentional difficulties (e.g., inattention) that are not accompanied by hyperactivity or impulsivity.

Nonverbal communication plays a significant role in qualitative aspects of communication such as voicing (e.g., pitch and volume), facial expressions, and eye contact. . An estimated 65% of communication is thought to be nonverbal. Rourke (1995) proposed that individuals with NVLD tend to communicate in a rote, repetitive manner and have difficulties in nonverbal problem-solving as well as struggles with communicating feelings and preferences. In addition, individuals with NVLD often present with poor social judgment, difficulty reading social cues, poor recognition of faces and emotional expressions, and poor adaptability in novel interpersonal situations. Rourke (1995) also identified a set of deficiencies commonly found in individuals with NVLD, including deficits in mechanical mathematics (computation), deficiencies in visual-spatial and organizational skills, bilateral tactile deficits and bilateral psychomotor coordination deficits (particularly on the left side of the body).

Needs and Resources

There are many wide-reaching impacts of learning disabilities (LD) beyond the performance within the classroom. For this reason, early identification and intervention are particularly important for learning disorders. Children with LD are much more likely to be successful when their academic difficulties are accurately assessed and when they receive appropriate and effective services and treatment options. Regardless of which specific learning disability is identified, individuals with LD often present with many of the same needs and underlying deficits. According to Goldstein (1997), factor-analysis research categorizes skills necessary for efficient learning into two broad processes—auditory-verbal processes and nonverbal processes. Weaknesses in the former result in reading disorders and other language-based learning problems, while weaknesses in the later may result in difficulties with handwriting, mathematics, and certain social skills. In addition to academic needs, individuals with LD have needs in several other areas of functioning: sensory processing, cognitive processing, and behavioral, social, and emotional difficulties. Each of these is described in more detail below.

Sensory Processing: Individuals with LD exhibit struggles with internal arrhythmia or dysrhythmia (Evans, 1986), which are attributed to the inability to inhibit motor responses. Self-control is a precursor skill to the development of higher executive functions. Dyslexia-related deficits have been theorized to be related to underlying visual and auditory perception problems, motor coordination problems, and difficulty with fluency. Based upon this framework, some authors suggested that music listening and music-making can increase auditory sensitivity and perception (Sutton, 1993) and discuss the use of singing as a way of slowing down and emphasizing phonological processes (Blythe, 1998). More recently, research has been conducted regarding the correlation between timing skills and LD that has applications related to music skills. These include difficulty with tapping rhythms (Wolff, 2002; Wolff, Michel, Ovrut, & Drake, 1990), rapid automatic naming (Wolf, 1991), pitch processing (Besson, Schön, Moreno, Santos, & Magne, 2007; Magne, Schön, & Besson, 2006; Schön, Magne, & Besson, 2004), and detecting complex timing patterns (Kotz & Schwartze, 2010; Kujala et al., 2000; Schmidt-Kassow, Rothermich, Schwartze, & Kotz, 2011).

Cognitive Processing: There are various forms of cognitive processing that are at work as children learn, any of which can lead to learning difficulties. These include deficits in phonological processing, attentional difficulties, metacognition, and working memory.

In spite of the approximately 80% to 90% of students with reading difficulties thought to have deficits in phonological processing (Fletcher et al., 1994), there are only a few theories that propose to describe the underpinnings for deficits in phonological skills, timing skills, and perceptual difficulties. Tallal, Miller, and Fitch (1993) theorized that deficits in rapid temporal processing can lead to auditory perception problems which, in turn, then cause specific phonological perception problems. Nicholson, Fawcett, and Dean (1995) proposed deficits in cerebellar processing which negatively impact development of automated motor skills, phonological awareness, and literacy skills.

Individuals with LD frequently present with difficulties with attention and concentration. Berninger and Abbott (1994) found that individuals with disorders in written expression have difficulty with attention, executive functions, and motivation. Hooper et al. (1994) found that individuals with writing disorders also tend to exhibit conduct problems and have a tendency to withdraw which is likely the result of attempting to avoid classroom embarrassment or humiliation.

Many individuals with LD have deficits in metacognitive skills. Metacognition refers to a level of thinking that involves active control over the process of thinking that is used in situations that involve learning, planning how to approach the learning task, monitoring oneself, and evaluating progress toward task completion. Research studies have shown that the inability to control one's train of thought has significant real-world consequences ranging from academic difficulties (e.g., reading comprehension) to emotional struggles (e.g., unhappiness). Metacognition helps people to perform many cognitive tasks more effectively. Related to metacognition is working memory that involves the ability to maintain and manipulate information in one's mind while ignoring irrelevant distractions and intruding thoughts. Passolunghi (2006) claimed that working memory problems are a central deficit in children with a mathematics disorder and that working memory plays a crucial role both in calculation and in solving arithmetic word problems (Passolunghi, 2006; Passolunghi & Siegel, 2001).

It has been suggested that working memory training programs are effective as treatments for attention-deficit/hyperactivity disorder (ADHD) and other cognitive disorders in children as well as a tool to improve cognitive ability and scholastic attainment in typically developing children and adults (Melby-Lervåg & Hulme, 2013). The effects of working memory training programs (such as Cogmed) on both verbal and visuospatial working memory skills are reliable for short-term improvements. Younger children (below the age of 10 years) showed significantly larger benefits from verbal working memory training than did older children (11–18 years of age).

It is important to keep in mind that working memory interventions may improve focus and attention but they are not intended to improve critical reasoning skills or magically alleviate all of the symptoms of a learning disability. Therefore, to address underlying symptoms of a learning disability, it's important to engage in comprehensive interventions that specifically target the symptoms (e.g., phonological decoding interventions for people with dyslexia). In addition, regardless of the method, working memory improvements are usually transient, meaning that repeated practice and ongoing challenges are needed in order to maintain improvements. In other words, individuals must implement habits of concentrating and mentally manipulating complex material in order to maintain improvements in focus and concentration.

Kaufman (2013) believes that there is an underestimation of the extent to which multiple aspects of development—cognitive, physical, social, and emotional—all feed off each other and argues that there is evidence to suggest that the strongest and most widespread effects on cognitive functioning result from those interventions that target the "whole person," such as traditional martial arts training and enriched school curricula.

> [I]ntelligence isn't a single ability. There is an emerging consensus among intelligence researchers that general cognitive ability is composed of multiple interacting cognitive functions, and working memory is one of those crucial intellectual functions (Kaufman, 2013).

Behavioral Difficulties: Behavior is a major challenge for many youth with learning disabilities. There is still no clear linear relationship between learning disabilities and behavioral difficulties. For example, it is not clear if the symptoms of ADHD and other disruptive problems lead to disabilities in language or vice versa. In a review of research, Spreen (1989) suggests that emotional problems likely occur as a secondary reaction to the stress and frustration of school demands. However, regardless of the relationship, learning disabilities and other disorders frequently coexist. In fact, individuals with LD represent a disproportionately high number of incarcerated juveniles (over 14%) and LD is the second most common disability found among incarcerated juveniles (Cortiella, 2011)

The U.S. Department of Education funded National Longitudinal Transition Study-2 (NLTS2), a follow-up of the original NLTS, which was data collected from parents, youth, and schools over a span of 10 years with intent to provide a national picture of the experiences and achievements of young people as they transition into early adulthood. The NLTS2 found that one-third of youths diagnosed with LD are suspended or expelled from school at some point. According to school-reported data, students with LD accounted for 52% of all students with disabilities who experienced disciplinary actions (in- or out-of-school suspension or expulsion) during the 2007–2008 school year. This represents approximately 24% of all students identified with LD as having some disciplinary action at school, essentially demonstrating that individuals with LD are two to three times more likely to be subject to discipline than students without disabilities.

Social Difficulties: There is research to suggest that social skills deficits exist at a significantly higher rate among children with LD (Gresham, 1986; Hazel & Shumaker, 1988). In general, social skills deficits include difficulties in pragmatics (e.g., social use of language to greet people, make small talk, making friends) was well as difficulties in cooperation, taking turns appropriately, and problem-solving with others. As a result of these deficits, individuals with LD experience more peer rejection, seek more help from others, and are more frequently the victims of bullying than their peers without LD (Nabuzoka & Smith, 1993). In addition, peers described children with LD as shy more often than they did their nondisabled peers.

Emotional Difficulties: Although emotional difficulties are not included in the definition of LD, individuals with LD frequently exhibit emotional problems. Symptoms of depression and anxiety can precede, follow, or occur at the same time as the LD. In addition, individuals with LD also have deficits in adaptive behavior. Individuals with LD were found to have a more external academic locus of control, lower expectations for themselves, and a poorer concept about their academic ability (Chapman, 1980). It is also important to note that the externalizing and internalizing problems in younger students with LD continue to persist as they mature (Fuerst & Rourke, 1995).

Referral and Assessment

The vast majority of children with LD receive other forms of treatment such as tutoring, speech therapy, occupational therapy, and psychological services. If medication is prescribed, it is usually intended to address associative symptoms of the LD (e.g., difficulties with attention, behavior, or mood) rather than core symptoms of the LD.

Within the public school setting, individuals with LD are often placed within a Response-to-Intervention (RTI) process. RTI is designed for making decisions in preschool, general education, and special education with intent to create a well-integrated system of instruction and intervention. RTI is guided by child outcome data and is a multitier approach to the early identification and support of students with learning and behavior needs. The RTI process begins with high-quality instruction and universal screening of all children in the general education classroom. Students who struggle are then provided with interventions at increasing levels of intensity intended to accelerate their rate of learning. These services may be provided by a variety of personnel, including general education teachers, special educators, and specialists.

Many children with LD have Individualized Education Plans (IEPs) designed to include academic, social, and emotional/behavioral goals. Music therapists working with children and adolescents with LD in school settings are considered part of a multidisciplinary team, and music therapy is considered a related service according to the IDEA. Most often, the music therapy goals included in a child's IEP address deficits in academic areas of functioning (most commonly reading).

Music therapists may often serve as a consultant to music educators dealing with children and adolescents with emotional/behavioral disorders in music education classrooms. The relationship between the music therapist and the music educator is often collaborative in that they work together to create meaningful activities to support the learning of musical concepts while supporting the needs of children with LD.

Referrals for music therapy often come from parents rather than other providers or teachers. Within the community, private music therapy services are frequently sought by parents or other therapists as an additional augmentative treatment after other more traditional therapies have been put into a child's therapy schedule. As such, the music therapist's role in the treatment of children with LD tends to be as part of a multidisciplinary team, but is dependent upon the setting, referral source, and clinical needs. Music therapy assessment can identify limitations and weaknesses in children, as well as their strengths and potentials. Yet, only a few formal music therapy assessment processes are cited in the literature.

Most music therapy assessments serve to determine eligibility for services, to gather information on levels of functioning, and to determine treatment goals. Most assessments are conducted through behavioral observation within the music-making session, assessing peer-to-peer social interaction, use of communication and language, or musical responses as indicators of developmental levels of functioning (Schwartz, 2008, 2011). Some music therapy assessments incorporate evaluation of musical skills (e.g., pitch discrimination, rhythmic accuracy, etc.). However, no specific music therapy assessment has been developed specifically for learning disorders.

Brunk and Coleman developed the *Special Education Music Therapy Assessment Process* (SEMTAP) (1999) to assess the functioning of children and adolescents who receive special education services. The purpose of the SEMTAP is to determine eligibility for music therapy services for children who have an Individualized Education Plan (IEP). The SEMTAP process allows for comparison of a client's responses with and without music.

Another assessment tool, from Baxter et al. (2007), is called the *Individualized Music Therapy Assessment Profile* (IMTAP); this assesses client functioning in several domains for individuals with a wide range of diagnoses, including physical disabilities, communication disorders, autism, emotional disturbances, social impairments, and learning disabilities, among others. The IMTAP allows music therapists to use their own repertoire of methods and experiences to conduct the assessment. It is intended to be used as a tool for treatment planning and goal development, providing a baseline of overall functioning for treatment, and as a communication tool for parents and other therapists. In addition, the IMTAP attempts to identify effective strategies for each client.

It is suggested that the music therapist have access to the student's treatment plan, prior evaluations, and IEP to prior to or after completing assessment to effectively plan and design music therapy sessions. Through assessment, the music therapist gains understanding of the individual's unique clinical profile, strengths, weaknesses, and priority needs. From the data gathered in the assessment, the music therapist can select appropriate methods for treatment. Music therapy goals then ideally should address the child's academic needs as well as support other concerns in behavioral, emotional, and social areas of functioning.

Guidelines for Music Therapy Methods

There are several common guidelines that music therapists should consider when conducting experiences for individuals with LD. Rationale for incorporation of music methods comes from the growing body of literature that supports specific music experiences and activities to teach and practice essential literacy learning components. Individuals with LD often present with distractibility and attentional difficulties and are likely to respond better to visual support during music therapy instruction (Shehan, 1981).

While techniques for implementing music therapy vary from therapist to therapist, there are numerous articles specifically examining re-creative interventions to address associative, cognitive, behavioral, and social deficits for individuals with LD. However, it goes without saying that music therapists need a high level of clinical musicianship and also interpersonal skills in order to be sufficiently flexible and spontaneous when working with this population. Music therapists should consider their client's unique individual and musical differences while engaging them in music.

There are numerous nonmusical suggestions applicable to music therapists working with individuals with ADHD or LD. Montello and Coons (1998) suggest that individuals with LD are likely to respond better to highly structured music experiences. It is advised that music therapists be knowledgeable about basic behavioral techniques and concepts of operant conditioning. Music therapists need to understand concepts such as types of reinforcement (stimuli that increase behavior), types of punishment (stimuli that decrease behavior), escape, avoidance, and simple schedules of reinforcement (e.g., continuous reinforcement, fixed and variable ratio, fixed and variable interval). In music therapy treatment, the effect of reinforcement may be measured as an increase in the frequency of its expression (e.g., demonstrating the behavior more frequently), duration (e.g., demonstrating the behavior over longer periods of time), or magnitude (e.g., demonstrating the behavior with greater force or intensity), or decrease in latency (e.g., demonstrating the behavior more quickly following the onset of an environmental event).

Previous research indicates that some specific musical elements may play a role in a music therapist's choice of intervention. For example, several sources cite music's role in increasing memory functions and auditory perception in learning (Morton, Kershner, & Siegel, 1990; Roskam, 1979; Shehan, 1981; Wolfe & Horn, 1993), increasing attention span (Cripe, 1986), serving as a contingent reinforcer (Reid, Hill, Rawers, & Montegar, 1975), and increasing academic task performance (Abikoff, Courtney, Szeibel, & Koplewicz, 1996). Regardless of the music therapy methods used in treatment, music therapists most often addressed behavioral goals, followed by psychosocial goals, and then cognitive goals (Jackson, 2003).

Overview of Methods and Procedures

The following methods and procedures are used most commonly with clients with learning disabilities.

Receptive Music Therapy

- Contingent Music: the playing of music dependent upon the absence of a nondesired behavior or in the presence of a desired behavior.
- Auditory Perception Training: the use of live or recorded music for perceptual and discrimination development.

Re-creative Music Therapy

- Musical Play: includes a wide variety of musical interventions, including action songs, playing instruments with songs, instrumental songs (not improvisation), and musical games.
- Adaptive Music Lessons: a form of individual music therapy in which the music lesson format (most commonly using voice, piano, or guitar) is used to accomplish therapeutic goals such as sequencing ability, self-awareness, and self-regulation.
- Structured Movement Songs: Children perform movements supported by musical elements of rhythm, tempo, and style to address goals primarily related to cognitive processing and motor coordination.

Compositional Music Therapy

- Songwriting: occurs when changes are made to some or all of the lyrics and/or music of an existing song, or when a new song is written in its entirety.

Guidelines for Receptive Music Therapy

Not surprisingly, the majority of music therapy literature focuses on the use of re-creative methods for individuals with LD to address specific underlying cognitive, behavioral, and social functioning. Receptive music therapy experiences are intended to engage the client in a musical experience designed to provide stimulation of sensory or cognitive processes. Yet, there is a wide range of applications of receptive music therapy experiences as well as purposes. Receptive music therapy interventions can be designed to attract, foster, and sustain children's engagement in any number of ways—socially, emotionally, cognitively, sensorially, and motorically, as well as musically. The use of familiar melodies and repetition may aid recall of new information by taking advantage of previously learned information (e.g., song's melody). Musical mnemonics may be a useful technique for individuals with LD as well as typical peers (Gfeller, 1983).

Contingent Music

Overview. Contingent music is defined as the playing of music dependent upon the absence of a nondesired behavior or in the presence of a desired behavior. There are many applications of playing music to increase wanted behaviors and decrease unwanted behaviors. The premise for effectiveness of contingent music is based upon the concepts of behavioral modification strategies, especially operant conditioning, wherein desired behaviors are either positively or negatively reinforced. There are no known contraindications for this method. Level of therapy: augmentative.

Preparation. In advance of applying contingent music, the music therapist needs to assess both the environment and the clients. Use of preferred music or musical styles is suggested due to increased motivation and saliency. Once this is determined, the music therapist needs to prepare the music—either via speakers or using live music. If using recorded music, the music therapist should have music selections organized into a playlist (e.g., downloaded onto an iPod, recorded onto a CD) and ready to be played and stopped easily using a handheld remote control (if possible). If live music is used, the instruments should be tuned and ready to be played. The target behavior and how the music will be administered must be decided prior to implementing contingent music in order to provide consistency of feedback and to strengthen associative qualities of music with the target behavior. Considerations for how the music is presented include determining the duration of the music. For example, will the music be played for duration of the targeted behavior (e.g., while children are walking in line) or will it be played only when all children are lined up at the door? The music therapist must also determine when the music will be stopped. For example, will the music stop if children are not on task during an independent academic task or will it be stopped once the child engages in disruptive or hyperactive behavior (e.g., getting out of his seat, calling out in class)?

What to observe. The music therapist will monitor the targeted behavior and will fine-tune the contingent use of music to produce the best results. Qualitative data about the child's affective experience to the music (e.g., Is it still motivating?) can be assessed through observation of the child's facial expression as well as verbalizations. The music used in the procedure should be changed and/or modified as needed to ensure saliency. Observation of the targeted behavior without music must also be made in order to evaluate for generalization of the behavior into nonmusical conditions and across settings.

Procedures. The music therapist determines the child's preferred music, asking for a selection(s) that he would like to hear. Recordings of that music are prepared and readied for play. With remote in hand, the music therapist informs the child of when the music will be played (e.g., "as long as you stay sitting in your seat") and when it will be stopped (e.g., "when you get out of your seat"). Once the child understands the conditions for the music to be played, the music therapist begins the procedure. Contingent music can be administered according to natural time frames in the child's day, such as during math class, while at recess, or during dinner. However, in order for there to be demonstrated improvement on the targeted behavior, the child must have sufficient opportunities for repeated practice. The length of treatment using contingent music can vary from several weeks to a period of months, depending upon the targeted behavior and the established threshold for mastery. Typically, behaviors are considered mastered when they occur in an average of 80% of trials or four of five opportunities. Once mastery has been reached, the music therapist will change to an intermittent application of the music treatment, meaning that music will only sometimes be presented during the targeted behavior. During this phase of treatment, the music therapist is still monitoring the target behavior to ensure that mastery is maintained.

Adaptations. Contingent music can be applied in individual situations as well as used in groups. It can be administered in any number of environments, including school, home, therapy office, playground, etc.

Auditory Perception Training

Overview. Auditory Perception Training (APT) is a Neurologic Music Therapy technique that uses live or recorded music for perceptual and discrimination development as described below (Thaut, 2005). APT has other applications that can be used in receptive music therapy processes: auditory localization and auditory discrimination. The ability to discriminate between sounds is the key to language learning and literacy. For individuals with LD, the music therapist assesses auditory perception and awareness skills. Auditory discrimination is fundamental to the development of language skills. Weaknesses in auditory discrimination contribute to phonological deficits and later to reading as well as possibly other learning tasks.

Preparation. In advance of presentation of any auditory perception task, the music therapist must have determined which equipment to use (including electronic devices for sound production), which instruments, and how the experience will be implemented. Most individuals with LD have adequate auditory awareness, meaning that they are able to perceive sounds. Most often, music therapists will design APT experiences to support the most common deficit areas, namely those skills related to phonological processing, auditory discrimination, and auditory processing. Because individuals with LD often have difficulty with attention and processing, it is advised that the room be free of both visual and auditory distractions.

What to observe. The therapist will observe the individual's level of attention, motivation, and interest in the musical task while also taking into consideration patterns of response errors and level of effort. It is suggested that the experience be simplified or the task demands made easier should the student become frustrated. Similarly, students who appear bored or who perform accurately on tasks should be afforded more challenging experiences. With opportunities for repeated practice across several sessions, it is expected that students will make positive changes/improvements over time. However, it is important to keep in mind that subtle differences in performance on APT experiences across sessions may be related to variability in level of energy, mood, and general disposition.

Procedures. The therapist presents the APT task and verbally explains the expectations. For example, if the child is working on auditory perception tasks in relation to discrimination of higher or lower pitches, the music therapist will instruct the student on how to identify each type of pitch. Then, the client is presented with the auditory stimulus (e.g., single keys played in succession on the piano) either recorded or played live. Students with LD may have trouble with pitch discrimination (e.g., being "higher" or "lower") due to the abstract nature of this concept. One strategy to try is to teach the "feel" of pitches as they are projected through an overhead or white board. Instruct children to use their hands to follow the motion of the notes as the music therapist points and sings at the same time. The "higher" the note climbs on the staff, the higher everyone's hands move, and the pitch of the sung note becomes higher as well. By helping children learn to associate written notes and pitches with physical height on their body, they have another sensory method to help them "feel" the vertical distances of different notes.

When teaching a melodic ostinato, start by notating the rhythm of the ostinato and clapping it. For the rest of this concept, consider a simple children's song (e.g., "Three Blind Mice") in the following example. Once the class has a solid rhythmic understanding of the ostinato, indicate pitches by placing the notes of the rhythm at different heights on the board. Assign different pitches to a different part of the body and then have children tap the correct area on their body, in rhythm, while singing the name of the associated body part.

Adaptations. When targeting a specific phoneme (speech sound), the music therapist can intone two words (the correct word and the incorrect word) using two or three tones (depending on the number of syllables). APT experiences can also be modified to be more challenging or to address multiple perceptual or processing components at the same time. For example, a student may be asked to tap out the rhythm of the three-note pattern heard while singing the melody. In another example, students may be asked to reproduce/play increasingly longer series of desk bells after the music therapist plays them out of the student's line of sight.

GUIDELINES FOR IMPROVISATIONAL MUSIC THERAPY

The musical experiences improvised during sessions typically arise from the vocal and motor output provided by the child. The child plays a central role in the creation of the music and is an active creator. The child plays various instruments that require no formal training or experience, while the music therapist improvises music that reflects and expands on the child's music-making, emotional state, and/or movements.

Some researchers describe music improvisation as a "right brain" activity that is related to feeling, creative expression, and artistic talent, while research is associated with typical "left brain" activities such as cognitive analysis, linear and sequential tasking, and numeric calculation. It is the intent of the music therapist to create a musical environment that is responsive to the dynamics of physiological measures and aimed at clinical goals (Miller, 2011).

Goals in improvisatory music therapy methods with individuals with LD are likely very similar to those designed for addressing deficits commonly found in persons with ADHD, such as improving impaired timing, decreasing impulsivity, enhancing self-organization, improving body awareness, and increasing self-control. Creating music with others requires considerable attention and self-control. Accuracy in the timing of motor responses (such as playing a drum during an improvisation) depends upon an individual's ability to plan and organize a response. It requires estimation of time and anticipation of future events. These skills are directly related to working memory, a cognitive process often impaired in individuals with ADHD as well as those with LD. The therapist's role during improvisational methods is to provide necessary structure, reinforcement, and organization to support clinical objectives and academic needs.

At the time of this publication, there were no articles describing the specific use of compositional methods in music therapy for individuals with LD. It is suspected however, that while not specifically discussed, compositional methods may have been incorporated into more eclectic studies (see Research Evidence).

GUIDELINES FOR RE-CREATIVE MUSIC THERAPY

Music therapists frequently design original music activities to address nonmusical goals. Active music approaches are inherently multisensory and naturally reinforcing, able to convey and teach many types of information. Singing, dancing, and action songs are common childhood experiences. Because re-creative music therapy methods are active and require accurate auditory and motor timing skills, they provide much needed multisensory training for persons with LD. In particular, songs have wonderful potential to teach vocabulary and word use, categorization, similarities, opposites, and many other concepts simply because singing them provides students with the opportunity for repeated practice. Singing songs also serves as a vehicle for practicing reading fluency and comprehension.

It has long been suggested that rhythm activities can facilitate internal organization (Gaston, 1968) and coordination of mind and body (Montello, 1996), as well as help control impulses by providing a sense of internal security (Bruscia, 1987). Music lessons were found to have a positive impact on students with poor reading (Douglas & Willatts, 1994). In addition, active music-making experiences were found to improve rapid temporal processing skills, phonological skills, and spelling in children with dyslexia (Overy, 2002).

Experiences such as musical play and group singing often pair music and information, while music and movement experiences address auditory perception skills and memory. It is important that the music therapist be familiar with current children's music groups, artists, and theme songs to popular children's programs as well as their clients' favorite musical songs and styles. Adaptations of familiar children's music provide opportunity for addressing clinical needs while taking advantage of the child's motivation and interest in his preferred music. Therapist-created songs are composed with specific therapeutic objectives in mind.

Musical Play

Overview. Musical play experiences include a wide variety of interventions, including action songs, playing instruments with songs, instrumental songs (not improvisation), and musical games. Most musical play experiences are highly structured activities that actively engage the client in playing along with a song or moving in time to music. The music therapist engages individuals in a musical experience that incorporates repetition and structure to promote development of underlying cognitive skills associated with the individual with LD's specific weaknesses.

Research has shown that music and movement activate both brain hemispheres (Hannaford, 1995; Morton, Kershner, & Siegel, 1990). In these methods, the client's response within music can be instrumental, verbal, vocal, or behaviorally oriented (e.g., movement). Some basic goals for musical play methods include foundational skills for communication such as awareness of and responding to environmental cues (e.g., starting and stopping, modulating play to match musical qualities, imitating rhythmic or melodic patterns), early play skills (e.g., engaging in reciprocal pattern play, mutual or joint play, playing in synchrony, responding to a music cue with learned rhythmic or melodic pattern), and more sophisticated responses that promote independence and creativity.

Musical play experiences can be used within both individual and group sessions. When used in group settings, the goals often include social skills development such as listening skills, direction-following, anticipation and motor planning of defined responses, and self-organization (e.g., impulse control). These methods may need to be modified in order to be used for children with severe behavioral or social difficulties. However, other than the possibility of the inability to adapt instruments to accommodate physical or sensory limitations, there are no known contraindications to using musical play experiences in therapy. Level of therapy: augmentative.

Preparation. The music therapist will need to spend some time setting up the room and gathering appropriate instruments prior to implementing this method, especially when more than one musical play experience will be used in the session. Considerations of possible therapeutic needs for space, seating, and safety should all be made. The choice of songs to be used should be made prior to the session as well. Choices of songs are made by keeping in mind the client's need for structure and stability, rhythmic sophistication, sound tolerance, and musical style and instrument preferences. Since many children with LD also struggle with impulsivity and hyperactivity, care should be taken to ensure that the musical experiences do not overexcite or overarouse the child. In addition, they may have difficulty in waiting to play the instruments, so it suggested that they be allowed to handle and try out any novel instruments prior to their use in the experience.

The music therapist should also consider the client's clinical profile when using musical play activities. In particular, the music therapist will consider the child's academic and behavioral needs to design musical play experiences. Since individuals with LD often have deficits with rhythmic reproduction, experiences that encourage repetition and offer repeated practice are highly suggested. The music therapist may choose songs that have accessible, familiar meter, repetitive rhythms, simpler instrumentation, and predictable structure. Songs that have multiple juxtaposing rhythms, thick harmonic structures, or sophisticated chord progressions might not be suitable for some clients with LD, since they may lack perceptual organization and can become overwhelmed or frustrated.

What to observe. The music therapist will pay attention to how the client interacts with the materials or instrument assigned, including whether the child is able to effectively find the beat, reproduce rhythms, match pitch, or perceive melodic elements in the music. The music therapist will also observe if there are misalignments in timing between vocal/verbal and motoric demands of the activity.

Deficits in temporal timing can be related to underlying cognitive processing or to motor coordination weaknesses. How the music therapist understands these misalignments determines where to intervene and support the individual with LD. Some individuals may require the activity to be slowed to half-time in order to be successful; others may need to have repeated practice in the mechanics of the musical experience. Overall, how well a child participates is often an indication of self-organization, self-regulation, awareness of others, and relatedness to the group as a whole.

Affective responses and range of creativity shown while playing are also important. When presented in a group setting, the music therapist will observe both intrapersonal and interpersonal responses and interactions.

Procedures. The music therapist can set up and direct musical play experiences in any number of ways. Initially, children with LD will perform best under highly structured conditions and when the music therapist is highly directive. For the child with LD, these experiences and skills serve to address key deficits in metacognition, working memory, and self-awareness.

When introducing a new song, game, or music and movement experience, the equipment can be placed in front of the child (but within easy reach) to minimize impulses to play while holding it. Instrumental songs most often focus on learning, remembering, and reproducing simple rhythmic or melodic patterns. It is advised that mastered experiences be modified slightly once the general concepts and goals for the song have been achieved. This can be accomplished by decreasing the amount of structure and control within the experience, providing clients an opportunity to lead or direct the activity, or modifying rules for play. To maintain the interest and motivation of children with LD during their favorite activities, assign different instruments, adjust one musical aspect of the song (e.g., tempo, key, etc.), or simply change the order of the instruments played.

Many musical play activities used primarily to address attention, cognitive processing, and impulsivity commonly found in individuals with ADHD can also be used for individuals with LD. Some examples of musical play activities include musical versions of "stop and go" activities, songs that require adjustments in playing as songs become faster/slower, louder/quieter, or change in style. Other musical play experiences include assigning children to play instruments at designated times (i.e., when they hear a word) during a song or story, doing seated rhythmic imitation using egg shakers to instrumental music, musical chairs, musical hot potato games (using directives to repeat a rhythm on the instrument passed around the circle), rhythm stick activities, and more.

Adaptations. The adaptations for using musical play in music therapy are countless. By incorporating movement paired with instrument-playing, the client gains practice in more sophisticated levels of responding and has opportunity for greater self-organization and self-regulation. Often, these activities can become a warm-up experience that leads into others. Similarly, it is quite common for music therapists to combine action or movement activities with instrument-playing and singing. By using virtual or electronic instruments rather than real instruments, the child with LD is given opportunities for expanded creativity, novel sensory experience, and adaptive use of technology.

Adaptive Music Lessons

Overview. Adaptive music lessons are a form of individual music therapy wherein the intent of instruction is on clinical goals rather than development of musical skill. While adaptive music lessons could be conducted on any instrument, the most common are typically voice, piano, guitar, and drums. During the adaptive music lesson, the therapist interacts with the client in the process of making music on a selected instrument. The intent of the session is to address clinical goals to improve the client's functioning. For students with LD, common therapeutic goals include addressing deficits in the following areas: verbal or auditory processing (including awareness and discrimination of pitch and rhythm), motor control and coordination (including left-right confusion), attention and concentration, sequencing, memory, and temporal processing.

In addition to addressing cognitive processes and motor skills, adaptive lessons may also improve metacognitive skills such as self-regulation and modulation, self-awareness, sequencing, working memory, and selective attention. In addition, adaptive music lessons also provide practice in considering others and adjusting behavior. It should be noted that referrals for adaptive music lessons often come from parents of children with LD or at the request of the child himself. For this reason, the music therapist will need to spend some time explaining the intent and purpose of the sessions to parents.

Individuals with dyslexia (in particular) may be strong kinesthetic learners (meaning that they learn by doing or touching) as a compensation for deficits in visual or auditory functioning. Taking this into consideration, Vance (2004) made several suggestions for adapting music instruction for these students. Most important, she suggests working with students individually and being alert for signs of frustration. Suggestions for accommodations during music lessons include:

- Having a student who struggles with learning rhythms clap, tap, or stomp a section until mastered before playing it on an instrument;
- Using the Kodály method of speaking rhythms as preassigned syllables (e.g., "ta," "ti") for teaching rhythm;
- Initially teaching using a "playing by ear" method (such as Suzuki method) prior to teaching how to read music notation;
- Marking keys or positions on an instrument using color-coded methods;
- Incorporate ear-training activities into each lesson (e.g., pitch discrimination, pitch matching, timing activities);
- Breaking physical movements into the smallest and simplest units possible;
- Saying note names out loud while playing;
- Singing or playing along with the student.

No contraindications are known for adaptive music lessons. Level of therapy: augmentative.

Preparation. The decision to engage in an adaptive music lesson requires preparations prior to the first session. The music therapist will need to assess the client's basic functioning level, ability to follow directions and self-correct, level of engageability and motivation, and physical or emotional barriers that may influence the choice of instrument. For example, a child with poor auditory discrimination skills and limited attention span might not be a good candidate for adapted violin lessons. Lessons on piano are suggested for individuals with low frustration, short attention span, or limited self-awareness. It is the music therapist's responsibility to help clients and their families make realistic instrument choices given the clinical needs and abilities as well as therapeutic goals.

Preparation for sessions needs to take into consideration the needs for physical space for the lesson and required equipment (e.g., music stand). The music therapist will have appropriate sheet music, CD player, and/or recording device, as well as other materials needed to conduct the session (e.g., tuners, metronome, extra strings for guitar, etc.). It will be particularly important for the child with attentional difficulties to have as few distractions in the room as possible. Therefore, do not conduct the lesson next to a window, near a fan, or near a cluttered table. If at all possible, the music and instrument should be the only things in his line of sight.

What to observe. The music therapist observes the client's quality of participation in the session, paying particular attention to frustration, ability to understand instructions, physical limitations, and coordination issues, as well as cognitive skills related to the process of learning music. Because the adapted music lesson involves more than simply playing the instrument, the music therapist must be able to communicate basic musical constructs to the child in a manner that supports their process. At some point, most clients will be expected to be able to play notes from a page of sheet music. Therefore, didactic instruction on ear-training, musical notation, music theory, and music history may all enter the session. The music therapist will also pay particular attention to the level of effort and motivation the client demonstrates. The music therapist will be interested in finding out if the client practices their instrument between sessions and their expectations for their lessons, as well as their progress in playing it.

Procedures. As with traditional music lessons, clients will spend at least some time with warm-ups, review of familiar materials, technical exercises, ear-training, and learning new information. While adaptive music lessons are conducted much like other music lessons, music therapists adapt procedures and devise teaching strategies according to the needs of the student. Some simple teaching strategies may include teaching rhythm or melody in isolation, the use of color-coded keys (e.g., on the piano), labeling notes with letters, using larger notation, or creating and improvising musical jingles to remember note names, key signatures, etc.

During the adaptive music lesson, the music therapist maintains an active and supportive role with the client by providing encouragement and gentle redirection and eliciting responses on the performance. The music therapist attempts to assist the client in improving underlying cognitive weaknesses by pointing out commonalities between errors, indicating aspects of playing to attend to, and providing assistance in how to overcome common hurdles. The music therapist may accompany the child by playing the same thing or providing harmonic structures in order to practice playing along with others. At the end of the session, the music therapist will identify tasks to practice at home, theory worksheets to complete, etc.

Structured Movement Songs

Overview. Structured movement songs are extremely common in childhood music experiences. All children can benefit from structured movement songs since movement, supported by music, can be a powerful combination for the child who is challenged developmentally. There are a wide variety of applications and objectives for structuring movement songs. They can be designed to incorporate practice in discrimination and ability to adjust to variations in tempo, rhythm, and style. They can also be designed to facilitate motor coordination and address deficits in temporal perception (e.g., timing) by having students starting and stopping movement with selected music, following directions for movement, moving cooperatively with a peer partner, or imitating another's movements. Movement songs can also be designed to facilitate practice in sequencing skills, improve auditory discrimination and phonological processing, address memorization of academic concepts, and support cognitive fluency (e.g., producing familiar actions fast).

Music therapists should monitor the level of participation and be alert to any indicators of decreased motivation and engagement. There are no known contraindications for movement songs aside from the possibility that those students with high levels of impulsivity and psychomotor activity may become overaroused. Level of therapy: auxiliary or augmentative.

Preparation. Structured movement songs can be implemented in a number of environments, depending upon the size of the available space. When space is constricted, students may participate in in-seat movement experiences (which, incidentally, provide better structure for students with higher levels of impulsivity). Children may also lie or sit on the floor if there is adequate space.

The music therapist carefully selects songs and musical material that support and enhance the desired movement or sequence of movements. Explore all the different types of movement as they connect to music. Duple meter is great for running; 6/8 is a jumping sound; 3/4 can be for rocking or swaying. 5/8 or 7/8 provide an opportunity for uneven duration of motions and can help to strengthen attention or muscle tone. Harmonic or melodic elements can create a mood or atmosphere that can help the children put learned movement patterns into a larger world context.

What to observe. Most typical children will make gains and benefit from watching movements being performed by others. However, for the individual with LD, active participation is key. Movement patterns, like music, develop sequentially in early childhood. Consult with a movement therapist or physical therapist for help in knowing which movement activities are developmentally appropriate for the child. The supporting music can help suggest movement vocabulary for the child.

Procedures. Structured movement songs can be a single element within a music therapy session or can be the entire focus of the session. Although movement is instinctual for young children, they will generally require modeling of movement or movement sequences within a structured format. Initially, music therapists will pair verbal directives and lyrics with the movement desired (as in pair-associated learning techniques). Movement activities that allow for both a verbal and motoric response are suggested for those individuals with LD who do not naturally find the pulse or meter of a song. During this level of intervention, music therapists are likely to use live music rather than recorded music to allow for individual differences in performance and to accommodate for slower processing and difficulties with motor coordination.

Movement songs for individuals with more severe LD are likely to use only body movements that are supported by the music therapist's singing. The supporting music can be provided with rhythmic percussion, voice only, harmonic progressions, or through recorded music. Exaggerated actions and affect often help a child to attempt new motions and build body awareness that supports sensory integration processes. If there is accompaniment, it is likely to be simple yet rhythmically strong and predictable (such as a march), in order to promote integration of cognitive and motoric responses. Once the student is able to accurately produce the movements, the additional task demand of verbalizing, vocalizing, or singing words can be added to the movements. To increase complexity and maintain interest, music therapists are encouraged to layer additional musical elements one at a time or to increase the difficulty of rhythmic components of the experience.

Adaptations. There are numerous ways to adapt structured music songs for both individual and group sessions. For individuals with LD, these adaptations are primarily determined by the type of goal being addressed. For individuals with needs related to cognitive processing, the music therapist may choose to lessen task demands by using instruments that do not require as much physical coordination to be successful to enable the focus to be on other aspects of the experience. When the focus is on sensory integration and processing skills that encompass motor skills, the music therapist may choose to use a variety of instruments that, over a series of music therapy sessions, become increasingly more sophisticated in order to allow the child to build on skills while still having success.

GUIDELINES FOR COMPOSITIONAL MUSIC THERAPY

Compositional methods focus on the use of therapist-generated or client-generated musical experiences to address nonmusical goals. Songs and instrumental compositions in therapy generally arise out of an identified clinical issue and/or the music therapist's desire to support therapeutic aims in a more structured manner. Sometimes the composition arises out of the client-therapist's musical interaction or musical themes from the session. At other times, the composition can arise out of a verbal discussion of interpersonal struggles or emotional difficulties.

When the music therapist creates compositional experiences for or with individuals with LD, the resulting composition likely contains lyrics that provide information on improving behavior, attention, and working memory. As with the use of compositions for individuals with behavioral and emotional needs arising from other clinical conditions, compositions may be created to address rules for good classroom behavior (e.g., staying in seat, raising hands to speak), using manners (e.g., recognizing when to use please and thank you), or basic life skills (e.g., understanding roles of community helpers such as police and firefighters, recognizing safety signs), etc. For higher-functioning individuals with LD, compositional themes of peer pressure, bullying, self-esteem, disappointment, competition, self-identity, problem-solving, and other psychological processes may be expressed.

Songwriting

Overview. Songwriting is simply the process of creating of lyrics set to melody. Of course, there are many variations in how songwriting is implemented, based upon the therapeutic intent of the experience, the needs of the client, and musical elements that support the goals for treatment. Songwriting may be indicated for children and adolescents with LD to address underlying deficits in phonological processing or cognitive fluency, to support learning academic concepts, or to address emotional/behavioral symptoms. For some individuals with LD, merely thinking of and suggesting words to fill in or replace those in a familiar song can be challenging (e.g., lyric substitution). However this method can foster cognitive and processing skills and encourage creativity.

Geist et al. (2008) used song language substitution to increase social greetings and support literacy. Song lyric substitution might also be designed to increase the use of novel language, to provide an opportunity for expression, and to encourage problem-solving and creativity. Songwriting may be used to provide personal reflection, encourage problem-solving, and promote emotional growth. Group songwriting can be used to develop problem-solving skills, increase group cooperation and participation, and improve tolerance and respect for others. Group songwriting helps develop shared responsibility and the ability to compromise and work cooperatively for a single purpose.

Songwriting may be contraindicated for individuals with severe communication disorders and may be too overwhelming for students requiring a higher degree of structure and support. Level of therapy: auxiliary or augmentative.

Preparation. In early intervention, the therapist will most often create or adapt a musical structure with enough flexibility for the child to contribute new song lyrics. Prior to beginning, the therapist determines the melodic, rhythmic, and structural format of the song. Lyrics allow for multiple responses so that every child's input can be incorporated. For children with limited speech, the therapist might have drawing materials or assistive technology available.

What to observe. Songwriting relies on active participation from the child, including singing, speaking, or drawing the new lyrics. However, the music therapist can modify task demands to allow for adequate processing time within the music for the child to independently answer. The music therapist will observe the client's level of participation, paying particular attention to struggles with word-finding or issues with sequencing or cognitive processing as it relates to producing rhythms, melody, and language-oriented tasks (e.g., writing, spelling, etc.). In addition, the music therapist is alert to indicators of frustration that may indicate the need to modify task demands.

Procedures. The therapist composes or adapts a song that has lyric content that is appropriate to the developmental level and needs of the child. Harmonic, melodic, or rhythmic elements should create a musical atmosphere that matches or enhances the concepts or themes chosen. The words offered are then incorporated into the melody, using similar melodic rhythm and melodic contour. The therapist can also suggest words or ideas and help make the cognitive, social, or emotional connection from the music to the child's new words and ideas. Language use can be reinforced by using melody and rhythm to support developmental syntax and grammar. For instance, to encourage lyric substitution about emotions, the therapist might change the mode of the melody to minor. The therapist will most often introduce the song either through words or by beginning to sing or play. The child will need to understand the expectation for adding lyrics. The therapist can do this through verbal directions or through using musical pauses and facial affect to indicate that they will wait for the child.

Adaptations. Because individuals with LD also have comorbid difficulties in motor coordination, cognitive processing, and behavior, the goals for song lyric substitution can be bolstered by combining the music with other artistic expression such as movement, drawing, or painting. The music therapist can collaborate or consult with educators or other arts therapists on developmentally appropriate methods. In addition, collaboration with the music teacher may prompt creative compositional methods that not only meet educational objectives, but also address related needs in social and behavioral areas of functioning. Because the majority of individuals with LD are served within the general education setting, positive experiences with typical peers may promote an increase in cooperative skills, improve peer relationships, and provide practice in relating to others.

Working with Caregivers

According to Jellison (2000), opportunities for the inclusion of music therapy services within Individualized Family Services Plans (IFSP) are increasing as a result of state and federal legislation that includes families in intervention. There are numerous opportunities for music therapists' collaboration with various professionals and educators within special education for individuals with LD. Some opportunities come from the ability to act within a consultative role to other professionals, while other opportunities arise from the ability to implement intervention.

When working with children with LD, consideration of the child as part of a larger system is essential. Music therapists are encouraged to recognize the essential role that parents and other family members play in children's development and their academic achievement. Music therapists have a unique opportunity to support and collaborate with teachers, especially music educators, and other therapists by listening and observing the interaction between the child and other colleagues while creating a musical environment that enhances the experiences of their interaction. By sharing music therapy strategies with others, children are afforded help to ensure generalization and opportunity for practice and retention of skills.

Within a consultative role to the music educator, the music therapist can serve as a resource for designing and implementing interventions to address the general classroom environment and support specific academic skills. For other therapists (e.g., speech/language pathologist, occupational therapist, behavior therapist, psychologist), a music therapist may guide and inform them regarding simple strategies to deepen their musical experience with their clients by using music intentionally, but within their scope of practice.

Although not specific to individuals with LD, music therapists can provide music therapy interventions within the context of the family. Music therapy interventions used in family sessions most often will include movement, instrument-playing, and singing songs. The goals for family music therapy interventions are often to increase positive parent/child interactions, to promote communication between family members, to provide an opportunity for generalization of skills, and to demonstrate techniques to family members (Allgood, 2005).

Research Evidence

It is widely assumed that music learning, music reading, and participation in music activities enhance academic achievement and cognitive development. Yet, there is a need for more specific research documenting the effectiveness of music therapy procedures and methods with children who have special education needs. The need for specific research on both the musical abilities and the effects of music therapy interventions for individuals with learning disabilities is even greater.

There are some studies investigating correlations between music abilities and academic abilities, particularly in the area of music and reading. For example, Cutietta (1996) found that music participants had better discrimination for perceiving language and were able to effectively transfer music skills to the development of language and reading skills. More specifically, these include phonological awareness (Anvari, Trainor, Woodside, & Levy, 2002), phonemic awareness, sight identification, orthographic awareness, pitch discrimination (Fisher & McDonald, 2001), and fluency (Register, Darrow, Stanley, & Swedberg, 2007).

Recent research suggests underlying difficulty with timing for persons diagnosed with dyslexia. Overy, Nicolson, Fawcett, and Clarke (2003) found that children with dyslexia demonstrated particular difficulties on tests involving rapid temporal processing. They also noted that individuals with dyslexia tended to score higher than control subjects on pitch skills (e.g., melody discrimination, pitch discrimination, and pitch matching) while performing more poorly than control subjects on tests of timing (e.g., tempo copying, tempo discrimination, and song beat). Their results suggest that rhythm skills and training in musical timing may be areas of focus for music therapy intervention.

Several case studies found positive outcomes in internal organization using creative or eclectic music therapy approaches (Aigen, 1997; Haines, 1989; Lefebvre, 1991; Robbins & Robbins, 1991). In addition, some research incorporated the use of both passive (music listening) and active music interventions (singing, instrument-playing, and movement) within the same study. Register, Darrow, Standley, and Swedberg (2007) found that students with reading disorders who participated in music therapy interventions made greater gains in word decoding, word knowledge (vocabulary), and reading comprehension than did students receiving the "normal" reading program over a four-week program.

Receptive Methods

It has long been known that the use of familiar melodies can aid in learning new information. For the past 40 years, researchers have demonstrated that paired associates embedded in stories or in sentences can assist students in learning them more quickly (Austen, 1977; MacMillan, 1970) and that the presentation of information in songs facilitates greater retention (Lathom, 1970). More recently, Shehan (1981) examined pair-associated learning using musical, verbal, musical/visual, and verbal/visual approaches to short-term memory tasks for children with LD. Specifically, within the musical conditions, she sang the word pairs using an ascending perfect fourth interval. She concluded that the music/visual and verbal/visual teaching strategies produced the best results.

Musical mnemonics are already used extensively in preschool and primary educational settings to teach concepts such as the alphabet (using the tune "Twinkle, Twinkle, Little Star"). Gfeller (1983) used a variety of experimental conditions to examine the effects of melodic-rhythmic mnemonics on students with LD's ability to learn multiplication facts. Conditions included verbal rehearsal with repetition, verbal rehearsal with repetition with modeling and cuing, musical rehearsal, and musical rehearsal with repetition with modeling and cuing. She found that using the melodic-rhythmic mnemonics condition produced the best results and significantly impacted retention of multiplication tables for students with LD as well as typical students.

Several studies have examined the therapeutic effects of various receptive methods of music therapy using operant learning paradigms. Contingent music listening can be used effectively for a variety of clinical purposes, including teaching social and adaptive skills, teaching academic skills, increasing motivation on nonpreferred tasks, and improving behavior. The flexibility of using contingent music as an effective technique for behavior change is demonstrated in numerous studies in the 1970s and 1980s (although the most were not specific to individuals with learning disabilities). Madsen, Smith, and Feeman (1988) found that students with behavior and/or learning problems were more motivated to volunteer to be tutors for younger children when they had the opportunity to earn a music tape.

Cripe (1986) examined the effects of contingent rock music on hyperactivity and attention span in children with ADHD. Music conditions were administered via headphones without options for volume control. During 20-minute sessions, clients either engaged in free play or were instructed to work on mazes and coloring pictures. Results were clinically significant and indicated that subjects engaged in more off-task behaviors during the nonmusic conditions of the study vs. the music conditions. Findings in Cripe's study can be applied to individuals with LD, given the associative behavioral difficulties that are often present.

Abikoff et al. (1996) compared the effects of "extra-task stimulation" on arithmetic task performance in boys with ADHD and typical peers (those without ADHD). Subjects' performance was evaluated across three conditions: high stimulation (preferred music), low stimulation (voice recording of an evening business report), and no stimulation (silence). The music was individually chosen for the subjects to ensure saliency. Abikoff and his colleagues found that the children without ADHD performed similarly under all three conditions, while those children with ADHD performed significantly better under the music condition than the other two conditions. Again, these findings can be applied to individuals with LD.

Improvisational Methods

At the time of this publication, there are no music therapy articles that specifically address the efficacy of improvisational methods for individuals with learning disabilities. However, it is assumed that some research already cited may have incorporated improvisational experiences within their methodologies. Unfortunately, none of the research highlighted improvisational methods.

Re-creative Methods

There are numerous research articles on the use of re-creative methods to address deficits and skills generally lacking in individuals diagnosed with learning disabilities. Researchers have investigated the relationship between Orff, Kodály, or Dalcroze instruction and participation in choral, band, or orchestral ensembles on reading achievement (Douglas & Willatts, 1994; Harris, 1977; Hurwitz, Wolff, Bortnick, & Kokas, 1975)

Overy, Nicolson, Fawcett, and Clarke (2003) found that children with dyslexia performed much more poorly on tasks of song rhythm and spelling. In the process of tapping a rhythm to a song, subjects with dyslexia had difficulty in tapping the rhythm that corresponds directly to the onset of syllables in a familiar song. They found that children with dyslexia do not automatically utilize syllable segmentation as a phonological strategy. Interestingly, poor performance on the tapping task was correlated to poorer spelling ability in children with dyslexia. They suggest that musical activities that focus on rhythm skills can have a positive effect on development of phonological skills and spelling abilities.

There is general agreement that rehearsal of rhythmic tasks is likely to lead to improvement in internal organization and impulse control (Gaston, 1968; Gibbons, 1983) and improve body awareness (Wigram, Pederson, & Bond, 2002) and motor coordination (Gibbons, 1983; Moore & Mathenius, 1987; Thaut, 1985). Children with and without disabilities tend to respond similarly to the same teaching techniques and methodologies. For example, rhythm duplication was increased when spoken syllables were added to tapped rhythms (Atterbury, 1983), and rhythm perception was improved with the addition of auditory prompts and cues (Larson, 1981). Goswami (2011) discusses the potential benefits of therapeutic interventions or educational practices based on rhythm and music. She suggests that remediation based on rhythm and music (e.g., matching syllable patterns to metrical structures in singing, playing instruments, or moving in time, working with metrical poetry, or singing nursery rhymes) might be beneficial in developmental language disorders.

Not specific to individuals with learning disabilities, several studies demonstrate the efficacy of music applications. When structured as a cue or prompt, music was found to have a positive impact on several learning tasks such as improved recall of multiplication facts (Gfeller, 1983), accuracy of paired-associate learning (Shehan, 1981), and rate of learning telephone numbers (Wolfe & Horn, 1993). In addition, contingent use of preferred music was found to improve arithmetic skills (Dorow, 1976; Miller, 1977).

Only a few studies have examined the correlation between the difficulties of musicians with dyslexia and reading difficulties. Researchers have found that individuals with dyslexia often experience difficulty in processing information that includes words and names referring to the pitch or the lengths of notes and musical symbols (Ganschow, Lloyd-Jones, & Miles, 1994; Hubicki, 1994). These difficulties are viewed as deficits in associative learning and are similar to the pattern of difficulties experienced in written language. They propose that problems with representation of time, rhythm, and sequencing are similar to the difficulties they have in identifying and representing phonological units. However, Jaarsma, Ruijssenaars, and Van den Broeck (1998) suggest that the explicit instruction of subskills in music instruction (e.g., adapting note reading with color coding) do not necessarily improve more integrated and automated processes. Instead, they propose putting more emphasis on helping students acquire subskills more implicitly by overlapping components of musical instruction.

Stanley and Hughes (1997) investigated the effects of a systematic music-reading intervention on prereading and prewriting skills of four-year-olds in an early intervention setting. They found that music therapy interventions significantly improved students' measures of print awareness, print concept, and developmental writing and language skills over a 15-week program when compared to students who did not participate in the intervention.

Bryan, Sullivan-Burstein, and Mathur (1998) found that when students with learning disabilities listened to music selected to promote positive affect, they interpreted social scenarios more positively and used more embellishments (details) as compared to students in the neutral or self-induced conditions.

Montello and Coons (1998) found improvements in attention, motivation, and emotional functioning following both active rhythm–based and passive listening–based group music therapy for individuals with emotional, learning, and behavioral difficulties.

Research on the musical abilities of individuals with learning disabilities is inconclusive. Atterbury (1983) found no significant differences in rhythm perception between students with LD and typical peers, although differences were observed in rhythm performance tasks. McGivern, Berka, Languis, and Chapman (1991) found that first, second, and third graders with reading impairments demonstrate difficulty in discriminating rhythm patterns as "same" or "different" on the Seashore Rhythm Test. These findings support previous research which demonstrated that students with disabilities exhibited disordered beating, inability to organize rhythms, and inability to sustain a steady beat (Hong, Hussey, & Heng, 1998; Moore & Mathenius, 1987).

Compositional Methods

Only few studies examined the use of songwriting experiences with children with social, emotional, and learning disabilities. Most recently, Rickson & Watkins (2003) incorporated both active and passive music therapy interventions in their treatment of boys with aggressive behaviors. While subjects' diagnoses were not limited to LD, the program was designed to use group music therapy experiences to increase subjects' awareness of others' feelings, decrease hostility, and provide practice in developing relationships based upon respect and trust. Results of their study found trends indicating improvement in peer relationships. However, the researchers used several group music therapy interventions, including group songwriting using a blues format. Therefore, it is difficult to determine the role that group songwriting may have had in the outcome of the study, given that there was no discussion of the impact on compositional methods in the results.

Summary and Conclusions

Over time, individuals with LD can learn to compensate for their weaknesses. With early, effective support, most people with LD can develop good academic and related skills and enjoy great success academically and professionally. There is growing interest in the use of music therapy methods to address metacognitive and behavioral difficulties found to underlie the academic difficulties in individuals with LD. Currently, the applications of music therapy interventions for children with LD are primarily focused on re-creative and receptive methods designed to address underlying deficits in cognitive processing that are purported to underlie difficulties in academic areas. However, there is growing evidence for cross-domain effects (from music to language) that supports the possibilities of using a wider range of music experiences to support learning, enhance training, and remediate associated difficulties in social and emotional functioning. In addition, music has the unique ability to stimulate impaired temporal processing networks while providing motivation and enjoyment to individuals with LD. There is also a need to explore improvisational methods of music therapy as well as to develop music therapy assessment procedures specifically for individuals with LD.

Given the neurological and musical deficits identified in the literature, there is the potential for music therapists to have both a diagnostic and a treatment role for individuals with LD. However, more research is needed on how the effects of music therapy intervention can be generalized to other settings for individuals with LD.

References

Abikoff, H., Courtney, M. E., Szeibel, P. J., & Koplewicz, H. S. (1996). The effects of auditory stimulation on the arithmetic performance of children with ADHD and nondisabled children. *Journal of Learning Disabilities, 29*(3), 238–246.

Allgood, N. (2005). Parents' perceptions of family-based group music therapy for children with autism spectrum disorder. *Music Therapy Perspectives, 23*(2), 92–99.

American Psychiatric Association (APA). (2000). *Diagnostic and statistical manual of mental disorders—Text revision* (4th ed.). (DSM-IV-TR). Arlington, VA: Author.

Anvari, S., Trainor, L., Woodside, J., & Levy, B. A. (2002). Relations among musical skills, phonological processing, and early reading ability in preschool children. *Journal of Experimental Child Psychology, 83,* 111–130.

Atterbury, B. W. (1983). A comparison of rhythm pattern perception and performance in normal and learning-disabled readers, ages seven and eight. *Journal of Research in Music Education, 31,* 259–270.

Austen, M. P. (1977). The effects of music on the learning of random shapes and syllables with institutionalized severely mentally retarded adolescents. *Contributions, 5,* 54–69.

Baxter, H. T., Berghofer, J. A., MacEwan, L., Nelson, J., Peters, K., & Robers, P. (2007). *The individualized music therapy assessment profile: IMTAP.* Philadelphia, PA: Jessica Kingsley.

Berninger, V. W., & Abbott, R. D. (1994). Redefining learning disabilities: Moving beyond aptitude-achievement discrepancies to failure to respond to validated treatment protocols. In G. R. Lyon (Ed.), *Frames of reference for the assessment of learning disabilities: New views on measurement issues* (pp. 163–184). Baltimore, MD: Brookes.

Besson, M., Schön, D., Moreno, S., Santos, A., & Magne, C. (2007). Influence of musical expertise and musical training on pitch processing in music and language. *Restorative Neurology and Neurosciences, 25,* 399–410.

Blythe, S. (1998). Music matters. *Music Teacher, 9,* 43.

Brooks, A., Berninger, V., Abbott, R., & Richards, T. (2011). Letter naming and letter writing reversals of some children with dyslexia: Symptoms of inefficient phonological and orthographic loops of working memory? *Developmental Neuropsychology, 36*, 847–868.

Bruscia, K. (1987). *Improvisational models of music therapy*. Springfield, IL: Charles C. Thomas.

Bryan, T., Sullivan-Burstein, K., & Mathur, S. (1998). The influence of affect on social-information processing. *Journal of Learning Disabilities, 31*, 418–426.

Chapman, J. W. (1980). *Affective correlates of learning disabilities*. Lisse, Netherlands: Swets & Zeitlinger.

Cortiella, C. (2011). *The state of learning disabilities*. New York, NY: National Center for Learning Disabilities.

Cripe, F. F. (1986). Rock music as therapy for children with attention deficit disorder: An exploratory study. *Journal of Music Therapy, 23*(1), 30–37.

Cutietta, R. (1996). Language and music programs. *General Music Today, 9*(2), 26–31.

Douglas, S., & Willats, P. (1994). The relationship between musical ability and literacy skills. *Journal of Research in Reading, 17*(2), 99–107.

Evans, J. R. (1986). Dysrhythmia and disorders of learning behavior. In J. R. Evans (Ed.), *Rhythm in psychological, linguistic and musical process* (pp. 249–274). Springfield, IL: Charles C. Thomas.

Fisher, D., & McDonald, N. (2001). The intersection between music and early literacy instruction. *Learning Disabilities Online*. Retrieved from www.ldonline.org-indepth/reading/cars

Fletcher, J. M., Shaywitz, S. E., Shankweiler, D., Katz, L., Liberman, I. Y., Steubing, K. K., ... & Shaywitz, B. A. (1994). Cognitive profiles of reading disability: Comparison of discrepancy and low achievement definitions. *Journal of Educational Psychology, 86,* 6–23.

Fuerst, D. R., & Rourke, B. P. (1995). Psychosocial functioning of children with learning disabilities at three age levels. *Child Neuropsychology, 1,* 38–55.

Ganschow, L., Lloyd-Jones, J., & Miles, T. R. (1994). Dyslexia and musical notation. *Annals of Dyslexia, 44,* 185–202.

Gaston, E. T. (1968). *Music in therapy*. New York, NY: McMillian.

Geist, K., Geist, E., & Kuznik, K. (2012). The patterns of music: Young children learning mathematics through beat, rhythm and melody. *Young Children, 67*(1), 74-79.

Gfeller, K. C. (1983). Musical mnemonics as an aid to retention with normal and learning disabled students. *Journal of Music Therapy, 20,* 179–189.

Gibbons, A. C. (1983). Rhythm responses in emotionally disturbed children with differing needs for external structure. *Music Therapy, 3*(1), 94–102.

Goldstein, S. (1997). *Managing attention and learning disorders in late adolescence and adulthood: A guide for practitioners*. New York, NY: John Wiley & Sons.

Goswami, U. A. (2011). Temporal sampling framework for developmental dyslexia. *Trends in Cognitive Sciences, 15,* 3–10. DOI:10.1016/j.tics.2010.10.001.

Gresham, F. M. (1986). Conceptual issues in the assessment of social competence in children. In P. Strain, M. Guralink, & H. Walker (Eds.), *Children's social behavior: Development, assessment, and modification* (pp. 143–186). New York, NY: Academic Press.

Hannaford, C. (1995). *Smart moves: Why learning is not all in your head*. Arlington, VA: Great Ocean.

Harris, M. (1977). Auditory training of learning disabled using Orff music. *Dissertation Abstracts International, Section A: Humanities & Social Sciences, 37,* 5036.

Hazel, S., & Shumaker, J. B. (1988). Social skills and learning disabilities: Recommendations for future research. In J. F. Kavanaugh & T. Truss (Eds.), *Learning disabilities: Proceedings of the national conference* (pp. 293–344). Parkton, MD: York Press.

Heikkila, E., & Knight, A. (2012). Inclusive music teaching strategies for elementary-age children with developmental dyslexia. *Music Educators Journal, 99*(1), 54–59.

Hong, M., Hussey, D. L., & Heng, M. (1998). Music therapy with children with severe emotional disturbances in a residential treatment setting. *Music Therapy Perspectives, 16,* 61–66.

Hooper, S. R., Montgomery, J., Swartz, C., Reed, M., Sandler, A., Levine, M., & Watson, T. (1994). Measurement of written language expression. In G. R. Lyon (Ed.), *Frames of reference for the assessment of learning disabilities: New views on measurement issues* (pp. 375–418). Baltimore, MD: Brookes.

Hubicki, M. (1994). Musical problems? Reflections and suggestions. In G. Hales (Ed.), *Dyslexia Matters.* London, England: Whurr Publishers.

Hurwitz, I., Wolff, P., Bortnick, B., & Kokas, K. (1975). Nonmusical effects of the Kodály music curriculum in primary grade children. *Journal of Learning Disabilities, 3*(3), 167–174.

International Dyslexia Association. (2008). *Definition of dyslexia: Fact sheet.* Retrieved from http://www.interdys.org/ewebeditpro5/upload/Definition.pdf

International Dyslexia Association. (2012). *Dyslexia basics.* Retrieved from http://www.interdys.org/ewebeditpro5/upload/DyslexiaBasicsREVMay2012.pdf

Jaarsma, B. S., Ruijssenaars, J. J. M., & Van den Broeck, W. (1998). Dyslexia and learning musical notation: A pilot study. *Annals of Dyslexia, 48,* 137–154.

Jackson, N. A. (2003). A survey of music therapy methods and their role in the treatment of early elementary school children with ADHD. *Journal of Music Therapy, 40*(4), 302–323.

Jellison, J. A. (2000). A content analysis of music research with disabled children and youth (1975–1999): Applications in special education. In *Effectiveness of music therapy procedures: Documentation of research and clinical practice* (pp. 199–265). Silver Spring, MD: American Music Therapy Association.

Kaufman, S. B. (2013, April 15). *In defense of working memory training.* (Web log post). Retrieved from http://blogs.scientificamerican.com/beautiful-minds/2013/04/15/in-defense-of-working-memory-training/

Kotz, S. A., & Schwartze, M. (2010). Cortical speech processing unplugged: A timely subcortico-cortical framework. *Trends in Cognitive Sciences, 14,* 392–399. DOI: 10.1016/j.tics.2010.06.005.

Kujala, T., Myllyviita, K., Tervaniemi, M., Alho, K., Kallio, J., & Naatanen, R. (2000). Basic auditory dysfunction in dyslexia as demonstrated by brain activity measurements. *Psychophysiology, 37,* 262–266.

Larson, B. A. (1981). Auditory and visual rhythmic pattern recognition by emotionally disturbed and normal adolescents. *Journal of Music Therapy, 18,* 128–136.

Lathom, W. B. (1970). *Retarded children's retention of songs, stories, and poems.* Doctoral Dissertation, University of Kansas. University Microfilms No. 71-06483.

Lyon, G. R. (1996). Learning disabilities. In Mash, E. J., & Barkley, R. A. (Eds.). *Child Psychopathology.* New York, NY: The Guilford Press.

MacMillan, D. L. (1970). Facilitative effect of verbal mediation on paired associate learning by EMR children. *American Journal of Mental Deficiency, 74,* 611–615.

Madsen, C. K., Smith, D., & Freeman, C. C. (1988). The use of music in cross-age tutoring within special education settings. *Journal of Music Therapy, 25,* 135–144.

Magne, C., Schön, D., & Besson, M. (2006). Musician children detect pitch violations in both music and language better than nonmusician children: Behavioral and electrophysiological approaches. *Journal of Cognitive Neuroscience, 18,* 199–211. DOI: 10.1162/jocn.2006.18.2.199.

McGivern, R. F., Berka, C., Languis, M. L., & Chapman, S. (1991). Detection of deficits in temporal pattern discrimination using the Seashore Rhythm Test in young children with reading impairments. *Journal of Learning Disabilities, 24,* 58–62.

Melby-Lervåg, M., & Hulme, C. (2013). Is working memory training effective? A meta-analytic review. *Developmental Psychology, 49*(2), 271–291.

Miller, E. M. (1977). Effects of music-listening contingencies on arithmetic performance and music preference of EMR children. *American Journal of Mental Deficiency, 81,* 371–378.

Miller, E. B. (2011). *Bio-guided music therapy: A practitioner's guide to the clinical integration of music and biofeedback.* Philadelphia, PA: Jessica Kingsley.

Montello, L. F. (1986). *A psychoanalytic music therapy approach to treating adults traumatized as children.* Paper presented at the World Congress of Music Therapy, Hamburg, Germany.

Montello, L. M., & Coons, E. E. (1998). Effects of active versus passive music group music therapy on preadolescents with emotional, learning and behavioral disorders. *Journal of Music Therapy, 35,* 49–67.

Moore, R., & Mathenius, L. (1987). The effects of modeling, reinforcement, and tempo on imitative rhythmic responses of moderately retarded adolescents. *Journal of Music Therapy, 24,* 160–169.

Morton, L. L., Kershner, J. R., & Siegel, L. S. (1990). The potential for therapeutic applications of music on problems related to memory and attention. *Journal of Music Therapy, 27*(4), 195–208.

Nabuzoka, D., & Smith, P. K. (1993). Sociometric status and social behavior of children with and without learning difficulties. *Journal of Child Psychology and Psychiatry, 34,* 1435–1448.

National Joint Commission on Learning Disabilities. (1990). *Learning disabilities: Issues on definition.* Retrieved from http://www.ldonline.org/about/partners/njcld/archives

Nicholson, R. I., Fawcett, A. J., & Dean, P. (1995). Time estimation in developmental dyslexia: Evidence of cerebellar involvement. *Proceedings of the Royal Society, 259,* 43–47.

Overy, K. (2002). *Dyslexia and music: From timing deficits to music intervention.* Unpublished doctoral dissertation. University of Sheffield.

Overy, K., Nicholson, R. I., Fawcett, A. J., & Clarke, E. F. (2003). Dyslexia and music: Measuring musical timing skills. *Dyslexia, 9,* 18–36.

Passolunghi, M. C. (2006). Working memory and mathematical disability. In T. P. Alloway & S. E. Gathercole (Eds.), *Working memory and neurodevelopmental condition* (pp. 113–138). Hove, England: Psychology Press.

Passolunghi, M. C., & Siegel, L. S. (2001). Short-term memory, working memory, and inhibitory control in children with difficulties in arithmetic problem solving. *Journal of Experimental Child Psychology, 80,* 44–57. DOI: 10.1006/jecp.2000.2626.

Przybylski, L., Bedoin, N., Krifi-Papoz, S., Herbillon, V., Roch, D., Léculier, L., ... & Tillmann, B. (2013). Rhythmic auditory stimulation influences syntactic processing in children with developmental language disorders. *Neuropsychology, 27*(1), 121–131.

Register, D., Darrow, A. A., Standley, J., & Swedberg, O. (2007). The use of music to enhance reading skills of second grade students with reading disabilities. *Journal of Music Therapy, 44*(1), 23–37.

Reid, D. H., Hill, B. K., Rawers, R. J., & Montegar, C. A. (1975). The use of contingent music in teaching social skills to a nonverbal, hyperactive boy. *Journal of Music Therapy, 12*(1), 2–18.

Rickson, D. J., & Watkins, W. G. (2003). Music therapy to promote prosocial behaviors in aggressive adolescent boys—a pilot study. *Journal of Music Therapy, 44,* 283–301.

Roskam, K. (1979). Music therapy as an aid for increasing auditory awareness and improving reading skill. *Journal of Music Therapy, 16,* 31–42.

Rourke, B. P. (1995). Syndrome of nonverbal learning disabilities: Neurodevelopmental manifestations. *Journal of Pediatric Psychology, 3,* 62–66.

Schmidt-Kassow, M., Rothermich, K., Schwartze, M., & Kotz, S. A. (2011). Did you get the beat? Late proficient French-German learners extract strong-weak patterns in tonal but not in linguistic sequences. *NeuroImage, 54,* 568–576. DOI: 10.1016/j.neuroimage.2010.07.062.

Schön, D., Magne, C., & Besson, M. (2004). The music of speech: Music training facilitates pitch processing in both music and language. *Psychophysiology, 41,* 341–349. DOI: 10.1111/1469-8986.00172.x.

Shehan, P. K. (1981). A comparison of mediation strategies in paired-associate learning for children with learning disabilities. *Journal of Music Therapy, 18,* 120–127.

Spreen, O. (1989). Learning disability, neurology, and long-term outcome: Some implications for the individual and society. *Journal of Clinical and Experimental Neuropsychology, 11,* 389–408.

Spreen, O., Risser, A., & Edgell, D. (1995). *Developmental neuropsychology.* New York, NY: Oxford University.

Stanley, J. M., & Hughes, J. E. (1997). Evaluation of an early intervention music curriculum for enhancing prereading/writing skills. *Music Therapy Perspectives, 15,* 79–85.

Sutton, J. (1993). The guitar doesn't know this song. An investigation of parallel development in speech/language and music therapy. In M. Heal & T. Wigram (Eds.), *Music therapy in health and education* (pp. 264–272). Philadelphia,PA: Jessica Kingsley.

Tallal, P., Miller, S., & Fitch, R. H. (1993). Neurological basis of speech: A case of the preeminence of temporal processing. *Annals of the New York Academy of Science, 682,* 27–47.

Tannock, R. (2013, May 1). *Rethinking learning disorders.* (Web log post). Retrieved from http://blogs.scientificamerican.com/mind-guest-blog/2013/05/01/rethinking-learning-disorders/

Thaut, M. (1985). The use of auditory rhythm and rhythmic speech to aid temporal muscular control in children with gross motor dysfunction. *Journal of Music Therapy, 22,* 108–128.

Thaut, M. (2005). Neurologic music therapy in speech and language rehabilitation. In *Rhythm, music and the brain: Scientific foundations and clinical applications (studies on new music research)* (pp. 165–178). New York, NY: Routledge.

U.S. Office of Special Education. (2002). *Facts from OSEP's national longitudinal studies.* Retrieved from http://www.nlts2.org/fact_sheets/nlts2_fact_sheet_2002_08.pdf

Vance, K. O. (2004). Adapting music instruction for students with dyslexia. *Music Educators Journal, 90*(5), 27–31.

Wigram, T., Pedersen, I. N., & Ole Bonde, L. (2002). *A comprehensive guide to music therapy: Theory, clinical practice, research and training.* Philadelphia, PA: Jessica Kingsley.

Wolfe, D. E. (1982). The effect of interrupted and continuous music on bodily movement and task performance of third grade students. *Journal of Music Therapy, 19,* 74–85.

Wolfe, D. E., & Horn, C. (1993). Use of melodies as structural prompts for learning and retention of sequential verbal information by preschool students. *Journal of Music Therapy, 30,* 100–118.

Wolff, P. (2002). Timing precision and rhythm in developmental dyslexia. *Reading and Writing: An Interdisciplinary Journal, 15,* 179–206.

Wolff, P., Michel, G. F., Ovrut, M., & Drake, C. (1990). Rate and timing precision of motor coordination in developmental dyslexia. *Developmental Psychology, 26,* 349–359.

Chapter 8

Behavioral and Interpersonal Problems in School Children

Patricia McCarrick

DIAGNOSTIC INFORMATION

Children with emotional/behavioral disorders demonstrate a wide range and variety of conditions, including a general disturbance of mood, conduct, and emotions and difficulty relating appropriately to others. Some emotional/behavioral disorders in children are severe enough to be classified as mental illness. The Centers for Disease Control and Prevention (CDC) estimate that approximately 8.3 million school children ages 4–17 have emotional or behavioral difficulties, and many have been prescribed medication as a result (2008). Given these statistics, it is expected that many of these individuals will meet diagnostic criteria for a mental illness or behavioral disorder.

There are a variety of agencies and organizations that offer definitions for mental disorders. The National Alliance on Mental Illness (NAMI) defines mental illness slightly differently, stating that they are "medical conditions that disrupt a person's thinking, feeling, mood, ability to relate to others, and daily functioning." Mental illnesses often result in a "diminished capacity for coping with the ordinary demands of life" (NAMI, 2010).

According to the American Psychiatric Association, a mental disorder is considered a "manifestation of a behavioral, psychological, or biological dysfunction of an individual" [*Diagnostic and Statistical Manual of Mental Illness, Fourth Edition, Text Revised (DSM-IV-TR),* 2000, p. xxxi] which is associated with a current disability or impairment in cognitive, social, emotional, or behavior difficulties. Often, children with mental disorders have poor social skills and difficulty relating appropriately to others as a result of their emotional and behavioral difficulties. Behaviorally, these children often struggle with hyperactivity, impulsivity, and a short attention span. They may demonstrate aggressive behavior and frequent tantrums, and exhibit poor coping and problem-solving skills.

Emotionally, they may seem immature, have excessive fears and anxieties, or experience mood swings. Severe forms of emotional disturbance may include distorted thinking. Research suggests that many children with emotional disturbance suffer from cognitive deficits in addition to behavioral disorders which then negatively impact learning and academic achievement. Some individuals may even meet criteria for a learning disorder which is characterized by "academic functioning that is substantially below expected given chronological age, measured intelligence, and age-appropriate education" (*DSM-IV-TR,* 2000, p. 39). Disorders of learning may include issues with reading, math, and written expression.

The Individuals with Disabilities Education Act (IDEA) defines emotional disturbance as "a condition exhibiting one or more of the following characteristics over a long period of time and to a marked degree that adversely affects a child's educational performance:

1) An inability to learn that cannot be explained by intellectual, sensory, or health factors.
2) An inability to build or maintain satisfactory interpersonal relationships with peers and teachers.
3) Inappropriate types of behavior or feelings under normal circumstances.
4) A general or pervasive mood of unhappiness or depression.
5) A tendency to develop physical symptoms or fears associated with personal or school problems." (National Dissemination Center for Children with Disabilities Fact Sheet 5, 2010)

The IDEA requires that all children with disabilities ages 3–21 receive a free, appropriate education within the least restrictive environment, meaning that children and adolescents with emotional and behavioral disorders are entitled to receive special education and related services in an appropriate educational environment. Depending upon the severity of the emotional disturbance, children may be educated in settings other than a public education one. These include mental health facilities, residential treatment centers, approved private schools, and alternative schools designed specifically for the education and treatment of emotionally disturbed children.

Educational programs for children and adolescents with emotional and behavioral problems are often designed to develop academic skills, improve social skills, and increase self-awareness, self-esteem, and self-control. Schoolwide and classroomwide methods of providing positive behavioral support are designed to minimize disruptive behaviors and develop appropriate behaviors. Individualized Education Plans (IEPs) are designed to include academic, social, and emotional/behavioral goals and are implemented by highly qualified special education teachers with strong behavior management skills. Related services usually include psychological/counseling services, social workers, and creative arts therapists.

Music therapists working with children and adolescents with interpersonal and behavioral problems in school settings are primarily considered part of a multidisciplinary team. Team members generally include special education teachers, school psychologists, social workers, counselors, behavior analysts, other therapists, and parents. Depending on the needs of the students, other therapists may include speech therapists, occupational therapists, physical therapists, and creative arts therapists. Music therapy may be considered a related service according to the IDEA, and therefore music therapy goals may be included in a child's IEP.

Music therapists may often serve as consultants to music educators dealing with children and adolescents with emotional/behavioral disorders in music education classrooms. Some music educators may feel uncomfortable dealing with children with such challenging behaviors and may request behavior management strategies and behavior modification techniques. The relationship between the music therapist and the music educator must be one of mutual respect, keeping the successful inclusion of the child in music as the primary goal. Not all children are appropriate for inclusion due to their social emotional needs. Some children may receive music therapy before being included in more inclusive settings.

The primary consideration when working as a member of a multidisciplinary team is working together to attain the best interest of the child. Working with others can be challenging, especially when each member has different concerns and interests. Team members must be willing to express their concerns as well as compromise with others. Working with parents of children and adolescents with emotional/behavioral problems can be extremely challenging considering the many issues involved. Families need empathy and support as well as constructive coping strategies in dealing with these challenging children.

Medication is often the primary treatment for children and adolescents with emotional or behavioral disorders due to the lack of treatment options available. An increase in insurance costs has resulted in a decrease in treatment options for these children and their families. Research reveals an increase in the use of antipsychotic medication in foster care in recent years. Children with ADHD, conduct disorders, and disruptive, aggressive behaviors are often treated with antipsychotics to manage behaviors and remain in school.

The issue of treating disruptive behaviors with psychotropic drugs has drawn recent attention due to the concerns of long-term effects of these medications on the brain and learning. Research suggests that behavior problems may be a manifestation of untreated traumas, and medication may be the only option if there are no other treatment programs available (Burling, 2012). More treatment options are needed for children and adolescents with emotional/behavioral disorders and their families.

Attention and Disruptive Behavior Disorders

There are several clinical diagnoses that fall under this category of disorders. These include disorders of attention, e.g., Attention-Deficit Disorder (ADD) and Attention- Deficit/Hyperactivity Disorder (ADHD), and disruptive behavior disorders, e.g., Oppositional Defiant Disorder (ODD) and Conduct Disorder. Disorders of attention and conduct are generally treated through a combination of medication, therapy, and/or behavior modification. These behaviors can be extremely challenging to deal with in a variety of settings, especially in public schools.

Attention-Deficit/Hyperactivity Disorders: According to the *DSM-IV-TR* (American Psychiatric Association, 2000), Attention-Deficit/Hyperactivity Disorder (ADHD) is characterized by a persistent pattern of hyperactivity and/or impulsivity that is inconsistent with peers of a comparable age and level of development. Symptoms must be present before the age of seven and present in two or more settings, such as home, school, work, etc., for at least six months. Symptoms need to be severe enough to interfere with appropriate family, academic, social, and occupational functioning.

Behavior characteristics of ADHD include distractibility, difficulty focusing and maintaining attention to task until completion, poor work ethic, and poor organizational skills. Students have difficulty listening to and following directions. They may appear restless, with excessive movements. This impulsivity causes great difficulty in academic, social, and occupational settings. Descriptive features of disruptive behaviors include constant demands for attention, low frustration tolerance, emotional outbursts, temper tantrums, and oppositional behavior. Children often have poorly developed social skills, resulting in poor peer relationships and low self-esteem. Great variability may exist in intellectual functioning. Some students may be above average or even gifted. A lower IQ is much more debilitating, impacting family, educational, and social functioning.

Approximately half of ADHD children and adolescents may have disruptive behavior disorders, such as ODDs or Conduct Disorders. Others may have a variety of mood disorders, anxiety disorders, communication disorders and substance-related disorders (*DSM-IV-TR,* 2000, p. 88). The presence of an additional behavioral disorder complicates treatment and makes prognosis much more guarded.

Disruptive Behavior Disorders: This classification of disorders includes both Oppositional Defiant Disorder (ODD) and Conduct Disorder (CD). ODD is characterized by a persistent and prolonged pattern of hostile, negative, and defiant behavior toward authority figures such as parents, teachers, and superiors. Behaviors must be present for at least six months and inappropriate for chronological age and development, leading to significant impairments in family, academic, social, and occupational settings. Behaviors are characterized by argumentative, defiant, and noncompliant behaviors. Children may appear irritable, angry, rude, and disrespectful. They may be unwilling to accept responsibility for their own behavior and often blame others, resulting in conflicts with parents, teachers, and peers. Children may have low frustration tolerance, poor self-esteem, and frequent conflicts with parents, teachers, and peers.

Defiance may appear as intentional annoyance of others, ignoring authority figures, limit-testing, and verbal abuse. Children may also deliberately ignore rules, violate curfews, and demonstrate reckless behaviors such as underage use of alcohol, tobacco, and illegal drugs. Some children diagnosed with ODD may also meet clinical criteria for ADHD, learning disabilities, or communication disorders (*DSM-IV-TR,* 2000, p. 101). Children and adolescents with Oppositional and Defiant Disorder (ODD) exhibit less severe behaviors than those with Conduct Disorders. Incidentally, ODD is not diagnosed if symptoms of Conduct Disorder are present.

Although oppositional behavior is common in preschool-age children, for children diagnosed with ODD, these symptoms become more prevalent and severe as they get older. Symptoms are generally present before the age of eight, with onset occurring no later than adolescence. Behaviors initially begin in the home and may appear in other settings, such as school. While ODD may precede Conduct Disorder, children with ODD do not necessarily develop Conduct Disorder. Symptoms for ODD are generally more prominent in males prior to puberty, but the male/female symptoms are more equal after puberty, with males demonstrating more confrontational and persistent symptoms of behavior.

Similar to individuals who eventually meet clinical criteria for CD, diagnosis of ODD is more prevalent in families with inconsistent, neglectful, or strict parenting; marital discord; or frequent changes in caregivers. In addition, familial history of ADHD, depression, conduct disorder, or substance abuse increases the likelihood of disruptive behaviors.

The number of children with Conduct Disorders (CD) appears to have increased over the past decades, occurring more often in urban settings than in rural, and involving more males than females. Conduct Disorders are characterized by a persistent pattern of behavior that violates the basic rights of others and major age-appropriate rules of society. Conduct disorders are the most frequently diagnosed conditions in outpatient and inpatient mental health facilities for children. Factors that may predispose an individual to CD may include parental neglect or rejection due to difficult infant temperament, lack of supervision, inconsistent or strict child-rearing practices, and physical or sexual abuse. Other issues may involve early institutional placement, frequent changes of caregivers, and a history of family psychopathology. The child may also experience neighborhood violence, peer rejection, and/or a delinquent peer group. In general, more damaging behaviors at an early age are predictive of a worse prognosis for treatment.

Behavior characteristics of children with conduct disorders include a lack of empathy and little concern for others, with no feelings of guilt or remorse. Behaviors may include intentional cruelty to animals and people, fire-setting, and destruction of property. They may have an inflated self-image to disguise feelings of low self-esteem. Other behaviors include hostility, irritability, poor frustration tolerance, and sudden temper outbursts. In addition, there may be an early onset of risk-taking behaviors and reckless acts, such as smoking, drinking, use of illegal substances, and sexual promiscuity. Such behaviors result in physical fights, truancy, frequent suspensions/expulsions from school, unplanned pregnancies and STDs, addictions, arrests, and legal problems. These individuals blame others and do not accept responsibility for their actions.

Children with CD may also have a low average intelligence and particularly weak verbal IQ. Academic achievement is generally below average for age and ability, especially in reading. This may result in an additional diagnosis of a learning disability or communication disorder. Their disruptive behaviors may be severe enough to prevent attendance in ordinary schools and living in their parental or foster homes. Refusal to comply with school rules may result in suspension or expulsion from public school settings, whereas explosive behavior at home may result in removal from family or foster home to a more restrictive environment such as a residential treatment facility. Children with CD may have a higher rate of suicidal ideation, attempts, and completions than other diagnosis (*DSM-IV-TR,* 2000, p. 96).

Conduct Disorders are one of the most difficult emotional/behavioral disorders to treat. Prognosis and treatment is also affected by age of onset and severity of behaviors. Services may include family therapy and parental training in behavior management. School-based programs include training in problem-solving, coping skills, and social skills with comprehensive treatment plans designed to improve individual behavior in addition to academic skills. Community-based programs may offer after school programs and occupational training.

Mood Disorders

Mood Disorders in children and adolescents include issues with anxiety and depression as well as specific disorders like eating disorders, obsessive-compulsive disorders, and post-traumatic stress disorders. Mood disorders are defined as having a prolonged disturbance in behavior including Depressive Disorders, Bipolar Disorders, Mood Disorders Due to a General Medical Condition, and Substance-Induced Mood Disorders.

Depressive Disorders: Depression is characterized by feelings of hopelessness, sadness, apathy, sleep disturbance, and feelings of irritability. However, rather than expressions of sadness, children and adolescents may display agitation, angry outbursts, low frustration tolerance, poor concentration, irritability, somatic complaints, and social withdrawal. These symptoms may or may not be accompanied by a sudden drop in grades and academic performance. Although symptoms of depression are the same for both children and adolescents, adolescents tend to have more prevalent symptoms of decreased energy, increased sleep patterns, and possible delusions. Depression is more common in the presence of other mental disorders such as ADHD and Disruptive Behavior Disorders, Anxiety Disorders, Substance-Related Disorders, and Eating Disorders (*DSM-IV-TR,* 2000, p. 354).

A Major Depressive Episode is characterized by extreme sadness for at least two weeks and a loss of interest in nearly all activities of daily life. Additional symptoms may include changes in appetite with sudden weight loss or gain, sleep disturbance, and decreased energy. There may be feelings of worthlessness, difficulty concentrating, and a preoccupation with thoughts of death or suicidal ideation. Symptoms may cause severe impairments in academic, social, occupational, and other areas of daily living.

Bipolar Disorders: Bipolar Disorders are characterized by one or more manic episodes usually accompanied later by major depressive episodes. A manic episode is described by an abnormal euphoric mood accompanied by increased activity, decreased need for sleep, rapid speech, and flight of ideas. Manic behaviors may also appear as a result of drug or alcohol intoxication (*DSM-IV-TR,* 2000, p. 360). Individuals may demonstrate dramatic mood swings, impulsiveness, poor judgment, and risky behaviors without regard for consequences. Behaviors may be severe enough to require hospitalization. Manic episodes in adolescents may be characterized by a history of behavior problems, truancy, school failure, antisocial behavior, and substance abuse (*DSM-IV-TR,* 2000, p. 360). Individuals with Bipolar Disorders may have a general mood of irritability accompanied by sudden fluctuations between euphoria and agitation.

Anxiety Disorders: Anxiety Disorders range in severity from mild to severe and also may be related to specific circumstances or stimuli or may be a general response to everyday occurrences. Some individuals may display excessive irrational fears of specific or ordinary life situations. Anxiety Disorders include separation anxiety, panic attacks, phobias, obsessive-compulsive disorders, post-traumatic stress disorders, and generalized anxiety disorders. Separation anxiety is characterized by inappropriate fear and anxiety regarding separation from home or a parental figure. Behaviors include irrational fears, school refusal, sleep disturbances such as nightmares, and physical symptoms resulting from separation. Symptoms result in significant impairment in social, academic, occupational, and other areas of functioning (*DSM-IV-TR,* 2000, p. 125).

Fears are very common in childhood, but are not usually diagnosed as a specific phobia unless the condition significantly interferes with educational, social, and occupational functioning. The condition must be present before the age of 18 and present for at least six months (*DSM-IV-TR,* 2000, p. 453). Children with emotional/behavioral disorders may exhibit specific phobias or social phobias, such as school phobia, which is characterized by excessive anxiety over a specific situation such as peer pressure or bullying, leading to avoidance behaviors. There may be a decline in educational performance, school refusal or avoidance, and reluctance to participate in age-appropriate social activities. To be diagnosed in children, there must be evidence of forming appropriate social relationships with familiar adults and evidence of social anxiety in establishing appropriate peer relationships. Childhood onset may prevent failure to achieve a developmentally appropriate level of functioning. In adolescence, phobias may lead to decreased social and academic performance.

Fear of failure in academic and social situations may lead to somatic complaints, frequent absences, and truancy to avoid school. Recurrent truancy can lead to legal complications and forced school attendance to be mandated.

Generalized Anxiety Disorder (GAD) is characterized by excessive worry or apprehension for a period of at least six months. Symptoms may include irritability, restlessness, fatigue, muscle tension, sleep disturbances, and difficulty concentrating. Constant worry impairs appropriate functioning in daily living skills. Children with this disorder tend to worry about personal competence and quality of their performance. They may be perfectionists and tend to redo tasks because of personal dissatisfaction with their performance. They may need to seek constant approval and reassurance regarding the quality of their work. GAD appears to be overly diagnosed in children. A thorough psychological evaluation must be done to determine if another childhood anxiety disorder may more accurately describe the symptoms of anxiety. Excessive fear of illness may actually represent anxiety, and OCD symptoms regarding school performance may represent a Social Phobia rather than GAD (*DSM-IV-TR,* 2000, p. 474).

Obsessive-Compulsive Disorder (OCD) is characterized by recurrent obsessions or compulsions that are time-consuming and cause significant impairment in daily living. Obsessions are defined as persistent thoughts or impulses that are inappropriate and intrusive, causing distress and anxiety. These recurrent ideas are excessive worries that are usually not related to real-life situations, such as monsters under the bed or fear of contamination. Compulsions are repetitive behaviors designed to reduce stress or anxiety. The most common compulsions involve washing or cleaning, counting, checking, ordering, and demanding reassurance. An individual who has an obsession with contamination may engage in compulsive hand washing.

Children with obsessive-compulsive behaviors usually lack cognitive awareness to realize that these behaviors are excessive and unreasonable. Obsessions and compulsions can be highly disruptive to overall functioning, as both can be extremely distracting, which disrupts the ability to complete tasks that require concentration (e.g., reading, computation) and frequently results in lower academic performance. Obsessions or compulsions are extremely time-consuming, often involving at least an hour a day, and interfere in appropriate daily academic, occupational, and social functioning (*DSM-IV-TR,* 2000, p. 458).

Post-Traumatic Stress Disorder (PTSD): The essential feature of PTSD is the development of symptoms following exposure to a perceived traumatic life event that the individual has either experienced or witnessed. Symptoms usually begin within three months of the trauma, although there may be a delay of months or years before they occur. Response to the event includes persistent anxiety, fear, horror, helplessness, and reliving or avoiding reminders of the trauma. Individuals may suffer from nightmares; appear anxious, irritable, or angry; and have difficulty concentrating or completing tasks. Behaviors must be present for more than one month and cause distress in cognitive, social, occupational, and other areas of daily functioning. In children, symptoms must involve disorganized or agitated behavior and may present as distressing dreams, reliving the trauma through repetitive play, or physical ailments such as head- or stomachaches (*DSM-IV-TR,* 2000, p. 466).

Eating Disorders

Eating Disorders are characterized by severe disturbances in eating behavior and include the specific diagnoses of Anorexia Nervosa and Bulimia Nervosa.

Anorexia Nervosa: Anorexia Nervosa is characterized by an individual refusal to maintain a normal body weight and is more prevalent in societies where food is abundant and society views attractive women as being thin. Eating disorders are more prevalent in females than in males and seem to have increased in recent decades. The illness rarely begins before puberty, but presence at an earlier age may be indicative of more severe mental disturbances. Onset is usually in mid- to late adolescence (13–18 years) and may be associated with a better prognosis for treatment.

Anorexia Nervosa is characterized by a refusal to maintain a normal weight, intense fear of gaining weight, and significant disturbance of body image. During childhood or adolescence, there may be a failure to make expected weight gains rather than excessive weight loss. Weight loss is viewed as self-discipline and therefore is accompanied by a reduction in total food intake. Weight gain is considered a lack of self-control. Those with anorexia are unable or unwilling to acknowledge the serious health complications caused by malnourishment. Individuals with anorexia may also reveal symptoms of depression, irritability, sleep disturbances, and social withdrawal. Obsessive-compulsive symptoms, related and unrelated to food, are often present. Other issues may include a strong need to control, rigidity in thinking, and perfectionism.

Bulimia Nervosa: This is defined by repeated episodes of binge eating and purging. A binge is defined as consuming excessive amounts of food in a limited time period, usually less than two hours. Binge eating appears to be characterized more by an abnormality in food consumption than a craving for a specific food, such as chocolate. Binge eating usually occurs in secrecy. Individuals may experience loss of control, followed by feelings of shame, depression, and self-loathing. Purging is characterized by self-induced vomiting, abuse of laxatives or diuretics, fasting, and excessive exercise. A disturbance in perception of body shape and weight is an essential feature of eating disorders.

Bulimia nervosa usually begins in late adolescence or early adulthood. Individuals are typically within the normal weight range, and may also exhibit depressive symptoms, mood disorders, and anxiety disorders. Substance abuse or dependency on alcohol and stimulants may begin as an attempt to reduce appetite and control weight gain. Disturbed eating may persist over a period of years, alternating between binge eating and periods of remission. Eating disorders are treated through a comprehensive program of psychotherapy and counseling, in addition to a thorough evaluation of medical and nutritional needs. A period of remission for longer than one year is associated with a better prognosis (*DSM-IV-TR,* 2000, p. 593).

Symptoms of bulimia nervosa include binge eating and inappropriate compulsive methods to prevent weight gain, such as self-induced vomiting, misuse of laxatives and diuretics, and excessive exercise. Behaviors must occur at least twice a week for a period of three months.

Needs and Resources

Personal characteristics of children and adolescents with emotional/behavioral disorders have been discussed more thoroughly in the diagnostic information section above. Disruptive Behavior Disorders may present with symptoms of inattention, impulsivity, hyperactivity, and restlessness. Children and adolescents with Conduct Disorders may be destructive, aggressive with sudden temper outbursts, and have poor peer relationships. Those with ODDs may be rude, disrespectful, and noncompliant. Students with Mood Disorders and Anxiety Disorders may appear as depressed and withdrawn and have low self-esteem.

Despite the symptoms of their emotional disorder, each child is a unique individual, with individual likes, dislikes, and musical preferences. Some students prefer singing while others prefer instrumental activities, improvisation, and songwriting. It is important to recognize and respect the individual differences each child possesses within the musical environment. Children with emotional/behavioral disorders vary in musical strengths and abilities, varying from little or no experience with music to having had musical training or participating in organized musical activities such as chorus, band, or orchestra.

Problem areas include impulsive behavior, noncompliance, and difficulty relating appropriately to others. Structure, limit-setting, and consistency are necessary in dealing with difficult behaviors. These children have difficulty forming trusting relationships and expressing feelings appropriately. Working with children with emotional/behavioral disorders requires patience, understanding, and compassion. Improvement in behavior and musical interaction can occur with time.

Many children and adolescents with emotional/behavioral disorders demonstrate a need for structure, predictability, and consistent routine. Familiarity with expectations can foster a sense of security, stability, and trust. Increased comfort allows for an increase in cooperation, participation, and self-expression.

Behavioral impulsiveness of emotionally disturbed children and adolescents may be related to motor timing deficits in the brain. Medication can increase a child's ability to regulate impulsive responses (Rickson, 2006). Transitions, those times between structured experiences (whether in the classroom or at home), can be difficult. Children with emotional/behavioral disorders are better able to sustain attention, concentration, and self-control during musical activities than in between. Improvements in organization and impulse control can be demonstrated over time (Rickson, 2006). Establish rules within a highly structured musical environment. Children and adolescents with emotional/behavioral disorders respond well to consistent routines, clear limits, and immediate consequences for inappropriate behavior (Birkenshaw-Fleming, 1993).

Trust is a major issue with children and adolescents with emotional and behavioral disorders due to feelings of abandonment, frequent changes in caregivers, facilities, schools, and teachers. It is difficult to develop and maintain trusting relationships with adults and peers. The therapist must establish a safe and secure musical environment in which feelings can be expressed and explored without judgment. A safe, consistent environment helps promote a trusting relationship and produces positive behavioral change in children and adolescents with emotional/behavioral disorders. Many are extremely reluctant to form trusting relationships due to issues of abandonment and frequent transitions to various schools, placements, and foster care settings. A nonthreatening musical environment can allow exploration of feelings and increase self-expression and self-esteem. Music therapy can promote positive social relationships through musical interaction.

Inclusion

Children and adolescents with emotional/behavioral difficulties are some of the most challenging students and have been one of the last populations to be involved in inclusion in public school settings due to their severe behavior problems. Regular educators often lack training regarding knowledge of emotional/behavioral disorders and behavior management skills. Classroom management strategies are needed in defining rules and expectations for behavior.

Inclusion is defined as placing special needs students in classrooms with typical peers in a regular education setting. It is believed that inclusion provides social and academic advantages for both special education and regular education students by fostering understanding, tolerance, respect, and appreciation for the differences of others, minimalizing segregation and the "labeling" of special needs students. However, regular education teachers often state that they need more information regarding special needs students, the amount of time required for successful inclusion, and the range of abilities in an inclusive classroom. Additional concerns educators have include the lack of training, negative attitudes toward students with disabilities, and fear that their special needs students' disruptive and inappropriate behaviors will impede the progress of regular education students (Darrow, 1999).

Limited research regarding music therapy with children and adolescents with emotional or behavioral problems currently exists (Layman & Hussey, 2002; Rickson & Watkins, 2003), and it is extremely limited regarding inclusive school settings. Few studies examine the inclusion of special needs students in a general music education setting (Jones et al., 1998). The music education classroom is a common placement for special needs students. Administrators may be unaware of the challenging academic environment of the music classroom and seem to believe that special needs students can just "listen" to music (Darrow, 1999). Academic and social challenges in the music classroom may be even more overwhelming to students with emotional/behavioral problems.

Children with emotional/behavioral problems respond well to a highly structured musical environment with rules that promote positive behaviors that can be observed and measured. Rules must be consistently reinforced with clearly defined consequences. Negative behaviors require immediate consequences. Positive reinforcement motivates students and decreases negative behaviors. Children with behavioral disorders respond well to consistent routines within a supportive environment.

Many music educators mentioned music therapy as a more appropriate setting for some special needs students or the need for a music therapy consultant to help transition special needs students into the music education classroom. The need for collaboration and consultation between the music educator and the music therapist was determined as essential for successful inclusion of special needs students in the music education classroom (Darrow, 1999). Preservice education and in-service training that involves special needs students is imperative for successful inclusion of children and adolescents with emotional/behavioral disorders in music education classrooms.

The role of the music therapist within inclusive school settings is continually evolving. Many music therapists provide services within a segregated environment but indicate a willingness to adapt practices to accommodate a changing school system and deliver services in integrated settings (Jones et al., 1998). The music therapist may serve as a facilitator and inclusion specialist for music education programs, providing in-service training for music educators. In-service training may include adapting curriculum, music, teaching strategies, and instruments, as well as behavior management strategies for children with emotional/behavioral difficulties. Support for music educators may create an inclusive music classroom appropriate for all students—even those with the most challenging behaviors.

Referral and Assessment

Referrals to music therapy services in school settings come from a wide variety of disciplines, including special education teachers, school counselors, psychologists, or other mental health professionals. Music teachers may also request music therapy services for children with more challenging or disruptive behaviors. In addition, parents may refer children and adolescents with emotional/behavior difficulties in school settings to music therapy.

Reasons for referral to music therapy for students with emotional/behavioral disorders in school settings can vary based upon the diagnosis and treatment plan of the individual. Children with extreme depression may be referred to music therapy sessions to increase self-expression and improve self-esteem. Music therapy may be used to reduce restlessness and channel excessive energy in children with extreme hyperactivity. Children and adolescents with severe anger issues may use music therapy to express negative emotions in a more positive manner. Children who have been abused, neglected, or abandoned can use music therapy to heal painful memories and establish more trusting relationships with others. Sexually abused children and adolescents may be referred to explore feelings of shame and violation and promote healing through self-expression and communication through music. Adolescents struggling with substance abuse issues may be referred to music therapy to explore dependency and sobriety through songwriting and improvisation. Students with eating disorders may be referred to music therapy to promote a healthy self-concept.

Reasons for referral should include the specific needs and behavior characteristics of the student involved. The person making the referral should describe the problems to be addressed by the music therapist, advise if special precautions are necessary, and provide any additional information that would be useful to the music therapist prior to scheduling the music therapy assessment. The music therapist should have access to the student's diagnosis, treatment plan, and IEP to prior to or after completing assessment to effectively plan and design music therapy sessions.

In designing a referral form, the music therapist should include identifying information, reasons for referral to music therapy, problems to be addressed by the music therapist, any special precautions needed, or any additional information regarding the student. Identifying information should include the student's name, age, home room teacher, and school location, and the person referring the student for music therapy services. Reasons for referral to music therapy should address the needs of the students as well as the concerns of the person making the referral and their relationship to the client. The special education teacher, school psychologist, social worker, parent, or other concerned school personnel may refer a student with emotional/behavioral disorders for music therapy services.

A music therapy survey or interest inventory may be an effective method of gathering information and determining musical preferences and characteristics of students with emotional/behavioral disorders. It may be designed to reflect the specific needs and interests of a specific population, such as hip-hop music with inner-city adolescents. Information can be gained regarding a student's musical background and experiences, such as participation in school-based performance groups and ensembles. Information should also be included to determine a student's likes, dislikes, and musical preferences. Interest in available performance groups can be determined through a music therapy interest inventory if the music therapist in the school setting organizes such groups.

Assessment within an educational context is an essential part of determining eligibility for special education services according to PL 94-142 (IDEA). The multidisciplinary team (MDT) is a group of specialists performing a variety of assessments with special needs children. Music therapy assessments with special needs children can be used for screening, referral, program planning, treatment, and evaluation of services.

According to the AMTA Standards of Clinical Practice, assessment is the first step in providing music therapy treatment (AMTA, 2000). A music therapy assessment is defined as "any music-based evaluation of a child's psychological, educational, social, behavioral, physiological, or musical functioning completed prior to the delivery of music therapy or other services/interventions" (Wilson & Smith, 2000, p. 99). Assessment was interpreted to mean "any evaluative measure where the response to a music-based stimulus or question (pretest, baseline recording, survey of musical preferences) was a major determinant for measuring success of a later intervention" (Wilson & Smith, 2000, p. 99).

Assessments provide information regarding different areas of functioning, such as physiological, psychological, cognitive, socialization, and communication (Layman & Hussey, 2002). A well-designed music therapy assessment helps the music therapist evaluate musical and nonmusical responses of the client in addition to determining needs and strengths, musical skills and preferences, and potential goals and objectives for treatment. Musical behaviors expressed may include musical aptitude, perception, and preferences. Nonmusical behaviors may include self-expression, communication, motor skills, cognitive development, social interaction, and behavioral responses. Assessment should be ongoing throughout the treatment process.

There is a lack of information and availability regarding existing music therapy assessment forms used by music therapists in school settings. Furthermore, research suggests that there is a lack of standardized music therapy assessment forms for special needs students in school settings. It appears that most music therapists use original assessment forms designed specifically for their unique setting and primary population (Wilson & Smith, 2000). Despite the existence of highly developed music therapy assessment forms, limited attempts have been made to create a standardized music therapy assessment in school settings (Wilson & Smith, 2000). Other disciplines, which provide services to special needs students in school settings, have standardized assessment forms, such as occupational, physical, and speech therapy.

Reliable assessments related to specific populations are rare in music therapy. Music therapists working with children and adolescents with emotional/behavioral disorders may benefit from an assessment instrument designed for the specific needs of this population. A reliable assessment form records concrete musical and nonmusical behaviors that are both observed and measurable. Subjective behaviors such as affect, social interaction, and communication are more difficult to measure, but offer valuable information to the music therapist and should be included. A standardized assessment form can serve as a valuable research tool, providing baseline functioning and measuring change over time.

A well-designed assessment form should evaluate the musical and nonmusical behaviors of the client as well as their musical and social interaction with the therapist. A music therapy assessment should include the physical characteristics and emotional responses of the client to music. The assessment should evaluate rhythmic and melodic characteristics as well as musical responses and abilities. Instrumental preferences and styles of music preferred and disliked can be determined during the initial assessment.

An assessment form can provide useful information such as the student's degree of musical involvement, use of musical experiences, and motivational level for attending and participating in music therapy. Degree of musical involvement can be used to determine the importance of music in relationship to the client's daily life. Music can be seen as a necessary part of life, and therefore music therapy may be an effective treatment modality. Music may serve more as a recreational activity or music may have little or no primary role in the student's life. The client can use music for a variety of reasons. Music can be used to reduce stress and increase relaxation. Some students use music to express feelings, release energy, or increase social interaction and enjoyment.

What is the client's motivation for attending music therapy sessions? Is music a necessary and important treatment modality, an essential part of daily life to the client? A student who is highly motivated to attend music therapy will actively participate. Some students may need encouragement to attend but cooperate when present. Other students actively avoid music therapy and resist participating in musical activities.

Social interaction with the therapist and with others in the musical environment must also be considered. Evaluate eye contact, verbal responses, and ability to communicate with others. Physical characteristics such as affect, appearance, and body image and posture can be indicative of a client's emotional state. A flat affect may reveal depression. A disorganized personal appearance may indicate a poor self-concept. Chaotic, disorganized drum beating may be reflective of internal disorganization.

A music therapy assessment should also record such information as the student disposition and reason for referral. Possible therapeutic goals and objections as well as music therapy methods should be evaluated. The therapist should consider how the client uses music, what feelings music evokes, and what issues could be addressed in music therapy. Assessment should be an ongoing process in music therapy and should be evaluated over time and throughout the treatment process.

A music therapy survey might also be helpful to assess the musical interest and background of incoming students for the purpose of program planning and possible inclusion in specific performance groups. Specific questions to ask should pertain to favorite music type, favorite artists, formal music training, ability to read music, participation in musical groups or ensembles, how music is used (e.g., leisure, relaxation), interest in learning an instrument, etc.

The growing trend of music therapists in school settings establishes a need for a standardized music therapy assessment form to establish credibility through accountability. A standardized music therapy assessment reflects the importance of music therapy as a profession and determines its ability to relate to other health care professionals. Standardization has the ability to allow for generalization of assessment results to other disciplines and other settings. Research suggests that a greater attempt must be made to compile, replicate, and evaluate existing therapist-made assessment forms (Wilson & Smith, 2000).

Additional research is suggested to determine whether a standardized music therapy assessment is even possible, given that some elements of music are considered to be subjective and difficult to measure. The existence of a standardized music therapy assessment in school settings may provide more consistency, validity, and reliability to the value of music therapy as a profession regarding the evaluation and treatment of special needs children and adolescents.

Overview of Methods and Procedures

The following methods and procedures are used most commonly with children and adolescents with behavioral and interpersonal problems:

Receptive Music Therapy

- Music Listening: engages the client in a process of listening to music chosen by the therapist or the client for purposes of relaxation and stress management, self-awareness, or problem-solving.
- Music and Imagery: The client is engaged in listening to music for purposes of eliciting mental imagery to promote personal insight.

Improvisational Music Therapy

- Individual Improvisation: spontaneously creating music alone or with support of the music therapist using instruments and/or voice.
- Group Improvisation: Therapist and clients use a combination of musical sound sources to create improvisations within a group.

Re-creative Music Therapy

- Individual Singing: Clients sing precomposed songs with or without instrumental accompaniment.
- Multicultural Group Music Therapy: structured or improvisational musical experiences facilitated by the music therapist to promote awareness, respect, and understanding of different cultures.

Compositional Music Therapy

- Songwriting: occurs when changes are made to some or all of the lyrics and/or music of an existing song, or when a new song is written in its entirety.

Guidelines for Receptive Music Therapy

Listening to music is almost an essential part of daily life. It evokes memories, elicits feelings, and promotes communication. It can reflect or heighten mood and provides insight into thoughts, feelings, and emotions. Passive or receptive music listening experiences can promote relaxation, lift spirits, and provoke discussion of lyrics. Music listening may be indicated for children and adolescents with emotional/behavioral disorders when verbal communication and self-expression are too difficult or too painful. Receptive listening may be less threatening than performance-based activities and may initially provide structure and security for more emotionally fragile individuals.

Children and adolescents with emotional/behavioral problems have varying needs for external structure to control behavior. The more severe emotional disturbances seem to require a greater need for external structure (Gibbons, 1983). These individuals may have difficulty listening, following directions, and attending to task. Keep verbal directions to a minimum. Modeling appears to be more effective in developing musical skills. There is a need for immediate gratification, with a preference for immediate rewards rather than long-term ones.

Receptive music therapy may be appropriate for more traumatized children initially to establish trust with the therapist and comfort within the musical environment before progressing to more performance-based musical activities. Listening activities within a group environment can promote respect for others and development of group cohesion. Listening to another group member's musical selection can improve and develop peer relationships and increase tolerance for differences. Music listening can be used to promote relaxation and stress reduction in children and adolescents with emotional/behavioral disorders.

Children with behavioral disorders have difficulty transitioning to and from music as well as between musical activities. Music listening can be used to assist in allowing children to transition more easily to music, between musical activities, and when returning to the classroom. Music therapists can assist special education teachers in using receptive music listening to reduce stress and increase relaxation in the classroom. Music can also be used as positive reinforcement for some children and adolescents with behavioral disorders.

Music Listening

Overview. Music listening is a very flexible technique that engages the client in a process of listening to music chosen by the therapist or the client for purposes of reflection, symbolic thinking, or gaining insight. Receptive music therapy strategies such as music listening may be included at the initial levels of therapy in order to establish a relationship and promote trust, safety, and security with the therapist and within the musical environment. Music listening may also afford a more advanced level of therapy for those individuals capable of symbolic thinking and gaining personal insight into their behavior.

Receptive music listening is often implemented at the augmentative level of treatment, given that it typically addresses goals to manage behavioral problems, promote social development, and build basic skills in communication. Music listening may be contraindicated for clients with extremely disruptive and hyperactive behaviors, as they may lack the attention span and internal controls to effectively listen to music. Discussion of lyrics may be contraindicated for lower-functioning students who are incapable of symbolic thinking or obtaining insight into thoughts and feelings.

Preparation. Many factors should be considered when preparing for a receptive listening experience. The size, comfort, lighting, and acoustics of the room should be evaluated. Depending upon whether music listening is done individually or in a group, the music therapist will set up the room to accommodate for space and sound needs. Depending upon the therapeutic intent of the music listening, the music therapist can determine whether clients will be seated or lying down on a mat or rug. If listening is to promote relaxation (for example), the lighting should dimmed, if possible, to promote an appropriate atmosphere. Complete darkness is not advisable, as it limits the therapist's ability to monitor clients' experiences and may be frightening to some children.

The selection of the music is extremely important to the listening experience. The therapist must be acutely aware of the client's or group's present emotional state and select music based upon their current needs. The therapist also must be aware of the changing needs of the client or group as the session progresses and be able to adjust the music accordingly when necessary.

The acoustics of the room must be conducive to listening, and the sound system should be of the best possible quality affordable to provide a positive experience for the listener. Distractions should be avoided to allow complete focus on the music. The therapist should have access to a wide variety of music, based on the interests and needs of the students involved. Students may also ask to bring selections for music listening to contribute to the group experience.

What to observe. It is important for the music therapist to be extremely observant of the client's physical and emotional responses to music. Physical responses include degree of relaxation, type of breathing, and degree of engagement with the music. The therapist must be aware of the client's or group's degree of relaxation by noticing clients' breathing, level of engagement, amount and quality of movement, facial expressions, and verbal responses.

Procedures. Music listening experiences may be presented in a number of ways depending upon the needs of the client or group, therapeutic intent, and the experience of the therapist. When used for relaxation, the procedure begins with the music therapist providing a verbal induction, which is followed by active listening. After the listening experience concludes, the music therapist provides verbal cues for clients to return their awareness to the present environment and their bodies. At this point, the music therapist can process the clients' experience. Verbal processing can be in the form of a discussion of the experience, facilitated by the therapist or group. Nonverbal processing may be represented in a drawing such as a mandala, which may be more effective for some children with emotional/behavioral disorders who are unwilling or unable to process feelings verbally.

The induction should be planned by the therapist and based upon the needs of the client or group. An induction may be physical (such as a gradual tensing and releasing of muscle tension throughout the entire body) or imaginal (such as calming or peaceful nature scenes) to promote a relaxed physical state. A physical induction may be more appropriate for more active children and adolescents, while an imaginal induction may be more appropriate for students capable of symbolic thinking, reflection, and providing insight into their behavior.

The therapist must be extremely aware of the sound, tone, and inflection of their voice. The therapist's voice must be calming and reassuring to the client, providing a sense of safety and security during the listening experience. The choice of music is based upon clients' musical preferences, musical structure (e.g., tempo, melody, harmony), and length of piece. A music therapist may choose a single three- to five-minute instrumental piece with a high degree of predictability when clients need a good deal of structure and have limited attention spans. Older clients and those with longer attention spans may benefit from having two or three musical selections pieced together to create an experience lasting up to 10 or more minutes.

When the music listening is completed, the therapist must gradually return the listener to the present. The therapist must allow the client or group adequate time to return before they are able to process the experience verbally or nonverbally. The therapist then facilitates discussion of the experience with the client or group, carefully guiding the direction of the discussion to promote positive insight or emotional growth.

Adaptations. Students with emotional, learning, and behavioral disorders may benefit from active music listening in a group (Montello & Coons, 1998) to address goals related to self-esteem and cohesion. Initially, the music therapist selects a variety of music designed to evoke meaning and share feelings. Discussion includes the mood of the music, meaning of the lyrics, favorite aspects of the music, and memories experienced. The therapist would observe and encourage student responses. Eventually, selection of music for group listening can come from group members, who present their own recordings of favorite songs to the group and facilitate the group discussion. Over time, group cohesion gradually develops, and group members may become more cooperative and willing to participate in discussion (Montello & Coons, 1998).

A safe musical environment can create a community of musical sharing and develop positive peer relationships. Listening to a peer's music can develop tolerance and acceptance for others. Children and adolescents with emotional/behavioral difficulties can increase positive feelings for others, appreciate differences, and recognize similarities, seeing that they are not alone in their experiences. The group may begin to find comfort and security within their shared musical experiences. Listening to the music of other group members, even those whom they may dislike, can increase tolerance and improve the security of the musical experience.

It is suggested that more passive music listening experiences be introduced first when working with preadolescents with emotional/behavioral disorders to establish trust and avoid issues associated with more performance-based types of music therapy. Students may have difficulty expressing feelings through singing, playing, and moving in front of others, especially children who were sexually abused or severely traumatized. These children may be extremely sensitive to loud, aggressive drum beating and may be unable to tolerate loud music until a sense of safety and security is established in the group. Passive music listening may prove to be a less threatening means of self-expression and communication.

Skills developed through passive listening music therapy may be transferred eventually to more active music-making and improvisation. Children and adolescents with severe disruptive behavior disorders have difficulty with active rhythm training and may benefit from more passive listening techniques initially. Extremely aggressive or hyperactive children may have difficulty functioning in less structured forms of music-making. Skills gained through passive listening, such as listening to others and waiting your turn, may be transferred to other types of musical intervention.

Finally, exposure to multicultural music may provoke feelings and promote acceptance of different forms of musical expression. For example, listening to African drumming may promote discussion of nonverbal communication through music. Moving beyond their comfort zone may provide further therapeutic insight into the needs of children and adolescents with emotional/behavioral disorders.

Music and Imagery

Overview. Music and imagery techniques may be an effective treatment strategy for aggressive adolescents over time to reduce stress and anxiety, decrease anger and frustration, and channel aggressive impulses into creativity and self-control. In a group setting, music can promote communication, foster respect, and increase group cohesion. In a group setting, music and imagery may be an effective treatment strategy for adolescents with disruptive behavior disorders. Music and imagery techniques may be used with aggressive adolescent males with anger management issues to promote relaxation and develop positive coping skills. Music can be used to reduce physical tension, decrease anxiety, and channel aggressive impulses.

Music and imagery is typically administered at the augmentative or intensive level of therapy. It may initially be contraindicated for hyperactive, aggressive adolescents; however, it is believed that relaxation techniques must be taught and practiced to promote trust and security in the therapist and in the therapeutic process. Initially, attempts may be met with resistance or refusal, but students may become more cooperative over time. Guided Imagery and Music is also contraindicated in cases of active psychosis or severe neurological impairments, or if a client lacks sufficient ego strength (Bonny, 1989).

Because sessions may be held in a classroom, students might be seated at desks and school lighting might not be adjustable. In these cases, students can be encouraged to put their heads down on the desk and close their eyes in order to relax as much as possible. The therapist must have access to a good-quality portable sound system and a variety of music. Consideration must be given to the type of induction as well as the musical selection. A physical induction such as a tense/release can reduce physical tension, decrease anxiety, and reduce aggressive impulses. Musical selections should be brief initially to increase focus of attention and promote physical relaxation.

Preparation. In preparing the session, the therapist must be aware of the size and comfort of the listening area. It must be equipped with appropriate lighting, a superior sound system, and a variety of music based on the perceived needs of the client. During the session, the therapist must be aware of the physical and emotional responses of the client as well as the degree of verbal interaction with the therapist. The therapist must be attuned to the needs of the client during the session and select and/or change music as the session progresses. After the experience, the therapist must facilitate discussion and aid the client in processing their experience.

What to observe. During the session, the therapist should be aware of the students' physical and emotional responses to music. Physical responses may include deep breathing, muscle relaxation, and degree of engagement. Emotional responses may include facial expressions, bodily responses, and involvement in processing the experience.

Procedures. Once clients are in a relaxed state and given a basic induction to increase relaxation and focus on the music, the music therapist begins playing the selected music. Brief excerpts of classical music such as Beethoven's "Moonlight Sonata" and Bach's "Jesu, Joy of Man's Desiring" may be appropriate. After the music has ended, the students are then given time to reenter their environment and process their experience either in a creative way (e.g., drawing mandalas) or a more cognitive way (e.g., writing descriptive words, or group discussion). Students should be encouraged to discuss their feelings and their experience with the group, if desired, as the therapist guides the discussion. Some students may be willing to discuss their "peaceful place" and their experience with the group, while the remaining group members should be encouraged to listen without judgment. Over time, clients will likely become more proficient at entering and returning from the imagery experience and report feeling that they are more fully engaged in the process.

Adaptations. When used within individual sessions, music and imagery may be used to promote relaxation and provide insight into thoughts, feelings, and behaviors. Listening may be receptive or passive, or active and intentional. Guided imagery may be indicated to increase personal exploration, explore interpersonal relationships, and resolve long-standing issues. Guided Imagery and Music is contraindicated in individuals that are actively psychotic or incapable of symbolic thinking. It can be a very effective treatment modality for receptive individuals. Guided Imagery and Music (GIM) involves four major components: the music, the client, the therapist, and the environment, with music being the most important element. Music is the catalyst for growth and change. Music is the link to an individual's psychoemotional state.

Case example—Troy. Troy was a 17-year-old male diagnosed with severe depression and referred to individual music therapy sessions to increase self-esteem and self-expression. Troy was on grade level academically, but seemed to have difficulty concentrating on his work due to his emotional issues. Troy initially participated in active music-making sessions that were more performance-based, such as playing the drums while the therapist played the piano, using improvisational and structured musical activities. Musically, Troy was very expressive, but he had great difficulty in discussing issues verbally and processing his feelings.

It was suggested that Troy might benefit from Guided Imagery and Music sessions, since he was capable of symbolic thinking, could differentiate between symbol and reality, and had a positive relationship with the therapist. Several individual sessions were used, with Troy using the Helen Bonny tapes and methods of induction. Mandala drawing was used to help reentry into a conscious state and serve as a more concrete, nonverbal means of self-expression. Although the process seemed to elicit relaxation, imagery, and discussion, Troy had difficulty using guided imagery experiences to fully achieve insight into his issues and develop problem-solving skills, and expressed a desire to return to active music-making within his music therapy sessions.

There could be several reasons for this outcome. It is believed that issues of depression require a longer series of sessions for clients to express feelings, evoke images, and resolve issues (Bonny, 1898). Troy initially participated in active music-making experiences with the therapist, and although he had developed a positive, trusting rapport with the therapist, GIM may have been too intense and personal for Troy to share with the therapist at this time. He may have encountered frightening imagery which he was unable or unwilling to share with the therapist. Requesting to return to the more familiar active music-making may have been Troy's way of avoiding the intensely powerful feelings elicited by Guided Imagery and Music. Troy may also have been resistant to exploring these feelings and emotions at that time.

Guidelines for Improvisational Music Therapy

Improvisational Music Therapy is defined as "the art of spontaneously creating music while playing, rather than performing a composition already written" (Bruscia, 1987. p. 5). Music therapists strive to create music of a high quality while accepting whatever response the client offers during the improvisation. Improvisations may be vocal, instrumental, or movement in response to the music. Improvisations may be active or receptive. Active improvisations involve participation of the client in the experience, while receptive improvisations involve the client observing or listening to the improvisation. Improvisational music therapy may be used with individuals or groups and should be based on the needs and capabilities of the clients.

Improvisations may be structured or free-flowing in nature. Structured improvisations are designed with a clear beginning, middle, and ending. Free-flowing improvisations flow naturally and are based on events as they occur in the session. Improvisational music therapy may be used with individuals or groups, but the therapist must be aware of the capabilities and challenges of the population. Children with emotional/behavioral disorders represent a wide variety of needs and challenging behaviors. Music can be the stimulus for change in children and adolescents with severe behavior problems.

Improvisation may serve as the initial level of therapy by establishing contact and musically establishing communication with an emotionally withdrawn child. Improvisational music therapy may serve as a more advanced level of therapy to promote nonverbal self-expression and communication. A higher-functioning child or adolescent may be able to begin to verbalize feelings and provide insight into behavior issues through improvisation. Improvisational music therapy may be contraindicated for emotionally fragile children who may be overwhelmed by the lack of structure initially. Improvisation may also be contraindicated for extremely hyperactive children and adolescents and those with disruptive behavior disorders or children requiring a higher level of structure and intervention.

Several successful music therapy approaches have been used with children and adolescents with emotional/behavioral difficulties. There are some indications that an instructional music therapy approach may help reduce impulsive behaviors in other settings, such as the classroom (Rickson, 2006). Some students with disruptive behavior disorders may have difficulty with rhythm training in a group setting (Montello & Coons, 1998). Improvisational music therapy with aggressive adolescent boys suggests that creative music-making may cause overarousal in some students with disruptive behavior disorders, suggesting that some children cannot tolerate the lack of structure. Some children and adolescents with disruptive behavior disorders may respond more positively to structured music therapy programs that are very predictable (Barkley, 1998). Music therapists working with children with emotional/behavioral difficulties may prefer to use highly structured rhythmic activities for individuals and small groups, at least initially.

Goals of improvisational music therapy are based upon the needs and interests of the client. Individual goals may be to increase awareness of self, others, and the environment. Some children may use improvisational music therapy for self-expression, communication, and exploration of feelings. Goals of group improvisation may be to increase group cooperation and participation and awareness of others. Improvisation may serve as the initial level of therapy by establishing contact and musically establishing communication with an emotionally withdrawn child. Improvisational music therapy may serve as a more advanced level of therapy to promote nonverbal self-expression and communication. A higher-functioning child or adolescent may be able to begin to verbalize feelings and provide insight into behavior issues.

In preparing the session, the music therapist must be aware of the lighting, acoustics, furniture, and arrangement of instruments and create a safe, secure musical environment for the client. The therapist must also be aware of the client's emotional and physical state before preparing for the music therapy session. The therapist should try to meet the child where they are at by matching their emotional or physical state musically.

Individual Improvisation

Overview. Individual improvisation is defined as spontaneously creating music based on the musical and emotional needs of an individual client in music therapy. After information is obtained through the initial referral, assessment, and background, it can be determined whether improvisational music therapy may be an effective modality of treatment for this client. Verbal therapy is contraindicated initially until a trusting relationship can be established with the therapist within a safe, secure musical environment.

The goals of improvisational music therapy are typically to increase nonverbal communication and self-expression. Improvisations were almost exclusively instrumental in nature and were both structured and free-flowing. Individual improvisation occurs at the augmentative or intensive level of therapy.

Preparation. In preparing the session, the therapist must be aware of the size and comfort of the listening area. It must be equipped with appropriate lighting, with a variety of instruments available to the client. Depending upon the needs of the client and the therapeutic objectives, the music therapist may arrange the room to have rhythmic and percussive instruments and/or melodic instruments present.

What to observe. During the session, the therapist must be aware of the physical and emotional responses of the client as well as the degree of verbal interaction with the therapist. The therapist must be attuned to the needs of the client during the session and select and/or change music as the session progresses. After the experience, the therapist must facilitate discussion and aid the client in processing their experience. During individual improvisations, it is important to be aware of the physical and emotional responses of the client. The therapist must be attuned to affect, facial expressions, bodily responses, and verbal interactions of the client. Musically, it is important to notice the instruments chosen or ignored and whether preferred instruments are melodic or rhythmic. Musical elements to be evaluated include rhythm, pitch, tempo, and dynamics.

Procedures. There are a variety of methods for implementing an individual music improvisation; however, the music therapist must first assess the emotional/physical state of the client before engaging in conversation and beginning the improvisation. By engaging the client in music-making either by initiating a musical conversation or allowing the client to initiate interaction, the music therapist may assess the level of support and structure the client needs in order to be successful. Music therapists are encouraged to be aware of any musical motifs or themes that may emerge to utilize in planning for future sessions.

Case example–Mark. Mark was a 12-year-old African-American male, diagnosed with severe depression. Mark's background was characterized by a history of abuse and neglect, and Mark was removed from the family of origin at an early age. He was placed in a variety of foster homes, special schools, and residential treatment facilities for children with emotional/behavioral problems. As a result, he had severe abandonment issues and an inability to trust or form appropriate relationships with others. Mark was extremely quiet and withdrawn and was unable to benefit from verbal therapy initially. The special education teacher referred him for individual music therapy sessions at his school, hoping that music therapy would allow Mark to increase self-expression and communication.

Mark's musical journey took an entire school year. His primary therapeutic need was to establish a trusting relationship with another person, and hopefully with the therapist, through music. During the initial assessment, Mark was quiet and cooperative, and responded appropriately to the therapist's requests. He responded to a wide variety of instruments and activities and indicated that he would be willing to attend music therapy sessions, although his affect remained depressed.

The initial assessment revealed that verbal communication and interactions were contraindicated, at least initially. It was believed that Mark might respond well to an entirely improvisational approach to music therapy. The session was prepared with a large variety of percussion instruments, to encourage musical exploration while the therapist improvised at the piano. Initially, Mark explored percussion instruments as the therapist improvised at the piano, reflecting Mark's musical responses. Mark seemed to maintain a physical distance from the therapist, as if evaluating the situation and his willingness to trust the therapist.

The course of therapy became dramatically different when Mark engaged in improvisations with the therapist at the piano. Initial improvisations reflected a melancholy, as well as deep pain, sadness, and longing. Music was improvised based on Mark's musical responses, and were generally in a minor key and very expressive. Piano improvisation became the primary means of communication between Mark and the therapist. The therapist would often vocalize along with the improvisation to establish and maintain a more nurturing, human connection with Mark, although little or no vocalization usually occurred in response. The musical environment was supportive and nonjudgmental. Musical responses were encouraged and nurtured by the therapist.

As Mark became more trusting of the therapist, musical motifs began to reoccur in his music, which the therapist acknowledged, repeated, and developed along with Mark. The music seemed to almost nurture Mark, filling within him a need that had long been denied, and allowing him to grow emotionally through the music. At times, if the improvisation seemed too intense, Mark would withdraw physically from the therapist and return to improvising on percussion instruments. This may represent resistance, as well as time needed for Mark to process musical and emotional growth occurring through creative improvisations.

Despite some resistance, which was necessary for musical and emotional growth, Mark remained committed to his music therapy sessions, and relied on the piano as his primary means of nonverbal self-expression and communication. Mark and the therapist developed a positive nonverbal relationship through the music, and emotional growth was observed both within and outside of the musical environment. Mark's music began to grow and change, at times reflecting a personal joy in his creative musical expression. His music began to express newfound feelings of happiness, self-confidence, and hopefulness.

Music empowered Mark to grow and change by providing new opportunities for positive social interactions. Mark's teacher reported more self-esteem and self-confidence in his academic work, and the establishment of more positive peer interactions. Music provided the means to integrate his past negative experiences and develop positive new experiences, as well as hope for potential future experiences. The "music child" within Mark had awakened and grown through creative improvisation.

Group Improvisation

Overview. During group improvisation, the music therapist leads group members in an improvisational music experience using a variety of instruments based upon therapeutic goals for increased social skills, behavioral objectives (e.g., responding to nonverbal cues), and emotional functioning. Group improvisations may be facilitated in a variety of ways. Sometimes music therapists may choose to provide a reference for the improvisation such as an emotion, a situation, a memory, etc. Sometimes, the music therapist may choose to limit the experience in some way to increase group cohesion and provide additional structures and limits, such as only providing percussive instruments, encouraging turn-taking or call-and-response techniques, or instilling time limits.

Although improvisational music therapy is generally contraindicated for children and adolescents with extreme hyperactivity and disruptive behavior disorders, highly structured group improvisational activities can be extremely effective with this population. Children and adolescents with severe emotional/behavior disorders respond well to a highly structured musical environment with clear expectations and firm and consistent limits. Structured group improvisational music therapy can be used to increase group cooperation and participation, improve impulse control, and develop appropriate peer relationships. Other goals may be to increase compliance with group expectations and work together to create a group musical product. Starting with highly structured improvisational activities that are therapist-led may progress to free-flowing improvisations, which are group-led in future sessions.

Preparation. Before the session, the therapist carefully evaluates the needs of the group, selects the music, and plans the session. The room must be carefully arranged and the instruments selected based upon the activities designed. The therapist plans, structures, and implements the session.

What to observe. It is important to observe and assess the physical and emotional state of the group immediately upon arrival in the music room. Evaluate group dynamics, affect, and interpersonal communication between group members. Assess group cooperation, willingness to participate, and focus of attention on task. The therapist must intervene when necessary to maintain a safe, secure musical environment where all group members can feel free to express themselves. Any attempts at threats and intimidation must not be tolerated. During musical interactions, the therapist must be aware of musical involvement and willingness to listen and follow directions, as well as individual frustration tolerance.

Procedures. Group improvisation activities should encourage personal freedom, increase appropriate social interaction, and develop group cohesion. When possible, groups should be organized according to the capabilities and personalities of group members to promote a safe experience where group members can communicate emotions through musical improvisation.

In structured improvisational activities, the therapist will introduce the activity and assign the parts based on knowledge of students' musical abilities and willingness to cooperate. Activities should be designed to allow students to be successful. The therapist will direct activities and conduct the session. After each session, the therapist should document the session and evaluate group progress to plan for future sessions. The intention is to move from highly structured group activities to free-flowing improvisations as group cohesion increases and peer relationships improve.

Free-flowing improvisations (those without a theme or referenced concept) should be attempted only after group cohesion has been established and the group has experienced success with structured improvisational activities. It is suggested that brief free-flowing improvisational activities be attempted initially and evaluated by the therapist before attempting longer improvisations.

Some children with severe hyperactivity, attention deficits, or disruptive behavior disorders may have difficulty dealing with a lack of structure in improvisational music therapy. Some children and adolescents with emotional/behavioral disorders need structure in order to experience success. A lack of structure can cause some children to feel overwhelmed and overstimulated. A return to a more predictable structured approach may be necessary for some children and adolescents with emotional/behavioral disorders. Structure and order in music can help reduce the internal chaos that some emotionally disturbed children and adolescents experience in their lives.

Case example—Josh. Josh was a 13-year-old African-American male diagnosed with a conduct disorder. He attended an alternative school for children and adolescents with emotional and behavioral disorders. Josh had been expelled from his previous middle school due to fighting, aggression, and a history of noncompliant and rebellious behavior. He was angry, aggressive, and disrespectful to peers, staff, and teachers. The alternative program had a strict, highly developed schoolwide behavior system designed to improve behavior, increase academic skills, and return students to a less restrictive school environment.

Josh attended group music therapy sessions with five male classmates. The group was assigned according to their special education class, and was not always a compatible group, musically and socially. Initially, Josh was loud, aggressive, disruptive, and attention-seeking. He rebelled against the structure imposed by the therapist, and engaged in power struggles with peers. Josh attempted to dominate others musically, blocking out or sabotaging group musical responses. Josh's controlling, dominant behavior interfered with the musical and social development of the group.

The music therapist consulted with the special education teacher regarding the social/emotional needs of the group to plan for music therapy sessions. Josh was of particular concern because of his attempts to dominate and control the group. Josh apparently had serious learning issues, which caused him to have low self-esteem. He often attempted to blame others for his mistakes, and developed an aggressive, intimidating nature to feel better about himself. Because of the intense nature of the school program, any attempts at threatening or intimidation on Josh's part had to be met with immediate consequences, with removal from the musical environment, if necessary.

The primary goal of music therapy within the group setting was to increase cooperation and participation, improve appropriate social interactions, and develop peer relationships. It was believed that a highly structured musical environment with clear and consistent expectations for behavior could improve group dynamics and increase musical self-expression. Music therapy sessions would be highly structured, at least initially, with emphasis on the group learning, performing, and responding to precomposed music to establish and develop musical relationships.

Musical activities with specific parts were designed to increase group cohesion and respect for others. Parts were assigned at random or by volunteer. To establish "fairness," parts could be picked out of a hat or a headed tambourine, allowing all group members to become proficient at each musical part. Successes through group musical activities would contribute to group cohesion as well develop group cooperation and participation. Group musical activities could also develop social interaction and peer relationships and increase individual self-expression and self-esteem.

Activities were selected to develop appropriate musical responses and increase group cooperation and participation. Each person had a specific musical part to play, and each musical part was essential to group's musical success. "Joshua Fought the Battle of Jericho" was a particular favorite of the group, and each person took turns being the musical director. As Josh experienced success within the musical environment, he was able to establish more appropriate peer relationships through the musical activities. As his hostility and aggression decreased, Josh became a more respectful, cooperative member of the group. Josh was able to learn how to reduce impulses and channel anger and aggression more appropriately through musical self-expression. As Josh learned to respect and appreciate other students' musical contributions, he earned the respect and appreciation of group members in return.

As the group progressed, improvisation was gradually added, primarily through instrumental improvisation or "drumming." A similar approach was used, and instruments were selected, as well as a musical director. Each group member was given an opportunity to direct an improvisation for a brief period. At the end of the improvisation, the director was to give one positive compliment to each performer, with no negative feedback permitted. The approach continued until all group members had the opportunity to perform as the musical director, allowing all group members the opportunity to participate in a leadership role.

Participation in structured improvisational musical experiences provided Josh with opportunity for personal and musical growth. Initially, the more structured musical environment allowed Josh to learn appropriate behavior within social situations and increase positive peer interactions. Over the course of treatment, he was able to develop more acceptable forms of self-expression and communication through group musical activities.

Group music therapy sessions helped Josh to accept responsibility for his actions rather than blame others for his mistakes. His role in the group progressed from "bully" or intimidator to becoming more of a "team player." He became gradually more willing to accept others' musical responses as well as his own. Josh seemed more able to accept constructive criticism from others and grow and develop his range of musical self-expression within the safety of the musical group. Improvement within the musical environment transferred to other group situations where Josh was able to be placed in a less restrictive school environment after leaving the alternative school setting.

Guidelines for Re-creative Music Therapy

Re-creative music therapy is defined as participation in previously precomposed music through singing, movement, and playing instruments. Re-creative music therapy may be initially indicated to establish structure and provide a sense of security in music. A predictable musical environment with consistent routines may create a sense of trust and help to establish a positive relationship with the therapist. Familiar music can create a sense of comfort and safety in which feelings can be expressed and explored. Performance-based activities may be contraindicated for extremely shy or withdrawn children initially. Too many instruments or activities may be overstimulating for students with hyperactivity or disruptive behavior disorders.

Participation in music-making demands attention and self-control. Music therapists have documented that children and adolescents with emotional/behavioral problems usually exhibit disordered beating and an inability to sustain a steady beat or rhythmic pattern due to poor impulse control (Merle-Fishman & Marcus, 1982; Nordoff & Robbins, 1977). A steady beat can be used to contain and hold a client and provide structure to disorganized musical responses. Music can be an organizing force providing structure and order to counteract internal chaos (Birkenshaw-Fleming, 1993). Research suggests that a link may exist between impaired timing and impulsive behavior. Creating organized music with peers can improve social skills and increase group cooperation and participation (Birkenshaw-Fleming, 1993). Rehearsal of rhythmic tasks can lead to improvement in organization and impulse control.

Motivation and immediate rewards of creative group music-making through improvisation could eventually enable children and adolescents with disruptive behavior disorders to benefit from group improvisation (Rickson, 2006). The immediate rewards inherent in music can provide a high degree of motivation for musical success (Aigen, 1997). Children and adolescents with disruptive behavior disorders demonstrated improvements in listening, attending, and engaging in group music-making activities (Rickson, 2006).

Frequent changes of instruments and activities can help to focus attention and increase participation. Movement activities can help to develop motor coordination and release physical energy in a constructive manner. Rhythm can be used to improve body awareness and motor coordination. Instrumental activities can improve group cooperation and participation. Structured group activities can vary in complexity, which allows for different levels of participation. Each child can have a different role in the group musical experience, creating a sense of responsibility and belonging.

Rhythm is defined as the most important and most dynamic element in music. Rhythm has the unique potential to energize and bring order. Without rhythm, there is chaos (Gaston, 1968). Nordoff and Robbins (1979) have diagnosed 13 categories of musical responses, with eight specific categories of rhythmic responses, and developed improvisational techniques to structure and integrate disorganized rhythmic responses. Merle-Fishman and Marcus (1982) determined that emotionally disturbed children demonstrated a higher incidence of impulsive, disordered beating. Improvements in rhythmic development may require more interventions by the therapist. Rhythm may be important and useful in the assessment and evaluation of music therapy programs for emotionally disturbed children and adolescents (Gibbons, 1983).

Singing can be a "direct extension of self" (Nordoff & Robbins, 1971). Singing both alone and with others can improve social relationships, stimulate speech and language development, and develop feelings of self-confidence and self-esteem. Singing allows an appropriate means of self-expression for children and adolescents with emotional/behavioral disorders. Songs with content they find meaningful allow children to explore and express difficult emotions in a nonthreatening manner. Certain songs may relate to a personal emotional need that is difficult to express verbally. Songs that explore feelings of sadness may allow development of an emotional experience through musical self-expression.

Group singing can increase awareness of others, social interaction, group cooperation, and participation. Many children and adolescents with emotional/behavioral disorders are extremely self-absorbed and have little concern or empathy for others. Group songwriting can promote listening and developing respect and caring for others. Working together toward a group goal can help develop a sense of belonging and allow students to compromise and substitute their own needs for the needs of the group. Compositional music therapy involves risk-taking, which can help develop leadership skills and increase cooperation and participation toward a common goal.

Participation is more important than performance with children and adolescents with behavioral and interpersonal problems. Singing can improve motivation, concentration, and focus of attention. Group performance creates a sense of purpose and pride in personal achievement. Music can provide unity to groups with difficult personalities and help improve group dynamics. Songs can have a purpose in the group. A "greeting song" can ease transition into music and provide a sense of unity in the group, and a "good-bye song" can provide closure and transition to other activities. Structure can impose order and a sense of purpose for children with emotional/behavioral disorders.

Re-creative musical activities can improve impulse control, develop appropriate rhythmic responses, and promote emotional growth. Playing instruments can improve motor coordination and improve attention to task. Group participation can increase cooperation and participation, improve social skills, and develop appropriate peer relationships. The immediate rewards of re-creative music therapy are appropriate for students with hyperactivity and disruptive behavior disorders. The long-term rewards of developing musical skills require hard work and determination, which can develop patience and improve frustration tolerance and pride in personal accomplishments for students with emotional or behavioral disorders

Individual Singing

Overview. Individual re-creative music therapy can be based on the needs and interests of the client. Singing can be used to increase self-expression and develop self-esteem. Lyric discussion can promote personal growth and provide insight into feelings and behaviors. Lyric analysis may provide the catalyst for change and emotional growth and development for students with severe behavioral disorders. Performances can develop self-confidence and pride in personal accomplishments.

There are no known contraindications for individual singing. This experience takes place primarily at the augmentative or intensive level of treatment, depending upon the therapeutic goals addressed.

Preparation. The music therapist should be familiar with a variety of music and musical styles geared toward the interests and needs of the client and have access to a piano or guitar to provide musical accompaniment. The room should be comfortable, adequate in size, and well-lit, and have good acoustics. The client or the therapist, based on the perceived emotional needs of the individual at the time, can initiate the choice of music. The therapist must be aware of the client's mood, affect, and degree of musical involvement. Singing can be evaluated on accuracy of pitch, tone, inflection, and degree of emotional expressiveness. Lyric analysis and discussion can be attempted based on the client's willingness to participate and ability to apply meaning to their personal life and real-life situations. Higher-functioning clients may be able to develop insight into their feelings and behaviors to promote emotional growth and change.

What to observe. It is important for the music therapist to be extremely observant of the client's physical and emotional responses to music, level of interest and motivation, frustration tolerance, and level of self-awareness. Of particular interest is the client's need for accompaniment, musical structure, and ability to accept feedback on his/her singing.

Procedures. The music therapist works with the client to choose a song that addresses underlying clinical objectives. Initially, singing songs chosen by the client may provide indicators of the client's emotional functioning, maturity level, and music preferences. Depending upon the client's age and ability, the music therapist may then provide printed lyrics or sheet music of the chosen song and may watch a performance of the song on video (such as YouTube) in advance of singing the song for the first time. Depending upon client need and preference, song accompaniment may be provided live by the music therapist on the guitar or piano, through a karaoke recording, or as the actual song (e.g., from a CD). Clients may request to sing alone or ask the music therapist to sing along with them. Oftentimes, music therapists can provide subtle support through singing along with their client to aid in keeping tempo and correcting melody, etc.

Music therapists may keep a binder of each client's song choices with copies of sheet music and lyrics. A song list at the front of the binder may assist clients in choosing songs to sing during their sessions. New songs can be suggested by either the client or the music therapist. It is also suggested that the music therapist make notation of any accompaniment rhythms and tempi used on electronic keyboards to ensure continuity of song presentation across sessions.

Case example—Holly. Holly was a bright, 16-year-old female diagnosed with bipolar disorder who was performing on grade level academically, but experienced dramatic mood swings that interfered with her academic performance. Holly attended a high school program for adolescents with emotional and behavioral problems and was referred for individual music therapy sessions because of her beautiful singing voice and interest in music. The treatment team believed that music therapy might help Holly increase self-expression and improve self-esteem. The initial assessment revealed that Holly preferred vocal activities.

Holly was raised in a very strict home environment by well-meaning but extremely overprotective parents. Her mental health issues were seen as a stigma upon the family, and Holly began requiring treatment during early adolescence. Academics and therapy seemed to be the primary focus of Holly's life, even though Holly longed to audition for chorus, plays, and musicals. Holly was not permitted to engage in sports or other age-appropriate extracurricular activities.

Holly had a beautiful soprano voice, with accurate pitch and inflection; however, her singing seemed empty and totally devoid of emotion. Holly was unable to connect the music to her emotions at this time. The primary focus of music therapy was to establish a trusting relationship with Holly which would support work on her emotional issues. Holly was extremely interested in musical theater and singing show tunes. The therapist initially served as the accompanist while Holly sang. As the musical relationship progressed, lyric discussion and analysis allowed Holly to connect her emotions to the lyrics she was singing and allow her more musical freedom and self-expression in her vocal responses.

Phantom of the Opera and *Les Misérables* were favorites because Holly had seen both musicals in the theater. The music of *Les Misérables* seemed to be of particular interest to Holly, especially "Castle on a Cloud" and "I Dreamed a Dream." At the time, Holly was trying to convince her parents to allow her to take private voice lessons and possibly audition for a local musical theater group. Holly's parents were reluctant out of the fear that failure might trigger additional mental health issues. The lyrics of both songs seemed to express feelings of loss and longing, as well a sense of determination. Holly was encouraged to discuss the lyrics and interpret what they meant to her. At a time when Holly was angry with her parents, the therapist encouraged Holly to put that feeling into the song and really allow herself to experience her anger. An excerpt from "I Dreamed a Dream" is included below.

I Dreamed a Dream

And still I dream he'll come to me,
That we will live the years together.
But there are dreams that cannot be,
And there are storms we cannot weather.

I had a dream my life would be
So different from this hell I'm living,
So different now from what it seemed,
Now life has killed the dream I dreamed.

The lyrics and the music gave Holly permission to be angry within the safety of the musical environment. Holly finally expressed her feelings appropriately and allowed herself permission to feel angry. The music empowered Holly to confront her parents and express her desire for private voice lessons. Although reluctant initially, Holly's parents finally agreed to honor her request. Once Holly convinced her parents that she was emotionally strong enough to take private voice lessons, she became more self-confident and self-assured. Music therapy sessions then revealed more appropriate emotional connection to the music and the lyrics as Holly revealed greater self-esteem and increased self-expression in her singing. Because of her increased self-confidence, Holly successfully auditioned for the high school chorus and became more active in the high school theater department. Holly felt more "normal" and was identified by her peers and her parents with her abilities rather than with her illness.

Multicultural Group Music Therapy

Overview. Multicultural music can be defined as using structured or improvisational techniques to promote awareness, respect, and understanding of different cultures. Multicultural music can be used to establish contact with clients of different nationalities and promote tolerance and respect for others. Multicultural music therapy can promote knowledge of different nationalities, beliefs, cultures, and religions. Students can be exposed to different tonalities, instruments, and languages to promote diversity and increase cultural awareness.

Multicultural songs and improvisations can be influential in establishing therapeutic relationships. Cultural empathy is becoming more essential in a mostly heterogeneous society. Those with different cultural identities can remain isolated in our society. Music therapists must remain open to exploring, learning, and interacting through multicultural music. Multicultural music can expand the musical and clinical consciousness of music therapists (Shapiro, 2005). Music therapists must become more aware of the needs and values of clients from other cultures.

Music can open the doors to communication in a culturally diverse society. Music therapists must become more aware of the specific role music plays within each culture. There is a need for the inclusion of multicultural music therapy in clinical training and research into multicultural clinical practice. Cultural considerations must also be included in music therapy assessments. Cultural considerations are important in assisting the therapist in effective planning and implementation of music therapy services (Chase, 2003). Participation in multicultural music therapy can increase self-expression and communication and develop social skills. Multicultural music can be adapted to provide different levels of therapy. It may be the initial form of establishing communication with a client with a different nationality.

In group therapy, multicultural music can be used in improvisational and performance-based activities. Singing in other languages may be difficult for clients with severe communication disorders. Multicultural activities must be highly structured, with fewer choices of instruments and activities to prevent overstimulation of children with severe hyperactivity and disruptive behavior disorders. The music therapist must research and prepare multicultural music based on the needs and goals of the individual or group. Careful consideration must be given to learning proper pronunciation and meaning of lyrics and the appropriate use and playing of multicultural instruments.

Preparation. Music therapists should be well acquainted with the music before presenting it to the group, introducing vocal and instrumental parts separately. Difficult parts should be introduced in small segments, with frequent review before proceeding. Additional concepts can be introduced in the same matter and continued until mastered by the group. The room size must be appropriate for the size of the group, with accurate acoustics. Instruments must be in tune and of the best quality affordable. The therapist must be aware of individual needs within the group, considering attention span, frustration tolerance, and musical abilities.

What to observe. The therapist must also be aware of group dynamics and willingness to cooperate. Parts can be simplified or adapted according to the needs and abilities of the group to ensure successful musical experiences and promote pride of accomplishment. Assess group cooperation, willingness to participate, and focus of attention on task. The therapist must intervene when necessary to maintain a safe, secure musical environment where all group members can feel free to express themselves. Any attempts at threats and intimidation must not be tolerated. During musical interactions, the therapist must be aware of musical involvement and willingness to listen and follow directions, as well as individual frustration tolerance.

Procedures. There are many ways to implement a multicultural music therapy experience. For example, group experiences can be organized by themes (e.g., diversity), country/nationality, or language. Regardless of the theme chosen, one of the main emphases of the group is respecting differences in others and appreciating and understanding different nationalities and cultures.

Adaptations. Performance-based classroom groups can be facilitated by the music therapist to increase group cooperation and participation and improve peer relationships. In keeping with the schoolwide theme of diversity, creative arts therapists explore multicultural art and music with students in arts festivals and holiday performances. A winter concert may include various holiday songs that acknowledge different cultural celebrations, such as Hanukkah, La Posada, Christmas, and Kwanzaa. A springtime performance may also be created to celebrate the academic and artistic accomplishments of the students throughout the school year and may incorporate seasonal themes such as spring themes of flowers, blooms, weather, etc. In this example, the music therapist may choose to feature a combined performance of the chorus with instrumental accompaniment to the Japanese song "Sakura" (which translates into "cherry blossoms" in English) because of its beautiful pentatonic harmonies. Performance-based groups may include chorus, hand bells, and recorder groups. The music therapist may choose to orchestrate an original accompaniment, which could include Orff instruments, resonator bells, Chinese bell tree, triangles, finger cymbals, cymbal, drum, gong, and piano.

By performing holiday and spring concerts at nursing homes and senior centers, clients with emotional and behavioral disorders become more caring, productive members of the community. Singing for the elderly allows these students to develop empathy, accountability, and respect for others. Despite their many personal problems, students learn that they can make a valuable contribution to the lives of others and become more productive members of the community.

Guidelines for Compositional Music Therapy

Compositional music therapy can provide a musical structure and elicit individual responses. Songwriting can provide the therapist with valuable insights into behavior and reflect individual as well as group issues. Creative songwriting can promote significant growth within an individual group member and within the group itself. Songwriting is a success-oriented process that is focused on increasing self-expression and developing group cohesion. Significant growth and change can occur in the therapeutic environment through songwriting (Edgerton, 1990).

Lyric writing can provide insight into personal and group issues. Lyric analysis can allow for the recovery or repressed material for children and adolescents who have experienced trauma (Edgerton, 1990). Songwriting and musical composition is included in improvisational music therapy (Bruscia, 1987). No specific agreement exists on the best approach to musical composition.

Goals of songwriting may include increasing group cohesion, exploring personal and group issues, and gaining insight through compromise and cooperation (Edgerton, 1990). Songwriting can improve positive self-concept, establish peer relationships, and promote successful experiences of emotionally disturbed children and adolescents to increase self-expression and improve self-esteem. Group songwriting can delay the need for immediate gratification, improve peer relationships, and establish group goal-setting. Group members can increase assertiveness and develop self-confidence (Haines, 1989).

Songwriting

Overview. Songwriting is defined as composing original music and lyrics to express feelings and emotions. Individuals can use songwriting in music therapy to release feelings, explore creativity, examine problems, and provide solutions in a positive manner. Past experiences and behaviors can be re-examined in a safe and secure musical environment. Group songwriting can promote group cooperation and participation. Songwriting can promote tolerance and respect for others through a shared group purpose. Songwriting can be an extremely personal form of self-expression and communication.

Songwriting may be inspired by a melodic fragment or rhythmic pattern initiated in an improvisation. Recurrent musical motifs or repeated rhythms may be inspiration for a melody or lyric. Lyrics may be based on personal or group experiences, past problems, or difficult relationships. Lyrics may be inspired by original poems or private journals that deal with personal experiences or painful memories.

Songwriting may be indicated for children and adolescents with emotional/behavioral disorders if they are able to express thoughts and feelings verbally and are capable of problem-solving and symbolic thinking. Songwriting may be contraindicated for children with psychosis and distorted thinking and those incapable of distinguishing fantasy from reality. Songwriting may be difficult for students with severe communication disorders and may be too overwhelming for students requiring a higher degree of structure and support.

Songwriting may involve a more intense and personal level of music therapy than receptive or re-creative music therapy for some individuals. It may be utilized after initial musical contact has been established and the therapist has developed a trusting relationship with the client and a deeper level of therapy is possible.

Individual goals for songwriting may include increasing self-expression and communication and improving self-esteem. Songwriting may be used to provide personal reflection, encourage problem-solving, and promote emotional growth. Group songwriting can be used to develop problem-solving skills, increase group cooperation and participation, and improve tolerance and respect for others. Group songwriting helps develop shared responsibility and ability to compromise and work cooperatively for a single purpose.

Preparation. Songwriting may occur spontaneously or have been previously discussed in therapy. What comes first, the melody or the lyrics? Either may provide the inspiration for songwriting. The music therapist must be aware of the needs of the individual or group and the goals for therapy. Musical themes, melodic ideas, or rhythmic patterns may have evolved in musical improvisations and can be utilized in songwriting. The room must be adequate in size for the needs of the individual or group, with a piano or guitar to provide accompaniment. Instruments should be of the highest quality affordable, and the room should have accurate acoustics. Paper and pen may be needed to transcribe or create lyrics, and staff paper or musical software is needed to notate music. A recording device is needed to record ideas and revisions. The final product may be videotaped, recorded, or performed.

The music therapist must be familiar with a variety of musical styles and accompaniments. The music therapist may facilitate the songwriting process or assist the client with the songwriting process by transcribing the melody and lyrics musically.

What to observe. The therapist must observe and assess the client's receptivity to expressing thoughts and feelings through songwriting, and observe the client's emotional state, affect, and willingness to cooperate. Be aware of any resistance or attempt at avoidance. Some students may not be ready to explore personal feelings or painful memories at this time. In a group setting, the therapist must evaluate group attitude and group dynamics to determine ability to participate in songwriting activities. Group cooperation and participation must be encouraged to participate in songwriting. The therapist must facilitate group discussion, at least initially.

Procedures. Songwriting may be approached in a variety of ways. Songwriting may be initiated by the individual or group or suggested by the therapist. A melodic motif or rhythmic pattern from an improvisational activity may be utilized in songwriting. A theme may be presented by the individual or group based on a present problem or past experience. The individual or a group member may base lyrics on an original poem or journal writing. Lyrics may be suggested by a personal or group experience or past memory.

Songwriting may occur spontaneously or be planned by the therapist. The therapist, individual, or group member may suggest a theme, which is utilized and developed. As the process unfolds, the lyrics may be written down to capture ideas to be developed and revised. The songwriting process may be recorded as it occurs and then transcribed to musical notation. The client may sing or suggest a melody, which can be further developed by the group and facilitated by the therapist. The song can later be videotaped, performed, or recorded by the individual or group.

Case example—Nathan. Nathan was a 10-year-old African-American boy diagnosed with depression and anxiety who attended a self-contained elementary class for children with emotional and behavioral disorders. Nathan was shy and quiet, and had difficulty establishing appropriate relationships with peers and teachers. Although suffering from some learning difficulties, Nathan was extremely creative, enjoying drawing, poetry, and music. The special education teacher believed that music therapy could increase appropriate self-expression and communication for Nathan.

During the initial assessment, Nathan was quiet and cooperative, and responded appropriately to all tasks presented. Nathan seemed to particularly enjoy piano improvisation with the therapist. The early stages of therapy were designed to establish a trusting relationship with the therapist. Initially, Nathan enjoyed singing and playing instruments, but as sessions progressed, Nathan expressed an interest in creating or composing his own music through songwriting. He composed poems or song lyrics and brought them to the music therapy session, where he would then create a melody by singing his lyrics. The music therapist transcribed Nathan's melody to the piano. Nathan and the music therapist collaborated in revising the melody until it met his expectations. Next, the therapist would harmonize Nathan's melody according to his specifications. When the melody and harmony played by the therapist met with Nathan's approval, the song was transcribed to music by the therapist. An excerpt of one of Nathan's songs is provided below.

Prejudice

Prejudice is something that is wrong,
That's why we sing this song.
Makes no difference if we're black or white,
There's no need for us to fight.

Nathan's song continued to explore and express the feelings that he must have experienced personally, even at a very young age. Nathan was able to use songwriting to express his thoughts, feelings, and personal experiences in an appropriate manner. Musical self-expression through songwriting enabled Nathan to develop feelings of worth and self-esteem as well as pride at his personal accomplishments. Nathan continued to use songwriting as his primary form of musical self-expression and communication throughout the school year.

Nathan's special education teacher was so impressed by his song that she requested permission to submit it to a statewide songwriting contest. Out of all the entries submitted, Nathan's won an award for his age group and he was permitted to perform his song at the award ceremony as well as at a schoolwide assembly dealing with "Respect." Nathan's song was well received by teachers and peers, and Nathan was congratulated on his accomplishments. Music therapy using songwriting enabled Nathan to become more accepted and less isolated from his peers, increasing opportunities for developing appropriate social interaction. Nathan was eventually able to attend more inclusive school settings with his same-age peers in music.

Adaptations. Group songwriting can be used to express feelings, explore problems, and brainstorm solutions in a creative manner. It can also increase group cooperation and participation and tolerance and respect for others, and improve peer relationships. Group cohesion can be achieved through compromise and a shared purpose. The final product can encourage feelings of self-esteem and pride of accomplishment.

Some groups may require a higher degree of structure and greater intervention by the therapist. A specific format such as the 12-bar blues may provide the structure and support needed by some groups initially. More advanced groups with a higher degree of group cohesion may not require such restrictions. Songwriting may be contraindicated for extremely impulsive groups that may require a more structured intervention, at least initially.

Group goals in songwriting may be to increase group cooperation and participation and improve positive peer relationships. Songwriting involves group relationships, working through issues, solving problems, and learning to compromise to create a group product. Group songwriting may focus on a shared experience while working toward a common goal. Shared issues such as addiction and substance abuse can provide a theme for group exploration through songwriting.

Ideas and themes for group songwriting may be initiated by a group member or by the therapist. Themes can be discussed and voted on by the group. The goals of the group can be explained and discussed. A melody or rhythm may be suggested by the group or be based on a previously learned song. Shared experiences such as anger, poverty, and loneliness may provide the inspiration for songwriting.

Once a theme is suggested, the group can brainstorm lyrics based on the theme in pairs or small groups. Lyrics can be combined to create verses, and the group can create a recurring chorus or refrain. The therapist can assist in the creation of the melody or allow the group members to create it, based on the needs and abilities of the group. Group members can create a group song utilizing ideas from all group members. The therapist can facilitate the process, providing as much guidance as necessary during the process. The therapist can help transcribe ideas musically if necessary.

Case example—"West Meade Blues." Andrew was a 14-year-old male with a long history of hyperactivity and disruptive behavior, complicated by a history of substance abuse. Andrew had an extensive history of attending various foster placements, residential treatment facilities, and special schools for children and adolescents with emotional/behavioral problems.

Andrew was below grade level academically, but was extremely likable and easily established positive relationships with peers, teachers, and staff. Andrew was seen in a music therapy group for adolescents with a dual diagnosis of mental health issues and addiction. Students were required to attend daily meetings with addiction counselors, as well as academic classes and therapy sessions. Often, addiction issues served as material for music therapy sessions. Music was often used as a means of group support for individuals struggling with drug and alcohol addiction. Songs such as "Lean on Me" were a frequent request in Andrew's music therapy group.

After a music therapy session in which the 12-bar blues format was explained and played musically, Andrew became inspired to write his own blues with the help of the music therapy group. Andrew wrote the lyrics with the help of the group members, and the therapist transcribed his melody to music. The entire group helped to develop the accompaniment through musical improvisation and writing additional verses. An excerpt of Andrew's blues is included below.

West Meade Blues

I got the West Meade Blues (group echo: West Meade Blues)
I got the West Meade Blues (group echo: West Meade Blues)
I got the West Meade Blues (group echo: West Meade Blues)
'Cause I can't get high no more! (group echo: No more! No more!)

Can't get high no more! (No more! No more!)
Can't get high no more! (No more! No more!)
Can't get high no more! (No more! No more!)
It's just so hard but I got to hang in for sure (For sure! For sure!)

The session continued, with other group members contributing additional verses to "West Meade Blues." Additional blues verses described individual as well as group struggles with substance abuse and mental health issues. This experience seemed to have a profoundly unifying effect on the group, developing group cohesion and social interaction through shared musical and emotional experiences.

Songwriting allowed Andrew the opportunity for appropriate self-expression and communication through music. Group members provided musical and emotional support, allowing Andrew to express his personal struggles within the safety of the musical environment. This experience allowed Andrew the opportunity to develop positive peer relationships and increase self-esteem and feelings of accomplishment.

WORKING WITH CAREGIVERS

Extremely limited research exists regarding working with caregivers and children with emotional/behavioral disorders in school settings. Music therapy can be highly effective in dealing with stress and reducing anxiety. Physiological responses to music therapy include reducing heart rate, lowering blood pressure, regulating breathing responses, and releasing muscle tension. Emotional responses include a positive change in mood and emotion, with decreasing feelings of hopelessness and helplessness. Music can empower the listener, providing a sense of safety and security. Music can allow the listener to develop positive coping strategies and promote emotional growth and change.

In a study with caregivers and psychiatric patients, music therapy improved the overall quality of life for families by improving mood and affective states and developing a safe and successful means of self-expression. Both caregivers and patients reported lower stress scores and high satisfaction with life. Caregivers reported an emerging sense of problem-solving techniques, flexibility, enjoyment, and appreciation (Silverman, 2011).

Music therapy was used with families of children and adolescents who had been placed in foster and adoptive homes due to issues with abuse, neglect, and abandonment. Such children are at risk for developmental delays, emotional/behavioral disorders, poor emotional health, and relationship issues (Seles, 2009). Music therapy in the family setting was used to foster trust, develop appropriate social behaviors, and increase appropriate family interactions. Music therapy sessions were structured toward specific skills and goals and designed to encourage engagement and build trust with the caregiver. Appropriate social behaviors can be taught, such as making eye contact, increasing touch, turn-taking, choice-making, and expressing emotions appropriately. Music therapy in the family setting can be beneficial in teaching and practicing basic attachment behaviors in children and adolescents in foster care and adoptive families who have suffered abuse and displacement (Seles, 2009).

Severe emotional/behavioral disorders may result in removal from the family or foster home to more restrictive environments such as residential treatment centers and hospitals. Information can be gained from evaluating the role of the music therapist with children and their parents facing the challenge of hospitalization. Whether the issues are physical or emotional/behavioral, the issues are comparable when supporting children and their parents. Hospitalization and removal from the family home can be extremely stressful for both the child and the parents (Ayson, 2008).

Emotional/behavior issues or mental illness can have a substantial impact on both the child and the family. Disruptive behavior can have a negative impact on the family and can influence family relationships and interactions. Each family has differing needs for structure and support influenced by the degree of coping and impact of crises each family experiences. In working with caregivers, the music therapist must consider the personality of the child and whether parental involvement is advisable. In situations of abuse, neglect, or abandonment, contact with the parent may be prohibited. The health and recovery of the child must remain the primary issue (Ayson, 2008).

The rights of the child must be a priority in treatment. The child has the right to confidentiality in therapy that may be inhibited by the presence of parent. The child may feel uncomfortable expressing difficult feelings and emotions through songwriting, for example, if the parents are present. If the presence of the parent will support recovery and promote a healthy family relationship, then that must be encouraged and supported by the music therapist.

Research Evidence

Receptive Music Therapy

Little research has been conducted in music therapy to determine which therapeutic approach would allow the maximum outcome for children and adolescents with severe behavioral disorders. Even fewer studies compare different approaches to determine the effectiveness of dealing with the problematic behaviors of children with emotional/behavioral disorders (Montello & Coons, 1998). However, music may be the preferred therapy and is often the only treatment with this population that enhances communication (Brooks, 1989).

A study comparing active rhythm-based music therapy vs. passive listening music therapy was done with emotionally disturbed preadolescents in school settings (Montello & Coons, 1998). Findings suggest that both approaches seem to facilitate self-expression and group cohesion. It is suggested that the music therapy approach should be based on the clinical diagnosis and personality types of group members. Different types of music therapy may affect observable behaviors in emotionally disturbed children and adolescents (Montello & Coons, 1998).

Lack of verbal communication with children and adolescents with emotional/behavioral disorders can prevent successful treatment through traditional methods. Choice of music represents power and control to the adolescent. Because adolescents relate personally to the music of their peer group, music therapy can be used to facilitate communication and self-expression. Because the music therapist utilizes music to establish communication, the music therapist enhances treatment (Brooks, 1989).

Group listening and song discussion without judgment develops appropriate social interaction and communication. The safety of the musical environment allows the adolescent to indirectly explore personal feelings within the context of lyric discussion. By giving control of song selection to the group members, the music therapist functions as a safe adult facilitator (Brooks, 1989).

A passive listening approach seems to increase the therapeutic relationship between the therapist and the group members, developing trust and an increased willingness to cooperate and participate. Passive listening experiences for adolescents can also increase self-esteem and improve group cohesion. Listening to the music of others can increase tolerance and respect for others, allowing adolescents to discover similarities and appreciate differences in others (Montello & Coons, 1998).

Montello and Coons (1998) suggest that passive listening–based music therapy may be used initially with children and adolescents with emotional/behavioral issues to develop trust and avoid issues associated with "performing." Performing may cause distress due to insecurity and the need to perform music "correctly." Students may be embarrassed or afraid to play, sing, or move in front of others, especially those who were severely traumatized or sexually abused. Listening can increase group cohesion and feelings of safety and security before exploring more active music-making activities.

Passive listening–based music therapy allows the child to use song lyrics to express thoughts and feelings in a safe, nonthreatening environment. Brooks (1989) suggests that the nonthreatening nature of music permits the therapeutic process to occur without adolescent resistance because the child is "tuned in" to the nature of the music and not the adult therapist. The music serves as the catalyst, and the therapist is the safe adult leading the adolescent through the process toward recovery.

Guided Imagery and Music techniques can be used to teach children and adolescents a coping strategy to decrease anger and frustration and find peace in a socially acceptable manner. GIM can be used effectively with children and adolescents with certain modifications in both goal and method (Wesley, 2002). Bonny and Savary (1973) originally used GIM with children in music appreciation classes. They believed that children and adolescents need a complete explanation of the process and an opportunity for discussion of concerns. The relaxation techniques should consider the interests and attention of the child. The selection of the music and the length of the program must be geared toward the age of the child, with younger children requiring shorter programs. The mood of the music should be consistent, with negative moods being avoided. Only high-quality recordings should be used (Wesley, 2002).

Elliot (1991) used GIM with hospitalized emotionally disturbed children to increase the number of hours spent in regular classrooms and inclusive settings. GIM was used to increase the ability to express and address issues affecting success in school settings. GIM was used to increase verbal self-expression and communication and decrease stress by increasing relaxation (Wesley, 2002).

Wagner (1992) used GIM with emotionally disturbed children in a special education setting to develop trust, express emotional issues, and reduce anxiety. The need for concrete explanations, step-by-step directions, and considerable time to teach progressive muscle relaxation was stressed. Wagner (1992) initially used music with little dynamic or timbre variation and later progressed to musical selections with a greater variety of musical variation, such as Bonny's Children's Imagery Tape. Wagner (1992) believed that individual GIM session could be effectively applied in assisting traumatized children work through painful past memories (Wesley, 2002).

Although limited research exists involving the use of Guided Imagery and Music with children and adolescents with emotional/behavioral disorders, use is contraindicated in clients with active psychosis, severe neurological impairments, and a lack of ego strength. Clients using Guided Imagery and Music must also be capable of symbolic thinking and able to differentiate between symbol and reality to achieve positive emotional growth (Bonny, 1989).

Although these criteria may prevent its use with some students with emotional/behavioral issues, it may also be prove to be highly effective with higher-functioning adolescents as a primary treatment modality to express feelings and resolve issues. Further research is recommended to explore the effectiveness of using Guided Imagery and Music in the treatment of adolescents with emotional/behavioral disorders.

Improvisational Music Therapy

Improvisation can serve as an effective means of nonverbal self-expression and communication for children and adolescents with emotional/behavioral disorders. Bruscia (1987) recommends using the Iso principle and beginning where the child is at emotionally, acknowledging and reflecting the mood or feelings of the child or group.

The physical environment must be conducive to therapy and may be structured or free-flowing. Structured improvisations must be highly planned and are effective for individuals and groups needing more structure. In free-flowing improvisations, the child determines the direction of the session. Improvisation may be active or receptive in nature. Active improvisation is when the child creates his/her own music, and receptive improvisation is when the child or group listens to others improvise. Active improvisation allows problems to be examined directly through the music. Receptive improvisation stimulates reflection, verbal discussion, and behavioral responses.

Improvisation must be based on the needs of the client and on the personal skills and preferences of the therapist. It is imperative that the improvisations reflect the musical and personal needs of the client rather than the musical and personal needs of the therapist (Bruscia, 1987).

Nordoff and Robbins used Creative Music Therapy, where music serves as the principal therapeutic medium, with minimal verbal interaction between the therapist and child. In Creative Music Therapy, the therapist continually observes the child's musical responses and responds through spontaneous musical improvisations. In Nordoff and Robbins music therapy, the therapist must meet the child where s/he is musically, and evoke musical responses. Through improvisation, the child can develop musical skills, establish communication, and increase self-expression. Musical communication between the therapist and the child allows acceptance, establishes trust, and creates rapport (Bruscia, 1987).

Bruscia (1987) discusses several Nordoff and Robbins models of therapy. Initially, 13 categories of response to spontaneous music-making through improvisation are presented. Next, the child's growth is analyzed according to scales describing progressive stages in the therapeutic relationship. Then, the client's music is analyzed according to the level of emotional engagement and responses. Tempo and dynamics are associated with different emotions.

Nordoff and Robbins believe that the environment must be prepared with high-quality instruments and appropriate acoustics. Tapes or transcripts of the session must be analyzed so that the therapist can vary and repeat musical motifs and phrases that occur in musical improvisations. The human voice should be used to establish contact and nurture the child. Using reflection, the therapist must represent the child musically. The musicianship of the therapist is extremely important. The therapist must be able to create tension and resolution through the music based on the client's music (Bruscia, 1987).

Nordoff and Robbins believed that the "music child" lies dormant within the handicapped child. Activation of the "music child" is awakened in the child through musical experiences with the therapist. Through the musical interactions, the ego develops and the child becomes a more thinking, feeling, willing person. The thinking child becomes more aware of impulses and the sensory environment. The feeling child reacts to the experiences of the inner and outer environments, and the willing child begins to make more intentional choices. The development of the ego allows for the integration of the "old" and "new" selves. The music is the primary catalyst for growth and change (Bruscia, 1987).

Bruscia (1987, p. 65) describes the five stages of therapeutic growth through Nordoff and Robbins creative music. They are as follows: (1) Musical Awakening while Establishing a Relationship; (2) Musical Responsiveness within an Activity Relationship; (3) Musical Involvement within a Working Relationship; (4) Musical and Interpersonal Independence; and (5) Assimilation and Closure. Because the goal of creative music therapy is to increase appropriate self-expression and communication, therapy ends when the child has reached their potential for musical and emotional growth, based on their musical ability and developmental level. Time is needed for the child to process the changes that have occurred and apply these new changes to daily life situations. The child may discontinue music therapy, be placed in a performance-based group, or receive formal musical instruction (Bruscia, 1987).

Nordoff and Robbins (1977) recommended clinical improvisation using a variety of multicultural influences such as pentatonic, modal, and Middle Eastern scales and folk music from various countries. Multicultural music with children and adolescents with emotional/behavioral disorders can increase exploration and appreciation of other cultures by interacting through different musical tonalities and instruments. Multicultural music can promote greater group acceptance, flexibility, and tolerance of others in our society.

Improvisational music therapy may be contraindicated for extremely withdrawn or extremely aggressive children (Bruscia, 1987). Children with severe disruptive behavior disorders and severe focus issues may find improvisational music therapy too threatening initially. Children and adolescents with disruptive behavior disorders and attention deficits seek structure and order in music to eventually begin to work together in a group (Barkley, 1998). Rickson (2006) suggests that beginning with improvisation may require more time for emotionally disturbed children to maximize the benefits of music therapy. Montello and Coons (1998) suggest that active music therapy may not be the best approach with severely disruptive and hyperactive children. Extremely withdrawn or regressed children may respond better to a receptive listening approach to create safety and group cohesion before pursuing a more active approach. Edison (1989) suggests that music may be helpful in structuring forms of interaction that go beyond verbalization.

Some emotionally disturbed children and adolescents lack the internal controls needed to regulate their impulses and control their behavior. They may demonstrate a need for external structure and require more frequent interventions by the therapist. Many may not be able to tolerate the lack of direction and become severely overstimulated. Merle-Fishman and Marcus (1982) reported that severely emotionally disturbed children reveal a higher incidence of disordered beating and impulsive rhythmic beating, with inconsistent tempo characterized by frequent stops/starts. This finding supports Nordoff and Robbins's (1971) association between disturbance and pathology. Gibbons (1983) suggests that rhythm may be a useful element in the assessment and treatment of children with emotional/behavioral disorders.

Differences in interpersonal group dynamics can influence the benefits of improvisational music therapy. Groups with more difficult personalities or a higher degree of hyperactivity and impulsivity may impact group cooperation and participation. Because improvisation relies more on group process to promote growth and change than an instructional approach, personalities can affect group outcomes. An evaluation of group dynamics in improvisational music therapy can assist the therapist in determining the most appropriate method of music therapy and assist in goal formation (Rickson, 2006).

Nordoff and Robbins believed that musical responses reveal the psychological development of the child (1971, 1977). The musical responses revealed through improvisation may be helpful in the assessment and evaluation of children and adolescents with emotional/behavioral disorders. Emotionally disturbed children can develop feelings of self-confidence and hope for the future. Abused and neglected children may find nurturing and fulfillment through the music and the therapeutic relationship. Traumatized children may be able to work through past traumas within the safe, nonjudgmental musical environment. Emotionally disturbed children and adolescents can achieve their full potential for emotional growth and development through music therapy.

Re-creative Music Therapy

Children and adolescents with emotional/behavioral problems have varying needs for external structure to control behavior. Students with moderate to severe needs for structure had less rhythmic success than those with little need for structure. Rhythmic imitation tasks may be an important and useful element in the assessment, evaluation, and treatment of children with emotional disturbance (Gibbons, 1983).

Barkley (1998) suggests it may be best to at least begin music therapy programs with a high level of structure. Children and adolescents with attention deficits and disruptive behavior disorders seek structure and order in music to eventually work together in the musical environment. Creation of organized music in a group setting demands attention to task and self-control. Rehearsal of rhythmic tasks can lead to improvement in organization and impulse control for children and adolescents with emotional/behavioral disorders (Rickson, 2006).

Music therapy is a preferred treatment method for adolescents. Behavior modification techniques within a concrete structure can help adolescents learn appropriate methods to deal with their problems in a safe environment. Music therapy can enhance treatment for adolescents with emotional/behavioral disorders (Brooks, 1989).

Merle-Fishman and Marcus (1982) reported that children with emotional/behavioral disorders had a higher incidence of disordered beating than normal children, and vocal expression was often absent during singing. Success or failure of rhythmic responses may be related to the internal behavioral controls of the child. A child's internal controls provide the organization necessary to perform rhythmic tasks. The degree of emotional disturbance defines the need for external structure. Children with a greater need for external structure may find musical success in simple rhythmic activities that increase in complexity based on improved internal controls (Gibbons, 1983).

Montello and Coons (1998) suggest that active rhythmic training may be too threatening for children and adolescents with emotional/behavioral problems, especially for those with severe attentional deficits and difficulty focusing. They may respond better to highly structured musical activities to avoid overstimulation. A highly structured approach to music therapy may be more appropriate than an improvisational approach with some children with hyperactivity and disruptive behavioral disorders. Some children become overstimulated in less structured settings (Rickson & Watkins, 2003). Children and adolescents with emotional/behavioral disorders may exhibit aggressive drum beating characterized by impulsivity and distractibility. Rhythmic tasks may be characterized by motor learning difficulties, which further increase anxiety and frustration. Children with behavioral disorders often cannot tolerate a lack of direction and structure and need more frequent interventions by the therapist (Merle-Fishman & Marcus, 1982).

Rhythmic activities may facilitate internal organization and improve impulse control. Music therapy can help children and adolescents with emotional/behavioral disorders to regulate and manage their own behavior in the musical environment. Skills learned in music therapy may eventually be transferred to other nonmusical environments (Montello & Coons, 2003). Edison (1989) reported higher levels of on-task behavior evident during musical vs. nonmusical intervals and believed that interpersonal skills developed in music may be transferred back to classrooms.

Participation in music therapy may encourage higher levels of on-task behavior, develop interpersonal skills, improve group cohesion, and increase positive self-esteem. In re-creative music therapy, students with emotional/behavioral disorders can be taught arrangements designed to structure success. Each student can be trained as the musical director to develop leadership skills and increase self-esteem (Edison, 1989).

Developing positive self-esteem is a major concern in the treatment of children and adolescents with emotional disturbance. Participation in performance-based groups develops peer acceptance and group cohesion (Haines, 1989). Singing in chorus demands attention to task, group cooperation, and participation. Learning new materials requires individual patience and determination to accomplish a group goal. Children must learn positive decision-making skills and channel inappropriate behaviors to achieve their goals. Instructional activities such as playing hand bells or structured instrumental parts improve attention span and increase self-esteem (Haines, 1989).

Certain musical forms require designated responses from the group to allow interpersonal contact through structure. Activities are not designed to teach skills but to serve as reflections of the emotional needs of the group (Aigen, 1997). Merle-Fishman and Marcus (1982) reported improvement in rhythmic beating, increased attention span, and more self-initiated musical activity with children with emotional/behavioral disorders in music over time. It is important for the therapist to recognize the "healthy"-functioning part of children and adolescents with emotional/behavioral disorders in music therapy.

Compositional Music Therapy

Songwriting can be a highly effective music therapy treatment method with children and adolescents with emotional/behavioral disorders. These children and adolescents often experience conflict within themselves and with others that are usually expressed in socially unacceptable ways (Edgerton, 1990). Songwriting with emotionally disturbed children and adolescents can increase appropriate self-expression and communication, promote problem-solving skills, and develop respect and tolerance for others.

The needs of the individual or group are more important than the songwriting process (Edgerton, 1990). Goldstein (1990) used songwriting as an assessment to measure hopelessness in depressed adolescents. Hopelessness was defined as a negative expectation toward the future, a primary characteristic of adolescent depression, and a predictor of suicidal behavior. Songwriting was used to promote healing, increase self-expression, and improve self-esteem after sexual abuse. Songwriting allowed the expression of painful emotions, allowing the composer to develop strength and become more assertive (Lindberg, 1995).

Group songwriting using a 12-bar blues format can provide the structure needed by some children and adolescents with emotional/behavioral problems. The blues contain short, repetitive ideas, which can be contributed by different individuals and be developed and supported by the group with resolution in the final phrase. Echoing short phrases in response can develop group support and affirmation (Rickson & Watkins, 2003).

Students with emotional/behavioral disorders may explore repressed feelings through lyric discussion and analysis after listening to songs involving difficult issues and past traumas. The songwriting group may allow opportunities to explore emotions and discussion of painful feelings within the safety of the musical environment. Edgerton (1990) used Creative Group Songwriting to increase self-expression, develop group cohesion, and increase self-esteem using a six-step process, which included lyric analysis and interpretation, music analysis, theme and style selection, lyric writing, music composition, and culmination through performance. Musical skills learned included lyric writing techniques, compositional skills, and musical analysis of rhythmic, melodic, and harmonic elements. Nonmusical skills learned included listening, decision-making, contributing, and compromising. Songwriting allowed students to increase appropriate self-expression, develop self-esteem, and improve peer relationships. Goldstein (1990) suggests that songwriting can provide an effective coping strategy, increasing appropriate self-expression and promoting healing in adolescents struggling with depression.

Compositional music therapy techniques using music technology and computer software with children and adolescents with spinal cord injuries may be applicable to children and adolescents with emotional/behavioral disorders. In this study, patients created different types of songs based on the degree of willingness to engage with the therapist interpersonally and intrapersonally. "Interpersonal" referred to how much the patients were willing to reveal their personal lives to the therapist, and "intrapersonal" referred to the patients' connections to their internal world during the songwriting process (Viega, 2010).

In this music-centered approach, music was the medium in which therapy took place. Songwriting was used to encourage and enhance musical participation, promote enjoyment, guide song creation, and build a musical partnership with the therapist. Using a resource-oriented music therapy framework, music helped strengthen the recovering patient toward health. Songwriting allowed patients to feel empowered, build resilience, and experience positive emotions (Viega, 2010).

Further research is needed using music technology and computer software in compositional music therapy with children and adolescents with emotional/behavioral disorders. It is believed that replicating a study such as the one above, which promoted physical healing with hospitalized children and adolescents, may be used to promote emotional healing in children who have suffered abuse, neglect, and trauma.

Summary and Conclusions

Mental illness is considered a stigma in our society. Many parents and caregivers are reluctant or embarrassed to seek services for children and adolescents with emotional/behavioral disorders. School administrators and regular education teachers are often resistant to having children with severe behavior problems attend their school and their classes.

There appears to be limited research in music therapy with emotionally disturbed children and adolescents in general, and most available research is related to residential treatment facilities and inpatient hospitalization settings. More research is needed regarding children and adolescents with emotional and behavioral disorders in both residential treatment facilities and inclusive school settings.

The music therapist can serve as a consultant to teachers and administrators in school settings regarding the specific characteristics of emotional/behavioral disorders and demonstrate behavior management techniques. Mental health professionals can provide parent training and coping strategies for families. Preservice training and in-service training programs can prepare music educators for the challenges presented by children and adolescents with interpersonal and behavioral problems.

Although the challenges presented by children and adolescents with interpersonal and behavioral problems may seem overwhelming initially, with courage, persistence, and determination, music therapy can have a profound effect in promoting emotional growth and change over time. Music therapy can empower children and adolescents with emotional/behavioral disorders to express the inexpressible, move beyond the traumas of the past, and look forward to the possibilities of the future.

References

Aigen, K. (1997). Here we are in music: One year with an adolescent creative music therapy group. *Nordoff & Robbins music therapy monograph series, 2*. Gilsum, NH: Barcelona Publishers.

American Psychiatric Association (APA). (2000). *Diagnostic and statistical manual of mental disorders—Text revision* (4th ed.). (DSM-IV-TR). Arlington, VA: Author.

Ayson, C. (2008). Child-parent wellbeing in a paediatric ward. *Voices: A World Forum for Music Therapy, 8*(1). Retrieved from https://normt.uib.no/index.php/voices/article/view/449/367

Barkley, R. A. (1998). Attention-deficit hyperactivity disorder. *Scientific American, 279*(3), 66–71.

Birkenshaw-Fleming, L. (1993). *Music for all: Teaching music to people with special needs*. Toronto, Canada: Gordon V. Thompson.

Bonny, H. L. (1989). Sound as symbol: Guided imagery and music in clinical practice. *Music Therapy Perspectives, 6*, 7–9. Abstract obtained from *Music Therapy Perspectives, 6* (1989).

Bonny,H.L. & Savary L (1973). *Music and your mind: Listening with a new consciousness*. New York, NY: Harper & Row.

Brooks, D. M. (1989). Music therapy enhances treatment with adolescents. *Music Therapy Perspectives, 6*, 77–87.

Bruscia, K. E. (1987). *Improvisational methods of music therapy*. Springfield, IL: Charles C. Thomas.

Burling, S. (2012, May 7). Antipsychotics and foster care. *Philadelphia Inquirer, check up*: The inquirer health blog. Retrieved from http://www.philly.com/philly/blogs/healthcare/

Centers for Disease Control and Prevention. Simpson, G.A., Cohen R.A., Pastor P. N., & Reuben C.A.(2008). *Use of mental health services 12 months aged 4-17 years: United States, 2005-2006*. NCHS Data Brief No. 8, 1-8. http.//cdc.gov/nds/databriefs/db08.pdf

Chase, K. (2003). Multicultural music therapy: A review of the literature. *Music Therapy Perspectives, 21*(2), 84–88.

Darrow, A. (1999, Winter). Music educators' perception regarding the inclusion of students with severe disabilities in the music classrooms. *Journal of Music Therapy, 36*(4), 254–273.

Edgerton, C. (1990). Creative group songwriting. *Music Therapy Perspectives, 8*, 15–19.

Edison, Jr., C., (1989). The effects of behavioral music therapy on the generalization of interpersonal skills from session to the classroom by emotionally handicapped middle school students. *Journal of Music Therapy, 26*, 206–221.

Elliot, A. (1991). *Guided imagery and music: An affective educational tool. Unpublished report*. Topeka KS: Capital City Schools.

Gaston, E. T. (1968). *Music in therapy*. New York, NY: Macmillan.

Gibbons, A. (1983). Rhythm responses in emotionally disturbed children with differing needs for external structure. *Journal of Music Therapy, 3*(1), 94–102.

Goldstein, S. (1990). A songwriting assessment for hopelessness in depressed adolescents: A pilot study and review of the literature. *Arts in Psychotherapy, 17*, 117–124.

Haines, J. H. (1989). Effects of music therapy on the self-esteem of emotionally disturbed adolescents. *Music Therapy, 8*(1), 78–91.

Hussey, D., & Layman, D. (2003, June). Music therapy with emotionally disturbed children. *Psychiatric Times*, June 2003 XX(6). Retrieved from http://www.vaccinationnews.com/DailyNews/2003/June/09/MusicTherapyWith Emotionally9.htm

Jones, L. L., & Cardinal, D. (1998). A description and analysis of music therapists' perception of delivering services in inclusive settings: A challenge to the field. *Journal of Music Therapy, 35*(1), 49–67.

Lindberg, K. (1995). Songs of healing: Songwriting with an abused adolescent. *Music Therapy, 13*(1), 93–108.

Merle-Fishman, C., & Marcus, M. (1982). Behaviors and preferences in emotionally disturbed and normal children. *Journal of Music Therapy, 2*(1), 1–11.

Montello, L., & Coons, E. (1998). Effects of active versus passive group music therapy on preadolescents with emotional, learning, and behavioral disorders. *Journal of Music Therapy, 35,* 49–67.

National Alliance on Mental Illness (2010). *What is mental illness: Mental illness facts*. Retrieved from http://www.nami.org/template.cfm?section=about_mental_illness

National Dissemination Center for Children with Disabilities. (2010, June). Emotional disturbance. In *Emotional Disturbance* [NICHCY Disability Fact Sheet 5 (FS5)]. Retrieved from http://file:///Emotional%20Disturbance.webarchive

Nordoff, P., & Robbins, C. (1971). *Music therapy in special education*. New York, NY: John Day.

Nordoff, P., & Robbins, C. (1977). *Creative music therapy*. New York, NY: John Day.

Nordoff, P., & Robbins, C. (1979). *Therapy in music for handicapped children*. New York, NY: John Day.

Rickson, D. (2006). Instructional and improvisational models of music therapy with adolescents who have ADHD: A comparison of the effects of motor impulsivity. *Journal of Music Therapy, 43*(1), 39–62.

Rickson, D., & Watkins, W. (2003). Music therapy to promote prosocial behavior in aggressive adolescent boys: A pilot study. *Journal of Music Therapy, 40*(4), 283–301.

Seles, K. (2009, November). *Effect of Mally music therapy on the attachment behaviors of children and adolescents in foster and adoptive families, abstract*. Presentation at the American Music Therapy Association Conference.

Shapiro, N. (2005). Sounds in the world: Multicultural influences in clinical practice and training. *Music Therapy Perspectives, 23*(1), 29–35.

Silverman, M. (2011, November). *Effect of caregiver-based educational music therapy on depression and satisfaction with life in acute care psychiatric patients and their caregivers, abstract*. Presentation at the American Music Therapy Association Conference.

Viega, M. (2010). *Compose yourself: A clinical approach to song writing in music therapy for children and adolescents in rehabilitation for spinal cord injuries and orthopedic challenges*. Unpublished manuscript. Temple University: Philadelphia, PA.

Wager, K. (1992). *Experiences, thoughts, and reflections on the use of GIM with emotionally disturbed children*. Unpublished manuscript.

Wesley, S. B. (2002). Guided imagery and music with children and adolescents. In K. E. Bruscia & D. E. Grocke (Eds.), *Guided imagery and music: The Bonny method and beyond* (pp. 137–149). Gilsum, NH: Barcelona Publishers.

Wilson, B., & Smith, D. (2000). Music therapy assessment in school settings: A preliminary investigation. *Journal of Music Therapy, 37,* 95–117.

Resources

Bonny, H. L. (1978). *Group experience program*. Federal Way, WA: Cassette Technologies.

Chatman, P. (1955). *Every day I have the blues*. Milwaukee, WI: Hal Leonard.

Hammond, S. (1994). *Classical kids: The classroom collection*. Pickering, ON: Children's Group.
Levin, G., Levin, H., & Safer, N. (1975). *Learning through music*. Boston, MA: Teaching Resources.
Nordoff, P., & Robbins, C. (1972). *Spirituals for children to sing and play*. Bryn Mawr, PA: Theodore Presser.
"Sakura." (1996). *Get America singing again! Volume 1: Traditional Japanese folk song*. Milwaukee, WI: Hal Leonard.
Schoenberg, C. M. (1980). *Les misérables*. New York, NY: Alain Boublil Music Ltd.
Weber, A. L. (1986). *Phantom of the opera*. London, England: The Really Useful Group, PLC.

Chapter 9

Children with Hearing Loss

Christine Barton

Introduction

Doing Deaf Differently©. That is the slogan emblazoned on T-shirts worn by hundreds of Hear Indiana supporters at the annual *Talk, Walk, Run* fund-raiser. Hear Indiana is a state affiliate of the Alexander Graham Bell Association for the Deaf and Hard of Hearing (AGBell), the national organization dedicated to supporting individuals with hearing loss (and their families) who wish to live and thrive in a listening and spoken language society. Its mission: *Advocating Independence Through Listening and Talking!* (AGBell, 2012). With the advent of sophisticated hearing technologies such as digital hearing aids (HA) and cochlear implants (CI), the goal of mainstreaming many children with severe to profound hearing loss with their age-matched hearing peers is now attainable. Through early detection and diagnosis, properly fitted and maintained hearing devices, and effective habilitation practices, many deaf children are finding themselves comfortably part of the hearing world.

This is in contrast to the approach of the *Deaf community*, or *culture,* which identifies itself with a capital "D" and takes pride in using American Sign Language (ASL) as its communication method while embracing its own rich and storied history. The Deaf culture is defined by its own language, values, norms, and social rules. It includes hearing family members, friends, and professionals who share the belief that being Deaf doesn't mean that an individual needs to be "fixed," but rather that he needs to be appreciated and respected for being differently abled (Gfeller, 1999). This author strongly believes that families should be made aware of all communication options, in an unbiased way, in order to make informed choices about which communication approach will best fit their child and family, and, furthermore, that music therapists who intend to engage deaf or hard-of-hearing children (D/HH) in therapy should be well versed in all the communication choices, as well as the culture to which the family belongs, in order to interact in an appropriate and respectful manner.

The clinical methods presented in this chapter reflect the author's expertise, developed through years of work with children engaged in the listening and spoken language approach (LSL) to education and life. Think of it as *Doing Music Differently*.

Diagnostic Information

Deafness occurs in approximately one out of every 1,000 babies born annually in the United States, while six out of a thousand have some degree of hearing loss (Beginnings, 2011). This means that roughly 24,000 infants are born every year in the U.S. with a hearing loss that will affect their development. Beginning in 1993, the National Institutes of Health (NIH) and the American Academy of Pediatrics (AAP) recommended that every newborn be screened for hearing loss before leaving the hospital. This Universal Newborn Hearing Screening (UNHS) is a noninvasive procedure completed in the hospital usually while the baby is asleep. Based on 2009 data by the Centers for Disease Control (CDC), 97% of U.S. infants were screened at birth. In 2007, the Joint Commission on Infant Hearing (JCIH) (ASHA,

2007) issued a policy statement proposing screening before one month, diagnosis by three months, and intervention by six months. That is the ideal; the reality is that almost half who fail the screening receive a timely diagnosis and only one third identified with a hearing loss receive appropriate intervention by the six-month timeline set forth by JCIH (NCHAM, 2003). There are many reasons for this disparaging fact, but that is for another discussion.

The Individuals with Disabilities Education Act (IDEA) definitions of disabilities guide individual state governments in determining who is a candidate to receive special education services. IDEA (2009) defines *hearing impairment* as "an impairment in hearing, whether permanent or fluctuating, that adversely affects a child's educational performance." Deafness is defined as "a hearing impairment that is so severe that the child is impaired in processing linguistic information through hearing, with or without amplification." Hearing impairment is the official term used by IDEA. However, because of the sensitive nature of the word *impairment*, current practice is to use *deaf and hard-of-hearing* (D/HH) or just *hearing loss (HL)*. (Note: The reader will find relevant organizational and instructional resources in Appendix E.)

Types and Degrees of Hearing Loss in Children

Hearing loss can occur *bilaterally* (both ears) or *unilaterally* (one ear). It can be *symmetrical,* meaning that both ears have the same degree and configuration of loss, or *asymmetrical,* wherein each ear is different. The *age of onset,* or the time when the hearing loss is first diagnosed, is a strong indicator of future prognosis. A loss can be present from birth *(congenital),* develop later in life *(acquired),* or worsen over time *(progressive).* Children with a congenital loss, or those who lose hearing before speech and language develops, have a *prelingual loss.* Those who lose hearing after speech and language develop have a *postlingual loss.* If a child has a congenital or prelingual loss, this means that they have been deprived of sound even while in the womb, and the implications for language development are far more challenging than for children with a postlingual loss. Postlingually D/HH children have an advantage because their language system was already in place before the hearing loss. However, there will likely be delays compared with their normal hearing (NH) peers, and care must be taken to provide adequate LSL intervention. A loss can occur suddenly or progress over a period of time and even fluctuate, as in the case of *otitis media,* a commonly occurring ear infection in young children. It is estimated that 30% to40% of individuals with a hearing loss have other complicating factors (Almond & Brown, 2009; Robbins, 2009).

The anatomical origin of the hearing loss defines its type. If there is an obstruction or anomaly in the outer or middle ear, it is referred to as a *conductive loss.* This could be the result of an infection, unusual construction or malfunction of the bones in the middle ear, or just a buildup of excessive earwax. Whatever the reason, sound is unable to reach the inner ear to then stimulate the hearing nerve. Often medication or surgery will correct the problem. A more serious condition is a *sensorineural loss,* which occurs in the inner ear, where the cochlea and auditory nerve are affected. Surgery will not correct the problem, and hearing aids may not mitigate the loss. A cochlear implant may be a viable option as long as the auditory nerve itself is not damaged. A *mixed loss* is a combination of a conductive and sensorineural loss, as in the instance of a child with a sensorineural loss who happens to also have a conductive loss due to an ear infection and fluid in the middle ear.

Measuring Hearing Loss

Hearing loss is measured by audiologists (Au.D.), hearing specialists with a doctoral degree in audiology and licensed by the state in which they practice. Their job is to determine a child's *hearing threshold,* or the softest sounds at different *frequencies* (pitches) a child will hear without amplification (HA or CI) about 50% of the time. This information is plotted on an *audiogram* according to *intensity* (loudness) and frequency. Intensity is measured in *decibels* (dB) and frequency, vibrations per second, is measured in *hertz* (Hz). The approximate range of "soft sounds" is 0 to 35 dBs, "moderate sounds" are 35 to 90 and "loud sounds" are 90 to 110. The approximate range of "low-pitched" sounds is 250 to 1060 Hz; high pitched sounds are 1060 to 8000.

An audiogram is useful because it provides a visual representation of:

1) The degree of hearing loss
2) Whether both ears have the same or different hearing thresholds
3) What frequencies are heard better than others
4) What residual hearing remains

Since frequency (pitch) is an important element in music, it is advisable that music therapists have a reference point when thinking about hearing loss. A typical ear hears anywhere from 20–2,000 Hz. Normal speech is in the 500–2,000 Hz range. A piano encompasses roughly 20–4,000 Hz, a very large *spectral range* (frequency). This is important to consider because some children have hearing loss in the upper range, but may still have access to the lower frequencies that the piano affords. A child's residual hearing will be utilized in the LSL approach.

Intensity also plays a role in music. Think of all the dynamic ranges possible within a given piece of music. A piece may go from *ppp* (pianississimo) at 30 dB up to *fff* (fortississimo) at 100 dB. Rock music tops out at 120 dB, or well above the safe listening zone. As you will see later in this chapter, louder is not always better when working with D/HH children. Figure 1 illustrates the decibel levels of commonly heard sounds. The smile-shaped gray region is called the speech banana and comprises the area where all the speech sounds of the English language would fall. It is especially helpful to compare the audiogram below with a client's audiogram to note exactly what speech or environmental sounds a child is capable of hearing through their HA or CI.

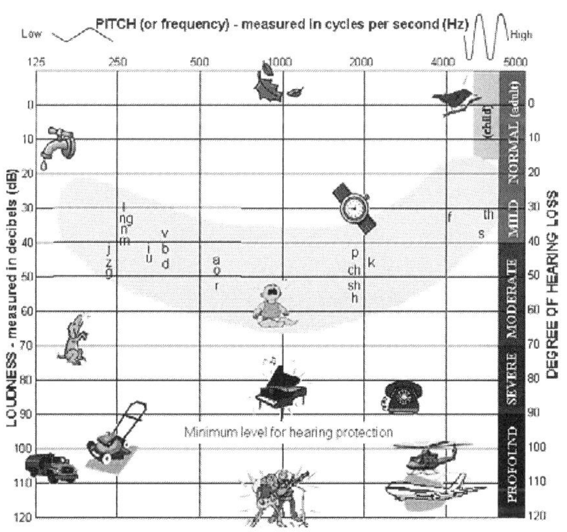

Figure 1. Interactive audiogram.

From "Interactive Audiogram," by First Years, 2009a,
http://firstyears.org/lib/interactiveaudiagram.htm. © 2009 by First Years. Reprinted with permission.

If the reader desires more information on specific frequency and intensity levels of common instruments, the PSB Speakers *Frequencies of Music: Ranges of the Fundamental Frequencies of Voices and Instruments* chart (PSB Speakers, 2005) may be useful.

Effects of Hearing Loss on Speech and Language

The path to spoken language begins *in utero* around five months (Locke, 1993). Hearing infants are born with a preference for their own mother's voice. By six months, they begin to interact with their caregivers through cooing and facial expressions. This sets the stage for future language acquisition, which is typically "caught, not taught." This means that a NH child immersed in a rich language environment of his or her own culture will eventually learn all the rules that govern that language without having been formally taught. For a child with a congenital hearing loss, he or she has not heard intrauterine sounds and most likely will have limited access to auditory stimuli early on, resulting in delayed auditory brain development (Madell & Flexer, 2012). This has a direct impact on the child's ability to learn language. The ability to *overhear* others' conversations and pick up language through *incidental learning* will not be the case. Rehabilitation will be required to train the auditory system by attaching meaning to sound and ultimately setting the stage for spoken language development to begin.

A child with any degree of hearing loss will be at a disadvantage for learning spoken language at the same rate as a NH peer. The good news is that D/HH children pass through the same developmental milestones as their NH peers, although in a delayed fashion. How much of a delay depends on the time of identification of the hearing loss, severity of the loss, whether there are other medical or developmental issues, and access to intervention. It is suggested that music therapists become familiar with language development timelines in order to address the therapeutic needs of their clients. Collaboration with the audiologist and speech language pathologist will be invaluable in providing an assessment of the child's *hearing age* vs. *chronological age*. If a child is chronologically two years old before cochlear implantation, once the CI is activated, his or her hearing age is said to be 0, because that is the point at which the child's hearing is "born." This is important to understand because a child may be eight years old, but have the language capabilities of a much younger child. When planning developmentally appropriate music experiences, this is an important consideration. As in the case of a NH child, first words will come about a year after implantation. The goal of LSL therapy is to close the gap between the hearing and chronological ages. Optimally, the aim should be one year of progress for every year of access to spoken language and then increasing the progress so that eventually the gap is closed (Sindrey, 1997). To gauge the impact that different degrees of hearing loss have on speech and language understanding, please see Table 1..

There are two main communication philosophies currently employed in the education of individuals with hearing loss: auditory and visual. Selecting the option that best fits each family is a decision that should be made based upon information about each of the approaches and careful consideration about which method is most compatible with the family and the child. This is a huge decision that all parents must face, so it is critical that all information be presented in an unbiased and clear manner. There are also variations on each philosophy, which are detailed below.

Auditory Approaches: Auditory Verbal (AVT). Through audition, or listening alone, a child develops communication without the use of sign or visual cues. It relies heavily on the child's residual hearing and the use of amplification. Parents attend one-on-one weekly sessions with a Certified Auditory Verbal Therapist (LSLS Cert. AVT™ or Cert. AVEd™). Its goal is to prepare the child for inclusion into the hearing community.

Auditory/Oral (AO): This approach maximizes the use of a child's residual hearing through the use of HA/CI and FM systems. No signs, except for the occasional gesture, are used. Visual aids may be used.

Visual Approach: American Sign Language (ASL)/English as a Second Language is the official language of the Deaf community. Its grammatical structure is not based on the English language, and there is no written equivalent. English is taught once the child becomes fluent in ASL. Amplification is not required, but may be used in this approach. Typically, most of these children attend state schools for the Deaf, with many being residential. However, budgetary constraints, plus advancements in hearing technologies, have caused many state schools to close. The goal of this approach is to prepare the child for inclusion into the Deaf community.

Table 1. Degrees of hearing loss in children.

Levels of Hearing Loss	Degrees of Hearing Loss	Effects on Language & Speech Understanding
Normal Hearing	0 dB–15 dB	None
Mild	16dB–30dB	May have trouble hearing faint or distant sounds
Moderate	31dB–50dB	Speech must be loud to be understood; will have increasing difficulty in group discussions. Speech likely to be defective. Language usage and comprehension deficiencies. Vocabulary limitations.
Severe	51dB–80dB	May be able to hear load voices about 1 foot from ear. May be able to identify environmental sounds. May be able to discriminate vowels but not consonants; speech and language will be affected if hearing loss is present before 12 months unless amplification is provided.
Profound	81+ dB	May be able to hear loud sounds more through vibrations than of tonal patterns. May rely on vision rather than hearing as the primary sensory channel for communication. Speech and language deficiencies.

From "Degrees of Hearing Loss in Children," by Beginnings, 2011, http://www.ncbegin.org/index.php?option=com_content&view=article&id=88&Itemid=142. Reprinted with permission.

Total Communication (TC): This philosophy uses all means available to teach communication skills to D/HH children. Unlike ASL, the sign language used in this approach is not its own language, but rather follows the English language rules of grammar. It is a see-and-say approach, where sign is used in conjunction with spoken language. Finger spelling, speech reading, gestures, and amplification are all part of the TC approach.

Cued Speech: This is a visual system composed of eight cues or hand shapes representing different speech sounds. The cues are placed at four locations around the face and are used simultaneously with speech. They enable the child to differentiate between similar speech sounds such as "p" and "b."

Hearing Technologies

When the parent of a D/HH child makes the decision to have their child pursue the listening and spoken language path, amplification technology is paramount. Depending on the severity and type of loss, a child will be fitted with either *hearing aids* (HAs) or *cochlear implants* (CIs). They are very different devices. A HA is an externally worn device that amplifies acoustic sounds through the ear canal to the brain (See Figure 2). Conversely, a CI has a surgically implanted electrode array, plus an externally worn sound processor and microphone. (See Figure 3.) Instead of sound traveling through the ear canal, it is digitally transmitted via electrical stimulation to the auditory nerve. A child may be a *unilateral* (one HA or CI), *bilateral* (two CIs or HAs), or *bimodal* (one HA and one CI) user.

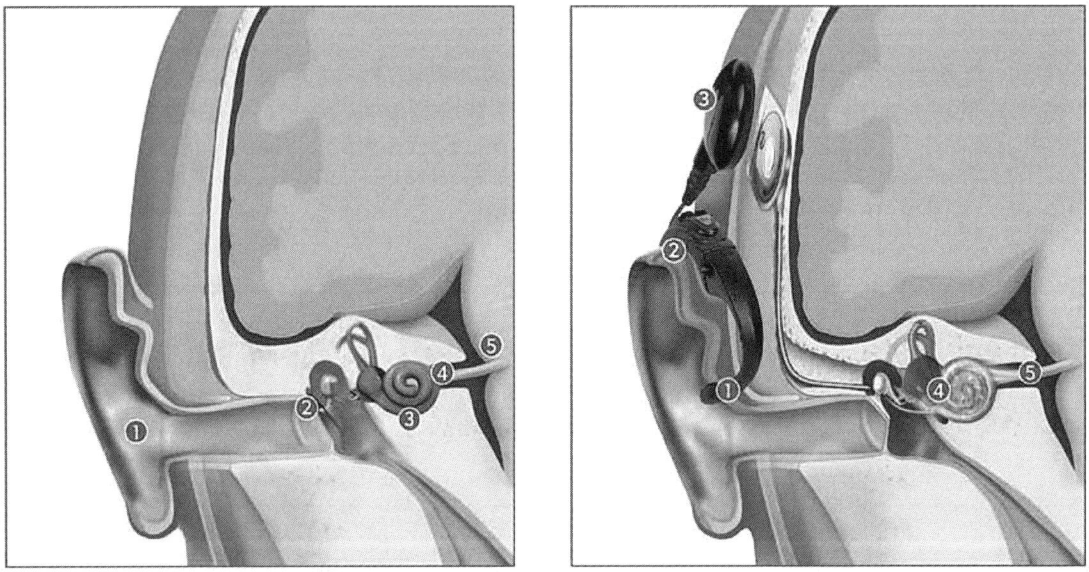

HEARING WITH A NORMAL EAR

1) The outer ear collects sound waves that pass through the air.
2) The sound waves vibrate the eardrum and the three tiny bones in the middle ear.
3) The vibrations move the tiny hairs of the sensory cells of the inner ear.
4) Sensory cells convert the vibrations to electric signals that are sent to the hearing nerve.
5) 5) The signals travel up the nerve and into the brain, where they are interpreted as sound.

HEARING WITH A BIONIC EAR

1) The sound processor microphone captures sound waves that pass through the air.
2) The sound waves are converted into detailed digital information by the sound processor.
3) The magnetic head piece sends the digital signals to the implant's electrode array in the inner ear.
4) The electrode array in the implant sends electrical signals to the hearing nerves.
5) The hearing nerve sends impulses to the brain where they are interpreted as sound.

Figure 2. How a CI works (Image provided courtesy of Advanced Bionics)

In the U.S., a child must first be fitted for a trial period with hearing aids. If the hearing aids fail to provide an audible, intelligible and comfortable listening condition, the child may benefit from a CI (Carpenter, 2009). That child will then be referred for an implant candidacy assessment administered by a multidisciplinary team consisting of medical, audiological, psychological, educational, and rehabilitation specialists. Candidates and their families must be willing to make long-term commitments to device management, auditory rehabilitation, and the resources necessary to support both.

A Frequency Modulation (FM) system (See Figure 3) is an additional technology that is especially useful in compensating for the distance between the speaker and listener, competing environmental noise, and less than optimal room acoustics, such as reverberation. The speaker (teacher, therapist, or parent) wears a small microphone that transmits his or her voice directly to the listener's HA or CI. Many D/HH children find them useful in the classroom or group setting, as well as in the noisy environs of a car. The music therapist will often be asked to wear a personal FM system. A classroom teacher, speech language pathologist (SLP), or audiologist (Au.D.) can provide the music therapist with hints on how to operate the equipment, as well as how to maximize its effects. Some classrooms will be equipped with a sound field FM system that amplifies the teacher's voice for all students to hear.

Figure 3. A Personal Frequency Modulation (FM) System
(Image provided courtesy of Advanced Bionics)

The CI Rehabilitation Process

One must remember that a CI is not an immediate fix for deafness. The sound transmitted through the CI is not the same as what a NH child will experience (Gfeller, Driscoll, Kenworthy & VanVoorst, 2011). However, studies have shown that a CI is very effective in conveying speech sounds, especially those of higher frequencies. They also increase the likelihood of overhearing others' conversations, which maximizes the potential for incidental learning (Robbins, 2009). Madell and Flexer (2012) state that NH infants and young children acquire 90% of what they know about the world through incidental learning. Once the CI is implanted, a child must learn to attach meaning to all of these sounds they begin to hear, from speech and environmental sounds to music. It is a long process that can have differing outcomes for children depending the age of implantation, cause of deafness, residual hearing, LSL experience, effective habilitation, and family support. Nicholas and Geers (2006) found that early implantation, when neuroplasticity in the brain is at its highest, along with quality auditory intervention, yielded the most positive spoken language outcomes for children. Some current studies have shown even more positive results for bilateral implantation (Litovsky et al., 2005).

Perhaps the greatest predictor in future language outcomes is the commitment made to wearing the hearing device(s). *Unless a child wears his/her hearing device every waking hour and is immersed in a rich language and sound environment, auditory brain development will be minimal* (Madell & Flexer, 2012). A child who wears his or her device only during school hours is missing out on hours and hours of listening. In other words, a child wearing hearing technology four hours a day will need six years to hear what a NH child hears in one year (Madell & Flexer, 2012). A very famous study by Hart and Risley (2003) revealed that by the age of four, a child should have heard 46 million words. If that is not the case, their language will be less than sufficient to communicate effectively, let alone to become literate.

Music and Language Development

Just as young children pass through certain language milestones on their way to becoming fluent communicators, they also follow a time-ordered sequence of *music milestones* (Barton, 2010). Because children are unique, the time frames for each milestone may vary, but the developmental sequence is the same. A D/HH child will pass through these milestones in a delayed fashion beginning from the time of amplification and access to music. Remember, in both language and music development, a child first needs to hear it, then speak it, and finally read and write it. Appendix A offers an at-a-glance chart of language and music milestones that NH children progress through. It is important that the music therapist working on speech and language goals become familiar with these milestones, especially when working with very young children. Again, the SLP, early interventionist (EI), and teacher of the deaf (ToD) are essential colleagues when considering using music to support LSL goals. Appendix B provides general tips for successfully integrating music into the lives of D/HH children.

Music and Language Similarities and Differences

Even though music and speech utilize different listening and processing strategies, improvements in one area often result in gains in the other (Kraus & Skoe, 2009). These specializations do not contradict the possibility of shared neural mechanisms (Patel, 2008), thus making music and speech harmonious partners. There are many ways in which they are similar:

- Both language and music are uniquely human and are found in every known culture.
- Music and language follow a sequential developmental path whereby mastery is built upon previously acquired skill sets.
- Children are born with the capacity to learn both music and language.
- Children must have access to spoken language and music in order to become fluent in each.
- Music and speech share pitch, timbre, and timing.
- Music and speech have *prosody* or melodic contour.

There are also ways in which they are different:

- Music encompasses a greater spectral range than speech.
- Music can be instrumental, thus not requiring language.
- Spoken language surrounds most children, whereas music may not.

Working with Caregivers

Because of earlier identification of D/HH children, due in large part to the UNHS, many more infants and toddlers make up the caseloads of practicing clinicians. Many of these children are followed through early intervention programs provided by individual states. In this context, the parent and family are at the center of the intervention and are considered to be the child's primary teachers, with the home as the place where most of the language learning takes place (Robbins, 2009). If one considers the fact that a music therapist may have contact with a D/HH child 30 to 60 minutes per week, this leaves thousands of hours per year when the child is not engaged in utilizing music to help promote LSL. By coaching the parents and having them practice under the therapist's supervision, the desired language behaviors can be supported outside the therapy session.

This *natural environment* approach may be mandated by a state, and when possible, a clinician should make the child's home the preferred place for intervention. However, that may not be an option because of time constraints and a lack of qualified therapists serving these families. Fortunately, there is no research to date that intervention provided in the home has a more positive effect on the D/HH child's outcome (Houston & Bradham, 2008). In fact, Robbins (2009) notes several advantages for both therapist and client seen in a clinical setting:

- The ability to control background noise and distractions (TV, radio, phone, computer, people talking).
- The ability to have use of all the equipment necessary for sessions. This is especially true for the music therapist who may rely on several large instruments in therapy.
- The availability of qualified professionals experienced in working with young D/HH children is limited. When travel time is factored in, the therapist will be forced to see a smaller caseload of children.

Regardless of where therapy takes place, it is imperative that parents and caregivers are provided strategies and techniques for nurturing LSL in everyday situations and settings. For a music therapist, this requires (1) stating the goal, (2) outlining the music experience and how it will target the goal, (3) strategies for implementation, (4) ideas for carryover to the home, and (5) evaluating and planning for the next goal.

A family-centered approach also requires an interdisciplinary team that is sensitive to cultural, ecological, and family issues (Sass-Lehrer, 2004). Changing demographics of children with hearing loss can present challenges to those working with their families:

- English may not be the primary language spoken in the home.
- Information presented may be misunderstood.
- Differing cultural and religious views of the hearing loss may also hamper effective collaboration.
- Distrust of professionals and government organizations may keep some families from seeking services.

- Limited resources, including lack of insurance, transportation, and paid time off from work, can also become barriers to accessing appropriate care.

It is imperative that all members of the team make every effort to effectively communicate with the family in a way that honors and respects the family's cultural norms and values.

Overview of Methods and Procedures

The following methods and procedures are used most commonly with children who have hearing loss.

Receptive Music Therapy

- Perceptual Listening: Client listens to music to develop skills in auditory attention, perception, discrimination, and conservation.
- Action Listening: Client exhibits target behaviors in response to lyrics or verbal cues in the music.
- Eurhythmic Listening: Client moves in time with the beat or rhythm of the music.

Re-creative Music Therapy

- Vocal Re-creation: Client sings, chants, or imitates precomposed melodies, rhythms, or songs.
- Instrumental Re-creation: Client plays or performs a precomposed instrumental piece or part.
- Musical Games: Client plays activities or games that are structured or accompanied by music.
- Musical Production: Clients prepare songs, pieces, or musical plays and perform or produce them for an audience.

Improvisational Music Therapy

- Instrumental Improvisation: Client makes up music extemporaneously on an instrument.
- Body Improvisation: Client makes up music extemporaneously, using body percussion.

Compositional Music Therapy

- Music Collage: Client creates a recording in which the client selects and sequences the music, songs, or sounds, most often with a personal life theme.
- Songwriting: Client composes lyrics, melody, and/or accompaniment to a song, with various levels of assistance. The product may or may not be notated or recorded.

Guidelines for Receptive Music Therapy

The development of listening skills is the first critical step toward spoken language acquisition. Auditory rehabilitation, defined by Cole and Flexer (2007) as the interventions aimed at teaching D/HH individuals to listen and talk, is a target for music therapy intervention. With children who are D/HH, receptive experiences are tantamount. Music therapists use *listening experiences* to address *listening problems* associated with auditory functioning, such as detection, discrimination, identification, and comprehension.

Erber (1982) outlined four Levels of Auditory Functioning: *Detection,* the ability to hear sound or no sound and demonstrate it by some sort of action (head turn, pointing to the ear); *Discrimination,* the ability to recognize difference and similarity between auditory stimuli (shaker vs. drum, high vs. low); *Identification,* the ability to demonstrate knowledge of what sound is heard (point to a picture, verbally express); and *Comprehension,* the ability to make meaning out of the sounds that are heard (hearing a certain song means that it is time to clean up). As noted previously, the D/HH child will progress through these stages in the fashion of his NH peers, albeit at a delayed pace. The child must acquire the skill sets associated with each level prior to moving to the next level. As referenced earlier in this chapter, many D/HH children, particularly those with CIs, may have difficulty with pitch discrimination tasks. However, some children can improve and even succeed with exposure and training.

Continual consultation with the SLP, ToD, Au.D., and/or parent is recommended in order to obtain the child's current listening level. Depending on the hearing age of the child and where he or she falls within Erber's levels of listening skills, the therapist will select and design receptive interventions to reinforce the current level of functioning with an eye toward the next level.

Perceptual Listening

Overview. Perceptual Listening involves a client listening to live or recorded music provided by the therapist in order to "improve skills in auditory attention, perception, discrimination, and conservation" (Bruscia, 1998, p. 120). Music selections should be developmentally appropriate to the HA of the D/HH child, with a sensitivity toward chronological age. So, if a child's HA is 1 year, but chronologically is 8 years, choose music that is simple, yet linguistically accessible and appealing. While it is possible for a client to receptively experience music, verbal responses are preferred to strengthen the expressive skills of the child. Music choice should encompass a wide array of genres, ethnicities, tempi and instrumentation. Use of this method is indicated when clients have difficulty with one or more levels of auditory functioning. Perceptual Listening exercises support the LSL approach and thus would be contraindicated for children and parents whose communication preference is that of the Deaf culture.

Preparation. With all music therapy methods, but especially with receptive experiences, it is imperative that the child be wearing operational hearing devices. If available, the use of a personal FM system is suggested. A quiet environment is critical to the success of these experiences. As possible, therapists should reduce or eliminate extraneous sounds such as ticking clocks, fans, outside noises, or any other sounds that could interfere with the child's ability to listen carefully. As important as hearing a sound in the environment, the ability to detect silence, or the absence of sound, is also critical. Receptive experiences can provide for the acquisition of these skills. When introducing novel sounds/instruments at the level of detection, it is important for the therapist to position herself on the side of the child with the most residual hearing. In a group setting, the therapist should be visible to all.

With young children, the temptation is to seat them on the floor "criss-cross applesauce"; however, this therapist finds that chairs for part of the session help to define personal space, thus avoiding potential disturbances between neighbors. Be sure the chairs are an appropriate size so that the children have their feet comfortably touching the floor.

Tune instruments and arrange those to be used in the session within easy reach of the therapist before the session begins. If using prerecorded music, check to see that the necessary equipment is operational. Queue up the CD or MP3 to the correct track, so all that is required is to press the Play button at the correct time. The volume should be at a comfortable listening level and should be adjusted down or up if the children are providing feedback.

The therapist may place pictures of instruments used on a bulletin board or classroom wall to reinforce learning. This also gives parents and teachers an opportunity to talk about the instruments and their characteristics with the child after the session has ended. In addition, the classroom teacher can use the pictures as a way of preparing children for the next session by reflecting on what instruments they believe the therapist will bring.

What to observe. At the detection level, the music therapist observes whether the child is able to demonstrate detection through audition alone. Detection experiences are designed to improve the child's ability to determine whether or not sound is present in the environment. The therapist may present a musical sound by playing an instrument out of the child's sight and watch for signs that the child has heard the sound (pointing to the ear or looking in the direction of the sound). If so, reinforce verbally that they have heard it (e.g., "Yes, you heard the drum!") and then show the child the source of the sound. Discrimination experiences require a child to correctly indicate, either verbally or by pointing to a picture, whether or not the auditory stimuli presented are the same or different. Once the child can accurately participate in discrimination exercises, the therapist can move to the identification level. If the therapist observes that the child can correctly identify the sound (instrument) presented by either pointing to a picture or responding verbally, begin to increase the number of instruments presented.

It is critical that the therapist be sensitive to the child's ability to perform pitch discrimination tasks. Some D/HH children readily engage in this game; others find it frustrating. Indications of frustration might include: hands over the ears, comments such as "I can't do it" or "it's too hard," or just a refusal to participate. The therapist should respond by returning to a familiar and successful level of auditory functioning in order to reengage the child and secure his or her trust.

Procedures. The therapist should first present the sounds/instruments through audition, then through audition and visual means, and then through audition again. For instance, the therapist says "Listen—what do you hear?" as a maraca is played out of the child's sight. If the child is unable to recognize and name the sound, the therapist shakes the maraca within the child's vision and names the instrument. Finally, the therapist again shakes the maraca out of sight and asks the child to name the instrument. This is a procedure in which the sound is "sandwiched" by auditory information (Koch, 1999). It gives the child a chance to hear the sound, compare the sound to what he or she has heard, and then hear it again, thus strengthening the connection between the sound and the sound source. Once the therapist observes signs that the child has heard the sound, she presents the instrument to the child and helps him or her figure out how it makes its unique sound.

For example, in a group situation, the therapist tells the children, "Play your instrument [or move] when you hear the music, and stop when the music stops." Initially within sight of the children, and later out of sight but within hearing range, the therapist plays live, instrumental music, forming predictable musical phrases. She then ceases playing until all children have stopped playing (or moving) and then verbally reinforces that they have stopped on cue. One adaptation of this intervention is modification of musical elements, such as tempo, dynamics, and register. In this case, for example, when the therapist plays music in a low range, the children would play (or move) in a low plane.

Another way to target detection is through the "No Peeking Game." This can be played either in individual or group sessions, with each student taking a turn. The therapist arranges a linear series of six to eight place markers on the floor (rings, dots) to indicate where the children are to move when they hear a certain sound. The therapist stands behind the children, out of view. She plays a single drumbeat, and the children move to the next marker. As with the intervention described above, it is important that the therapist verbally reinforce the children's success.

Adaptations. The music therapist can easily adapt interventions to address other levels of auditory functioning. For example, when helping a child at the discrimination level, it is advised to begin with instruments that have dissimilar timbres and later move toward instruments of a similar timbre.

Once a child is ready for pitch discrimination experiences, the therapist can demonstrate same and different pitches on a visually accessible instrument such as a keyboard. As the child watches, the therapist says something akin to, "I am going to play two notes that are the same." After several demonstrations, ask the child to play two more notes that are the same. Once the child is able to play many pairs of notes that are the same, introduce notes that are widely different. Again, say, "Now, I am going to play two notes that are different." Have the child demonstrate that he or she can play pairs of different notes. The therapist may now request the child to play two notes that are the same and/or two notes that are different. When the child is capable of accurately playing pairs of same and different notes, the therapist can turn the keyboard around, so that the child can't see the notes as they are played, and ask him or her to name what was heard. Prompt the child by saying, "Tell me if you think the two notes are the same or are different. Here is the first note *[play note];* here is the second note *[play note]."* After the child provides an answer of same or different, play the notes again within view of the child to support or correct the response.

When the child is able to hear and respond to a single instrument (e.g., a drum), a second instrument of distinctly different timbre (e.g., cymbal) can be introduced. As in the previous version of the "No Peeking Game," children move forward and backward on the markers placed on the floor, with instruments of dissimilar timbre being used to indicate direction of movement (e.g., cymbal and drum). Once the children demonstrate the ability to discriminate between two or more instruments, timbres, or even pitches, they are ready to move to the identification level (accurate indication or naming of source of sound). There are many experiences targeting these skills. In noncompetitive "Instrument Bingo," children place markers on their bingo card with pictures of familiar percussion and tonal instruments if they hear the corresponding sound.

Games like "Doggie, Doggie, Where's Your Bone?" can target peer voice identification. Children sit in a circle with eyes closed and hands behind their backs. One child walks around the circle and deposits the bone into a classmate's waiting hands. When the therapist sings, "Who has the bone?," the child with the bone responds, "Me" or "I do." The children then guess whose voice they heard and the game begins again, with the selected child moving around the circle and depositing the bone.

Pitch identification can proceed from the same/different realm to the high/low arena. The therapist will present the experience in similar fashion by visually playing high and low notes on a keyboard and having the child do the same. Once the child can accurately play high and low notes, turn the keyboard around and present one at a time and have the child name it as "high" or "low." As in instrument identification, choose pitches that are either very high or very low at first to avoid confusion. It may also be useful to practice talking or singing in high or low voices to add another dimension to this experience.

Finally, when children have successfully mastered identification, the therapist can design experiences that support the development of listening comprehension skills. Emotion conveyed by speech and music requires the ability to perceive complex cues, with which some D/HH children struggle (Darrow, 2006). Two prominent elements that enable one to recognize happy and sad music are mode and tempo. A recent study (Hopyan, Gordon, & Papsin, 2011) found that CI children use tempo cues better than NH peers to discriminate happy vs. sad music. The music therapist can facilitate the discrimination and ultimately comprehension of the emotional intent of a piece of recorded or live instrumental music by labeling and talking with the children about the feelingful quality of that piece of music. The therapist should choose dramatically disparate examples of music that reflect diverse emotions. Providing cards with matching facial expressions can add a visual connection to the auditory examples. Ideally, the music therapist is encouraged to improvise or play precomposed music in the moment. If recorded pieces are required, select sparsely recorded instrumental music (e.g., ethnic folk), which uses few instruments but many different scales, modes, and tempi.

Action Listening

Overview. Bruscia (1998) defines Action Listening as a method that reinforces daily living skills and elicits verbal and motor behaviors in response to lyrics embedded in a song or to specific musical cues. D/HH children can benefit from simple directives given as a chant (e.g., "take two sticks and pass the rest, uh, huh") or sung to a familiar tune such as "If You're Happy and You Know It"("Put the shaker in the bag, in the bag"). Action Listening exercises support the LSL approach and thus would be contraindicated for children and parents whose communication preference is that of the Deaf culture.

Preparation. The session room should provide ample space, be void of extraneous environmental sounds, and have adequate lighting and optimal room acoustics. All equipment used should be operational and within reach of the therapist. The therapist should be aware that some children will use an FM system, which will require the therapist to wear a small microphone. Classroom teachers and even the children can assist the therapist in proper placement of the microphone and correct settings of the FM system. When using recorded music, call attention to when the music begins (point to the ear and say, "Listen") and when it stops (point to the ear and say, "The music stopped"). Select music that has a simple accompaniment and strong pulse. Labeling the constructs for the children will reinforce their ability to discern these same constructs in a variety of musical selections.

What to observe. Pairing words to the motions of a musical selection (up and down, round and round, wiggle, wiggle, turn and turn) linguistically reinforces how the child is moving. Observe the child's ability to imitate the therapist's movements, first with visual modeling and then through audition alone. Provide ample opportunities for each child to demonstrate a specific movement of his or her choosing and label it for future reference, e.g., "Johnny is moving his arms up and down."

Procedures. Select a precomposed action song or create one that specifically targets body movements. Children will perform body movements (clap hands, stomp feet) as the song directs. Choose movements that are developmentally appropriate for the group. The therapist may initially want to model the movements for the children, but eventually phase them out so that the children have to rely on audition to perform the correct action. It may be helpful to insert a "stop" or "freeze" between movements. As children become comfortable with this experience, have them offer different ways to move their bodies and insert them into the experience. Encourage them to name their movement and be prepared to offer suggestions if they can't respond verbally.

Adaptations. Using a similar approach as the one presented above, provide rhythm instruments to the group and have them play according to the directives embedded in a song. Musical constructs such as fast and slow, loud and soft, and high and low can easily be targeted. Select music that is simple, preferably in the moment, and highlight dramatic differences between the musical constructs. Begin by having all children respond as a group and move toward an identification experience by requiring certain instruments to play. For example, the therapist may say, "Only the shakers will play" or "Only the girls will play." These directives can become more complex (only girls who are wearing red and have a shaker may play) as children's listening skills increase.

Eurhythmic Listening

Overview. Eurhythmic Listening (Bruscia, 1998) is defined as using the beat and rhythm of music to help organize motor behaviors. These behaviors may include speech, fine and gross motor sequencing, breathing, exercising, and structured dance steps. Contrary to Action Listening, Eurhythmic Listening does not require extraction of cues by the child in order to indicate which motor behavior is to be executed. Because movement follows a developmental trajectory similar to language and music development, use of this method is indicated for children whose chronological age is two or more years.

Because the inner ear contains both the auditory nerve as well as the vestibular system, many D/HH children are at risk for balance and gross motor delays. Goals of eurhythmic listening in this particular situation include helping the child to move rhythmically in nonlocomotor fashion with an eventual progression to balanced and free locomotor movement.

Weikert (1987) has extensively researched stages of aural, visual, and tactile/kinesthetic decoding in young children. She provides guidelines for presenting movement experiences that align with children's development needs with respect to motor function. According to Weikert's model, there are five sequential stages in movement development, each of which could be supported through Eurhythmic Listening experiences. These include Stage 1: Single Bilateral Symmetrical Movement; Stage 2: Single Predictable Alternating Movements; Stage 3: Single Asymmetrical Movements; Stage 4: Single Asymmetrical Tracking Movements; and Stage 5: Sequenced Bilateral Symmetrical Movements. Once children have mastered these nonlocomotor stages, they are deemed *beat competent* and are ready to move with others to a common beat.

Preparation. Provide a space free of obstacles and clutter with ample room to move. Position the CD or MP3 player close to the group and play at a volume that is comfortable for the music therapist. Do not play at a loud volume, as it may sound distorted to amplified ears. Select music with a prominent steady beat or pulse. This author has found folk dance music from around the world to be ideal, because it is usually performed on acoustic instruments with the primary aim of eliciting synchronized movement. Do not use music that reinforces the offbeat or back beat.

Children with poor balance must be closely supervised when engaged in any movement where a risk of injury is present. The music therapist should consult with the OT, PT, etc., about the child's capabilities prior to using movement in this way. This is typically one intervention within a session rather than the focus of a complete music therapy session.

What to observe. When the music therapist observes children starting to move in their seats spontaneously in response to music vs. spoken language, this is likely an indication that they are able to discriminate music from speech or environmental sounds and will thus be ready to respond to the musical elements through bodily movement. The experiences presented are designed to facilitate a child's ability to move to a common beat. This is a skill that develops sequentially over time. The therapist should become familiar with these movement milestones and observe when children pass through them and select music experiences that support success and the progression to the next developmental skill set. Young children can respond to movement experiences in many ways, some appropriate and some not. Invading a neighbor's space or becoming overstimulated or silly can often derail an experience. The therapist needs to carefully monitor the group and be ready to redirect undesirable behaviors so that the experience will be successful.

Procedures. Children can be seated on the floor or in chairs. Be sure there is ample space between each child. Using either rhythm sticks (cut them in half so they are easier for little hands to manipulate) or small paper plates, begin with a piece of lively (120–136 bpm) instrumental recorded music and invite the children to synchronize with a series of bilaterally symmetrical movements (e.g., tapping the knees with both sticks/plates simultaneously, pushing out and in with paper plates under the feet). Change the movement patterns every 16 beats to start so that all children have a chance to synchronize with the movement. Ultimately patterns can be altered every eight beats, aligning with musical phrasing. Saying the word "watch" on beat 15 (or 7) serves as a verbal prompt for when the movement is about to change. Once the children have demonstrated the ability to synchronize with the therapist's patterns and have a "vocabulary" of movements from which to choose, they should be able to confidently lead the group with their own movement patterns. Changing with the phrases will come with continued practice and listening and spoken language development.

Movement through space (locomotor movement) can take many forms and address various therapeutic aims. When targeting moving to a common beat, Weikert (1987) advises having the children first alternate feet while seated, then walk or march in place, walk in a forward direction in a straight path, and finally walk backward and sideways. Remembering also that many motor behaviors develop in a sequential manner and that some D/HH children will have significant delays, be sure to assess the motor abilities of the group members before introducing locomotor movements. For example, jumping with two feet is easier than hopping with one, and galloping is a prerequisite skill to skipping.

Adaptations. Since music is a multisensory experience, young children tend to respond with the whole body and not just with the ears (Schwartz, 2008). Nonlocomotor movement with streamers, scarves, stretchy bands, and other props can provide an opportunity to focus on imitation (therapist or child leads the group), echo (therapist or child presents a movement and group echoes), mirroring (one partner moves while the other mirrors the movements exactly), and creative expression.

GUIDELINES FOR RE-CREATIVE MUSIC THERAPY

Mithen (2006) argues that speaking and singing are instinctual behaviors that are inexorably linked. Indeed, singing to infants is a universal behavior that exists in all cultures and has been documented throughout time (De L'Etoile, 2006). There is even evidence to suggest that mothers will adjust their vocal style to match the hearing age of their D/HH child (Bergeson, Miller, & McCune, 2006). This deep-seated connection can be used advantageously to support spoken language in very young children with hearing loss.

The current available research on the development of pitch production in D/HH children is limited. Nakata, Trehub, Mitrani and Kanda (2006) found that while congenitally deaf children sang with the same enthusiasm as their NH peers, the direction of pitch changes was often unrelated to the pitch changes in the songs. Chen et al. (2010) was the first study to report improvement in pitch perception in prelingually deafened CI children after a period of musical training. The researchers speculate that auditory plasticity may have been a factor. With earlier and bilateral implantation, improved hearing technology, and ample exposure to music (and, perhaps, intervention and music training), there exists optimism that the tuneful D/HH singer will become less the exception and more the rule (Kraus & Skoe, 2009).

Vocal Re-creation

Overview. Singing, chanting, vocal imitation, and learning melodies are all examples of vocal re-creation (Bruscia, 1998). Performance for an audience is not required, but may be included in this method. Goals areas for D/HH children may include: vocal prosody, increased attention, memory and sensorimotor development, and expressive language skills. The novice listener may have limited expressive language, but nursery songs can provide some of the earliest vocabulary. Finger plays and gestures that accompany the songs are also recommended.

Preparation. As explained above, singing on pitch may pose a challenge for many D/HH children. *Prosody,* the lyrical nature of speech, may also be lacking in some D/HH children. Vocal exercises that require a child to explore the full range of his or her voice can be helpful in raising a child's awareness of the different voices he or she is capable of producing (e.g., shout, whisper, speak, and sing; high and low). This author has found that the Feierabend (2004) *Pitch Exploration Pathways* are helpful visual aids for encouraging the client to warm up the vocal muscles prior to singing. As with any method employed, all hearing technologies should be fully operational and worn. Personal FM systems may be useful, and environmental noises should be minimized.

What to observe. With very young listeners, the therapist will want to check for song identification. One way to do this is to observe whether or not the child will imitate the motions of simple songs such as "Twinkle, Twinkle, Little Star" or "Itsy, Bitsy Spider" as the therapist sings. Once the child is successful with several songs, the therapist should try singing one without the hand motions and wait to see if the child begins the gestures on his/her own. The therapist should observe when the child begins to "ask" for certain songs by making the hand motions. Parents and teachers can provide this information to the therapist as well. As the child progresses through the various auditory levels, the therapist will be looking for spontaneous singing while at play, singing along with others, and whether or not the child has preferences for certain songs and genres.

Procedures. It is important for the D/HH child to realize that a singing voice is different from a speaking voice. Vocal imitation of the changing pitch of a slide whistle or the movement of a ball thrown in the air, while moving the body up and down with the pitch change, are some ways to integrate the voice with the body. Begin by demonstrating the slide whistle to the children. Have each child move his or her body up and down while vocally mimicking the sound of the whistle by using a vowel such as /u/ or /a/. Vary the tempo so that sometimes they will pop up quickly and other times very slowly. Be sure to label the movements for them. Sing "The Grand Old Duke of York" and play the whistle at the appropriate place as all the children vocally mimic and move up and down with the whistle. Once they are familiar with the game and can successfully vocally imitate the slide whistle, the therapist can move out of sight, but within hearing range of the children, and play the whistle. Observe whether the children are able to correctly label the sound as moving up or down.

Adaptations. The Feierabend *Pitch Exploration Pathways* (2004) are a series of 11 charts that visually represent the notion of moving the voice up and down. Each has an engaging illustration with a single movement line, such as a hot air balloon rising up into the sky. These drawings provide an enjoyable way for children to make sliding sounds that explore the vocal muscles used to sing in the upper register or *head voice*. The music therapist and children can also make their own drawings.

Drawing lines of differing lengths but on a similar plane on a chalkboard or white board can be a way to visually represent duration, i.e., long and short. This procedure, often paired with a motion, is employed frequently in auditory oral approaches as a precursor to learning multisyllabic words. Have the child trace the line with a finger and say or sing a syllable or vowel that is in his or her repertoire. As an example, for a long line, one would say "baaaaaaaaaaaaaaaa"; for short lines, "baa"; and for staccato dots, "ba, ba, ba."

Rhymes, with their phonologic elements, are necessary for learning language and ultimately prepare the road toward literacy. Nursery rhymes, chants, and songs provide a rich treasure trove that can strengthen the conceptualization of rhyme. One suggestion is to leave off the final lyric in a phrase of a familiar song and listen for the child to supply the missing correct lyric. Or, alternatively, to insert the wrong lyric and see if the child notices and corrects. Echo songs such as "Charlie Over the Ocean," "Down by the Bay," and "Kye, Kye, Kule" have short phrases and limited pitch range, making them ideal resources for beginning singers.

This author has also found *solfège* to be a very useful tool when teaching interval singing. Pairing solfège with hand signs, which correspond in space to the distance of the interval, has proven successful for some D/HH children. A suggestion is to begin with so-mi, then so-mi-la, then so-mi-la-do. Pictures of the Curwin/Kodaly hand signs adorn the eight steps leading to this therapist's music therapy clinic. The children sit on each step and sing the corresponding syllable after the therapist first models it. A suggestion when singing outside the vocal range of a child is to lean in close to the hearing device and softly sing the pitch, encouraging the child to mimic the singing voice as opposed to the speaking voice. Often, children confuse "sing higher" with "sing louder."

Microphones, either real or pretend, can be used as vocal prompts. If the therapist expects the child to imitate her pitch or vocal phrase, the microphone will indicate whose turn it is to sing. As an example, the therapist would sing into the microphone and then place it in front of the child's mouth when the appropriate response is desired. Many D/HH children like to hear themselves amplified through a speaker. Be sure to adjust the volume to a comfortable listening level. Some children with personal FM systems like to hear themselves sing or speak into their microphones for enhanced auditory feedback.

Instrumental Re-creation

Overview. When children are involved in playing or performing precomposed instrumental pieces, possibly using some kind of notation, either in a group setting or by themselves, they are engaged in Instrumental Re-creation (Bruscia, 1998). The structure of such a method can be useful for children who need to develop certain sensorimotor, memory, attention, and social skills. Many more D/HH children are engaged in taking private music lessons today as a result of advanced hearing technologies and interaction with NH peers.

Preparation. The music therapist should offer D/HH children a variety of pitched and nonpitched instruments to play. It is advisable to introduce instruments one at a time and for the therapist to model the correct way to play it. Take time to talk with the children about how it is constructed, what part of the world it comes from, and how it makes its sound. General principles such as the longer the instrument, or string, the lower the sound, and vice versa, will enable the children to predict what sound an instrument might make even before they hear it. A phrase this therapist uses as a mnemonic is, "The longer the flute, the lower the toot." Older children can be introduced to additional sound qualities such as resonance and timbre. It is also helpful to talk about instrument families, so that every time an instrument is introduced, children can compare its sound to those of other family members. Pictures of instruments arranged by families can be placed on the therapy wall for all to see and discuss.

Before beginning an Instrumental Re-creative experience, be sure all hearing and sound devices are functioning. Reduce any extraneous environmental sounds that could clutter the sound field.

What to observe. It is advisable that the music therapist ask each child to demonstrate the correct technique used to play the instrument they will be using during the music experience. The therapist will need to monitor each child as the experience unfolds to ensure that no damage comes to the instrument or the child. Take note of the instruments the children tend to prefer and which may pose challenges either because of the motor skills required to play them or because of their timbre. Some children may cover their ears when introduced to novel sounds, and the therapist should use care when introducing potentially invasive sounding instruments such as a cymbal or thunder tube. Offering the child the opportunity to explore the offending instrument on his/her own will often mitigate the problem.

Procedures. A logical place to start an Instrumental Re-creative experience is by selecting a piece of music that lends itself to starts and stops at predictable moments, such as the end of a musical phrase. The group members should sit in chairs or on the floor in a semicircle, with the therapist visible by all members. Either assign or have the children select an instrument and demonstrate proper technique required to play it. The therapist will explain that the children will play when they hear the music, but stop playing when the music stops. This will reinforce the notion of presence or absence of sound—so crucial to the LSL approach. Once the children are accurately starting and stopping with the therapist, turn around so that the children will need to rely on audition alone to provide the cues. Take note of which children are able to be successful through listening and which are merely following their peers' actions. It may be useful to have each child take a turn, so that the music therapist has an accurate way of knowing who is successful.

Adaptations. Once the group is successful at starting and stopping through audition alone, add another dimension to the experience. Begin by having the children match the therapist's style of playing, e.g., fast, slow, loud, soft, as she models with visual cues. Once they demonstrate accuracy, the therapist will turn around and present the experience through audition. As before, observe which children are able to master the experience.

A logical next step is to use an instrumental re-creation of a song or tune in which each child has a specific role or part to play. For example, the therapist can either assign students resonator bells that have been color-coded with stickers or use the color-coded KidsPlay® handbells. The children are then required to follow a color-coded chart that the therapist has prepared that provides either the chords or melody of a song. This experience offers children the opportunity to function as a member of a musical ensemble, to hear when their individual part is to be played, and to play it in just the right way.

Musical Games

Overview. Bruscia defines Musical Games as "participation in any activity that is structured by music" (1998, p. 120). American traditional singing games provide ample opportunities for following directions embedded within the lyrics. "In and Out the Window,""Bluebird Through My Window," and "The Farmer in the Dell" are just a few examples. In addition, they are a wonderful means of supporting the development of social skills (everyone has a job to do, everyone gets a turn). Singing the songs over and over while everyone plays the game facilitates quick learning and often becomes a favorite playground activity, because they can be led by solely by the children.

Preparation. The music therapist will want to select a singing game that is developmentally appropriate for the HA and CA of the group. She may want to change the lyrics to adapt the game either up or down to the listening level of the group. Provide a space that is free of clutter and ample enough to accommodate the group size. At the same time, be aware of room acoustics and determine if an additional sound system may be required. All hearing devices should be operational and worn by the children. Any props should be gathered ahead of time and within easy reach of the therapist. It is best to have the therapist sing and play in the moment to provide an appropriate tempo and vocal range.

What to observe. The therapist should observe that all members of the group are able to hear the directives embedded in the lyrics of the singing game and are actively engaged. Remind the group that everyone will have a turn and be ready to facilitate that promise.

Procedures. The therapist will learn the singing game "Bluebird Through My Window" and be prepared to sing it for the group. She should provide a prop, either a bluebird puppet, stuffed animal, or paper representation. This therapist prefers the Audubon Plush Bird Toys with real birdcalls that are activated by squeezing the toy. Begin by having the children seated in a circle either on the floor or in chairs, with enough space between them for a child to pass through. Keeping the bird out of sight, play the birdcall for the children and see if they recognize it as a bird sound. Then, present the bird to them and play the call again. Taking the bird with her, the therapist will sing the song while weaving in and out of the circle and pretending to make the bird fly through the air. At the last line of the song, the therapist will present the bird to a child and say, "Squeeze the bird." The child will make the bird sing and then it is his/her turn to go in and out of the circle and present it to another child, giving the same directive. The game ends when every child has had the chance to make the bluebird fly in and out of the window (circle). The therapist may wish to add a child's name to the last line, "Sing a song for____," and see whether the child with the bird can give it to the correct peer.

Musical Productions

Overview. The focus of a Musical Production is planning an event with the intention of performing for an audience (Bruscia, 1998). Many facilities and schools prepare celebrations that highlight the progress children have made throughout the year. Music is almost always a featured component of those celebrations. Parents and potential donors are appreciative of the effort put into such presentations.

Preparation. When very young children are involved in a performance, one must prepare for the unexpected, e.g., stage fright, running to Mom or Dad, "forgetting" to sing. Therefore, using musical selections that come out of the therapy sessions and the classroom experience will support the children because of their familiarity with the process. This approach may be preferable to learning a prewritten play/musical that is not contextually relevant to the goals of the classroom.

The music therapist should be cognizant of the sound requirements of the performance space and assess what additional sound equipment will be required. Because many children are involved in the performance, it will be impossible for the therapist to wear individual FM systems. Lighting should be sufficient for the audience to see each child on the stage. It is also recommended that the house lights remain on so the children can spot their parents and avoid the fears that can accompany a darkened room. If the children are assigned specific places to stand, it is a courtesy to let parents know in advance, so they can seat themselves in proximity to their child, allowing for the best picture and video opportunities. If risers are used, be sure the children have ample opportunities to practice standing on them in advance. Do not require students with balance issues to stand on the risers. Be sure the path to the stage is free of clutter and well lit.

If the performance space is off-site, take pictures of the space and share with the students in advance. Plan to have at least one rehearsal in that space because the acoustics and logistics will be different from what the students are used to. If microphones are used, be sure to model the correct way to speak or sing into one. Practice repeatedly.

Hearing technologies should be operational and worn at all times. If additional equipment is required, e.g., PA system, CD or MP3 players, be sure that the volume is adequate for the space.

What to observe. Anything can happen during a performance involving young children, so the therapist will do well to keep a lighthearted attitude. Children will sense when the therapist is nervous or upset. Watch for signs like tears, silliness, or a refusal to go up on stage and plan to have an adult ready to sit with the child while the performance continues. Upset tummies are not uncommon, so provisions for dealing with them should be made ahead of time. Again, if the performance comes out of what the children have done in music therapy sessions, they will be comfortable with the program.

Procedures. The therapist will want to gather input from classroom teachers and other members of the hearing team to select a theme or purpose for the program. It is imperative that everyone feel comfortable with the selections chosen. Select a date, performance space, and travel arrangements to and from the site. Gather all props, supplies, instruments, costumes, and music necessary for the program and make arrangements to transport them to the performance space. Make and print programs if desired and arrange to have volunteers hand them out before the performance. Accept any help that is offered.

The therapist should plan for activities for the children to be engaged in while waiting for the performance to begin. Movies or stories work well to calm nerves and focus attention. Plan enough adult supervision so that the therapist is free to prepare and to take care of last-minute issues for the performance.

It is advisable to have adults organize the students in the correct order and facilitate the entrance to and exit from the stage. Some may even want to remain on the stage with the children for moral and technical support. Have students or a designated adult announce the selections. If students come to the stage by class, be sure to have a space with adult supervision where the remaining students can wait. The music therapist should be prepared (or assign someone) to perform musical selections during lengthy transitions. Often, these pauses will afford an administrator or parent the opportunity to talk positively and supportively about the school. Video montages of the children taken throughout the year can also be presented and are often a highlight of the celebration.

Once the performance is over, thank the audience for their attendance and be on hand to answer any questions or just to talk with family members. Receptions are a nice finish to a program. Arrange for transportation of students and all supplies back to school. Thank all volunteers and others involved with the production. Start planning for the next celebration!

GUIDELINES FOR IMPROVISATIONAL MUSIC THERAPY

When a client (either alone or with others) creates a melody, rhythm, song, or instrumental piece in the moment, it qualifies as an improvisatory experience (Bruscia, 1998). For D/HH children with limited expressive language abilities, this method can afford a nonverbal means of self-expression and communication. Young NH children often create spontaneous songs while at play (Barton, 2010). This author has found that the D/HH child who has been offered a musically rich environment will also pass through this important developmental stage, albeit at a slower pace. It is advised that the music therapist ask parents and teachers for their observations regarding a child's play habits, as well as his or her access and exposure to music experiences.

Instrumental Improvisation

Overview. Bruscia (1998) suggests two possible types of improvisation; *referential* and *nonreferential*. Referential provides a nonmusical theme upon which music is created. This could include anything that the client has had experience with: birthday party, shopping, playground, feelings, etc. Nonreferential improvisations are those created without a referent, or theme, resulting in a purely musical meaning. Gardstrom (2007) suggests two types of referents, *static* and *dynamic*. Static referents are those concepts conveyed by the music that don't change over the course of the improvisation. An example could be "sleepy" or "lonely." Dynamic referents change considerably throughout the improvisation. A "rainstorm" or "going to the beach" would be examples of dynamic referents. These referents are sometimes used together to reinforce opposite concepts and are known as *continuum referents*. Going from "happy to sad" or "playtime to quiet time" are examples of continuum referents. Referents are important because they lend support and focus to a musical improvisation. Depending on the language and developmental level of the child, these referents can be chosen by the music therapist or the child.

While no studies on music improvisation and young D/HH children exist in the current literature, several music pedagogies and models embrace exploration and improvisation as a critical component to developing and manipulating the language of music (Campbell & Scott-Kassner, 1995). Even before the advent of sophisticated hearing technologies, Robbins and Robbins (1980), pioneers in Creative Music Therapy, encouraged D/HH children to sing, play, and dance freely while the therapist provided a rhythmically flowing accompaniment. *Orff* instruction may feature invention of a melody on a C pentatonic scale, while a *Kodaly* approach may involve creation of rhythmic or pitch patterns for an echo response. The long-term success of these methods in helping children achieve a sense of form, genre, structure, musical expression, and concepts speaks to the importance of improvisation within a creative music process.

Preparation. When developing an instrumental nonreferential improvisation experience for the very young D/HH child, the therapist should engage a parent, older child, or any other member of the hearing team to model the process for the child. All hearing technologies must be fully operational, employed and functioning. The music therapist should also minimize any extraneous noises in the session or therapy room to ensure an optimal listening environment. Provide drums and other percussion instruments such as xylophones or metallophones tuned to specific pentatonic or modal scales.

What to observe. The therapist will want to monitor carefully how the child engages in the improvisation experience. Is he/she aware that the therapist is an integral part of the improvisation or merely self-absorbed in his/her own music-making? The therapist's playful demeanor will help engage the child. First experiences will tend to be exploratory in nature, but imitation, mirroring, and turn-taking can be addressed through this method.

Procedures. The therapist will provide for or allow the child to choose an instrument for improvisation. Ample opportunities to explore the sound of his/her instrument should be given before embarking upon the improvisation. The therapist will want to provide a "vocabulary" of rhythm or tonal ideas through re-creation and imitation until the child feels comfortable choosing from the "palette" of sound possibilities for the improvisation. It is important for the therapist and/or child to decide how to begin and end the experience and whether or not other rules apply, such as turn-taking or imitation. The therapist and/or student may count "One, two, three, go" to begin and "Three, two, one, stop" to bring the improvisation to a close. Maintain close proximity to the child throughout the experience. After the experience, even if short-lived, the therapist should talk with the child about the process. Conversation starters may be questions such as, "How did you like the music we made? Did it put a picture in your head and if so, what was it? Can you think of a title or name for our song?" After successful duet experiences, try a trio or quartet and include siblings, parents, and any other team member involved in the session.

Adaptations. Once a child has had plenty of opportunities to engage in nonreferential improvisation, the therapist may wish to try a referential experience. Special consideration and care should be taken when choosing a referent. It is crucial that it be an idea or concept with which the child is familiar. Not all children have had the same experiences or opportunities. Parents can help guide the therapist in choosing an appropriate referent. Emotions tend to work especially well. Using picture cards of children displaying different facial emotions can be helpful when choosing a specific emotion as a referent. If the picture is that of a crying child, why not develop a narrative of why that child might be sad? The more the emotion is explored before the improvisation begins, the higher the probability that it will be conveyed throughout the improvisation.

Body Improvisations

Overview. This variation employs the use of body percussion (patting, clapping, stomping) as an improvisatory experience (Bruscia, 1998). Solos, duets, and even small groups can utilize this method.

Preparation. Provide ample space and an optimal acoustic environment with adequate lighting. All hearing technologies should be operational and worn by the children. The therapist should be prepared to utilize an FM system, if required. Assemble a list of various body sounds that young children can produce. Collect precomposed or therapist-developed songs or music that can be accompanied by body percussion.

What to observe. The therapist should spend time observing the children in various settings to see what kinds of body sounds they spontaneously make and incorporate them into the body improvisation experiences that she designs for the children. The OT and SLP may also have some recommendations for oral motor sounds targeted in their therapies. Because many body percussion sounds appear silly to some children, extra care should be taken to keep the experience structured enough to keep everyone on track.

Procedures. By initially providing students with a *body percussion vocabulary,* a series of developmentally appropriate options, they are then free to select from these options during an improvised experience. As a way to introduce the children to this vocabulary, have them seated in chairs arranged in a semicircle, taking care that the therapist remains visually accessible by all. A simple directive, "Follow me," is given. The therapist chants "Monkey see, monkey do, what I do, you can, too!" and then models a percussive body sound while observing the students for successful imitation. Once the children are able to successfully imitate the therapist's sounds, the chant can be changed to "Monkey see, monkey do, what you do, we will, too!" and each child can be allowed to model a percussive body sound of his or her choosing. For the child who is reluctant to share on the spot, a simple default sound (clap) can be agreed upon before beginning the experience. Mouth sounds (raspberries, tongue clicks) can be incorporated into the experience and double as an oral motor exercise. "Riddle, riddle, riddle, ree/Do what I do after me" (Nash & Rapley, 1990) also works well for this experience.

Guidelines for Compositional Music Therapy

For some children, Music Composition experiences can be a highlight of music therapy sessions. This author has found that for D/HH children who are advanced listeners and comfortable and fluent with expressive language, a composition provides a finished product that can be shared with family and friends. Such a product can serve as a record of the child's current skills, with future compositions providing evidence of developmental progress. Bruscia (1998) suggests that clinical goals for such experiences can be: documentation of inner thoughts and feelings, retelling and re-creating a life event or experience, integrating separate thoughts and parts into a whole, developing planning, and learning organizational skills and self-responsibility, particularly if the client works singly on the composition outside of the actual music therapy session.

Music Collages

Overview. Bruscia (1998) defines Music Collages as any recording in which the client selects and sequences the music, songs, or sounds, which can reflect a personal experience or a therapeutic aim. For children, a personal experience could involve a birthday, family outing, vacations, or even a music therapy session. Eliciting parents' input can help guide the process for young children.

There is historical evidence to support the fact that D/HH children are at risk for serious reading delays (Geers & Moog, 1989). The "fourth grade slump" is the term used to describe the reading plateau that above which many high school students with hearing loss have difficulty rising. However, Robertson (2009) argues that higher literacy levels are possible for those children who are involved in the LSL approach from an early age. *Phonological awareness,* or the ability to learn pronunciation of the sounds of a language, is best served through listening (Perigroe, 2001) and is fundamental to reading acquisition (Goswami, 2009). If we agree that the purpose of language is to create meaning, then we begin to understand something we hear or read about as we connect it to something we already know. To that end, Robertson (2009) developed the concept of *Language Experience Books.* This is an approach to reading instruction that focuses on the child's current vocabulary and language capabilities. Because this approach uses stories created using the child's own words, the element of predictability emerges. The child tells his or her story to a caregiver and that person writes it down; then the child draws a picture to accompany the story. Over time, the child will learn to do the printing as well. This author believes that music can enhance the effectiveness of these books and thus has developed *Music Experience Books* (MEBs) (Barton, 2011). MEBs provide a unique way to bring children and parents together to create a personalized resource that will have lasting appeal and benefit.

Preparation. The therapist will want to explore with the child and parents a theme for the *Music Experience Books.* Once a theme is agreed upon, parents will help the child gather visual and tangible objects to include as part of the composition. Songs, instruments, and other music recordings can be chosen. It is realistic to plan for several sessions to pull the entire project together.

What to observe. MEBs should be child-centered and -directed. The therapist may need to remind overly helpful parents that their purpose is to assist the therapist in facilitating the process. Watch for indications that the child is fully engaged and happy with the process as it unfolds. At the same time, some decisions will require certain technical abilities and thus will need to be made by the therapist, such as how to record the child's narration or how to facilitate the addition of music to the book.

Procedures. What follows is a procedural example of a MEB created by an eight-year-old child about a typical music therapy session. Parents took digital pictures of the child engaged with the music therapist in singing, playing instruments, moving to music, and, in some cases, writing music. The parent then shared the photos with the child and had the child narrate each picture in his or her own words. Parents then wrote down the child's narration and sent the pictures and narration to the therapist. Using the Tar Heel Reader (THR), http://tarheelreader.org/, a free online book publishing program developed at UNC–Chapel Hill, the therapist would upload all the pictures and enter the text for each. The unique book was then produced and available to view on the THR website. Subsequently, using the Tar Heel Player (THP; http://gbserver.cs.unc.edu/TarHeelPlayer/setup.html), audio was added, thus enabling the child to narrate, sing, and provide musical accompaniment to his or her book. A link to an example of a *Music Experience Book* and a direction sheet for using the THP can be found at http://firstyears.org/lib/thp.htm. Since the development of the THP, many other similar programs have been created and are readily available over the Internet for free.

Adaptations. It is also possible to create a story or event and tell it through environmental or musical sounds, which this author calls a *SoundStory.* The therapist and client choose a topic such as a trip to a haunted house or the experience of being in a rainstorm. The child and therapist develop the sequence of events. Once the sequence is finalized, the therapist writes a narrative to assist with selecting an instrument or sound to represent that narrative, e.g., knock on the door, wind, thunder, bats screeching, etc. The SoundStory is recorded and, upon playback, the listener is able to follow the premise of the tale through the audio alone. See Appendix C for an example of a SoundStory.

Songwriting

Overview. Songwriting and working toward developing a product can be a focus of the music therapy session or may evolve out of a song a child composed at home and then brought into the session. In the latter instance, the therapist can assist the child in flushing out the lyrics and melody. Often, a song will take the form of a rap or chant, not only because these are popular genres, but also because, as previously stated, pitch and melody might be problematic for D/HH children. Once completed, it can be notated and recorded, thus allowing the child to share it with family and friends. There are other instances when writing a song about a memorable event, such as the loss of a loved one or a pet, a week at camp, or the dog that ate the child's hearing aid, will provide good material for a song. These then provide the germ for a more formal composition. See Appendix D for an example of a song created during music therapy sessions.

Preparation. Topics or themes for the song need to be developed. The therapist can facilitate choosing a subject with the child, but ultimately, the process will unfold smoothly if the child has a major stake in the topic. Parents can aid the child and therapist in choosing an appropriate topic and the vocabulary needed to write the song. Decisions about the best way to record and/or notate the song should be made before embarking on the actual songwriting experience. The therapist will either want to have staff paper, a computerized notation program, or a recording device to collect initial ideas, which are referred to as the songwriting process unfolds. It may be useful to have some drawing paper and markers for the child to make illustrations for the piece.

What to observe. If a child brings a composition to a session, or if parents report that the child is creating songs at home, these may be indications that the child is ready to engage in songwriting. Once the process is begun, the therapist will need to monitor the child's behavior and watch for signs that the process is a positive one. If a child seems impatient, distracted, or disengaged, it might be best to put the song "on hold" and come back to it at a later date.

Procedures. The therapist should have a knowledgeable understanding of the child's language abilities before starting to help him or her write a song. It is important to let the child know that songwriting is a multistep process and may require several sessions to complete. Once a subject is chosen, a narrative can be written with a sequence of events unfolding in a logical order. If the child is young, he or she may dictate the narrative to the therapist. For an older student, the music therapist can help the child decide on a rhyming scheme if desired and what form the song should take. For instance, will there be verses and choruses, or will it be through-composed? Some children relish the idea of writing lyrics at home and bringing them into the session for use in collaborating with the music therapist. Once the text is formed, a melody is created. This therapist has found that using a C pentatonic scale (do-re-mi-so-la) can assist the child in creating a pleasing melody with an accessible vocal range. The student will need the therapist's musical guidance to help develop a melody that can be sung with accurate phrasing, rhythmic flow, and contour. When the melody and lyrics are complete, the chordal accompaniment is created. The therapist can offer the child a number of possibilities from which to choose. However, if the child is eager to play the accompaniment by himself or herself, the therapist will need to consider the musical abilities of the child when presenting harmonic options. Choosing the instrumentation for the song is the next step in the process. The therapist offers the student a selection of developmentally appropriate instruments. Possibilities include a keyboard with an automatic chord function, a Q-Chord™, autoharp, and Orff instruments. If the child currently is taking private instrumental music lessons, find every opportunity to include the instrument in the accompaniment. Keep the arrangement simple. Once the song is complete and has been rehearsed adequately, it can be recorded and/or notated, if desired. The child composer typically delights in sharing his or her song with friends and family.

Research Evidence

One might question the fact that many children with hearing loss could be musical. However, many D/HH children enjoy and participate in music informally as well as formally (Gfeller, 2000; Mitani et al., 2007; Trehub, Vongpaisel, & Nakata, 2009; Vongpaisel, Trehub, & Schellenberg, 2009). While the majority of research involving music and D/HH listeners has focused on adults, there is a growing body of research examining music perception and enjoyment in children, particularly CI users. With a trend toward earlier implantation, some researchers have examined using music as an integral part of the habilitation process (Abdi, Khalessi, Khorsandi, & Gholami, 2001; Chen et al., 2010; Peterson, Mortensen, Gjedde, & Vuust, 2009; Yuba, Itoh, & Kaga, 2007). What follows is a review of current research on music and D/HH children engaged in the LSL approach.

Several researchers have found that D/HH children perceive *rhythm* nearly as well as their NH peers, and rhythm-based music activities, because of their multisensory nature, afford children an outlet for successful participation (Kraus, Skoe, Parbery-Clark & Ashley, 2009; Gfeller, 2000; Gfeller et al., 2011).

Pitch and *timbre* tasks pose the greatest challenge to D/HH children, particularly to CI users (Kraus et al., 2009). This is due in part to the underlying CI processing strategies, which are designed to replicate speech and not the fine-grained spectral cues that music demands. Pitch and *melody* perception studies have shown that CI users perform poorly compared to their NH peers (McDermott, 2004; Nakata, Trehub, Mitani, & Kanda, 2006). However, music training and experience can improve outcomes (Chen et al., 2010; Galvin, Fu, & Shannon, 2009). Stordhal (2002) and Vongpaisal, Trehub, and Schellenberg (2006) found that CI children had difficulty recognizing familiar songs in the absence of lyrics, when compared to their NH peers. Thus, the addition of lyrics is helpful for engaging young CI children in music-making (Gfeller et al., 2011; Trehub et al. , 2009).

Recognition and discrimination of musical instruments may also pose a problem to D/HH children, particularly CI users (Galvin et al., 2009). Much of the research regarding pitch and timbre perception through the CI has focused on postlingually deafened adults who respond poorly when compared to NH listeners. Their enjoyment of music wanes postimplantation, perhaps because music through the CI pales in comparison to their auditory memory of music (Galvin et al., 2009). Fortunately, the current data seem to support the notion that children with CIs find music to be more engaging and enjoyable than their adult counterparts (Galvin et al., 2009; Trehub et al., 2009). Perhaps this is because early implanted children have only experienced music through their bionic ears and have no reference as to how music "should sound."

Singing tunefully requires the ability to match pitch, melodic contour, and rhythmic patterns. Given the difficulty that many D/HH children experience with pitch perception, it may be that "carrying a tune" is outside the realm of their music capabilities. That being said, singing is an important part of childhood and provides rich opportunities to develop vocabulary, practice prosodic speech production, reinforce culture, learn social skills, and create bonds with peers. Singing also offers a way to reinforce listening skills and enjoyably rehearse vocalizing. This author has encountered many D/HH children who possess excellent pitch discrimination and production.

Summary and Conclusions

There is no doubt that D/HH children today are *Doing Music Differently* than their D/HH counterparts from a decade ago. The world of music has been opened to many children with hearing loss as a result of current sophisticated hearing technologies. Once relegated to playing and experiencing instruments of a sensory and rhythmic nature, D/HH children are now learning to play the piano, violin, guitar, and anything else they are motivated by or have access to. In addition, many are accompanying themselves while they sing. Parents of children immersed in the LSL approach are eager to expose them to all of the experiences that their NH siblings or friends enjoy. Programs such as *Music Together®*, *Kindermusik®*, and *Music Playhouse* have emerged on the scene and increased awareness of the importance of early childhood music for many families. IPods and digital downloads, music video games, and DVDs are now an integral part of their lives just as they are for their NH peers. For many, music provides a conduit to a larger social community.

However, as important as these changes are, it is appropriate to remember and recognize the music therapists who served D/HH children before the advent of sophisticated hearing technologies. Pioneers such as Carol and Clive Robbins (1980) developed a curriculum that was experiential in nature and focused as much on the music as speech and language, social awareness, and auditory training goals. Claus Bang (2012), considered by many to be the father of music therapy in Denmark, has carefully archived his 40-year tenure at the Aalborg School and the Guidance Center for deaf, hearing-impaired, and deaf-blind children. Darrow and Adamek (2005) and Kate Gfeller (1999) have conducted extensive research on music and deafness and contributed vastly to the music therapy canon.

It is the case that there will be some D/HH children who do not enjoy music. (Let us not forget that this is true also for some in the NH population.) Their less than positive appraisal may be due to many factors; late diagnosis and access to sound, lack of exposure to music from an early age, familial indifference to music, refusal to wear hearing devices during all waking hours, and inability to access the whole spectral and rhythmic array afforded by current hearing technologies. This author's experience tells a much different story.

Acknowledgment

The author wishes to acknowledge with gratitude Susan Gardstrom for her assistance in preparing this chapter.

References

Abdi, S., Khalessi, M. H., Khorsandi, M., & Gholami, B. (2001). Introducing music as a means of habilitation for children with cochlear implants. *International Journal of Pediatric Otorhinolaryngology, 59*, 105–113.

AGBell. (2012). *Mission statement*. Retrieved from http://www.listeningandspokenlanguage.org/Document.aspx?id=36

Almond, M., & Brown, D. J. (2009). The pathology and etiology of sensorineural hearing loss and implications for cochlear implantation. In J. Niparko (Ed.), *Cochlear implants: Principles and practices* (pp. 39–81). Philadelphia, PA: Lippincott Williams.

Association for Speech and Hearing (2007). Executive Summary, JCIH, Year 2007. *Position statement: Principles and guidelines for early hearing detection and intervention programs*. Retrieved from http://www.asha.org/uploadedFiles/advocacy/federal/ehdi/JCIHExecutiveSummary.pdf#search =%22JCIH%22

Bang, C. (2012). *A world of sound and music*. Retrieved from http://www.clausbang.com/

Barton, C. (2010). *Music, spoken language, and children with hearing loss: Development and definitions*. Retrieved from www.speechpathology.com

Barton, C. (2011). *Music experience book. First years*. Unpublished Manuscript.

Barton, C., & Robbins, A. M. (2007). *TuneUps: A music program designed to foster communication development*. Valencia, CA: Advanced Bionics.

Beginnings. (2011). The importance of early diagnosis/intervention. Retrieved from http://www.ncbegin.org/index.php?option=com_content&view=article&id=73&Itemid=193

Bergeson, T. R., Miller, R. J., & McCune, K. (2006). Mothers' speech to hearing-impaired infants and children. Infancy, 10, 221–240.

Bruscia, K. E. (1998). Defining music therapy (2nd ed.). Gilsum, NH: Barcelona Publishers.

Campbell, P. S., & Scott-Kassner, C. (1995). Music in childhood: From preschool through elementary grades. New York, NY: Schirmer Books.

Carpenter, R. M. (2009). Correlates of sensorineural hearing loss and their effects on hearing aid benefit and implications for cochlear implants. In J. Niparko (Ed.), Cochlear implants: Principles and practices (pp. 83–87). Philadelphia, PA: Lippincott Williams.

Centers for Disease Control. (2009). *Summary of 2009 national CDC EHDI data*. Retrieved from http://www.cdc.gov/ncbddd/hearingloss/2009-Data/2009_EHDI_HSFS_ Summary_508_OK.pdf

Chen, J. K., Chuang, A. Y., McMahon, C., Hsieh, J. C., Tung, T., & Li, L. P. (2010). Music training improves pitch perception in prelingually deafened children with cochlear implants. *Pediatrics, 125*(4), 793–800.

Cole, E., & Flexer, C. (2007). *Children with hearing loss: Developing listening and talking birth to six*. San Diego, CA: Plural Publishing.

Darrow, A. A. (2006). The role of music in deaf culture: Deaf students' perception of emotion in music. *Journal of Music Therapy, 43*(1), 2–15.

Darrow, A. A., & Adamek, M. S. (2005). *Music in special education*. Silver Spring, MD: American Music Therapy Association.

De L'Etoile, S. K. (2006). Infant-directed singing: A theory for clinical intervention. *Music Therapy Perspectives, 24*(1), 22–29.

Easterbrooks, S. R., Lederberg, A. R., Miller, E. M., Bergeron, J. P., & Connor, C. M. (2008). Emergent literacy skills during early childhood in children with hearing loss: Strengths and weaknesses. *The Volta Review, 108*, 91–114.

Erber, N. (1982). *Auditory training*. Washington, DC: AGBell.

Feierabend, J. (2004). *Pitch exploration pathways*. Chicago, IL: GIA Publications.

First Years. (2009a). *How to read an audiogram: Auditory thresholds*. Retrieved from http://firstyears.org/lib/howtoread.htm

First Years. (2009b). *Developmental milestones: Birth to 8 years*. Retrieved from http://firstyears.org/miles/chart.htm

First Years. (2009c). *Speech banana*. Retrieved from http://firstyears.org/lib/banana.htm

Galvin, J. J., Fu, Q., & Shannon, R. V. (2009). Melodic contour identification and music perception by cochlear implant users. *The Neurosciences and Music III—Disorders and Plasticity: Ann. N.Y. Acad. Sci., 1169,* 302–319.

Galvin, J. J., Fu, Q. J., & Nogaki, G. (2007). Melodic contour identification by cochlear implant listeners. *Ear & Hearing, 28,* 302–319.

Gardstrom, S. C. (2007). *Music therapy improvisation for groups: Essential leadership competencies.* Gilsum, NH: Barcelona Publishers.

Geers, A. S., & Moog, J. S. (1989). Factors predictive of the development of literacy in profoundly hearing-impaired adolescents. *Volta Review, 91,* 69–86.

Gfeller, K. (2000). Accommodating children who use cochlear implants in music therapy or educational settings. *Music Therapy Perspectives, 18,* 122–130.

Gfeller, K. E. (1999). Music therapy in the treatment of sensory disorders. In W. B. Davis, K. E. Gfeller, & M. H. Thaut (Eds.), *An introduction to music therapy: Theory and practice* (2nd ed.). (pp. 179–203). Boston, MA: McGraw-Hill.

Gfeller, K., Driscoll, V., Kenworthy, M., & Van Voorst, T. (2011). Music therapy for preschool cochlear implant recipients. *Music Therapy Perspectives, 29*(1), 39–49.

Gfeller, K., Knutson, J.F., Woodworth, G., Witt, S., & DeBuss, B. (1998). Timbral recognition and appraisal by adult cochlear implant users and normal-hearing adults. *Journal of the American Academy of Audiology, (9),* 1-19.

Gordon, E. (2003). *A music learning theory for newborn and young children.* Chicago: GIA Publications.

Goswami, U. (2009). The basic processes in reading: Insights from neuroscience. In D. Olson & N. Torrance (Eds.), *Cambridge handbook of literacy* (pp. 134–151). Cambridge, UK: Cambridge University Press.

Hart, B., & Risley, T. R. (2003). The early catastrophy: The 30 million word gap by age three. *American Educator, 27*(1), 1–6.

Hopyan, T., Gordon, K. A., & Papsin, B. C. (2011, February). Identifying emotions in music through electrical hearing in deaf children using cochlear implants. *Cochlear Implants International, 12*(1), 21–26. DOI: 10.1179/146701010X12677899497399.

Houston, K. T., & Bradham, T. S. (2008). Service delivery in natural environments: Evaluating the most appropriate treatment setting for infants and toddlers with hearing loss. *The ASHA Leader, 13*(16), 5–7.

Individuals with Disabilities Education Act (IDEA). (2009). Categories of disability under IDEA. Retrieved from http://nichcy.org/disability/categories#hearing

Joint Committee on Infant Hearing (JCIH). (2007). Year 2007 position statement: Principles and guidelines for early hearing detection and intervention. Retrieved from www.asha.org/policy. DOI: 10.1044/policy.PS2007-00281

Kraus, N., & Skoe, E. (2009). New directions: Cochlear implants. *The Neurosciences and Music III—Disorders and Plasticity: Annals of the New York Academy of Science, 1169,* 516–517. doi: 10.1111/j.1749-6632.2009.04862.x

Locke, J. L. (1993). *The child's path to spoken language.* Cambridge, MA: Harvard University Press.

Madell, J., & Flexer, C. (2012). Beyond ANSI standards: Acoustic accessibility for children with hearing loss. *Audiology Online Live Expert eSeminar.* Retrieved from http://www.audiologyonline.com/ceus/enterRecording.asp?class_id=19866&member_id=53532&pid=1

McDermott, H. J. (2004). Music perception with cochlear implants: A review. *Trends in Amplification, 8*(2), 49–81.

MENC. (2010) *Performance standards for music: Prekindergarten* (Ages 2-4). Retrieved on January 25, 2010 from http://www.menc.org/resources/view/performance-standards-for-music-standards-publications.

Mitani, C., Nakata, T., Trehub, S., Kanda, Y., Kumagami, H., Takahasaki, K., et al. (2007). Music recognition, music listening, and word recognition by deaf children with cochlear implants. *Ear and Hearing Supplement, 28*(2), 29S–33S.

Mithin, S. (2006). *The singing Neanderthals: The origins of music, language, mind, and body.* Cambridge, MA: Harvard University Press.

Moog, H. (1976). *The musical experience of the pre-school child.* London, England: B. Schott.

Nakata, T., Trehub, S. E., Mitani, C., & Kanda, Y. (2006). Pitch and timing in the songs of deaf children with cochlear implants. *Music Perception, 24*(2), 147–154.

Nash, G. C. & Rapley, J. (1990). *Music in the making: OptimaLearning® in speech, song, instrument interaction and movement for grades K-4.* Van Nuys, CA: Alfred Music Publishing.

National Center for Hearing Assessment and Management (NCHAM). (2003). *Universal newborn hearing screening fact sheet.* Retrieved from http://www.infanthearing.org/newsletter/backissues/si_v5n3.pdf

Nicholas, J. G., & Geers, A. E. (2006). Effects of early auditory experience on the spoken language of deaf children at 3 years of age. *Ear and Hearing, 27,* 286–298.

NIDCD. (2001) *Speech and language developmental milestones.* Retrieved on January 25, 2010, from http://www.nidcd.nih.gov/health/voice/speechandlanguage.asp#mychild

Patel, A. D. (2008). *Music, language and the brain.* New York, NY: Oxford University Press.

Perigroe, C. (2001, Fall). Listening: The road to spoken language. *The Listener,* 43–46.

Peterson, B., Mortenson, M. V., Gjedde, A., & Vuust, P. (2009). Reestablishing speech understanding through musical ear training after cochlear implantation. *Annals of the New York Academy of Sciences, 1169,* 437–440.

PSB Speakers. (2005). *Frequencies of Music; Ranges of the Fundamental Frequencies of Voices and Instruments.* Retrieved from http://www.psbspeakers.com/articles/The-Frequencies-of-Music

Robbins, A. M. (2009). Rehabilitation after cochlear implantation. In J. Niparko (Ed.), *Cochlear implants: Principles and practices* (pp. 267–312). Philadelphia, PA: Lippincott Williams.

Robbins, C., & Robbins, C. (1980) *Music for the hearing impaired and other special groups: A resource manual and curriculum guide.* St. Louis, MO: MagnaMusic-Baton.

Robertson, L. (2009). *Literacy and deafness: Listening and spoken language.* San Diego, CA: Plural Publishing.

Sass-Lehrer, M. (2004). Early detection of hearing loss: Maintaining a family-centered perspective. *Seminars in Hearing, 25*(4), 295–307.

Schwartz, E. (2008). *Music, therapy, and early childhood: A developmental approach.* Gilsum, NH: Barcelona Publishers.

Sindrey, D. (1997). *Listening games for littles.* London, Ontario: Wordplay Publications.

Stordhal, J. (2002). Song recognition and appraisal: A comparison of children who use cochlear implants and normally hearing children. *Journal of Music Therapy, 39*(1), 2–19.

Trehub, S., Vongpaisal, T., & Nakata, T. (2009). Music in the lives of deaf children with cochlear implants. *The Neurosciences and Music III—Disorders and Plasticity: Annals of the New York Academy of Science, 1169,* 534–542.

Vongpaisal, T., Trehub, S. E., & Schellenberg, E. G. (2006). Song recognition by children and adolescents with cochlear implants. *Speech, Language, and Hearing Research, 49,* 1091–1103.

Vongpaisal, T., Trehub, S. E., & Schellenberg, E. G. (2009). Identification of TV tunes by children with cochlear implants. *Music Perception, 27*(1), 17–24.

Weikart, P. S. (1987). *Round the circle: Key experiences in movement for children.* Ypsilanti, MI: High Scope Press.

Yuba, T., Itoh, T., & Kaga, K. (2007). Unique technological voice method (the YUBA method) shows clear improvement in patients with cochlear implants in singing. *Journal of Voice, 23*(1), 119–124.

APPENDIX A

MUSIC AND LANGUAGE MILESTONES IN NH CHILDREN

Music milestones have been adapted from Campbell & Scott-Kassner (1995), Gordon (2003), MENC (2010), Moog (1976), and Schwartz (2008). Language milestones have been adapted from ASHA (2009), CDC (2009), First Years (2009c), NIDCD (2001), and Sindrey (1997).

Birth to 3 Months:

- Music: Alerts and calms to music; prefers infant-directed singing; coos and cries
- Language: Moves to the sound of a familiar voice, looks at speaker's mouth; coos and cries

3 to 6 Months:

- Music: Musical babbling; repetitive movements in response to music; turns to the source of music; prefers higher-pitched voices
- Language: Babbles, laughs, smiles, vocalizes pleasure and displeasure

6 to 9 Months:

- Music: Occasionally matches pitch; larger repetitive movements; recognizes familiar melodies; uses descending vocalizations
- Language: Smiles at speaker; uses voice and gestures to show displeasure; responds to own name

9 to 12 Months:

- Music: "Sings" spontaneously; recognizes and attempts to sing along with familiar songs
- Language: Recognizes names of family members; waves bye-bye; says one or two words; responds to "no"; babbles with inflection

12 to 18 Months:

- Music: Dances to music; pays attention to lyrics; sings snippets of learned songs; more pitch matching; starting to match movements to music
- Language: Jargonlike utterances with some words included; follows one-step directions; 20–100 words

18 to 24 Months:

- Music: Looks for dance partner; spins; marches to music; spontaneous songs have steady rhythm; able to initiate songs; lyrics more accurate than pitch
- Language: Two-word phrases; uses question intonation; repeats overheard words; starts using pronouns; understands "where" and "what's that?"; >200 words

2–3 Years:

- Music: Learns singing vs. speaking voice; sings in different keys and meters; matches pitches consistently; some instrument discrimination
- Language: Three-word phrases; refers to self as "me"; starts to use verbal endings; answers questions with yes or no; follows two-step command; >900 words

3–4 Years:

- Music: Begins to discriminate between familiar instruments; uses instruments to accompany own songs; melodic contour is intact; makes up songs
- Language: Uses many more pronouns; names colors; sentences of five or six words; tells stories; expresses feelings; enjoys pronouns; sense of humor starts to develop; >1,500 words

4–5 Years:

- Music: Larger purposeful movements; imaginative songs and stories; beginning to recognize familiar melodies without lyrics; matches beat to others
- Language: Asks what, why, who, where questions; answers why and how questions; uses future tense; tells name and address; uses longer sentences: >2,500 words

5–6 Years:

- Music: Maintains steady beat while moving to music; sings melody with pitch accuracy; plays melodies on simple instruments; can remember songs in head; begins to read and write rhythmic notation
- Language: Uses past tense, verbs, pronouns, prepositions correctly; sentences much longer; begins to read and write; knows more sequences like rhymes; >2,800 words

6–7 Years:

- Music: Develops tonal center; starts to sing harmony and rounds; vocal range focused around five or six notes; expands rhythmic and melodic written notation
- Language: Uses many more verb tenses; can tell right from left; makes comparisons; tells well-crafted, imaginative stories; >13,000 words

7–9 Years:

- Music: Vocal range expands; uses more complex meters and harmonies; demonstrates music preferences
- Language: Exaggerates; explains ideas in detail; likes vocabulary and word play; understands jokes, riddles, and idioms; >20,000 words

---

Appendix B

TuneUps! Teaching Tips

Christine Barton, MT-BC, and Amy M. Robbins, CCC-SLP

1. *Your voice is the most important instrument you can own!*

   It is not necessary to be able to play an instrument when singing with children. In fact, for our implanted kids, it may be difficult for them to separate instrument from voice at first. Teach them the song, and then if you are willing and able, add the accompaniment, being careful to acquaint them with the instrument before you sing.

2. *Don't reserve singing for "music time."*

   A child's day offers many opportunities to break into song: bedtime, car rides, snack time, changing diapers, you name it! Use it often, like seasoning, interspersed throughout the day.

3. *Use music purposefully and not as "background."*

   It's one thing to play soothing music during naptime, but quite another to leave the radio on all the time. Normally, we turn off background noise during speech and language activities because its presence may create a poor signal-to-noise ratio. If you intentionally play background music with an older child to teach listening in noise, we recommend this only for children with advanced levels of auditory development.

4. *Always introduce the CD player and any other electronic music equipment before you use it.*

   Kids need to know where the music is coming from. When using electronic equipment, CDs, or DVDs, be sure to introduce the equipment before you start the activity. So many times, our CI children are left in the dust as the teacher puts in a CD and the music "appears" out of nowhere. Take them through every step from opening the CD case to inserting it into the player. And then ask them, "Do you hear the music?" Likewise, when the music stops, make a big deal out of the "nothing" or silence factor.

5. *Experiment with using different "voices."*

   For instance, sing a familiar song in a voice like a lion or a kitten, or like a big dog or a little dog, or a mommy or a daddy. Children find this very comical. What you are actually doing is teaching them about timbre and that they have many different voices. They are also learning to recognize others' voices based upon individual characteristics, what are referred to as "indexical features" of speech. The result can be better prosody and more expressive, spontaneous language from our children with implants.

6. *Turn-taking is essential.*

One of the foundational skills of communication that children learn through music is taking turns: I speak or sing, then you speak or sing. Many of the songs on the *TuneUps!* CD provide turn-taking opportunities. When you hold a pretend microphone in front of the child, you are indicating that it is his or her *conversational turn,* just as you would in spoken conversation. Be sure to wait longer for a response than you would with a child with normal hearing. Children wearing CIs, especially novice listeners, need more processing and response time. Be certain to make direct eye contact with that child as an additional cue that indicates, *It's your turn, we're waiting on you.*

7. *Turn any important phrase into a song.*

If you are struggling to teach a young child to use an important phrase such as *Open the door*, *There it is*, or *What's in the bag?*, add a simple melody to it and use it every time you say the phrase. Don't force the child to sing it—just model it yourself each time you use it and encourage parents to do the same. This technique actually has a name: melodic intonation.

8. *Rhythm is a powerful cue for spoken language.*

As in the case with melody, adding a rhythmic pattern to a spoken phrase that a child is trying to master will increase his/her attention, give order and structure to perception, and enhance memory. Metrical organization makes it easier to remember verbal material. When modeling a rhythmic phrase, combine it with a movement or tap the phrase on a table or child's arm to add an additional sensory cue.

Appendix C

SoundStory: The Rainstorm

1. The wind blows and the clouds roll in (make wind sounds)
2. Distant thunder is heard (thunder tube)
3. Rain starts to fall gently (rain stick)
4. Rain falls harder (pat knees and hands)
5. Thunder is closer (thunder tube, low notes on piano)
6. Lightning (cymbal crash)
7. Pouring rain (marimba, piano, pat hands and knees)
8. Booming thunder (thunder tube, low notes on piano, contrabass)
9. Very windy (make wind sounds, use bull roarer)
10. Lightning (cymbal crash)
11. Pouring rain (marimba, piano, pat hands and knees)
12. Booming thunder (thunder tube, low notes on piano, contrabass)
13. Rain lessens (marimba, piano)
14. Distant thunder (thunder tube)
15. Raindrops as clouds move out (marimba, tap fingers together)
16. Sun comes out and a rainbow appears (bell tree, rainbow streamers)

Appendix D

Bad Dog, Ophie!

Ophie, my dog, is very cute.
Ophie, my dog, is very bad.
While I was busy counting sheep,
She ate my hearing aid without a peep!
Chorus:
OH, NO! OH, YES!
Bad dog, bad dog, what did you do?
Bad dog, bad dog, what did you chew?
Bad dog, bad dog, you're making me blue.
You are in the doghouse!
Leslie, my mom, is usually nice.
Leslie, my mom, rarely gets mad.
But when she saw what Ophie had done,
She blew her top and we all had to run.
Chorus:
Ben, my brother, is pretty cool.
Ben, my brother, is pretty nice.
He knew Ophie was in big doo-doo.
And he wanted to undo her bad boo-boo.
So he called to Isaac, my other bro.
He's really smart, my other bro.
They found Ophie hiding under the bed
With a stash of stuff all torn to shreds!
Chorus:
Then Nathan, that's me, with only one ear
Said, "Hey, guys, come look under here!
I found mom's phone and her diamond ring
Ophie's been guarding them since way last spring!"
Then, Tim, our dad, came running in
And mom too, when she heard the commotion
"My ring!' she squealed, "and my cell phone, too!
"Ophie, what would we do without you?"
OH, YEAH? OH, YEAH!
Good dog, good dog, what would we do?
Good dog, good dog, without you?
Good dog, good dog, we love you!
You are out of the doghouse!
And even though I only have one ear,
If I put it on her tummy, I can hear loud and clear!!
OH, YEAH? JUST KIDDING!

Appendix E

Resources

- Currently there are three cochlear implant manufacturers worldwide. Each offers a wealth of habilitation resources available at their respective websites: Advanced Bionics (www.advancedbionics.com), Cochlear Americas (www.cochlearamericas.com), and Med-El (www.medel.com).
- There are many hearing aid companies that also offer resources for individuals with hearing loss. Information about personal and soundfield FM systems can also be found at these websites: Oticon (www.oticon.com), Phonak (www.phonak.com), and Starkey (www.starkey.com) are just a few.
- The Listening Room™, www.hearingjourney.com, sponsored by Advanced Bionics, offers free listening, language, and learning activities. Developed by Dave Sindrey, M.Cl.Sc., LSLS Cert. AVT, these activities change weekly and monthly. This author regularly contributes music activities to the site.
- The *TuneUps!* CD, winner of the 2009 MVP Award from Therapy Times, was developed by Amy McConkey Robbins, CCC-SLP, and this author as a music program designed to foster communication development. There are 19 songs and activities, a booklet for parents and teachers/therapists, and a music listening game included in the package. For ordering information, go to www.advancedbionics.com.
- *Hear & Listen! Talk & Sing!* and *Songs for Listening! Songs for Life!* are two songbooks/CDs edited by noted Canadian LSLS, Cert. AVT Warren Estabrooks and music educator Lois Birkenshaw-Fleming. *Hear & Listen!* is geared to very young D/HH children, while *Songs for Listening!* appeals to children four to eight years old. They are available through the AGBell Bookstore:

    https://netforum.avectra.com/eweb/shopping/shopping.aspx?pager=0&site=agbell&cart=0 &shopsearchCat=Merchandise.

There are a number of organizations dedicated to supporting families and individuals with hearing loss. Among them are:

- The Alexander Graham Bell Association for Deaf and Hard of Hearing Individuals (AG Bell), http://agbell.org, is an organization that provides extensive advocacy work, educational training materials and programs, research and financial aid. It is named for its founder, Alexander Graham Bell, whose wife and mother were both deaf. Its mission remains, "Advocating independence through listening and talking!" There are many state and worldwide chapters.
- The Listening and Spoken Knowledge Center, launched by AGBell in May, 2012, offers visitors the "go-to" place to access a wealth of listening and spoken language resources for D/HH individuals and those who support them: www.listeningandspokenlanguage.org/.
- To obtain more information about this author's music therapy practice, publications, recordings, presentations and performances, please explore her website:

    http://christinebarton.net.
- Beginnings, http://www.ncbegin.org/, is a nonprofit agency located in North Carolina. It provides a nonbiased approach to helping parents find the right resources and services for their children with hearing loss. Their knowledgeable staff and abundant resources provide technical as well as emotional support for families and professionals.
- The Better Hearing Institute, http://betterhearing.org, is an organization dedicated to erasing the stigma of hearing loss. They have solicited the help of many celebrities who are willing to share their

own stories of living with a hearing loss. They have a number of educational materials available, provide resources to medical professionals, and operate a call center for consumers.

- FIRST Y*EARS*, http://firstyears.org, is a graduate, distance education, certificate program committed to enhancing the knowledge and skills of professionals practicing in the fields of deaf education, speech-language pathology, audiology, and early intervention. FIRST Y*EARS* combines clinical mentorships with cutting-edge academic training, from counseling to speech acoustics, to audiology diagnostics, to sensory technology, to speech-language development, to emergent literacy. This author is a graduate of the program.
- Gallaudet University Research Institute (GRI) conducts and disseminates data related to demographics and educational issues that affect individuals with hearing loss and those who interact with and support them. It is affiliated with Gallaudet University, the premier university for education and career development for D/HH individuals. See: http://www.gallaudet.edu/gallaudet_research_institute.html
- John Tracy Clinic, http://jtc.org, was founded in 1942 by Spencer and Louise Tracy after their son was found to have a severe hearing loss. It is a worldwide organization and provides, without fee, educational services to young children, their parents, and educators. Many of their educational materials have been translated into other languages.
- My Baby's Hearing, http://babyhearing.org., is sponsored by Boys Town National Research Hospital and the National Institute on Deafness and Communication Disorders (NIDCD). Its esteemed contributors include: audiologists, speech-language pathologists, teachers of the deaf, geneticists, physicians, and parents. The website is also available in Spanish.
- NCHAM, http://infanthearing.org, is located on the campus of Utah State University and serves as a multidisciplinary National Resource Center that oversees the Early Hearing Detection and Intervention (EHDI) systems. Their goal is to effectively identify infants with hearing loss before three months of age and ensure audiological, educational, and medical intervention before six months of age.
- The National Institute on Deaf and other Communication Disorders (NIDCD): http://www.nidcd.nih.gov, is an arm of the National Institutes of Health (NIH) and is committed to conducting research that has the potential to improve the health of those living with communication disorders. Information about their past and present research, as well as educational resources, can be found at their website.

Chapter 10

Visually Impaired School Children

Paige A. Robbins Elwafi

Introduction

It was during a music therapy session that I had a unique experience coleading a music therapy session with a group of visually impaired and blind teenagers. My cotherapist was an experienced music therapist who is also blind. I quickly realized that I experienced interaction, social nuances, nonverbal language, and communication in a much different way than that to which I was accustomed.

One day in group, after listening to a blues progression and exploring it musically, the conversation took a turn toward mobility experiences. These were primarily the challenges involving mobility for the group members and my blind cotherapist. The discussion became energetic and somewhat cathartic for the group members as they expressed deep frustrations in a safe place where others could relate.

As the group members and my cotherapist shared their struggles of mobility, I realized that I had never considered this issue and felt that I had little to contribute to the songwriting experience that followed. As the discussion transformed into laughing and jokes, I struggled with finding my "voice" as a group member and coleader. Because I was having such a difficult time relating to the topic both personally and professionally, I focused on something I knew, which was providing a musical structure for the songwriting. I hoped that my providing a blues pattern on the guitar would enable me to be a part of the group process; however, the group's energy completely consumed the space as well as my energy. In spite of my efforts to provide an accompaniment, I was disengaged from the discussion. It later occurred to me that their experiences were as vitally exclusive to their individual struggles and accomplishments as people who were visually impaired, that no matter how I tried, I could not enter their world. For the first time in my work as a music therapist, I felt excluded and isolated during a music therapy session. It was very frustrating as it was happening, but I came to realize later that the experience was valuable in giving me a small glimpse into the world of my clients. I continue to see the differences and values in having *sight* with the eyes, and possessing *vision* to truly see.

With encouragement from my cotherapist, I shared my personal experience with the rest of the group. We continued our work together for several months to complete the *Mobility Blues* song (2012):

Running into walls, tripping down the halls
I can't see a thing so I might as well use my cane
I've got the mobility blues. How about you?

Tap, tap, tapping from room to room
While all the sighted kids get to zoom, zoom, zoom!
I've got to swing my cane every day

I wish those kids would move out of my way.
I've got the mobility blues. How about you?

Kids trip on my cane and it drives me insane.
Getting around can be a real pain!
Trippin' over desk legs, falling over book bags,
Running into door frames, this is such a drag!
I've got the mobility blues. How about you?
Even though we've been complaining this whole song,
Our canes are what help us get along.

Diagnostic Information

When working with blind and visually impaired children, the music therapist needs a basic understanding of "normal" functioning vision. The eyes are primarily connected to the terms "vision" or "sight," but the eyes are only one part of the complex system of vision (Roman-Lantzy, 2007). This system consists of the eyes, the optic nerves, and the brain (Clark, 2012). Vision begins with the eyes as the receptors that take in light and images, and send that information, via the retina and optic nerves, to the brain. There are additional protective structures of the eye that include the orbit, orbital fat, eyelids, eyelashes, eyebrows, and tears (Codding, 1984).

The three parts of the visual system—the eyes, optic nerves, and the brain—work together, each serving a unique purpose, but all creating a dynamic and fascinating sensory input. Once the eye has fulfilled its ocular functions and passed that information along to the retina and optic nerves in the back of the eye, the brain interprets the information (Clark, 2012). Vision is processed in different parts of the brain. Dutton (2002) explains that primary visual processing (acuity, field analysis, color, contrast, and perception of movement) occurs in the occipital lobe, whereas recognizing the visual information takes place in the temporal lobes. The posterior parietal lobes allow us to deal with visual complexity and help us to make accurate visually guided body movements (Dutton, 2002).

Visual Impairment

Very few visually impaired individuals are totally blind or unable to see anything with either eye (AFB, 2008). Vision loss is when a person is having trouble seeing, even if wearing contact lenses or glasses. Vision loss can be self-reported or clinically diagnosed by an optometrist or ophthalmologist. Legal blindness is a level of vision loss that is clinically diagnosed and "... refers to the central visual acuity of 20/200 or less in the better eye with the best possible correction, and/or a visual field of 20 degrees or less" (AFB, 2008). This legal definition of blindness is generally used to determine a person's eligibility for benefits and resources. A person with low vision will present with acuities from 20/70 to 20/200 in the best eye with best possible correction (Clark, 2012). Low vision is defined as a visual impairment that is severe enough to significantly affect a person's ability to independently complete daily activities while maintaining some degree of usable vision (AFB, 2008).

The prevalence of visual impairment in the United States is generally better documented amongst adults than school-age children. Even though Congress is informed of the number of children ages 3–21 receiving special education services by the U.S. Department of Education, these numbers are not a true representation because the child can only be counted in one category of disability (AFB, 2009). Many children who are visually impaired also have additional disabilities. LaVenture and Allman (2007) estimate that that approximately 100,000 visually impaired students receive special education services in the United States.

While visual impairment is considered a low incidence disability in the United States (LaVenture & Allman, 2007), it is more prevalent throughout the rest of the world. According to the World Health Organization (WHO, 2011), 285 million people are visually impaired worldwide and 39 million are estimated to be blind. Approximately 90% of these people live in developing countries. The leading causes of visual impairment include nearsightedness, farsightedness, and astigmatism, followed by cataracts, and glaucoma. The WHO reports that 80% of all visual impairment can be avoided or cured, for example, in the case of blindness caused by infectious disease and cataracts. Concentrated efforts in public health education and governmental funding in countries such as China, India, Oman, Brazil, and Morocco have significantly decreased the occurrence of blindness over the past 20 years (WHO, 2011).

Although public awareness about blindness and prevention worldwide has increased, many challenges still exist. The social stigma and lack of educational opportunities for blind children remain prevalent. A number of humanitarian organizations are working to improve the lives of blind and visually impaired children. One of those organizations, UNICEF (2012), is working to increase inclusion, education, and access to Braille for children in countries like Sierra Leone and Zimbabwe.

Categories of Visual Impairment

Problems can arise anywhere in the visual system, including the eyes, the optic nerves, or the brain. It is possible for one, two, or all three parts of the visual system to be affected (Clark, 2012). Visual impairment is a purely individual experience based on the child's history and/or medical problems. As the visual system is composed of three parts, the categories of visual impairment can also be thought of as three parts (Clark, 2012). The three categories of impairment include acuity loss, field loss, and processing difficulties. Because visual impairment can occur at different levels of the visual system, the effects and level of impairment can vary greatly from one child to the next.

Acuity loss. Visual acuity is defined as a measurement of the eye's ability to distinguish objects and details by the smallest object seen at a specific distance (Cassin, 2001). Acuity loss affects the sharpness and clarity of images. Also referred to as ocular problems, acuity loss can usually be corrected by the proper refraction with glasses (Clark, 2012). Normal visual acuity is described as 20/20. The top number refers to the distance that the object is being viewed, and the bottom number is the distance that a normal eye could be away from the object to see it (Simmons & Stout, 1993). For example, a person who has an acuity of 20/200 can see at 20 feet what a person with normal vision can see at 200 feet The person with 20/200 acuity can still see, but what is seen is very blurry. Although the acuity for a legally blind person is 20/200, acuity loss can be much greater and variable (Clark, 2012). Simons and Stout (1993, p. 25) explain that when visual acuities exceed 20/400 or 20/600, vision may be documented as (1) hand motion (see movement of object), (2) object perception (see an object), (3) light perception (perceive presence of light), and (4) light projection (where the light is coming from).

Field loss. The second category of visual impairment is field loss. Visual field is defined as the "full extent of the area visible to an eye that is fixating straight ahead" (Cassin, 2001, p. 108). A person who is visually impaired can have a loss in any part of the visual field. Significant visual field loss of 20 degrees or more can be defined as legally blind (Simmons & Stout, 1993). Loss in a child's visual field can greatly affect his or her functional vision, or how the child uses his or her vision. Some examples of field loss include central loss with tunnel vision, half field loss, partial field loss, light perception, and total field loss (Clark, 2012). Retinal detachment can also lead to field loss.

Field loss can often be accompanied with different types of posturing of the head (Clark, 2012). This is an appropriate and accommodative visual behavior that the child may utilize in order to focus or find their null-point or null zone. Head posturing can also been seen when a child has nystagmus, which is eye movement that is involuntary and often side-to-side or up-and-down (Cassin, 2001). Vision professionals may work to capitalize on any vision that the child possesses, unless it is too much work for the child to access (Clark, 2012).

Processing difficulties. The third category of visual impairment involves processing difficulties. Problems with visual processing are the result of damage to the visual processing centers and pathways in the brain (Roman-Lantzy, 2007). The damage can occur before, during, or after a child is born. Roman-Lantzy describes cortical visual impairment (CVI) as "... a condition when a child or adult is visually unresponsive but has a normal eye examination or an eye exam that cannot explain the individual's significant lack of visual function ..." (2007, p. 5). *Cortical visual impairment* is the term used primarily in North America to describe the condition, while *cerebral visual impairment* is used more in Europe (Roman-Lantzy, 2007). CVI will be discussed in greater detail later in this section.

Common Visual Impairments Involving the Eyes

There is a large variety of ocular disorders that can cause visual impairment. Visual acuity, visual field, color perception, and detecting movement are all associated with ocular pathologies of the eyes (Dutton, 2002). Some of the leading ocular impairments include cataracts, microphthalmos, anophthalmos, coloboma, cytomegalovirus (CMV), glaucoma, aniridia, Retinopathy of Prematurity (ROP or RoP), albinism, and Leber's Congenital Amaurosis (Clark, 2012). These visual impairments were reported by Ferrell (1998) in a longitudinal study called the PRISM Project. The study looked at the development of over 200 visually impaired young children who were receiving services from vision professionals in more than seven states over a five-year period.

Ocular visual impairments can affect a child's vision in a variety of ways. The impairment may result in quite functional vision in one or both eyes for some children, while others can experience a total vision loss. Vision may change over time due to the process of some types of visual impairments, either improving or slowly worsening. Cataracts in children can be congenital, but are often repaired or improved by surgical options with positive and negative effects on visual acuity (Clark, 2012). Anophthalmos is a condition where the child is born without one or both eyes. This condition can often be accompanied with additional motor challenges. Microphthalmos is when one or both eyes are abnormally small, and may not always result in blindness, but often does (Simmons & Stout, 1993). While there is no cure for anophthalmia or microphthalmia, prosthetic eyes can be used to address cosmetic issues (NEI, 2009).

Coloboma is a structural abnormality that can occur in any part of the eye (Simmons & Stout, 1993). It occurs when two layers of tissue fail to complete growth during fetal development and can result in minor to severe visual impairment, depending upon the location of the coloboma (Simmons & Stout, 1993). Cytomegalovirus, or CMV, is a congenital condition that is contracted during gestation (Clark, 2012). CMV results in cataracts, cortical visual impairment, hearing loss, and additional multiple physical disabilities. Glaucoma is the buildup of intraocular pressure when the draining of fluid inside the eye is disrupted (Clark, 2012). The presence of glaucoma is very serious and needs to be closely monitored because the effects are irreversible and result in field loss. Aniridia is a condition where the iris is missing or only partly developed in the eye (Simmons & Stout, 1993). The iris is a muscle that plays the essential role of contracting the pupil in response to light. Damage can easily occur to the eye when the iris is not functioning properly. Leber's Congenital Amaurosis (LCA) is a genetic condition that is caused by a congenital abnormality in the retina. Resulting visual impairment and nystagmus for an individual with LCA can be visual acuities ranging from 20/80 to only light perception (Simmons & Stout, 1993).

Retinopathy of prematurity or (ROP) emerged in the 1940s and 1950s in children who were born prematurely (Clark, 2012). Although the condition was quite common in the past, the occurrence has slowly decreased with increased awareness of the early exposure to harsh lighting in the NICU and better regulation of oxygen in premature infants. Albinism is a hereditary condition in which pigment is deficient (Simmons & Stout, 1993). Two forms of albinism exist: *complete albinism,* affecting the whole body, and *ocular albinism,* resulting in normal or greatly reduced vision (Simmons & Stout, 1993). Nystagmus is usually present in all types of albinism, as well as light and ultraviolet sensitivity. Especially among dark-skinned individuals, albinism may be associated with increased social stigma and isolation. One particularly disturbing example is that in some parts of Africa, adults and children with albinism are at risk for murder and mutilation due to cultural beliefs that their body parts may give good luck (UNICEF, 2012). Special protection centers have been created for albinos in countries such as Tanzania, which has one of the largest populations of individuals with albinism in the world.

Common Visual Impairments Involving the Optic Nerves

Optic nerve hypoplasia (ONH), septo-optic dysplasia (SOD), and optic atrophy are three common visual impairments of the optic nerves (Clark, 2012). Optic nerve hypoplasia (ONH) is underdeveloped optic nerves, resulting in fewer nerve fibers carrying visual information to the brain. ONH can occur in one or both eyes, and vision can vary greatly with severe to minimal effects on acuity and/or visual field (Simmons & Stout, 1993). Septo-optic dysplasia, or SOD, is when the underdevelopment of the optic nerve is accompanied with additional medical issues and midline brain abnormalities (Simmons & Stout, 1993). The medical concerns associated with SOD are quite serious and include problems with metabolism, growth hormone, pituitary gland, and thyroid hormone. Children who have ONH and SOD are often characterized as having unique behaviors that may, in some situations, resemble autism spectrum disorder. These behaviors include sensory sensitivity, perseveration, echolalia, and difficulty in relating to others, as well as expressive and receptive language delay (Slott, 2005).

Optic atrophy is when the optic nerve dies and changes color from a healthy pink color to pale (Simmons & Stout, 1993). The atrophy of the optic nerve can be partial or complete, and is caused by congenital infections, major head trauma, or hydrocephalus. Visual problems resulting from optic atrophy can be progressive and include loss in visual acuity, visual field loss, and color perception.

Common Visual Impairment Involving the Brain

Cortical visual impairment is a complex visual condition, often accompanied by additional physical disabilities and neurological problems, including seizure disorder, cerebral palsy, cognitive impairment, and sensory sensitivities (Roman-Lantzy, 2007). Although CVI is still viewed as a questionably "legitimate" type of visual impairment by some eye care specialists, it remains the most common cause of visual impairment in the United States among children (Roman-Lantzy, 2007).

The causes and conditions associated with a diagnosis of CVI are still being discovered through ongoing research. Some of these include cerebral vascular accident, asphyxia, periventricular leukomalacia, structural abnormalities, central nervous system infection, intrauterine infection, and head injury. One very serious brain injury that results in CVI is Shaken Baby Syndrome (SBS). SBS is a brain trauma that causes visual impairment (cortical, and sometime ocular) and is characterized by a variety of conditions including bleeding in the brain, bone fractures, and retinal hemorrhages following violent shaking and/or other severe trauma to the head (Kivlin, 1999). The child is usually three years of age or younger at the time of the injury, but some cases have been documented up to five years of age (King et al., 2003).

It is difficult to fully meet the visual needs of a child with CVI, as each child is affected differently and vision can vary from one day to the next (Clark, 2012). Children with CVI have strong color preferences (red and yellow), find visual complexity difficult, experience visual field loss as well as preferred fields, and enjoy light gazing (Roman-Lantzy, 2007). Visual latency is often quite pronounced, resulting in delayed visual response, as well as the inability to look at and touch an object at the same time. Visually guided reach is a complex task for a child with CVI that requires the child to coordinate visual, auditory, and motor abilities. Its absence is a primary characteristic of CVI and should be adapted for when working with a child with CVI. Specifically in the music therapy session, it will often be easier for the child with CVI to attend to the music auditory first, before looking and reaching to play the instrument, because listening is more easily accessed than vision. Depending on the goal in music therapy treatment, addressing auditory skills can be helpful. However, providing a place for the child to work on vision goals and coordinating visually guided reach might also be beneficial. The world we live in for the child with visual impairment is highly auditory, especially for the child with CVI. Visual information is often presented so quickly that the child with CVI is not given adequate time to access his or her vision, and then to process the information. The music therapy session, also usually very auditory-directed, is a place that, with planning, can be controlled enough to provide opportunities for work on vision-related goals, such as visually guided reach.

Visual Behaviors and Mannerisms

Blind and visually impaired children can present with a variety of visual behaviors and mannerisms. Many of the behaviors have a purpose in aiding the child's access to his or her functional vision or in providing neurological input (Jan & Groenveld, 1995). Some of these behaviors include nystagmus, close viewing, and light gazing. Nystagmus, or the involuntary jerking of the eyes from side to side or up and down, can provide some clues into the child's visual impairment, onset, and involvement when observed by a trained vision professional. Nystagmus can interfere with the child's vision and can often indicate that the child is trying to use his or her functional vision.

Close viewing is a technique that individuals with visual impairment may use to adapt. Jan and Groenveld (1995) state that close viewing is most often seen with ocular disorders, where magnification can be obtained simply by leaning in close to the object or bringing the object close to the face. Close viewing has been documented in children with CVI also. When presenting objects and or instruments, the music therapist should understand where the child's preferred visual field or fields are, as well as the appropriate viewing distance to support the child's functional vision. These behaviors should not be reduced, as long as they are fulfilling an important visual function.

Blind and visually impaired children may exhibit behaviors that are stereotypical in nature and referred to as *blindisms, blind mannerisms,* or *mannerisms.* Some of these behaviors include eye pressing, light gazing, and flickering fingers in front of the eyes (Jan & Groenveld, 1995). These behaviors typically fulfill a function important in providing neurological and visual input. The nature of these behaviors may bring unneeded social attention to the child or may be somewhat harmful, as in eye pressing. The decision to manage or change these behaviors should be made in coordination with a vision professional, the caregivers, and, if possible, the child, and should be addressed per the individual needs of the child. If the behavior interferes with learning, it is important to substitute those with more appropriate sensory stimulation (Hughes & Fazzi, 1993).

Eye pressing is common among children who are blind and visually impaired. This is most often associated with ocular visual loss, especially retinal disorders (Jan & Groenveld, 1995). Eye pressing can be done with fingers, knuckles, and backs of the hands, and can increase in intensity so much that some bruising can occur. Jan and Groenveld (1995) explain that totally blind children do not press their eyes and that eye pressing can provide helpful information about the child's vision. Over time, the child who chronically and actively presses his or her eyes will develop darker pigmentation around the eye, as well as deep-set eyes.

Light gazing is when a child intently visually seeks out sources of light and engages with that source for periods of time. It is often prolonged and compulsive, and is most commonly a feature of a brain-based (cortical) visual impairment (Jan & Groenveld, 1995). Rarely is light gazing seen with children who have ocular defects, although finger flicking in front of the eyes with a light source can be seen in these children as well. As the cortical visual impairment improves, light gazing can also improve and sometimes stop altogether.

Some behaviors of children who are blind or visually impaired can look similar to behaviors observed with a child who has autism. One of these behaviors is rocking. The difference is the function of the behavior. We can try to differentiate the function of this behavior between the child who is visually impaired and the child who has an autism spectrum disorder, in addition to assessing other areas of development. Jan and Groenveld (1995) explain that children who are visually impaired may sway, excessively rock, and flap hands when they need more movement.

Impact of Visual Impairment in Children

Visual impairment and blindness has the potential of having a tremendous impact on the development and learning of a child. The development of the child who is blind or visually impaired is very much like that of a typically developing child (Codding, 1984). Just as in typical development, it is essential that the visually impaired child have access to a rich learning environment filled with opportunities to play, explore, and interact with his or her internal and external world. We live in a highly visual world. The amount of information that we learn with the use of our vision is astounding (Clark, 2012). *Incidental learning* is responsible for a great deal of information that we learn through the eyes. The size of a bus, the placement of a violin on the shoulder, or how to use social and nonverbal cues are just a few examples of incidental learning that sighted individuals may often take for granted. The development of a blind or visually impaired child is directly affected by his or her sight, or lack thereof (Codding, 1984). Additional physical, medical, neurological, cognitive, and emotional problems can cause further challenges. Nurturing healthy attachment to parents and caregivers, building early social skills, and exploring the immediate environment and outside world are important in the development of a child who is blind or visually impaired. Early intervention for infants and young children are important because the plasticity of the brain enables the development of new vision skills with the facilitation of appropriate interventions (Roman-Lantzy, 2007).

Environmental restrictions externally imposed on the child based on his or her disability impact the development of the visually impaired child (Codding, 1984). As is human nature, we often interact with others based on our stereotypical preconceptions, especially in the case of individuals with special needs. Visual impairment is a handicap that is widely misunderstood and feared in society. The independence of blind and visually impaired children is often significantly limited by these fears and preconceptions. Codding (1984) stresses the importance of providing opportunities to exercise independence, which will also encourage feelings of self-worth. Codding recommends providing the child with "concrete growth experiences" that will aid in general development, as well as allow the child to compensate for the direct and indirect effects of his or her disability. This approach can also be applied with caregivers, teachers, and family of the blind or visually impaired child, as these individuals have the most influence on the child's development (Darrow & Johnson, 1994).

Many children with multiple disabilities may also have a visual impairment. Moving the head, neck, trunk, and arms can become a very complicated activity for a visually impaired child with multiple disabilities. Blind and visually impaired children with diminished head and neck control can encounter a significant restriction in their visual environment (Jan & Groenveld, 1995). For example, if the child has specific visual field preferences, but can only access that vision by tilting his head a certain way, this requires much coordination and concentration to maneuver. If the same child is in the music therapy session and working to stabilize his trunk to reach out and hit the drum, this could be extremely exhausting. Due to the impact that multiple disabilities have on the visually impaired child, appropriate and supportive seating, positioning, and environments must be provided. The child will be better able to access his functional vision when he feels physically supported. This is something the music therapist should work to address and support in the music therapy session, to ensure that the child's access to functional vision is best supported.

Finally, for people who may be unfamiliar with the effects of visual impairment, some form of simulation might be helpful. A Zimmerman Low Vision Simulation Kit is a product that includes goggles that can be worn to simulate different types of visual impairment that affect acuity and the optic nerves. Blindfolds can also be used to simulate no vision. While use of these tools professionally could be very helpful, their use with families of a child who is blind or visually impaired is cautioned (Clark, 2012). This may not be appropriate and could even be detrimental for the well-being of the family.

NEEDS AND RESOURCES

For the visually impaired child, learning is the primary goal that fuels their development. Just as in typically developing children, learning is the key to becoming independent, contributing members of society. I have found it helpful in my work to focus on the child and not the visual impairment, although this may seem clinically counterintuitive at times. This approach to working with children who are blind and visually impaired supports the natural development of the child as a whole person, while allowing the *possibilities* to overshadow the *impossibilities*. Looking at the whole child and not focusing on the visual impairment also facilitates independence and can begin to prepare the child for the challenges to come as he or she goes out into the world. Education, auditory awareness, social development, emotional adjustment, mobility, and accessibility and technology are some needs of visually impaired school children. Resources will be discussed as well.

The educational needs of blind and visually impaired children are complex, as they need to learn additional skills outside of the typical things that sighted children learn (LaVenture & Alman, 2007). LaVenture and Alman state, "When a child is unable to gather information through his or her sense of sight, it is essential to help the child obtain that information in other ways" (2007, p. 13). Some of these specific skills include learning Braille, orientation and mobility skills, developing the use of functional vision, and the use of technology and assistive devices.

Provisions and access to special education services and accommodations for children with visual impairment is mandated in the United States by IDEA (Individuals with Disabilities Education Act), which was enacted in 1975 (LaVenture & Alman, 2007). Some options in educational placement for visually impaired children might include regular classrooms with the support of a teacher of the visually impaired (TVI), neighborhood schools with specialized rooms and instruction for children with disabilities, and special state schools specifically for visually impaired students.

Depending upon the child's educational placement, a variety of professionals can be a part of his or her team. Some of these professionals might include the classroom teacher, a teacher of the visually impaired (TVI), an orientation and mobility (O&M) instructor, a teaching assistant, an occupational therapist, a speech therapist, a physical therapist, an ophthalmologist, and an optometrist. The child's parents or caregivers should be the primary advocates for the visually impaired child's education.

The assessment of the visually impaired child's educational needs should be based on his or her visual impairment and how it affects the child (LaVenture & Alman, 2007). An Individualized Education Plan or IEP will be written, detailing the types of accommodations and services that can benefit the child's education. IDEA also provides specialized vision-related services, accommodations, and modifications that children who are visually impaired need for learning. Some of these might include Braille, large print, magnification devices, voice output programs, and a note taker like a BrailleNote.

One evaluation that is completed in the educational setting by a TVI and can also be completed in a medical setting with an eye doctor and a low-vision therapist is a functional vision assessment or evaluation. The functional vision assessment can be a very important tool for the music therapist because it can be a guide to understanding the child's vision. For example, if the child has a specific visual field preference, or if close viewing is an effective technique for the child to access his or her usable vision, the functional vision evaluation should detail this information. Simple adaptations can be provided during the music therapy session so that the child may have some opportunities to work on his or her functional vision. Further consultation with the vision professional is recommended for the music therapist to provide increased opportunities for working on functional vision.

Developing auditory awareness for children who are blind and visually impaired is important for a number of reasons. Because the visual sense is impaired or not present, the other available senses must be utilized to help the visually impaired child meet daily life needs. When developed, individuals who are blind or visually impaired can develop refined auditory skills. Gougoux, Lepore, Lassonde, Voss, Zatorre, and Belin examined the auditory spatial localization abilities of blind and sighted individuals judging the direction of changes in pitch. The onset and duration of the visual impairment when present was documented as well (e.g., early-blind vs. late-blind). The researchers found that the earlier the onset of blindness, the better the individual was able to determine the direction of pitch changes. These results support the importance of early learning and the role of cerebral plasticity in early developmental stages

For individuals who are blind and visually impaired, information in the environment can be gained easily through the tactile and auditory senses. At the same time, the auditory environment can sometimes provide too much information if there is extraneous noise, which can lead to overstimulation. Providing the child who is blind or visually impaired with a simplified auditory environment during the music therapy session is ideal.

Narration or providing a verbal description of visual images, movements, and activities in the environment is a technique that can be helpful for individuals who are blind and visually impaired. When working with children who are visually impaired, especially those with low vision or those who are Braille readers, it is very important to provide a running narration of the activities happening in the surrounding environment. This technique adequately informs the child of what is going on around him or her, can refine listening skills, and creates a learning opportunity.

Due to the strong reliance on listening, the auditory sense can sometimes take over the visual sense, if the child has usable vision. The use of silence is recommended when a visually impaired child is working to access his or her functional vision. This can be challenging in the music therapy context, but music therapy can be easily adapted with the use of silence. Children with cortical visual impairment (CVI), especially, can benefit from the use of silence and space in the music for visual processing. Adaptations in the sound environment for children with CVI are important when dealing with challenges with visually guided reach.

Silence can also be a useful technique to utilize when dealing with delays in visual, auditory, and cognitive processing. The presence of multiple disabilities creates many challenges for the child, often accompanied by cognitive and communication delay. This is why it is in the child's best interest for the therapist to provide space and time for processing.

Children who are blind and visually impaired face challenges in developing social skills. Robb (2003) relates that approximately 85% of what sighted individuals learn is with the eyes. For a child who is visually impaired, social skills can be difficult to understand and put into practice due to the lack of incidental learning opportunities. This is one reason why a delay in social development is a common issue among children who are blind and visually impaired. A delay in social development can also affect other areas of development, such as communication. Because of these challenges, unless the child who is visually impaired or blind is provided with adapted learning opportunities in the social realm, a delay will occur in this mode of development (Codding, 1984).

Early intervention can be of great importance in providing appropriate social skills activities and training for young children (Robb, 2003). As children grow, it is common to see anxiety or a lack of interest with social interaction. Rainey Perry (2003) documented this observation in her qualitative research study with children who were multiply handicapped and visually impaired. Children who are blind and visually impaired may exhibit behaviors or mannerisms that may seem odd or alarming to sighted individuals. Behaviors such as light gazing, rocking, and lack of eye contact can sometimes be mistaken for autism spectrum disorder.

Social skills for blind and visually impaired children are very important to model, teach, and practice. Social gestures, nonverbal language, and social nuances can be difficult to understand and incorporate into daily social interaction. The music therapy environment is a nonthreatening and creative place to provide opportunities for addressing these issues of social development.

Social acceptance of individuals who are blind and visually impaired is a problem. The visually impaired child's social development can be seen as a foundation for life and viability. Acceptance is an issue, especially given that many visually impaired children are capable and able-bodied individuals who will one day grow up into physically, mentally, and emotionally independent, contributing members of society. The approximate rate of unemployment among blind and visually impaired individuals in the United States is 70% (Nyman, 2009). This number is alarming, but an accurate indicator of the connection between the social integration and lack of acceptance of blind and visually impaired individuals in general society.

A child's visual impairment is most often accompanied by a wealth of complex emotions. The emotional impact of the child's visual impairment can differ from a congenital or acquired problem. Family and emotional grieving will be present in these situations. The occurrence and timing of the visual impairment may have some effect on the child's ability to cope and adjust. In the case of retinitis pigmentosa, for example, the child can lose a significant amount of vision at a young age. This loss can be exceptionally difficult for the child, as well as his or her family. Children who undergo trauma such as Shaken Baby Syndrome will often experience significant changes in their immediate family and may experience a major change in caregivers, such as through adoption. The music therapist can provide support during times of emotional adjustment for children who are visually impaired and their families.

Many children who are visually impaired experience other special needs that may require medical care. Codding (1984) discusses the importance of the development of a strong bond between the visually impaired child and his/her parents or caregivers in infancy. This may be difficult for the child who begins life undergoing medical procedures, hospitalizations, and doctor appointments. It may be necessary to support this bond in music therapy treatment if appropriate.

A child's visual impairment directly affects the ability and motivation to explore his or her environment. *Orientation* is knowing where one's body is in space and where one would like to go (Martinez & Moss, 1998). *Mobility* is carrying out the plan to move. These are unique needs of a child who is blind or visually impaired. An orientation and mobility (O&M) instructor, formerly known as a *peripatologist,* teaches safe and efficient travel through various methods. This can include direct instruction, consulting with school professionals, teaching family members, and educating the public (Hill, n.d.). Orientation and mobility is recognized as a related service through IDEA. Therefore, O&M instructors are a part of the multidisciplinary team and contribute to the development of the child's IEP and education. An O&M teacher or specialist must complete specific degree requirements and obtain certification through the Academy for Certification of Vision Rehabilitation & Education Professionals (ACVREP).

Some goals for O&M instruction include spatial concepts, sensory awareness, independent movement, cane skills, and sighted guide (Martinez & Moss, 1998). O&M instruction also involves teaching safe and independent street crossings and use of public transportation systems (Hill, n.d.). O&M instruction is known to influence cognitive, perceptual, social, self-help, and language development. The development of independence in orientation and mobility is stressed.

Encouraging independent movement and exploration during the music therapy session can be beneficial for the visually impaired or blind child. A simple technique such as exploring the instrument closet together can provide the child with an opportunity to practice orientation and mobility skills. The music therapist can also coordinate with an O&M instructor when specially designed music experiences could be of benefit to the child. Perhaps the child is struggling with learning a concept such as appropriate use of the elevator. The music therapist can write a song with the help of the child and the O&M specialist to highlight the essential steps the child will need to follow to complete the task. O&M instructors can also be a reliable resource in learning about visual impairment and adapting the music therapy session for the child's vision-related needs.

Sighted guide technique is an important mobility and orientation technique for people who are blind and visually impaired. A sighted guide "… accompanies a blind person in a travel situation so that faster and more efficient locomotion can be accomplished …" (Codding, 1984). This technique can also be used when the environment is congested or unfamiliar, making safe travel difficult for the child who is visually impaired or blind. Codding points out that the age in which children should begin utilizing sighted guide technique is after second grade. Prior to that age, the preschool- and early elementary-age child can hold the guide's hand. Learning the sighted guide technique would be a helpful and important skill for the music therapist to obtain.

The visually impaired child's IEP and education should address accessibility and technology. Specially trained Internet and technology professionals who specialize in accessibility programs and devices designed for blind and visually impaired individuals provide adaptive vision-related services as needed. These specialized professionals can usually be found at agencies or schools who serve blind and visually impaired individuals. These professionals are trained to assess the needs of clients and provide training on the appropriate software or devices that can make the visually impaired person's education or job more accessible, which can include everything from a smart phone to gaining access to voice output software for a desktop computer to using special scanners that can read print. A variety of software programs can provide enlargement and voice output, to name two possibilities, to increase accessibility. With the fast-paced nature of technological development, accessibility options are continuing to increase for blind and visually impaired individuals.

Much like the developing multicultural issues in music therapy, the vision profession is becoming more aware of a significant void between the culturally sensitive services recommended to children and the actual training and abilities of professionals (Gallimore, 2005). While the information available and research are quite limited, especially for blind and visually impaired students, the need is quite great. Gallimore (2005) points out the importance of understanding the cultural attitudes and acceptance of visual impairment, especially among minority families. She encourages adapting to these attitudes, especially if they are different from the majority culture. The music therapist should pay special attention to the role of music in a client's culture. However, when working with children who are blind and visually impaired, the therapist should also consider the role of disability and visual impairment in the client's culture.

Referral and Assessment

Referral and assessment procedures in music therapy with children who are blind and visually impaired are limited. One dissertation was found on the topic, by Browne (1984). This music-based assessment was created for music therapists and related professionals for assessing cognitive functioning in children who are nonverbal, multihandicapped, blind, or visually impaired. The Auditory Perception Cognition Profile (APCP) was administered twice to a group of 54 children. The author reported that reliabilities were reported at acceptable levels, indicating a pattern of development in the children. This included imitation, discrimination, imagery, seriating, conservation, and class inclusion (Browne, 1984).

It is important to get an idea of where the child is cognitively, but music therapy treatment should not be based on that primarily. The child's cognition can be affected by the developmental delays. Even if the child is typically developing but is visually impaired, he or she will likely have some delay due to the role of visual and incidental learning in childhood. An effective music therapy referral and comprehensive assessment for a child who is blind or visually impaired should encompass an integrative approach. A variety of information can be gathered in the assessment process. The therapist's theoretical and clinical orientation will likely play a role in the assessment process. A general guide for music therapy referral and assessment with blind and visually impaired children is provided in Appendix A.

Overview of Methods and Procedures

Receptive Music Therapy

- Moving to Music: Children listen to live or recorded music and move expressively in response to different aspects of the music.
- Song Discussion: a listening experience that provides an opportunity for children to be exposed to new types of music and songs, reflect on the meaning of a particular song, and build connections with others.
- Meet the Instrument: Children are introduced to orchestral instruments through performances, improvisations, demonstrations, discussion, and opportunities to handle and play the instruments themselves.

Improvisational Music Therapy

- Instrumental Improvisation—Follow the Leader: Children improvise on "accompaniment" instruments, following the solo improvised by the therapist or other child on a different instrument.

Re-creative Music Therapy

- Adaptive Music Instruction: The therapist teaches a child how to sing or play an instrument, with the aim of identifying special needs and developing the accommodations the child will need to pursue further study with a music teacher.
- Group Singing and Playing: Children re-create a precomposed song or piece of music together by singing, playing instruments, or both singing and playing.
- Performance in a Music Recital or Production: Children prepare for a recital or music production, and then perform it for an audience, with emphasis on the child's participation rather than the musical product.

Compositional Music Therapy

- Songwriting: Children participate in creating any or all aspects of a song with the assistance of the therapist.

GUIDELINES FOR RECEPTIVE MUSIC THERAPY

For the child who is blind or visually impaired, the auditory world plays a major, if not primary, role in learning. This role varies for each child, depending upon the amount and quality of functional vision he or she possesses. Therefore, the use of receptive music experiences should be evaluated with attention to minimizing auditory distraction and overstimulation. Listening is one of the primary modes of taking in information for the blind or visually impaired child. Presenting too much auditory stimulation at one time, or giving instructions while a piece of music is playing, for example, can cause confusion. Each child may experience different challenges with participating in receptive music therapy experiences, depending upon his or her developmental concerns.

Free or structured movement with a parachute or scarves accompanied by music encourages independent movement, body awareness, social interaction, and spatial awareness for the visually impaired child. Song discussion can address self-awareness, social interaction, and refinement of listening skills. Last, "meeting" an instrument and exploring it can be a meaningful hands-on learning experience for blind and visually impaired children.

Moving to Music

Overview. Motor, orientation, and mobility skills are often a serious need for blind and visually impaired children. Learning how to move your body to music is typically thought of as a visual learning experience. Therefore, blind and visually impaired individuals may lack this connection with movement. Music experiences designed in coordination with appropriate materials can facilitate body connection. Using a parachute works well to facilitate a social connection to others.

This experience is appropriate for a variety of ages and abilities, including nonambulatory as well as ambulatory. Encouraging independent movement, listening and auditory skills, spatial awareness, and social interaction are some possible goals of the "listen and move" experience. The level of therapy for the experience is augmentative.

Blind and visually impaired children who have significant sensory involvement could be contraindicated for the "listen and move" experience. Children who have difficulty being in a group of people may also not be appropriate for this experience. However, these children could possibly participate in an adapted experience designed for the individual.

Preparation. An open area with adequate space to move is required for the "listen and move" experience. A parachute is needed, and these come in varying sizes, depending upon the needs of the group. Different-size parachutes can have various benefits for the group members and meeting the goals of the experiences. Recorded or live music should be prepared as well. The piece of music should be contrasting and move between various tempi and dynamics. Additional small instruments like small jingle bells or brightly colored balls can be gathered as well. These objects can be placed inside of the parachute to stimulate visual attention, as well as create a challenge of keeping them in the parachute during the experience.

What to observe. The "listen and move" experience in a group session can become quite lively, producing lots of sounds and stimulation. This can be a joyful experience for some children because they are allowed, while still in a structured environment, to vocalize, kick, jump, laugh, and yell. The parachute connects them to others. They can feel that connection and the effects of their movement on the parachute, and on the additional objects if applicable. However, this experience can result in overstimulation and become uncomfortable for some children. It's important for the therapist to monitor the activity and engagement of the group as a whole, as well as individual participants. Adjusting the volume of the music, redirecting boisterous vocalizations, or taking a break are some ways that multisensory stimulation can be readjusted.

Procedures. After preparing the appropriate space and gathering the materials for the experience, the following procedure can be used. These steps may be adapted as needed:

1) Gather the children in a circle; using a parachute will connect the participants to one another, because it takes participation from everyone to move the parachute.
2) Provide recorded or live music. It needs to be a piece of music that has contrast between soft, loud, fast, and slow. Begin presenting the experience with simple differences in the music, but as the children gain experience with listening and moving their bodies in response to the music, complexity can be increased.
3) The children should be directed to listen to the music and move the parachute the way that the music sounds. Give examples like, "When you hear the music go fast, move the parachute fast" and "When the music is quiet, you can move the parachute quietly or softly." The therapist can problem-solve with the children and talk about ways to express with movement of the parachute the changing dynamics and tempo of the song.
4) After giving the directions for the experience, the music therapist should ask if anyone needs clarification or has a question. Tell them that when the music stops, you can all sit down and talk about the experience.
5) During the "listen and move" experience, objects can be put in the parachute to create visual and auditory stimulation, such as brightly colored balls with jingles inside or small jingle bells. Make sure that the object that is put into the parachute is not heavy or dangerous, in case it were to become "launched" during the movement of the parachute.
6) Take a break to regroup and bring their attention back to the goals at hand. The highly social aspect of this experience often gets the children excited and laughing together. Adjusting the volume, stopping the music briefly to check in, or asking the children what they hear in the music to refocus on the auditory aspect can be helpful. Resume the music for another few minutes or so.
7) Following the experience, it is helpful to have a short discussion about what it was like for the children. In an effort to increase awareness and connections directly related to the goals of the experience, the music therapist can facilitate processing of the experience by asking questions like: What did you hear? How did you move the parachute in response to the music? What did you see? How many other people were moving the parachute with you? Could you feel anyone else moving the parachute along with you? What was that like?

Adaptations. The "listen and move" experience can be adapted for the use of scarves or streamers. Using these materials or something similar focuses more on facilitating individual creative and free movement. This is a need for children who are blind and visually impaired also. This adaptation can also be used in an individual music therapy session or small group session to address gross motor movement, body awareness, spatial awareness, and listening skills.

Song Discussion

Overview. Song Discussion is a listening experience that provides an opportunity for participants to be exposed to new types of music and songs, reflect on the meaning of a particular song, and build connections with others. Children who are blind and visually impaired can benefit from the song discussion experience, with varying levels of adaptations.

Song Discussion is indicated for individuals who are able to listen, attend to the music and the words of the song, and participate in a discussion. Participants should possess some insight into their lives and be able to express that awareness to others. Possible goals include increasing self-awareness, improving listening skills, communicating thoughts and feelings and how they relate to the song, and developing social connections to other group members (Bruscia, 1998). The level of therapy for song discussion experience can be augmentative or intensive.

Song Discussion would not be appropriate for the child who is not able to attend, sit quietly, and listen to a piece of music. Ideal participation during the song discussion experience requires maturity, recognition of social roles, selective attention, and self-awareness. If the child is not able to sit and listen to a piece of music, as well as work through a group discussion, then the experience is contraindicated.

Preparation. Because blind and visually impaired children receive much information from the auditory sense, to enhance their ability to focus on the song and words, it is important to provide a calm and quiet environment during the song discussion experience. The therapist should decide on the song to be presented, and if a live or recorded version will be used. Lyric sheets should be provided to older participants when appropriate. Providing lyrics prior to the actual session can be helpful for visually impaired children. Reading can sometimes be labor-intensive for children who are blind or visually impaired, especially when they have additional disabilities. Therefore, the therapist should make sure to have the lyrics available in print or Braille or provide a recording of the lyrics for individuals who learn better by listening. An electronic file of the lyrics can be provided if the therapist does not have access to a Braille embosser.

What to observe. The music therapist should monitor the engagement and participation of the children during the Song Discussion experience to ensure that the goals for the experience are being met. The therapist should monitor the sounds in the environment, because extraneous unrelated noise can be quite distracting for a blind or visually impaired child. Talking or activity during the song should be minimized to create an optimal listening environment with little distraction. Offer to play the song again in case something was missed between reading the lyrics and listening. The therapist can ask questions like: How was that? Can I do anything to make this more meaningful for you? Should we listen to it again?

Procedures. The following steps can be followed when conducting a Song Discussion with blind and visually impaired children:

1) Preparation for the experience should be completed, including song choice and mode of playing the song. If using lyric sheets (recommended for older children) the therapist should make available copies, whether in large print, Braille, or recorded.
2) Prior to playing the song, the therapist can structure the experience by giving certain themes or ideas for which to listen. The therapist can also make this an unstructured listening as well, depending upon the needs and goals of the clients.
3) The therapist should play the song, either by recording or live. Monitor the client's engagement during the listening portion of the experience.
4) The discussion can be started by the therapist or, even better, by a participant. Be open to talking about the lyrics and the musical elements of the song.
5) Play the song again if needed for review and expansion on ideas or themes that were discussed.
6) Wrap up the discussion by reviewing significant themes or issues that came up in the discussion.
7) Offer to play the song one last time for final processing and closure of the experience.

Adaptations. The song discussion experience can be shortened and made into a purely rote experience for younger blind and visually impaired children. The experience can also be adapted into a song communicatio*n,* where the therapist asks the client to select a piece of music that expresses something about him or her (Bruscia, 1998). A song communication experience can be further adapted and expanded to a group experience, where each group member is given the opportunity to share with others. Last, the song discussion experience can be transitioned into a compositional music therapy experience. A *song parody* can be created when "the client changes words, phrases, or the entire lyrics of an existing song, while maintaining the melody and standard accompaniment" (Bruscia, 1998, p. 120). This gives the client a chance to contribute his or her own voice to a song that has meaning.

Meet the Instrument

Overview. One day, my cotherapist and I were asking some parents who attend a small music therapy group what they would like to gain from group. One parent explained that she would like her child, who is visually impaired and has multiple disabilities, to have access to more instruments. After asking a few questions, we realized that many of the blind and visually impaired children we work with have never been exposed to orchestral instruments. They have heard their sounds, but not touched or been able to explore instruments such as the violin, cello, or clarinet. The role of incidental learning is a repeating theme when working with blind and visually impaired children. Sighted children learn about these instruments by seeing them in books, playing with instrument-themed puzzles, or seeing them on children's shows. This type of incidental learning is not available for blind and visually impaired children. Thus, my cotherapist and I created the following experience to introduce our clients to various instruments that we do not typically use in the music therapy session.

The Meet the Instrument experience is indicated for individuals with a variety of needs and abilities. The experience is designed as a group music therapy experience, so the child should be able to participate with or without assistance in a group of people. The experience requires the ability to touch and explore a variety of instruments, so the child should exhibit minimal tactile defensiveness. Goals of the Meet the Instrument experience are to increase exposure to various instruments and provide a learning opportunity to children who are blind and visually impaired. The level of therapy for the experience can be auxiliary, augmentative, or intensive, depending upon the needs or the clients, setting, and presentation.

Clients who are significantly tactile-defensive and who suffer from significant sensory dysfunction will be contraindicated for participation in the Meet the Instrument experience. The experience is designed to be presented during a group music therapy session, so if the child has difficulty in participating in group experiences, this experience would not be appropriate.

Preparation. The music therapist should be prepared to conduct the Meet the Instrument experience over the course of several music therapy sessions. Repeated exposure to each instrument's sounds, the role it plays in an ensemble (band, orchestra, etc.), and hands-on exploration will contribute to learning. This is especially true for children who are developmentally delayed and who are totally blind.

The therapist should determine the instrument to be looked at before the session. Playing a couple of performances by the instrument (solo and ensemble) for clients adds to the multisensory learning opportunity. Try to find contrasting listening examples to illustrate the instrument's range and capabilities. These recordings should be gathered and prepared prior to the session.

The actual instrument should be collected to present to clients during the music therapy session. Tactile discovery is essential for making connections to what is heard for blind and visually impaired children. It may be a challenge to locate and borrow an instrument whose owner will allow the children to touch and explore it. Donated or secondhand instruments are ideal for presenting during this part of the experience. For more fragile things such as the bow, it would be helpful to have a used bow that the children can freely explore. If the therapist is not proficient on the instrument, a volunteer will be needed to play a brief musical excerpt live during the session.

What to observe. During the tactile exploration portion of the experience, the therapist should monitor the child's interaction with the instrument. The exploration of the instrument should include detailed opportunities for touch, close viewing, description, and narration. These opportunities will provide the client with adequate time for processing and exposure to the instrument.

Procedures. The following steps can be followed to conduct the Meet the Instrument music therapy experience. The steps do not need to be followed in this exact order. These can be adjusted depending upon the needs of the clients.

1) The therapist should make the appropriate preparations for the experience. These include gathering the instrument, appropriate recordings, and a proficient performer to play a brief excerpt or improvisation on the instrument.
2) Gather the clients and provide a brief overview of the experience and play one of the recordings, preferably something featuring the instrument like a solo piece or concerto.
3) Make the official introduction to the clients by introducing the performer (if appropriate) and the instrument. The instrument can be presented to the children by passing it around the group for tactile exploration. This process should be closely monitored by the therapist to ensure that sufficient time is given to learn about the instrument, including feeling the size of the instrument, the textures, the strings or keys, the weight, etc. If touch should be limited due to the condition of the instrument, close viewing can be used. Close viewing and narration when appropriate should also be provided during the exploration of the instrument.
4) A live musical performance or improvisation on the instrument should be played for the children. If a proficient musician is not available to play the instrument, another recording can be played as a substitute. However, a live performance is ideal.
5) Provide the opportunity for additional tactile or visual access to the instrument if needed. The therapist should facilitate verbal discussion about the qualities of the instrument and the observations made by the clients.

Adaptations. The Meet the Instrument experience can be adapted to include a group improvisation lead by the featured instrument. This is a creative way of expanding the goals of the experience in a musical opportunity. The accompanying instruments should complement the featured instrument, yet not overshadow it.

Guidelines for Improvisational Music Therapy

Improvisational music experiences can be quite meaningful for children who are blind or visually impaired. The structure provided by the rhythmic, harmonic, melodic, and form of the music can be grounding. Musical expression during improvisational music experiences can give the blind or visually impaired child a unique connection to others.

Instrumental Improvisation—Follow the Leader

Overview. When introducing improvisation to blind and visually impaired children, structured and semistructured improvisational music therapy experiences can be a good place to begin. One learns much of what is expected of his or her role in the improvisation through exposure to the experience of improvising. A significant amount of information is communicated during improvisations through nonverbal language. Therefore, it may take more time for blind and visually impaired children to become comfortable with the musical roles during an improvisation, especially within a group setting. However, this is purely based on the musical responses of clients. The lack of sight may very well contribute positively to the improvisational experience in music therapy for blind and visually impaired children.

The Follow the Leader improvisation is indicated for a variety of ages, abilities, and needs. Clients can participate on any level they are able to, with or without assistance. Possible goals that can be addressed include social interaction, communication, and listening. It should be designed specifically for the needs of the client and can be utilized in individual or group settings. This is a very unintrusive music experience for parents or caregivers to participate in, and can be an ideal introduction to the power of improvisation. The level of therapy for the Follow the Leader improvisation can be augmentative or intensive.

Children who are blind or visually impaired who have severe sensory dysfunction may not be appropriate for the Follow the Leader improvisation. Also, children who have multiple sensory impairments as well as significant medical problems and physical disabilities may require intensive adaptations before participation in the experience would be beneficial.

Preparation. The structured nature of the experience will require some preparation. The therapist should choose the leading instrument he or she will play, as well as the mode or key most appropriate for the improvisation. Accompanying instruments should be chosen to complement the timbre, quality, and range of the leading instrument. The choir chimes, tone bars, stringed instruments, and small percussion instruments function well as accompaniment. Stringed instruments will need to be prepared with the alternate tunings prior to the session. If using choir chimes, tone bars, or other Orff instruments, the therapist should make sure the tones work well within the chosen key or mode for the improvisation. The therapist should assess the client's needs prior to the experience, to ensure that the instrument will be manageable. This is especially important with the client who has additional multiple disabilities. Challenges in handling and manipulating certain instruments can arise for these children specifically. Be sure to provide adaptive equipment or physical assistance for maximum success and participation for the child. The therapist should also keep in mind the visual needs of the client and if he or she would benefit from a specific viewing distance, angle, or task lighting.

What to observe. During the Follow the Leader improvisation experience, the music therapist should monitor the musical interaction of the clients. The therapist should practice creative problem-solving and make adjustments within the experience to better meet the specific goals for each child. This might include providing a different positioning option, placing the instrument in a more visually accessible or physical accessible location, or trying another instrument.

Procedures. The following steps provide a general outline for conducting the Follow the Leader improvisational experience:

1) Pass out the accompanying instruments to clients or the client if designed for an individual session. Ensure proper tuning if appropriate.
2) Provide appropriate assistive devices and positioning for participants, with attention paid to creating the maximum amount of independent play.
3) The therapist should briefly explain that she will play an improvised melody on her instrument, and that everyone can follow along with their instruments.
4) The leading instrument should create an improvisation in the designated key or mode. After three to five minutes of music, the improvisation can come to a close. The length of the actual musical improvisation is not set, and should feel natural within the structure of the experience. You should be able to sense the level of engagement from the clients, and this should guide the length of the improvisation.
5) If appropriate for the clients and the goals set for the experience, a short discussion can follow the music.
6) Feel free to repeat the improvisation. Clients can choose a different instrument or exchange with a neighbor within a group session.

Adaptations. Follow the Leader improvisation can be adapted for vocal improvisation, wind instruments, or drums. The role of *leader* can be shared between the therapist and another client, or exchanged with another participant. Keep in mind that the leader should have a good sense of musicality and be able to lead the group with assistance from the therapist.

GUIDELINES FOR RE-CREATIVE MUSIC THERAPY

Re-creative music therapy experiences are effective for children who are blind or visually impaired because they provide a balance of creativity and structure. Codding (1984) states, "Music activities provide a structure to promote the synthesis of sensory information and allow for development of socially appropriate skills" (p. 60). Re-creative music therapy experiences are beneficial because they provide structure for clients who require it when developing various skills and roles (Bruscia, 1998). Adaptive music instruction is often one of the primary reasons for music therapy referral in my work with children who are blind and visually impaired. "Group singing and playing" is another re-creative music therapy experience that provides a space for creativity, while addressing developmental goals. Last, performing in a music recital or production provides a unique opportunity for blind and visually impaired children to demonstrate independence, practice social skills, and increase their sense of self-worth.

Adaptive Music Instruction

Overview. While adaptive music instruction is often a primary reason for referral, it is rarely the only goal we address in music therapy. As the assessment progresses, additional needs and concerns arise that are often deeper, including emotional adjustment and coping with vision loss. Adaptive music instruction can be a controversial topic amongst music therapists; however, Bruscia (1998) defines re-creative experiences as those in which "... the client learns or performs precomposed vocal or instrumental music ..." (p. 117). In my clinical work, I have found it helpful to set a long-term goal of preparing the child to eventually participate in private music lessons or school and community ensembles. This easily creates the boundary of what I, as the music therapist, can provide therapeutically, and puts responsibility on the client (and caregivers) for pursuing future music education if so desired. I do always explain that I am available for consultation or assistance in the future for the child or his future teachers. This consultative role is especially important for the child who is learning Braille music notation and will need music transcribed into Braille.

Learning how to play a musical instrument has numerous benefits. For the child who is blind or visually impaired, adaptive music instrument can develop auditory skills, build confidence and independence, and provide a positive coping outlet. Adaptive music instruction can also lead to increased social opportunities, thus developing the skills needed in interacting with others, including sighted and visually impaired peers. To benefit from adaptive music instruction, the child should be able to attend to the experience for an appropriate length of time, as well as be able to practice at home, with or without prompting from family or caregivers. Most importantly, the child should indicate an interest in the instrument and in spending time learning how to play. The level of therapy of the adaptive music instruction can be auxiliary or augmentative.

The therapeutic goals for adaptive music instruction are important to keep in mind when assessing the child's needs, designing proper instruction methods, and evaluating progress. The music therapist is well prepared to utilize his or her clinical knowledge and training in adapting instrumental or vocal instruction. However, consultation with a vision professional such as a low-vision therapist, teacher of the visually impaired (TVI), or orientation and mobility (O&M) instructor could be quite helpful for the music therapist.

If the child's musical ability is beyond what the therapist can provide, where the goals have been met or there are no therapeutic needs, the child may not be appropriate for adaptive music instruction.

Preparation. It is important for the music therapist to understand the visual needs of the child. The proper adaptations can be made when this information is clearly communicated by the child, the vision professional who works with the child, and his or her caregivers. The design of the instruction, adaptation of materials, and lighting are some important ways to prepare for the session and the environment. The general design of adaptive music instruction for the blind or visually impaired child should be based on his or her visual needs. The child's primary mode of learning is another important consideration. With the help of a low-vision therapist or teacher of the visually impaired (TVI), a blind or visually impaired child will typically learn to read by using large print or Braille. The materials for music instruction can be adapted to include (1) large print with enlargement on a copy machine, (2) proper magnification of printed music with a magnification device, such as a CCTV, (3) auditory or rote learning, and (4) Braille music notation.

A child who has low vision but still quite a bit of functional vision can benefit from enlargement or magnification. Siligo (2005) points out that some individuals with low vision prefer "reversed" background display (black background with white print). However, magnifying printed material will not be helpful for a child who has visual field losses, because the enlargement can expand outside of the child's visual field.

For the child whose vision is very low or is a total loss, the music therapist can teach by ear or rote learning. Finally, for the more advanced musician who is blind or significantly visually impaired, he or she can learn Braille music notation. If the therapist has limited knowledge or is not comfortable with teaching Braille music notation, he or she may refer to someone in the community with the expertise.

Recording the music being learned in the session can be beneficial for children who are blind and visually impaired. Siligo (2005) indicates this practice works well with both vocal and instrumental pieces and can be provided as a CD, MP3 file, or other compatible media files. I have used recording in conjunction with large print and magnification of music. When creating audio recordings for the visually impaired individual, the therapist can provide a variety of recordings of the piece that will meet the child's musical needs. Some of these may include a slower version while speaking the note names or chord names to be played, explanation of the rhythms or strumming patterns with counting as they fit into the song, and a version of the entire song without breaks, as it is typically played.

Lighting is another important consideration for the child who is visually impaired. Adjusting the lighting in the room can positively or negatively affect the child's vision. By lowering the lighting, some children with CVI respond positively, while a darker room for a child with retinitis pigmentosa (RP), for example, may make it more difficult to see. Proper task lighting (with special lamps) can make reading music much more effective. Task lighting in addition to magnification can also be helpful during adaptive music instruction.

Some information on Braille music. Braille music is composed of a series of raised dots like literary Braille, but uses a completely different code (Siligo, 2005). Braille music does not use a grand staff, but instead octave marks and interval signs. Because Braille music is learned tactilely, the way that it is learned and the way that it is played are different from how sighted individuals use print music. Braille music is typically used for memorizing, and the process of learning is slower than the process of learning print music. Braille music readers will need music that has been transcribed into Braille (Siligo, 2005). Some special software programs like Goodfeel allow the transcription from print music to Braille music. Transcription services are also available for a fee.

Braille music can be embossed by a Braille embosser or by hand, using a Braille writer, which is similar to a typewriter. Adaptive magnification devices can be used as well for musicians with low vision. The problem that many musicians run across is the amount of money some of these devices cost, which can be thousands of dollars. Special grants are sometimes available for purchasing assistive devices for students. Various guides and how-to books that can be used by sighted or visually impaired individuals are available for learning Braille music. Some of these will be listed in the resource section at the end of this chapter. Books containing tactile graphics can be helpful for children to understand what print music notation looks like.

What to observe. The impact of the child's visual impairment should guide the music therapist's choices in presenting materials, techniques for instruction, and evaluation of progress. The child's vision is very important to understand, in order to adapt instruction and materials properly. The impact of the child's visual impairment will indicate the most appropriate path for learning music, via large print, auditory learning, or Braille music. It is helpful for the music therapist to have a working knowledge of a variety of visual impairments and how vision is affected. Keep in mind that visual impairment can be a uniquely individual experience and can affect acuity, visual fields, and processing in various combinations or in only one area. If the acuity is not good, magnification could be a simple adaptation of printed materials. However, if there is field and acuity loss, enlarging or using magnification such as a CCTV might not be as effective. Problems in visual processing may require auditory or rote learning, or possibly Braille music notation. The music therapist can work with the child, caregivers, and vision professionals to evaluate the effectiveness of adaptive music instruction.

Procedures. Once the music therapist has thoroughly assessed the child's needs, the following procedures can be used to conduct the adaptive music instruction experience:

1) Prepare the proper lighting and materials. A quiet environment with little sensory distraction will be helpful.
2) Provide the option for a warm-up, with the therapist's participation or without. The goal is to engage the child and prepare him or her for learning.
3) Present the adapted materials to the child. This can be in the form of large print or Braille music notation. Magnification devices may also be used in this process. If utilizing auditory training or rote learning, recording parts of the session will be helpful. Make sure to have the recording device (i.e., digital voice recorder, etc.) ready.
4) Review and learn materials. Match the child's pace in learning and provide many opportunities for repetition.
5) Evaluate the child's progress, as well as the effectiveness of the adaptive materials and instruction. Be open to using description and narration, as well as appropriate tactile cues. Be sure to ask permission before providing tactile or physical prompts or cues to the child.
6) Ask the child questions to assess his or her understanding of the musical concept you are teaching during the session.
7) Provide adequate time for auditory and/or visual processing. Also allow the child to take breaks as needed.

Adaptations. The adaptive music instruction experience can be adjusted to a variety of instruments and learning styles. Various cues and prompts play an important role in conducting adaptive music instruction. Tactile, physical, visual, auditory, verbal, and musical cues or prompts can be effective for children who are blind and visually impaired. The child's vision and sensory involvement can guide the therapist in choosing the most effective cues. A combination of prompts, depending upon the child's preferences, can be helpful, and may vary depending upon the instrument. For example, it can be confusing when teaching fingering for a chord on the guitar using only verbal description. Pairing that verbal description with physically moving the child's fingers on the fret board could be more effective. It is important to ask permission before touching the child's hands, or giving a verbal warning like, "I'm going to touch your hand to show you how to play the chord—is that okay?" Creativity and flexibility are necessary when conducting adaptive music instruction.

Structured Singing and Playing

Overview. Structured Singing and Playing is often an ideal place to begin when assessing a child and developing the therapeutic relationship. It can provide a safe yet creative environment to assess the child's strengths, needs, and vision. It involves the therapist and the client re-creating a precomposed song or piece of music together (Bruscia, 1998). It can include only singing, only instrument play, or singing with instrument play. Some thought should go into the instrument choice. When working with visually impaired children, certain instruments can be presented that can create increased visual attention or facilitate increased musical interaction.

A wide range of abilities, ages, and needs of children with visual impairment can benefit from Structured Singing and Playing experiences. It can provide a safe space for the child to experience new sounds and instruments. Meaningful boundaries can be created to allow the child to explore and engage the music environment while accessing his inner world to build a connection to his inner voice (Bruscia, 1998). Structured Singing and Playing may be used to get to know a new client or as a warm-up. To participate, the child should be able to attend and interact vocally or with instruments with or without assistance. Some possible goals for Structured Singing and Playing may include increasing communication, developing fine motor skills, improving social interaction within a group, and enhancing listening and auditory skills. The levels of therapy can be augmentative or intensive.

Children who are blind and visually impaired may have increased sensitivity to sounds in the environment, especially certain types of instruments. Sensory deficits and sensitivity should be taken into account when choosing the music and instruments. If the child is sensitive to metallic, high-pitched sounds, for example, the use of wind chimes would be contraindicated, unless the goal was to decrease sensitivity. The therapist's accompanying instrument can sometimes cause unwanted distraction in a sensory or neurologically involved child with visual impairment. Listening, visual processing, and playing may not be developed enough for the child to interact musically while an accompanying instrument is played. These children may require a more "hands on" approach. Structured Singing and Playing is not directly contraindicated for this type of child, but the use of an accompanying instrument might not be effective initially.

Preparation. The music therapist should prepare the session and environment to meet the needs of the child and goals for the experience. Preparing a list of songs from the therapist's own repertoire would be helpful. Also, the therapist can assess the child's music preferences and prepare some of his or her preferred songs. This is an especially important step to take when developing the therapeutic relationship or working with a child with low musical responses (needing much prompting, etc.). The therapist can also provide a songbook for the child to choose songs. Try to adapt this if the print is not large enough for the child to read or if he or she is a Braille reader. For example, the therapist could read some song choices from which the client could choose.

The therapist can prepare the instruments before the session by setting the needed instruments out and making them readily available. However, the therapist may choose to have the client search and find instruments, either in an instrument closet or a certain part of the room, to address orientation and independent movement.

What to observe. It is important for the therapist to observe the child's musical interaction and engagement. The child's interaction can be indicated by the specific goal of the experience, and if he or she is meeting that goal. For example, if the goal is to increase vocalizations within the song, the therapist can be specifically looking for that response in the music. If the child is not singing along, the therapist should respond and provide the prompting or "space" in the music to encourage the child.

I have found in my work that simple manipulation of sound, time, and silence can increase musical responses in the child who is blind or visually impaired. Creating tension and anticipation in the music has sometimes been one of the only ways I have been able to elicit musical responses, especially with severely visually impaired children who also have multiple disabilities. Rainey Perry (2003) also discovered and documented the effectiveness of some of these techniques.

Procedures. The following steps provide a general outline to use when conducting a Structured Singing and Playing experience:

1) Prepare the environment, with special consideration of how instrument choice, lighting, and supportive seating or positioning work to create an appropriate environment. Some nonambulatory children may benefit from freedom of movement during the experience. If the child requires special positioning or will benefit from independent movement, provide a safe a comfortable place for this.
2) The therapist can gather the instruments with the client. If chosen prior to the session, talk to the child about the instruments you will be playing today. Taking some time to introduce the child to the instrument can be beneficial for the blind or visually impaired child. Visual learning or incidental learning opportunities are greatly reduced for visually impaired children, so taking time to describe the instrument and ways in which it can be played can be very beneficial. Give the client a couple of minutes to freely explore the instrument and ask questions. This approach could also decrease tactile defensiveness with some children.
3) The music therapist can work together with the child to choose the song to re-create, or the child can make the choice. The therapist may take the initiative to choose the song at times to direct work on the goals.
4) Eliminating downtime where there is no music or verbal exchange is ideal. The therapist should provide narration of the nonverbal activity when possible, especially for the blind or severely visually impaired child. Narration is essential in creating an environment where the visually impaired child is aware and informed.
5) If addressing a vision goal, the therapist should try to manage the sound that is produced to allow for adequate silence while the child is processing visual information. The auditory stimulation of the music or verbal prompting can be very visually distracting when a child is learning to access his or her functional vision.
6) The music therapist should evaluate the activity and engagement of the child throughout the experience. Monitoring whether the child is meeting the goals set for the experience is important in assessing its overall benefit and effectiveness.

Adaptations. Structured Singing and Playing can be adapted to increase independence and social interaction between children. In a group music therapy session, social interaction can be addressed by passing the instruments around the circle or sharing a large community instrument, such as a gathering drum. Structured musical play may also be expanded into an improvisatory experience. Instead of focusing the musical play on a specific song, the client and therapist would extemporaneously create music in the moment using a variety of musical media (Bruscia, 1998).

Performance in a Music Recital or Production

Overview. Performing in a music recital or production is something that can be therapeutic and meaningful for the school age child who is blind or visually impaired. Our focus in music therapy is on the process of preparing for and participating in the experience, rather than the musical product. The process involved in performing holds many opportunities for addressing a variety of goals for the visually impaired child. It can also function as an effective advocacy tool and educate the public about the abilities of children who are blind and visually impaired.

Performing in a music recital or production can be a positive experience for the blind or visually impaired child. While keeping in mind that the process is the focus and not the product, performing a song can work to improve self-esteem and develop a sense of accomplishment. Social interaction goals can also be addressed when the child performs in a group song, as well as being a member of the audience.

To participate comfortably in the music recital or production, the child should be able to be in a large group of people, tolerate noise, adjust to an unfamiliar environment with or without assistance, and demonstrate adequate maturity to focus on the task of performing. It is important to make this a successful experience for the child. The level of therapy for performing in a music recital or production is augmentative.

It is not recommended that a child who has much difficulty with unfamiliar environments, noise, and large groups participate in a music recital or production. Some children who have additional neurological and multiple handicaps may have sensory sensitivities that trigger unwanted neurological problems, such as seizures. Some visually impaired children may "shut down" in this type of busy or overwhelming environment. Participation in this type of experience is something that can slowly be introduced over time, but because the success of the child is one of our main concerns, it may be best that these children not be exposed to the setting of the musical recital.

Preparation. Preparing the environment for the music recital or production with children who are blind and visually impaired involves writing a program explanation, setting up the performance space, arranging the instruments, making plans for navigation and mobility of participants, and preparing for video and audio recording. The program can include the name of the performer and song. Also, a brief explanation of something the child has been working on or why he chose that particular song can be helpful in giving the audience a sense of the role of music therapy in the performance.

Setting up the performance space and arranging the instruments in ways that are quickly accessed during the performance is essential in creating smooth transitions between each song. The performance space may likely be a novel and unfamiliar space, thus creating orientation and mobility challenges for the blind and visually impaired performers. The therapist can introduce the performers to the space before the performance to aid in orientation. However, this may not be possible. Making plans with the performers as well as consulting with an O&M specialist is a proactive way to be prepared for possible challenges. Be prepared to use a sighted guide with some children with very low vision or who are totally blind, and make sure to have other staff or volunteers available to provide assistance as well.

It may be helpful when arranging a group of performers to create a simple diagram to share with a person who can help to arrange the performers and instruments during the actual performance. Finally, being able to document the performances with a good-quality audio and/or video recording can be very meaningful to the participants and their families. The appropriate releases or permissions for video, audio, and multimedia uses should be obtained from the participants and their families.

What to observe. During the performance, it is important to monitor the stimulation and participation of the performers. Making sure the performers get the correct instruments, are seated in appropriate supported positions, and have assistance playing the instruments if needed are additional things to watch for during the performance. Finally, maintaining manageable transitions between each song is important. As the main facilitator of the performance, the music therapist will have many duties to maintain, so designating fellow staff members to assist is essential.

Procedures. The procedures for conducting the music recital or production will need to be planned and implemented to meet the needs of the performers and space to be used for the performance. The following are general procedures to use:

1) The therapist should make sure that the performance area is arranged and all preparations have been completed.
2) Explain to participants that prior their performance they can share their name, age (if appropriate), and song they are going to perform. Performers can be encouraged to bow after the song.
3) Welcome the audience. A warm-up or greeting song can be offered.
4) Proceed through the program of songs. As it is each person's turn to perform, he or she should be assisted as needed up to the performance space. Use of the sighted guide technique can ensure efficient and quick travel, as well as proper positioning in the performance space. If the performer uses a white cane, he or she can decide whether or not to bring the cane.
5) When the performer is finished, he or she should be assisted back to his or her seat.
6) The process involved in setting up for each song and transitioning to the next one can seem tedious and long for audience members. Providing some narration, a verbal explanation of the song, and a short amount of information about the performer during transitions between songs can improve this experience.
7) Providing refreshments at the end of the recital gives the performers and families a time to share their accomplishments and socialize with others.

Adaptations. Performance in a music recital or production can be adapted in a variety of ways. The experience can be adapted into a musical play, such as the wonderful works by Paul Nordoff and Clive Robbins (1995). The performance experience can also be adapted to various venues, including public spaces and performance halls. Last, the music recital performance can be adapted for a smaller audience and a more informal presentation. The music therapist should ensure that the adaptations made will meet the needs of clients and the goals for music therapy treatment.

GUIDELINES FOR COMPOSITIONAL MUSIC THERAPY

Compositional music therapy experiences can provide an ideal balance between creativity and structure for children who are blind and visually impaired. A variety of compositional experiences described by Bruscia (1998), such as song parodies and instrumental compositions, can be adapted to meet the needs of visually impaired children. A songwriting music therapy experience will be presented.

Songwriting

Overview. There is a variety of approaches to writing songs with clients in music therapy. Bruscia (1998) describes the process of songwriting as one where "the client composes an original song or any part thereof (e.g., lyrics, melody, accompaniment) with varying levels of technical assistance from the therapist" (p. 120). The final product is documented in a form of notation or recording.

Songwriting is indicated for individuals who are able to communicate their thoughts and feelings, make decisions, and assist in determining the overall structure of the song with or without assistance. The client should demonstrate musical interaction without needing very much prompting because the songwriting process requires creativity and engagement in the music. Goals for songwriting may address communication skills, cognitive abilities, and coping. Songwriting can also address social interaction as a way of creating connections between group members (Bruscia, 1998). The level of therapy for songwriting can be augmentative or intensive.

It is important that clients participating in the songwriting experience engage easily and actively in the music setting. Individuals that require a significant amount of structure and prompting to interact musically may be contraindicated for the songwriting experience. A songwriting experience may not be appropriate for an individual who has not developed a voice of insight and awareness, although this may be adapted. Also, it may be difficult to complete this experience with a visually impaired child who has sensory dysfunction and sensitivities to various sounds present in the music therapy environment.

Preparation. There are many different techniques the music therapist can use to facilitate a songwriting experience. The techniques and approach should be comfortable and effective for the client and therapist. When preparing the session and environment for songwriting, the therapist should have access to an accompanying instrument, such as a guitar or piano. In the beginning of the songwriting process, providing the client with an accompanying instrument is an option, although this could become a distraction. Set the stage and prepare the client for the songwriting experience. The topic can be determined beforehand by the music therapist or decided with the participant. Brainstorming or writing down ideas to stimulate the songwriting process is often helpful.

The therapist will need something to document the words, music, and harmonic structure of the song. The therapist may prefer to transcribe in the moment with paper and pencil or on a white board or large paper. With the increased use of tablets and electronic devices, these can be utilized as well. Recording the experience to transcribe later or in addition to writing everything down can be effective in preserving the words as well as the melody and chord progression. The client can participate in documenting the song as well; however, it may be difficult for a child writing in Braille to play an instrument and write or read at the same time because these are both tactile tasks.

What to observe. The music therapist should monitor the engagement of the child during the songwriting experience. Observe if the child is meeting the goals set for the experience. Sensory-wise, is the therapist providing enough stimulation, or is the client struggling with focusing on the task? Is the child able to process everything appropriately, or is writing the music with lyrics at the same time too much? The typical songwriting process for a sighted individual may need to be adjusted to meet the needs of the blind or visually impaired child.

Procedures. There are a variety of different approaches and techniques that the therapist can utilize during a songwriting experience. The procedures that will be provided here encompass techniques that I have used clinically and are my preference. However, the therapist can utilize these techniques or substitute his or her own preferred approach to songwriting.

1) Decide on the method of documenting the components of the song, including lyrics, melody, chord progression, rhythm, etc. If using paper, white board, or something similar, make these available. If the child's vision is good, the therapist can make this visual so the child can read along. Or, if the therapist will be using an electronic device to write the words or record the song, make sure these materials are readily available as well.
2) If a topic for songwriting wasn't determined earlier, work with the client to designate a few ideas. Then work together to narrow the ideas down to one topic that is appropriate and therapeutic.
3) Begin the writing with the child, depending upon the approach to the songwriting experience, with the lyrics, music, or both. Evaluate if the approach is beneficial for the child. Ongoing assessment is recommended during the songwriting experience to ensure success.
4) On an accompanying instrument, provide a musical background or structure using a simple and repeating chord progression throughout the experience. The therapist can accompany the songwriting on a guitar in a repeating pattern to stimulate continued engagement in the songwriting experience, while encouraging additional meaningful input from the client.

5) As the client and therapist work together to write the song, the therapist can repeat each line or two lines that was written until a verse (or the first section of the song) is created.
6) Once the first verse or section is completed, musically review it, then transition into the second section or chorus. Repetition of the chord progression and the written lines as they fit into the gestalt of the song can help to encourage creativity and smooth transitions between the different sections of the song.
7) The therapist can reflect on the client's contribution and provide positive feedback during the songwriting experience. Consistently reinforcing the child's contribution and participation is important. It isn't easy for many people to write a song, and it is especially challenging if it is about a difficult topic, such as vision loss. Additional reinforcement can be helpful for the child.
8) Continue to repeat the process of writing, reviewing, and reflecting while providing the musical background or structure as the songwriting experience continues.
9) Provide the child with an opportunity to take a break if needed. Come back to the song later in the session or in the next session.
10) To complete the songwriting experience, the therapist can write or type the song and present it to the child as a finished product. Recording a performance of the song can document the client's accomplishment in a way that he or she will be able to review in the future.

Adaptations. Songwriting is a compositional music therapy experience that can be easily adapted for differing ability levels. Bruscia (1998) describes song parodies as when "[t]he client changes words, phrases, or the entire lyrics of an existing song, while maintaining the melody and standard accompaniment." (p. 120). If the child needs additional structure to meet the goals of the songwriting experience, this can be a beneficial adaptation. Songwriting experiences can also be adapted to include the participation of nonverbal children. Bertolami and Martino (2002) shared a technique of adapting a songwriting experience by working with the caregivers of the individuals who spend a lot of time with the children and who have insight into their lives. Adapting a songwriting experience in this way involves the children meaningfully because the caregivers are able to contribute in partnership with the child and therapist.

WORKING WITH CAREGIVERS

Blindness and visual impairment is documented as a low-incidence disability, yet the people affected by the disability are quite sensitive (LaVenture & Alman, 2007). Reliable information is limited for families to educate themselves on blindness and visual impairment. Even some ophthalmologists do not give the family the appropriate information regarding a child's visual impairment (Roman-Lantzy, 2007). Some doctors may tell a family that their child is blind and "will never see," but this is difficult to judge in infants and very young children. Depending upon the child's diagnosis, his or her vision could improve over time as the child grows or learns to use his or her functional vision. This is especially true for children with cortical visual impairment (Roman-Lantzy, 2007). Once this type of information is given to the family, it can stimulate additional guilt and grieving over their child's visual impairment.

Although the music therapist is not a vision professional typically, the therapist is able to observe the client in the session. The therapist should offer observations of the positive things happening with the child, especially if he or she is engaged in music experiences. The music therapist can be an advocate for the child, communicating as much as possible to the caregivers, including how he or she is meeting the goals in the music therapy session. Especially when working with visually impaired children who have multiple disabilities, it is important to take the time to communicate the accomplishments and intentionality of a client's "work" in the music therapy session as an effort to educate the family or caregivers and influence greater emotional acceptance of the child.

Advocacy can be an important role for the music therapist to play when assessing and evaluating the strengths and needs of a child who is blind or visually impaired. Taking into account the emotional undertones of the family, their available resources, and their additional needs are some valuable ways to assess the whole child. The needs of the parents or caregivers are important to consider, as they help to shape the child's worldview and self-concept. Family, friends, and peers create the inner social circle for individuals with special needs (Darrow & Johnson, 1994). Rehabilitation professionals and the general public make up the second and third circles. The inner social circle has the greatest impact on the development of the disabled person's self-concept and social acceptance (Darrow & Johnson, 1994). The authors point out that while the music therapist may have little impact on the attitudes of the person's family and peers, he or she can play an important role in monitoring and facilitating positive interactions. If the parents see the possibilities in their child's handicap, then the child will also see the possibilities in his or her challenges. Last, the music therapist can refer the family to a local community agency that specializes in visual impairment. These resources can function as a valuable support for families of children who are blind and visually impaired.

Research Evidence

When working with blind and visually impaired children, the music therapist should be open to considering the multiple connections to music that are gained by vision. As sighted individuals, we build many connections to melody, rhythm, and harmony through incidental learning. This shapes our understanding of musical concepts, movement, sound, and instruments. When working with children who are blind and visually impaired, the therapist should be open to thinking about music in different ways. The music therapy literature addresses this issue as well as others that can provide some research guidance to clinical practice. However, statistically significant research is lacking due to a focus toward case studies and small group experimental research. Survey research provides some very interesting information on the perception of blind individuals in society.

Codding (1984) contributed a significant amount of information to the field with a book chapter about music therapy for visually impaired children. The chapter provided a comprehensive guide to important issues relating to visual impairment, as well as applications for music therapy. Codding's (2000) literature review on music therapy with the visually impaired reviewed 17 case studies and 27 data-based research studies. The review provided a much needed foundation for music therapists working with individuals who are visually impaired.

Madsen and Darrow (1989) examined the perception of music and musical concepts. The authors provided 32 blind and visually impaired subjects with two tests, each looking at music aptitude and the understanding of musical concepts such as frequency, duration, and amplitude. Subjects responded in a lower score than what was expected on the musical concept questions. The difference in the way the subjects perceived the sound examples and the tactile representation of those sounds could explain the lower musical concept scores. Madsen and Darrow caution the music therapist not to make presumptions about how sound or musical concepts are perceived by visually impaired individuals.

The perception of sound and imagery in music with visually impaired and hearing-impaired children was investigated by Darrow and Novak (2007). Listening excerpts from Saint-Saëns's "Carnival of the Animals" were played for children who were visually impaired, hearing-impaired, and typically developing. The children were also asked to identify the image of the animal portrayed in the music. Darrow and Novak found that the sensory-impaired participants struggled with agreeing on the composer's intended meaning, whereas the participants with typical hearing and vision were able to do this more often. The authors discuss the compositional dimensions of music such as rhythm, timbre, texture, or pitch, and how these influenced the participants' imagery. The subtle nuances of "Carnival of the Animals" may be easily lost for the visually impaired child who has likely had limited exposure to an elephant, a mule, and a kangaroo, just to name a few. Darrow and Novak's (2007) findings show the importance of concept development and exposing children who are blind or visually impaired to the outside world. Last, the authors share their observation that imagery is rarely used with children who are visually impaired.

The difficulties that blind and visually impaired individuals face in regard to social acceptance and inclusion are pervasive. Even in a modern society that outwardly seems to value diversity, the covert fear and ignorance of blindness and visual impairment are present. Darrow and Johnson (1994) examined the attitudes of junior and senior high school music students toward people with a variety of impairments including amputation, blindness, cosmetic conditions, deafness, paralysis, epilepsy, and health-related disabilities like cancer and AIDS. A total of 699 completed surveys were analyzed. The authors state that the three most accepted disabilities were visible scars, heart condition, and deafness. Among the three least acceptable disabilities were paralysis, AIDS, and blindness. It is significant to note here that blindness was ranked last in the list of ten, meaning it was the least accepted disability. The authors attributed this to the possibility that personal mobility, which is valued highly among young people, can be significantly affected by blindness. In my opinion, the social stigma and archetypal nature of visual impairment had some effect as well. Darrow and Johnson (1994) state that these results illustrate the importance of nurturing and encouraging the acceptance of individuals with disabilities, which as music therapists we have the capability of doing. Some interesting significant findings were that high school students and females tended to express more accepting attitudes.

A case study by Salas and Gonzalez (1991) documented the therapists' work with a young child who was blind and had multiple disabilities. Prior to music therapy treatment, one of Gabriella's main struggles was connecting with the outside world. This resulted in helplessness, vulnerability, and struggling with interpersonal interactions. The authors explain that in the improvisation-based music therapy environment, Gabriella was able to develop strengths, connection, and communication with herself and the people in her outside world.

Rainey Perry's (2003) study examining the communication development of children with multiple disabilities is relevant when looking at communication skills of visually impaired children. Nine out of the 10 participants were noted to have vision problems. Nine of the 10 participants also had a medical diagnosis of cerebral palsy, while one participant had a genetic condition called Norrie's Disease. Evidence of the high rate of children with multiple disabilities, especially including cerebral palsy, who also have a visual impairment is something that is seen quite often.

Improvisational music therapy was used to explore the communication abilities of the participants in the qualitative case study approach (Rainey Perry, 2003). The author provided observations of some of the visually impaired participants. The children's disabilities affected their ability to communicate at times during the music therapy session. The visual impairments of three participants caused them to be reluctant to touch and manipulate objects and instruments in the session. The author reported that when assistance was provided, the children resisted those attempts. The children's visual impairments also made anticipating when others were going to assist them difficult. These are common issues with visually impaired children, but can be addressed with narration techniques, like giving a verbal warning before providing assistance. Musical cues given in anticipation of the physical assistance, as well as introducing objects slowly, were helpful in dealing with tactile defensiveness (Rainey Perry, 2003).

Rainey Perry (2003) also reported that some children with visual impairment had difficulty in exploring the environment and efficiently using eye gaze in communication. The visually impaired child's ability to use eye gaze and explore the environment are directly related to the child's vision problems. Because a child's environment can be difficult to access due to his vision, they will likely be much less motivated to independently explore things in their environment. This is why a lot of physical prompting such as hand over hand or, even better, hand under hand or touch prompting is really important for children with visual impairment. Some techniques that Rainey Perry (2003) found to be helpful in musically engaging and stimulating communication with the children were techniques that built up the level of musical tension and anticipation. Using different styles of music, media, and activities also helped to maintain the child's musical interaction. Overall, the participants' communication development was delayed and significantly affected by their visual impairments and multiple disabilities.

Appropriate assessment and design of music therapy experiences should meet the developmental needs of children who are blind and visually impaired. The effect of visual impairment on development is such that even a typically functioning child who is visually impaired will likely be delayed in many areas. In their study examining the participation of a young child with visual impairment on a school playground, Kern and Wolery (2001) tested the developmental age of the child. They found that David, who was 40 months old, scored well under his chronological age. The developmental age scores ranged from nine months for play skills to the highest, which was 36 months for grooming. His general age equivalent based on the rating scale used in the study was 23 months, illustrating some of the developmental effects of visual impairment.

While this study examined the behavior of a preschool child on the playground, there is some applicable information for school-age children who are blind and visually impaired. Open spaces can often be difficult for children with visual impairments to navigate and explore, thus reducing engagement and interaction with people and objects in the environment. Kern and Wolery (2001) adapted a school playground with developmentally appropriate multisensory instrument stations, a tactile walkway, and a pushcart. David's play and social interactions prior to the adaptation were not meaningful, but after the adaptations, some changes were documented in engagement and stereotypical movements. However, the staff development activities, in addition to the physical adaptations of the playground, brought about the most changes in David's interactions, engagement, and stereotypical movement.

Robb (2003) measured the group participation skills of six visually impaired young children enrolled in early-intervention classrooms. The ABBA design included two 30-minute play-based sessions and two 30-minute music-based sessions. Diagnostic information included in the article noted a diverse group of visual impairments, including three children with cortical visual impairment (CVI) with other disabilities. Participation skills that were measured included attentive behavior, following one-step directions, remaining seated, facing the speaker, and functional object manipulation. Results of Robb's study found that most participants exhibited equal or improved performance on all behaviors that were measured during the music-based sessions.

Robb (2003) attributed much of her study's results to theories of arousal: "Given that the processing of music stimuli occurs in the same centers of the brain associated with emotion, arousal, and pleasure, it would appear reasonable to consider that in this study, music may have functioned to induce optimal levels of arousal in participants" (p. 278). It can be difficult to engage young visually impaired children during group activities due to multiple vision-related issues, including the auditory environment, listening skills, tactile engagement, and selective attention (Robb, 2003). Therefore, the increased participation among the young group members in Robb's study is a positive result. However, with an increase in these outward signs of group participation, visual attention and use of the child's functional vision will likely be ignored. Especially in a multisensory environment like music therapy, a visually impaired child's behavior and participation increases. At the same time, the child may not be using the functional vision that he or she possesses. Often when auditory modes of learning are accessed, the child will attend to the auditory mode over the visual because it is more easily accessed than vision. While the music therapist may not typically address vision issues, the music therapy session can be a place where the visually impaired child can be given that opportunity to utilize functional vision, even if it is low, i.e., as long as it is a functional and practical thing for that child. If using his or her vision is too exhausting, then there is no reason to address this goal in the music therapy session.

Bertolami and Martino (2002) share some of their clinical work at a private school for children with multiple handicaps and visual impairment. The music therapists address specific goals as part of an integrative team of professionals and teachers, but also value the therapeutic nature of making music with others and nurturing the innate musicality of each child. Bertolami and Martino explain that songwriting has been particularly effective with their clients. They explain that the experience can be easily adapted for nonverbal and cognitively less aware children as well. The authors give detailed ideas on ways to adapt a songwriting experience and share that "... what is moving about it is that we see children beginning to notice each other and acknowledge each other through these individual expressions" (p. 2). They also mentioned the positive impact that the songwriting experiences had on the staff, which saw the children and their lives in a more positive way.

Summary and Conclusions

There are multiple layers of information to consider when working with school-age children who are blind and visually impaired. The innermost foundation is the child, free from impairment or dysfunction. This child possesses all of the same desires, hopes, learning, exploration, and educational needs of typical children. The next layers around the child can include family, friends, and community. Some important considerations within this layer include culture, health, religion, spirituality, and support. If blindness or visual impairment significantly affects the child's life, it would be a part of the third layer. This is due to the pervasive nature of visual impairment. The fourth layer can include additional challenges the child may face. These might be medical, physical, and cognitive disabilities. The additional layers are where intervention, access to education, technology, and adaptation are integrated.

While music therapy can be a vital contribution to the development of children who are blind and visually impaired, it is just one part in this complex puzzle to be solved. The music therapist should work to maintain this perspective and respect the role with which we have been entrusted. My work with blind and visually impaired individuals has taught me how much I take my sight for granted. The amount of information that I have learned from simple observation and modeling during my life seems too expansive to even quantify when I reflect on the things with which I see clients struggle. When working with blind and visually impaired children, the music therapist should practice empathy and be open to "seeing" things in new and different ways. Although one's sight may not be usable, his vision can be priceless.

References

American Foundation for the Blind (AFB). (2008, September). *Key definitions of statistical terms.* Retrieved from http://www.afb.org/section.aspx?SectionID=15&DocumentID=1280

Bertolami, M., & Martino, L. (2002). Music therapy in a private school setting for children with multiple handicaps who are visually impaired or blind. *Voices: A World Forum for Music Therapy, 2*(1). Retrieved from https://normt.uib.no/index.php/voices/article/view/69/59#

Browne, N. J. (1984). *A music-based cognitive assessment procedure for nonhandicapped, nonverbal, and blind young children.* Dissertation Abstracts International: Section B. Health and Medicine, 45(8), 2709.

Bruscia, K. (1998). *Defining music therapy* (2nd ed.). Gilsum, NH: Barcelona Publishers.

Cassin, B. (2001). In M. Rubin (Ed.), *Dictionary of eye terminology* (4th ed.). Gainesville, FL: Triad.

Clark, K. (2012, June). *"Fingering" it out! Emergent literacy for infants and toddlers, including those who are blind or visually impaired.* Cincinnati, OH: Bureau of Early Intervention Services Training.

Codding, P. (1984). Music therapy for visually impaired children. In W. B. Lathom & C. T. Eagle (Eds.), *Music therapy for handicapped children. Volume I: For the hearing impaired, visually impaired, deaf-blind* (pp. 43–96). Washington, DC: National Association for Music Therapy.

Codding, P. (2000). Music therapy literature and clinical applications for blind and severely visually impaired persons: 1940–2000. In C. Furman (Ed.), *Effectiveness of music therapy procedures: Documentation of research and clinical practice* (pp. 159–198). Silver Spring, MD: The American Music Therapy Association.

Darrow, A., & Johnson, C. (1994). Junior and senior high school music students' attitudes toward individuals with a disability. *Journal of Music Therapy, 31*(4), 266–279.

Darrow, A., & Novak, J. (2007). The effect of vision and hearing loss on listeners' perception of referential meaning in music. *Journal of Music Therapy, 44*(1), 57–73.

Dutton, G. (2002). Visual problems in children with damage to the brain. *Visual Impairment Research, 4*(2), 113–121.

Ferrell, K. (1998). *Project PRISM: A longitudinal study of developmental patterns of children who are visually impaired.* Retrieved from http://www.unco.edu/ncssd/research/PRISM/ExecSumm.pdf

Gallimore, D. (2005). Multiculturalism and students with visual impairments in New South Wales, Australia. *Journal of Visual Impairment and Blindness, 99*(6), 345–354.

Gougoux, F., Lepore, F., Lassonde, M., Voss, P., Zatorre, R. & Belin, P. (2004). Pitch discrimination in the early blind. *Nature, 430*(6997), 309-310.

Hill, E. (n.d.). *The role of the orientation and mobility teacher in the public schools*. Retrieved from http://tsbvi.edu/orientation-a-mobility/2110-the-role-of-the-orientation-and-mobility-teacher-in-the-public-schools

Hughes, M., & Fazzi, D. (1993). Chapter five: Behavior management. In (No Ed.), *First Steps: A handbook for teaching young children who are visually impaired.* Los Angeles, CA: Blind Children's Center.

Jan, J., & Groenveld, M. (1993). Visual behaviors and adaptations associated with cortical and ocular impairment in children. *Journal of Visual Impairment & Blindness, 87*, 101-105.

Kern, P., & Wolery, M. (2001). Participation of a preschooler with visual impairments on the playground: Effects of musical adaptations and staff development. *Journal of Music Therapy, 38*(2), 149–164.

King, J., MacKay, M., & Sirnick, A. (2003). Shaken baby syndrome in Canada: Clinical characteristics and outcomes of hospital cases. *Canadian Medical Association Journal, 168*(2), 155–159.

Kivlin, J. (1999). A 12-year ophthalmologic experience with the shaken baby syndrome at a regional children's hospital. *Transactions of the American Ophthalmological Society, 97*, 545–581.

LaVenture, S., & Allman, C. (2007). Special education services: What parents need to know. In S. LaVenture (Ed.), *A parents' guide to special education for children with visual impairments* (pp. 3–35). New York, NY: AFB Press.

Madsen, C., & Darrow, A. (1989). The relationship between music aptitude and sound conceptualization of the visually impaired. *Journal of Music Therapy, 26*(2), 71–78.

Martinez, C., & Moss, K. (1998). Orientation and mobility training: The way to go. *See/Hear, 3*(4). Retrieved from http://www.tsbvi.edu/seehear/fall98/waytogo.htm

National Eye Institute (NEI), (2009). *Facts about anophthalmia and microphthalmia.* Retrieved from http://www.nei.nih.gov/health/anoph/anophthalmia.asp.

Nordoff, P., & Robbins, C. (1995). In C. Robbins (Ed.), *Music therapy in special education* (2nd ed.). Gilsum, NH: Barcelona Publishers.

Nyman, J. (2009). Unemployment rates and reasons: Dissing the blind. *Braille Monitor, 52*(3). Retrieved from http://www.nfb.org/images/nfb/publications/bm/bm09/bm0903/bm0903tc.html

Rainey Perry, M. (2003). Relating improvisational music therapy with severely and multiply disabled children to communication development. *Journal of Music Therapy, 40*(3), 227–246.

Robb, S. (2003). Music interventions and group participation skills of preschoolers with visual impairments: Raising questions about music, arousal, and attention. *Journal of Music Therapy, 40*(4), 266–282.

Roman-Lantzy, C. (2007). *Cortical visual impairment: An approach to assessment and intervention.* New York, NY: AFB Press.

Salas, J., & Gonzalez, D. (1991). Like singing with a bird: Improvisational music therapy with a blind four-year-old. In K. Bruscia (Ed.), *Case studies in music therapy* (pp. 17–27). Gilsum, NH: Barcelona Publishers.

Siligo, W. (2005). Enriching the ensemble experience for students with visual impairments. *Music Educators Journal, 91*(5), 31–36.

Simmons, S., & Stout, A. (1993). Chapter three: The eye. In (No Ed.), *First Steps: A handbook for teaching young children who are visually impaired.* Los Angeles: Blind Children's Center.

Slott, G. (2005). Speech and language development in children with ONH. In (No Ed.), *A unique way of learning; Teaching young child with optic nerve hypoplasia.* Los Angeles, CA: Blind Childrens Center.

UNICEF, (2012). *UNICEF calls for social inclusion of children with disabilities in Africa*. Retrieved from http://www.unicef.org/media/media_62646.html.

World Health Organization. (WHO). (2011, October). *Visual impairment and blindness fact sheet No. 282.* Retrieved from http://www.who.int/mediacentre/factsheets/fs282/en/

Resources

Information on Blindness and Visual Impairment

- Zimmerman Low Vision Simulation Kits: www.lowvisionsimulationkit.com
- American Foundation for the Blind (AFB): www.afb.org
- National Industries for the Blind (NIB): www.nib.org
- Association for Education and Rehabilitation of the Blind and Visually Impaired (AER): www.aerbvi.org

Information on Braille Music

- Braille Music Texts
  - Jenkins, E. (1960). *The primer of Braille music.* Louisville, KY: American Printing House for the Blind.
  - Krolick, B. (1998). *How to read Braille music: An introduction.* San Diego, CA: Opus Technologies.
  - Taesch, R. (2001). *An introduction to music for the blind student.* Valley Forge, PA: Dancing Dots.
- Transcription Software
- Goodfeel and Dancing Dots: www.dancingdots.com/main/goodfeel.htm
- Transcription Services
  - Computers to Help People: www.chpi.org
  - Dancing Dots: www.dancingdots.com
  - Valley Braille Service: www.valleybraille.com

Appendix A

Music Therapy Referral and Assessment Questionnaire For School-Age Children with Visual Impairment

Basic Information

Reason for Referral:

Child's Name:

Parents or Caregivers:

Age and DOB:

Address:

Phone:

Email:

Siblings, family members, or other individuals living in the home:

Any other family members who are visually impaired also:

Eye and Medical Information

Vision Diagnosis or Diagnoses:

Other Health Conditions:

Other Relevant Medical Information:

Allergies:

Vision Concerns:

Visual behaviors in which the child engages:

Functional Low-Vision Assessment or Evaluation Completed:

If so, where can a copy of the report be obtained?

Quality of Functional Vision:

Independent use of functional vision or are prompts and support needed?

Color Preference:

Visual Complexity Ability:

Educational Information

Current Grade Level:

Mode of Learning (Braille, large print, auditory):

Reading ability:

Accommodations received in school:

Accommodations that would be helpful in music therapy (magnification device, lighting):

Therapies (OT, PT, Behavioral, Speech, etc.):

Names and Contact Information for Therapists:

Vision-Related Services Received:

Names and Contact Information for Vision Professionals/Instructors:

Developmental Information

Parents' developmental concerns for the child:

Does the child receive/participate in music education at school?

Name of the teacher and contact information:

Participation in Group Setting:

Approximate Developmental Age:

Presence of cognitive, visual, or motor processing delay:

Sensory Sensitivities:

If sensitivities are present, how is it addressed?

Music Therapy Considerations for Assessment

Is the child currently receiving or has the child in the past received music therapy services?

If relevant, name and contact information of therapist:

Musical Responses:

Music Genre Preferences:

Instrument Preferences:

Instrument or Sound Sensitivities:

Other Relevant Information:

Chapter 11

Mild to Moderate Intellectual Disability

Douglas R. Keith

Diagnostic Information

Intellectual Disability (ID) is a relatively common and familiar condition. The American Association on Intellectual and Developmental Disabilities (Schalock et al., 2010) includes the following criteria in its definition: significant limitations in intellectual functioning (criterion A) and adaptive behaviors (criterion B). Adaptive behaviors cover three types of skills:

1) Conceptual skills (language and literacy; time and number concepts, etc.)
2) Social skills (interpersonal skills, social responsibility, self-esteem, etc.)
3) Practical skills (activities of daily living)

These limitations occur in at least two of the following areas:

communication	self-direction
self-care	work
home living	leisure
social/interpersonal skills	health
use of community resources	safety
functional academic skills	

In order to diagnose intellectual disability, these deficits must occur before age 18 (criterion C). Criteria A and B benefit from further elaboration.

"General intellectual functioning," for purposes of diagnosis, is defined as Intelligence Quotient (IQ), and "significantly subaverage" is defined as two standard deviations below the mean. Intelligence tests used to test IQ, such as the Fourth Edition of the Wechsler Intelligence Scales for Children (WISC-IV) Wechsler et al., 2004), have a standard error of measurement of about five points. Intelligence quotients alone do not define intellectual disability, as there must also be existing deficits in adaptive behavior. For example, some people with an IQ of 70–75 may be diagnosed with intellectual disability, while others with a lower IQ (e.g., 65–70), may not be so diagnosed, based on the presence or absence of deficits in adaptive behavior.

Adaptive behaviors are an indication of how well people cope with demands of daily life and how independent they are given their chronological age and expectations of the environment in which they live. The measurement of both intelligence and adaptive behaviors can be complicated by cultural differences, language barriers, physical handicaps, or sensory limitations. In any case, music therapists typically focus on improving adaptive skills, because cognitive function is difficult to improve. In very young children, adaptive behaviors are usually the initial symptoms of intellectual disability, because cognition is not easily evaluated.

Individuals with intellectual disabilities have been given many different diagnostic labels throughout history. These changes are often driven either by what is considered socially acceptable (with changes in language usage) or by educational policy. Diagnostic labels were used inconsistently from place to place. Early music therapy references from the 1950s still contain terminology such as "moron" and "imbecile" (Smith, 1953). With shifting language use, these terms became used as insults, and the diagnostic term "mental retardation" was seen as an improvement. The current *Diagnostic and Statistical Manual of Mental Disorders (Fourth Edition – Text Revision)* (American Psychiatric Association, 2000) includes four subcategories or levels, defined by IQ.

Mild Mental Retardation	50–55 to approximately 70
Moderate Mental Retardation	35–40 to 50–55
Severe Mental Retardation	20–25 to 35–40
Profound Mental Retardation	Below 20 or 25

The word "retarded" has been used so often as an insult that many places of employment prefer terms such as "special needs learner," "developmentally delayed," or "intellectually disabled." However, "mental retardation" remains a diagnostic category at this point in time. Readers should note that different countries use different terms for mental retardation. For example, one encounters the term "learning disability" in the music therapy literature from the UK, where it seems to refer to "mental retardation" (Bunt, 1994). In the US, "learning disability" has an entirely different meaning. The former American Association for Mental Retardation (AAMR) has become the "American Association on Intellectual and Developmental Disabilities" (AAIDD), and refers to mental retardation as "intellectual disability" (AAIDD, no date). It is predicted that the next version of the *Diagnostic and Statistical Manual of Mental Disorders (Fifth Edition)* will shift to this term. In any case, this chapter focuses on the first two levels of intellectual disability in the current US classification system: mild and moderate intellectual disability.

In the first half of the 20th century, policies and practices varied widely in the education of children with intellectual disability. The White House Conference on Child Health and Protection (1930) solidified the term "educable," setting a limit on what children schools were expected to educate. Most schools were allowed to exclude children they deemed "ineducable," that is, incapable of benefiting from education. This report encouraged increased resources for children considered "trainable," that is, children with more severe cognitive impairments. It is noteworthy that at this time, IQ was usually the only criterion used to define intellectual disability (White House Conference).

The largest number of individuals with intellectual disability falls into the "mild" category, which constitutes approximately 85% of all individuals with intellectual disability. People with mild ID are often indistinguishable from their peers during the early developmental period (i.e., before age five) and have few motor, social, or communication problems. Typically, they are able to attain the academic skills associated with the sixth grade (i.e., ages 11–12) by the end of their formal education. In adulthood, they can often live relatively independently, but may need supervision and guidance when under stress (American Psychiatric Association, 2000, p. 43).

The next largest group of individuals with intellectual disability falls into the "moderate" category—about 10% of people with ID. Children with moderate ID may show signs of cognitive impairment at a younger age than children with mild ID, but they typically develop basic receptive and expressive language skills (i.e., understanding and speaking simple sentences) during the early childhood years. While unlikely to develop academic skills beyond second-grade level (i.e., ages 7–8), vocational training often helps individuals with moderate intellectual disability attain a certain level of independence and ability to live in the community. Adolescence can be particularly difficult for children with moderate intellectual disability because of the complex social conventions among teenagers (American Psychiatric Association, 2000, p. 43).

Needs and Resources

By definition, children with intellectual disabilities have cognitive impairments; this is one of the key criteria for diagnosis. Children with mild intellectual disability may learn reading, writing, and math skills up to about a sixth-grade level, and children with moderate intellectual disability may learn basic reading skills, number concepts, and basic verbal communication skills. While the diagnostic criteria for intellectual disability include "deficits in adaptive behavior," the presence of adaptive deficits varies. Most children will exhibit strengths in some areas and limitations in others.

Children with intellectual disabilities often exhibit markedly poor communication skills. Language develops later, children use less language, its structure is more rudimentary, and its content is typically poorer than that of children without similar impairment. This creates an unfortunate circular effect. With some syndromes, such as Down's syndrome, children may have hearing impairments (Roizen, Wolters, Nicol, & Blondis, 1993), which can affect development of communication skills. Generally, more severe impairment means more problems in this area.

In terms of emotional and social skills, children with intellectual disability have a limited ability to understand their emotions, while they may feel them just as strongly as children without impairments. This imbalance can lead to problems in the social area as well, because children often misunderstand and are misunderstood by others. This can lead to social isolation, compounded by deficits in communication skills. Generally, one can assume greater challenges in these areas with a higher degree of impairment. As with all children, the early experiences of children with intellectual disability influence the development of their personal characteristics. Neglect, abuse, or belittling will have negative effects on the personal characteristics of children with intellectual disability, while support, care, and encouragement will have positive effects. However, since young children cannot understand much of the experiences that shape their later development, and since intellectual disability is associated with lower cognitive skills, children with intellectual disability can be expected to be *even more* influenced by early life experiences, because they are cognitively less able to process and understand them. Thus, positive early childhood experiences are critical for children with intellectual disability.

In terms of motor skills, children with intellectual disability often have lower gross motor, fine motor, and balance skills (Vujik, Hartman, Scherder & Visscher, 2010). As in other areas of adaptive functioning, the level of impairment is typically correlated with cognitive functioning.

In terms of musical characteristics, some evidence suggests that children with intellectual disability have vocal ranges that are narrower and lower than comparable children without intellectual disability (Larson, 1977). Music therapists should take this into account when planning vocal activities. Early research in music therapy suggests that some children with moderate intellectual disability (specifically, Down's syndrome) are less skilled at imitating rhythms presented to them than children without ID, likely correlated with their overall lower IQ (Peters, 1970). Level of activity (i.e., energy level) also correlates with preferences for music experiences; children who have a high energy level tend to prefer high-energy music therapy experiences, such as moving to music, while children with lower levels of activity tend to activities that require less energy, such as listening to music (Humphrey, 1981). This seems very similar to the tendencies and preferences of children who do not have intellectual disability.

Several different syndromes are associated with mild or moderate intellectual disability, including Down's syndrome (Lagasse, 2011) Williams syndrome (Lenhoff, 1988), Tuberous Sclerosis, Klinefelter syndrome, Turner syndrome, and Phenylketonuria (PKU) (Lathom-Radocy, 2002). Children with Williams syndrome are often musically and socially gifted, while exhibiting cognitive levels typical of children with mild to moderate intellectual disability. While it is important to assess each child individually, it is wise to keep in mind that some syndromes have associated strengths and needs. Children and adolescents with Williams syndrome, for example, may be vulnerable because they often cannot identify dangerous behaviors in people: Healthy suspicion may be absent. Williams syndrome is also associated with a certain degree of anxiety and impulsivity, which can lead to some behavioral problems (Levine, n.d.).

When working with children and adolescents with mild and moderate intellectual disability, music therapists address multiple goal areas, most of which fall in the category of "adaptive functioning," because changing intelligence level is unreasonable. For some music therapists, the overarching goal of music therapy for children with intellectual disability is normalization, or developing skills appropriate for integrated and learning environments (Lathom-Radocy, 2002, p. 41). It is helpful to think of adaptive behaviors or skills in this way. Most people with mild or moderate intellectual disability have a typical life span. Thus, music therapists are wise to consider the long-term impact of their work. This includes cultural surroundings, community resources, and vocational expectations, among others. Where will this client live as an adult? What does the client's local culture expect? What kinds of resources are available to adults with intellectual disability in the community? Will the client potentially hold a job someday? All of these questions can help guide the work of the music therapist working with any child with intellectual disability.

Assessment and Referral

Although music therapy was established as a profession over 50 years ago, relatively few formal, standardized assessment tools have emerged. This is not limited to any particular clientele. In 1978, Cohen, Averbach, and Katz analyzed the spectrum of roles and responsibilities of music therapy and music therapy assessment with clients with developmental disabilities. They underscored the specialized contributions that music therapists can make to the assessment process, not only for the services music therapists provide to clients, but also to its effects on the profession. More recently, in 2004, Sabbatella noted that in comparison with other related professions, publications in the areas of assessment and evaluation were relatively weak. The next section will discuss several music therapy–based assessment tools and give basic information on several other assessment tools used commonly in settings where music therapists work with children and adolescents with mild/moderate intellectual disability.

Grant (1995) developed a music therapy assessment tool for children and adolescents with developmental disabilities (intellectual disability), based on an earlier publication that outlines a curriculum for children with developmental disabilities (Grant, 1989). The assessment tool is laid out in outline form, with six example assessments given at the end. It seems to have been developed for children who are lower-functioning (i.e., with more severe forms of intellectual disability), but can be adapted for use with children and adolescents with mild or moderate intellectual disability.

This assessment focuses on four domains in which music therapists can make unique contributions to the assessment process: sensorimotor, cognitive, communication, and social. Each domain includes pitfalls to avoid and things to keep in mind. For example, music therapists assessing sensorimotor skills, rather than simply asking clients to play music, should make music and invite clients to play along. The section on social skills reminds the reader to keep in mind the developmental levels of play, which children with intellectual disability also progress through, albeit at a delayed and slower rate.

In the late 1990s, Brunk and Coleman developed the Special Education Music Therapy Assessment Process, or SEMTAP (Brunk & Coleman, 1999). SEMTAP, as the name suggests, is specifically designed to assess the functioning of children and adolescents who receive special education services, with the purpose of determining eligibility for children who have an Individualized Education Program

(IEP). The SEMTAP process includes a review of client records, interviews with professionals who work with the client (e.g., speech therapists, physical therapists), observations of clients, and direct assessments of clients. The music therapy–specific portion of SEMTAP is designed by the assessing music therapist, and a thorough description of the assessment session(s) is an important part of the report.

The SEMTAP process allows a comparison of client responses with and without music, based on benchmarks from the client's IEP. The results help determine whether music therapy is required for an individual to benefit from an educational program and whether music therapy ought to be added to their IEP. The SEMTAP manual provides examples of clinical contracts, written communication, and assessment reports.

While not specific to children and adolescents with mild or moderate intellectual disability, the SEMTAP is designed for those students who have an IEP, and most (if not all) children with ID fall into this category. As such, it is a potentially useful and valuable tool for music therapists working with these clients, especially in the process of qualifying children for music therapy services under their IEP.

A more recent assessment tool, the Individualized Music Therapy Assessment Profile, or IMTAP (Baxter et al., 2007) assesses client functioning in ten domains:

Gross motor
Fine motor
Oral motor
Sensory
Receptive communication/auditory perception
Expressive communication
Cognitive
Emotional
Social
Musicality

IMTAP defines each domain and its subdomains, and provides musical examples for most. Users can rate the client being assessed on four levels, each representing a level of functioning within a domain. Additionally, IMTAP includes four levels of consistency, ranging from "never" to "consistent," which indicate how reliably a client performs within a domain at a given level.

Music therapists who use IMTAP will find helpful examples of an intake form, a session outline, a scoring sheet, and a list of cross-domain skills, since many skills are relevant to more than one domain. For example, the skill "follows one-step verbal direction" (p. 32) is indicative of functioning in the domains "cognitive," "receptive communication/auditory perception," and "social." The output of IMTAP is a summary sheet and graph, which depict the functioning level of the client being assessed in written form and graphically. Users may choose to graph domains or subdomains, allowing music therapists to focus in on particular areas of interest. An additional "quantification module" thoroughly describes how to quantify the results of the assessment, when exact measurements are required. Two sample case studies provide contrasting examples of how music therapists use IMTAP. The book closes with examples of music notation for assessment purposes. While the IMTAP, like SEMTAP, is not specifically designed for children or adolescents with intellectual disability, it is a thorough and flexible tool for music therapists who work with these clients.

Of course, music therapists work in settings where other assessment tools are used, and can often incorporate information from these into their own assessment of the children and adolescents with whom they work. This section gives several examples of assessment tools commonly used in educational settings, focusing particularly on adaptive functioning.

The *Vineland Adaptive Behavior Scales (Second Edition)* (Sparrow, Cicchetti, & Balla, 2005) are a general assessment of personal and social skills of individuals. These scales are adaptable for all ages. The Vineland Scales assess communication, daily living, socialization, and motor skills. The scales have undergone extensive validity and reliability testing (Icabone, 1999). The American Association on Intellectual and Developmental Disabilities (AAIDD, n.d.) has published the Diagnostic Adaptive Behavior Scale (DABS), which provides a comprehensive standardized assessment of adaptive behavior.

The DABS measures the three domains of conceptual skills, social skills, and practical skills, and functions to rule in or rule out a diagnosis of intellectual disability, thus determining eligibility for various services. The DABS is based on an earlier scale, the Adaptive Behavior Scale (AAIDD, n.d.).

Music Therapy Methods

This chapter focuses on music therapy for children and adolescents with mild and moderate intellectual disability. While "mild" and "moderate" represent two distinct diagnostic categories, children and adolescents in these categories exhibit shared needs and strengths that distinguish them from lower-functioning clients, often diagnosed as having severe or profound intellectual disability. Generally, children and adolescents in these categories have stronger adaptive skills, such as language, gross and fine motor, and social skills, than individuals with severe or profound intellectual disability. These adaptive skills make it easier for them to be a part of the community.

Gaston, an early pioneer and theorist in the profession of music therapy, recognized the benefits of music therapy for children with intellectual disabilities (1968). Music activities provide opportunities for children with ID to learn group skills, which they often lack. Music circumvents challenges associated with verbal communication and accesses various nonverbal means of communication. The structure of music provides security and a degree of predictability, thus reducing anxiety. Children can contribute to a musical experience on many levels, and the gratification from success leads to self-esteem. Finally, children *need* the aesthetic sensory experience of music, because it makes them more fully human (Gaston, 1968, pp. 50–52).

Music therapists should be ready to adjust the methods presented in the following sections according to their assessment of the needs and skills of the clients with whom they are working. Additionally, music therapists need to be cognizant of the age-appropriateness of any and all music therapy experiences used with adolescents. It is important for adolescents to feel a part of their peer group, and this is particularly difficult for adolescents whose cognitive and adaptive behaviors are significantly below that of their peers. The following sections of this chapter focus on the four main methods used in music therapy: re-creative, receptive, improvisation, and composition. The methods are prioritized according to their suitability, given common needs and goals for these clients.

Overview of Methods and Procedures

Re-creative Music Therapy

- Picture Songs: Clients sing precomposed songs while using pictures to support concept development.
- Instrumental Play-Songs: consist of musical pieces with accompaniment and assigned instruments for clients to play parts.
- Music Ensembles: Clients are active participants in groups that learn and perform musical pieces that may consist of singing and instrument playing.
- Adaptive Music Lessons: a form of individual music therapy where the music lesson format (most commonly using voice, piano, or guitar) is used to accomplish therapeutic goals such as sequencing ability, self-awareness, and self-regulation.
- Developmental Speech and Language Training through Music: the systematic use of musical cues within speech-language lessons to address common goals related to speech production, intelligibility, and communication skills.

Receptive Music Therapy

- Action Listening: using recorded or live music to cue specific behaviors such as gross or fine motor movements, verbal responses, or activities of daily living.
- Contingent Music Listening: Music is played when a client demonstrates a desired behavior and is removed when the behavior is not present.

Improvisational Music Therapy

- Nonreferential Group Improvisation: Group members improvise music, usually on instruments, using nonreferential experiences such as "call and response" or imitation for the purposes of establishing greater communication, self-awareness, or cooperation.
- Referential Improvisation: Clients participate in improvised music structured around a nonmusical theme or idea using musical concepts of rhythm, dynamics, and tonality.

Compositional Music Therapy

- Group Songwriting: occurs when changes are made to some or all of the lyrics and/or music of an existing song, or when a new song is written in its entirety.
- Sound Poem: The client creates musical sounds in response to a poem, using the rhythm and rhyme of the words as a guide.

Guidelines for Re-creative Music Therapy

In re-creative methods, clients learn, perform or reproduce any kind of musical form. This method also includes any structured music activities or games wherein clients have a specifically designated role (Bruscia, 1998, pp. 117–118). Re-creative methods focus on goals such as sensorimotor skills, adaptive behavior, reality orientation, role behaviors, and cooperation, because these are basic requirements for singing or playing precomposed music (Bruscia, 1991, p. 7). Many of these, especially adaptive behavior, are primary goal areas for children and adolescents with mild and moderate intellectual disability. Many key developments in the practice of music therapy with children with intellectual disabilities involved re-creative music therapy (Nordoff & Robbins, 1971; Alvin, 1976).

Picture Songs

Overview. Picture songs involve singing a song while using pictures (often laminated) to display a concept. Picture songs are a group experience and are most often used in a classroom or small group setting. They are indicated for younger children with intellectual disabilities. The primary goals for picture songs are academic: to improve sight recognition, to develop prereading skills, to develop premath skills, etc. Specific goals will depend heavily on the verbal content and structure of the song. Behavioral goals, especially impulse control and appropriate group behavior (e.g., taking turns), may serve as secondary objectives in this method. Picture songs are on the augmentative level of music therapy, because the music therapist usually consults with a classroom teacher or other professional (e.g., speech therapist) and augments their work. In some cases, the music therapist may develop songs for other professionals to use in the absence of the music therapist to practice and reinforce skills gained. In these cases, the activity moves to the auxiliary level. There are no contraindications for using this method. However, blind children will benefit less from visually oriented experiences like this. Skilled music therapists can adapt the experience to incorporate other sensory stimuli, such as touch or smell.

Preparation. Preparation requires familiarity with the lessons and learning goals of the classroom, and selecting a song that supports these. Picture songs will almost always have a component of visual identification in the experience. They may involve visual materials for the children to identify or manipulate within the context of the musical experience. Some picture songs involve laminated images on a board or a folder that are distributed to or displayed by the therapist for children to point to or move from one place to another. Other songs add small pictures that can be attached (using Velcro, etc.) to a board or folder.

Many songs consist of verses with minor differences from one verse to the next. The main topic or teaching concept of the picture song is often embedded into the verses. These topics often include goals to make associations, discriminate, categorize, or sequence information. Many times, the themes within the songs include academic concepts, support behavioral objectives, and facilitate development of cognitive skills. For example, if the goal is to facilitate understanding of animals and their associated sounds, each verse may focus on a different animal. During each verse, a different animal picture is presented for the child to move from one location to another specified spot such as a larger laminated board depicting a farm scene. One such example is the song "One Wide River to Cross," which tells the story of odd pairs of animals being brought onto Noah's ark and offers fun and stimulating opportunities, especially for young children. Many such songs can be found at Prelude Music Therapy (preludemusictherapy.com), which has well-organized and creative visual aid kits.

In another example, verses may focus on the building of a sequence of steps to complete a life skill such as counting, tying a shoe, crossing the street, etc. Other traditional or children's songs involve sequencing, such as "There's a Hole in the Bucket." This song is about a problem, and each verse of this song presents a short lesson in problem-solving and cooperation, along with a dose of humor. Music therapists can easily find similar "problems" or challenges that children face, conduct a task analysis, and write a song that includes verses for each step.

Preparation of the environment is likely minimal, as this experience typically occurs in a classroom or other room familiar to the children. The children should be located so that they can easily see the music therapist.

What to observe. During picture songs, music therapists observe whether children follow directions, receptively identify pictures (i.e., point), expressively label pictures (i.e., give a verbal response), and match, categorize, or sequence objects. Because this experience primarily focuses on pre-academic and academic skills, the music therapist needs to know whether the children are making progress toward the academic goals in place, such as identifying familiar objects or animals, recognizing sight words, or sequencing, as well as how progress is documented and mastery of concepts is determined.

Procedures. Assume that this session is the first time the music therapist introduces a new picture song. Having prepared the visual materials, the music therapist considers whether to introduce the visual or musical materials first. A few things to take into consideration include the complexity of the song, the distractibility of the children, and their relationship to the therapist. Most children will be distracted if the visual materials are presented first, so in most cases, it is preferable to introduce the song (or at least part of it) first, and then introduce the visual materials. In this way, the music supports the visuals. If the visual materials are essential in helping the children learn the song, then consider introducing them first.

Lead the children in the song using the visual aids. Depending on the song, they may be asked to identify body parts, items of clothing, animals, foods, etc. The visual aids should support and not distract from this process. For example, any visuals given to children should be relatively simple and easy to hold. If the song asks them to place objects on a board, match similar objects, etc., teach the children how to do this. Expect some "competition" for prized objects; ignoring minor problem behaviors may extinguish them. While leading picture songs, the music therapist may use an accompanying instrument (e.g., guitar), but the primary focus should be on helping the children participate. When children become more familiar with the materials, they may become more independent.

Adaptations. Picture songs are illimitably adaptable, because they depend on the creativity of the music therapist and the repertoire of songs that can be adapted for appropriate use. Instead, it may be more useful to discuss different types of picture songs. Prelude Music Therapy's Visual Aid Kits (Coleman & Brunk, 2001) include picture songs with directions (e.g., point to this item of clothing), categories to identify (e.g., modes of transportation), and items to match and put in place on a board or folder (e.g., barnyard animals). Other adaptations might include pieces of a puzzle or puppets. In all cases, the experience should support and enrich learning goals.

Instrumental Play-Songs

Overview. Instrumental play-songs consist of musical pieces with accompaniment and parts for instruments. The music therapist typically provides the accompaniment, with instrumental parts assigned to members of the group. Group members may rely on cues from the music therapist or may read modified music notation, depending on skill levels. Instrumental play-songs have been used with children with intellectual disabilities since the early days of music therapy (Gaston, 1968; Nordoff & Robbins, 1971). Many examples are found in Levin and Levin (1998, 2004, 2005, 2006), Ritholz and Robbins (1999, 2003), and Robbins and Robbins (1980). They are indicated for children who have at least rudimentary group skills (e.g., taking turns, basic impulse control) and adequate motor skills (both fine and gross). Goals include improving social skills, behavioral skills such as improving impulse control and self-regulation, motor skills (fine and gross), enhancing self-confidence, and, in some cases, improving academic skills. Instrumental play-songs are on the augmentative or intensive level, depending on how they are practiced. No contraindications are known, beyond an absence of group skills.

Preparation. Instrumental play-songs can be the focus of part of a session or of a whole session. Play-songs, in this case, refer to any song or piece that involves instruments. Music therapists can also arrange existing pieces for small groups with relative ease. This is a creative way to incorporate music that clients like, but which may not yet be published. Most songs of this type use percussion instruments.

Prepare for the session by learning the music that is to be used. Important questions include:

- Is there an accompanying instrument? If so, who leads the group?
- Will the players read notated music or rely on cues from the music therapist?
    - Is the music notation simple enough for the clients to read it? If not, can it be adapted?
    - Can the music therapist provide cues from the keyboard, guitar, or other accompanying instrument?
- What instruments will the group members play?
    - Do the group members have adequate impulse control? If not, can you work to improve this skill?
    - Do the group members have adequate fine motor skills? For example, can they hold the drumstick effectively with a palmar grasp? Can they use a pincer grasp to hold a small mallet?
- How complicated are the parts that group members will play?

What to observe. During instrumental play-songs, observe group members' skills and performance using instruments. Are they able to manipulate instruments adequately? Are they able to play when cued? Do they adjust their playing appropriately? Observe group dynamics as well: Are the group members working well together? Pay attention to how individual members contribute to the group sound: Are they part of the group, or do they stand out in some way? Observe how flexible group members are. Sometimes children can become perseverative with their music, and this repetitive, inflexible playing can cause problems in group music experiences. Overall, what needs to change in order to improve the music experience?

Procedures. The first time the group encounters the piece, be sure to introduce it to the group, possibly by playing a recording (if available), teaching the song if it includes lyrics (some do), or playing it through on a keyboard.

Decide which group members play which instruments. This will depend to a certain degree on the skills required to play the instrument. If skills need rehearsing, see this as an opportunity to extend the work of music therapy. For example, if one part requires the player to play a drum for four beats, and then rest for four beats, the player must be able to (a) hold a drumstick, (b) use appropriate gross motor skills to strike the drum, (c) remember to play four (and only four) beats, and (d) maintain tempo during the rests while not playing (that is, internalize the beat). Each of these subskills is worth spending time on for some children.

Teach the parts of the song that involve all group members, then teach individual or small-group sections. Little by little, assemble the piece, taking care to avoid boredom. Here, excursions to other music experiences can be helpful. For example, take a break and do some movement to music.

Ideally, group members should all learn to play all parts, if possible, because different parts require different skills (e.g., waiting long times between cues, playing repetitive patterns, listening closely for auditory cues). The session, like most sessions, may run better if the music therapist alternates between focused work and more leisurely experiences.

Many client groups enjoy performing instrumental play-songs at school events such as seasonal concerts and graduations. For example, the author worked with a group of young children to perform a simple song with bells during a preschool graduation. In weeks of low-intensity preparation, the children (all of whom had mild intellectual disabilities) developed the motor skills and emotional stability in order to perform this at this event. If a performance is part of the process, the music therapist should take into account the many distractions that will inevitably occur. The focus of therapy may shift toward maintaining focus on a motor task in differing conditions.

Adaptations. Adaptations will be based on the specifics of different play-songs, as well as the abilities of the group. In general, adaptations can be made in the format of the experience, as well as within the difficulty of the rhythms or melodies performed. For example, having all children play the same instrument in unison reduces distraction; later, the music therapist can add in other parts to play simultaneously. Some play-songs use notation that can be read by children with basic reading skills, while others require more intensive cuing on the part of the therapist. In all cases, the music therapist needs to adapt the experience to the needs and skills of the clients. In another adaptation, clients may be involved in basic steps of arranging existing music for an instrumental play-song; in this case, the experience includes a compositional element.

Music Ensembles

Overview. Here, music therapy clients are active members in ensembles such as a rock band, chorus, drum corps, concert band, etc. The goals of a regular music group include experiencing pleasure, developing self-confidence, improving hand-eye coordination, mastering music skills, and improving social skills. Music ensembles are a common leisure activity for many people in communities, and acclimating children and adolescents to participating in them is a valuable contribution to their integration in broader society. Schalkwijk (1994, pp. 14–17) has described the benefits and possible structures of this type of music experience. Music ensembles are indicated for children and adolescents who are capable of working together as a group; this includes most individuals with mild (and many with moderate) intellectual disability. No contraindications, per se, exist for participation in music ensembles. However, members of a treatment team may determine that individual clients are not suited for being in an ensemble, e.g., because of perseverative musical behavior (e.g., spinning cymbals or tapping on drums) that would interfere with the music-making within the group. Being in a music ensemble is on the auxiliary level of practice.

Preparation. Some versions of this music experience do not require the specific skills that a music therapist brings. The person leading the session prepares by becoming familiar with the strengths and needs of the individuals who participate and by learning appropriate music to practice with members of the group. In some cases, musical roles will be assigned to individual members ahead of time. For example, in a rock band, the leader or music therapist may decide to assign specific instruments to individual group members, based on their skills. In other cases, the group members themselves may decide. In larger ensembles, such as a marching band, children or adolescents may choose their own instruments, depending on their strengths and interests, and in some cases, on the needs of the group. It is not uncommon for an adolescent with mild intellectual disability to be a member of a school performing group.

Preparation of the environment will vary substantially, depending on the type of group. A chorus should have chairs placed so that members can see the conductor and possibly each other. A rock band requires an open stage so that members can move around as needed, and instruments, amps, etc., set up to facilitate communication among members.

What to observe. In any ensemble, the focus is primarily on learning and preparing music: what parts are working and what parts are not. Thus, the leader or music therapist needs to be able to identify musical problem areas as they occur, such as balance, tempo, tuning, etc., and work with group members to correct problems that arise. This is a long-term process and will likely involve helping members learn to recognize when they are having a problem musically. This in itself is a valuable goal.

Procedures. Sessions for music ensembles will be conducted more like a rehearsal than a traditional music therapy session, because the primary objectives are musical rather than therapeutic. Rehearsal styles will vary, depending on the type of ensemble. However, the music therapist or leader should take the varying needs of members into consideration. For example, a chorus teacher may pair a child with intellectual disability with a "buddy" who helps during rehearsals.

Adaptations. It is impossible to list all possible adaptations. Higher-functioning children in music ensembles may function in a very nonrestrictive environment, while some children or adolescents may need more direct 1:1 attention. In this light, "adaptations" represent a spectrum of attention required by clients in music ensembles.

Adaptive Music Lessons

Overview. Adaptive music lessons are a form of individual music therapy, and consist of private lessons on voice or an instrument, adapted to the needs and goals of a child or adolescent with a disability. As such, they are indicated for clients who need individual therapy. This approach is common in community music schools, which frequently offer private lessons to students with disabilities of various kinds. Adaptive music lessons address a broad variety of goals, but therapeutic goals are primary, while music learning is secondary. Primary goals include self-awareness, cognitive skills (i.e., sequencing, divided attention), development of leisure skills, and improving frustration tolerance. Other goals include improving motor skills (i.e., fine motor control, eye-hand coordination, etc.), enhancing social skills, and increasing self-esteem. Adaptive music lessons are theoretically available on all instruments, but seem to be most common on voice, piano, guitar, and drums. Adaptive music lessons are on the augmentative level of music therapy. No contraindications are known for adaptive music lessons.

Preparation. Sessions take the form of individual music lessons, adapted to the preferences and strengths of the student. In some cases, the music therapist may be asked to help the child select an instrument. Here, an initial assessment is very valuable. In particular, does the child have good fine motor skills? Does the child have good oral motor skills and breath support (for voice and wind instruments)? On the other hand, many students (and parents) come to music lessons with an instrument already picked out. The sensitive music therapist can assess how realistic the choice of instrument is and advise the family accordingly. For example, an instrument like violin, while very popular, requires strong fine motor skills and has a high frustration level at the beginning. In many cases, an instrument that provides more immediate positive feedback is preferable. The music therapist should use quality music education materials (e.g., method books) and information from the assessment of the client to develop and adjust the student's curriculum. The environment will likely be the same as a music studio, with some adaptations as necessary. For example, the music therapist may need to provide adaptive supports for larger instruments (e.g., cello, trombone). Some children (irrespective of disability!) need to alternate between focused work and more diversionary experiences.

What to observe. Observe the student's skill and performance level during each aspect of the lesson. Regular lessons are an opportunity to conduct ongoing assessment. Evaluate levels of frustration, self-awareness, openness to correction, physical endurance, listening skills, etc. If possible, learn how much time children are spending on music outside of the lessons. Children who are naturally attracted to music may wish to be part of an ensemble, and music may become a valuable part of their lives. In lessons, when children are at the edge of their frustration tolerance, move on to something simpler and familiar. Be sure to work at the threshold between areas of mastery and areas that are less familiar, a practice that is valuable with most young learners.

Procedures. Adaptive music lessons are conducted similarly to most standard music lessons, but music therapists adapt the procedures according to the needs of the student. Remember that while music learning lays the foundation for accomplishing therapeutic aims, learning itself is secondary to these. As with standard music lessons, spend time with warm-ups, familiar materials, technical exercises, and new materials. These procedures hold true for both instrumental and vocal lessons, but different types of instruments challenge students in different ways. For example, string instruments require more finely tuned fine motor skills and auditory discrimination abilities than brass instruments, while all wind instruments require more oral-motor skills than strings. Vocal lessons focus more on expressive language production than instrumental lessons.

Adaptations. Adaptive music lessons are by their nature an adaptation. Specific examples of adaptations might include using adaptive tools (drum holders, larger picks, etc.) to help students with motor challenges play instruments, blocking holes on woodwind instruments (e.g., clarinet) to make fingering easier, using tape and other visual signals on string instruments, and using EZ-chord (or similar tools) for guitar. Further, simplified notation systems are helpful to children with limited or basic music reading skills.

Music Therapy in Special Education

Overview. Music therapy in special education (Bruscia, 1998, pp. 182–183) represents a broad category of practices, all generally focused on the use of music in special education settings to help students (clients) gain nonmusical knowledge and skills that are important for their development. It is indicated for clients who have developmental challenges that respond well to musical intervention, and is appropriate for self-contained classrooms or groups that are homogenous in developmental needs (Bruscia, 1988, p. 182). No general contraindications exist for music therapy in special education; specific contraindications may exist for certain approaches. For example, some clients with very poor motor skills may not be suited for instrumental work, but would benefit from vocal work. However, some apparent contraindications are actually areas that benefit from focus. Goals include improving functioning in any area, but especially in the areas of social skills, communication skills, cognitive skills, and motor skills. While Bruscia categorizes this as music therapy, Schalkwijk (1994, pp. 17–25) uses the term "remedial music-making" to describe a similar practice, but excludes it from his definition of music therapy. Schalkwijk also categorizes a great deal of the classical music therapy literature (Alvin, Nordoff and Robbins, Lecourt, etc.) as "remedial music-making." Music therapy in special education is practiced on the augmentative level.

Preparation. Begin preparation by selecting and learning music that is appropriate for the group. The environment should be conducive to working musically with a group; it should include all musical instruments (if any), and probably some other instruments to explore options. It should include seating that facilitates successful participation.

What to observe. When doing music therapy in special education, observe the students for mastery of the skills required to successfully make the music. For example, clients asked to play a xylophone should have adequate visual and fine/gross motor skills to be able to play the correct notes. Clients who are singing should be able to recognize and understand spoken words. It is important to observe client behavior (both individual and group), because the dynamics in a group affect the success of the experience for the children. For example, children who are withdrawn may need special attention to reach their potential. Other children may exhibit behaviors that need shaping. It is wise to use behavioral techniques wisely, because it is likely that teachers and others use these. In special education settings, consistency may be an important factor.

Procedures. Music therapy in special education is a spectrum of different experiences; different procedures will emerge for specific versions. In general, start with some form of opening and preparation to work. This may be a "hello song" and "warm-up," or it may be a series of exercises to introduce and practice specific skills, e.g., following gestures made by the conductor or leader. It is a good idea to establish a predictable pattern.

Introduce new materials step by step, making sure that clients have mastered individual sections, parts, or voices before moving on. While working, be aware of the amount of time and effort spent on a particular section or piece. Remember that in general, children and adolescents with mild or moderate intellectual disability have less patience and experience more frustration than other children. Alternating between focused work and other types of more relaxed experiences is suggested in order to avoid frustration and boredom.

Adaptations. The practices of music therapy in special education are similar in some ways to the group work of Nordoff and Robbins (1971, 1977), but Bruscia (1998, p. 1989) categorizes these practices as "developmental music therapy," placing it on the intensive level because of its broad concern for various therapeutic needs of the client (1998, p. 189). When the practices shift to this broader approach, the music therapist takes more of the client's personal history into account, and the goals may be broader, moving into areas of personality development and self-fulfillment. The practice of music therapy in special education may include performance, which would necessitate some adaptations to prepare students for the pressure of a performance setting. It is entirely possible that children with mild intellectual disability may enjoy performing.

Developmental Speech and Language Training through Music

Overview. Developmental Speech and Language Training through Music (DSLM) (LaGasse, 2011; Lim, 2011) is a music therapy practice designed to help children (typically younger children) develop speech and language. It uses cues within music (e.g., a regular tempo) to prompt children to use expressive language. DSLM was originally developed for children on the autistic spectrum, but is also used to help children with mild and moderate intellectual disability, because speech and language problems are also common for these children. While DSLM is a scientific (that is, standardized) approach, music therapists adjust it to the individualized goals of the clients they serve. Typical goals include improving speech production and intelligibility. DSLM is on the augmentative level of therapy. No contraindications are known, except possibly for individuals with profound deafness.

Preparation. Developmental Speech and Language Training through Music (DSLM) is an example of a technique codified by practitioners of Neurologic Music Therapy (NMT). Neurologic Music Therapy is defined as "the therapeutic application of music to cognitive, sensory, and motor dysfunctions due to neurological disease of the human nervous system (Thaut, 2005, p. 126). Like all NMT techniques, DSLM involves a thorough assessment and planning process. The music therapist should prepare by reviewing the client assessment and relevant scientific literature, from any and all relevant fields (speech therapy, etc.).

Be aware of the sequence of sound development in children. For example, consonants such as /p/, /b/, and /n/ are typically among the earliest to develop in most children, but /k/ and /d/ develop later, /s/ and /z/ still later, and finally (in most cases), more complex consonants such as /j/ and /th/ (Lehr, 2000). Speech/language pathologists are typically excellent resources for this information.

The therapist should develop a series of musical interventions specific to the goals of the client. For example, if a client needs to improve production of initial consonants in words, such as /b/, the music therapist should create songs that cue and require that sound. If the client needs to learn to ask "w" questions (what, who, where, etc.), the therapist should create music experiences that require the client to form questions. DSLM often incorporates a metronome as a regular, predictable cue; this should be present in the session. Ideally, everything in the session room should contribute to (and not distract from) the focused work on communication.

What to observe. During the music experiences, observe the client's performance on tasks, as well as affective and behavioral responses. This practice is driven by data; thus, it is of prime importance to observe carefully and collect data on progress toward goals and objectives. Affective and behavioral responses are important for helping the music therapist decide the next steps of intervention. For example, if a child's affect changes negatively, the music therapist should consider whether or not to change course during the session.

Procedures. The procedures involved in DSLM are specific to the clients, but the same theoretical basis underlies them all. The procedures involve embedding a desired response into an exercise and pairing this exercise with a musical stimulus. This stimulus, which may include a metronome to provide a temporal cue, helps the client produce the desired response. For example, if a child has a series of target words to develop (a common goal), the music therapist may incorporate them at predictable times in a song (e.g., at the end of a phrase). Over time, the cues fade and the client begins to take on more control of her speech and language production. Sessions may include greetings and good-byes, which focus less on the specifics of speech and language production, but the primary focus of the work is speech and language. The session may include breaks from focused work, where the client is allowed to explore other musical experiences. These breaks can be seen as an integral part of the flow of DSLM sessions.

Adaptations. Because DSLM is a standardized procedure, most adaptations are based on the results of the assessment of a particular child (client). Sometimes DSLM uses nonmusical elements, such as picture communication systems (Lim, 2007). This underscores similarities between DSLM and other practices described here and elsewhere (e.g., "picture songs.").

Guidelines for Receptive Music Therapy

In receptive methods, clients listen to music and respond in some way: silently, verbally, or in some other modality (i.e., by making art, moving, etc.). The music used in receptive experiences may be live or recorded improvisations or performances, and may be of any type. Receptive experiences for children and adolescents with mild or moderate intellectual disability focus on goals such as improving receptive language skills, improving physical coordination, developing or improving auditory-motor skills, and changing desirable or undesirable behaviors.

Action Listening

Overview. Action Listening consists of using recorded or live music (with or without lyrics) to cue specific behaviors, such as gross or fine motor movements (e.g., lifting one foot), verbal responses (e.g., saying hello), or activities of daily living (e.g., brushing teeth) (Bruscia, 1998, p. 123). Thus, children should be able to hear and have at least basic receptive language skills or the ability to differentiate among different sounds. Children who have not yet developed these skills can benefit from this experience by following cues from the therapist or of other children. As with most behavioral techniques, no contraindications exist for an activity of this type, except possibly for children with severe sensory integration or sensory processing challenges. In these cases, the music therapist would consider whether using music as a cue is likely to be effective at helping the client reach the desired behavioral response. Note that in Action Listening, the music only cues—and does not structure—the response of the client.

Goals of Action Listening include improving receptive and expressive language skills, improving self-care, and following directions. This type of music therapy experience is typically at the augmentative level of therapy.

Preparation. Prepare by examining the behavior that the music should cue. How long should the behavior last? How many times should the behavior occur? How natural is it for the child(ren) with whom you are working? Choose music to cue the desired behavior.

Therapists who are well versed in the musical details and/or lyrics of the music can easily adapt to unpredictable changes in a group of children, such as interactions between children, external distractions, and mood changes. How long is the music? What does it contain? Are there sections? Is it easy to follow? Is there a strong melody or rhythm? Typically, the music will include verbal cues, but sometimes, musical features (e.g., a change in tempo) may also serve as cues. Be very familiar with the music so you can demonstrate it and the desired behavior in context. For example, if the desired behavior is for a child to identify body parts by touching them, you might choose the song "Over My Head" (traditional) and plan for the child to point to the head, feet, heart, and eyes, as the verses progress.

Set up the room so that all members can hear the music equally well, and ideally see each other. Consider placing children with behavior problems close to the therapist. What types of behavior response does the experience include? If members will be walking or dancing, consider whether chairs are appropriate. If members will not be moving around (i.e., sitting or standing only), consider the benefits of chairs: They often serve as place markers and provide physical reminders of one's space.

If using a recording, be familiar with the technology available and have it ready (test it!) before the session. Technological challenges are common, but proper preparation can help prevent many issues from arising. For example, are you using an MP3 player? Where are the speakers and how does the MP3 player attach to them? Are batteries charged?

What to observe. In this experience, observe first of all how children respond to the presentation of music. Can they focus their attention well enough to follow the music? Observe whether they respond predictably with the desired behavioral response. Observe language responses, especially if you change the lyrics: Do children indicate that they understand the lyrics? Observe physical coordination: Are clients responding when the music cues them? Does this matter for the purposes of this experience? Many children will be able to approximate a movement and obtain just as much benefit. Observe how children respond to one another in a group: Do children pick up on cues from their peers? Do they imitate?

Procedures. This experience may be part of a session or a whole session. Choose music that is age-appropriate for the group members. The music should have some elements (lyrics, timbre, instruments) that cue or give direction. When listening to the music, the children follow the cues in the words, music, or both. A very familiar example of a song used in this type of experience is the "Hokey Pokey." In this example, the lyrics tell the listeners to put their legs, arms, head, and so forth into the center of the circle. Of course, songs with lyrics may also elicit verbal and other types of responses.

Music without lyrics calls on a different set of skills from children, such as identifying and responding to changes in music. Music with obvious contrasts is particularly appropriate. For example, instrumental music often includes changes of mood, tempo, key, instrumentation, etc. Music therapists who use live music can use all the elements of music at their disposal to cue movements, including lyrics.

This activity is likely more appropriate for younger children than for older children or adolescents, but can be adapted for any age. For example, elements of this activity might help teenagers with cognitive impairments participate in certain types of performance groups, such as show choirs.

Depending on the group's familiarity with the music, the therapist may wish to play the music first and ask group members to listen closely for cues built into the song or music. Children may listen multiple times and may wish to practice identifying the cues and rehearsing their responses to them. Higher-functioning or older children may want to develop their own responses to cues in the music, depending on the focus of the experience. The therapist should move from simpler to more difficult responses in this experience; like all children, children with intellectual disability need time to learn sequences.

Adaptations. In one adaptation, eurythmic listening, the music is used to structure the response from the children, rather than simply cuing it. Here, the goals may include promoting physical coordination, improving physical endurance, increasing physical activity, and improving impulse control. Eurythmic listening may more commonly use recorded music, in which case the music therapist should be very familiar with the music chosen. Familiarity allows the music therapist to adapt easily to unpredictable changes in a group of children, such as interactions between children, external distractions, and mood changes.

Adaptations may be required for children who are profoundly deaf or developmentally unable to participate in group activities. Children who are profoundly deaf may still benefit from a modification of this experience, and children who do not yet have adequate group skills may benefit from the experience in an individual setting. Even children with sensory processing challenges could benefit if the steps are broken down even further.

Contingent Music Listening

Overview. Contingent music listening, in which music is played when a client performs a desired behavior, is a classic example of behavioral music therapy. It is indicated for children or adolescents for whom listening to preferred music is a clearly identified reinforcement for desired behavior. Few contraindications are imaginable for contingent music listening or for any behavioral music therapy experiences. One might think about children who, when they hear music, behave in an undesirable way, but with appropriate behavioral techniques and adequate time, a music therapist could conceivably extinguish these negative behaviors and replace them with more desirable ones. However, it is questionable whether this approach is the most effective in terms of effort and cost. The goal of contingent music listening is to increase desirable behavior or to reduce less desirable behavior. Synonyms such as "adaptive behavior" are also commonly used.

Preparation. Because contingent listening is a broad category of experiences, music therapists must operate from behavioral techniques, that is, by conducting a thorough analysis of the client(s) and the environment, including effective reinforcers, distractors, and other features. The environment should be conducive to attaining the stated outcomes of therapy, and the therapist should choose music that is proven to be an effective behavioral motivator for the client(s).

What to observe. Primarily, the therapist should closely observe the behavior of the client. Particular behaviors to be observed will differ from one client to the next, but first, the therapist needs to observe whether the client is exhibiting the behavior which is required to "earn" music listening, and second, whether the music listening (the "contingency") continues to have the desired behavioral outcome. For example, when working to increase on-task behavior of a child in a classroom setting, the music therapist should observe the level of on-task behavior, to determine if the client has reached the desired level, and then, after providing the reinforcer (music), observe the same behavior to see if the reinforcer is having the desired effect of increasing that on-task behavior.

Procedures. As mentioned above, procedures will vary substantially from one client or client group to another, because contingent music listening is a highly adaptable behavioral technique. The main principle is that listening to music serves as a reinforcer for the client(s). All details, including whether this experience occurs in the context of a traditional music therapy "session," depend on the context in which the desired behavior is to occur.

In a traditional music therapy setting, contingent music listening might be used to help children or adolescents of any age to improve social behaviors. The music therapist, after determining which music is a most effective reward, engages with clients in a music therapy session, carefully measuring the amount of social behavior that the clients are exhibiting. At the end of the session, or at the time agreed upon with the clients, the clients are allowed to listen to their preferred music. The music therapist should be familiar with behavioral principles such as different reinforcement schedules.

In a slightly different example, contingent music listening was used to reinforce the desired behavior of following directions during adaptive piano lessons for a child with mild to moderate intellectual disability (Jorgenson, 1974). When the client followed directions and did not exhibit stereotypical behaviors (e.g., slapping legs), he earned 30-second segments of time that he could use for listening to music he enjoyed.

In an example from a work setting (Bellamy & Sonntag, 1973), contingent music served to reinforce a manual task (stuffing envelopes) that students with intellectual disability were asked to complete. In this example, the therapist played student-preferred music when a student successfully completed the task of stuffing an envelope.

Adaptations. Contingent music listening is adaptable in myriad ways, as long as the music listening is contingent in some way upon demonstration or presence of a desired behavior. It is conceivable that for some clients, playing music is a stronger reinforcer than listening to music. In this case, this experience would likely be categorized as re-creative.

Instead of specific adaptations, the music therapist may think about adaptations of the *role* of music therapist in this type of experience. In some cases, the music therapist is in a primary role, leading a traditional session and taking observational data. In other cases, the music therapist may only be in an auxiliary role. These differences will depend on and influence the behavioral plan developed for the client.

Guidelines for Improvisational Music Therapy

In improvisational methods, clients make up music extemporaneously. Clients may play or sing, and may create melody, rhythm, spontaneous song, or instrumental music. Clients may improvise alone, in a duet, or in a group; the therapist may improvise as well, or not. Clients may use any musical resources within their capabilities, including voice, instruments, body percussion, etc. The therapist typically helps by providing instructions and demonstrations, offering musical examples or structures as a basis for the improvisation, providing accompaniment, or presenting nonmusical ideas to stimulate improvising (Bruscia, 1998, p. 116). Improvisational experiences for children and adolescents with mild or moderate intellectual disability focus on goal areas such as verbal and nonverbal communication, sensory skills, sensory-motor skills, self-awareness, and self-esteem.

Nonreferential Group Improvisations

Overview. In nonreferential group improvisations, clients (and usually therapists) improvise music together on instruments, interacting mostly through music. Instead of organizing improvisations around some nonmusical idea (e.g., "feelings"), the therapist provides some degree of musical structure for clients. For example, the music therapist may provide a harmonic structure while clients play melodic instruments. In another example, she may create a rhythmic ostinato while clients take turns improvising on percussion instruments. These types of improvisations are prominent in both Nordoff-Robbins and Orff music therapy practices. They are indicated for children who have any number of challenges, including communication, physical coordination, self-awareness, and behavioral problems. Children should be able to manipulate instruments physically. No contraindications are known, but children and adolescents who are unable to function in groups may need to start with individual sessions before being in a group.

Goals for nonreferential group improvisations include improving nonverbal communication skills, eye-hand coordination, and sensory-motor skills (Harris, 1977); developing self-confidence (Robbins & Robbins, 1991); and improving social skills (Nordoff & Robbins, 1971). Instrumental improvisations can occur on different levels of therapy, depending to a certain degree on whether they occur in individual sessions, dyads, or groups.

Preparation. The practice of improvisation of this type requires substantial training and education. Because of the prominence of music and musical materials in nonreferential improvisations, music therapists must be skilled in using a broad array of musical materials, from traditional styles to modern genres.

Prepare by selecting instruments for the client(s) and therapist(s). The therapist will likely need an instrument to lead from, commonly piano or guitar, but may choose another instrument instead. For clients, choose instruments that the clients will be able to play, including percussion and some simplified wind or string instruments if desired. This will depend to a large degree on the clients and their abilities and interests.

The therapy room should have enough room for client(s) and therapist to play the instruments. Some children may avoid the instruments; for this reason, consider removing extra items from the room that may distract clients. Provide seating for instruments that are played sitting down, but some instruments are best played standing (e.g., some tall drums). For some young children, a chair can provide helpful support, and in some cases, a gentle reminder to stay "on task."

What to observe. During nonreferential instrumental improvisations, the therapist primarily observes how clients interact with music, including music instruments. Do clients indicate any interest in making music? Do clients accept instruments presented to them, or do they pick their own? Do clients play the instruments in a conventional way? Observe what clients do (and do not do) when playing. Observe the relationship of the clients' playing to yours. Observe what happens when clients play alone or with each other without the therapist. Above all, observe the music that clients make and respond to it with clinical musicianship (Cooper, 2010).

Procedures. Improvisations of this type can make up the bulk of a music therapy session or only a part. Have instruments ready when clients enter the room, but possibly out of reach or sight, depending on what the clients need. Model how to play the instruments, if needed, and allow clients to explore making sounds. Show conventional and novel ways to play the instrument, if appropriate (Gardstrom, 2007).

A nonreferential improvisation typically starts with music, rather than with nonmusical ideas. This leaves several options to start, including simply starting to play or asking clients to play in a certain order, at a certain volume or speed, with certain people, or using specific procedures. These are often called *givens*. Because of the wide variety of possible improvisations of this type, a few examples follow.

A group of young children (under five years) with intellectual disability were seated in a circle on the floor and asked just to play one person at a time. The music therapist provided a handheld instrument to one child, who played it briefly and passed it to the next child, etc. The next step involved placing an instrument in front of each child, and asking each child to play alone, then return the instrument to its place. The next step asked the children to hold their own instrument while another child took a turn. These steps were introduced over several sessions and were interspersed with segments of group play and other activities.

A boy in elementary school with moderate intellectual disability came to individual music therapy. The therapist provided a drum and other percussion instruments, while playing the piano herself. The therapist began by observing the boy's manner, movements, etc., as he entered the room, and creating sounds to match her observations or to set the tone of the session. If necessary, she directed the boy (by singing, speaking, or gesture) to play the drum and other instruments available, and the therapist and he played together for an undetermined period of time. Sometimes the client and therapist played, and sometimes they did not. Sometimes the client left the proximity of the therapist and explored other things in the room or simply became distracted, but typically the therapist tried to keep the child engaged in joint music-making.

A group of middle schoolers (i.e., ages 11 to 14) with mild intellectual disability came together for group music therapy weekly. Each had established basic skills on pitched and nonpitched percussion instruments. The music therapist often provided a rhythmic and harmonic structure for group improvisations, while group members improvised rhythms, phrases, etc. Sometimes group improvisations developed into songlike materials, and the group decided to compose a song. This is an example of how the process of improvising can subtly shift into the process of composing.

Adaptations. It is easy to structure nonreferential improvisations like a game, where the play rules or givens function as rules of the game. Children enjoy the excitement of a stop/go game, for example, and in their excitement, lose inhibitions that may have kept them from reaching their potential previously (Nordoff & Robbins, 1971, pp. 75–78). Improvisation experiences of this type are infinitely adaptable. Consult Bruscia (1987) for the many types of givens—both musical and nonmusical—that can be used in the various types of improvisations.

Referential Improvisations

Overview. Themed (referential) improvisations consist of improvised music, structured around a nonmusical theme or idea, sometimes called a "referent." They are indicated for those clients who are able to use language effectively, and who have the cognitive capacity to translate words and thoughts into actions, and vice versa. They challenge clients to translate between two different media, in both directions. On the one hand, clients translate thoughts, concepts, feelings, ideas, etc., into music. On the other, clients are often asked to listen to others' music, and think about its relationship to a concept, idea, etc. In particular, they are indicated for children and adolescents who need to develop their sense of self, establish channels of communication, and develop perceptual and cognitive skills. Goal areas are directly related to these: self-expression, self-awareness and self-esteem, communication skills, sensory (perceptive) skills, and cognitive skills. The goals differ from those of nonreferential improvisations to a certain degree, because clients are asked to connect their thoughts to music and their music to their thoughts.

Preparation. To prepare for referential improvisations, consider the primary goal(s) of the experience. The themes that the music therapist chooses should relate directly to these. For example, if a goal is to improve social skills, then the therapist should consider themes that are relevant to the emotional and social domains, such as feelings and social themes (e.g., "meeting new people"). It is easy to find flash cards that include emotion words on them, and these are useful props for this type of experience.

The session should include a wide enough array of musical instruments to allow for contrast among sounds. Gardstrom (2007) recommends having a mix of instruments played by shaking, striking, and scraping. The therapy room should not include too many distractions, but neither should it be free of other objects, because often objects in the therapy room themselves can stimulate ideas for improvisations.

What to observe. During themed improvisations, observe clients' musical and nonmusical behavior. Do they seem to understand the process? Do they have adequate symbolic thinking to participate meaningfully? In a group, how do the group members interact with one another?

Procedures. Themed (referential) improvisations can take many forms. Perhaps the most common is a basic "round robin," where group members and the therapist take turns (e.g., asking clients in a group to play how they are feeling that day). In some cases, therapists may initiate themed improvisations where all children play together as a group.

Themed improvisations can be simply a part of a session, or the main experience in a music therapy session. In most cases, themed improvisations start with a nonmusical idea, which is then expressed musically in some way. For example, with a group of children, the music therapist may introduce the idea of playing a "storm." Ask the children what they know about storms. Do they start slowly or suddenly? Are they loud or soft, or do they change? Next, ask children to select instruments they want to use to "play a storm." From this point, there are many options; children can enter one by one to create the impression of a storm approaching; they may start all at once to resemble a sudden storm; or they may be given the choice to play as they wish. After playing, the therapist may initiate discussion of the music, but it can also be insightful when group members generate ideas on their own.

Depending on the nonmusical idea chosen and the purpose of the experience, the improvisation may take the form of short individual improvisations, group improvisations of varying lengths, dyad or small-group improvisations, or any combination of these. Depending on the choice of materials provided, this will either be an instrumental, body percussion, or vocal improvisation. For some adolescents, vocal improvisations may not be appropriate, simply because of social expectations among teenagers. However, considering that children with Williams syndrome often enjoy singing (for example), and the history of successful implementation of vocal improvisation with children of many ages (Nordoff & Robbins, 1977), it is important to base decisions like this on a thorough assessment.

Adaptations. Because of the improvisational nature of this experience, adaptations are endless. One "spectrum" of variation is the types of instruments provided and the way they are played. Consider the effect of selecting instruments of varying vs. similar timbres, varying vs. similar means of sound production, etc. Another spectrum would be the types of nonmusical stimuli used to stimulate improvisations. By varying the types of nonmusical stimuli presented to the group, the music therapist can stimulate group members' creativity and self-expression skills. Another spectrum would be the types of interpersonal relationships that clients can explore by playing together. Adaptations here would be related to the goals of therapy and the "referents" chosen. For example, if a music therapist wants to help an adolescent client improve interpersonal skills, she might choose referents that emphasize interpersonal interaction (e.g., "meeting someone for the first time"), and deliberately work in dyads.

GUIDELINES FOR COMPOSITIONAL MUSIC THERAPY

In compositional music therapy experiences, the therapist helps the client to write songs, lyrics, or instrumental music, or to create any kind of musical product (i.e., music videos, playlists, mix tapes, music apps). The client typically engages in the simpler aspects of the experience, while the music therapist takes responsibility for the more challenging musical aspects (Bruscia, 1991, p. 6).

Group Songwriting

Overview. In group songwriting, clients contribute various elements, usually with significant organizational input from the music therapist, to create a song together. Group songwriting is indicated for clients who need to work on making decisions, expressing themselves in words and music, and working together as a group. No contraindications are known for group songwriting, but clients who have few group skills or who have trouble working together with others may be a challenge for the music therapist, and may benefit less from the experience than others. It is a flexible method, but is generally more effective with adolescents than with children of elementary school–age. Goals of group songwriting include improving decision-making skills, increasing group cohesion, and improving verbal skills.

Preparation. Before the session, decide what level of structure the group needs to be successful. Some children and adolescents with intellectual disability need the music therapist to provide the musical structure, to facilitate the positive aesthetic experience that is in itself a motivator. Others enjoy developing the sounds on their own. With computer applications such as GarageBand, it is increasingly easy for people of very diverse skill levels to create their own music.

The environment should contain musical instruments (acoustic, electronic, or both), a means of displaying the song materials visually (white board, projector, chalk board, etc.), and seating. All group members should be able to see the musical and lyric materials presented, and have access to instruments, when appropriate.

What to observe. Primarily, the music therapist should observe the group members for their level of participation. Group songwriting is a group process that results in a product. Both process and product bring benefits for group members. It is particularly important to value the contributions of all members.

Procedures. The process of group songwriting may take more than one session, depending on the group, the session length, etc. Therefore, it is important to keep a record of all materials (musical and lyrical) that the group develops.

Begin with a discussion about the focus of the session: writing a song. Solicit ideas, words, images, etc., for the topic of the song. In some cases, topics will emerge naturally; in others, clients may need prompts such as images, stories, or topic suggestions. Eventually, choose a topic for the song and write it on the board.

After choosing a topic, work with the group to develop ideas and phrases around the topic. For example, if the topic is "vacation," the group may develop phrases like "I'm going to the beach," "My family loves to go on vacation," etc. Depending on what the group develops, the music therapist may group the materials in a meaningful way, e.g., thoughts about vacation, things that happened on vacation, and memories of vacation.

Work with the group to assemble the ideas or phrases into a lyric structure that makes sense. Be sure to seek consensus from group members on all decisions. Add music to the lyrics. During the first stages, the music therapist should be developing musical materials that are age-appropriate, culturally and stylistically relevant, and suitable for the lyric ideas that emerge. For example, rap music represents one of the easiest types of songs, because the main focus is on rhythm, and melody and harmony play a reduced role. With access to technology, the group members can make increasingly complex additions to the music without necessarily having the musical skills to play them. Perform the song, for the group or for others. Recording (audio or video) makes it possible for group members to experience and share their contributions with others.

Adaptations. In a simpler version, the music therapist provides examples of lyrics that the clients can put in order. These lyrics may already have music associated with them, or the music therapist can let the clients select musical materials. This version is possibly better for clients with more limited language skills.

Another version begins with the music therapist introducing the music first and then working with clients to create lyrics that fit the existing music. This is a slightly more difficult process for some clients, because it requires clients to force their ideas into an existing structure, no matter how flexible that structure is. To extend this version and give the clients more ownership of the music, the experience could start with improvisation, so that the clients first create the music, solidify it into a structure (e.g., 12-bar blues), and then create lyrics to fit the structure.

Sound Poem

Overview. In "sound poem" (C. Mercado, personal communication, March 1, 2007), clients set sounds or music to a poem, as opposed to setting the words of a poem to music. It is indicated for clients who are capable of understanding spoken language (written language, optional), who can make basic choices, and who have basic impulse control. No contraindications are known, except possibility the inability to function in a small-group setting. Goals for "sound poem" include improving comprehension of the spoken word, enhancing group skills, and developing creativity. "Sound poem" is on the augmentative level of music therapy practice.

Preparation. Prepare by selecting a poem that is appropriate for the children or adolescents in the group. It should be age-appropriate and of a topic that will hold their attention. Children with intellectual disability often have a complicated relationship with language, because it is typically an area that is difficult for them. For this reason, consider length, complexity, presence of symbolism, etc. In the beginning, a short, familiar poem is a good choice.

Sound poems benefit from contrasting sounds, particularly sounds that the clients can associate to words or phrases in the poem. By providing a broad variety of instruments and sound-makers for the clients, music therapists can stimulate interest in the process and engage clients in the creative process more effectively.

It is a good idea to have a white board or chart handy to notate the parts of the poem and the associated sounds or music.

What to observe. During the creation of a sound poem and its performance, observe to make sure the clients understand the purpose and the process. Do they understand the words you are using? Are they engaging in the creative process? Are they listening to and watching their peers? Are they able to "read" the notation that the music therapist creates on the board? Can they read written language?

Procedures. Start by introducing the poem. Read the poem to the group, and it may be good to provide a printout of the words for clients who can read. Some music therapists may choose to teach the poem (if short enough) to clients. The purpose of this stage is to help the clients become familiar with the meaning and content of the poem.

Next, divide the poem into lines. The purpose of this step is to encourage creativity, so it is a time for clients to think about the words, sounds, associations, and/or meanings of individual lines. The therapist may wish to ask individual clients to create sounds for each line. Alternately, the group can work together to make these decisions. By the end of this step, each line (phrase, etc.) will have one or more sounds associated with it.

Next, rehearse the poem. The purpose of this step is to think about the aesthetics of the sounds, particularly in sequence. Help the group decide whether they like the sequence, whether the sounds make sense and are a "good fit" for the poem, etc. Remind clients that they can make changes, because the process is theirs.

Finally, perform the poem. The purpose of this step is to experience the aesthetic product the group created. If possible, make an audio or video recording of this poem or perform it in front of others (e.g., during a class play). The clients can experience a sense of pride in their work.

Adaptations. Sound poems are very adaptable. Some music therapists engage the group in writing the poem first, starting with a general theme and then asking clients to contribute words, phrases or sentences about that theme. This process engages clients in the creative process even more broadly. Some groups may wish to create a metered sound poem, which could lead to a more "rap"-like product. Others may choose unmetered sounds, or a combination. Other musical elements, such as melody, timbre, or texture, will also have a greater or lesser role, depending on the poem, the wishes of the group members, and other factors. While this experience focuses predominantly on the product (the sound poem), the process of creating the poem is very important to the experience, because it is there where much of the work occurs.

Working with Caregivers

Children and adolescents with intellectual disability have many caregivers, including family members, classroom teachers, and providers of other therapeutic services (e.g., occupational therapists). Some music therapists work in a consultative model to teach caregivers (in particular, teachers and teacher assistants) how to use music within the classroom to support learning. This occurs most commonly by embedding academic (or pre-academic) skills, behavior cues, etc., into songs that are used in the classroom. This is obviously an auxiliary practice, but it can reinforce learning in many settings.

Another type of consultative work occurs when music therapists work with school music teachers to integrate children with special needs into music classes. General music classes are often well suited for children with mild and moderate intellectual disability, especially during elementary school, where these classes provide hands-on music-making experiences and introduce children to basic music-reading skills. The physical coordination that comes from playing basic instruments, the language practice that occurs naturally when singing songs, and the sensory integration of music and movement games all contribute to the general development of children with special needs.

When children have the opportunity to be in performing groups (e.g., chorus, band, orchestra), the work tends to become more focused, and the music therapist may work individually with children or adolescents or consult more closely with the music teacher. Children with intellectual disability benefit potentially from participating in ensembles in many ways, from the fine-motor skills and auditory discrimination skills required to play most instruments, to the visual discrimination skills involved in reading music, to the emotional and social benefits of being an integrated and vital part of a group, especially a group that performs. A music therapist who facilitates such experiences for children and adolescents with intellectual disability (or any handicapping condition) has the potential to make significant impact on these young people's lives.

RESEARCH EVIDENCE

Music therapists have been practicing music therapy and conducting research with children with intellectual disability since the early days of the profession. The first volume of the *Journal of Music Therapy* includes a bibliography of music therapy practices. The section of this bibliography that focuses on intellectual disability (intellectual disability) includes 31 references, an astonishing number at that early date. However, many of the clients or students referenced in this bibliography were likely lower-functioning (e.g., with severe or profound intellectual disability).

Re-creative Music Therapy

In a great deal of writing on re-creative methods with children with mild and moderate intellectual disability, music serves as a reinforcer. Standley (1996) conducted a meta-analysis on the effects of music initiation, interruption, or performance as a contingency for behavior change. Results underscored the effectiveness of music as a reinforcer: Benefits were almost three standard deviations greater than control or baseline conditions, but pairing other stimuli (food, approval, etc.) decreased music's effectiveness as a reinforcer. Interestingly, music served simultaneously as a reinforcer and subject matter. This section includes a selection of published literature on music therapy in its role as a reinforcer.

Jorgenson (1970) used music listening to motivate a nine-year-old child with moderate intellectual disability who exhibited stereotypical behaviors that interfered with his learning. For each segment of time that he followed directions and exhibited no stereotypical behaviors (hitting palms together or on his legs) during his piano lessons, he earned 30 seconds of music listening. This double baseline study indicated improvement in behavior for this child as a result of the behavioral plan.

Four children with moderate intellectual disability, ages eight and nine, participated in a music therapy group designed to improve their social behaviors (Jorgenson & Parnell, 1970). After taking a baseline, the music therapists used points and candy to reinforce behavior that improved group music activities and to decrease behavior that interfered with group music activities. Children with the most points were also allowed to choose a record for the group to listen to, during which they could complete any activity they wished. The program resulted in decrease in all undesirable behaviors and increases in all positive behaviors.

Dileo (1975) studied the use of a token economy with institutionalized children with intellectual disability. The children earned and lost tokens in a group chorus class by showing appropriate and inappropriate behaviors, respectively, and used the tokens to gain access to preferred group and individual activities, such as playing instruments, participating in field trips, or snacks. The token economy effectively increased the rate of appropriate behaviors and reduced the rate of inappropriate behaviors.

Re-creative music experiences also serve as carriers of information to be learned. Music therapists often use songs to teach words and concepts. Bokor (1976) studied the responsiveness of children with intellectual disability to series of musical and spoken letters and notes. Testers used simple letter and note sequences consisting of the vowels a, e, i, o, and u, sung to the major scale. No visual cues were present. Children responded equally well to spoken and musical stimuli. When visual cues or actual objects of focus are used, children may learn concepts better (Hoshizaki, 1983).

Re-creative music experiences may serve as a cue for developing and practicing particular skills. For example, practitioners and researchers in the area of Neurologic Music Therapy (NMT) have developed "Developmental Speech and Language Training through Music" (DSLM). This protocol mimics speech therapy approaches by incorporating aspects of play and interaction, combined with cues for responses within the play experience. LaGasse (2011) described a course of music therapy with a child with Down's syndrome and concomitant moderate intellectual disability who experienced frustration with expressive language, while exhibiting fairly strong receptive language skills. The course of therapy consisted of simple songs that structured and accompanied the interactions between client and therapist. All interventions included a metronome set at a constant tempo as an auditory cue. LaGasse also developed exercises for the client's parents to use at home. Over time, melodic cues were faded and only rhythmically spoken cues remained. After success with this fading, cues external to the client were faded. The therapist taught the client to provide his own motor cues by tapping himself on the leg. At the end of music therapy, the child had substantially improved the volume and intelligibility of his speech. When he was not understood, he used signs or a visual communication system to communicate more consistently. His frustration incidents decreased substantially as well.

Re-creative music experiences also serve as a context in which certain skills are to be learned, often social skills. This is often the case when working with children with intellectual disability in a performance setting. Robbins and Robbins (1991) also used re-creative experiences with an adolescent girl with moderate intellectual disability, brain injury, and emotional instability to develop her sense of self and the ability to communicate her self with the world. In a group project, the client took on a role in a production of a Christmas play, where she developed self-confidence and enjoyed a sense of pride. The changes generalized to school and home, where she was able to socialize with her peers, and she was less sensitive to sudden and loud noises. Humpal (1991) found that children with intellectual disability interacted more with peers in an integrated early childhood music program that incorporated re-creative experiences.

Receptive Music Therapy

Relatively little has been published about receptive music therapy methods with children with intellectual disability. The relative weakness in this area is likely due to several factors. First, receptive music experiences may be more difficult for children with intellectual disability, because they ask the client to listen actively, which is often difficult for children and adolescents with cognitive impairments. Second, receptive experiences do not seem to be a natural match for the educational goals of music therapy with children with intellectual disability. Listening has often been used as a type of reinforcer (see the section on research in re-creative methods), but not as a primary, independent method. Thus, research that includes music as a reinforcer has been organized under the section for the primary music therapy method used. However, foundational research on hearing, music listening preferences, etc., may be of interest.

Like most children, the musical preferences of children with intellectual disability are informed by multiple influences. In the presence of socially influential adults, children with intellectual disability may change their stated music preferences, but these changes are often not maintained in the absence of these adults (Steele, 1967). In other words, when music therapists ask children about their musical preferences, they are probably influencing the results.

The sound level (i.e., loudness) is of concern in almost all music therapy experiences. Children with Down's syndrome, which is typically associated with moderate intellectual disability, are often described as being "good candidates for music therapy," for a variety of reasons. Notably, these children are reported to be more sensitive to sound and to prefer music activities with quiet volume.

Another syndrome associated with moderate intellectual disability is Williams syndrome. Children and adolescents with Williams syndrome often exhibit highly developed musical, verbal, and social skills, with significant deficits in other areas. Individuals with Williams syndrome who listen to music are reported to have fewer problematic externalizing symptoms, such as aggression, than those who do not listen to music.

One relatively common receptive approach to music therapy with children and adolescents with intellectual disability is the Rhythmic Auditory Stimulation (RAS)—the Neurologic (sic) Music Therapy term for listening to music that has rhythm—in this case, music of different speeds. Soraci, Deckner, McDaniel, and Blanton (1982) tested the effects of RAS on the level of stereotypical behaviors exhibited by children with intellectual disabilities (mild-severe). The speed of the recorded music was positively correlated with the rate of stereotypes to a certain point, at which time the correlation reversed. In other words, fast music may overwhelm children's ability to carry out stereotypical behaviors.

Improvisational Music Therapy

The research base on improvisational music therapy with children with mild and moderate intellectual disability is relatively limited, especially in terms of quantitative research. The reason for this seems obvious. At first glance, improvisation does not seem to meet one of the basic requirements of quantitative research: It is difficult to standardize or replicate, a challenge that Aldridge (1996) faced in a study on the effects of creative music therapy on communication skills of children with developmental delays. However, there is much writing on the practice of improvisation with these clients from the early days of published literature in music therapy.

Paul Nordoff and Clive Robbins (1971, 1977) describe their work with many children who would be classified today as having mild or moderate intellectual disability. Their publications include extensive case histories and descriptions of the process of improvising music as therapy. Juliette Alvin, while focusing mostly on her work with children with autism, also wrote of her work with children with intellectual disability (1965, 1976, 1978).

Boxill (1981) describes an improvisational approach to working with a child with a developmental disability. While this child probably had a severe developmental disability, it is nonetheless useful to consider the three phases or strategies Boxill describes: reflection, identification, and our contact song. Each of these is founded on improvisation, and each has its own purpose: laying the groundwork for contact, developing self-awareness, and establishing a relationship.

Gunsberg (1988, 1991) describes "improvised musical play," a strategy to encourage social interaction between young children (i.e., preschoolers) with intellectual disabilities and those without. Children in a classroom where IMP was implemented participated in social interaction for longer periods of time, and these social interactions included larger numbers of children. Notably, IMP accommodated participation by children with widely varying play styles and skills. Children who were higher-functioning (i.e., with mild developmental delay) gravitated toward the more verbal aspects of the experience and were able to follow the "plots" that developed. Lower-functioning children tended to mimic the actions of other children.

Robbins and Robbins (1991) used improvisation with an adolescent girl with moderate intellectual disability, brain injury, and emotional instability to develop her sense of self. In individual music therapy, improvisation helped the client develop trust in the therapists, the music, and herself. The physical activity of improvising at the drum had a profound effect on the client's self-confidence. When she played, she created sounds that normally would frighten and overstimulate her. The act of playing, however, was physically liberating, and the loud sounds she created had no repercussions for her. In fact, the music therapist accepted them and supported them from the piano. The experience of creating music all her own led her to a greater degree of self-confidence.

In more recent years, technology has made it easier to record and analyze improvised music, and, as a result, foundational quantitative research has emerged on the characteristics of music improvised by various client groups. Miller and Orsmond (1994) and Orsmond and Miller (1995) analyzed improvisations by children with disabilities, including intellectual disability. When the children were asked to improvise at the piano with very few instructions, they improvised with widely varying complexity and coordination. Interestingly, greater prevalence of harmonic and melodic elements was correlated with lower problem behaviors, such as irritability, crying, stereotypical behavior, and hyperactivity.

Luck, Riikkilä, Lartillot, Erkkilä, Toaviainen, Mäkelä, et al. (2006) used a computer model to determine which musical factors of improvisations best predicted level of intellectual disability. The children improvised jointly with a music therapist at a MIDI keyboard. In general, temporal (time-related) factors are the strongest predictors, and pitch-related elements (melody, tonality) are weak predictors. Specifically, improvisations by children and adolescents with milder forms of intellectual disability, on average, are characterized by shorter periods of silence, shorter note duration, less variation in note duration, lower average note density, higher variation in note density, more legato playing, higher integration of articulation with the music therapist, lower integration of tempo with the therapist, and more difference in volume with the therapist (p. 44). This suggests that children with mild and moderate intellectual disability are able to organize their playing on their own than children with more severe forms of intellectual disability, and are more independent from the music therapist playing with them.

Summary and Conclusions

Children and adolescents with mild or moderate intellectual disability exhibit deficits in cognitive functioning and adaptive skills. With this population, music therapy helps clients improve adaptive skills and facilitates the generalization of these skills to various settings (Dileo, 1989). The practice of music therapy with children and adolescents with mild and intellectual disability includes all music therapy methods, with re-creative methods predominating. Depending on the goals, which are typically either educational (didactic) or social, the music has three possible roles. In the first, music serves as a reward for behavior desired by the therapist. In the second, practicing the elements of music serves to stimulate the development of various skills. In the third, information is embedded in music. Naturally, some examples of music therapy will not fit neatly into these categories, but the bulk of practice and research seems to fall into these three methodological approaches.

A strong behavioral research base underscores the effectiveness of music therapy, particularly contingent music, with this population. Music serves an effective reinforcement on its own, because it serves as its own reinforcement. However, much of the published research is not method-specific, and only recently have researchers been able to conduct foundational research in certain methods, such as improvisation. Future research should be more specific about the music therapy methods used (even in strictly behavioral studies), in order to begin to establish which methods are effective and appropriate when working on specific therapeutic goals.

References

Aldridge, D. (1996). Creative music therapy in the treatment of children with developmental delay. *Music therapy research and practice in medicine: From out of the silence* (pp. 243–271). Philadelphia, PA: Jessica Kingsley.

Alvin, J. (1963). Music therapy for the mentally retarded child. *Bulletin of the National Association for Music Therapy, 12*(4), 7-12.

Alvin, J. (1976). *Music for the handicapped child.* London, England: Oxford University Press.

Alvin, J. (1978). *Music therapy for the autistic child.* London,England: Oxford University Press.

American Association on Intellectual and Developmental Disabilities. (n.d.). *Diagnostic adaptive behavior scale.* Retrieved from http://www.aaidd.org/content_106.cfm

American Psychiatric Association (APA). (2000). *Diagnostic and statistical manual of mental disorders—Text revision* (4th ed.). (DSM-IV-TR). Arlington, VA: Author.

Baxter, H. T., Berghofer, J. A., MacEwan, L., Nelson, J., Peters, K., & Roberts, P. (2007). *The individualized music therapy assessment profile.* Philadelphia, PA: Jessica Kingsley.

Bellamy, T. & Sontag, E. (1973). Use of group contingent music to increase assembly line production rates of retarded students in a simulated sheltered workshop. *Journal of Music Therapy, 10*(3), 125-136.

Bokor, C. (1976). A comparison of musical and verbal responses of mentally retarded children. *Journal of Music Therapy, 13*(2), 101–108.

Boxill, E. H. (1981). A continuum of awareness: Music therapy with the developmentally handicapped. *Music Therapy, 1*(1), 17–23.

Bruscia, K.E. (1987). *Improvisational models of music therapy.* Springfield, IL: Charles C. Thomas.

Bruscia, K.E. (Ed.) (1991). *Case studies in music therapy.* Gilsum, NH: Barcelona Publishers.

Bruscia, K.E. (1998). *Defining music therapy* (2nd ed.). Gilsum, NH: Barcelona Publishers.

Bunt, L. (1994). *Music therapy: An art beyond words.* London, England: Routledge.

Cohen, G., Averbach, J., & Katz, E. (1978). Music therapy assessment of the developmentally disabled client. *Journal of Music Therapy, 15*(2), 88–99.

Coleman, K., & Brunk, B. (1999). *SEMTAP: Special education music therapy assessment process.* Grapevine, TX: Prelude Music Therapy.

Coleman, K., & Brunk, B. (2001). *Visual aid kits: Volumes 1 & 2.* Grapevine, TX: Prelude Music Therapy.

Cooper, M. (2010). Clinical-musical responses of Nordoff-Robbins music therapists: The process of clinical improvisation. *Qualitative Inquiries in Music Therapy, 5,* 86–115.

Dileo, C. L. (1975). The use of a token economy program with mentally retarded persons in a music therapy setting. *Journal of Music Therapy, 12*(3), 155–160.

Dileo, C. M. (1989). The California symposium: Summary and recommendations. *Music Therapy Perspectives, 6,* 82–84.

Gardstrom, S. (2007). *Music therapy improvisation for groups: Essential leadership competencies.* Gilsum, NH: Barcelona Publishers.

Gaston, E. T. (1968). *Music in therapy.* New York, NY: MacMillan.

Grant, R.E. (1989). Music therapy guidelines for developmentally disabled children. *Music Therapy Perspectives, 6,* 18-22.

Grant, R. E. (1995). Music therapy assessment for developmentally disabled clients. In T. Wigram, B. Saperston, R. West, T. Wigram, B. Saperston, & R. West (Eds.), *The art and science of music therapy: A handbook* (pp. 273–287). Chur, Switzerland: Harwood Academic.

Gunsberg, A. (1988). Improvised musical play: A strategy for fostering social play between developmentally delayed and nondelayed preschool children. *Journal of Music Therapy, 25*(4), 178–191.

Gunsberg, A. (1991). A method for conducting improvised musical play with children both with and without developmental delays in preschool classrooms. *Music Therapy Perspectives, 9*, 46–51.

Harris, M. A. (1977). *Auditory training of learning-disabled children using Orff music.* Dissertation Abstracts International, *37*, 5036A.

Hoshizaki, M. (1983). Music in language and speech development. In *Teaching the mentally retarded children through music* (pp. 90–95). Springfield, IL: Charles C. Thomas.

Humpal, M. (1991). The effects of an integrated early childhood music program on social interaction among children with handicaps and their typical peers. *Journal of Music Therapy, 28*(3), 161–177.

Humphrey, T. (1981). Selection of music therapy activities by mentally retarded young adults of low, moderate, and high activity. *Perceptual and Motor Skills, 53*(3), 905-906.

Icabone, D. G. Vineland adaptive behavior scales. *Diagnostique, 24*(4), 257–273.

Jorgenson, H. (1974). The use of contingent music activity to modify behaviors which interfere with learning. *Journal of Music Therapy, 11*(1), 41–46.

Jorgenson, H. (1974). The use of a contingent music activity to modify behaviors which interfere with learning. *Journal of Music Therapy, 11*(1), 41-46.

Jorgenson, H., & Parnell, M. K. (1970). Modifying social behaviors of mentally retarded children in music activities. *Journal of Music Therapy, 7*(3), 83–87.

LaGasse, B. A. (2011). Developing speech with music: A neurodevelopmental approach. In A. N. Meadows (Ed.), *Developments in music therapy practice: Case study perspectives* (pp. 166–181). Gilsum, NH: Barcelona Publishers.

Lathom-Radocy, W. (2002). *Pediatric music therapy*. Springfield, IL: Charles C. Thomas.

Lenhoff, H.M. (1998) Information sharing: Insights into the musical potential of cognitively impaired people diagnosed with Williams syndrome. *Music Therapy Perspectives, 16*(1), 33-36.

Levin, H., & Levin, G. (1998). *Learning through music*. Gilsum, NH: Barcelona Publishers.

Levin, H., & Levin, G. (2004). *Distant bells*. Gilsum, NH: Barcelona Publishers.

Levin, H., & Levin, G. (2005). *Let's make music*. Gilsum, NH: Barcelona Publishers.

Levin, H., & Levin, G. (2006). *Symphonics r us*. Gilsum, NH: Barcelona Publishers.

Levine, K. (n.d.). *Williams syndrome information for teachers*. www.williams-syndrome.org. Retrieved from http://www.williams-syndrome.org/teacher/information-for-teachers

Lim, H. A. (2007). *The effect of "developmental speech-language training through music" on speech production in children with autism spectrum disorders*. Doctoral dissertation. Available from http://scholarlyrepository.miami.edu/cgi/viewcontent.cgi?article=1062&context=oa_dissertations

Lim, H. A. (2011). *Developmental speech-language training through music for children with autism spectrum disorder*. Philadelphia, PA: Jessica Kingsley.

Luck, G., Riikkilä, K., Lartillot, O., Erkkilä, J., Toiviainen, P., Mäkelä, A., et al. (2006). Exploring relationships between level of mental retardation and features of music therapy improvisations: A computational approach. *Nordic Journal of Music Therapy, 15*(1), 30–48.

Luckasson, R., Borthwick-Duffy, S., Buntinx, W.H.E., Coulter, D.L., Craig, E.M., Reeve, A., . . .Tassé, M.J. (2002). *Mental retardation: Definition, classification, and systems of support* (10th ed.). Washington, DC: American Association on Mental Retardation.

Miller, L. K., & Orsmond, G. (1994). Assessing structure in the musical explorations of children with disabilities. *Journal of Music Therapy, 31*(4), 248–265.

Nordoff, P., & Robbins, C. (1971). *Therapy in music for handicapped children*. London, England: Victor Gollancz.

Nordoff, P., & Robbins, C. (1977). *Creative music therapy: Individualized treatment for the handicapped child*. New York, NY: John Day.

Orsmond, G., & Miller, L. K. (1995). Correlates of musical improvisation in children with disabilities. *Journal of Music Therapy, 32*(1), 152–168.

Over my head. (1998). In P. Hackett (Ed.), *The melody book* (3rd ed.) (p. 227). Upper Saddle River, NJ: Prentice Hall.

Peters, M.L. (1970). A comparison of the musical sensitivity of mongoloid and normal children. *Journal of Music Therapy, 7*(4), 113-123.

Ritholz, M., & Robbins, C. (Eds.). (1999). *Themes for therapy from the Nordoff-Robbins center for music therapy at New York university*. New York, NY: Carl Fischer.

Ritholz, M., & Robbins, C. (Eds.). (2003). *More themes for therapy from the Nordoff-Robbins center for music therapy at New York university*. New York, NY: Carl Fischer.

Robbins, C., & Robbins, C. (1980). *Music for the hearing impaired: A resource manual and curriculum guide*. St. Louis, MO: Magnamusic-Baton.

Robbins, C. M., & Robbins, C. (1991). Self-communication in creative music therapy. In K. Bruscia (Ed), *Case studies in music therapy* (pp. 55–72). Gilsum, NH: Barcelona Publishers.

Roizen, N. J., Wolters, C., Nicol, T., & Blondis, T. A. (1993). Hearing loss in children with Down syndrome. *The Journal of Pediatrics, 123*(1), S9–S12.

Sabbatella, P. E. (2004). Assessment and clinical evaluation in music therapy: An overview from literature and clinical practice. *Music Therapy Today, 5*(1). Retrieved from www.musictherapyworld.net

Schalkwijk, F. W. (1994). Care through the medium of music-making. In A. James (Trans.), *Music and people with developmental disabilities: Music therapy, remedial music making and musical activities* (pp. 7–31). Philadelphia, PA: Jessica Kingsley.

Schalock, R. L., Borthwick-Duffy, S.A., Bradley, V.J., Buntinx, W.H.E., Coulter, D.L., Craig, E.M., . . .Yeager, M.H. (2010). *Intellectual disability: Definition, classification, and systems of support* (11th ed.). Washington, DC: American Association on Intellectual and Developmental Disabilities.

Smith, A. G. (1953). Music methods and materials for the mentally retarded. In E. G. Gilliland (Ed.), *Music therapy 1952: Proceedings of the national association for music therapy, II*, 139–144. Lawrence, KS: National Association for Music Therapy.

Soraci, S., Deckner, C. W., McDaniel, C., & Blanton, R. L. (1982). The relationship between rate of rhythmicity and the stereotypic behaviors of abnormal children. *Journal of Music Therapy, 19*(1), 46–54.

Sparrow, S.S., Cicchetti, D.V., & Balla, D.A. (2005). *Vineland adaptive behavior scales* (2nd ed.). Circle Pines, MN: AGS Publishing.

Standley, J. M. (1996). A meta-analysis on the effects of music as reinforcement for education/therapy objectives. *Journal of Research in Music Education, 44*(2), 105–133.

Steele, A. (1967). Effects of social reinforcement on the musical preference of mentally retarded children. *Journal of Music Therapy, 3*(2), 57–62.

Thaut, M.H. (2005). *Rhythm, music and the brain*. London, England: Taylor & Francis.

Vuijk, P. J., Hartman, E., Scherder, E., & Visscher, C. (2010). Motor performance of children with mild intellectual disability and borderline intellectual functioning. *Journal of Intellectual Disability Research, 54*(11), 955–965.

Wechsler, D., Kaplan, E., Kramer, J., Morris, R., Delis, D., & Maerlender, A. (2004). *Wechsler intelligence scale for children* (4th ed). San Antonio, TX: Harcourt Assessment.

White House Committee on Special Classes. Section III F, *Special education of the handicapped and gifted*. 1930 White House conference on child health and protection (pp. 439ff).

Chapter 12

Severe to Profound Intellectual and Developmental Disabilities

Donna W. Polen

Diagnostic Information

The American Association on Intellectual and Developmental Disabilities (AAIDD) defines Intellectual Disability (ID) as "characterized by significant limitations both in *intellectual functioning* and in *adaptive behavior,* which covers many everyday social and practical skills. This disability originates before the age of 18" (AAIDD, 2011). According to the AAIDD (2011), intellectual functioning "refers to general mental capacity, such as learning, reasoning, problem-solving, and so on." The AAIDD is clear that "Intellectual Disability" is the preferred term, but vernacular changes evolve slowly. Changes need to occur in numerous venues, including legislative and regulatory areas, agencies and support groups, and others. Change in language impacts change in perception, expectation, and supports and services. The devastating impact of the previous terms (including "imbecile," later referred to as moderate and severe mental retardation, and "idiot," later referred to as profound mental retardation), is still felt today. The reader may find the content of Dave Hingsburger's blog post titled "The People Who 'ARE' the R Word" (2010) to be of interest.

According to the *Diagnostic and Statistical Manual of Mental Disorders,* Fourth Edition, Text Revision (DSM-IV-TR) (APA, 2000), mental retardation (or intellectual disability in the changing terminology) is "significantly subaverage general intellectual functioning that is accompanied by significant limitations in adaptive functioning in at least two of the following skills areas: communication, self-care, home living, social/interpersonal skills, use of community resources, self-direction, functional academic skills, work, leisure, health, and safety" (DSM-IV-TR, 2000).

Intellectual functioning, or intelligence, is often evaluated using an Intelligence Quotient (IQ) test (such as the Wechsler Intelligence Scales for Children—Fourth Edition (WISC-IV), Stanford-Binet, or the Kaufman Assessment Battery for Children). Intellectual assessments are standardized and normed by age. Average standard scores range from 90 to 110 and have an accompanying percentile of 25% and 75% respectively. Therefore, a score of 90 reflects that the individual's score is better than 25% of same-age peers. The numerical rating scale assigned to individuals with mental retardation (according to the DSM-IV-TR) is as follows:

317	Mild Mental Retardation	IQ level 50–55 to approximately 70
318.0	Moderate Mental Retardation	IQ level 35–40 to 50–55
318.1	Severe Mental Retardation	IQ level 20–25 to 35–40
318.2	Profound Mental Retardation	IQ level below 20 or 25
319.0	Severity Unspecified	

The DSM-IV-TR goes on to say that individuals diagnosed at the severe level constitute 3% to 4% of all individuals with mental retardation. For individuals at this level of cognitive functioning, language skills emerge late, if at all, and they garner limited benefits from traditional academic methods and instruction. During adulthood, these individuals may be able to learn simple tasks under close supervision and training. Individuals diagnosed at the profound level represent approximately 1% to 2% of all people with mental retardation. There are often significant sensorimotor challenges present early in their childhood, but improvements are possible with ongoing training and support. Significant impairments are present across all domains, but people can learn some simple tasks under close supervision.

The causes of ID range from medical to social to behavioral and educational, and can occur as a prenatal, perinatal, or postnatal event. IDs are one form of Developmental Disability (DD), which the AAIDD defines as "severe chronic disabilities that can be cognitive or physical or both. The disabilities appear before the age of 22 and are likely to be lifelong" (2012). Previously referred to as "mentally retarded," individuals with these cognitive and related challenges are now considered to have a developmental disability (DD).

Adaptive behavior generally refers to three areas, that of conceptual skills (basic academics and cognitive concepts, including literacy, numbers, time, self-direction, etc.), social skills (such as the ability to interact and form social relationships, self-responsibility, self-esteem, and the ability to function in society according to norms and laws), and activities of daily living (ADLs), including basic self-care (such as bathing, dressing, transportation, self-medication, safety, etc.).

Needs and Resources

The focus of this chapter is on individuals whose intellectual functioning is estimated to be at the "severe" or "profound" level, meaning their IQ standard scores fall at or below 40 on a standardized measure of intelligence. It is important to keep in mind that there isn't a distinct line between these two levels in terms of their strengths, needs, and interests. In addition, these individuals may possess "splinter skills" (high-level ability in isolated skill areas); may seek out and prefer experiences in areas of interest and/or motivation; and may also possess "natural musicianship," just as others do. The skilled music therapist will assess each individual as just that: an individual with a personal history, a musical history, an affinity for or aversion to varying types of music and ways of experiencing music, etc. There must be a detailed examination of the person's strengths and challenges in a variety of domains.

Keeping in mind the diagnostic information and definitions of intellectual and developmental disability, it's clear that this population brings with it a range of challenges which must be overcome by the client and therapist alike. These challenges include issues in the areas of sensorimotor development (gross motor, fine motor, visual motor, diaphragmatic motor), communicative development (preverbal, nonverbal, expressive, and receptive language skills), cognitive development (ability to attend, choice-making, cause-and-effect, basic concepts related to time, space, color, etc.), and affective/emotional development (verbal and/or nonverbal expression of emotion, ability to perceive emotion in music, ability to engage in interpersonal relationships, behavioral stability). Many individuals at the severe and profound levels of IDD are also dually diagnosed with psychiatric or behavioral disturbances, making the process of assessment and treatment planning more complex. Clinicians must also take into account environmental factors such as residential history and current placement, program services, medical status and the accompanying impact of medications, family and support network, etc., along with the immediate environment (the actual therapy space, equipment, and the person's ability to engage in the session).

The AAIDD stresses that, when working with individuals with IDD, it is crucial to maintain a broad view and give equal consideration to community, cultural, and environmental factors. They emphasize that the process of assessment must not focus solely on a person's limitations and challenges but also seek out their strengths. It is only since 1992 that the focus has started to shift from viewing those with an intellectual disability as being subjected to a lifelong, unchanging range of function to someone having the capacity to grow and change when provided the necessary services and supports. Of course, this is always the perspective of the ethical music therapist when approaching assessment with any individual with whom they may work, and an attitude of clinical curiosity informs the process in a way that allows that therapist to uncover a wide range of abilities as well as potentials.

Referral and Assessment

There are numerous ways in which a client may be referred for music therapy assessment, and it is not uncommon for the referral to be provided in an informal manner, such as verbally, through a direct email correspondence, or as a result of discussion at a team meeting at which the music therapist is typically not present since the client is not yet receiving services. Often, the initial referral is made by a family member or team member, and the reason for referral may not necessarily be based on true clinical need but more because a particular person "loves music" or "sings along with the radio all the time," or perhaps because "they're not responding to any other therapies." While a love of music can be helpful in a person's motivation to participate in music therapy, it is not an indicator of their actual *need* for music therapy, nor is it a dependable gauge of their likelihood to succeed in achieving new or expanded skills. If a client is unresponsive to other services they are receiving, they might indeed find music therapy to be more motivating or stimulating in helping them to work toward their outcomes.

There are also instances in which a client may self-refer. Although this is somewhat rare in the course of working with people functioning at the severe or profound level of intellectual and developmental disability, it is not out of the realm of possibility. In some cases, the individual may offer similar reasons for seeking music therapy ("I love music!" or "I know all the songs on the radio"). In some work settings, a client might observe that several of their peers go with the music therapist every Wednesday and Friday afternoon and decide, simply based on that, that they would like to go as well. It is the music therapist's ethical responsibility to follow up on all referrals received.

Music therapists should always strive to help family and staff members understand the potential benefits of music therapy and, subsequently, to help people learn to make informed referrals. Toward that end, development of a referral form for use in your own work setting(s) can be an invaluable tool in obtaining the sort of information that can help you prioritize scheduling and be alert to important cues in the assessment process with each individual.

Types of information to seek on the referral form include date of birth; primary and secondary diagnoses; current medications; current residential and/or treatment settings; other services (clinical and other) the individual is receiving; goals being addressed in other clinical services; special interests and particular dislikes; previous participation in music therapy and, if so, access to those records or contact information for the therapist; any known musical interests or skills; specific reason(s) for referral; name and title of person(s) making the referral; etc. This will of course need to be customized for each setting in which you work.

The American Music Therapy Association (AMTA) states that assessment with this population should include consideration of the following (from the *Standards of Clinical Practice*, November, 2011): "[T]he general categories of psychological, cognitive, communicative, social, and physiological functioning focused on the client's needs and strengths. The assessment will also determine the client's responses to music, music skills, and musical preferences." The *Standards* document goes on to also discuss areas of culture, age, diagnoses, and functioning level.

Although music therapy assessments for individuals with IDD have not been standardized, there are assessments that other music therapists have designed, and there are many resources available for therapists to use in creating original assessment tools and procedures. In relation to individuals with severe-profound IDD, some of these include Boxill (2007), Coleman and Brunk (2003), Grant (1995), Nordoff and Robbins (1971, 2007), Polen (Wheeler et al., 2005), and Wigram (1995).

Assessment can encompass a range of procedures, including review of client records; interview of family, friends, and staff; and observation of the client in other (non–music therapy) settings. Ultimately, the music therapist must engage the client in a wide range of music experiences to assess the person's strengths, needs, interests, and potentials, and then make recommendations based on those findings. Is direct music therapy recommended? If so, what should be the format (i.e., individual, group, a combination thereof)? What is the recommended frequency and duration of treatment? And perhaps most importantly, what are the targeted areas for skill development, and how will this be documented (goal/treatment plan, data collection, ongoing evaluation of response to therapy, etc.)?

Equally important is being able to determine if music therapy is *not* recommended. This is sometimes more elusive, and it is essential that a therapist not jump to this conclusion based on issues of resistiveness, aggression, or agitation on the part of the client. It is not uncommon for an individual with severe to profound IDD to be hesitant to engage with the therapist in an initial assessment session, to appear disinterested, or to be overwhelmed with the possibilities available to them to the point of becoming hyperstimulated and disorganized. It is for this reason that assessment should ideally occur over several sessions over the course of several weeks. Keeping in mind the basis for the referral, a helpful foundation upon which to determine the appropriateness for recommending inclusion in music therapy is the following: Is the client able to use the music therapy environment to establish a relationship with the music and/or the therapist, and/or are they able to use the music therapy environment to develop and/or expand their ability to engage in expressive communication (verbal, vocal, nonverbal, musical)? If the therapist determines that either or both of these scenarios are a possibility for the client, then a recommendation for inclusion is appropriate. If the therapist feels that either or both of these scenarios are not a possibility, then noninclusion is likely the more appropriate recommendation. There are instances, however, in which a clear distinction is not evident; at these times, the possibility for inclusion on a short-term, trial basis may be the best strategy.

The significance of eliciting and interpreting *music* responses during music therapy assessment cannot be overstated. Too often, music therapists spend their time reporting on nonmusical responses and behaviors (e.g., in-seat behavior, following directions, etc.). Of course, issues related to in-seat behavior and following directions can be addressed in music therapy, but it is more clinically relevant and valid to focus on the *music* experience of the client that may lead to improvements in other areas of therapeutic concern (e.g., in-seat behavior, following directions). In other words, why not describe how the client was able to follow changes in tempo while sustaining engagement in a drumming experience for eight minutes? Can we then deduce from that (and it can be stated in just this way in an assessment report) that the person remained seated through that experience and was clearly following directions (nonverbally, *musically*) by demonstrating the ability to synchronize with the therapist's improvised music?

In considering an individual's response to music, the music therapist must be alert to the manner in which a person responds to music. Are they someone who primarily moves to music? Is this movement obvious, perhaps dramatic? Or is it more subtle, such as changes in respiration or a slight change in eye gaze? In contrast, perhaps the person responds vocally, by humming, grunting, vocalizing on nonsense sounds, or spontaneously engaging in lyric improvisation. Or does the individual express their connection with the music instrumentally, perhaps just percussively through clapping, stomping, knee patting, drumming, or maybe more melodically by playing the piano, tone chimes, horns, etc. Many individuals with IDD demonstrate all modes of response (kinesthetic, vocal, and instrumental), while others may only demonstrate one; still others may vacillate in their response mode over time, within a session or across sessions. And the person who quickly demonstrates a range of responses and a deep connection to music may suddenly become overwhelmed and lose control, emotionally or behaviorally. Clearly, determining an individual's strengths, needs, and interests is paramount to identifying the course of treatment. While there are many who believe that individuals with IDD do not or cannot live a rich, musical life or are unable to adequately process musical material in a way that they can access it and use it for emotional expression and interpersonal connection, this is clearly not the case. It is crucial, and especially so in working with people functioning at the severe or profound level of intellectual and developmental disability, to be able to get to this point in our assessment, documentation, treatment planning, implementation, and evaluation, so that we can communicate to our colleagues and others the unique knowledge we possess regarding the way our clients respond to music and how we use that in our work with them.

General Considerations for Implementation of the Methods

In considering specific components of each of the four main methods (receptive music therapy, improvisational music therapy, re-creative music therapy, and compositional music therapy), the reader is cautioned to keep in mind the fact that each method can grow from another or one can be included in the midst of another; while each can be planned and implemented on its own, they typically don't function in isolation. If this were the case, it would more resemble activity therapy in which the therapist would plan to "play a Name That Tune game" followed by "an improvisation activity" and then, perhaps, "do a movement to music activity." The implementation of the four main methods is more organic and dynamic in nature, and in the hands of a skilled therapist they support the moment-to-moment flow of a session.

For example, a therapist is engaging a client in a drumming improvisation in which the therapist is presenting changes in dynamics for the client to follow. The therapist observes that the client is more successful in following a change in dynamics if it occurs immediately following an ascending glissando and a tremolo in the music. As a result, the therapist starts to incorporate an ascending glissando and tremolo each time they want the client to follow a change in dynamics, resulting in the improvisation becoming more structured and moving into a re-creative experience. Over the course of several sessions, the therapist notates this improvisation and thus begins to move toward a compositional experience (initially a theme-based composition, completed *for* the client). Finally, the client becomes somewhat familiar with the general structure and expectation ("I listen for those sounds and then the piano music changes and I change my drumming"), incorporating a receptive experience for the client. Ultimately, the therapist may then introduce change to the structure by perhaps introducing a descending glissando and tremolo to signal a dynamic change, moving back to a more improvisational experience. Over time, the therapist may pair the ascending glissando with changes to a louder dynamic level and the descending glissando with changes to a softer dynamic level, again changing the emphasis in method.

The descriptions below are written in isolation in reference to each specific method indicated in an effort to present clear and specific examples, but the reader is encouraged to remember that this is not a reflection of the way these methods are typically implemented in therapy. In summation, each of the four types of music experiences or methods (receptive music therapy, improvisational music therapy, re-creative music therapy, and compositional music therapy) can function as an independent or principle tool in therapy, but they are more often a component of, precursor to, or successor to the other methods.

OVERVIEW OF METHODS AND PROCEDURES

Receptive Music Therapy

- Listening to Live, Therapist-Provided Music: The client listens to live music (precomposed or improvised) provided by the therapist, with specific responses and outcomes targeted for response.
- Listening to Peer(s) in a Group Setting: The therapist facilitates a group music experience in which group members may play or sing with or without the support of the therapist accompanying them, or in which some group members are solely engaged in an active listening experience while just one group member is actually producing music.
- Somatic Listening: The client listens to recorded music while also feeling its vibrations.
- Listening to Precomposed Songs from the Clinical Repertoire: The therapist selects and presents precomposed songs from the clinical repertoire with specific goals and outcomes in mind for the client. These songs contain certain concepts as an integral part of the lyrics or are structured as question/answer learning songs or fill-in-the-blank songs.

Improvisational Music Therapy

- Instrumental Improvisation: The client(s) spontaneously make up and play music on instruments while the therapist accompanies or listens.
- Vocal Improvisation: The client(s) spontaneously vocalizes while the therapist accompanies or listens.
- Song/Lyric Improvisation: The client(s) spontaneously make up and sing songs or lyrics, while the therapist accompanies or listens.

Re-creative Music Therapy

- Instrumental Re-creation: The client learns precomposed instrumental music through a process of repetition and practice.
- Vocal Re-creation: The client learns precomposed vocal music through a process of repetition and practice.
- Performance Re-creation: The client learns precomposed vocal or instrumental music through a process of repetition and practice and then performs in front of an audience.

Compositional Music Therapy

- Composition Experiences with a Client: The therapist helps the client to create original songs, lyrics, or instrumental pieces.
- Composition Experiences for a Client: The therapist creates original songs, lyrics, or instrumental pieces that target specific skills and/or issues unique to a particular client.
- Song Parody: The therapist helps the client to create original lyrics within the structure of a precomposed song which may or may not be familiar to the client.

- Theme-Based Composition: As certain themes (melodic, rhythmic, stylistic, lyrical, etc.) evolve organically over time in therapy, the therapist works with the client to create more structure, resulting in an original composition.

GUIDELINES FOR RECEPTIVE MUSIC THERAPY

Bruscia (1998) defines receptive experiences as those in which "the client listens to music and responds to the experience silently, verbally, or in another modality. The music used may be live or recorded improvisations, performances, or compositions by the client or therapist, or commercial recordings of music literature in various styles. ... The listening experience may be focused on physical, emotional, intellectual, aesthetic, or spiritual aspects of the music, and the client's responses are designed according to the therapeutic purpose of the experience (pp.120–121)." These experiences are sometimes also simply referred to as listening experiences.

Some of the main clinical goals of receptive experiences include promoting receptivity (an emphasis on external environment), evoking specific body responses (e.g., changes in muscle tone, respiration rate, positioning, etc.), stimulation or relaxation, as well as evoking changes in emotional state, exploration of ideas, stimulating reminiscence, evoking imagery, supporting a connection to a particular social group, and others (Bruscia, 1998).

The music used can be live or recorded music; it can be familiar or unfamiliar to the client; it can be of any style; it can be an original composition written by the client or written by the therapist for the client. The options are limitless, but of course must be based on careful consideration of the strengths, needs, and interests of the client; the anticipated outcomes for therapy; previous interventions; and the relationship between the client and the therapist.

Receptive experiences are a highly internal process for the client. If the client doesn't express their experience through physical changes and/or movement and is unable to communicate their experience verbally, it can be challenging for the therapist to adequately observe and interpret the effectiveness of the intervention and use that information to plan future experiences. If the therapist and the client have a deep understanding of each other within the context of their relationship, this might be less of a concern. In working with people functioning at the severe or profound level of intellectual and developmental disability, there is also the possibility that they may not possess the degree of cognitive processing or conceptualization in order to fully participate in and benefit from extensive listening experiences.

Listening to Live, Therapist-Provided Music

Overview. The therapist presents live music for an active, receptive experience. The music might be instrumental (piano, guitar, percussion), vocal (lyrical or nonlyrical), or a combination of both; it may also be precomposed or improvised. The expectation for the client is to listen actively and respond as indicated. The client's response to the experience might occur concurrently with or following conclusion of the music. Listening to live, therapist-provided music may be indicated for a client who needs to work on increasing awareness of external stimuli and other environmental factors, for someone who is working on general listening and attending skills, and for an individual who is working on impulse-control issues. The goals of therapy in these instances may include having the client respond in specific ways to cues or directives in the music or extending the period of time that someone is able to listen. This experience is primarily provided at the augmentative and intensive levels; in some cases, it may progress to the primary level.

There are no obvious contraindications for use of this method, although particular consideration needs to be given to the efficacy of implementing this method when working with clients who have profound hearing impairments or who are deaf. For those individuals, somatic listening experiences may be more appropriate and meaningful.

Preparation. Positioning of the client in relation to the therapist and any instruments being used is important to ensure that the client can see any cues or prompts the therapist might provide. It is important that the client be comfortable so that they can concentrate on their listening experience without distractions. Whenever possible, make certain that the session room is free of visual and auditory distractions (windows, loudspeaker announcements, noise from neighboring rooms, other instruments within visual or physical range that are not included in the listening experience, etc.) to ensure that the client's participation and success are optimized.

What to observe. The therapist is to observe the client for any targeted responses as well as secondary responses. For example, if one of the goals being addressed is for the client to strike a crash cymbal each time there is a rest in the music, the therapist is observing for the cymbal strike, and may also observe that the client turns their head sharply to the right following each cymbal strike. This may be reflective of a wide range of possibilities: Perhaps the client has a severe hearing loss in their right ear and they are turning their head to the right in order to receive more vibratory stimulation in their left ear resulting from the cymbal strike, or perhaps the client feels a need to disengage from direct contact with the therapist following their successful cymbal strike due to issues with self-confidence and a concern that their effort was not "good enough"—or any number of other possibilities. The therapist must not only watch for the response they are trying to elicit, but also always observe the complete experience of the client.

Procedures. Depending on the degree of receptive language skills of the client, the therapist might provide initial verbal instructions to the client about what to listen for and what, if anything, the client is to do in response. Modeling of any physical, instrumental, or vocal/verbal response expected of the client might be necessary. The therapist may determine that, as the listening experience progresses, changes in the music are warranted, based on observed responses or reactions from the client.

Listening to Peer(s) in a Group Setting

Overview. The therapist facilitates a group music experience in which the music might be instrumental (piano, guitar, percussion), vocal (lyrical or nonlyrical), or a combination of both; the music may also be precomposed or improvised. Group members may play or sing without the support of the therapist accompanying them, or with therapist accompaniment; there may also be instances in which some group members are solely engaged in an active listening experience while just one group member is actually producing music. The therapist will always provide the necessary structure and cuing to ensure that group members are aware of the expectations for their participation and response. The client's response(s) to the experience might occur simultaneously or following conclusion of the music. Listening to peer(s) in a group setting may be indicated for a client who needs to work on increasing awareness of external stimuli and other environmental factors; for someone who is working on general listening and attending skills; for an individual who is working on impulse-control issues; and for a client who is working on developing social communication skills. The goals of therapy in these instances may include having the client respond in specific ways to cues or directives in the music, extending the period of time that someone is able to listen, contributing to the completion of a shared outcome, and learning basic accepted methods of recognizing the musical effort of another. This experience is primarily provided at the augmentative and intensive levels.

This method is only appropriate for those clients who are capable of functioning in a group setting in terms of their cognitive, emotional, and behavioral functioning. This method might naturally follow the previously described method (listening to live, therapist-provided music) for a client who achieves a certain level of competency in the individualized therapy setting and then transitions into group work. Furthermore, as indicated earlier in the discussion of listening to live, therapist-provided music, consideration needs to be given to the efficacy of implementing this method when working with clients who have profound hearing impairments or who are deaf. For those individuals, somatic listening experiences may be more appropriate and meaningful.

Preparation. Positioning of the client in relation to the therapist, any instruments being used, and the other group member(s) is important to ensure that the client can see any cues or prompts the therapist might provide. It is important that the client be comfortable so that they can concentrate on their listening experience without distractions. Whenever possible, make certain that the session room is free of visual and auditory distractions (windows, loudspeaker announcements, noise from neighboring rooms, other instruments within visual or physical range that are not included in the listening experience, etc.) to ensure that the client's participation and success are optimized. In group settings, it is also crucial that adequate space is provided between the group members so that everyone has enough space in which to respond without imposing on others while also being close enough to the other group members to facilitate any direct interaction that might be expected (e.g., handshakes, passing an instrument, etc.).

What to observe. The therapist is to observe the client for any targeted responses as well as secondary responses. For example, if one of the goals being addressed is for the client to cease drumming and listen when cued that it is their peer's turn to solo on the hanging chimes, the therapist is watching to make sure the client is not playing and is listening to their peer play the hanging chimes. The therapist may also observe that the client holds the mallets in the air in anticipation of playing, or perhaps places the mallets on the floor. This may be reflective of a wide range of possibilities: Perhaps the client is unsure of what to do with their mallets when not actually engaged in drumming; or they may feel anxious about not playing, thinking it appears that they are not fully participating; or they may feel bored or uninterested in the experience unless they are more actively engaged in music-making; or any number of other possibilities. The therapist must not only watch for the response they are trying to elicit, but also always observe the complete experience of the client.

Procedures. Depending on the degree of receptive language skills of the client(s), the therapist might provide initial verbal instructions to the group about what to listen for and what, if anything, each individual is to do in response. Modeling of any physical, instrumental, or vocal/verbal response expected of the group members might be necessary.

Somatic Listening

Overview. In somatic listening interventions, the therapist presents recorded music to the client through use of a Somatron or other type of vibroacoustic equipment, providing the client with a full-body experience of the music. The selection of the music is based on the therapist's knowledge of the client's preferences and the targeted outcomes for the experience. Somatic listening to recorded music via Somatron or similar vibroacoustic equipment may be indicated for a client who needs to work on increasing awareness of external stimuli and other environmental factors; for someone who is working on general listening and attending skills; for an individual who is working on impulse-control issues; for an individual who is working on increasing or decreasing muscle tone; to support a client with profound hearing loss or deafness to experience music; to stimulate respiratory, verbal, or vocal responses; to stimulate gross motor movement; and for a client who is working on learning relaxation techniques. The goals of therapy in these instances may include having the client respond in specific ways to cues in the music or suggestions from the therapist; extending the period of time that someone is able to listen; increasing or decreasing respiration rate; expanding pitch range and duration of verbal or vocal responses; increasing range of motion by playing specially positioned instruments while listening; and learning to follow basic instructions and modeling of progressive relaxation strategies. This experience is primarily provided at the augmentative and intensive levels, and in some cases progresses to the primary level.

This method has very broad applications. In one application, it might be highly effective with a multiply-challenged individual in order to provide a deep level of sensory stimulation to support a decrease in muscle tone and an increase in range of motion. In another scenario, it can provide an individual with profound hearing loss or total deafness with their only authentic experience of music. In another application, it could provide a tangible experience of physical relaxation for an individual with minimal physical challenges but complicated emotional/behavioral issues. Some individuals with severe and profound IDD may not possess the cognitive ability to garner benefits from the use of somatic listening experiences, while others might find it to be a very powerful tool. The therapist must make an informed choice in this regard.

Preparation. When using recorded music in session, it is important to have the possible music selections organized and available in order to minimize disruption and distracting the client by looking through CDs, etc. It is also important to ensure that all equipment is in working order, the Somatron or similar vibroacoustic equipment has been cleaned prior to bringing the client into the therapy space, and volume settings are appropriate; the therapist must already be familiar with the music selections and equipment in order to provide an experience that is safe as well as effective. Make sure that adequate seating is available for the therapist so that full access to the equipment as well as the client is facilitated with minimal extraneous movement. It is important that the client feel safe in the Somatron or similar vibroacoustic equipment and be comfortable so that they can concentrate on their listening experience without distractions. When working with those with severe physical disabilities, the use of adaptive seating arrangements (pillows, bolsters, etc.) may be indicated. Whenever possible, make certain that the session room is free of visual and auditory distractions (windows, loudspeaker announcements, noise from neighboring rooms, other instruments within visual or physical range that are not included in the listening experience, etc.) to ensure that the client's participation and success are optimized.

What to observe. The therapist is to observe the client for any targeted responses as well as secondary responses. For example, if one of the goals being addressed is for the client to increase vocal responses, the therapist watches and listens for these responses. The therapist may also observe that the client demonstrates a change in respiration rate immediately prior to producing a vocal response. This is likely indicative of the stimulation of the overall respiratory system and the client's anticipation of vocalizing. The therapist may want to pay particular attention to what types of music elicit this response in order to more effectively support the client in achieving success over time by providing suitable music. The therapist must not only watch for the response they are trying to elicit, but also always observe the complete experience of the client.

Procedures. The therapist assists the client into the Somatron or similar vibroacoustic equipment, ensuring their safety and comfort. Depending on the degree of receptive language skills of the client, the therapist might provide initial verbal instructions about what to listen for and what, if anything, the client is to do in response. Modeling of any physical, instrumental, or vocal/verbal response expected of the client might be necessary. Particular attention must be given to the selection of musical material as well as the volume settings in order to ensure a full musical experience without damaging the client's hearing. Knowledge of the client's musical preferences, always a crucial component in all clinical work, may be of particular importance in the selection of recordings for use in somatic listening experiences. For example, the therapist may be working with someone on increasing relaxation and may have a recording of music specifically produced for this purpose. However, if the client's favored style of music is disco dance music from the 1970s, this might actually be more effective than the therapist's selection. Therapists should pay attention to components of novelty and familiarity in selecting recordings for somatic listening experiences. For example, when working on increasing verbal/vocal production, it may be more effective to use recordings of vocal music in a language unfamiliar to the client; this provides the model of the human voice without the additional content of the message of the lyrics.

Adaptations. Often, a client may respond especially well and in a consistent manner to a particular recording or series of recordings. If a routine selection or sequence of selections becomes a grounding tool for a client working on, for example, learning self-relaxation techniques, the therapist may determine after a period of time that it could benefit the client to have access to the same music at their home. The client may be able to transfer the experience and the strategies they have learned in music therapy and use these to their benefit in other settings. For example, a client may have particular difficulty upon arriving home in the afternoon from their program setting and reentering the less structured environment of their home. Having the familiar music from their somatic listening experiences available may provide them with a tangible tool to use in making this transition.

Careful consideration must be given to the possibility, however, that use of the same music which is so powerful in the music therapy environment and within the context of the clinical relationship *outside* of that context could actually decrease the effectiveness of that music within therapy.

Listening to Precomposed Songs from the Clinical Repertoire

Overview. The therapist selects and presents precomposed songs from the clinical repertoire with specific goals and outcomes in mind for the client. These songs may contain certain concepts as an integral part of the lyrics (e.g., Nordoff-Robbins Play Songs such as "I'm Mad Today," "Shoe-Tying Song," "The Penny-nickel-dime-quarter-dollar Song," etc.) or are structured as question/answer learning songs or fill-in-the-blank songs (e.g., "What Day Is It Today?" or "A Rainy Day," etc., by Nordoff and Robbins, or "What's In Your House?" or "What Do You Say?," etc., by Herbert and Gail Levin). Listening to precomposed songs from the clinical repertoire may be indicated for a client who needs to work on increasing awareness of external stimuli and other environmental factors; for someone who is working on general listening and attending skills; for an individual who is working on learning a variety of adaptive behavior skills; for a client who needs to work on learning social interaction skills; and for someone who needs to address issues of self-confidence and self-esteem. The reader is reminded of the description of *adaptive behavior* as it relates to this population: conceptual skills (basic academics and cognitive concepts, including literacy, numbers, time, self-direction, etc.); social skills (such as the ability to interact and form social relationships, self-responsibility, self-esteem, and the ability to function in society according to norms and laws); and activities of daily living (ADLs), including basic self-care (such as bathing, dressing, transportation, self-medication, safety, etc.). The goals of therapy in these instances may include having the client respond in specific ways to cues in the song, having the client sing along with the song or fill in answers or the end of sentences, and ultimately having the client sing the song independently (transitioning from a receptive experience to a re-creative experience). This experience is primarily provided at the augmentative and intensive levels, and sometimes at the auxiliary level.

There are no obvious contraindications for use of this method, although particular consideration needs to be given to the efficacy of implementing this method when working with certain clients with severe and profound IDD who may not possess the cognitive ability to garner benefits from this method. In addition, this would be an inappropriate and ineffective method to employ with nonverbal clients if a verbal or vocal response is required (as is often the case when using precomposed songs from the clinical repertoire), although there will be instances in which a nonverbal client can benefit from internalizing the general content and structure of a song. The therapist must be sensitive in this regard.

Preparation. When using precomposed songs from the clinical repertoire in session, it is important to have the song selections memorized and/or to have the music available and organized in order to minimize disruption and distracting the client by looking through books, etc. Ensure that any supporting materials being used (e.g., photographs, picture communication symbols, other manipulatives, etc.) are also readily available. Whenever possible, make certain that the session room is free of visual and auditory distractions (windows, loudspeaker announcements, noise from neighboring rooms, other instruments within visual or physical range that are not included in the listening experience, etc.) to ensure that the client's participation and success are optimized.

What to observe. The therapist is to observe the client for any targeted responses as well as secondary responses. For example, if one of the goals being addressed is for the client to learn how to plan a healthy breakfast meal in order to be more involved in managing diabetes, the therapist watches, listens, and may also observe that the client repeatedly identifies foods that, while qualifying as healthy choices, are more appropriate for an evening meal. This may be reflective of a wide range of possibilities: Perhaps the client is unsure of the distinctions between different meals based on their typical names (i.e., breakfast, lunch, dinner) and might be more successful with descriptors of each meal (e.g., "What do you like to eat in the morning when you wake up?" "What do you bring to program in your lunch pail?" "What's one of your favorite things to eat at your house at night after you're home from program?"); or it may be that they don't typically have the opportunity to participate in meal planning and therefore don't have an understanding of being able to make independent selections of favorite foods and might be more successful if they were provided with pictures of possible answers from which to choose; or any number of other possibilities. The therapist must not only watch for the response they are trying to elicit, but also always observe the complete experience of the client.

Procedures. The therapist presents the targeted song. In many cases, it assists the client to succeed if the song is first presented as a complete structure and then presented a second time, during which the client is supported in singing along and/or providing responses to answer the questions posed in the song. Intentional use of pauses, tremolos, suspended chords, dominant sevenths, etc., can serve to regain attention and motivate the client to maintain active engagement in the experience.

Adaptations. If a client responds especially well and in a consistent manner to a particular precomposed song or songs used in therapy to support their learning of self-care strategies or activities of daily living, providing a recording or series of recordings of these songs for listening in other settings can help to concretize the concepts and support the client in transferring these skills. These recordings may already exist, or the therapist may need to produce them for the client. For example, having a recording of the familiar song from their therapy sessions available to them in the actual environment in which they can apply the information (e.g., a song about bathing playing while they are bathing) may provide them with a tangible tool to use in making the transition from singing about a concept in a song to functional application of a skill in their life.

Guidelines for Improvisational Music Therapy

Bruscia (1998) defines improvisational experiences as those in which "the client makes up music while playing or singing, extemporaneously creating a melody, rhythm, song or instrumental piece. The client may improvise alone, in a duet, or in a group which includes the therapist, other clients, and sometimes family members. The client may use any musical medium within his/her capabilities. … The therapist helps the client by providing the necessary instructions and demonstrations, offering a musical idea or structure upon which to base the improvisation, playing or singing an accompaniment that stimulates or guides the client's improvising, or presenting a nonmusical idea (e.g., image, title, story) for the client to portray through the improvisation" (p. 116).

Some of the main clinical goals of improvisational experiences include establishing a nonverbal channel of communication or a bridge to verbal communication, providing a means of self-expression, exploring aspects of self in relation to others, developing interpersonal intimacy and/or group skills, stimulating the senses, and developing perceptual and cognitive skills (Bruscia, 1998).

While it may seem that a client's response while engaging in improvisational experiences is easily observable, the therapist must remain cognizant at all times that there is a simultaneous internal process occurring for the client. The therapist must be alert to both dramatic and subtle shifts in the client's playing; changes in body positioning, facial affect, and breathing; verbal and vocal responses, including the content, timbre, pitch range, etc.; and also silences or ceasing of activity. All of these elements provide critical information for the therapist in interpreting the effectiveness of the intervention and using that information to plan future experiences. Often, when working with people functioning at the severe or profound level of intellectual and developmental disability, there is a degree of freedom experienced during improvisational experiences which can provide a path of communication and relationship with the therapist that might otherwise be unavailable.

Instrumental Improvisation

Overview. In instrumental improvisation experiences, the therapist is responsible for providing environmental and musical structures which facilitate a successful process for the client. Selection and positioning of instruments and determination of style(s) of improvisation are important considerations, as is the level of modeling and prompting employed in supporting the client in entering into instrument play. Instrumental improvisation may be indicated for a client who needs to work on increasing awareness of external stimuli and other environmental factors; for someone who is working on general listening and attending skills; for an individual who is working on impulse-control issues; for someone who is nonverbal or for whom verbal communication poses unique challenges; and for someone who needs to work on developing leadership and self-confidence. The goals of therapy in these instances may include having the client respond in specific ways to cues or directives in the music, extending the period of time that someone is able to sustain active engagement in improvising, and having the client follow therapist-introduced changes or initiate changes. This experience is primarily provided at the augmentative and intensive levels and in some cases progresses to the primary level.

Consideration needs to be given to the efficacy of implementing this method when working with clients with severe and profound IDD who may not possess the physical ability to actively engage independently in playing an instrument. The use of special positioning and various adaptations (adaptive mallets with built-up handles or straps, oversized guitar picks, horn stands, wheelchair clips for securing paddle drums, switches, etc.) can help to maximize the independence of a client with physical challenges as they engage in instrumental improvisation experiences. Providing extensive physical assistance, such as hand-over-hand assistance, is contraindicated in such situations, as the client is no longer exerting their own effort and intention.

Another consideration is the use of this method in group work with individuals with severe/profound IDD. Generally speaking, individuals functioning at this level of cognition have both attentional deficits and impulse-control challenges which often prevent them from achieving independent instrumental improvisation while others are also playing, with the exception of grounding and structuring as provided by the therapist. While group instrument play can be an effective social tool in group sessions, it is rare that the playing would reach the level of true improvisation. This is not to say that group instrument playing is not a viable and valuable part of group work with this population, but the outcome may not be one of great depth, although it can provide a rich experience of shared effort and productivity.

Finally, many clients functioning at this level of IDD may feel intimidated or uncertain about improvising alone. It will likely be most effective for the therapist to improvise with the client(s), at least initially, until they develop a level of self-trust, trust in the therapist, and trust in the music.

Preparation. Positioning of the client in relation to the therapist and any instruments being used is important to ensure that the client can see any cues or prompts the therapist might provide. The therapist may want to have access to paper or a recording device (audio or video) in order to capture the client's efforts for future notation or for playbacks. Whenever possible, make certain that the session room is free of visual and auditory distractions (windows, loudspeaker announcements, noise from neighboring rooms, other instruments within visual or physical range that are not included in the improvisation experience, etc.) to ensure that the client's participation and success are optimized.

What to observe. The therapist is to observe the client for any targeted responses as well as secondary responses. For example, if one of the goals being addressed is for the client to experience tempo mobility by following changes in tempo as presented by the therapist in a piano improvisation, the therapist observes whether the client is able to synchronize with any changes. The therapist may also observe that the client ceases beating for the approximate equivalent of one measure each time the therapist presents a gradual tempo change, while in contrast the client is able to follow tempo changes without ceasing their activity when the tempo change presented is sudden and dramatic. This may be reflective of a wide range of possibilities: Perhaps the client is becoming engrossed in their own beating effort and therefore doesn't notice a subtle change in the music but is drawn back to awareness when an abrupt change occurs, or perhaps the compulsive character of the individual is so strong that a gradual change isn't powerful enough to move them off course. The therapist must not only watch for the response they are trying to elicit, but also always observe the complete experience of the client.

Procedures. Depending on the degree of receptive language skills of the client, the therapist might provide initial verbal instructions to the client about what is expected of them; more often, however, the therapist will simply organize the instrument(s) being used, provide some modeling as needed, and allow the experience to unfold. Particularly when working with individuals with severe/profound IDD, the concept of providing more specific ideas (i.e., such as a referential improvisation) is too complex and abstract and would serve only to confuse the client and undermine their confidence. As the improvisation progresses, the therapist determines, on a moment-to-moment basis, how and when to try to guide the improvisation by presenting changes (e.g., tempo, meter, dynamic, style, phrasing, etc.) or using various techniques such as imitating, synchronizing, reflecting, exaggerating, etc., in order to try to move the client's playing in a particular direction, as appropriate and as indicated by the course of treatment.

Vocal Improvisation

Overview. In vocal improvisation experiences, the therapist is responsible for providing musical structures which facilitate a successful process for the client. Determination of style(s) of improvisation, including tonal centering and pitch range, are important considerations, as is the level of modeling and prompting employed in supporting the client in entering into vocal play. Vocal improvisation may be indicated for a client who needs to work on increasing awareness of external stimuli and other environmental factors; for someone who is working on general listening and attending skills; for someone who is nonverbal or for whom verbal communication poses unique challenges; and for someone who needs to work on developing leadership and self-confidence. The goals of therapy in these instances may include having the client respond in specific ways to cues or directives in the music, extending the period of time that someone is able to sustain active engagement in improvising, and having the client follow therapist-introduced changes or initiate changes. This experience is primarily provided at the augmentative and intensive levels and in some cases progresses to the primary level.

This would be an inappropriate and ineffective method to employ with clients who are incapable of producing vocal sounds, but this must not be confused with those who may be nonverbal but are able to vocalize. Indeed, this can be an especially powerful method for just such a client.

Another consideration is the use of this method in group work with individuals with severe/profound IDD. Generally speaking, individuals functioning at this level of cognition have both attentional deficits and impulse-control challenges which would preclude the use of group vocal improvisation. While group singing can be an effective social tool in group sessions, actual vocal *improvisation* would likely be unproductive at best and perhaps result in agitation for some group members.

Finally, many clients functioning at this level of IDD may feel intimidated or uncertain about improvising alone, especially with the most personal of all instruments: their voice. It will likely be most effective for the therapist to improvise with the client, at least initially, until the client develops a level of self-trust, trust in the therapist, and trust in the music. Help the client to understand that what matters most is how they *feel* when they are singing, not how they sound.

Preparation. Positioning of the client in relation to the therapist is important to ensure that the client can see any cues or prompts the therapist might provide. It is important that the client be comfortable so that they can concentrate on their vocal improvisation experience without distractions. The therapist may want to have access to paper or a recording device (audio or video) in order to capture the client's efforts for future notation or for playbacks. Whenever possible, make certain that the session room is free of visual and auditory distractions (windows, loudspeaker announcements, noise from neighboring rooms, instruments within visual or physical range that are not included in the experience, etc.) to ensure that the client's participation and success are optimized.

What to observe. The therapist is to observe the client for any targeted responses as well as secondary responses. For example, if one of the goals being addressed is for the client to experiment with producing various nonsense sounds by dropping their jaw to allow for a relaxed sound, the therapist observes whether the client vocalizes with an open mouth; however, the therapist may find that the client instead clenches their teeth and vocalizes through tense muscles around the mouth, jaw, and throat area. This may be reflective of a wide range of possibilities: Perhaps the client is feeling anxious about opening their mouth because they have poor oral hygiene and relate opening their mouth with painful dental procedures; or perhaps they are so accustomed to keeping their mouth tightly shut that relaxing the muscles in that area feels unnatural and makes them feel vulnerable; or any number of other possibilities. The therapist must also closely observe related responses including breathing, facial affect, overall body position, etc., to ensure the client's comfort and safety. The therapist must not only watch for the response they are trying to elicit, but also always observe the complete experience of the client.

Procedures. Depending on the degree of receptive language skills of the client, the therapist might provide initial verbal instructions to the client about what is expected of them; more often, however, the therapist will simply organize the environment, provide some modeling as needed, and allow the experience to unfold. Particularly when working with individuals with severe/profound IDD, the concept of providing more specific ideas (i.e., such as a referential improvisation) is too complex a concept and would only serve to confuse the client and undermine their confidence. As the improvisation progresses, the therapist determines, on a moment-to-moment basis, how and when to try to guide the improvisation by presenting changes (e.g., tempo, meter, dynamic, style, phrasing, pitch range, timbre, nonsense sounds, etc.) or using various techniques such as imitating, synchronizing, reflecting, exaggerating, etc., in order to try to move the client's vocalizing in a particular direction, as appropriate and as indicated by the course of treatment.

Adaptations. The concept of vocal improvisation may be fairly elusive for many individuals with severe/profound IDD, especially since it is (at least initially) a very internalized process in addition to the fact that the therapist might actually be supporting natural vocal production from the client that is more typically ignored, interrupted, or halted. The use of instruments as stimulators for vocal production can be very effective in these situations. In particular, use of reed horns, kazoos, harmonicas, and even vocalizing through boom whackers can all stimulate vocal response and lead the client into more outward vocal improvisation.

Song/Lyric Improvisation

Overview. In song and/or lyric improvisation experiences, the therapist provides musical structures which facilitate a successful process for the client. Determination of style(s) of improvisation, including tonal centering, pitch range, and phrasing, are important considerations, as is the level of modeling and prompting employed in supporting the client in entering into singing. The therapist may need to model words or phrases for the client to sing, or structure the improvisation more as a question/answer or call-and-response intervention. Song/lyric improvisation may be indicated for a client who needs to work on increasing awareness of external stimuli and other environmental factors; for someone who is working on general listening and attending skills; for an individual who is working on impulse-control issues; for an individual who is working on learning a variety of self-care skills and activities of daily living; and for someone who needs to address issues of self-confidence and self-esteem. The goals of therapy in these instances may include having the client respond in specific ways to cues or directives in the music, extending the period of time that someone sustains active engagement in improvising or having them contribute additional phrases/lyrics over time, and having the client follow therapist-introduced changes or initiate changes. This experience is primarily provided at the augmentative and intensive levels and in some cases progresses to the primary level.

This would be an inappropriate and ineffective method to employ with clients who are nonverbal. Another consideration is the use of this method in group work with individuals with severe/profound IDD. Generally speaking, individuals functioning at this level of cognition have both attentional deficits and impulse-control challenges which would preclude the use of group song/lyric improvisation. While group singing and group songwriting can be effective social tools in group sessions, actual song/lyric *improvisation* would likely be unproductive at best and perhaps result in agitation or frustration for some group members.

Finally, many clients functioning at this level of IDD may feel intimidated or uncertain about improvising lyrics alone, especially with the most personal of all instruments: their voice. It will likely be most effective for the therapist to improvise with the client, at least initially, until the client develops a level of self-trust, trust in the therapist, and trust in the music.

Preparation. Positioning of the client in relation to the therapist is important to ensure that the client can see any cues or prompts the therapist might provide. It is important that the client be comfortable so that they can concentrate on their experience without distractions. The therapist may want to have access to paper or a recording device (audio or video) in order to capture the client's efforts for future notation or for playbacks. Whenever possible, make certain that the session room is free of visual and auditory distractions (windows, loudspeaker announcements, noise from neighboring rooms, other instruments within visual or physical range that are not included in the listening experience, etc.) to ensure that the client's participation and success are optimized.

What to observe. The therapist is to observe the client for any targeted responses as well as secondary responses. For example, if one of the goals being addressed is for the client to improvise lyrics about people who hold importance in their life, the therapist is observing for the identification of such people and perhaps also for indications from the client regarding why particular people are held in high regard by the client. Let's say the client improvises lyrical content regarding a favored staff person from their residence and how that person helps them feel good about themselves when helping them learn how to do their laundry, etc. The therapist may also observe that the client begins to sing about a family member that the client has not seen or had contact with for many years. This may be reflective of a wide range of possibilities: Perhaps the client has made a connection in their memory about their feelings for their relative after expressing their closeness to the staff who assists them with activities of daily living (ADLs) at their current residence and is expressing a desire to reconnect with the relative as a result; or perhaps the client used to help or watch their relative do the laundry or other household chores before they moved into their community housing and the actual process of doing ADLs stimulates those memories; or any number of other possibilities. The therapist must not only watch for the response they are trying to elicit, but also always observe the complete experience of the client.

Procedures. Depending on the degree of receptive language skills and level of cognitive function of the client, the therapist might provide initial verbal instructions to the client about a topic or subject on which to concentrate (referential) or may leave this open (nonreferential). This will be due, in large part, to how directive the therapist feels they need to be; they may be trying to help the client to use the process of lyric improvisation to work through a particular situation or challenge, or they may simply be helping the client to explore whatever comes up in the clinical moment. Modeling of verbal material/lyric improvisation may be necessary to support the client in entering the experience. Supportive music provided by the therapist will be crucial in helping the client feel safe and confident enough to participate: Consideration should be given to styles of music used in previous sessions and what the client's reaction has been; awareness of the client's vocal range should guide the determination of tonal centering; intentional use of chordal movement vs. melodic content can stimulate variations in phrase length produced; and providing a musical structure that has a songlike quality to it can help support the client's effort. For example, given the mood of the client and the anticipated outcomes and goals, would a blues structure be appropriate? A choral structure? '50s rock-and-roll?

Guidelines for Re-creative Music Therapy

Bruscia (1998) defines re-creative experiences as those in which "the client learns or performs precomposed vocal or instrumental music or reproduces any kind of musical form presented as a model. Also included are structured music activities and games in which the client performs roles or behaviors that have been specifically defined. The term re-creative is used here rather than performing because the latter often implies singing or playing a piece before an audience. Re-creative is a broader term which includes rendering, reproducing, realizing, or interpreting any part or all of an existing musical model, whether done with or without an audience" (pp. 117–118).

Some of the main clinical goals of re-creative experiences include developing sensorimotor skills; fostering adaptive, time-ordered behavior; improving attention and reality orientation; developing memory skills; and learning specific role behaviors in various interpersonal situations (Bruscia, 1998).

Re-creative experiences can provide particular challenges when working with individuals with severe to profound IDD. Most individuals functioning at this level have limited or no ability to read and many are challenged even with following adaptive charts such as those that might use a color-coding system or some other form of notation or symbol communication tools. Frequent cuing or conducting on the part of the therapist is often warranted. However, it is also possible for many individuals to internalize the structure of precomposed material (instrumental or vocal) and then retain, retrieve, and utilize the structure during a re-creative experience, resulting in an intense experience of accomplishment and pride. This process often begins with participation in receptive experiences (particularly Method One: Listening to Live, Therapist-Provided Music and Method Four: Listening to Precomposed Songs from the Clinical Repertoire) discussed earlier in this chapter, and is then strengthened through focused participation and practice in various re-creative experiences. As with all other methods, the therapist needs to be alert to the strengths, needs, and interests of their client(s), make adaptations as necessary to ensure success, and also recognize and respect that, for some people, certain experiences are not beneficial, purposeful, or productive.

Instrumental Re-creation

Overview. In instrumental re-creation experiences, the client learns precomposed instrumental music through a process of repetition and practice. The therapist may present the chosen musical selection in parts or as a whole, and may or may not use supportive tools such as adapted music charts to provide additional guidance to the client in learning their part. Attention to detail during repetitive practice is crucial in helping the client to achieve success. Instrumental re-creation may be indicated for a client who needs to work on increasing awareness of external stimuli and other environmental factors; for someone who is working on general listening and attending skills; for an individual who is working on impulse-control issues; for someone who is nonverbal or for whom verbal communication poses unique challenges; for someone who needs to increase functional motor skills and/or range of motion; for someone who needs to work on sequencing skills; and for someone who needs to work on developing self-confidence. The goals of therapy in these instances may include extending the period of time that someone is able to maintain active grasp of instruments, expanding the amount of space that someone uses to play instruments, and having the client respond to and follow specific cues or directives (whether introduced musically, verbally, visually, gesturally, or through direct physical assistance). This experience is primarily provided at the augmentative and intensive levels, and sometimes at the auxiliary level.

As with Method One: Instrumental Improvisation discussed earlier in this chapter in the section on Improvisational Music Therapy, consideration needs to be given to the efficacy of implementing this method when working with clients with severe and profound IDD who may not possess the physical ability to actively engage independently in playing an instrument. The use of special positioning and various adaptations (adaptive mallets with built-up handles or straps, oversized guitar picks, horn stands, wheelchair clips for securing paddle drums, switches, etc.) can help to maximize the independence of a client with physical challenges as they engage in instrumental re-creative experiences.

Another consideration with the use of this method with individuals with severe/profound IDD was alluded to earlier in the section on guidelines for Re-creative Music Therapy: Generally speaking, individuals functioning at this level of cognition have both attentional deficits and impulse-control challenges which may prevent them from achieving independent instrumental re-creation. As discussed earlier, many have limited or no ability to read and are challenged even with following adaptive charts, requiring frequent cuing or conducting on the part of the therapist. However, it is also possible for many individuals to internalize the structure of precomposed material by repetition, sometimes referred to as rote learning.

Finally, many clients functioning at this level of IDD may feel intimidated or uncertain about the expectations inherent in having to re-create a precomposed or predetermined structure, as this holds with it the inherent possibility of failure, of making mistakes, of being wrong, or of not being good enough. Particularly when working with individuals who may have endured years of institutionalization, the therapist must be especially sensitive to providing a safe and supportive environment in which the client can feel confident that their efforts are valued, even if they don't achieve the targeted outcome. Of course, this is true in all areas, methods, and levels of work with individuals with severe to profound IDD, but it may be of particular importance when working on re-creative experiences.

Preparation. Positioning of the client in relation to the therapist and any instruments or cuing tools being used is important to ensure that the client can see any cues or prompts the therapist might provide. If one of the targeted outcomes is for the client to increase range of motion, make certain that there is adequate space available in the room so that the instruments can be positioned to facilitate this. Whenever possible, make certain that the session room is free of visual and auditory distractions (windows, loudspeaker announcements, noise from neighboring rooms, other instruments within visual or physical range that are not included in the improvisation experience, etc.) to ensure that the client's participation and success are optimized.

What to observe. The therapist is to observe the client for any targeted responses as well as secondary responses. For example, if one of the goals being addressed is for the client to play two resonator bars in sequence followed by playing a single beat on a timpani drum, the therapist is observing for the client to sequence these instruments accurately and at the indicated time in the composition. The therapist may observe, however, that the client consistently plays two beats on the timpani drum instead of one. This may be reflective of a wide range of possibilities: Perhaps the client is becoming engrossed in their own effort and therefore doesn't notice the cues in the music; perhaps the client is internalizing the two-beat sequence from the resonator bar phrase and unintentionally transferring it to the timpani drum (which could be a compulsive rhythmic response or a processing issue); perhaps the client just enjoys the sound of the timpani drum and would like it to last longer; or any number of other possibilities. In this case, the therapist must determine if they should strive to have the client achieve accuracy with the precomposed structure, or to alter the structure to add a second beat on the timpani drum. The therapist must not only watch for the response they are trying to elicit, but also always observe the complete experience of the client.

Procedures. Depending on the degree of receptive language skills of the individual, the therapist might provide initial verbal instructions to the client about what is expected of them. Regardless of the amount of verbal instruction, modeling and cuing [verbal, visual (including charts, etc.), gestural, tactile] will be crucial in supporting the client in learning their part. Extensive repetition and practice over time will help the client to learn the overall structure as well as their specific contribution(s), and will assist the client to retain, retrieve, and apply the information and skills. The therapist must be careful to present the structure with tremendous attention to accuracy each time; changes, even subtle ones, in tempo, dynamics, phrasing, etc., or more dramatic changes such as in tonality, can entirely alter the ability of the client to recognize something previously learned in a different way.

Adaptations. For some clients, providing a recording of the piece for them to listen to outside of the music therapy environment can further strengthen their internalization of the structure and support their learning of their part. Using a recording of the piece (with or without the client's part included) can also be a supportive technique within the actual music therapy session, allowing the therapist to provide increased cuing and assistance to the client as necessary.

Vocal Re-creation

Overview. In vocal re-creation experiences, the client learns precomposed vocal music through a process of repetition and practice. The therapist may present the chosen musical selection in parts or as a whole, and may or may not use supportive tools such as adapted music charts or lyric sheets to provide additional guidance to the client in learning their part. Attention to detail during repetitive practice is crucial in helping the client to achieve success. Vocal re-creation may be indicated for a client who needs to work on increasing awareness of external stimuli and other environmental factors; for someone who is working on general listening and attending skills; for an individual who is working on impulse-control issues; for someone who needs to increase expressive communication skills (for language development and/or emotional expression); for someone who needs to work on sequencing skills; and for someone who needs to work on developing self-confidence. The goals of therapy in these instances may include having the client respond in specific ways to cues or directives in the music, extending the period of time that someone is able to sustain breath support or pitch focus, expanding vocal range and melodic intonation, and having the client follow directives (whether introduced musically, verbally, visually, gesturally, or through direct physical assistance). This experience is primarily provided at the augmentative and intensive levels, and sometimes at the auxiliary level.

As with Method Two: Vocal Improvisation discussed earlier in this chapter in the section on Improvisational Music Therapy, this would be an inappropriate and ineffective method to employ with clients who are incapable of producing vocal sounds, but this must not be confused with those who may be nonverbal but are able to vocalize. Indeed, this can be an especially powerful method for just such a client.

Another consideration with the use of this method with individuals with severe/profound IDD was alluded to earlier in the section on guidelines for Re-creative Music Therapy: Generally speaking, individuals functioning at this level of cognition have both attentional deficits and impulse-control challenges which may prevent them from achieving independent vocal re-creation. As discussed earlier, many have limited or no ability to read and are challenged even with following adaptive charts, requiring frequent cuing or conducting on the part of the therapist. However, it is also possible for many individuals to internalize the structure of precomposed material by repetition, sometimes referred to as rote learning.

As is the case with instrumental re-creation, many clients functioning at this level of IDD may feel intimidated or uncertain about the expectations inherent in having to re-create a precomposed or predetermined structure, as this holds with it the inherent possibility of failure, of making mistakes, of being wrong, or of not being good enough. Particularly when working with individuals who may have endured years of institutionalization, the therapist must be especially sensitive to providing a safe and supportive environment in which the client can feel confident that their efforts are valued, even if they don't achieve the targeted outcome. Of course, this is true in all areas, methods, and levels of work with individuals with severe to profound IDD, but it may be of particular importance when working on re-creative experiences.

Finally, many clients functioning at this level of IDD may feel intimidated or uncertain about singing alone, as the voice is the most personal of all instruments. Some clients might worry that, since they don't sound like the people they hear on the radio (or like their music therapist), their singing is not worthwhile. It will likely be most effective for the therapist to sing with the client, at least initially, until the client develops a level of self-trust, trust in the therapist, and trust in the music.

Preparation. Positioning of the client in relation to the therapist and any cuing tools being used is important to ensure that the client can see any cues or prompts the therapist might provide. It is important that the client be comfortable so that they can concentrate on their vocal experience without distractions. Whenever possible, make certain that the session room is free of visual and auditory distractions (windows, loudspeaker announcements, noise from neighboring rooms, other instruments within visual or physical range that are not included in the improvisation experience, etc.) to ensure that the client's participation and success are optimized.

What to observe. The therapist is to observe the client for any targeted responses as well as secondary responses. For example, if one of the goals being addressed is for the client to sing the days of the week in correct sequence within the structure of a precomposed learning song, the therapist is observing for the client to sequence the days accurately and at the indicated time in the composition. The therapist may observe, however, that the client consistently omits "Tuesday." This may be reflective of a wide range of possibilities: Perhaps the client is anxious about a particular event that happens on Tuesdays and thinks that not singing the name of the day might help them avoid that event; perhaps the client is becoming engrossed in their own effort and therefore doesn't notice the cues in the music; perhaps the tongue placement for the "t" sound is uncomfortable due to poor oral hygiene or an oral-motor anomaly, so the client intentionally avoids producing the sound; or any number of other possibilities. The therapist must not only watch for the response they are trying to elicit, but also always observe the complete experience of the client.

Procedures. Depending on the degree of receptive language skills of the individual, the therapist might provide initial verbal instructions to the client about what is expected of them. Regardless of the amount of verbal instruction, modeling and cuing [verbal, visual (including charts, lyric sheets, etc.), gestural, tactile] will be crucial in supporting the client in learning their part. Extensive repetition and practice over time will help the client to learn the overall structure as well as their specific contribution(s), and will assist the client to retain, retrieve, and apply the information and skills. The therapist must be careful to present the structure with tremendous attention to accuracy each time; changes, even subtle ones, in tempo, dynamics, phrasing, etc., or more dramatic changes such as in tonality, can entirely alter the ability of the client to recognize something previously learned in a different way.

Adaptations. For some clients, providing a recording of the piece for them to listen to outside of the music therapy environment can further strengthen their internalization of the structure and support their learning of their part. Using a recording of the piece (with or without the client's part included) can also be a supportive technique within the actual music therapy session, allowing the therapist to provide increased cuing and assistance to the client as necessary. When working on vocal re-creation experiences that include lyrics, providing copies of lyric sheets for the client to use in learning the lyrics, with the support of staff or family members, can tremendously enhance the success level for the client. Finally, it is important to bear in mind that group singing can be an especially powerful social tool, so working on vocal re-creation (sing-alongs, adapted choral settings, etc.) can be highly motivating when working with individuals functioning at the severe or profound level of intellectual and developmental disability.

Performance Re-creation

Overview. Performance re-creation experiences can sometimes evolve naturally over time out of instrumental and/or vocal re-creative experiences undertaken within the confines of traditional therapy sessions. However, there are numerous elements to consider in performance re-creation that are not present during re-creative experiences within a session. A client might be very successful with and garner tremendous benefits from re-creative experiences within the confines of a session but could be devastated by trying to take that to a performance venue, so the therapist must proceed with caution when considering this undertaking and be prepared for possible adverse effects. Performance re-creation may be indicated for a client who needs to work on increasing awareness of external stimuli and other environmental factors; for someone who is working on general listening and attending skills; for an individual who is working on impulse-control issues; for an individual who is working on learning a variety of self-care skills and activities of daily living; and for someone who needs to address issues of self-confidence and self-esteem. The goals of therapy in these instances may include having the client respond in specific ways to cues or directives in the music, extending the period of time that someone sustains active engagement in playing or singing, contributing to the completion of a shared outcome, and learning basic accepted methods of recognizing the musical effort of another. This experience is primarily provided at the augmentative and intensive levels, and sometimes at the auxiliary level.

This method is appropriate only for those clients who are capable of functioning in a public performance setting in terms of their cognitive, emotional, and behavioral functioning. This method might naturally follow other methods over time for a client who achieves a certain level of competency with particular skills and for whom a performance opportunity could prove beneficial. Great care must be taken in determining if this is in the best interest of the client and what outcomes might be achieved. It must serve a purpose in the client's treatment.

Preparation. Performance re-creation occurs outside of the typical session structure and environment. Preparation for the performance re-creation would begin within the typical session structure and environment, drawing heavily on client experiences from a range of other methods described in this chapter. As it becomes apparent that a performance re-creation experience could be of benefit for a client, further preparation can occur in the physical space in which the performance will occur in order to familiarize the client with the environment and reduce subsequent anxiety. Positioning of the client in relation to the therapist is important to ensure that the client can see any cues or prompts the therapist might provide, along with minimizing distractions as much as is feasible given the setting. It is important that the client be comfortable so that they can concentrate on their experience without distractions. The therapist may want to have access to a recording device (audio or video) in order to capture the client's efforts for playbacks, and perhaps to provide a copy of the performance re-creation to the client and, when appropriate, their family. Whenever possible, make certain that the performance space is free of visual and auditory distractions (windows, loudspeaker announcements, noise from neighboring rooms, other instruments within visual or physical range that are not included in the listening experience, etc.) to ensure that the client's participation and success are optimized.

What to observe. The therapist is to observe the client for any targeted responses as well as secondary responses. A performance re-creation experience can present unanticipated challenges for client and therapist alike; audience members may interrupt a performance, cell phones might ring, the room might be unexpectedly hot or cold, etc. It is the therapist's responsibility to be alert to their client's reactions to all of these factors in order to ensure the most successful outcome possible. As with traditional session-based experiences, the therapist must not only watch for the response they are trying to elicit, but also always observe the complete experience of the client.

Procedures. As performance re-creation experiences are not music therapy sessions and typically occur in a location other than the actual therapy room, the points indicated in the earlier section on "Preparation of Session and Environment" are of utmost importance as part of the actual event. Once the performance event has started, it is the therapist's responsibility to ensure an atmosphere of respect for the performer(s). As is common in other performance settings, serving as an emcee of sorts and informing the audience members of basic concert etiquette (silencing cell phones, holding applause until the end, waiting to enter or exit until in between performances, etc.) can help to ensure a more pleasurable experience for performers and audience members alike. Within such a setting, the music therapist also assumes the role of "accompanist" and must ensure that no matter what happens, the performer(s) feel proud of their achievement.

Adaptations. In a performance setting, there is always the possibility that the performer(s) may react in an entirely different manner than that which they have prepared. In the case of performance re-creation experiences with clients, this might take the form of a client improvising new material in the moment within the context of a prepared piece (instrumental or vocal); it might also be the case that someone becomes overwhelmed by the intensity of the experience and "freezes" or becomes hyperexcited. The therapist may find that they need to alter the planned performance in any number of ways, including by eliminating a particular pieces or pieces; moving into a supportive improvised performance; changing the sequence of pieces and/or performers; changing from a performance style to a group participation experience; and/or making other adaptations as necessary and appropriate.

The therapist may want to have access to a recording device (audio or video) in order to provide a copy of the performance to the client(s) and their family members and other significant people, and to capture the client's efforts for playbacks and as part of their clinical record.

Guidelines for Compositional Music Therapy

Bruscia (1998) defines compositional experiences as those in which "the therapist helps the client to write songs, lyrics, or instrumental pieces, or to create any kind of musical product such as music videos or audiotapes. Usually the therapist takes responsibility for the more technical aspects of the process, and gauges the client's participation to his/her musical capabilities. For example, the client may generate the melody on a simple bar instrument, while the therapist provides the harmonic accompaniment, or the client may produce the lyrics while the therapist composes the melody and harmony to go with them" (p. 119).

Some of the main clinical goals of compositional experiences include developing organizational and planning abilities, working on creative problem-solving, promoting self-responsibility, communicating inner thoughts and experiences, and developing the ability to integrate and synthesize parts into wholes (Bruscia, 1998).

When working with individuals who function at the severe to profound level of IDD, composition experiences present a range of unique opportunities as well as challenges. Generally speaking, compositional music therapy with this population is most successful when focused on song composition and rarely addresses instrumental composition. Thus, the methods presented below describe implementation strictly for song composition unless otherwise indicated.

Composition Experiences *with* the Client

Overview. In composition experiences with a client, the therapist helps the client to create original songs, lyrics, or instrumental pieces. Receptive and expressive communication abilities of the client will determine the level of prompting and leading required on the part of the therapist to access material for use in the composition. Composition experiences completed with a client may be indicated for a client who needs to work on increasing awareness of external stimuli and other environmental factors; for an individual who is working on impulse-control issues; for someone who needs to work on sequencing skills; for someone who needs to increase expressive communication skills (for language development and/or emotional expression); for an individual who is working on learning new strategies for responding to challenging situations; and for someone who needs to work on developing self-confidence or enhancing self-esteem. The goals of therapy in these instances may include having the client respond to open-ended or yes/no questions, having the client dictate thoughts/lyrics to the therapist on specific topics, having the client engage in song/lyric improvisation (see Method Three: Song/Lyric Improvisation in the "Improvisational Music Therapy" section earlier in this chapter), and assuming a leadership role in approving the final product (lyrical content, ordering of lyrics, style of music). This experience is primarily provided at the auxiliary, augmentative, and intensive levels.

Consideration needs to be given to the efficacy of implementing this method when working with clients with severe and profound IDD who may not possess the cognitive capacity to actively contribute to the process of composition. For song composition, the therapist may need to structure the process so that the client can choose from between two options presented verbally or perhaps with visual aids, or to present yes/no choices. In cases in which the client is nonverbal or has limited language, they may need to respond through sign, gestures, behaviorally (i.e., eye blinks, head nods, etc.), or use of an augmentative communication device (e.g., Dynavox).

Preparation. Positioning of the client in relation to the therapist is important to ensure that the client can see any cues or prompts the therapist might provide. It is important that the client be comfortable so that they can concentrate on their composition experience without distractions. The therapist should have access to paper and/or staff paper and/or a recording device (audio or video) in order to capture the client's efforts for future notation and for playbacks. Whenever possible, make certain that the session room is free of visual and auditory distractions (windows, loudspeaker announcements, noise from neighboring rooms, instruments within visual or physical range that are not included in the experience, etc.) to ensure that the client's participation and success are optimized.

What to observe. The therapist is to observe the client for any targeted responses as well as secondary responses. For example, if the goal being addressed is for the client to develop strategies to learn how to increase independence when doing their laundry, the therapist is observing for the client to contribute ideas about recognizing that their clothes are dirty, accepting guidance from staff or family members, learning how to measure detergent, understanding the sequence of using the washing machine and dryer, etc. The therapist may observe, however, that the client frequently comments that they don't know how to unbutton buttons or unzip zippers, and that they ask one of their housemates to help them change into their pajamas at night. This is a clear signal to the therapist that there are multiple layers of learning involved in this topic, and they may need to accommodate this by also working on ancillary goals such as addressing fine motor skill development as well as privacy issues.

The therapist may want to consult other team members to provide additional support to the client (for example, to speak with an occupational therapist regarding the fine motor issues, and to speak with the client's advocate or psychologist to begin work on ensuring that they have adequate assistance and privacy when changing their clothes, and to help them learn about personal boundaries). Of course, the music therapist can address these skill areas as well, but if the immediate goal in music therapy is sequencing a complete laundry task, it's best to not confuse the client with working on too many concepts simultaneously. The therapist must not only watch for the response they are trying to elicit, but also always observe the complete experience of the client.

Procedures. Keeping in mind the contraindications discussed earlier for this method and depending on the degree of receptive and expressive language skills of the individual, the therapist should provide instructions to the client about what is expected of them, including presenting the focus topic for the composition, i.e., learning how to do their laundry. In most situations, simply starting with a conversation during which the therapist presents targeted questions and records the client's responses is a good beginning. For example:

Therapist (T): "What do you with your dirty clothes when you take them off?"
Client (C): "Put them in the laundry basket."
T: "When the basket is full, what do you do with it?"
C: "Ask staff to help me carry it to the laundry room."
T: "What do you use to wash your dirty clothes?"
C: "The machine."
T: "The machine? Do you remember what that machine is called?"
C: "It's the clean-the-clothes machine—with the water, with the soap."
T: "It's the washing ...."
C: "The washing machine!"
T: "Yes, very good. Now, what do you put in the washing machine first, your clothes or that special soap—the de-ter ...," etc.

This is an example of a highly structured conversation and does not include music at the outset. Another approach could be simply to engage the client in a more open discussion about doing laundry and see what comments are offered spontaneously; this could be done with a musical background provided on guitar or piano as more of a song/lyric improvisation, or without music. Perhaps the client presents a free-flow of thoughts on the topic, such as: "I like the smell of clean clothes; I spill my coffee a lot; the laundry room is in the basement and it scares me; we shop at Target for soap; I want new sneakers for my birthday," etc. The therapist can then work with the client on expanding the range of lyrical content, perhaps using the idea of "I like the smell of clean clothes" as the recurring theme and perhaps even as the title for the song.

Determining the style of music for a composition experience completed with a client is equally important. The therapist must draw on their knowledge of the client's relationship with music, particular styles of music that are especially motivating or stimulating for the client, and tonal centers that will encourage and support the client's natural intonation and vocal range, as well as give consideration to elements such as meter, phrase length, instrumentation, etc.

Adaptations. For some clients, providing a recording of the piece for them to listen to outside of the music therapy environment can further strengthen their internalization of the structure and support them in using the song in other settings. For example, if the song is focused on the correct sequencing of tasks involved in doing laundry, actually listening to a playback at their house while doing their laundry can be a supportive tool; if the song is about responding to stressful situations, knowing they have access to it (through a recording or internally) in settings other than their music therapy session can be comforting. In some cases, providing a hard copy of the song itself, or just the lyrics, is also helpful and can allow staff and/or family members to reinforce the content of the song. Finally, some clients greatly value creating a collection of favored songs (precomposed as well as original compositions) to keep in the music therapy room and sometimes at their home. It provides a tangible, external container for the internal containers provided by the songs and, for those individuals who choose to share this with others, it can create a mechanism for social interactions.

Similar strategies as described above in working with an individual client are easily adapted and implemented for composition experiences when working with a group.

Composition Experiences *for* a Client

Overview. Composition experiences *for* a client are distinctly different from composition experiences *with* a client, in that a therapist may find it necessary to engage in a composition experience separate from a client in order to meet a specific need demonstrated. It may be that a therapist has exhausted precomposed repertoire on a particular topic or area of skill development, or that a client is in a crisis situation which demands very individualized music and lyrics, or any number of other circumstances for which existing music or improvisatory approaches are not indicated or determined to be adequate. Composition experiences completed by the therapist for a client may be indicated for a client who needs to work on increasing awareness of external stimuli and other environmental factors; for someone who is working on general listening and attending skills; for an individual who is working on impulse-control issues; for someone who needs to work on sequencing skills; for someone who needs to increase expressive communication skills (for language development and/or emotional expression); for an individual who is working on learning new strategies for responding to challenging situations; and for someone who needs to work on developing self-confidence or enhancing self-esteem. As the bulk of this process occurs outside of the session, the goals of therapy in these instances may be more similar to those articulated earlier in this chapter in Method Two: Vocal Re-creation in the "Re-creative Music Therapy" section, including having the client respond in specific ways to cues or directives in the music, extending the period of time that someone is able to sustain breath support or pitch focus, expanding vocal range and melodic intonation, and having the client follow directives (whether introduced musically, verbally, visually, gesturally, or through direct physical assistance).

However, it is often the case that a therapist may undertake a composition experience for a client who has especially unique affective/emotional needs that are not adequately addressed by any precomposed song from the clinical or popular repertoire. Thus, the process of composing a song for a particular client is frequently driven by, and requires, a deep understanding of the client on the part of the therapist. This experience is primarily provided at the augmentative and intensive levels, and yet may sometimes be implemented at the auxiliary and primary levels, as diverse as they are.

There are, of course, exceptions to this line of thinking and instances in which a therapist might engage in a composition experience *for* a client about a topic that is much less emotionally charged (for example, the earlier scenario in the section on Composition Experiences with a Client that focused on a song about learning laundry skills). It is also not uncommon for a therapist to compose songs about specific topics or skills for more general application in their work and not necessarily written for one particular client. For example, many publications of Nordoff-Robbins compositions such as "Children's Play Songs" (Books 1–5) and others, and compositions by Herb and Gail Levin such as "Learning Through Music," "Learning Through Song," and "Learning Songs," contain compositions about topics as diverse as crossing the street safely; learning how to tie shoes; working on identifying coins and their values; addressing concepts such as colors, opposites, weather, etc.; and others, as well as instrumental compositions. At the same time, it is quite possible for a therapist to engage in composition experiences *with* a client on a topic of much more emotional volatility. For the purposes of this chapter, however, a distinction is made simply in the hope of providing clarity of clinical focus, and the remaining discussion of composition experiences *for* a client concentrates on topics of an emotional nature that are also highly individualized for a specific client.

Generally speaking, composition experiences completed by a therapist for a client are undertaken at the point when a therapist realizes that a particular client has a specific area or areas of need that are not addressed (or not adequately addressed) in the existing repertoire and that the client involved is not capable (due to language or cognitive limitations or emotional/behavioral complications) of participating in a meaningful way in composing the song in a collaborative manner.

Preparation. As composition experiences for a client are not music therapy sessions and typically occur as a solitary pursuit for the therapist, preparation of the session and environment is not a consideration in this case. The therapist should work on the composition in whatever setting is most effective and productive for their compositional efforts. Staff paper, instruments, and recording devices should be available in order to retain and refine the composition over time.

What to observe. As has already been discussed, this approach in therapy is one which the therapist undertakes outside of the session and apart from the client. However, when presenting the song to the client, the therapist will want to be particularly alert to any overt or subtle reactions on the part of the client that are being stimulated by the very personal content of the composition.

Procedures. The therapist must be sensitive to when they present the composition and how much they present. Is it appropriate and beneficial to present the entire composition all at once, or perhaps should it initially just be presented without the lyrics (or vice versa), so that the client can internalize parts of the whole? The therapist must also determine the frequency and duration of presenting the composition over time, and proceed cautiously.

Depending on the degree of receptive language skills of the client, the therapist might provide initial verbal instructions to the client about what is expected of them. In some cases, the composition might be clearly introduced to the client, e.g., "I'm going to play a song for you now, John. You can just listen to it and tell me what you think." In other cases, the composition might be woven into a session in a more subtle manner, e.g., at a point in the session when the client starts expressing concern about when they might talk with their family again, the therapist can transition into the song on the piano and perhaps use the music as a way of holding the client in the moment, eventually incorporating some of the lyrics until slowly, over time, the song emerges in full. Regardless of the manner in which the song is initially presented, prompting, modeling, and cuing [verbal, visual (including charts, etc.), gestural, tactile] will be crucial in supporting the client in learning the song. Extensive repetition and practice over time will help the client to learn the overall structure as well as the lyrics and will assist the client to retain, retrieve, and participate in the song in future sessions.

Adaptations. Over time, the client may intentionally or spontaneously create additional original lyrics for the song as their life experiences impact the content and function of the song. For example, a song that is written addressing a client's weekly phone conversations with their mother may have additional verses included to recognize phone conversations with other relatives or important people in the client's life; or it may be that a verse is created that describes an actual visit with family; or, should the client experience the death of a relative, the song can take on a different function in supporting the client through the grieving process.

As with Composition Experiences with a Client (above), providing a recording of the song for a client to listen to outside of the music therapy environment can provide them with a strategy to access the comfort of the form and function of the song at times when they wish to seek it out. Although composing a song for a client can also provide a primarily receptive experience, if the client is verbal and is capable of learning the song (even if not completely), the process of learning and singing such a composition can be quite a powerful process for the client to undergo. However, even for clients who are verbal and capable of learning and singing a song that their therapist has written for them, there may very well be instances when a therapist composes a song for a client for the simple act of providing a musical offering to the client, and the expectation of the client learning to sing the song is secondary.

Depending on the needs of a particular client, they may choose at some time to use the song in another setting. This may be as part of a larger event, such as a recital or community music therapy experience, or it may be more private, such as performing the piece as a musical gift for their family. Finally, there may be instances in which the therapist composes an instrumental piece for a particular client, perhaps to address individualized needs for range of motion development or sequencing skills development; this may be indicated for a client who is notably motivated by a certain instrument.

Song Parody

Overview. In song parody experiences, the therapist helps the client to create original lyrics within the structure of a precomposed song which may or may not be familiar to the client. The purpose of this process can be to support the learning of new skills and information or to reinforce existing knowledge and skills, or for emotional expression. It is important for the therapist to give careful consideration to the selection of precomposed song(s) for use in this method, as the use of familiar songs might prove confusing for the client. Much of the information discussed in the earlier methods applies to this area as well. Song parody experiences may be indicated for a client who needs to work on increasing awareness of external stimuli and other environmental factors; for an individual who is working on impulse-control issues; for someone who needs to work on sequencing skills; for someone who needs to increase expressive communication skills (for language development and/or emotional expression); for an individual who is working on learning new strategies for responding to challenging situations; and for someone who needs to work on developing self-confidence or enhancing self-esteem. The goals of therapy in these instances may include having the client respond to open-ended or yes/no questions, having the client dictate thoughts/lyrics to the therapist on specific topics, and having the client engage in song/lyric improvisation. The therapist assumes a leadership role in approving the final product (lyrical content, ordering of lyrics). This experience is primarily provided at the auxiliary, augmentative, and intensive levels.

Consideration needs to be given to the efficacy of implementing this method when working with clients with severe and profound IDD who may not possess the cognitive capacity to actively contribute to the process of song parody. The therapist may need to structure the process so that the client can choose from between two options presented verbally or perhaps with visual aids, or to present yes/no choices. In cases in which the client is nonverbal or has limited language, they may need to respond through sign, gestures, or behaviors (i.e., eye blinks, head nods, etc.). The therapist must also be sensitive to the fact that, for some clients, song parody can be a confusing concept; especially if the song being used is very familiar to them, they may not be able to understand the idea of singing it with different words. The structure and lyrical content of the original song may be too ingrained and internalized in the individual for them to be able to learn it with new lyrics. All too often, therapists think that using a familiar song, one in which the client is already very familiar with the melodic phrasing and harmonic structure, will support the client in learning new lyrics since they won't have to also learn the melody, etc. On the contrary, people who function at severe to profound levels of IDD may simply be confused or frustrated by this attempt at combining novelty with familiarity. If a therapist is struggling to create original harmonic and/or melodic material for a song parody experience, it might be more effective to seek out a precomposed song with which the client is not familiar, in order to lessen their confusion regarding the original lyrics.

Preparation. When using precomposed music, it is important to have the music memorized or to have hard copies organized and available in order to minimize disruption and distracting the client by looking through songbooks, etc. Positioning of the client in relation to the therapist is important to ensure that the client can see any cues or prompts the therapist might provide. It is important that the client be comfortable so that they can concentrate on their song parody experience without distractions. The therapist should have access to paper and/or staff paper and/or a recording device (audio or video) in order to capture the client's efforts for future notation and for playbacks. Whenever possible, make certain that the session room is free of visual and auditory distractions (windows, loudspeaker announcements, noise from neighboring rooms, instruments within visual or physical range that are not included in the experience, etc.) to ensure that the client's participation and success are optimized.

What to observe. The therapist is to observe the client for any targeted responses as well as secondary responses. This may take many different forms, depending on the subject matter of the song. For example, if the goal being addressed is for the client to learn strategies for responding to stressful situations or about privacy issues related to dressing and undressing as opposed to one in which the client is contributing to a song about places in the community they like to visit, the therapist will likely be much more directive in the first scenario than in the second one. The first goal area (stressful situations or privacy issues) may require the therapist to provide a lot more support and guidance to the client, as this is a process geared toward the actual learning of new information, behavior, and skills; the second goal area (fun places to visit) can be more spontaneous and celebratory in nature, and can also incorporate places the client has never visited but might like to visit, including their ideas (realistic or not) about what it would be like. The therapist must not only watch for the response they are trying to elicit, but also always observe the complete experience of the client.

Procedures. Song parody can be achieved through use of an existing song from virtually any period of music or through what is referred to here as "modified song parody," in which the therapist develops a general song structure and then asks the client to fill in the blanks. As mentioned earlier in regard to contraindications, the therapist must be sensitive to the fact that using a familiar song might be confusing to the client; in these cases, creating an original song structure for the song parody will provide a more fulfilling and successful experience for the client. For example, consider a client who often responds to stressful situations with physical aggression or property destruction, which of course leads to negative attention from staff and likely also a loss of some freedoms or special activities. It may even be that the anticipation of the special activity—let's say a breakfast outing with a favored staff person—is what creates the stress for the client.

The therapist should consider creating a song structure that is focused on the desired outcome for the client, e.g., a successful and enjoyable breakfast outing; this can be the "A" section of a song. The "B" section might concentrate more on some of the stressors leading up to the breakfast outing, e.g., displaying positive behavior toward peers all week; having to wake up earlier than usual on the day of the outing; dressing in special clothes; etc. The "C" section of the song can offer strategies for getting past these stressors, such as going to a different room if one of the client's housemates is making the client nervous; asking to go to bed early the night before and asking staff for help in setting an alarm clock to an earlier time than is typical; picking out an outfit the night before and making sure that everything is clean and ready to wear, etc. The return of the "A" section brings everything back to the goal: a successful and enjoyable breakfast outing with a favored staff person.

Adaptations. Strategies as described above in working with an individual client are easily adapted and implemented for song parody experiences when working with a group, with care given to the topic of the song. However, the therapist must be sensitive to the fact that, in a group setting, not all group members may have a frame of reference for certain topics, and the focus topic of the song parody experience needs to be carefully selected to be inclusive of all members. It may be helpful to provide a recording of the song for a client to listen to outside of the music therapy environment, which can provide them with a strategy to access the support of the form and function of the song at times when they wish to seek it out.

Theme-Based Composition

Overview. Certain themes (melodic, rhythmic, stylistic, lyrical, etc.) evolve organically over time in therapy, and in some cases the therapist determines that a theme can or should be moved to the more permanent format of an original composition. Theme-Based Composition experiences tend to emerge naturally over the course of therapy. The process may more accurately be referred to as "thematic development," and it frequently arises as a result of the repeated presentation of improvisational themes (harmonic, melodic, rhythmic, lyrical) over time that continue to deepen, expand, and gradually grow into recognizable structures and songs. Theme-based composition may be indicated for a client who needs to work on increasing awareness of external stimuli and other environmental factors; for someone who is working on general listening and attending skills; for an individual who is working on impulse-control issues; for someone who needs to work on sequencing skills; for someone who needs to increase expressive communication skills (for language development and/or emotional expression); for an individual who is working on learning new strategies for responding to challenging situations; and for someone who needs to work on developing self-confidence or enhancing self-esteem. The goals of therapy in these instances typically include having the client respond in specific ways (instrumentally, vocally, verbally, or through movement) to cues or directives in the music (whether introduced harmonically, melodically, rhythmically, instrumentally, or lyrically). This experience is primarily provided at the auxiliary, augmentative, and intensive levels.

There are no obvious contraindications for use of this method, although consideration needs to be given to the efficacy of implementing this method with clients with severe and profound IDD who may not possess the cognitive capacity to accurately internalize themes. These cases are rare. In fact, thematic development is often one of the most powerful methods in establishing initial and ongoing communication and a relationship of trust and intimacy with individuals who may otherwise struggle with receptive language skills.

Preparation. As theme-based composition experiences typically occur spontaneously and frequently develop organically over time, preparation of the session and environment is not as clear-cut as is the case with many other methods. As the therapist becomes aware of the ongoing thematic development, they should ensure that the work is captured through notation and/or recording in order to retain and refine the developing composition over time.

What to observe. The therapist is to observe the client for any targeted responses as well as secondary responses. As this method is one that typically begins in an unplanned and truly spontaneous manner, the therapist will need to observe the client's response to the thematic development over time. For example, if the goal being addressed is for the client to use both hands functionally for increasing lengths of time during a drumming experience, the therapist may develop a brief directive (e.g., "Two hands now! Two hands now! Two hands now on that drum!") and pair it with a specific melodic phrase within the context of an overall improvisation. Each time the theme is introduced, the therapist observes for the client to continue or resume use of both hands for drumming. The therapist must not only watch for the response they are trying to elicit, but also always observe the complete experience of the client.

Procedures. Depending on the degree of receptive language skills of the client, the therapist might provide initial verbal instructions to the client about what is expected of them; this would happen after the theme has already started to emerge in earlier sessions. In some cases, the theme might be clearly introduced to the client, e.g., "Kathy, I'm going to play something for you now. Listen carefully!" In the case of the "two hands now" example mentioned earlier, there may be instances in which the therapist might actually invite the client to sing the theme with them. It might help the client to internalize the theme as well as practice the expected response if they sing it while also sharing a drum with the therapist, each of them playing with both hands as they sing or chant the theme. In other cases, the theme might be woven into a session in a more subtle manner, e.g., at a point in the drum improvisation when the client starts using only one hand, the therapist can incorporate the theme into an ongoing improvisation. When the client responds by resuming the use of both hands, celebratory praise can be provided; this might actually become a secondary theme. Extensive repetition of the theme over time will help the client to learn the overall structure as well as any accompanying lyrics and will assist the client to retain, retrieve, and participate in the theme in future sessions.

Adaptations. Over time, as the client fully internalizes a theme such as the "two hands now" example, the therapist may slowly eliminate the actual singing of the lyrics and have only the melodic, harmonic, and rhythmic content of the theme function to prompt the client to demonstrate the targeted response.

There are many instances in which theme-based composition is the first step toward Method One: Composition Experiences with a Client and/or Method Two: Composition Experiences for a Client, and the reader only need refer to the clinical repertoire (especially much of the song collections of Nordoff and Robbins, Herb and Gail Levin, and others) to find songs that began as improvisations and over time developed into complete songs through the process of thematic development.

Research Evidence

Hooper, Wigram, Carson, and Lindsay (2008a; 2008b) provided an extensive literature review of both descriptive/philosophical and experimental writings related to a broad range of clinical approaches in working with individuals with intellectual disabilities. While it is not possible within this chapter to review all of the ideas and outcomes covered in their two articles, the reader is encouraged to consider referring to the articles as a starting point for further research regarding receptive, improvisational, re-creative, and compositional methods, as well as others not addressed in this chapter.

Receptive Music Therapy

In their chapter on vibroacoustic therapy, Skille and Wigram (1995) review a variety of clinical applications with a wide range of populations. They report on early discussions of vibroacoustic therapy between Skille and Juliette Alvin and the subsequent creation of equipment which they referred to as a "music bath." Contemporary versions of this include the Somatron. The use of this early "music bath" was overseen by Skille at a day program for children with IDD and physical challenges, specifically seeking outcomes of decreasing muscle tone and spasticity in individuals with cerebral palsy. The results were clear and quick, and follow-up work also incorporated movement experiences facilitated by the therapist. Additional applications discussed in their chapter which support Method Three: Somatic Listening to Recorded Music via Somatron or Similar Vibroacoustic Equipment from the section on "Receptive Music Therapy" include the use of vibroacoustic therapy for children with autism and its effectiveness in decreasing tactile defensiveness, thus allowing more direct intervention by the therapist.

Also supportive of Method Three: Somatic Listening to Recorded Music via Somatron or Similar Vibroacoustic Equipment from the section on "Receptive Music Therapy," Persoons and De Backer (1997) discuss the use of vibroacoustic therapy in working with individuals with multiple challenges and point to the efficacy of its application purely as a relaxation method as well as a preparation for more active experiences in music therapy. They speak to the importance of working in a client-centered way and highlight their success with using receptive relaxation experiences as a preliminary portion of a session, leading to an increase in client receptiveness to interpersonal interactions during more active portions of their sessions.

From the same publication, Wigram, McNaught, Cain, and Weekes (1997) provide further support for this method, specifically discussing the use of somatic listening in their work with two individuals with severe-profound IDD. One of the clients, Gregory, also had epilepsy and cerebral palsy. The focus of therapy for Gregory was on decreasing spasticity and increasing awareness and interaction. Results indicated that these goals were achieved, along with an overall increase in active range of motion and more receptivity in physical therapy. The other case discussed involved Adam, who, while having no physical disabilities, engaged in severe self-injurious behavior, including face slapping and biting himself on the arms and wrists. The focus of somatic listening for Adam was to decrease the self-injury, and the results indicated overall success although not complete elimination of the self-injurious behavior. Adam was generally noted to be calmer, more receptive to verbal or physical interaction with staff, and gentler with himself.

Improvisational Music Therapy

Boxill (1981) described a continuum of clinical process highlighted by "(1) Reflection—the mirroring of the here-and-now client; (2) Identification—the symbolic representation, in musical forms, of the here-and-now client and therapist; (3) Our Contact Song—a composed or improvised song that serves as an affirmation of the client-therapist relationship." She highlighted the clinical efficacy of vocal and/or instrumental improvisation in helping the therapist to recognize the client in a holistic state and, by doing so, support the client in experiencing a change in their own perception of themselves and how they relate to others and to their environment. Boxill emphasizes the importance of the immediacy provided by the moment-to-moment improvisation in helping the client to individuate, thus providing a strong argument for the power of improvisation to help clients with severe to profound IDD address goals such as increasing awareness of external stimuli, improving impulse-control issues, and developing self-awareness and self-confidence.

In her article discussing the Nordoff-Robbins case of Edward, Rolvsjord (1998) questions the basis of the therapists' decision to not comfort the screaming child, discovering through ongoing review of the case how this ultimately results in Edward's success in developing communication skills. As Nordoff and Robbins interpret the screams within an improvisational context, a musical interaction unfolds that grows into a musical interaction among the three. It expands to incorporate turn-taking as well as synchronizing. The improvisation of the therapist incorporates a tonal center, rhythmic and melodic themes, and ongoing development of theme and variations. Rolvsjord concludes that this process of improvisation which incorporates and expands the communicative efforts of Edward results in his growing awareness of self, differentiated from others, and ultimately allows for him to enter into a social relationship and shared communication with the therapists. This strongly supports the use of improvisation in working with individuals with severe to profound IDD—even those who are nonverbal and may initially be resistive in therapy.

Pavlicevic (2000) discussed distinctions between the functions of music improvisation and music therapy improvisation. She concluded that "MT improvisation taps a natural communicative resource: the mechanisms of nonverbal communication." She went on to affirm the power of improvisation in music therapy to create intimacy between the client and the therapist.

Rainey Perry (2003) describes a qualitative research project with 10 children with severe IDD and related challenges such as cerebral palsy, epilepsy, visual and hearing impairments, and others. The focus of the study was to look at the impact of improvisational methods on the development of communication and, subsequently, social interaction and relationship. Various improvisational techniques were implemented, along with the use of precomposed and thematically developed songs, and both instrumental and vocal experiences. Rainey Perry discerned that the experience of improvisation in music therapy provided motivation for participation, allowed for the children to exert a degree of control over their environment, and generally supported the development of trust and intimacy that resulted in improvements in social interaction and communication.

Specifically describing the effectiveness of Method Two: Vocal Improvisation, Graham (2004) discussed her work with a woman ("O") with numerous challenges including cerebral palsy, visual impairment, microcephaly, minimal motor function, and apparently minimal understanding of language. "O" often cried for reasons that were not apparent to her caregivers, and she was frequently moved to another room and isolated as a result. Graham worked with the crying vocalizations of "O" in an improvisational manner, supported with a piano accompaniment. The results of the work indicated that "O's" crying held expressive, communicative intent, and "O" changed her vocal productions in response to the therapist's singing and playing. Another client, "J," was diagnosed with autism and demonstrated a wide range of behavior challenges. Although nonverbal, "J" produced two distinct vocalizations, one which was a quiet humming and the other a high-pitched screaming. Analyzing the two vocalizations, Graham determined that "J's" humming was a method of self-calming whereas the screaming was expressive and communicative in nature. She worked to connect with "J's" screaming through vocal improvisation and, over time, "J" was able to alter his pitches, vocal range, and dynamics in order to engage in more collaborative vocalization with the therapist. In both cases, the implementation of vocal improvisation methods resulted in the development of relationship in therapy, and relatives and staff members noticed improvements in social interaction and communicative efforts.

Re-creative Music Therapy

Curtis and Mercado (2004) discuss a community music therapy "Performing Arts Program" held at a university campus whose members were those with and without developmental disabilities. Two groups were formed: a handbell choir and chorus, and an American Sign Language (ASL) and Music group. The groups met weekly and practiced, with the goal of a public performance at the end of the semester. Ratings of the experience were completed by participants and caregivers at the end of each semester, as well as by audience members, with five semesters of performances discussed in the article referenced here. The ratings from both groups of respondents were overwhelmingly positive and supportive of continuation of the project. The experience of all participants and the results of the survey evaluations speak to the efficacy of all three methods of Re-creative Music Therapy with individuals with severe to profound IDD discussed in this chapter, and particularly to Method Three: Performance Re-creation.

Hooper (2001) discussed his research describing the use of group music therapy to increase social interaction among recently deinstitutionalized adults with developmental disabilities. The primary experiences presented in the sessions were those of Re-creative Music Therapy Method Two: Vocal Re-creation. Hooper concentrated on presenting action songs such as "If You're Happy and You Know It" and familiar songs such as "When the Saints Go Marching In." He also implemented Re-creative Music Therapy Method One: Instrumental Re-creation, and Compositional Music Therapy Method Three: Song Parody. He concludes that music therapy clearly assists individuals with IDD to navigate the complexities of social interaction, and that it can be especially successful in helping those who are working to connect with others in new environments as a result of deinstitutionalization.

Aigen (1995) describes a process of Compositional Music Therapy Method Four: Theme-Based Composition, or thematic development, moving to Re-creative Music Therapy Method One: Instrumental Re-creation in his analysis of the well-known case of Nicole. In her first session with Carol and Clive Robbins, Nicole is greeted in the music therapy room by hearing Carol singing to her, "here we are in music." This recurring theme, with its consistent tonality and phrasing, served to help orient Nicole to the opening of each of her sessions. Over time, the phrase developed from a theme to a greeting song. Nicole initiated playing the melodic rhythm of the phrase on the piano, and ultimately Carol helped Nicole to play the actual melody with hand-over-hand assistance. The learning of this skill provided immense pleasure to Nicole and helped to further strengthen the intimacy and trust between Nicole and her therapists.

Clarkson (1991) discusses the case of a young man named Jerry diagnosed with autism who is said to function at anywhere from the mild to profound levels of mental retardation, with a mental age estimated to be between 2 and 8 years old. Jerry was also nonverbal and could be violent. Clarkson's work with Jerry included both improvised and structured instrumental and vocal experiences. It took some time for Jerry to trust his therapist, but as their work continued, it seems that Instrumental Re-creation took on a large role. A variety of instruments was used, including drumming with drumsticks and resonator bars. Clarkson worked with Jerry on "Fun for Four Drums" by Nordoff and Robbins, a piece introduced in the first few months of music therapy. After six months, Jerry recognized the four different patterns and learned to play the response. As he moved through his first year of therapy and into his second, Jerry began learning a system of musical notation with color-coding and learned a variety of bell accompaniments. This experience of learning precomposed music and re-creating it opened an expansive range of musical experiences for Jerry, with an accompanying growth in social skills.

Compositional Music Therapy

Farnan (1987) discusses key components that relate to Method Two: Composition Experiences for a Client, differentiating therapist-composed songs into two categories: songs that are specific to an individual and those that are created with a group in mind. For individual song composition, she indicates a general structure of targeting a specific task, constructing lyrics, defining success criteria, and then setting the words to music. For a group composition, the structure includes targeting a task, constructing simple sentences, and setting the words to music. She suggests that the group song is focused on more general responses and thus does not need to include specific criteria such as an individualized composition might.

Fischer (1991) illustrates the power of Compositional Music Therapy methods in her case study discussion outlining 11 months of individual and group music therapy with Albert. Developmentally disabled and autistic, Albert struggled with issues related to self-image, impulse control, and an inability to connect in a meaningful and positive way with others. While improvisation and instrument playing were also components of Albert's therapy, Fischer found that Methods One and Four (Composition Experiences with a Client and Theme-Based Composition, respectively) were the entry point into her work, starting with a very "safe" topic (foods that Albert liked to eat) and resulting in the composition of the "Food Song." After three weeks, they entered into a deeper area of concern and work began to focus on Albert's fears, some superficial (such as those related to television cartoons) and others more intense (such as those related to dark closets). Fischer continued to implement Methods One and Four and, after 15 weeks, the eight-verse "Fear Song" was completed. For the remaining 12 weeks of therapy, Fischer sought to move Albert to an active phase of working toward a more positive self-image. In order to accomplish this, she implemented Methods Two and Three (Composition Experiences for a Client and Song Parody, respectively). The therapist created the "Self Song," which included blanks for the client to fill in. Although challenging for Albert to do, with the support of his therapist he succeeded in moving toward a positive perspective of himself by starting to identify negative things he did not do; he celebrated the moments in group therapy when his peers sang the lyric contributed by the therapist, "Albert is a fine young man."

Summary and Conclusions

As discussed earlier in this chapter, there are those who believe that individuals with severe to profound intellectual and developmental disabilities do not or cannot live a rich, musical life; that they are unable to adequately process musical material in a way that they can access it and use it for emotional expression and interpersonal connection; and that they cannot enter into work that originates from a music-centered and humanistic perspective. This is clearly not the case. It is the responsibility of the music therapist serving these individuals to strive to understand their clients through their music; to use this understanding to inform their work; and to communicate the unique knowledge we possess regarding the way our clients respond to music *and* how we use that knowledge in our work to help others see the whole person.

References

Aigen, K. (1995). Cognitive and affective processes in music therapy with individuals with developmental delays: A preliminary model for contemporary Nordoff-Robbins practice. *Music Therapy, 13*(1), 13–46.

American Association on Intellectual and Developmental Disabilities. (2011). *Definition of intellectual disability.* Retrieved March 13, 2012 from http://www.aaidd.org/content_100.cfm?navID=21

American Music Therapy Association. (2011). *Standards of clinical practice.* Retrieved May 8, 2012 from http://www.musictherapy.org/about/standards/#DEVELOPMENTAL_DISABILITIES

Boxill, E. (1981). A continuum of awareness: Music therapy with the developmentally handicapped. *Music Therapy, 1*(1), 17–23.

Boxill, E. (2007). *Music therapy for developmental disabilities* (2nd ed.). Austin, TX: Pro-Ed.

Bruscia, K. (1998). *Defining music therapy* (2nd Ed.). Gilsum, NH: Barcelona Publishers.

Clarkson, G. (1991). Music therapy for a nonverbal autistic adult. In K. Bruscia (Ed.), *Case studies in music therapy* (pp. 373–385). Gilsum, NH: Barcelona Publishers.
Coleman, K. A., & Brunk, B. K. (2003). *SEMTAP: Special education music therapy assessment process handbook* (2nd ed.). Grapevine, TX: Prelude Music Therapy.
American Psychiatric Association. (2000). *Diagnostic and statistical manual of mental disorders (4th ed., text rev.). Washington, DC: Author.*
Farnan, L. (1987). Composing music for use in therapy. *Music Therapy Perspectives, 4,* 8–12.
Fischer, R. (1991). Original song drawings in the treatment of a developmentally disabled, autistic young man. In K. Bruscia (Ed.), *Case studies in music therapy* (pp. 359–371). Gilsum, NH: Barcelona Publishers.
Grant, R. (1995). Music therapy assessment for developmentally disabled clients. In T. Wigram, B. Saperston, & R. West (Eds.), *The art & science of music therapy: A handbook* (pp. 273–287). Chur, Switzerland: Harwood Academic Publishers.
Hooper, J. (2001). Overcoming the problems of deinstitutionalization: Using music activities to encourage interaction between four adults with a developmental disability. *Music Therapy Perspectives, 19*(2), 121–127.
Hooper, J., Wigram, T., Carson, D., & Lindsay, B. (2008a). A review of the music and intellectual disability literature (1943–2006): Part one—Descriptive and philosophical writing. *Music Therapy Perspectives, 26*(2), 66–79.
Hooper, J., Wigram, T., Carson, D., & Lindsay, B. (2008b). A review of the music and intellectual disability literature (1943–2006): Part two—Experimental writing. *Music Therapy Perspectives, 26*(2), 80–96.
Nordoff, P., & Robbins, C. (1971). *Therapy in music for handicapped children.* New York, NY: St. Martin's Press.
Nordoff, P., & Robbins, C. (2007). *Creative music therapy: A guide to fostering clinical musicianship* (2nd ed.). Gilsum, NH: Barcelona Publishers.
Pavlicevic, M. (2000). Improvisation in music therapy: Human communication in sound. *Journal of Music Therapy, 38*(4), 269–285.
Persoons, J., & De Backer, J. (1997). Vibroacoustic therapy with handicapped and autistic adolescents. In T. Wigram & C. Dileo (Eds.), *Music vibration* (pp. 143–148). Cherry Hill, NJ: Jeffrey Books.
Rainey Perry, M. (2003). Relating improvisational music therapy with severely and multiply disabled children to communication development. *Journal of Music Therapy, 40*(3), 227–246.
Skille, O., &Wigram, T. (1995). The effect of music, vocalisation and vibration on brain and muscle tissue: Studies in vibroacoustic therapy. In T. Wigram, B. Saperston, & R. West (Eds.), *The art & science of music therapy: A handbook* (pp. 23–57). Chur, Switzerland: Harwood Academic Publishers.
Wheeler, B. L., Shultis, C. L., & Polen, D. W. (2005). *Clinical training guide for the student music therapist*. Gilsum, NH: Barcelona Publishers.
Wigram, T. (1995). A model of assessment and differential diagnosis of handicap in children through the medium of music therapy. In T. Wigram, B. Saperston, & R. West (Eds.), *The art & science of music therapy: A handbook* (pp. 181–193). Chur, Switzerland: Harwood Academic Publishers.

Resources

Information Resources

Aigen, K. (1996). *Being in music: Foundations of Nordoff-Robbins music therapy*. Gilsum, NH: Barcelona Publishers.

Aigen, K. (1997). *Here we are in music: One year with an adolescent creative music therapy group.* Gilsum, NH: Barcelona Publishers.
Aigen, K. (1998). *Paths of development in Nordoff-Robbins music therapy*. Gilsum, NH: Barcelona Publishers.
Aigen, K. (2005). *Music-centered music therapy*. Gilsum, NH: Barcelona Publishers.
Baker, F., & Wigram, T. (2005). *Songwriting: Methods, techniques and clinical applications for music therapy clinicians, educators and students*. Philadelphia, PA: Jessica Kingsley.
Boxill, E. (1989). *Music therapy for living: The principle of normalization embodied in music therapy*. St. Louis, MO: MMB Music.
Boxill, E. (1997). *The miracle of music therapy*. Gilsum, NH: Barcelona Publishers.
Bruscia, K. (1987). *Improvisational models of music therapy*. Springfield, IL: Charles C. Thomas.
Chase, M. P. (1974). *Just being at the piano*. Culver City, CA: Peace Press.
Dileo, C. (2000). *Ethical thinking in music therapy*. Cherry Hill, NJ: Jeffrey Books.
Grocke, D., & Wigram, T. (2007). *Receptive methods in music therapy: Techniques and clinical applications for music therapy clinicians, educators and students*. Philadelphia, PA: Jessica Kingsley.
Hibben, J. (Ed.). (1999). *Inside music therapy: Client experiences*. Gilsum, NH: Barcelona Publishers.
Maslow, A. H. (1999). *Toward a psychology of being (3rd ed.)*. New York, MY: John Wiley & Sons.
Wigram, T. (2004). *Improvisation: Methods and techniques for music therapy clinicians, educators, and students*. Philadelphia, PA: Jessica Kingsley.

Music Resources

Levin, H., & Levin, G. (1977). *A garden of bell flowers*. Bryn Mawr, PA: Theodore Presser.
Levin, H., & Levin, G. (1981). *Learning songs*. Gilsum, NH: Barcelona Publishers.
Levin, H., & Levin, G. (1997). *Learning through songs*. Gilsum, NH: Barcelona Publishers.
Levin, H., & Levin, G. (1998). *Learning through music*. Gilsum, NH: Barcelona Publishers.
Levin, H., & Levin, G. (2005). *Let's make music!* Gilsum, NH: Barcelona Publishers.
Nordoff, P., & Robbins, C. (1962). *The first book of children's play songs*. Bryn Mawr, PA: Theodore Presser.
Nordoff, P., & Robbins, C. (1968). *The second book of children's play songs*. Bryn Mawr, PA: Theodore Presser.
Nordoff, P., & Robbins, C. (1969). *Pif-paf-poltrie*. Bryn Mawr, PA: Theodore Presser.
Nordoff, P., & Robbins, C. (1972). *Spirituals*. Bryn Mawr, PA: Theodore Presser.
Nordoff, P., & Robbins, C. (1979). *Fanfares and dances*. Bryn Mawr, PA: Theodore Presser.
Nordoff, P., & Robbins, C. (1980). *The third book of children's play songs*. Bryn Mawr, PA: Theodore Presser.
Nordoff, P., & Robbins, C. (1980). *The fourth book of children's play songs*. Bryn Mawr, PA: Theodore Presser.
Nordoff, P., & Robbins, C. (1980). *The fifth book of children's play songs*. Bryn Mawr, PA: Theodore Presser.
Nordoff, P., & Robbins, C. (1995). *Greetings and goodbyes*. Bryn Mawr, PA: Theodore Presser.
Ritholz, M. S., & Robbins, C. (1999). *Themes for therapy*. New York: Carl Fischer.
Ritholz, M. S., & Robbins, C. (2002). *More themes for therapy*. New York: Carl Fischer.

Chapter 13

Physical Disabilities in School Children

Jennifer M. Sokira

Diagnostic Information

Special education law in the United States provides that every child ages 3 to 21 years receives a free and appropriate education. According to the Individuals with Disabilities Education Act (IDEA), which was reauthorized in 2004, the broad category of "physical disabilities" may fall under the definitions of "orthopedic impairment" or "other health impairment."

Children with physical disabilities may have any number of conditions, including orthopedic disabilities (cerebral palsy, spina bifida, muscular dystrophy, juvenile arthritis), congenital disorders (cleft lip or palate, Moebius Syndrome, Apert Syndrome), or other health impairments (asthma, epilepsy, hemophilia, sickle-cell anemia, cystic fibrosis, hydrocephalus). Each category of disorder comes with its own complex set of clinical and educational needs. Orthopedic disabilities are defined by the IDEA as a severe:

> impairment that adversely affects a child's educational performance. The term includes impairments caused by a congenital anomaly, impairments caused by disease (e.g., poliomyelitis, bone tuberculosis), and impairments from other causes (e.g., cerebral palsy, amputations, and fractures or burns that cause contractures). (IDEA Part B, n.d.)

For the purpose of this chapter, the diagnoses of cerebral palsy, spina bifida, muscular dystrophy, juvenile rheumatoid arthritis, osteogenesis imperfecta, severe accidental injury, and congenital disorders are included in the category of orthopedic impairment.

Cerebral palsy (CP), which occurs in approximately two in 1,000 live births, is caused by "injury or abnormalities of the brain" which occur prenatally or during the first two years of life. CP may be caused by low levels of oxygen (hypoxia) or as a result of brain injury or infection, and it affects cognitive, motor, and sensory functions (Cerebral Palsy, n.d.). Subtypes of CP include spastic, athetoid, ataxic, and mixed. Regardless of subtype, symptoms may be diverse among clients and range from mild to severe. Abnormal movements and tremors may occur, as well as seizures, speech disorders, learning difficulties or disabilities, hearing and vision difficulties, swallowing and digestive problems, drooling, slow growth, breathing problems and urinary incontinence (Cerebral Palsy, n.d.). Symptoms of spastic CP include tight muscles, abnormal gait, toe walking, scissorlike leg movements, joint contracture, muscle weakness, or loss of movement in one side of the body (hemiplegia), both legs (diplegia), or both arms. Spastic CP comprises approximately 50%–75% of all CP cases, while Athetoid or Dyskinetic CP comprises 10%–20%

of all cases. Symptoms of Athetoid or Dyskinetic CP include involvement of the whole body, including slow or uncontrolled movements, low muscle tone, and difficulty with walking and postural control.

Spina bifida (SB) is a neural tube defect that affects 1,500 babies in the United States each year (Spina Bifida, n.d.). It is a condition wherein a baby's spine does not close completely during the first several weeks of pregnancy and results in nervous system damage. Three subtypes of SB exist: spina bifida occulta, meningocele, and myelomeningocele.

Muscular dystrophies (MD) are a "group of more than 30 genetic diseases characterized by progressive weakness and degeneration of the skeletal muscles that control movement." Subtypes vary based upon the "distribution and extent of muscle weakness (some forms of MD also affect cardiac muscle), age of onset, rate of progression, and pattern of inheritance" (NIH), and other symptoms can include muscle spasms, stiffness, vision, heart, gastrointestinal problems, deformity of limbs, loss of mobility, and decreased life expectancy [NINDS Muscular Dystrophy Information Page, n.d.; What Should You Know about Muscular Dystrophy?, n.d.; Understanding Muscular Dystrophy, n.d.].

Juvenile arthritis (JRA) is an autoimmune disease which has an onset between birth and age 16 years. It affects twice as many females as males. While some children experience the effects of arthritis through their lives, others go into remission. Symptoms include joint pain and swelling, fever, anemia, eye problems, mobility problems, loss of strength and endurance, weakened fine motor skills, and impaired growth and development. Additional accompanying symptoms include fever and rash and may involve internal organs, including the lymph nodes, spleen, liver, and heart. School-age children who have JRA may also experience isolation, insecurity, pain and fatigue, and related psychosocial effects of the limitations of JRA (Childhood Arthritis, n.d.; Juvenile Rheumatoid Arthritis, n.d.; School Success, n.d.). There are three main types of JRA: paurciarticular, polyarticular, and systemic (also known as Still's Disease), the difference between these being primarily related to the number of joints affected, symmetricality, and whether it is likely to be outgrown.

Osteogenesis imperfecta (OI) is a genetically inherited disease present at birth and characterized by extremely weak bones which easily fracture. Children with OI may also have shorter stature; early hearing loss; a light blue tint to the whites of their eyes, known as blue sclera; loose joints; bowed legs; kyphosis; and/or scoliosis. Dependent on the genetic variant, life expectancy is shortened or near normal. In addition, respiratory problems, pneumonia, spinal cord problems, and deformities are additionally associated with all types of OI (Osteogenesis Imperfecta, n.d.).

Severe accidental injuries among school children may occur for a variety of reasons, including falls, sports injuries, car accidents, burns, and other reasons. They may impact a student in a variety of ways, including loss of limb, loss of sensory input (e.g., hearing, vision), and loss of cognitive function. It is to be assumed that severe accidental injuries impact a student's school performance physically, emotionally, and cognitively, based upon the individual situation.

Congenital deformities are those with which an individual is born and can include a variety of disabilities including cleft lip and/or palate, Moebius Syndrome, and Apert Syndrome. Cleft lip is a notch or split in the lip; cleft palate is a notch or split in the palate. The length and size of the cleft varies. It occurs in approximately 1 out of every 2,500 people and is usually surgically repaired during the first year of life; however, additional dental, orthodontal, speech-language, and hearing intervention may be warranted (Cleft Lip and Palate, n.d.). Cleft lip and palate affect the appearance of the face and nose, cause problems with feeding and therefore growth, cause ear infections, and cause problems with speech.

Moebius Syndrome is a congenital neurological disorder in which the muscles which control facial and eye movement are paralyzed, resulting in the individual being unable to create facial expressions or raise their eyebrows. Feeding, speech, eye movement, and blinking difficulties also co-occur, as well as hand and feet deformities and developmental delays. Moebius Syndrome may also co-occur with intellectual disability and with autism spectrum disorder, although "most affected individuals have normal intelligence" (Moebius Syndrome, n.d.).

Apert Syndrome is a congenital genetic disorder in which the skull bones fuse earlier than normal. It is characterized by ear infection, hearing loss, webbing of the fingers and/or toes, bulging eyes, abnormalities in facial development, differences in intellectual development, and short stature. Usually, surgery is performed to correct bone growth problems (Apert Syndrome, n.d.).

Other Health Impairments

According to IDEA, the term "other health impairment" is used to describe chronic or acute health problems that adversely affect a child's educational performance. These may include asthma, attention deficit disorder or attention deficit hyperactivity disorder, diabetes, epilepsy, a heart condition, hemophilia, lead poisoning, leukemia, nephritis, rheumatic fever, sickle-cell anemia, and Tourette Syndrome.

Childhood Asthma, estimated to affect up to 7.1 million children under 18 years old, causes swelling of the airways, resulting in wheezing, coughing, difficulty breathing, and chest tightness. Asthma symptoms are caused by allergens, irritants, weather, exercise, and infections, and serious symptoms are called attacks. Asthma is controlled by "rescue" medicines for quick relief and control medicines which prevent symptoms in the long term (Asthma in Children, n.d.). According to the American Lung Association, asthma is "one of the leading causes of school absenteeism" (Asthma in Children Fact Sheet, 2012).

According to the National Institutes of Health, "Epilepsy is a brain disorder in which a person has repeated seizures (convulsions) over time. Seizures are episodes of disturbed brain activity that cause changes in attention or behavior" and may be caused by a stroke, brain injury or infection, congenital brain defects, birth injury, metabolism disorder, or problem with brain blood vessels or tissues (Epilepsy, n.d.). The three main types of seizures are absence (petit mal), tonic-clonic (grand mal), and partial (focal). Absence or petit mal seizures are characterized by brief staring spells, sudden stoppages in walking or speaking, eye fluttering, and chewing. Although absence seizures may be frequent, they may not be noticed because of the short duration and fleeting symptoms. Absence seizures "may be mistaken for lack of attention or other misbehavior" and may "interfere with school and learning" (Petite Mal Seizure, n.d.).

Tonic-clonic or grand mal seizures are characterized by unconsciousness and full body involvement in muscle contractions. During the seizure, symptoms may include incontinence, biting of tongue, stopped breathing, and/or changes in skin color. Following the seizure, the client may be tired, have memory loss, headache, and confusion (Generalized Tonic-Clonic Seizure, n.d.). Partial or focal seizures are limited to one area of the brain and may cause "muscle contraction/relaxation," affect one side of the body, "forced turning of the head," and other head movements, staring spells, other repetitive face and eye movements, sensations of numbness or tingling, hallucinations, pain, sweating, and nausea (Partial Focal Seizure, n.d.).

Two blood disorders are included in the definition of Other Health-Impaired disorders. These are hemophilia and sickle-cell anemia. Hemophilia is a blood disorder in which clotting takes longer than typically expected. While many individuals with hemophilia are able to lead normal lives, they are at risk for excessive bleeding following an injury. Therefore, individuals with hemophilia need to be particularly careful to avoid injury and typically require additional IV infusions to replace their missing clotting factor (Hemophilia, n.d.).

Sickle-cell anemia is a genetically acquired disease characterized by red blood cells that are abnormally crescent- or sickle-shaped and therefore negatively affect oxygen delivery and blood flow. It is more common in people of African and Mediterranean descent. Symptoms include abdominal, chest, and bone pain; breathing problems; rapid heart rate; delayed growth; fatigue; fever; jaundice; urinary symptoms; skin ulcers; and strokes (Sickle-Cell Anemia, n.d.).

Cystic fibrosis (CF) is a chronic, genetically inherited, life-threatening disorder which causes mucus buildup in the lungs and digestive system. The result of this mucus buildup is serious breathing and digestive issues, including delayed growth, abnormal weight gain, constipation, and/or gas/bloating. Respiratory issues include coughing, congestion, sinus pressure, recurrent pneumonia with fever, coughing, shortness of breath, and increased sputum. Individuals with CF are treated for both digestive and respiratory problems. For digestive problems, they are given pancreatic enzymes, vitamin supplements, and high protein and calorie diets. For respiratory problems, they receive antibiotics either regularly or during an infection. They also receive medications to open airways, enzymes to thin mucus and increase expectoration, and oxygen therapy as needed. Therapies to assist with loosening lung mucus include "Percussion Vest, manual chest percussion, A-Cappella, or TheraPEP device." Life expectancy for individuals with CF has increased significantly and is currently approximately 37 years, with lung complications increasing significantly in adulthood (Cystic Fibrosis, n.d.).

Hydrocephalus is caused by blockage, absorption, or production problems with cerebrospinal fluid, causing it to accumulate in the skull, resulting in brain swelling. It may begin prenatally and it is common among children with myelomeningocele spina bifida. It may also result from meningitis or nervous system infections, brain bleeding or injury, tumors, injury, or trauma. Symptoms include seizures, vomiting, eye gaze problems, sleepiness, vomiting, high-pitched cry, headache, temper, coordination, and bladder control and growth problems. The head may appear enlarged. Life-threatening without treatment, hydrocephalus is treated by medicines, or a shunt may be surgically inserted to reroute cerebrospinal fluid to another part of the body. Physical and intellectual disabilities may result as complications of hydrocephalus (Hydrocephalus, n.d.).

Needs and Resources

In order for students with physical disabilities to access this education, they often require specialized services, called "Related Services." Related services are based upon the individual student's need, are provided in the least restrictive environment (Coleman & Brunk, 1999), and may be provided by physical therapists, occupational therapists, speech-language pathologists, and music therapists. These therapists may serve as a consultant to a student or to their program as well as providing direct service to the student either individually or in a group as required by a student's Individualized Education Plan (IEP).

School children with physical disabilities possess needs which directly and indirectly result from their disabilities. Direct physical outcomes from an individual's physical limitations pose immediate needs in the areas of fine and gross motor skills such as ambulation, self-care, and communication. Secondary impacts from physical limitations include academic performance (often resulting from excessive absences for medical reasons), psychological well-being (e.g., anxiety, depression, self-esteem), social isolation, and behavioral difficulties (resulting from struggles with coping skills and development and maintenance of hope) (Anbar & Murthy, 2010).

It is important for the MT and the special education team to take into consideration these secondary effects and their impact upon the child's overall well-being. For example, when working with a student with cystic fibrosis, decreasing isolation, improving socialization, increasing confidence in self-expression, processing personal/social issues, coping skills, decreasing anxiety, exercising control, working through body image issues, and empowering the client to face existential issues may be necessary for the client to cope with his or her illness (Fenton, 2000).

There is no specific research studying the personal or musical resources of this diverse population; however, anecdotal descriptions in the music therapy literature and clinical experience have borne out that despite physical challenges or limitations, children with physical disabilities often have or may develop a resilient personality, allowing them to create and maintain relationships and meet the multiple challenges which confront them in the school setting. Musically, children with physical disabilities have preferences and interests in music as diverse as the typical population of students. It remains that each client should be considered as an individual first and that no diagnosis will fully define an individual's character, needs, or musical preferences.

REFERRAL AND ASSESSMENT

In public school settings, two types of assessments may be used. The first is an eligibility assessment, which determines the student's eligibility to receive music therapy as part of their educational program. The second is a clinical assessment, which is used to determine specific goals and objectives for MT-related service or particular foci for MT as consultation or educational enrichment.

Eligibility Assessment

In the United States, related services are provided in order to remediate needs and allow students to benefit from public education in the least restrictive environment (LRE). Therefore, therapy is provided within the natural context of the classroom as appropriate, and no more therapy is provided than warranted. The Special Education Music Therapy Assessment Process (SEMTAP) (Coleman & Brunk, 1999), aided by the Music Therapy Special Education Assessment Scale (MT-SEAS) (Bradfield, Carlenius, Gold, & White, 2008) allows the music therapist to determine if a student is eligible to receive music therapy services. After determining target IEP objectives in which the client is not making reasonable progress, music therapy and non–music therapy interventions which address these target objectives are compared. Should the music therapy intervention prove to be more effective, then MT as a related service is warranted for work in that area (Bradfield, et al., 2008).

Clinical Assessment

When a student is approved for music therapy services, therapist-created or standardized assessments may be utilized as appropriate to determine goals, objectives, and direction for therapy in the school setting. Wilson and Smith (2000) report that there is limited consistency in the published research with regard to assessment tools being commonly used among music therapists with a variety of populations, and that both named and therapist-created assessments are being used to assess a wide variety of musical and nonmusical areas of need. The Individualized Music Therapy Assessment Profile (IMTAP), developed by Baxter et al. (2007), is a multiuse tool which can guide initial assessment and treatment planning in various domains and subdomains pertinent to school children with physical disabilities, including gross motor, fine motor, oral motor, sensory, receptive communication/auditory perception, expressive communication, cognitive, emotional, social, and musicality.

Another form of assessment that has been described for people with physical disabilities is "Identity Structure Modeling," described by Clarkson and Robey (2000) in a case study of a young woman with severe physical disabilities for whom the roles of composer and music listener were central to her identity. Although not a music therapy–specific assessment, this computer-generated model organizes "self-reported qualitative information" and could be used to help the therapist better understand a client's personality, as well as facilitate client self-awareness. The "Categories of Response" described by Nordoff and Robbins (1971) have been reported to be used as an assessment tool improvisational musical therapy (Lem & Paine, 2011), and this tool provides insight into the musical and personal responses of the client.

Additionally, Improvisational Assessment Profiles (IAPs), developed by Kenneth Bruscia, are an assessment model which is applicable to school children with physical disabilities in assessing "musical tendencies and their significance in musical development and learning; inferences regarding the client's musical tendencies in terms of their generalizability to and significance for nonmusical areas of functioning" (Bruscia, 1987, p. 411).

Based upon the overall needs of the various diagnostic profiles, the areas of Cognitive Skills/Academic Learning, Communication, Gross Motor, Fine Motor, and Social and Emotional Skills should be considered in developing a music therapy treatment plan for school children with physical disabilities.

While each client should be evaluated on an individual basis, school children with physical disabilities may have needs beyond the areas of physical rehabilitation and/or adaptation. Secondary symptoms, for example, associated learning disabilities, may warrant assistance from the music therapist, as well as the communicative and social needs which may arise from the student's particular situation. As discussed above, music therapy provided in the public school setting, whether as related service or as consultation or educational enrichment, is intended to specifically assist a student in making reasonable academic progress. Assessed needs in the above areas may or may not qualify as clinical needs which must be met in order to assist a student in achieving this reasonable progress on his or her IEP. Regardless, an assessed need may be highly relevant for a child's personal, emotional, cognitive or social growth, and development or well-being, and therefore may be referred to private outside music therapy by the Planning and Placement Team as appropriate.

Technology

The use of Electronic Music Technology has greatly developed and is being included in the MT treatment of school children with physical disabilities. Applications such as Wii games, iPod and iPad applications, and computer programs can be utilized to address a wide variety of physical needs, such as hand and arm use, finger isolation, strength and endurance, leg function, sequencing, straight-building, endurance, and visual motor coordination (Whitehead-Pleaux, Clark, & Spall, 2011), as well as to develop musical skills (Spitzer, 1989). Applicable to re-creative, improvisational, and compositional experiences, EMT is cited in a qualitative study by Magee and Burland (2008), who describe the process of "applying EMTs in practice," which includes assessing available resources, understanding the client's movements, establishing the client as musician, establishing cause and effect, and musical play.

This use of technology may be contraindicated if the frustration level is too high or if the client is unable to understand cause-and-effect (Magee & Burland, 2008; Whitehead-Pleaux, et al., 2011).

Overview of Methods and Procedures

The following methods and procedures are used most commonly with school-age children with physical disabilities.

Receptive Music Therapy

- Relaxation: use of music to promote relaxation and/or reduce physical tension and/or emotional anxiety
- Music Procedure Support: use of music to structure, guide, or aid administration of a nonmusical procedure such as stretching muscles or gait training.

Improvisational Music Therapy

- Mixed Media Improvisation: Therapist and client use a combination of musical sound sources to create improvisations individually or within a group.

Re-creative Music Therapy

- Instrumental Re-creation: The client re-creates precomposed songs or parts of instrumental pieces, using instruments.
- Vocal Re-creation: The client participates by vocalizing or singing experiences using precomposed music either individually or in a group.
- Musical Games: These come in many forms, but typically consist of turn-taking activities that require cause-and-effect interactions, active participation, and some element of competition based upon musical elements.
- Music Ensembles: The client learns precomposed vocal or instrumental music through a process of repetition and practice and then performs in front of an audience.

Compositional Music Therapy

- Songwriting: occurs when changes are made to some or all of the lyrics and/or music of an existing song, or when a new song is written in its entirety.
- Instrumental Compositions: Clients create musical pieces using instruments, with support from therapists for development of melody, harmony, notation, and recording.

GUIDELINES FOR RECEPTIVE MUSIC THERAPY

Receptive music experiences may be used with school children with physical disabilities in order to support relaxation, decrease anxiety, and structure movement responses and routines. The client may respond by listening, moving, and relaxing (Bruscia, 1998). While there is little literature describing receptive music therapy techniques for children with physical disabilities in school settings, specific techniques of relaxation and music procedure support are described anecdotally and may be extrapolated from other areas of music therapy practice.

The receptive technique of relaxation is described by Grocke and Wigram, who describe its use among pediatric patients and children in school settings for a variety of clinical uses (2007). As a broader approach, relaxation experiences may be incorporated as inductions to music psychotherapy methods like the Bonny Method of Guided Imagery in Music or used as a stand-alone method to decrease anxiety (Grocke & Wigram, 2007).

Grocke and Wigram describe the vocal quality that is appropriate when conducting relaxation experiences, stating that it should be midrange, with a warm, comforting, and consistent tone, in order to convey that the therapist has "quiet control." Specific to working with children, they go on to state that dynamics of the voice may be required to be used to keep a child "focused on the music, or the relaxation/imagery script." Attention should also be given to the pacing of the voice and amount of repetition and pacing of spoken words and modeling of the breath.

Music procedure support is characterized by using music to structure, guide, or aid a nonmusical procedure. Goals include increased quality of life (Grasso, Button, Allison, & Sawyer, 2000), improved self-regulation (Ball, et al., 1975; Neilson & McCaughey, 1982), improved gross motor coordination (Peng et al., 2011), and increased strength (Pearce, 1981). In some instances, interventions incorporating music procedure support can be created by the music therapist in the clinical setting, for example, when a music therapist creates a musical schedule to help a client remain motivated to follow an educational routine. In other instances, the music therapist may be assisting with more complex physical movements, for example, sit-to-stand procedures or gait control. In these instances, techniques specific to Neurologic Music Therapy (Kwak, 2007; Peng et al., 2011; Thaut, 1985, 1988), may be employed, and it is noted that additional training is required. For client and therapist safety purposes, it is crucial to note that a music therapist should receive client-specific training prior to moving or physically manipulating any client with a physical disability.

Relaxation

Overview. Relaxation experiences are utilized when a client's physical tension or emotional anxiety are such that they are unable to benefit from the educational environment or function optimally in the classroom. (Yu, Liu, Li, & Ma, 2009; Yu, Liu, & Wu, 2009). The use of music to promote relaxation may be called for among clients who have physical or emotional tension and respond positively to music for these purposes. Goals for relaxation include improved physical state, lower muscle tone if appropriate, and improved ability to focus. In addition, goals of relaxation in the classroom setting include relieving tension and stress, educating about becoming calm when overactive, providing a "time out" from focused concentration, introducing creative thinking and engaging imagination, and providing pleasure (Grocke & Wigram, 2007). In the school setting, relaxation may take place at the augmentative level, depending on the severity of the client's need. Relaxation may be contraindicated among clients who are unable to follow verbal directions or who become overstimulated with live or recorded music. The client's physical therapist should be consulted prior to participation in relaxation experiences in the school setting. It is noted that relaxation is not intended to induce an altered state in the client or clients.

Preparation. The music therapist should prepare a therapeutic environment conducive to relaxation, and consideration should be given to the physical setting within the school with regard to noise level and space. Grocke and Wigram suggest that students may utilize mats on the floor of a movement space or that children in a classroom setting could put their heads on their desks. They also suggest that consideration be given to the light level, and while a more darkened room might be preferable, some younger children may not be comfortable—therefore, the MT should follow their preference. Recorded music choices should be preselected using the criteria described above and/or instruments for live, therapist-created music similarly prepared. Shanahan (in Grocke & Wigram, 2007) describes preparation of young children with disabilities which is also pertinent to work with children with physical disabilities in school settings. She describes using a Boardmaker™ schedule to prepare and teach the students about the relaxation routine, the use of weighted blankets to provide both sensory support as well as to indicate each child's personal space, dimming of the lights, and the incorporation, in collaboration with the occupational therapist, of sensory strategies such as joint compressions.

What to observe. The music therapist should be prepared to observe the client's responses to music and verbal directions as well as be prepared to process the experience with the client and observe changes in their physical or emotional state. When working with young children, the therapist should be aware of their responses to the light level, as well as any behavioral responses. When working in a group of children, the therapist should also be prepared to provide developmentally appropriate behavioral expectations for the relaxation experiences.

Procedures. The following procedures may be used when implementing relaxation experiences:

1) Greeting/Evaluation: The music therapist greets the clients and evaluates their level of tension by observation of and discussion with them.

2) Selection of Music: Based on the client's preferred music and the therapist's evaluation, music is selected using the criteria described above. Recorded music or live music may be used.
3) Induction: With consideration for the clients' ability to understand, the music therapist explains to the client what will be happening during the intervention, and the goal of the intervention as appropriate. The therapist then provides verbal cues to assist the client in beginning to relax.
4) Relaxation Experience: The clients may be led in a structured experience with concrete verbal directions set to live or recorded music from the therapist, e.g., progressive muscle relaxation. The music therapist may utilize a precomposed script to elicit relaxation and imagery. Depending on client need, therapist directiveness may vary.
5) Closure: The music therapist brings the music to appropriate closure. The therapist may ask the client to report on their physical state after the intervention.

Adaptations. Several adaptations of relaxation are mentioned in the literature. Grocke and Wigram (2007) include a discussion on the incorporation of tactile and sensory experiences. Another adaptation to this method is the use of relaxation to provide a "cooldown" after a music and movement experience.

Music Procedure Support

Overview. Music procedure support is characterized by the use of music to structure, guide, or aid a nonmusical procedure. The method is indicated when a client has physical or emotional difficulty participating in an educational or therapeutic routine or procedure, and when a musical structure and/or accompaniment created by the music therapist can assist or motivate the client to participate. As with other receptive methods mentioned above, their adaptations, increased quality of life, improved self-regulation, improved gross motor coordination, and improved strength are potential goal areas. Music procedure support in the school setting takes place in collaboration with other aspects of a client's treatment plan or in collaboration with other treatment team members; therefore, it would be considered to take place on the augmentative level of music therapy. Music procedure support may also be considered to be on the auxiliary level, depending on the level of the client/therapist musical relationship. For example, Music Procedure Support would be considered at the augmentative level when the music therapist is creating live music for the client to listen to as they practice walking with a steady gait, but it might be considered to be at the auxiliary level if the client uses a recorded tape without the physical presence of a music therapist. This type of intervention is contraindicated if the addition of music to the nonmusical procedure is not helpful in improving some aspect of the procedure's efficacy.

Preparation. The session environment is prepared based upon the nonmusical goal which is being assisted by music and the music therapist. This may take place in a clinical treatment room or classroom which is not the normal music therapy environment; therefore, recorded music or instruments may be required to be transported. Collaborative planning between the music therapist and other professionals involved is essential. This type of planning happens either individually with the collaborating therapist or in a, interdisciplinary team meeting which involves teachers, therapists, parents, and sometimes the student. In public school settings in the US, consultative or educational enrichment music therapy could be used to assist the student in meeting a particular IEP objective. For example, the music therapist may work closely with a physical therapist in order to assist the client in making progress with balance, gait, or compensatory skills. The therapists would work together to incorporate music into the PT interventions to provide structure, time orientation, anticipation, or motivation as needed to maximize the client's participation.

What to observe. The music therapist should be prepared to observe the effect of the music on the efficacy of the routine and procedure being supported. The music therapist should be aware of the client's participation and the level of effectiveness of the non–music therapy intervention before and after the addition of the music. The music therapist should also be attentive to the client's affect, motivation, and musical responses as they inform the intervention as it is carried out.

Procedures. The following procedures may be used in developing and conducting musical procedure support:

1) Greeting: The music therapist greets the client and any other professionals and caregivers.
2) Review of the procedure to be conducted without music: The music therapist observes the client and other professional participating in the procedure to be musically adapted, noting the movements, timing, and rhythms of the procedure.
3) Development of Musical Support: The music therapist, with assistance from the client, creates either live or recorded accompaniment to the specific procedure. This could include, for example, instrumental sounds which match spatial movements, rhythmic accompaniment for walking movements (Kwak, 2007), multipart music to match multistep actions (Peng et al., 2011), and recordings of set length to assist with timing of a routine (Grasso, Button, Allison, & Sawyer, 2000).
4) Evaluation and Adjustment of Musical Support: The music therapist and other professional, with the client's input, evaluate and adjust the music procedure support to maximize the client's outcome. This step is repeated as often as necessary.

Adaptations. Techniques specific to Neurologic Music Therapy, in which music is providing a structure or foundation for a nonmusical procedure, may be considered adaptations of Music Procedure Support. These techniques require additional training (Clair & Pasiali, 2004; Kwak, 2007; Peng et al., 2011; Thaut, 1985, 1988). For client and therapist safety purposes, it is crucial to note that a music therapist should receive client-specific training prior to moving or physically manipulating any client with a physical disability.

Guidelines for Improvisational Music Therapy

In improvisational music therapy methods, clients, individually or in groups, extemporaneously create music, in the form of melody, rhythm, song, or instrumental piece, using their voices or instruments (Bruscia, 1998). Among the literature addressing improvisation with children with physical disabilities in school settings, most descriptions combined use of various media, including instruments, voice, and technology; therefore, the method of mixed media improvisation is described below, as well as its various adaptations, which include Dynamic Sonification, (Lem & Paine, 2011), "Adapted Use Musical Instruments" (AUMI) (Oliveros, Miller, Heyen, Siddall, & Hazard, 2011), and Improvised Musical Play (Gunsberg, 1988).

Mixed Media Improvisation

Overview. In the improvisational method of mixed media improvisation, the therapist and client may use a combination of musical sound sources, including instruments, voice, body percussion, and technology in individual, dyad, or group settings (Bruscia, 1998). Mixed media improvisation may be is used with school children with physical disabilities for a variety of reasons, working toward achieving several goal areas concurrently. Possible goal areas include gross motor skills, verbal and nonverbal communication skills, social skills, awareness of self and others, self-expression, and awareness. Mixed media improvisation may take place at the augmentative level of music therapy. Mixed media improvisation may be contraindicated if a client is sensitive to instrumental sounds produced or if the client requires more structure than can be provided with this intervention.

Preparation. In preparing for the session, the therapist should consider the accessibility of the session environment and instruments. In addition, a selection of instruments and equipment should be available and adaptations should be made as appropriate to the client or clients participating. Recording equipment should be available as appropriate. Depending upon clinical goals and orientation, the therapist should also be prepared to musically support their client(s) in a variety of musical styles and keys.

What to observe. As in the above methods, the music therapist should be prepared to observe the client's musical participation with the therapist and others, in relation to the goals and objectives toward which the client is working. Specific to improvisation, the therapist should pay close attention to the various musical efforts of the client, for example, in the areas of tempo, rhythm, tone, timbre, melody, harmony, and volume, as these can be used to provide the musical and the clinical direction of the improvisation, the therapists' music, and clinical and emotional material pertinent to the client's work to meet their clinical objectives. In addition, the therapist should observe the movements, facial expressions, and nonverbal communication of the client, from which inferences may be made regarding the physical and emotional experiences of the client.

Procedures. Mixed media improvisation can be utilized in a variety of ways, based upon clinical need. It can constitute the only intervention within a session or it can be one of several that take place. The following procedures may not be applicable to every situation; however, the format of greeting, selection of media, improvisation, and closure, as with formats listed above, may be applicable. Specific procedures for improvisation will vary based upon setting; however, established models of Creative Music Therapy by Nordoff & Robbins (1980) and Free Improvisation Therapy by Juliette Alvin (Bruscia, 1987) may provide guidance into specific procedures, as described below.

Adaptations. The model of Creative Music Therapy created by Nordoff and Robbins is applicable to multimedia improvisation with school children with physical disabilities. In this music as therapy model, music is used to "motivate the physically disabled child to use his limbs or voice expressively; its rhythmic-melodic structures then support his activity and induce an order in his control that promotes coordination" (Nordoff & Robbins, 1971, p. 16). In this type of session, improvisation is the only intervention within the session, and the greeting and closing songs will be incorporated into the overall musical experience. This type of improvisation was originally created to involve two music therapists and one client, using piano, voice, and percussion as instrumentation. The session may vary in length based upon the client's musical participation. In school settings, further adaptations may include variances from the two-to-one therapist-client ratio and the session length, and client makeup could include individual, dyad, group therapy, musical instruction, and musical performances (Bruscia, 1987).

The improvisational model of Free Improvisation Therapy created by Juliet Alvin is also applicable to mixed media improvisation in music therapy with school children with physical disabilities in addressing goals of gross and fine motor skills, sensory-motor coordination, etc. (Bruscia, 1987). Initially used in individual and dyad sessions and with groups used when clients were developmentally ready, Free Improvisation Therapy utilizes a wide variety of instruments, and while piano may be used, it is not a focal point in the same manner as in Creative Music Therapy described above.

Two technology methods have been described to enhance the improvisation experiences of children with physical disabilities in improvising music. The first is Dynamic Sonification, in which sounds are improvised through client movements within the context of creative music therapy improvisation (Lem & Paine, 2011). The second is "Adapted Use of Musical Instruments" (AUMI), as described by Oliveros et al. (2011), which provides for a client's horizontal or vertical movements to be translated into keyboard or percussive sounds. These technologies allow for individuals with severely restricted movement to improvise creatively. One additional adaptation is described by Gunsberg (1988). In "Improvised Musical Play," the teacher leads music improvisation for preschool children of varying needs. Vocal and instrumental improvisation is facilitated by a teacher with the goal of increasing the amount of time children focus on social play and combines vocal/instrumental improvisation.

Guidelines for Re-creative Music Therapy

In Re-creative Music Therapy, children with physical disabilities sing or play precomposed music or participate in "structured music activities and games in which the client performs roles or behaviors that have been specifically defined" (Bruscia, 1998). Re-creative music therapy methods used with this population include instrumental re-creation, vocal re-creation, and musical games and activities. These methods have been described to address physical and attentional goals (Berel, Diller, & Orgel, 1971; Herron, 1970; Kennedy & Kua-Walker, 2006; Nasuruddin, 2010) as well as musical (Howell, Flowers, & Wheaton, 1995; Kennedy & Kua-Walker, 2006; Spitzer, 1989), emotional, and social goals (Gilboa & Roginsky, 2010) with children with physical disabilities in various settings. While there are potentially many adaptations to the methods described, the present author contends that, in light of the collaborative nature within the public educational setting in the United States, Re-creative Music Therapy methods may provide an excellent avenue for music therapist consultation, collaboration, and cotreatment with educational and therapeutic professionals on the interdisciplinary team.

Instrumental Re-creation

Overview. Instrumental re-creative experiences involve the client in re-creating precomposed songs or parts of instrumental pieces using instruments. This can include playing specific rhythms on rhythmic instruments, playing instruments from musical notation, playing in a musical ensemble like a band or orchestra, participating in melodic or rhythmic imitation, and taking private lessons (Bruscia, 1998). These experiences take place primarily at the auxiliary and augmentative levels of music therapy. The music therapist's consultation in the music education ensemble would be considered auxiliary, whereas individual adaptive lessons given by the music therapist would be considered augmentative.

Instrumental re-creation may be used to address multiple goals of children with physical disabilities in school settings, including improved adaptive skills, improved attention, development of fine and gross motor coordination, improved breath control and lung function, enhanced social skills, and facilitation and understanding of nonverbal communication. Instrumental re-creation may be contraindicated if physical adaptations cannot be made to allow for meaningful or independent participation, or if a high level of frustration occurs which is in conflict with the therapeutic outcome being sought.

Preparation. In preparing the school environment, consideration should be given to physical space needs, and all physical adaptations to instruments and equipment should be prepared prior to the session with assistance from an occupational or physical therapist as needed. Supplies needed are instruments with appropriate adaptions, and any sheet music or lead sheets, again with any adaptations needed, for example, larger print.

What to observe. The music therapist should be prepared to observe the physical efforts of the client in relation to their specific goals and objectives. As many clients with physical disabilities may be playing an instrument in an ensemble, this may require clinical observation of a student with follow-up consultation with the student and his or her music teacher. When conducting instrumental re-creation experiences in music therapy individual or group sessions, the music therapist observes the client's participation in relation to the clinical goal being addressed. For example, a client who is working on visual motor coordination may focus on accuracy in following her sheet music, whereas a client who is addressing his fine motor coordination may require the therapist to provide physical modeling and decreased tempo to accommodate for response delays and the development of muscle memory. The therapist should remain alert to any physical discomfort experienced by the client or any secondary behavioral responses that may indicate frustration.

Procedures. The following procedures may be used in conducting instrumental re-creation:

1) Warm-Up: The client(s) and therapist participate in exercises to physically and emotionally prepare the client for playing an instrument. Warm-ups could include stretching, finger exercises, and physical movement.
2) Song/Composition Selection: The client and therapist select the song or composition to be re-created. In an individual setting, the song may have a theme that is pertinent to the client's therapeutic goals. In a group setting, the group may work together or take turns selecting songs. In an ensemble setting, the leader or conductor of the ensemble is most likely to make the song/composition selections.
3) Instrument Selection: In school settings, the client may select an instrument to study in depth and the music therapist may provide assistance with any physical adaptations needed. In an individual music therapy setting, the client or therapist may select which instruments will be played. The therapist may encourage the client to provide input or direction regarding the tempo, dynamics, and other musical aspects of the song. In group music therapy, the clients may be assigned instruments or select them independently.
4) Role Assignments: The therapist or the client(s) may be assigned a musical role (e.g., leader, rhythm section, soloist, conductor).
5) Performance: The client(s) may elect to participate in a performance of their instrumental re-creation and may be involved by the therapist in various aspects of preparation, including creating a program, planning and setting up the performance space, and inviting attendees.

Adaptations. Instrumental re-creation may take place as the only music therapy intervention during a session, or as one of several interventions used as appropriate. Traditional instruments may be adapted to accommodate for children with physical disabilities (Clark & Chadwick, 1979).

Vocal Re-creation

Overview. In the re-creative method of vocal re-creation, using precomposed music, the client vocalizes, sings, chants, participates in voice lessons, or participates in vocal ensembles (Bruscia, 1998). Vocal re-creation takes place primarily at the auxiliary and augmentative levels of music therapy for school children with physical disabilities. Whereas this method may include participation in vocal ensembles (auxiliary level), some may participate instead in individual music therapy or in voice lessons, addressing areas of physical, communicative, or emotional need as part of the interdisciplinary team (augmentative level) or as "stand-alone" music therapy (intensive to primary levels).

Vocal re-creation may address a variety of clinical goals for this population, including improved lung function, communication, social interaction, and self-expression. It may be contraindicated if the client significantly struggles with vocal production and adaptations cannot be made for meaningful or independent participation.

Preparation. As with other music therapy methods described, preparation of the session requires planning of specific interventions by the therapist ahead of time, gathering any accompaniment instruments, needed lyric sheets, etc. It may also require preprogramming of assistive technology and preparation of the physical space to accommodate clients' physical needs.

What to observe. The music therapist observes the client's vocal efforts in relation to their clinical goals. This may vary based upon the client's specific needs, for example, for a client addressing social interactions, the music therapist may need to observe the client's interaction with peers in an ensemble setting and make recommendations to the music teacher and client. Alternatively, for a client working on improved lung function, the music therapist would make observations of the client's breath support while participating in vocal re-creation and then design exercises to specifically address their needs.

Procedures. The procedures listed above for Instrumental Re-creation may be adapted for Vocal Re-creation. These include, first, Warm-Up, in which the client(s) and therapist participate in exercises to vocally prepare the client for singing. Next, Song Selection takes place appropriate to the individual, group or ensemble setting. Third, the therapist or clients are assigned a role, for example, leader, voice part, soloist, conductor, or accompanist. Then the clients may elect to participate in a performance of their vocal re-creation and may be involved by the therapist in various aspects of preparation, including creating a program, planning and setting up the performance space, and inviting attendees.

Adaptations. Vocal re-creation may take place as the only music therapy intervention during a session or as one of several interventions used as appropriate. Individuals with physical disabilities may include using assistive technology or voice output as needed to produce words or vocal sounds.

Musical Games

Overview. In the re-creative music therapy method of musical games, individuals participate in experiences which are structured by music (Bruscia, 1998). In work with school children with physical disabilities, musical games and activities take place at the auxiliary and augmentative level of therapy. Musical games and activities may be used to meet the following therapeutic goals: improved social skills, improved fine motor coordination, improved gross motor coordination. Musical games and activities may be contraindicated if the client has a high frustration level with the structure or materials of the game, or with the technology being used (Whitehead-Pleaux, Clark, & Spall, 2011).

Preparation. In order to prepare the environment for musical games and activities, the music therapist should consider any physical adaptations required for the client, for example, adapted seating arrangement or adaptations to specific materials. Some experiences may be simple games which don't require additional materials; however, activity-specific materials such as an MP3 player/speaker, musical flash cards, etc., should be prepared. Additionally, many technology-based musical games are available and may require specific computerized instruments, television, controllers, computers, floor mats, etc., all of which should be prepared prior to the session.

What to observe. The music therapist should be prepared to observe the participation and interaction of all clients; clients' emotional and social reactions to the games, therapist, and other clients; and the ways in which the client is able to access the materials available, noting additional adaptations required.

Procedures. The following procedures may be utilized for conducting musical games and activities. First, during Introduction/Rules: The therapist introduces the game or activity and explains the specific rules and procedures. Any client questions are answered. Next, the game or activity takes place. Common musical games include variations of other non–musical quiz-like games such as Jeopardy!, Hangman, Family Feud, or Wheel of Fortune. Common musical games also include variations of other nonmusical games that require active participation from all clients at the same time, such as Simon Says, Charades, Pictionary, or Scattergories. After the game concludes, the therapist facilitates a brief discussion with the clients regarding their experience, the music, and their interactions. Finally, the clients may be involved with putting away equipment or otherwise cleaning up as appropriate.

Adaptations. While musical games and activities lend themselves to group experiences, options are available for individuals to participate in order to practice for group intervention at a later time.

Music Ensembles

Overview. Participation in a music ensemble may be indicated for school-age children in general, but can serve as a means of significant clinical benefit for children with physical disabilities. The therapeutic goals addressed through participation in a music ensemble include gross and fine motor skill development, self-awareness, and improvement of emotional functioning. This experience is primarily provided at the augmentative and intensive levels, and sometimes at the auxiliary level. Contraindications include use for those for whom performing may be prohibited due to limitations in mobility (e.g., unable to be transported to the performance location) or for whom the performance environment poses a possible threat or injury (e.g., too hot, too long a time without required equipment). This method is appropriate for only those clients who are capable of functioning in a public performance setting in terms of their cognitive, emotional, and behavioral functioning. This method might naturally follow other methods over time for a client who achieves a certain level of competency with particular skills and for whom a performance opportunity could prove beneficial.

Preparation. Performing in a musical ensemble typically occurs outside of the typical session structure and environment; however, the preparation for the actual performance takes place within the usual therapeutic setting. Preparation for the performance requires not only practice of the actual pieces to be performed, but also adjustments during final rehearsals so clients are prepared for their positions in relation to the therapist. It is important that the client be comfortable so that they can concentrate on their experience without distractions. The therapist may want to record (audio or video) the client's efforts for playbacks and provide a copy of the performance to the client. Whenever possible, make certain that the performance space is free of visual and auditory distractions (windows, loudspeaker announcements, noise from neighboring rooms, other instruments within visual or physical range that are not included in the listening experience, etc.) to ensure that the client's participation and success are optimized. The actual performance can present many unanticipated challenges for client and therapist alike (e.g., cell phones might ring during the performance, the room might be unexpectedly hot or cold, etc.). The therapist should take time to prepare clients for possible distractions, problems, and other mishaps and instruct them on the expected behaviors should they occur.

What to observe. The therapist observes the client for any targeted responses as well as secondary responses. As with traditional session-based experiences, the therapist must not only watch for the response they are trying to elicit, but also always observe the client's responses. Children may express concerns regarding transportation, remembering their parts, or worries about making mistakes. Therapists are advised to notice when clients are not participating at their optimal levels and determine appropriate interventions to make improvements. These might include changing a child's physical location in the ensemble, providing additional supports or cues, or reordering pieces in the actual performance to account for fatigue, as well as lessening attention and concentration over time.

Procedures. Once the performance event has started, it is the therapist's responsibility to ensure an atmosphere of respect for the performer(s). As is common in other performance settings, serving as an emcee of sorts and informing the audience members of basic concert etiquette (silencing cell phones, holding applause until the end, waiting to enter or exit until in between performances, etc.) can help ensure a more pleasurable experience for performers and audience members alike. Within such a setting, the music therapist also assumes the role of "accompanist" and must ensure that no matter what happens, the performer(s) feels proud of their achievement.

Adaptations. In a performance setting, there is always the possibility that the performer(s) may react in an entirely different manner than that which they have prepared. A client may improvise new material in the moment within the context of a prepared piece (instrumental or vocal) or may become overwhelmed or hyperexcited. The therapist may find that they need to alter the planned performance in any number of ways, including eliminating a particular pieces or pieces; moving into a supportive improvised performance; changing the sequence of pieces and/or performers; changing from a performance style to a group participation experience; and other adaptations as necessary and appropriate.

The therapist may want to have access to a recording device (audio or video) in order to provide a copy of the performance to the client(s) and their family members and other significant people, and to capture the client's efforts for playbacks and as part of their clinical record.

Guidelines for Compositional Music Therapy

In Compositional Music Therapy, the therapist assists the client in creating a musical product including songs, instrumental pieces, lyrics, and recordings. When participating in a compositional experience, clients may brainstorm themes, write lyrics, develop melodies and harmonies, and take part in creating a recording (Bruscia, 1998). For school children with physical disabilities, the methods of songwriting and instrumental composition are primary methods of compositional intervention. Both songwriting and instrumental composition experiences take place primarily on the augmentative level of therapy and serve to support the development of physical or academic/cognitive skills. Opportunities in the school setting, such as consultative music therapy within a music education classroom, would be considered to be on the auxiliary level. Instrumental composition and songwriting are less likely to take place at the intensive and primary levels, based upon the team approach used in public schools in the United States and limitations upon related services.

Songwriting and instrumental composition may be used to address multiple goals of children with physical disabilities in school settings, namely: improved fine and gross motor coordination via instrument playing and notation, development of abstract thinking, listening skills, choice-making, and social skills. Additional goal areas include improved self-expression, development of a "container" for an experience of loss, improved body image, improved social connectivity, improved self-awareness, and exploration of therapeutic themes through lyrics (Bruscia, 1998).

The following compositional interventions of songwriting and composing are reported in the literature or used in clinical practice.

Songwriting

Overview. In the compositional method of songwriting, the therapist and client work together to develop lyrics and musical accompaniment. Based upon the client's abilities and needs, the therapist may take a more significant role in assisting with "the more technical aspects" of melody, harmony, and accompaniment (Bruscia, 1998). Further, Baker and Wigram 2005) provisionally define songwriting as "the process of creating, notating, and/or recording lyrics and music by the client or clients and therapist within a therapeutic relationship to address psychosocial, emotional, cognitive, and communication needs of the client" (2005). Since these areas of therapeutic need are applicable to school children with physical disabilities, it is important to explore songwriting as a compositional method for this population.

In work with school children with physical disabilities in a school setting, songwriting may take place on the augmentative level, in which the music therapist is working together with other team members to contribute to the client's overall treatment plan (Bruscia, 1998).

Songwriting may be utilized to meet one of a variety of goals as referenced above. Songwriting with school children with physical disabilities may be contraindicated if adaptations are not available to allow the client to participate meaningfully or to experience success if appropriate. Clients should be able to minimally answer yes/no questions and make a choice between two symbols indicating possible lyrics.

Preparation. In order to prepare the environment for songwriting intervention, the music therapist should consider any physical adaptations required for the client, for example, adapted seating arrangement and availability of typing or dictation technology rather than writing implements. Materials needed include computer or pencil/paper for writing lyrics and notation; instruments including guitar, piano, and percussion; and recording equipment, for example, a digital recorder.

What to observe. During songwriting interventions, the music therapist should be prepared to observe and respond and adapt to the client's physical and communicative needs as well as the client's emotional responses. As the client responds and participates, the therapist should observe the client's physical participation, adjusting to allow the client to take a procedural and/or musical role in the song creation process to the extent to which they are physically able or desire to do so. For example, this could involve the creation of adaptations which facilitate the client typing lyrics, notating melodies and harmonies, and playing instruments. The therapist should observe the client's communicative participation, creating adaptations to the intervention to allow the client to verbalize or utilize assistive technology independently, to the extent of their ability to do so in order to sing or create melodies, develop lyrics, and give the therapist or others musical instructions. The music therapist should also observe the client's emotional responses by way of affect, verbal comments, and body language in order to inform the direction of the songwriting intervention as they relate to the client's present experiences and their responses to the musical and lyric materials.

Procedures. Wigram describes the following six-stage "Flexible Approach to Songwriting in Therapy (FAST)" (Baker & Wigram, 2005).

Stage 1: Introduction to Songwriting. This stage can include the methods of improvising, incorporating story creation, the therapist proposing song ideas via discussion, and clients requesting ideas as a result of song singing.

Stage 2: Formulation of Lyrics. This stage includes the methods of client-therapist brainstorming, spontaneous suggestion of words by the client or therapist, suggestion of words relating to client issues by either the client or therapist, and the client's proposal of precomposed lyrics.

Stage 3: Development of Music. This stage includes the method of improvising music, improvising melody over a structured harmonic frame by the client and/or therapist, creation of melody and harmony by the client, and therapist offering musical ideas to be accepted or rejected by the client.

Stage 4: Writing Down a Song. This stage includes methods of writing down lyrics only; writing down lyrics and melody; writing down lyrics, melody, and basic chordal structure; or writing down a full version including lyrics, melody, harmony and accompaniment.

Stage 5: Performing of Song. This stage includes the performance of the song by the client and therapist together, performance of the song to staff and other clients, and performance of the song to family and friends.

Stage 6: Recording of Song. This stage includes methods of recording the song in its original form, creating a group recording, and/or transcribing and orchestrating the song for a professional recording.

The following procedures for conducting songwriting intervention are described by Federico and Niedenthal (2011), specific to their work with a student with cerebral palsy:

1) Selection of Theme and Style: The music therapist guides the client(s) in determining a song theme. The theme may be therapist- or client-initiated.
2) Development of Lyrics (Brainstorming): The therapist assists the client in writing lyrics. This can take place in a variety of ways, using an idea bubble or mind map, writing full lyrics and editing. The therapist may assist with this process depending upon the needs of the client. Clients with less developed language may require a more structured approach offering developed lyric choices, while clients with a greater or typical language skills may need only guidance and suggestions.
3) Development of Melody: Based upon the client's needs, the music therapist may create all, some, or none of the melody. Clients may independently develop the melody or contribute to it either vocally or with an instrument.
4) Development of Harmony and Accompaniment: Again, based upon the client's needs, the music therapist may create all, some, or none of the harmony/accompaniment. Clients may develop the harmony either vocally or with an instrument.
5) Integration of Parts: The client and therapist put the melody, harmony, and lyrics together in order to create the final product.
6) Notate and/or Record: The song may be recorded or notated for future use.

Adaptations. Steps 2–4 may take place in any order and songwriting interventions may span several sessions. Songwriting can take place in individual, dyad, or small group sessions, including groups of children who have disabilities alongside of their typical peers. Clients may come to their sessions with developed themes or lyrics. Recordings of the song may be provided to the client on CD as appropriate. Clients may choose to perform their song for others.

Instrumental Composition

Overview. In the compositional music therapy method of instrumental composition, the music therapist works with the client to develop a musical piece using instruments. Based upon client needs and ability, the therapist may provide assistance in the development of the melody, harmony, notation, and recording of the composition (Bruscia 1998). Instrumental composition may take a variety of forms within a music therapy session; the client may actively create music using a variety of instruments, or the therapist may create or assist the client in this endeavor, checking in with the client to ensure that the composition is aligned with the client's wishes and preferences. The client may take an active role in notation and recording of the composition or the therapist may assist with notation and recording in full (Bruscia, 1998; Wigram, 2005).

Composition experiences take place primarily on the augmentative level of therapy in the school setting, potentially addressing multiple goals, as described above. As with songwriting, clients who are unable to musically demonstrate or verbally or symbolically express their desires for the composition, through traditional or technological means, may become overly frustrated, and therefore composition experiences may be contraindicated.

Preparation. As in songwriting, in order to prepare the environment for composition intervention, the music therapist should consider any physical adaptations required for the client, for example, adapted seating arrangement and availability of typing or touch screen technology rather than writing implements. Materials needed include computer or pencil/paper for recording and notation, instruments, and recording equipment, for example, a digital recorder. Appropriate electronic music technology such as a computer or tablet with software capabilities for recording/mixing such as GarageBand™ or others is also needed.

What to observe. As in songwriting, during composition interventions, the music therapist should observe and respond and adapt to the client's physical and communicative needs as well as to the client's emotional responses. The therapist may take an active or supportive role in both music-making and logistics, based upon the client's abilities to musically create the composition on instruments or vocally, notate the music, and participate in other aspects of the recording and performing process. For example, the therapist may help the client by playing music to the client's specifications and facilitating the notation, or the therapist may notate the client's composition.

Procedures. The following procedures may be used in conducting composition interventions. First, during instrument selection, the therapist guides the client(s) in selecting instruments for the composition. In school settings, these could include percussion, piano, guitar, band, orchestral, or electronic music technologies. Second, the composition is developed in one of several ways. These include trial-and-error through improvisation, notation of melodic and harmonic ideas as they are created, and music technology to develop melodic and harmonic aspects of the composition. Next, during integration and notation, the different parts of the composition are brought together and notated. Finally, during recording, the composition may be recorded for the client and clinical record.

Adaptations. Composition interventions may span several sessions. Composition can take place in individual, dyad, or small group sessions, including groups of children who have disabilities alongside their typical peers. Recordings of the composition may be provided to the client on CD as appropriate, and clients may choose to arrange their composition for performance for others.

Case example: An 8th grader, who had suffered the loss of his arm in a car accident, was referred to music therapy due to his unwillingness to participate in his physical education class. The school psychologist and several regular education teachers reported that although previously bright and social, he had stopped responding in class and appeared withdrawn from his classmates. The student had previously played bass in a band with several friends. The music therapist employed songwriting to assist him with emotional expression. The resulting songs expressed emotions regarding feeling different, his fears of rejection from peers, and his frustration with the changes in his ability to create music. In addition to recording the songs with the music therapist, he began to arrange the songs for his band and requested that the MT assist them in rehearsing the songs together. He also expressed interest in using touch screen tablet applications to be able to continue to create bass music as well as interest in developing his vocal skills. The education team reported increased participation in his classes.

Working with Caregivers

There is very little research regarding the music therapist's role in working with caregivers with children with physical disabilities. However, within the school setting, the music therapist needs to understand their role on the educational team and their potential role as a consultant to other team members, as well as their potential role as a clinical collaborator in therapy. Because special education takes place in the least restrictive environment in the United States (LRE) (IDEA, n.d.), students with physical disabilities are included alongside their nondisabled peers, so music therapists should be prepared to provide services appropriate to inclusive environment. In a survey of music therapists working with people with disabilities, Jones and Cardinal (1998) reported that music therapist respondents were knowledgeable and supportive of inclusion and willing to work in inclusive environments. It is clear that it is essential for music therapists to work alongside the teachers, special education teachers, paraprofessionals, occupational therapists, speech therapists, physical therapists, and specialist teachers (e.g., music education, art, physical education).

In the school setting, it is important that the music therapist be able to both support and be supported by fellow team members. Davis (1990) emphasizes the importance of collaboration with Occupational Therapy, Physical Therapy, and Speech-Language Pathology in order to optimize success with children with physical disabilities. May (1956) noted that music therapy "[in] conjunction with the work of speech and physical therapists, may aid materially with problems of speech and of physical co-ordination." Music therapists therefore may fulfill one or several roles in the educational environment: direct service provider (utilizing the methods described above), as well as consultant and collaborator.

Consultation

As a consultant to the special education team, the music therapist assists the team members in implementing music techniques into other professionals' work (Coleman & Brunk, 1999). While the music therapist is not teaching other professionals to engage clients in music therapy techniques, non–music therapy techniques can be adapted to include music (Bruscia, 1998). Consultation is often a strategy that schools use when direct, individual-related service is not required for a student to benefit from special education. Consultation allows students with physical disabilities to benefit from the incorporation of music into non–musically therapeutic strategies, and it allows the special education team to benefit from the music therapist's knowledge and skills.

Chester (1999) described a consultative model of music therapy in special education, stating benefits which include service delivery to more students, teacher use of music therapist–generated strategies, collaboration, and maximal use of the music therapist's time. More than half of board-certified music therapists working in educational settings collaborate and consult regularly with other professionals including OT, PT, Speech, and Special Educators (Register, 2002).

Collaboration with Other Educational and Therapeutic Disciplines

Clinical goals in the school setting may include overlap between disciplines; therefore, team collaboration and cotreatment may be warranted, with the music therapist offering important contributions (Johnson, 2002). Music therapists work with speech-language pathologists to assist with improved expressive and receptive communication. One study offers suggestions for facilitating better communication through the author's description of the use of Blissymbols with nonverbal children with CP (Herman, 1985). Although not widely used in the US, Blissymbols is an alternative graphic form of notation used to symbolize words and ideas. Herman suggests allowing the child to initiate topics or to give a cue as to what topic s/he wishes to pursue, asking questions that need more than a "yes" or "no" response, being sensitive to the child's need to organize his/her thoughts, and allowing time to finish, not interrupting with interpretation. He also suggests articulating slowly and clearly when giving instructions since some children process information slowly (Herman, 1985).

While music therapists could benefit from using augmentative and assistive communication in music therapy sessions, many report not using it regularly or having received specific training (Gadbury, 2011). It is crucial that music therapists utilize a collaborative team approach and receive training and consultation from the speech-language pathologists with whom they work (Gadbury, 2011; McCarthy, Geist, Zojwala, & Schock, 2008).

Music therapists may have the opportunity to work closely with occupational and physical therapists as well as special educators in their work with children with physical disabilities in school settings (Johnson, 2002). Despite this likelihood, there is little research outlining best practices specifically with this population. Some guidance may be provided in the literature addressing multiple disabilities and Rett Syndrome (Elefant & Lotan, 2004); however, future studies are recommended in this area to provide music therapists specific recommendations on collaboration in these important areas.

The music therapist may be called upon to collaborate with music educators in school settings. Many music educators have positive attitudes regarding inclusion, their level of support for teaching in inclusive environments, and outcomes for learners with special needs (Scott, Jellison, & Chappell, 2007), and many have received training in teaching music to children with physical disabilities (Colwell, 1995; Colwell & Thompson, 2000). Despite this, music educators may require assistance with preparing for students with physical disabilities, creating adaptations, and understanding their needs. Darrow (1999) describes one role of the music therapist as being "inclusion facilitator," collaborating with the music educator to facilitate a positive inclusion experience for the student with special needs in music education. The responsibilities of this role could include scheduling consultations, sharing and disseminating student-specific information, facilitating communication among team and family members, providing in-service training for music teachers, and providing direct classroom assistance to the student.

Research Evidence

Receptive Music Therapy

Behaviorally, receptive music has been shown to physically affect individuals both with and without disabilities. Pearce (1981) studied the effect of musical style on arousal measured by grip strength of undergraduate students. Comparing initial grip-to-grip strength while listening to stimulative, sedative, and no music, she found that strength decreased in the silence condition although the stimulating music did not affect grip strength. Several studies examined the effect of music on the behaviors of children with CP. Given client-preferred music, children with cerebral palsy have been shown to "self-regulate spasm and spasticity at the elbow and to regulate tonic stretch reflex sensitively independently of contraction level" (Neilson & McCaughey, 1982) and maintain neck posture without dropping their heads (Ball, McCrady, & Hart, 1975; Wolfe, 1980).

There are several examples of evidence for the use of receptive music therapy with school children with physical disabilities. In order to support a therapeutic routine, the music therapist may study the treatment and compose and record a "treatment tape" or CD for the client to use independently, outside of MT or in another therapeutic or educational setting. A "treatment tape" of therapist-composed music was shown to be effective in increasing the enjoyment of the daily cystic fibrosis chest physical therapy routine undertaken by caregivers and children with CF (Grasso, et al., 2000). When creating music for procedural support in special education, occupational therapy, physical therapy, speech-language pathology, and other educational areas, it is important to collaborate closely with the other professionals involved, as well as with the client with physical disabilities. Receptive listening of client-preferred music has been described as decreasing anxiety and increasing relaxation among children with CP receiving acupuncture (Yu, Liu, Li, & Ma, 2009; Yu, Liu, & Wu, 2009), and there are many anecdotal reports which support the use of client-preferred music to support relaxation. Among children with physical disabilities, physical muscle tension, and tightness, pain and stress responses may occur in response to the school environment and expectations; therefore, the special education team should be available to provide intervention should relaxation be needed for a student to participate meaningfully in school. Among a small group of clients with CP, Scartelli (1982) showed that the use of sedative instrumental background music added to EMG biofeedback relaxation was more effective than EMG biofeedback alone. Although further research is needed, this supports the use of music within relaxation experiences.

Peng et al. (2011) describe therapist-composed music for assisting clients with cerebral palsy with significantly improving their sit-to-stand movements, demonstrating music procedure support. Also, "Rhythmic Auditory Stimulation" (RAS), in which the therapist is providing rhythm to support gait training, has been shown to improve several aspects of gait of people with cerebral palsy (Kim et al., 2011; Kwak, 2007). In Kwak's study (2007), the greatest effect was shown with the therapist's presence in the session and social support of parents. When providing live procedural support, it is important for the music therapist to work closely with the other professionals involved with the particular therapeutic area. For example, an MT should be trained in positioning and moving a child with CP safely so as to not injure the student or self. If a particular clinical need or necessary intervention is not within an MT's area of competence, an appropriate referral should be made and additional training should be pursued.

Improvisational Music Therapy

Various types of improvisation are discussed in the music therapy literature studying children with physical disabilities, primarily combining the media of voice, instrumental, and technology. Specific technology programs have been created to assist children with physical disabilities in improvising music, as described above, including Dynamic Sonification (Lem & Paine, 2011) and "Adapted Use Musical Instruments" (AUMI) (Oliveros, et al., 2011), which provide for horizontal or vertical movements to be translated into keyboard or percussive sounds. These technologies allow for individuals with highly limited movement to improvise creatively, and the music therapist should be aware of the continued growth in this area and incorporate technology as appropriate.

While not specific to clients with physical disabilities in school settings, Gunsberg (1988) describes "Improvised Musical Play" as teacher-led music improvisation to increase the amount of time children focus on social play; this combines vocal/instrumental improvisation. In a similar vein, while the broad work of Nordoff and Robbins (1971, 1980) focuses upon clients who have multiple disabilities which move beyond the realm of physical disabilities, their work may also inform the music therapist using improvisation with school children with physical disabilities. Also, Alvin's model of Free Improvisation Therapy may inform music therapy with school children with physical disabilities in addressing goals of "gross and fine motor skills, sensory-motor coordination, etc." (Bruscia, 1987, p. 80), although it was not created expressly for this population. While these methods are described in the literature, additional studies are warranted in order to expand music therapists' understanding of the use of improvisational methods with clients with physical disabilities in school settings.

Re-creative Music Therapy

Within the music therapy literature, research studies evaluate the impact of re-creative music therapy methods on motor skills, coordination, self-help skills, and lung function, as well as relatedness, attention, self-confidence, and motor skills. Instrumental re-creation can be used to improve or support the fine and gross motor skills and coordination of children with various physical disabilities, as well as increase attention and self-confidence (Berel, et al., 1971; Herron, 1970; Nasuruddin, 2010). In a school setting, this has generalization to self-help skills, writing skills, and typing skills, all of which are essential to academic progress.

It has been shown that students with even significant physical disabilities are able to learn and improve musical skills (Howell, et al., 1995; Kennedy & Kua-Walker, 2006; Spitzer, 1989), and from this perspective, improved coordination also provides an individual with opportunities to express their creativity, inner experience, etc., with greater accuracy. For example, the use of weighted mallets may support improved hand strength, and the use of keyboard instruction can support posture, bilateral coordination, and finger isolation (Spitzer, 1989).

Children with physical disabilities may wish to play instruments in the band or orchestra or sing in music education classes and in school choir or chorus, or participating in school musicals or performances. These settings provide natural and age-appropriate opportunities for social development, improved lung capacity, listening, attention, and memory. This type of inclusion in ensembles and in music education not only benefits the individual with physical disabilities with regard to their physical coordination and social skills (Humpal, 1991), but also improves the attitude of the typical peers who are participating toward their peers with disabilities (Darrow and Johnson, 1994; Gregory, 1997, 1998). A physical disability does not preclude a child from participating in ensembles, as adaptations, including technology, can be used to promote this inclusion (Magee et al., 2011). The music therapist may play an essential role in assisting the music educator in making appropriate instrument choices, creating physical adaptations to instruments, and adapting lesson plans (Register, 2002).

Instrumental re-creation has also been used as part of the bonding work in mother and child dyads in which the child has CP. Since it has been reported that individuals with CP may experience attachment difficulties, instrument-playing was used, along with other music interventions, and resulted in increased relatedness (Gilboa & Roginsky, 2010). The use of wind instrument–playing has been shown to support lung function in individuals with asthma (Eley & Norman, 2010), and the use of singing has been hypothesized to improve lung function of individuals with cystic fibrosis (Irons, Kenny, & Chang, 2010) and physical disabilities in general (Batavia & Batavia, 2003).

Compositional Music Therapy

Although mentioned anecdotally, within the music therapy literature, there are limited studies supporting outcomes for the method of songwriting for use with clients with physical disabilities in school settings. Maddick (2011) describes the use of songwriting in music therapy–social work collaboration with individuals after acquiring a severe injury. They reported that songwriting assisted with improved body awareness and social connection, as well as acted as a "conduit" for emotional expression. This implies that in work with school children with physical disabilities, the music therapist may work individually with or in collaboration with a school counselor or psychologist in assisting with adjustment post–serious injury. Songwriting may be used with technology adaptations to aid with both physical and choice-making tasks, providing for increased independence. Federico and Niedenthal (2011) discuss the use of songwriting with technology adaptations for people with cerebral palsy, including physical, musical, instrumental, and technological means. While some conclusions may be drawn from these clinical descriptions and small studies, further research is warranted to expand the understanding of the use of songwriting in school settings and clinical outcomes of songwriting specific to children with physical disabilities.

There are no studies expressly studying the outcomes of instrumental composition with clients with physical disabilities in school settings at this time; therefore, additional research is recommended in this area.

Summary and Conclusions

School children with physical disabilities benefit from receptive, improvisational, re-creative, and compositional music therapy experiences to address their motor, communication, cognitive, social, and emotional needs. In school settings, the music therapist works as part of a team by providing direct service or by serving in a consultative role to teachers and other allied professionals, which assists the student in making reasonable academic progress. Music therapy can play an important part in meeting overarching needs in areas of fine and gross motor skills, communication skills, and social and emotional skills. While these needs arise directly or indirectly from the client's physical disability, support in these areas is essential to ensure that the student benefits from their educational program.

References

Anbar, R. D., & Murthy, V. V. (2010). Reestablishment of hope as an intervention for a patient with cystic fibrosis awaiting lung transplantation. *Journal of Alternative and Complementary Medicine, 16*(9), 1007–1010.

Apert Syndrome. (n.d.). In *ADAM medical encyclopedia*. Retrieved from http://www.ncbi.nlm.nih.gov/pubmedhealth/PMH0002548/

Asthma in Children. (n.d.). Retrieved from http://www.nlm.nih.gov/medlineplus/asthmainchildren.html

Asthma in Children Fact Sheet. (2012). Retrieved from http://www.lung.org/lung-disease/asthma/resources/facts-and-figures/asthma-children-fact-sheet.html

Ball, T., McCrady, R., & Hart, A. (1975). Automated reinforcement of head posture in two cerebral palsied retarded children. *Perceptual and Motor Skills, 40*(2), 619–622.

Batavia, A., & Batavia, M. (2003). Karaoke for quads: A new application of an old recreation with potential therapeutic benefits for people with disabilities. *Disability and Rehabilitation, 25*(6), 297-300.

Baxter, H., Berghofer, J., MacEwan, L., Nelson, J., Peters, K., & Roberts, P. (2007). *The individualized music therapy assessment profile*. Philadelphia, PA: Jessica Kingsley.

Berel, M., Diller, L., & Orgel, M. (1971). Music as a facilitator for visual motor sequencing tasks in children with cerebral palsy. *Developmental Medicine and Child Neurology, 13*(3), 335–342.

Bradfield, C., Carlenius, J., Gold, C., & White, M. (2008). *MT-SEAS: Music therapy special education assessment scale*. Grapevine, TX: Prelude Music Therapy.

Bruscia, K. (1987). *Improvisational models of music therapy*. Springfield, IL: Charles Thomas.

Bruscia, K. (1998). *Defining music therapy*. Gilsum, NH: Barcelona Publishers.

Cerebral Palsy. (n.d.). In *ADAM medical encyclopedia*. Retrieved from http://www.ncbi.nlm.nih.gov/pubmedhealth/PMH0001734

Chester, K. K. (1999). A program-based consultative music therapy model for public schools. *Music Therapy Perspectives, 17*(2), 82–91.

Childhood Arthritis. (n.d.). Retrieved from http://www.cdc.gov/arthritis/basics/childhood.htm

Clair, A. A., & Pasiali, V. (2004). Neurological music therapy. In A. A. Darrow (Ed.), *Introduction to approaches in music therapy* (pp. 143–157). Silver Spring, MD: American Music Therapy Association.

Clark, C., & Chadwick, D. (1979). *Clinically adapted instruments for the multiply handicapped.* Westford, MA: Modulations.

Clarkson, A., & Robey, K. (2000). The use of identity structure modeling to examine the central role of musical experience within the self-concept of a young woman with physical disabilities. *Music Therapy Perspectives, 18*(2), 115–121.

Cleft Lip and Palate. (n.d.). In *ADAM medical encyclopedia*. Retrieved from http://www.ncbi.nlm.nih.gov/pubmedhealth/PMH0002046/

Coleman, K., & Brunk, B. (1999). *Special education music therapy assessment process.* Grapevine, TX: Prelude Music Therapy.

Colwell, C. (1995). Adapting music instruction for elementary students with special needs: A pilot. *Music Therapy Perspectives, 13*(2), 97–103.

Colwell, C., & Thompson, L. (2000). "Inclusion" of information on mainstreaming in undergraduate music education curricula. *Journal of Music Therapy, 37*(3), 205–221.

Cystic Fibrosis. (n.d.). In *ADAM medical encyclopedia*. Retrieved from http://www.ncbi.nlm.nih.gov/pubmedhealth/PMH0001167/

Darrow, A. (1999). Music educators' perceptions regarding the inclusion of students with severe disabilities in music classrooms. *Journal of Music Therapy, 36*(4), 254–273.

Darrow, A., & Johnson, C. M. (1994). Junior and senior high school music students' attitudes toward individuals with a disability. *Journal of Music Therapy, 31,* 266–279.

Davis, R. (1990). A model for the integration of music therapy within preschool classrooms for children with physical disabilities or language delays. *Music Therapy Perspectives, 8,* 82–84.

Elefant, C., & Lotan, M. (2004). Rett syndrome: Dual intervention—music and physical therapy. *Nordic Journal of Music Therapy, 13*(2), 172–182.

Eley, R., & Norman, M. (2010). Music therapy to manage asthma symptoms in young indigenous people in urban settings. *Islander Health Worker Journal, 34*(3), 20–22.

Epilepsy. (n.d.). In *ADAM medical encyclopedia*. Retrieved from http://www.ncbi.nlm.nih.gov/pubmedhealth/PMH0001714/

Federico, G., & Niedenthal, R. (2011). *Music therapy & cerebral palsy: Songwriting with technology adaptations*. Proceedings of XIII World Congress of Music Therapy, Seoul, Korea.

Fenton, J. F. (2000). Cystic fibrosis and art therapy. *The Arts in Psychotherapy, 27*(1), 15–25.

Gadberry, A. (2011). A survey of the use of aided augmentative and alternative communication during music therapy sessions with persons with autism spectrum disorders. *Journal of Music Therapy, 48*(1), 74–89.

Generalized Tonic Clonic Seizure. (n.d.). In *ADAM medical encyclopedia*. Retrieved from http://www.ncbi.nlm.nih.gov/pubmedhealth/PMH0001715/

Gilboa, A., & Roginsky, E. (2010). Examining the dyadic music therapy treatment (DUET): The case of a CP child and his mother. *Nordic Journal of Music Therapy, 19*(2), 103–132.

Grasso, M. C., Button, B. M., Allison, D. J., & Sawyer, S. M. (2000). Benefits of music therapy as an adjunct to chest physiotherapy in infants and toddlers with cystic fibrosis. *Pediatric Pulmonology, 29*(5), 371–381.

Gregory, D. (1997). Before and after the Americans with Disabilities Act: An analysis of attitude and knowledge of undergraduate music majors. *Journal of Music Therapy, 34,* 119–128.

Gregory, D. (1998). Reactions to ballet with wheelchairs: Reflections of attitudes toward people with disabilities. *Journal of Music Therapy, 35*(4), 274–283.

Grocke, D., & Wigram, T. (2007). *Receptive methods in music therapy: Techniques and clinical applications.* Philadelphia, PA: Jessica Kingsley.

Gunsberg, A. (1988). Improvised musical play: A strategy for fostering social play between developmentally delayed and nondelayed preschool children. *Journal of Music Therapy, 25,* 178–191.

Hemophilia. (n.d.). In *ADAM medical encyclopedia.* Retrieved from http://www.ncbi.nlm.nih.gov/pubmedhealth/PMH0001564/

Herman, F. (1985). Music therapy for the young child with cerebral palsy who uses blissymbols. *Music Therapy, 5*(1), 28–36.

Howell, R. D., Flowers, P. J., & Wheaton, J. E. (1995). The effects of keyboard experiences on rhythmic responses of elementary school children with physical disabilities. *Journal of Music Therapy, 32*(2), 91–112.

Herron, C. J. (1970). Some effects of instrumental music training on cerebral palsied children. *Journal of Music Therapy, 7*(2), 55–58.

Humpal, M. E. (1991). The effects of an integrated early childhood music program on social interaction among children with handicaps and their typical peers. *Journal of Music Therapy, 28,* 161–177.

Hydrocephalus. (n.d.). In *ADAM medical encyclopedia.* Retrieved from http://www.ncbi.nlm.nih.gov/pubmedhealth/PMH0002538/

IDEA Part B (n.d.) Retrieved from http://nichcy.org/laws/idea/partb/subparta#300.8

Irons, J. Y., Kenny, D. T., & Chang, A. B. (2010). Singing for children and adults with cystic fibrosis. *Cochrane Database of Systematic Reviews* (Online), *5,* CD008036.

Johnson, F. (2002). Models of service delivery and their relation to the IEP. In B. Wilson (Ed.), *Models of music therapy interventions in school settings* (pp. 83–108). Silver Spring, MD: American Music Therapy Association.

Jones, L., & Cardinal, D. (1998). A descriptive analysis of music therapists' perceptions of delivering services in inclusive settings: A challenge to the field. *Journal of Music Therapy, 35*(1), 34–48.

Juvenile Rheumatoid Arthritis. (n.d.). Retrieved from http://www.webmd.com/rheumatoid-arthritis/guide/juvenile-rheumatoid-arthritis

Kennedy, R., & Kua-Walker, Y. (2006). Movement, singing, and instrument playing strategies for a child with myotonic dystrophy. *Music Therapy Perspectives, 24*(1), 39–51.

Kim, S. J., Kwak, E. E., Park, E. S., Lee, D. S., Kim, K. J., Song, J. E., & Cho, S. (2011). Changes in gait patterns with rhythmic auditory stimulation in adults with cerebral palsy. *NeuroRehabilitation, 29*(3), 233–241.

Kwak, E. E. (2007). Effect of rhythmic auditory stimulation on gait performance in children with spastic cerebral palsy. *Journal of Music Therapy, 44*(3), 198–216.

Lem, A., & Paine, G. (2011). Dynamic sonification as a free music improvisation tool for physically disabled adults. *Music and Medicine, 3*(3), 182–188.

Maddick, R. (2011). "Naming the unnameable and communicating the unknowable": Reflections on a combined music therapy/social work program. *The Arts in Psychotherapy, 38,* 130–137.

Magee, W. L., Bertolami, M., Kubicek, L., LaJoie, M., Martino, L., Sankowski, A., & Zigo, J. B. (2011). Using music technology in music therapy with populations across the life span in medical and educational programs. *Music and Medicine, 3*(3), 146–153.

Magee, W. L., & Burland, K. (2008). An exploratory study of the use of electronic music technologies in clinical music therapy. *Nordic Journal of Music Therapy, 17*(2), 124–141.

May, E. (1956). Music for children with cerebral palsy. *American Journal of Physical Medicine, 35,* 320–323.

Moebius Syndrome. (n.d.). Retrieved from http://ghr.nlm.nih.gov/condition/moebius-syndrome

Nasuruddin, M. G. (2010). The confluence between arts and medical science: Music and movement therapy for children with cerebral palsy. *The Malaysian Journal of Medical Sciences: MJMS, 17*(3), 1–4.

Neilson, P., & McCaughey, J. (1982). Self-regulation of spasm and spasticity in cerebral palsy. *Journal of Neurology, Neurosurgery and Psychiatry, 45*(4), 320–330.

NINDS Muscular Dystrophy Information Page. (n.d.). Retrieved from http://www.ninds.nih.gov/disorders/md/md.htm

Nordoff, P., & Robbins, C. (1971). *Music therapy for handicapped children.* London, England: Victor Gollancz.

Nordoff, P., & Robbins, C. (1980). *Creative music therapy.* New York, NY: New York University.

Oliveros, P., Miller, L., Heyen, J., Siddall, G., & Hazard, S. (2011). A musical improvisation interface for people with severe physical disabilities. *Music and Medicine, 3*(3), 172–181.

Osteogenesis Imperfecta. (n.d.). In *ADAM medical encyclopedia.* Retrieved from http://www.ncbi.nlm.nih.gov/pubmedhealth/PMH0002540/

Partial (Focal) Seizure. (n.d.). In *ADAM medical encyclopedia.* Retrieved from http://www.ncbi.nlm.nih.gov/pubmedhealth/PMH0001717/

Pearce, K. A. (1981). Effects of different types of music on physical strength. *Perceptual and Motor Skills, 53*(2), 351–352.

Peng, Y., Lu, T., Wang, T., Chen, Y., Liao, H., Lin, K., & Tang, P. (2011). Immediate effects of therapeutic music on loaded sit-to-stand movement in children with spastic diplegia. *Gait & Posture, 33*(2), 274–278.

Petit Mal Seizure. (n.d.). In *ADAM medical encyclopedia.* Retrieved from http://www.ncbi.nlm.nih.gov/pubmedhealth/PMH0001716/

Register, D. (2002). Collaboration and consultation: A survey of board-certified music therapists. *Journal of Music Therapy, 39*(4), 305–321.

Scartelli, J. (1982). The effect of sedative music on electromyographic biofeedback assisted relaxation training of spastic cerebral palsied adults. *Journal of Music Therapy, 19*(4), 210–218.

School Success. (n.d.). Retrieved from http://www.arthritis.org/ja-school-success.php#1

Scott, L. P., Jellison, J. A., & Chappell, E. W. (2007). Talking with music teachers about inclusion: Perceptions, opinions and experiences. *Journal of Music Therapy, 44*(1), 38–56.

Sickle-Cell Anemia. (n.d.). In *ADAM medical encyclopedia.* Retrieved from http://www.ncbi.nlm.nih.gov/pubmedhealth/PMH0001554/

Thaut, M. H. (1985). The use of auditory rhythm and rhythmic speech to add temporal muscular control in children with gross motor dysfunction. *Journal of Music Therapy, 22*(3), 108–128.

Thaut, M. H. (1988). Rhythmic intervention techniques in music therapy with gross motor dysfunctions. *The Arts in Psychotherapy, 15*(2), 127–137.

Spina Bifida. (n.d.). In *ADAM medical encyclopedia.* Retrieved from http://www.ncbi.nlm.nih.gov/pubmedhealth/PMH0002525/

Spitzer, S. (1989). Computers and music therapy: An integrated approach: Four case studies. *Music Therapy Perspectives, 7,* 51–54.

Understanding Muscular Dystrophy. (n.d.). Retrieved from http://www.webmd.com/parenting/understanding-muscular-dystrophy-basics

What Should You Know about Muscular Dystrophy? (n.d.). Retrieved from http://www.cdc.gov/ncbddd/musculardystrophy/index.html

Whitehead-Pleaux, A. M., Clark, S. L., & Spall, L. E. (2011). Indications and contraindications for electronic music technologies in a pediatric medical setting. *Music and Medicine, 3*(3), 154–162.

Wigram, T. (2005). Music and sound vibration: Testing hypotheses as a series of case studies. In D. Aldridge (Ed.), *Case study designs in music therapy* (pp. 163–189). Philadelphia, PA: Jessica Kingsley.

Wilson, B. L., & Smith, D. S. (2000). Music therapy assessment in school settings: A preliminary investigation. *Journal of Music Therapy, 37*(2), 95–117.

Wolfe, D. E. (1980). The effect of automated interrupted music on head posturing of cerebral palsied individuals. *Journal of Music Therapy, 17*(4), 184–206.

Yu, H., Liu, Y., Li, S., & Ma, X. (2009). Effects of music on anxiety and pain in children with cerebral palsy receiving acupuncture: A randomized controlled trial. *International Journal of Nursing Studies, 46*(11), 1423–1430.

Yu, H., Liu, Y., & Wu, L. (2009). Acupuncture combined with music therapy for treatment of 30 cases of cerebral palsy. *Journal of Traditional Chinese Medicine, 29*(4), 243–248.

Chapter 14

Individuals with Severe and Multiple Disabilities

Barbara L. Wheeler

Diagnostic Information

The American Association of Intellectual and Developmental Disabilities (AAIDD) states that intellectual disability is characterized by "significant limitations both in intellectual functioning and in adaptive behavior, which covers many everyday social and practical skills. This disability originates before the age of 18" (http://www.aaidd.org/content_100.cfm?navID=21). The Individuals with Disabilities Education Act (IDEA), defines a person with multiple disabilities as having "concomitant impairments (such as mental retardation–blindness or mental retardation–orthopedic impairment), the combination of which causes such severe educational needs that they cannot be accommodated in special education programs solely for one of the impairments. Multiple disabilities do not include deaf–blindness" (http://nichcy.org/disability/categories#multiple).

Although *multiple disabilities* can technically refer to any combination of disabilities (other than deaf–blindness), it is typically applied to people for whom one of the disabilities is a severe or profound intellectual disability (ID) along with another disability. This is how the term will be used in this chapter. Although a few instances in which intellectual disability is not one of the multiple disabilities included in this chapter, most of the people described have a severe or profound intellectual disability in addition to at least one additional disability.

Needs and Resources

While people with ID have a variety of abilities and disabilities, they share the need for support in many aspects of their functioning. Because their disabilities are both multiple and severe, they affect many areas of their lives, leading to their problems being interactive rather than additive, and making instruction and learning complex (*Education Encyclopedia,* n.d.). Their behavioral, emotional, and social needs are complicated by the complexity of their disabilities and their complex medical needs, and their education must take into account their multiple and severe disabilities.

The severity of the disabilities has a pervasive effect on the lives of people with severe and multiple disabilities. Although there is considerable evidence that musical aptitude can occur independent of disabilities, the studies that conclude this have generally been in areas other than intellectual disability, such as communication disorders (Cassidy, 1992), normal and hearing-impaired individuals with cochlear implants (Darrow, 1984; Stordahl, 2002), and blind and sighted children (Flowers & Wang, 2002). Hooper, Wigram, Carson, and Lindsay (2008) state that "studies that assessed musical aptitude by using subtests from [several standard batteries of musical aptitude] typically detected a lower level of performance among those with intellectual disability compared to samples without intellectual disability, or to published norms" (p. 81). One well-designed study (Zenatti, 1975) found clear differences in performance on melodic memory tests between young people of normal and lower-than-normal intellectual functioning. In a related study, DiGiammarino (1990) examined performance of functional music skills in individuals with ID. She found that the number of functional music skills performed was significantly and inversely related to level of intellectual disability and site of residence, but not to sex or severity of problem behavior. Fewer skills were demonstrated as the severity of intellectual disability increased.

Music therapists find and develop a person's resources, musical and otherwise, which often means tapping musical aptitude or other potential skill or ability. For example, children with ID who have unusual musical talent are sometimes called *musical savants* (Charness, Clifton, & MacDonald, 1988; Miller, 1987, 1999; Owens & Grimm, 1941). Music therapy pioneers Juliette Alvin, as well as Paul Nordoff and Clive and Carol Robbins, addressed this innate interest or aptitude and potential. Alvin (1959, in Hooper, Wigram, Carson, & Lindsay, 2008) spoke of the responses of 24 children with mild to severe intellectual disability (and we can assume some multiple disabilities) to short cello concerts that she played. The *music child,* developed as part of the Nordoff-Robbins Creative Music Therapy approach (Nordoff & Robbins, 2007; Robbins & Robbins, 1991), refers to the musical part of a child, unhampered by his or her disabilities. The music child can be musically expressive and is undamaged. The music child is seen as the child within the *condition child,* the child with the problems, and the Nordoff-Robbins music therapist works to develop this healthy music child.

Through *Sounds of Intent,* Welch, Ockelford, Carter, Zimmerman and Himonides (2009) attempted to develop a framework "to inform and underpin the construction and implementation of effective music intervention strategies in schools and to enhance the capacity of the mainstream sector to include children with complex needs in the early years" (p. 35). The framework includes three dimensions: (a) *reactive* (in response to another)—encounters sounds; shows awareness of sound and silence; attends and responds to a variety of sounds; attends and responds to simple patterns in sound; makes distinct response to familiar short pieces, fragments, or features of music and/or anticipates clear contrast within a familiar piece; (b) *proactive* (initiating behavior without an obvious external prompt)—makes sounds accidentally; makes sounds intentionally; makes a variety of sounds; produces simple patterns by repeating sounds; repeats short groups of sounds, which may incorporate recognizable fragments or features of music; and (c) *interactive* (with another)—chance interactions; makes sound in response to external stimulus and/or to stimulate response; takes turns, neither copying what is heard nor reacting differently if own sounds are copied; takes turns, copying individual sounds that are heard and/or relishing own sounds being copied; takes turns, copying short patterns in sound and/or anticipating own short patterns being copied (p. 359). Their initial research found support for the framework through 630 systematic observations in relation to the musical behaviors of 68 children and young people with complex needs, ages approximately 4½ to 19 years (average age, 13 years).

Later research indicated that the framework can be used to chart incremental progress over time (Ockelford, Welch, Jewell-Gore, Cheng, Vogiatzoglou, & Himonides, 2011). In the final phase of the project (Vogiatzoglou, Ockelford, Welch, & Himonides, 2011), an interactive software package based on the framework and containing video, photographs, and descriptions of children's musical engagement is being produced. This Web-based software package "will allow practitioners to assess their pupils' level of musical development, record their attainment and progress as individual profiles, and have ready access to curriculum materials" (p. 189).

Johnson (2002) developed hierarchies of responses that can guide music educators and therapists in helping children with severe and multiple disabilities in acquiring music skills. These are related to the National Standards for Music Education (National Association for Music Education [NAfME], n.d.). Responses are categorized into four areas—singing, playing, movement, and listening—each with a progression, beginning with the simplest response. Those that are most appropriate for children with severe and multiple disabilities are outlined in Table 1, Range of Singing, Playing, Movement, and Listening Responses.

Table 1.
Range of Singing, Playing, Movement, and Listening Responses

Range of Singing Responses	Range of Playing Responses	Range of Movement Responses	Range of Listening Responses
Produce vocal sounds (by chance or on purpose)	Produce sounds that may be rhythmic (clap hands, pat knees, tap feet, etc.)	Respond to music physiologically (via heart rate, breathing patterns, body temp., etc.)	Regard sounds (notice sounds)
Imitate vocal sounds (copy voice sounds or mouth sounds)	Produce sounds on an instrument (act to make a sound repeat the action)	Regard music (notice musical stimuli)	Act to repeat sounds (interact with auditory environment)
Sustain or repeat vocal sounds (play with the voice)	Explore playing techniques (discover different sways of playing, discover different sounds)	Localize the source of the music (turn or move toward the sound source)	Develop discrimination of sound characteristics (form concepts, generalize)
Imitate the musical contour of sounds (copy the phrasing or melodic shape of sounds)	Play an instrument musically (manipulate instrument with expression)	Respond to music with the body (change posture, facial expression, show a "feel" for the music)	Listen to a music selection as a unit (listen for overall effect)
Sing by imitating phrases	Maintain a part independently	Imitate the movements of others	Develop discrimination of music characteristics
Sing to self	Play a part in sequence	Isolate movement	Develop directed listening skills
Sing in presence of others	Respond to musical characteristics	Coordinate movement	Select music for free time listening
Perform music in a classroom setting	Use practice techniques	Imitate dancelike movements	Develop audience skills
Perform music in a performance setting	Perform music in the classroom	Move rhythmically	Attend musical events at school or in community
	Perform music in a performance setting	Dance in response to music	Function as a consumer of music

From Johnson (2002), pp. 96–99.

Referral and Assessment

A child may be referred to music therapy by the school team responsible for determining the child's educational program or by an individual, perhaps a family member, educator, or other professional. A child with ID would typically be referred to music therapy if it is felt that he or she might benefit from music therapy. Since these children typically have many needs, the music therapy might be thought to help in any of them.

Although music therapists working with these clientele certainly use assessments, only one formalized music therapy assessment procedure specific to people with severe and multiple disabilities was found. The Betz Held Strengths Inventory (Betz & Held, 2012) uses formalized music therapy assessment procedures to assess children with severe and multiple disabilities up to age 18 as measured by their developmental stage in sensory-motor, perception, language, and psychosocial domains. Each domain contains developmental benchmarks and strength indicators from which a strength profile emerges when the child reacts to cues and stimuli provided by the music therapist and the reactions are compared to the strength indicators. The child's strengths profile can then be used to communicate findings to other therapeutic disciplines.

Assessments developed and used with individuals with severe and profound IDs may also be applicable to these clienteles. One of these is the Music Therapy Assessment Profile for Severely/Profoundly Handicapped persons, Research Draft III (0–27 Months Level) (Michel & Rohrbacher, 1982). The developmental areas included are gross motor, fine/perceptual motor skills, communication, cognition, and social/emotional. Sample musical procedures to assess each level of development are included. They may be used as suggested, or the music therapist can devise other musical procedures to assess the child's functioning in each area.

The assessments by Michel and Rohrbacher (1982) and Farnan (2002) contain areas of focus consistent with those most commonly assessed in a survey of music therapists (Chase, 2004): (a) motor (fine and gross motor skills); (b) communication (expressive language/verbal skills; receptive language; nonverbal communication); (c) social (peer/adult interaction; attending skills; sharing/turn-taking); (d) cognitive (concepts; sequencing/memory; auditory perception/discrimination); and (e) music (rhythm/beat; melody/tonal; instrument exploration; interest/preference).

Farnan and Johnson (1988b) say: "At the *center* of all the activities, plans, and music *is a person*. If you want to develop a good music program, plan to systematically assess the individual's needs and abilities and then set achievable and measurable goals. Be aware of each person's response in order to develop future activities, plans, and music. How do you assess and monitor individual response to music?" (p. 50). They then suggest the following steps: (a) assessment, a process of determining the individual's needs by gathering information; (b) setting a long-term goal; (c) establishing short-term objectives; (d) data collection to determine progress toward the objective.

The three Nordoff-Robbins scales, developed to assess musical responses of children with disabilities, could also be used with this population. The early scales (Nordoff & Robbins, 1977, 2007) are: Scale I, Child-Therapist Relationship in Coactive Music Experience; Scale II, Musical Communicativeness; and Scale III, Musicking: Forms of Activity: Stages and Qualities of Engagement (Nordoff & Robbins, 2007).

The Special Education Music Therapy Assessment Process, or SEMTAP (Brunk & Coleman, 2000; Coleman & Brunk, 2003), is used to assess whether music therapy, as a *related service,* is required for certain students to benefit from public school special education programs. While this assessment does not focus on people with multiple disabilities or even ID, it can be used with these clients. Chase (2004) found the SEMTAP to be the most commonly used assessment (N = 23; 70%) by respondents who worked with children with developmental disabilities.

The Individualized Music Therapy Assessment Profile, or IMTAP (Baxter et al., 2007), was designed to assess the skills of children and adolescents with multiple severe physical disabilities as well as other disabilities. The authors say, "As a criterion-based assessment, the information resulting from the IMTAP process does not serve as a comparison of one client to another, but rather provides a deeper understanding of client functioning and the ability to track progress over time" (p. 26). It assesses 10 domains: gross motor, fine motor, oral motor, sensory, receptive communication/auditory perception, expressive communication, cognitive, emotional, social, and musicality, with subdomains under each.

Overview of Methods and Procedures

The following methods and procedures are used most commonly in music therapists' work with persons with severe and multiple disabilities.

Receptive Music Therapy

- Sensory Stimulation: use of musical experiences to arouse, excite, and activate the client.
- Musical Movement: use of background music to support clients' physical movement.
- Contingent Music: use of music as either a positive or negative reinforcement to increase targeted client behavior.
- Vibroacoustic Therapy: use of preselected frequencies played through specially designed recliners or pads to create sympathetic somatic resonance.
- Music Listening: use of music to support client gains in environmental awareness, attention, and discrimination skills.
- Music-Assisted Relaxation: use of background music as a stimulus or to facilitate relaxation interventions implemented by the music therapist.

Improvisational Music Therapy

- Møller's Level of Contact 1–5: The therapist uses musical elements to facilitate greater client awareness, engagement, and communicative intent across increasingly more structured improvisational experiences.
- Orff-Schulwerk: use of musical elements of singing, chanting, clapping, and keeping a beat to develop the cognitive and emotional skills.
- Orff Rondos: use of a musical rondo form to promote a variety of client responses.

Re-creative Music Therapy

- Songs with Instrumental Responses: use of precomposed songs to prompt client responses on instruments often to support basic academic and behavioral skills.
- Songs with Vocal Responses: use of precomposed songs to encourage client responses consisting of voice.
- Songs with Movement Responses: use of precomposed songs to encourage client responses consisting of nonlocomotor, locomotor, or cooperative group movement. Directives for client participation are often embedded within the song.

- Musical Song-Games: These come in many forms, but typically consist of turn-taking activities that require cause-effect interactions, active participation, and some element of competition based upon musical elements.

Compositional Music Therapy

- Songwriting: lyrics and/or music are created for entirely new compositions or for precomposed musical pieces. Lyrics substitution may take the form of single words or whole pieces.

Guidelines for Music Therapy Methods

Considerations in working with adults with ID, presented by Galerstein, Martin, and Powe (1998) in *Age Appropriate Activities for Adults with Profound Mental Retardation,* follow:

- Prompting: Levels of assistance. They suggest providing the least amount of assistance possible initially and then gradually increasing or layering prompts as needed. From least to most, they suggest: verbal prompt, gestural prompt, tactile prompt, faded physical prompt (hand-over-hand assistance, slowly removed as response occurs), and physical prompt.
- Communication: They suggest speaking to adult clients in the same way that one speaks to other adults. Although they may not understand everything, this may facilitate a sense of inclusion.
- Socialization: Utilizing opportunities to encourage clients to socialize with one another as well as with others with whom they come into contact.
- Adaptations: They advise getting to know client needs, adapting interventions to meet their needs, and consultation with other professionals when needed.
- Safety: Knowledge of client behaviors that might pose a safety risk.
- Inclusion: Creating opportunities to include clients in as many activities as possible regardless of ability. (pp. 16–17)

Galerstein, Martin, and Powe (1998) provide guidance for working in groups with people with profound intellectual disabilities that may apply to those with ID. They suggest seating people in a circle so that all members can see one another, the leader can see the members, and all members will be involved by virtue of being a part of the circle, even if they do not actively participate in any other way. They suggest:

- Encouraging Interaction and Inclusion: All members should listen to or watch the person of focus, providing prompts as needed. For example, if you are encouraging a particular group member to hit a tambourine and she is taking a while to do that, you might say, "Be sure to watch Jane, she about to play something."
- Using people's names as often as possible. Incorporate people's names into songs, such as "He's Got the Whole World in His Hands." Refer to people when possible, such as pointing out that Jim is wearing a long-sleeved shirt while Frank is wearing a shirt with short sleeves.
- Encouraging individuals to interact, talk, and ask questions of each other in addition to staff.

- Minimizing interruptions. Try to ignore if possible and redirect the individual back to what is occurring in the group. Positively reinforcing group members who are cooperating often motivates others who are not on task to make positive changes. Therapists must intervene if there is a serious disruption to the group but should return to the intended activity as soon as possible.
- Using different reinforcers for different people. Let others in the group know when a person is being reinforced for good behavior.
- Allowing more time to process information than those who do not have disabilities.
- Providing simple and clear directions using a calm and pleasant voice. Do not say, "Sally, I hope that you will be able to take both sticks, one in each hand, and play the drum using both hands." Do say, "Sally, play the drum, please."

Finally, two commonly used techniques applicable to multiple improvisational and re-creative methods are: (a) leave spaces in the music in which the person can respond; and (b) alternate between group response and individual responses, enabling all to be a part of the group but also providing an opportunity for individuals to respond.

Guidelines for Receptive Music Therapy

In receptive music therapy, the therapist engages the client in any kind of listening experience (Bruscia, 1998). The experience may focus on physical, emotional, intellectual, aesthetic, or spiritual aspects of the music, and the client may respond through activities such as relaxation or meditation, action sequences, structured or free movement, perceptual tasks, free association, storytelling, drawing or painting, dramatizing, reminiscing, imaging, and so forth. The music used for such experiences may be live or recorded improvisations, performances, or compositions by the client or therapist, or commercial recordings of music literature in various styles. The music should be from the client's culture when appropriate.

The following goals have been used in receptive music therapy: (a) decrease impulsivity; (b) increase response to one-step and two-step directions; (c) increase social interactions; and (d) reinforce a sense of rhythmic control (Goodman, 2007); (e) increase the frequency and variety of spontaneous vocalizations; (f) repeat simple words or sounds on cue; (g) increase attention span; (h) increase appropriate use of objects; (i) manipulate instruments; (j) decrease impulsive behaviors; (k) increase interaction with others (Wheeler, 1999a, 1999b).

Sensory Stimulation

Overview. Meadows (1997) said, "Sensory stimulation refers to the therapist's use of musical and other media to arouse, excite, and activate the child" (p. 12), and suggests that it is one of the main receptive methods described in the music therapy literature for this clientele. Farnan (2003) describes sensory stimulation and processing in which music-based sensory programs, designed in conjunction with OTs and employing principles from the sensory integration literature, pair OT principles of vestibular stimulation with rhythmic and auditory stimulation in prescribed protocols for activities. Farnan (2010) also describes techniques identified in Neurologic Music Therapy (NMT) approaches to sensorimotor rehabilitation (Thaut, 2005), including Patterned Sensory Enhancement (Thaut, pp. 149–154) and Musical Sensory Orientation Training techniques for sensory stimulation and arousal orientation (Thaut, p. 196).

Sensory stimulation is appropriate to use when the client is not responsive to environment with normal stimulation. The therapist should be aware of the client's responses and cautious about any that seem to indicate pain or other reasons that the client may not be responding. Caution should be used with physical stimulation, both to be sure that the client is not responding negatively (perhaps due to being hurt or to having sensory issues that make stimulation unpleasant) and to remain within whatever guidelines for physical contact are in place in the agency in which the therapy is taking place.

Sensory stimulation is used at the augmentative level of practice. The goals generally are to engage the client in any type of response that will foster activity and awareness of him- or herself, objects, and others. Through this increased awareness, the client may experience lessened effects from their complex clinical conditions and build basic skills for improving activities of daily living.

Preparation. The client should be in a comfortable position and able to see the therapist; the therapist should also be able to see the client and to make physical contact. The room should have as few distractions as possible to ensure that the client can focus on the music and the therapist. In a group setting, there should be room for all group members to respond and for the therapist to move from person to person. As much as possible, group members should be able to see one another in addition to the therapist; a semicircle is usually the ideal arrangement.

What to observe. Look for any response from the client, however small. This may include changes in breathing or eye contact as well as more overt responses such as moving or reaching toward the stimulus, vocalizing, laughing, words, and so forth.

Procedures. As suggested by Meadows (1997), any of the following may be done, briefly or over an extended period of time: (a) auditory stimulation, the therapist's attempts to stimulate the individual through various receptive musical means; (b) the use of textures, fabrics, and so forth to provide physical stimulation; and (c) physically stimulation and manipulation of the child's body by touching, massaging or carefully moving body parts (e.g., the therapist may massage the child's hand as a way of making contact or as a preparation for instrument-playing). Farnan (2003) suggests that music therapists use: (a) tactile desensitization techniques with fabrics and the physical vibration of low tones (62–110 Hz) and (b) range of motion activities (pairing rhythmic stimuli with specific movements provides multisensorial stimulation and improves sensory processing and integration). Coleman (2002) suggests puppets that are colorful and have interesting fabric textures; perhaps making silly sounds or performing silly actions may be included.

Adaptations. Farnan (2010) and an OT colleague utilized NMT techniques in their intervention entitled "Sit and Spin," which is described as a "sequential session plan for the pairing of movement-based therapeutic interventions within a rich multisensorial (auditory, vestibular, tactile, visual) environment with rhythmic structure. This approach necessitates active presence of both disciplines of OT and MT. The use of low-pitched tone bars accompanies the interventions, allowing participants to feel the vibration of the sound" (p. 1).

Several other strategies using active, live music for sensory stimulation are found in the literature. Find the Harp, from *Music Is for Everyone* (Farnan & Johnson, 1988b), can be used to promote sensory awareness. In its most basic form, it provides an autoharp and has the words "Find the harp ... and touch." Listen to the Sound of the Drum, from the same book, can also be used to encourage sensory awareness, as can Touch the Drum from *Everyone Can Move* (Farnan & Johnson, 1988a). Ghetti (2002) attempted to modulate behavior states using singing and multirhythmic stimulation.

Musical Movement

Overview. Movement is used here to refer to movement that is facilitated by the therapist or an assistant, sometimes in conjunction with a PT and, because it is a type of receptive music therapy, is done with background music. If needed, the therapist may need to move the child's body in a musical context to meet his or her physical and developmental needs. Movement activities are often specifically designed for children who have little or no voluntary control over their bodies or who lack the understanding to move in purposeful or controlled ways. Meadows (1997) believes that the two main functions of the music therapist in these programs are to provide structure within the sessions and to directly work with the child in providing physical interventions. Movement was used by Crowe (1999), whose client enjoyed walking and dancing to her favorite tune, out of her wheelchair and supported by the therapist; Krout (1987), who included a movement-to-music activity in two parts, first moving to recorded music to *loosen up,* and then wheelchair dancing with the therapist and then with each other; and Wheeler (1999a, 1999b), whose client enjoyed dancing to recorded music. Meadows (1997) suggests that:

> Movement programs have three related elements. The first of these is to focus on maintaining the child's physical functioning, including range of movement, muscle tone, and body symmetry (for example, maintaining posture). Secondly, an emphasis is placed on the quality of the interactions between therapist and child .... Thirdly, while the adult moves the child's body, independent movement is encouraged and supported at all times. (pp. 12–13)

Meadows (2002) also suggests two ways of implementing music and movement programs. For those who can move their bodies independently or with minimal assistance, activities are designed to maintain or increase the ability to move spontaneously and independently. For those with very limited motor abilities or who cannot move their bodies at all, the adult helper plays a very active role in manipulating the client's body through a sequence of movements that will maintain or increase the range of movement, stimulate spontaneous movement, and develop self-awareness. Providing physical assistance may be contraindicated if the client has fragile bones, structural reasons for not being able to move in certain ways, tight or restricted muscles, or other physical problems that restrict movement. Consultation with an OT or PT before and during embarking on such a program is crucial. In the absence of information about a client's physical functioning, it is wise to be conservative in movements that are requested or prompted. Any indication of pain or discomfort should be noted and the movements that were associated with it avoided, at least until additional information is acquired.

Goodman (2007) lists the following goals for movement activities: Decrease impulsivity, increase response to one-step and two-step directions, increase social interactions, and reinforce a sense of rhythmic control (p. 8). Additional goals might be to increase attention span or develop gross motor skills. It is used at the augmentative or intensive level of practice.

Preparation. The client should be in a comfortable position and able to see the therapist; the therapist should also be able to see the client and to make physical contact. The room should have as few distractions as possible to ensure that the client can focus on the music and the therapist. In a group setting, there should be room for all group members to respond and for the therapist to move from person to person. As much as possible, group members should be able to see one another in addition to the therapist; a semicircle is usually the ideal arrangement. It is important that there be room for the movement to occur.

What to observe. Look for any response from the client. Sometimes a movement may occur by chance, but the alert therapist can pick up on it and help to develop it. If others are providing assistance for the client's movements, it will be important to be sure that they are giving only the amount of assistance required and not overhelping.

Procedures. One common procedure involves movements that the therapist suggests, with recorded music that matches the rhythm or the movements as background. The music chosen should be in a tempo and style that supports or reinforces the planned movements. The therapist should have movements in mind that will be possible to be done by the client(s) and may model the movements and/or give verbal instructions. The therapist should provide guidance to assistants so that they provide an appropriate level of assistance as well as fading assistance as the client becomes more proficient. There should be a way to slow the pace of the movements if needed. If it is not possible to slow the music, it may be helpful to perform the movements in half-time and/or practice the movements without music first.

Adaptations. Movement can be accompanied by live as well as recorded music, and the music can be improvised or composed. More independent movement may be dancing, which might also be enjoyed at the auxiliary level of practice. Wheelchair dancing (Krout, 1987) provides an opportunity for people in wheelchairs to move and participate in a normal social activity. Wigram and Weekes (1985) present some advantages of using live, improvised music, which can be tailored to the exact needs of the clients. Some songs give cues for movement; examples of these are included under Guidelines for Re-creative Music Therapy.

Contingent Music

Overview. In contingent music, the music therapist uses music as a reward when the client makes a desired response (positive reinforcement) or, alternatively, discontinues the music when the client ceases doing something (time out from reinforcement). Precomposed live music is often used, although it may also be improvised or recorded, and the client may perform (re-create) it or be involved with it in some other way, or listen to it (a receptive technique, discussed under Guidelines for Receptive Music Therapy). Steele (A. L. Steele, personal communication, May 28, 2012) spoke of behavioral music therapists as using music, based on its general and specific reinforcement value, to: (a) draw a client into a relationship with the music therapist; (b) create an opportunity to work on, and reinforce, therapeutic, nonmusical responses; and (c) provide an opportunity for self-expression.

Rainey-Perry and Ri (2005) described strategies that included the music therapist responding to the use of gaze as communication, for example, by offering a student the guitar when he looked at it, or stopping the music when the student looked away, thus reinforcing the student looking at the guitar. Roberts (1986) used two behavioral techniques with a child. A microphone was used as reinforcement when he was allowed to sing into it as long as he sat upright in his wheelchair. Later, they worked on where he positioned the microphone, which he tended to put too close to his mouth, by allowing him to continue to use it as long as it was positioned correctly.

Indications for using reinforcement are difficult to identify, since reinforcement can be used with anyone and probably is used more often than many music therapists realize. While some therapists, who may identify themselves as behavioral music therapists or as following behavioral principles, use it intentionally, others use it without being aware of it. Anytime a music therapist praises or otherwise rewards a client, he or she is using reinforcement. Music therapists are encouraged to become aware of their use of reinforcement and use it intentionally. There are some instances in which reinforcement will have an effect when other techniques do not. One of these might be with a person at a very low level of awareness who may respond to reinforcement provided through music. No contraindications are known, although some approaches to music therapy would discourage using music contingently in favor of involving the client in the musical experience, regardless of his or her responses. In these approaches, it would be considered wrong to withhold music from a client who is behaving inappropriately or to provide music only when behavior is appropriate.

Contingent music is used at the augmentative level of practice. Goals may include to decrease impulsivity, increase response to one- and two-step directions, increase social interactions, increase the frequency and variety of spontaneous vocalizations, repeat simple words or sounds on cue, increase attention span, increase appropriate use of objects, manipulate instruments, decrease impulsive behaviors, and increase interaction with others.

Preparation. The client should be in a comfortable position with the ability for the therapist and client to see one another and make physical contact. The room should have as few distractions as possible to ensure that the client can focus on the music and the therapist. In a group setting, there should be room for all group members to respond and for the therapist to move from person to person. As much as possible, group members should be able to see one another in addition to the therapist; a semicircle is usually the ideal arrangement. Any device that is needed to help to deliver the reinforcement will also need to fit into the arrangement.

What to observe. A wide range of behaviors and responses may be used with this method. Regardless of the targeted objective, Madsen (Madsen, 1981; Madsen & Madsen, 1998) suggests a four-step approach to increasing its occurrence: *Pinpoint* the behavior of interest, *record* how often the behavior occurs, *consequate* to change the behavior, and *evaluate* the success of the procedures.

Procedures. There are no specific procedures for conducting a session that employs the contingent use of music. Contingent music can be both an application/method within a session or the underlying principle for the music therapy session. In the latter, the four-step approach should be applied to the methods that are used in the session.

Vibroacoustic Therapy

Overview. Vibroacoustic therapy (VAS; Skille, 1989) involves having the client lie on a specially designed bed or multiple transducer bed pad or sit in a VAT recliner. Preselected frequencies are played through speakers or transducers, allowing the body to vibrate in sympathetic resonance with the sound waves. A number of research studies using VAS are described later in the chapter, under Research Evidence, Receptive Music Therapy.

VAS is useful for people with a wide range of needs, including those who need to reduce pain or stress or who need to relax. People with sensory issues will need to be evaluated for their reaction, as some of the vibrations may affect them in unusual ways or increase hypersensitivity. Goals may include: Increase sensory stimulation, reduce pain, reduce stress, decrease muscle tone, increase range of motion, increase relaxation. It is used at the augmentative or intensive level of practice. For those clients seeking to minimize physical or medical problems, VAS may be considered as an intensive-level method, especially if it is used as a primary method for addressing the concern (e.g., pain reduction).

Preparation. The client should be in a comfortable position and able to get to (perhaps be moved to or placed upon) the chair or mat that is used for delivering the sounds and vibrations. The therapist and client should be able to see each other and make physical contact. The room should have as few distractions as possible, and preferably light that can be reduced to ensure that the client can focus on the music and the therapist. VAS is most likely to be done in an individual setting, but if a group is involved, there will need to be room for all group members and their vibroacoustic devices.

What to observe. The therapist needs to observe the client's responses, particularly as they relate to the goals. Any unexpected increase in tension, for instance, should be noted and adjustments made in the music when possible. In addition, all responses should be noted and taken into account in planning for future sessions.

Procedures. Client should be seated or lying in proper position. Therapist should select the music in advance and take client's preferences into account in the selection. Sometimes music is prepared specifically for a client, taking into account that client's musical preferences; at other times, the music is not individualized. Frequencies rather than music are often used. Skille (personal communication, Feb. 8, 2013) reports having analyzed the music that had been used in VAS and being "left with hundreds of frequencies that had been used, and end[ing] up with seven basic frequencies that alone, or in combinations, could be used [to meet] most of the issues" ... [and finding that] "one low frequency octave between 40 Hz and 80 Hz without any overtones" [is sufficient and effective]. Some sessions are specified to be 30 minutes long, although 23 minutes has been found to be sufficient (personal communication, O. Skille, Feb. 8, 2013). Care should be taken to insure that the volume of the music is appropriate for the client. Client should be oriented to what will occur through instructions by the therapist. According to Skille, the founder of VAS, a session "once a week is better than none at all" (personal communication, Feb. 8, 2013).

Adaptations. Vibroacoustic devices may be made by the therapist with the assistance of technicians. Others are purchased commercially and include Somatron® products such as mats, mattresses, or chairs.

Music Listening

Overview. Recorded music is pervasive in the environments of almost everyone, including people with disabilities. Listening to music is also something that most people do for entertainment and enrichment. Music listening is appropriate for those who function well enough to be aware of the music to any extent. Some people will be very responsive to music listening, and they are those for whom the technique is most appropriate. It is appropriate for those who need to work on attending behavior, develop listening skills for social situations, increase sensory stimulation, or provide an opportunity for social interaction. If recorded music is used, it is important that both the music recording and the equipment upon which it is played are of good quality, including the speakers. If clients cannot focus on the music in any way, this would not be a useful technique, especially because listening is often a passive experience. Some people with ID require more active involvement with a stimulus in order to be aware of or engage with it.

Music listening is often used at the augmentative level of practice and is often a part of a music therapist's session. Goals for music listening may include developing awareness of environment, increasing sensory awareness, improving listening skills, improving ability to attend, increasing attention span, decreasing impulsive behaviors, increasing interaction with others, and increasing the frequency and variety of spontaneous vocalizations and/or words.

Preparation. The client should be in a comfortable position and able to see the therapist; the therapist should also be able to see the client and to make physical contact. The room should have as few distractions as possible to ensure that the client can focus on the music and the therapist. In a group setting, there should be room for all group members to respond and for the therapist to move from person to person. As much as possible, group members should be able to see one another in addition to the therapist; a semicircle is usually the ideal arrangement.

What to observe. Look for any response and, if even a small response occurs, pay attention to it and work to increase it. Note the client's response to the music and make changes in the music if the reaction is not positive or if there are other indications that different music may be useful. If the client is responsive but needs to behave more appropriately, look for and work with (or reinforce) more appropriate responses.

Procedures. Music listening may be the primary focus of the session, or it may provide only a small portion of the content, as did Crowe's (1999) work in which sessions concluded by listening to music. In sessions for which listening to music is the focus, the therapist should introduce the listening in some way, providing the client with some background about the music and what to listen for. The main idea is for the music therapist to choose music that is both accessible and in a style that the client will relate to and enjoy. To maximize the possibility that this will occur, the therapist should have several selections from which to choose, including backup music in case responses to the intended music is not what is desired or needed. Wigram's (1981) findings, described under Research Evidence, Receptive Music Therapy, may provide guidance in selecting and presenting music for listening.

Adaptations. Improvised or live re-creative music may also be used for listening experiences. Music therapists may also be called upon (or should volunteer) to give input into music in the general environment. This may be background music that is played in public areas or suggestions for music to purchase for a particular client's personal listening. There may also be occasions in which the music therapist plays a role in bringing live music entertainment to the setting.

Music-Assisted Relaxation

Overview. Music-assisted relaxation uses background music as a stimulus or tool to promote relaxation. Relaxation to music may be the primary focus of the session, or it may provide only a small portion of the content. Sometimes it may be useful to begin or end the session with relaxation to music. It is indicated for clients who need to relax (due to stress or tension). It would be contraindicated for a client for whom music increases tension, who appears to be unaware of the music, or who cannot focus on the music in any way.

Goals may include increasing relaxation, increasing attention span, decreasing impulsive behaviors, reducing pain and stress, and decreasing muscle tone. It is used at the augmentative or intensive level of practice.

Preparation. The client should be in a comfortable position and able to see the therapist; the therapist should also be able to see the client and to make physical contact. The room should have as few distractions as possible to ensure facilitating focus on the music and the therapist. In a group setting, there should be room for all group members to respond and for the therapist to move from person to person. As much as possible, group members should be able to see one another in addition to the therapist; a semicircle is usually the ideal arrangement.

What to observe. Look for any type of response that indicates relaxation, including slower or deeper breathing, closed eyes, decreased muscle tension, and/or sleeping. It is also important to note responses that indicate that the person is not relaxing and, if these occur, to find alternate ways of promoting relaxation or simply allow more time.

Procedures. Regardless of when in the session the relaxation is to occur, the therapist will introduce it in simple language to ensure the client's understanding. The therapist should have several selections of music from which to choose to ensure that the music that is used will be relaxing to those in attendance. There are numerous ways of promoting relaxation, most of which employ some type of verbal guidance. The instructions with this population should be fairly concrete, as they would probably not be able to comprehend abstract imagery. One example would be to suggest that they breathe in and out, timing the breathing with the therapist's words and then focusing their attention on various body parts (often beginning at the feet and moving up to the head), suggesting that each be relaxed in sequence. This may be too abstract or complex for many with severe and multiple disabilities, but the music may guide them toward a more relaxed state, even if not exactly as the therapist suggests. If it is appropriate in the setting, some type of simple massage of clients' limbs, back, neck, and so forth may accompany and reinforce the relaxation. (Note, though, that in some settings and with some clientele, touching is not permitted.)

Adaptations. Live music, improvised or composed, can also be used to promote relaxation. Songs to promote and guide resting and relaxation are included in *Everyone Can Move* (Farnan & Johnson, 1988a) and in *Music Is for Everyone* (Farnan & Johnson, 1988b). Sekeles (1996) used improvised music so that she could follow her client's activity in helping him to achieve relaxation. An example of the use of relaxation music to decrease bruxism (teeth grinding) (Caron, Donnell, & Friedman, 1996) is presented later in the chapter, under Research Evidence, Receptive Music Therapy.

GUIDELINES FOR IMPROVISATIONAL MUSIC THERAPY

Improvisational music therapy is an important and commonly used method for working with people with ID (Crowe, 1999; Goodman, 2007; Hooper, 1993; Møller, 1996, n.d.; Nordoff & Robbins, 2007; Nowikas, 1999; Oldfield, 2006; Perry, 2003; Pfeifer, 1989; Rafieyan, 2003; Rainey-Perry & Ri, 2005; Ritchie, 1993; Salas & Gonzalez, 1991; Sekeles, 1996; Shoemark, 1991; Voigt, 1999; Watson, 2002, 2007; Wheeler, 1999a, 1999b). Improvisation is probably the most commonly used method for this population because it can be modified in the moment to allow people more time to process, initiate, and coordinate their responses.

In improvisational music therapy, the client *makes up* music while playing or singing, extemporaneously creating a melody, rhythm, song, or instrumental piece (Bruscia, 1998). (This and the other definitions of methods included in this chapter, all from Bruscia [1998], are generic descriptions of the methods and thus apply to how the methods are used with clients with all types of disabilities and at all levels of functioning. People with ID will not be able to do all of the things that are described.) The client may improvise a *solo,* or participate in a duet, trio, or ensemble, which also includes the therapist, relatives, or other clients. The client may use his/her voice, or any musical instrument of choice within his/her capability. The therapist facilitates the client's improvisation by presenting a nonmusical idea or a musical theme or structure upon which to base the improvisation. Often, therapists create an ongoing musical accompaniment that stimulates, guides, or supports the client's sound productions.

Improvisational music therapy may address diverse goals, including to increase the frequency and variety of spontaneous vocalizations; initiate communication; establish the prerequisite skills for intentional communication; increase interaction with others; indicate preferences; follow one- or two-step directions; increase attention span; increase appropriate use of objects; decrease impulsive behaviors; increase vocal projection; decrease auditory processing time; use arms and hands in a purposeful way; increase reciprocal musical exchanges such as turn-taking, responding to musical suggestions, and initiating musical ideas; and share and express personalities and feelings (Goodman, 2007; Rainey-Perry & Ri, 2005; Wheeler, 1999a, 1999b; for additional goals, see Oldfield, 2006; Rafieyan, 2003; Watson, 2007).

Electronic or adaptive technologies (Ellis, 1995, 1997; Magee & Burland, 2008a, 2008b; Magee et al., 2011; Martino & Bertolami, in press; Zigo, in press; www.ablenetinc.com; www.adaptivation.com; www.drakemusic.org; www.helpkidzlearn.com) have enabled people with severe and multiple disabilities to be involved in making music and can be used in various types of improvisations. The technological application becomes the person's way of being able to make the music that is used in the improvisation.

Møller's (1996, n.d.) five Levels of Contact when working with children and adults with ID will be used to present/divide initial uses of improvisation. Although discrete changes in improvisation do not occur from one level to the next, there are differences in client response and thus what the therapist does. This should clarify how improvisation can be used with clients at each level. It provides a framework for understanding how individuals who function at a very low level may progress in their responses.

Møller's Level of Contact 1:
"I sense contact between us occasionally."

Overview. At this level of improvisation, the therapist can sense occasional contact with the client. Contact between client and therapist may be tentative and may be elicited by the therapist's improvisation, which both supports and leaves space for the client. The improvisation may stimulate a response or foster interaction. This is similar to Level 2 (levels of participation: wary ambivalence, tentative acceptance; qualities of resistiveness: anxious uncertainty, tendency toward rejection) from the Nordoff-Robbins Child-Therapist Relationship in Coactive Musical Experience Rating Form (Nordoff & Robbins, 2007, p. 374). This level is indicated when the client appears generally unresponsive or exhibits only occasional or fleeting attention. It is contraindicated when the client responds consistently to the therapist's improvising. The main goals are to respond to music or therapist in any way and increase sensory awareness. This level of contact is primarily at the augmentative level of practice.

Preparation. The client should be seated in a comfortable position and able to see the therapist; the therapist should also be able to see the client and to make physical contact. Ideally, they sit near one another with the client facing therapist as much as possible. If the therapist is at the piano, the bench should be at a slight angle so that the therapist is facing slightly toward the client and can make eye contact and assist physically as needed. The room should have as few distractions as possible.

What to observe. Look for any type of response, musical or nonmusical, from the client and build on it. Notice everything. All responses are significant, including but not limited to changes in facial expression, respiration, or body posture.

Procedures. The therapist can improvise on any instrument. Improvise minimally to allow space for the client to respond. Use music of the client's culture when appropriate. Support the client in any response, no matter how small.

Adaptations. The therapist should be open to adapting to what happens in the moment. This could be an increase in the client's response, which would suggest to the therapist to move to the next Level of Contact and expect more response from the client, or a decrease in response, which would necessitate remaining longer on techniques designed to elicit a response, slowing the music, or changing to other music. The specifics cannot be spelled out in advance but are dependent upon the therapist's observations and the client's responses to changes in the music.

Møller's Level of Contact 2: "I see and hear the contact."

Overview. The client responds to improvisation at this time, but the response is not overtly interactive. He or she vocalizes, moves, or plays an instrument with some relationship to what the therapist is improvising (perhaps it fits rhythmically or in spaces within the music), but the responses do not alternate from client to therapist. The therapist improvises similarly to what was done in the previous level, but the client is somewhat more responsive so that the therapist does *see and hear the contact.* Responses at this level would probably be evaluated on the Nordoff-Robbins Child-Therapist Relationship in Coactive Musical Experience Rating Form (Nordoff & Robbins, 2007, p. 374) as Level 3 (levels of participation: limited responsive activity; qualities of resistiveness: evasive defensiveness).

This level is indicated when the client shows some responsiveness to music or to the therapist, but the responses are fleeting or inconsistent. It is contraindicated if the client interacts during the responses, in which case he or she should be encouraged to improvise at the next level. The therapist should ensure that mallets and instruments are used safely. This level of contact is at the augmentative or intensive level. Goals may be to increase the number and consistency of responses; vocalize, play, or move to musical or verbal cues; increase attentiveness to the therapist; and increase attention span.

Preparation. The room setup is the same for all five of Møller's Levels of Contact.

What to observe. At this level, children often respond during breaks in the music. They are likely going to be generally short. Therapists look for any vocalizations, movements (i.e., looking toward the music), changes in facial expressions, and affective responses, such as crying and laughing. The therapist should keep in mind that expressions and utterances do not yet have communicative intent but may simply be an emotional response to sensory impressions of music. The intent is that the therapist's responses to client behavior will gradually and eventually lead to the recognition of the outside world.

Møller (n.d.) identified three ways that a child is likely to respond to music at this level:

> (a) sound-reacting behavior; (b) sound-seeking behavior: The child turns his head/body in the direction of the sound; (c) sound-creating behavior (making sounds on instruments etc. and vocalizing) ... Development can be seen in (a) faster reactions and shorter pauses; (b) more significant reactions; (c) recognition of the place, the sounds, the instruments, the voice of the therapist. This indicates a growing awareness and an ability to form experiences. (p. 2)

When the responses become more interactive than solitary, the client is probably moving into Møller's Level of Contact 3.

Procedures. The therapist can improvise on any instrument, but should improvise minimally to allow space for client to respond. The therapist attempts to musically imitate or match the expressions or utterances of the child and then waits for him or her to perceive, adapt, and respond to the stimulus. Nordoff and Robbins (1977) suggest that the following may be used to elicit vocal responses: (a) making vocal sounds while musically reflecting the child's emotional state; (b) singing phrases that describe what the child is doing, feeling, or experiencing; (c) imitating the child's vocal sounds or words, matching the musical and emotional qualities; (d) providing opportunities to complete phrases and/or add sounds, syllables, or words; and (e) combining vocalizing with movement or instrument-playing. Any responses from the child may be incorporated into the improvisation.

Adaptations. It is better to work individually with a person at this level, but improvisation could be done in a group. Electronic or adaptive technology enables people with ID to be involved in making music and may become the person's way of being able to make the music that is used in the improvisation.

Møller's Level of Contact 3:
"You [the child] control the contact."

Overview. This level of contact would be similar to Nordoff-Robbins Child-Therapist Relationship in Coactive Musical Experience Rating Form (Nordoff & Robbins, 2007, p. 374) Level 4 (levels of participation: activity relationship developing; qualities of resistiveness: perversity and/or manipulativeness). This level is indicated when the client becomes more intentional about gaining the therapist's attention and participating in the interaction. The therapist therefore wants to engage the client and encourages participation. It is contraindicated if the client's responses are above or below those that are appropriate for this level, in which case work should be at a different level. This level is primarily at the augmentative or intensive level of practice. Goals may be for the client to increase number and consistency of responses; vocalize, play, or move to musical cue or in space in music; increase the frequency and variety of spontaneous vocalizations; increase attentiveness to the therapist; increase attention span; and initiate communication.

Preparation. The room setup is the same for all five of Møller's Levels of Contact. Allowing the client some options for movement may be preferable for at least part of the session.

What to observe. The therapist should be aware of responses by the client and work to develop them. Møller (n.d.) suggests that the child is now conscious of being able to gain the attention of others and uses vocal sounds, banging, clapping, and so forth, as well as an intense gaze to do so. The child's actions are more intentional and often have a social purpose. The client is not yet ready to engage in interactions but can be actively involved in making music. The way the client plays the instruments becomes more relevant, has intent, and incorporates new patterns of movement. The quality and duration of participation are important aspects in the client's development.

Procedures. The therapist should have a variety of instruments available and be ready to help the client to utilize them, although vocal or movement responses may also occur. At this time, the music therapist bases her interaction based upon the initiatives of the client and therefore the music created is in response to the client's expressions. The client's attention is likely on the therapist and on evoking a reaction from her, but there is likely no recognition of a turn-taking process or the basic structure of communication.

At this stage, improvisation serves to increase the client's awareness that he or she is communicating and to motivate him/her to initiate interaction. The client's progress at this level can be seen in an increasing activity in the musical interactions. Therefore, way the client plays instruments becomes more relevant and the quality and duration of participation also develop. Møller (n.d.) says:

> When he moves, plays on an instrument, looks at me, etc., then I start to play or vocalize. Sometimes it is most adequate to play/sing simultaneously with the child. Other times it works better to respond subsequently. (This may seem to be a dialogue but it is not....) The playrule is seen from the child´s perspective: "When I make my sound/movement, the therapist starts to play." I pick up the tempo of beats, vocal sounds and other expressions of the child and as a start I shape it musically so that my responses are fairly predictable and recognizable. Later I may try out other ways of responding—for instance move away and come back to the child or dance to his playing." (p. 2)

Use music of the client's culture when appropriate. The therapist should be flexible and ready to change the improvisation as the client changes.

The therapist should be open to adapting to what happens in the moment. This could be responses that indicate interaction, which would suggest to the therapist to move to the next Level of Contact, or a decrease in responses, which would necessitate remaining longer on techniques designed to sustain a response, slowing the music, or changing to other music. The specifics cannot be spelled out in advance but are dependent upon the therapist's observations and the client's responses to changes in the music.

Adaptations. This may be adapted to a group. As stated earlier, electronic or adaptive technology enables people with ID disabilities to be involved in making music and may become the person's way of being able to make the music that is used in the improvisation.

Making up song lyrics spontaneously is useful to either elicit or reflect responses and can be used at this and other Levels of Contact. Galerstein says, "I typically use traditional folk-type songs because our clients know them, and many lend themselves well to the type of lyric improvisation that I do. Examples are 'Michael, Row the Boat Ashore,' 'When the Saints Go Marching In,' 'He's Got the Whole World in His Hands,' and 'You Are My Sunshine'" (personal communication, Nina Galerstein, July 22, 2012).

Møller's Level of Contact 4: "Our contact takes the form of dialogue."

Overview. This level of contact would be somewhat equivalent to Nordoff-Robbins Child-Therapist Relationship in Coactive Musical Experience Rating Form (Nordoff & Robbins, 2007, p. 374) Level 5 (levels of participation: assertive coactivity, working relationship, self-confident purposefulness;

qualities of resistiveness: perseverative compulsiveness, assertive inflexibility, contest). This level is indicated when the client is responsive enough to initiate some musical interactions, thus beginning to participate in a dialogue with the therapist. It is contraindicated if client's responses are above or below those that are appropriate for this level, at which point work should be at a different level. Ensure that mallets and instruments are used safely.

The work at this level is generally augmentative or intensive. Goals may be for the client to increase number and consistency of responses; vocalize, play, or move to musical cues or in spaces in music; increase the frequency and variety of spontaneous vocalizations; increase attentiveness to the therapist; increase attention span; initiate and respond to communication with therapist; indicate preferences; increase appropriate use of objects; manipulate instruments; decrease impulsive behaviors; provide opportunities to make choices; and increase interaction with others.

Preparation. The room setup is the same for improvisations at all five of Møller's Levels of Contact. If the client can stand, it may be preferable to stand for at least part of the session.

What to observe. Sometimes there may not be a balance in our dialogue, but the child is conscious of the interaction between himself and the therapist. The child does not yet fully understand the idea of turn-taking, yet is taking turns listening and making sounds. He or she is developing joint attention and is able to focus on him-/herself, the therapist, and on the instrument. Gradually, the child understands the basic rule of communication, and turn-taking. Møller (n.d.) says that there is mutuality in the rules of play, namely: "We take turns at producing sounds and listening" (p. 3).

Procedures. At this level, the music therapist is working to facilitate reciprocal communication between herself and the client. The therapist works to create opportunities for the client to understand that their mode of expression has communicative intent. This can be accomplished by passing a small drum back and forth with the client as a means of objectifying the dialogue and creating symmetry between the interactions. The musical interaction may also shift from taking place on a shared drum, for example, to each person playing an individual instrument with a greater distance between them. Some children also begin to explore dynamics at this level. Møller (n.d.) says:

> Children with a very limited vocabulary can unfold their communicative skills in the music. It is often surprising in the music therapy to see that the principle of turn-taking is fully established even though they have had very little opportunity to practice it. ... At Level 4, the music basically has three forms: (a) as a dialogue, (b) as games of imitation, (c) as musical interaction where the child is capable of playing the basic beat of a melody. ... Some children master all three forms; others can only take part in one of them. Development shows in the awareness of the dialogue—expectation of taking turn and signals of giving turn. (p. 3)

Adaptations. The therapist should be open to adapting to what happens in the moment. This level may be adapted to a group. The therapist's observations and the client's responses to changes in the music allow for options to adapt. As stated earlier, electronic or adaptive technology may be used and may be adapted to a group.

Møller's Level of Contact 5:
"We communicate in the improvised music."

Overview. This level would be similar to Nordoff-Robbins Child-Therapist Relationship in Coactive Musical Experience Rating Form (Nordoff & Robbins, 2007, p. 374) Level 6 (levels of participation: mutuality and co-creativity in the expressive mobility of music; qualities of resistiveness: crisis—toward resolution, no resistiveness) or Level 7 (levels of participation: stability and confidence in interpersonal musical relationship; qualities of resistiveness: through identification with a sense of accomplishment and well-being, resists own regressive tendencies).

This level is indicated when the client is able and willing to participate, initiates and responds, and brings ideas to the improvisation. He or she is involved both with the therapist and the music. No contraindications are known, but the therapist should ensure that instruments are used safely.

This level of contact is primarily at the augmentative or intensive level of practice. Goals may include that the client increase number and consistency of responses; vocalize, play, or move to musical cues or in spaces in music; increase the frequency and variety of spontaneous vocalizations; increase attentiveness to the therapist; increase attention span; initiate and respond to communication with the therapist; indicate preferences; increase appropriate use of objects; manipulate instruments; decrease impulsive behaviors; increase interaction with others; increase expressive/receptive language; increase vocal projection; decrease auditory processing time; improve fine and gross motor coordination; and provide opportunities to make choices.

Preparation. The same room setup for improvisations is used at all five of Møller's Levels of Contact. Allowing movement may be allowed for at least part of the session.

What to observe. The client's musical and nonmusical responses should expand beyond those at previous levels, and it is important that the therapist pick up on these and help to develop them.

Procedures. At this stage, it is expected that the client interact with other people as well as the initial skills for verbal communication. There is both an ongoing exchange and reciprocal influence on the musical interaction. Within the musical experience, the client may demonstrate greater focus and communicative skills not otherwise observed. Møller (n.d.) says:

> Music provides a non-confronting space for the child to experience independency and autonomy. In the musical interaction he may further develop communicative skills such as sensitivity, flexibility, creativity, listening and responding to what you hear, etc. The improvised music blurs the aspects of timing and rules that [are] predominant in verbal communication. Thus music is free from demands and expectations that these children are very sensitive to. It is my impression that music represents a safe world with logical and meaningful structures that resonates with their perception of life and confirms their relationship with another human being. (p. 3)

Adaptations. Hooper's (1993) work with a woman with severe and multiple disabilities over an 18-month period illustrates each of Møller's Levels of Contact:

- Level 1: Describing the first three sessions, Hooper says: "She withdrew into a corner of the treatment room, her head turned away and her back to me. I sang quietly to her for about 20 minutes, lightly tapping a tambourine. Elizabeth remained withdrawn, intently studying her hands" (p. 209).
- Level 2: In the fourth and fifth sessions, Hooper describes Elizabeth as beginning the

session by again being withdrawn and unresponsive, but she began responding after a period of time. Ten minutes into session four, "She turned her head around, looked at me, and smiled. I gently took Elizabeth's hands and began stroking and patting them, singing quietly to her. Elizabeth did not resist, and when I introduced the tambourine, she smiled and laughed as I shook it" (p. 209). Session five began without visible response. "After five minutes, she turned round, smiling as before. She took hold of the tambourine and flicked at or pushed over the jangling metal discs. I copied this response and continued to sing quietly, reinforcing her response" (p. 209).

- Level 3: Hooper encouraged Elizabeth to sit on a chair, as recommended by her physical therapist, and shortly after this, she began sitting on a chair. He says: "In this new position, she acknowledged me almost immediately. I sang a lively greeting song to her. Elizabeth enjoyed this, becoming very animated. She clapped her hands and clapped her hands off mine. When I introduced the tambourine, she struck it excitedly. All this time I had been singing offering encouragement and supporting her responses" (p. 210).
- Level 4: Hooper says of the sessions, which have been occurring over a period of 18 months, "Elizabeth continues to enjoy clapping. She is keenly aware of imitation, which motivates and excites her. I spend long periods of the session singing to Elizabeth and responding to her clapping" (p. 210).
- Level 5: Hooper states: "Often she holds a lengthy musical conversation with me, either clapping her own hands together or clapping her hands off mine" (p. 210). For Elizabeth and at her level of functioning, this description appears to be communicating in the improvised music, Møller's description of Level 5.

Orff-Schulwerk

Overview. Orff-Schulwerk was developed by Carl Orff as a way to learn music and is based on things that children like to do such as singing, chanting rhymes, clapping, dancing, and keeping a beat. Instruments that can be played without training, some of which have been developed for Orff-Schulwerk, are often used. Orff-Schulwerk and Orff Music Therapy are used often in music therapy with children with severe and multiple disabilities. Orff-Schulwerk has been adapted for music therapy and used with a variety of clientele, including people with severe and multiple disabilities (Bitcon, 1976, 2000; Orff, 1974; Voigt, 1999). Many music therapy clinicians have been trained in Orff-Schulwerk and use it in their work.

Orff-Schulwerk is intended to be a creative process, and there are no set ways to use it. Therefore, what is listed here is only an example of how it might be used, one of many that could be developed. An Orff specialist said: "Many lessons I do begin with simple or elemental motifs or a folk tune or story. I build from that piece to see what inspires the people I am working with. When I work with my students, I emphasize the words invite, explore, choose, alternative pathways" (personal communication, Robert Amchin, June 10, 2012).

Orff-Schulwerk is indicated for people at all levels, of functioning, with the therapist providing more assistance and cues for those at lower levels of functioning and assuming that those at higher levels of functioning can do more with less or no assistance. No contraindications are known, but the therapist should ensure that mallets and instruments are used safely. Goals may include to increase vocalizations; develop one-word response; respond to one- or two-step directive (or more, if appropriate); increase eye contact; increase social interaction; increase appropriate use of objects; increase attention span; and encourage creative responses.

Preparation. The client should be in a comfortable position and able to see the therapist; the therapist should also be able to see the client and to make physical contact. The room should have as few distractions as possible to ensure that the client can focus on the music and the therapist. In a group setting, there should be room for all group members to respond and for the therapist to move from person to person. As much as possible, group members should be able to see one another in addition to the therapist; a semicircle is usually the ideal arrangement.

What to observe. It is important that the responses requested from a client be at an appropriate level, so the therapist should have a sense of what the client can do. As the client responds, the therapist should be aware of what the client is doing and adjust expectations so that the client will be successful. Following the response, the therapist should evaluate what occurred and make plans for the next desired response as well as how it should be supported.

Procedures. Since Orff-Schulwerk is improvisational, it is impossible to specify exactly what will occur. The therapist will observe and listen to the client(s) and base the procedures on what the client presents. Use music of the client's culture when appropriate.

As an example of what could occur, we might picture a situation in which a child with severe and multiple disabilities begins to make some vocal sounds and, at the same time, moves her body in rhythm with the sounds. This could be the beginning of what develops into an Orff-inspired music therapy procedure. Perhaps the child is saying/singing "wa wa waaa wa" on mi sol la sol. The therapist may use both the tonality and the rhythm, singing with the child and moving her (the therapist's) hands to the child's hands and feet in rhythm. This becomes the beginning of a student-inspired chant. Later, the rhythm could be transferred to various instruments, initially held by the therapist, to the child's hands or feet and eventually (perhaps after several sessions) held by the child herself, perhaps with assistance. Although at a very basic level, this has become an Orff activity for this child with severe disabilities. The child has been involved in a creative process, has experienced music as an outgrowth of speech and movement, and has developed some musical skill along the way.

With a higher-functioning individual, as another example, the music therapist may begin by playing an ostinato on a bass xylophone, inviting the client to join in as he (or she) likes. A selection of instruments could be available, although there is no reason that instruments need to be used, as the client and therapist could also use their bodies as percussive or vocal "instruments." Perhaps the ostinato consists of a slow C C moving up to G G, then repeating. The client may choose another melodic instrument, perhaps a metallophone, and play one or more notes. These can be developed over time, with the encouragement of the therapist. The therapist at some point might reflect what the client is doing by singing a *situation song* (Voigt, 1999): "Aaron plays all the sounds, listen as he plays." Aaron, the client, might eventually join in with part of the vocal melody, which could develop into a musical piece. In the same session or over time, the parts could change, the music can develop, and Aaron can explore new aspects of his musical and creative self.

Adaptations. These are just two examples of how the concepts of Orff-Schulwerk might be used in a music therapy setting. The Orff literature is extensive and has many examples of adaptations, including chants and songs as well as instrumental pieces. Music therapy literature and adaptations of Orff were presented earlier in this section. The process should always be creative and exploratory.

Orff Rondos

Overview. Orff rondos use the rondo form (A-B-A-C, etc.) so that a chant (A) is repeated, while each individual then has an opportunity for an individual response (B, C, etc.). The rondos are only one part of Orff-Schulwerk but may be particularly good for people with severe and multiple disabilities because they allow for individual as well as group responses. The following quote about Orff-Schulwerk (Bitcon, 2000) applies to people with severe and multiple disabilities: "Open-ended material should be presented to whatever degree possible. There may be a requirement for a specific response, but then expansion on that response is allowed. For individuals with extremely limited ability to participate, the material presented might at first be very controlled, requiring little—if any—expansion on a theme. This control will lessen as the participants understand the process and are better able to participate" (p. 11).

Orff rondos are indicated for people at all levels, with the therapist providing more assistance and cues for those at lower levels of functioning and assuming that those at higher levels of functioning can do more with less or no assistance. Bitcon (2000) suggests that an individual should be able to respond to the following basic commands in order to participate: "Look at me!" " Come to me!" "Sit down!" "Stand up!" "Give me your hand!" (p. 316). It is also possible to use Orff rondos with people who cannot respond to these commands, provided they receive additional assistance. No contraindications are known, but the therapist should ensure that mallets and instruments are used safely. Client goals may include increasing vocalizations; developing one-word response; responding to one- or two-step directives; increasing eye contact; increasing social interaction; increasing appropriate use of objects; increasing attention span; and encouraging creative responses. This level is primarily at the augmentative or intensive level of practice.

Preparation. As much as possible, group members should be able to see one another in addition to the therapist; a semicircle is usually ideal. The room should have as few distractions as possible to ensure that the client can focus on the activity.

What to observe. The therapist should be aware of responses by the client and work to develop them. The client may not be ready to engage in interactions but can be actively involved in music making. The way the client plays the instruments becomes more relevant, and new patterns of movement are incorporated. The quality and duration of participation are important aspects in the client's development. It is important that the responses requested from the clients be at an appropriate level, so the therapist should have a sense of what the client can do. During the client's response, the therapist should be aware of what the client is doing and adjust the expectations so that the client will be successful. Following the response, the therapist should evaluate what occurred and make plans for the next desired response as well as how it should be supported.

Procedures. Bitcon's (2000) book, *Alike and Different,* contains hundreds of Orff rondos. The rondos alternate between a group chant (A) and individual response (B, C, etc.). Therapists introduce the group chant, usually by saying or singing it, and repeat it until it is familiar. Depending upon the level of functioning, group members may be able to chant along with the therapist, but this is not essential. Then the first individual (B) is given an opportunity to respond, and this person should be supported in whatever response is given, including expanding it as much as possible. Then the A chant is repeated, again encouraging all to participate. It generally works well to go around the circle in order, so the second individual response (C) will be a person sitting on one side or the other of the first individual responder. The same process to elicit a response is repeated with this person, then the entire group does the group chant, and so forth. At the end, the therapist indicates that it is time to finish by a slight change in the chant, a change of movement, and/or dropping the vocal cadence, with exactly how this is done being up to the therapist.

Adaptations. A few of the many rondos that Bitcon (2000) suggests and that work well for these clients are:

- Name, name, what's your name? Name, name, what's your name? (p. 19)
- I've got a name and it sounds like this, I've got a name and it sounds like this. (p. 13)
- Listen, listen, listen to the sounds [instrument's name] makes. (p. 40)
- I can dance, I can sing, Can you make this little bell ring? (p. 41)
- We're having a party, who will come, and sit with me, and play on my drum? (p. 43)
- Sounds, sounds, all around. Choose an instrument and make your sounds. (p. 45)
- Copycat is the name of the game. Anything you do, we'll do the same. (p. 52)

GUIDELINES FOR RE-CREATIVE MUSIC THERAPY

In re-creative music therapy, or music therapy that involves performing precomposed music, the therapist engages the client in vocal or instrumental tasks that involve reproducing music in some way (Bruscia, 1998). This may include learning how to use the voice or produce sounds on an instrument; imitating melodies or rhythms; learning to sing by rote, learning to use musical notation, participating in a sing-along, rehearsing, taking music lessons, performing a song or instrumental piece from memory, working out the musical interpretation of a composition, performing in a musical show or drama, and so forth. Many re-creative techniques are likely to have begun as improvisations. It is common to evoke a response through improvisation and develop it over one or several sessions, then use it as a re-creative method.

Re-creative methods are used often with people with severe and multiple disabilities (Coleman, 2002; Crowe, 1999; Farnan, 2003; Ghetti, 2002; Goodman, 2007; Hooper, 2002; Krout, 1987; Magee et al., 2011; Nordoff & Robbins, 2007; Perry, 2003; Pfeifer, 1982, 1989; Rainey-Perry & Ri, 2005; Roberts, 1986; Salas & Gonzalez, 1991; Shoemark, 1991; A. L. Steele, personal communication, May 28, 2012; Stevenson, 2003; Wheeler, 1999a; 1999b; Witt & Steele, 1984). Hooper (2002) became aware of the value of activities (and thus the use of re-creative music therapy) compared with improvisation with clients with severe disabilities. He says, "Because of their level of musicianship and/or degree of learning disability, it may not be appropriate for some clients to develop the musical content through improvisation" (p. 166). Rather, Hooper presents music within the context of an activity, or series of activities, which are structured to encourage the development of particular nonmusical skills.

In addition to the goals that were listed under improvisational music therapy, re-creative music therapy may address the following goals: imitate gestures; reach for and touch objects; recognize voices and faces; show awareness of self; localize sound; make choices between several items; match items, shapes, colors; sort items; indicate specific words (finished, hello, good-bye, more, yes/no); access and operate a pressure switch; and utilize simple augmentative communication devices (e.g., Big Mack) (Coleman, 2002). Given that the vast number of goals that may be addressed, examples of goals that are considered primary for each method are listed under that method

Songs with Instrumental Responses

Overview. In these songs, cues or directions for playing or singing may be provided through the music, or the music and therapist may leave a space in the music for the client to respond with an instrument, giving an opportunity to complete or fill in a phrase. This will often begin in an improvised song and progress to what becomes a composed song. It can be in response to a musical cue (or space) or to a verbal/sung cue and may include a physical prompt. The client may have an instrumental part in a composition; depending upon the level of the client(s) and purpose of the activity, the parts may be rehearsed for a later performance of some sort.

Some instruments are easier to play and have a more satisfying sound than others. It is important to take this into account when selecting instruments for those with severe and multiple disabilities, for whom playing even simple instruments may be challenging. Farnan and Johnson (1988b) rank the difficulty of common rhythm instruments. They suggest the following instruments: (a) require minimum effort and achieve maximum sound: maracas, wrist bells, jingle bells with handle, puili sticks, school bell, bass drum, conga, suspended cymbal, hand drum; (b) require medium effort: tambourine, wood blocks, afuche, handheld drum with mallet; and (c) require maximum effort: cymbals (2 hands), rhythm sticks (2 hands), resonator bells, xylophone, claves, sand blocks, jingle sticks, handle castanets, guiro (p. 45).

Songs with instrumental responses are indicated when client has made no or only an occasional response. They may be particularly useful when client shows an interest in instruments or similar objects, although this is not necessary. There are no contraindications as long as the therapist is able to provide as much support as the client needs.

Songs with instrumental responses are used primarily at the augmentative or intensive level of practice. Client goals may be to attend to a task; increase appropriate behavior; develop or reinforce fine motor skills; learn or increase adaptive behaviors; work cooperatively toward a common goal; increase interaction with others; improve eye-hand coordination; develop imitative behavior; take turns; follow directions; indicate preferences; follow one- or two-step directions; increase attention span; manipulate objects/instruments; decrease impulsive behaviors; increase interaction with others; increase eye contact; make choices between several items; and match items, shapes, colors, and so forth.

Preparation. The client should be in a comfortable position and able to see the therapist; the therapist should also be able to see the client and to make physical contact. The room should have as few distractions as possible to ensure that the client can focus on the music and the therapist. In a group setting, there should be room for all group members to respond and for the therapist to move from person to person. As much as possible, group members should be able to see one another in addition to the therapist; a semicircle is usually the ideal arrangement. Instruments that will be used should be on a table or somewhere else that is accessible to the client(s). The therapist should sort the instruments in advance and only have available those instruments that will be used. For example, if only certain xylophone bars or resonator bells are to be used, only those should be displayed.

What to observe. Look for any response and work with it. For some, the response may be just a movement in the direction of an instrument. There may be a most appropriate time to encourage the response—as the client looks at the therapist or instrument, for instance. Others will be at a much higher level, so the work with them is to increase the consistency or quality of the response.

Procedures. There are many ways to conduct a session using precomposed or re-creative instrumental music. Some of the books from which the recommended music comes include instructions, and Nordoff and Robbins (2007, Chapter 12) provide suggestions for leading into instrumental activity that, although they are focused on improvisation, apply to precomposed songs also. In general, after seeing that clients are positioned so that they and the therapist can see one another, the therapist introduces the plan. In some situations, participants should be allowed to choose their instrument, although at other times, the therapist may decide what instruments should be played by whom, based on the clients' needs and abilities.

The clients may require assistance to hold the instrument. This can be provided by an assistant, but care should be taken not to assist too much: The client should hold and play the instrument, or do as much as possible, without assistance. It is helpful if someone other than the therapist can either provide the accompaniment or lead the song, although the music therapist can adapt to a situation in which only one person is available.

The therapist will probably need to cue participants so that they know when to play, a sign of progress being when fewer cues are needed. Every effort should be made to make the song musical, including keeping it moving forward, although there may be times that it is necessary to slow down or pause to enable someone to respond. Clients with severe and multiple disabilities may need extra cues and motivation to respond. The therapist's affect can encourage responses, sometimes creating a sense of suspense or surprise. It is usually a good idea to repeat the song more than once, as the experience will be more successful with repetition. In this type of session, as in all work with those with ID, the focus of the session should be on maximizing successful participation rather than completing the song or doing it perfectly.

Examples of composed music with spaces for instrumental responses can be found in Levin and Levin *Learning Through Music* (Levin & Levin, 1998), *Let's Make Music* (Levin & Levin, 2005), *The First*

Book of Children's Play-Songs (Robbins & Nordoff, 1962), *Music Is for Everyone* (Farnan & Johnson, 1988b), *Themes for Therapy* (Ritholz & Robbins, 1999), *More Themes for Therapy* (Ritholz & Robbins, 2003), and several *Play Songs* publications (Robbins & Nordoff, 1968, 1980a, 1980b; Robbins, 1995).

Adaptations. It may be necessary to adapt mallets, picks, and instruments so that clients can hold and play them. Many excellent suggestions for adapting instruments, including how they are placed in relation to the client and suggestions for adapting two-handed instruments to be played with a single hand, are provided by Clark and Chadwick (1980), Coleman (2002), Knoll (2012), and Farnan and Johnson (1988b).

Numerous technological adaptations can enable people with severe and multiple disabilities to participate more fully in instrumental activities (Magee & Burland, 2008a, 2008b; Magee et al., 2011; Martino & Bertolami, in press; Zigo, in press; www.ablenetinc.com; www.adaptivation.com; www.drakemusic.org; www.helpkidzlearn.com). Some clients will work better using a color-coded chart or otherwise matched to instruments. If using a chart is feasible, it should be large enough for all to see and hung somewhere or otherwise shown to participants.

Songs with Vocal Responses

Overview. In these songs, cues or directions for singing may be provided through the music; the music and therapist may leave a space in the music for the client to respond with the voice, giving an opportunity to complete or fill in a phrase; or the client may simply sing along with the song. This will often begin in an improvised song and progress to what becomes a composed song. It can be in response to a musical cue (or space) or to a verbal/sung cue and may include a physical prompt.

Songs with vocal responses are particularly useful when the client needs to develop verbal or vocal responses or shows pleasure in using voice. There are no contraindications as long as the therapist is able to provide as much support as the client needs. Goals may be for the client to localize sound; initiate communication; increase the frequency and variety of spontaneous vocalizations; repeat simple words or sounds on cue; increase expressive/receptive language; increase vocal projection; increase appropriate behavior; learn or increase adaptive behaviors; work cooperatively toward a common goal; develop imitative behavior; take turns; indicate preferences; increase social communication; follow one- or two-step directions; increase attention span; decrease impulsive behaviors; increase interaction with others; decrease auditory processing time; increase eye contact; and increase interaction with others. Songs with vocal responses are used primarily at the augmentative or intensive level of practice.

Preparation. The client should be in a comfortable position and able to see the therapist; the therapist should also be able to see the client and to make physical contact. The room should have as few distractions as possible to ensure that the client can focus on the music and the therapist. In a group setting, there should be room for all group members to respond and for the therapist to move from person to person. As much as possible, group members should be able to see one another and the therapist; a semicircle is usually the ideal arrangement.

What to observe. Look for any response and work with it. There may be a most appropriate time to encourage the response—as the client looks at the therapist or instrument, for instance. Clients who respond should then be encouraged to respond more consistently or at a higher level.

Procedures. There are many ways to conduct a session using precomposed or re-creative vocal music. In general, after seeing that clients are positioned so that they can see the therapist and the therapist can see them, the therapist introduces the plan using simple language If possible, someone other than the therapist may either provide the accompaniment or lead the song. The therapist should encourage participants to sing or participate in some other way vocally. Although their focus is improvised music, Nordoff and Robbins (2007; Chapter 10, Stimulating free singing—nonverbal or verbal) provide a number of suggestions for encouraging vocal responses. They also give suggestions for using singing and songs (Chapter 11). Every effort should be made to make the song musical, including keeping it moving forward, being mindful to slow down or pause to enable responses. Clients with ID may need extra cues and motivation to respond. The therapist's affect can encourage responses, sometimes creating suspense or surprise. Success may increase with each successive repetition. In this type of session, the focus of the session should be on maximizing successful participation rather than completing the song or doing it perfectly. Examples of composed music incorporate or encourage singing with spaces for vocal responses can be found in several publications, including Robbins and Nordoff (1962, 1968), Levin and Levin (1998, 2005), Ritholz and Robbins (1999, 2003), and Farnan and Johnson (1988b).

Adaptations. Coleman (2002) suggests the following adaptations:

- Vocal imitation or singing using voice-activated device: Select a song that has a recurring line. Coleman suggests "Train Is a-Coming," which has "oh yes" as a reoccurring line, or "I Get By With a Little Help from My Friends," which repeats the word "friends." Record this line on a voice-activated device such as a Big Mack. Prompt the students to depress the device at the correct time, thus allowing them to *sing* along.
- Tagboard books can be made to illustrate the words to a familiar song. Attach small pieces of sponge between the pages to make them thicker and easier to turn. The therapist can draw or use magazine pictures or other pictures to illustrate the song. The client can be prompted to turn the pages as the song is sung.
- Song file folders can also be used to illustrate songs. Pictures can be drawn or taken from magazines or other sources to illustrate key words in a song, preferably a song with basic, concrete words. Black-and-white pictures illustrating these words can be attached to the file folder, and clients can match the colored version of the picture to the folder as the song is sung. Clients with severe physical disabilities may indicate the correct picture to match with eye gaze or other alternative means of communication.

Songs with Movement Responses

Overview. In these songs, cues or directions for moving may be provided through the music, or the music and therapist may leave a space in the music for the client to respond with a movement, giving an opportunity to complete or fill in a phrase. This will often begin in an improvised song and progress to what becomes a composed song. It can be in response to a musical cue (or space) or to a verbal/sung cue and may include a physical prompt. Farnan and Johnson (1988a) divided movement into nonlocomotor (moving the body in place), locomotor (moving the body from place to place), cooperative group movement (moving together), and expressive (moving the body creatively).

Songs with movement responses are indicated when the client has made no or only an occasional response and so can benefit from making a brief response or developing a longer response. They are particularly useful when the client responds well to movement and seems to enjoy it, although such pleasurable responses are not necessary in order to use movement. Using songs with movement responses in a manner that does not follow any treatment protocols that have been put in place by occupational or physical therapists is contraindicated, and the music therapist should be trained by and/or work closely with these therapists. They are used at the augmentative or intensive level of practice. Client goals may be to attend to a task; increase appropriate behavior; learn or increase adaptive behaviors; improve receptive language; improve gross motor skills; work cooperatively toward a common goal; develop imitative behavior; take turns; indicate preferences; increase social communication; follow one- or two-step directions; increase attention span; decrease impulsive behaviors; decrease auditory processing time;

increase eye contact; develop/increase focus of attention; increase interaction with others; and show awareness of self.

Preparation. The client should be in a comfortable position and able to see the therapist; the therapist should also be able to see the client and to make physical contact. The room should have as few distractions as possible to ensure that the client can focus on the music and the therapist. In a group setting, there should be room for all group members to respond and for the therapist to move from person to person. As much as possible, group members should be able to see one another in addition to the therapist; a semicircle is usually the ideal arrangement. There will need to be room for movement to take place.

What to observe. If client is initially unresponsive, look for any type of response, encourage (reinforce) it, and build upon it. With clients who are already responsive, the focus will often be on increasing the strength and quantity of whatever responses are made. Observe how much the client is able to move without assistance and provide assistance only to increase that level.

Procedures. There are many possible ways to conduct a re-creative music movement session. Much of the music that will be used gives the instructions for the movement as part of the music, although the therapist will generally need to reinforce the words verbally and by providing a model in addition to providing physical assistance at times. These procedures may be followed: After being sure that all are positioned so that they can see and hear the therapist and hear the music, the therapist will want to let those in attendance know what they will be doing. This may be through brief verbal instructions and should be at the level that the members can comprehend. The therapist may then initiate the music to direct the movement, being careful that it is at the correct tempo. If the therapist is the only person providing the music, the songs may need to be sung without accompaniment so that he or she is available to assist with the movements. It is ideal to have someone who can provide accompaniment on piano/keyboard, guitar, or some other instrument so that the therapist can sing and provide verbal cues and physical assistance to clients. Since it is likely that clients will need extensive physical assistance, the session will work best if additional staff are available to help.

Much of the suggested re-creative music for movement includes the words/instructions as part of the music, so the therapist will need to give additional verbal instructions only as extra prompts. If the song does not include instructions for movement, as in "Punchinella," for example, clients will need assistance imitating and also verbal prompts. In this type of session, the focus of the session should be on maximizing successful participation rather than completing the song or doing it perfectly.

Meadows (2002) suggested structured music and movement as an often motivating experience for people with ID; however, he recommends having a PT present as much as possible during this type of session since music therapists will need to follow treatment protocols. Meadows's sequence is: (a) preparation, during which clients and helpers enter the room and are positioned comfortably on mats; the music therapist may be improvising or playing recorded music to create a suitable atmosphere from which to begin the session; (b) greeting song/orientation to session, including a song welcoming all to the session; (c) whole-body awareness, during which the adult helpers stimulate the children's bodies by massaging body parts with the intent of increasing body awareness and preparing the body to move; the music therapist improvises music to match the interventions and may also provide guidance to the helpers; (d) gross motor activities such as hip extension and flexion and feet stomping, with the assistance of the helpers and with the music therapist singing a song to describe the movement or improvising music to match the movements; (e) upper-body work such as arm stretches, elbow rotation, and wrist rotation, using similar procedures to those just outlined; (f) hand and finger massage, also following similar procedures; (g) moving while sitting on a roller or other aid, incorporating whole body movements such as rotation at the hips, reaching forward and stretching back, and touching body parts; the music therapist will probably sing songs that describe the movement; (h) massaging the clients' bodies, with clients on the mats and receiving the massage without needing to respond; accompanying music mirrors a quiet, peaceful place; (i) closure, usually some type of closing song. The music therapist should be aware of the policy of the institution or employing agency as far as touching (massaging) clients, as there may be restrictions on this.

Examples of composed music with spaces for movement include songs such as the "Hokey Pokey," "Punchinella," and "Head, Shoulders, Knees, and Toes." Other experiences can be found in Levin and Levin (1998, 2005), Robbins and Nordoff (1980a, 1995), Ritholz and Robbins (1999, 2003), and Farnan and Johnson (1988a, 1988b).

Adaptations. Improvised music may be used in much the same way that precomposed (re-creative) music is used. Meadows (2002) suggests that improvised music may be more appropriate at times than the more structured approach described; he said that his clinical team had seen the limitations of working in a predetermined sequence of movements. He said that many children, particularly those who had little self-awareness or were very sensitive to touch, tended not to respond well to structured forms of movement, especially when those movements did not reflect their emotional state, and that the work was more successful when the adult helpers began working more spontaneously with these children, trying to engage them in movement experiences based on their immediate needs.

Coleman (2002) recommends the incorporation of manipulatives (e.g., beanbags, plastic hoops, or yarn balls). Students can be encouraged to pick them up and manipulate them according to directions in a song.

Musical Song-Games

Overview. Some musical song-games could also be described as composed songs that include movement. Others might be improvised initially and function later as composed song games. A key element that distinguishes a song-game from a song that includes gamelike elements or movement is some type of surprise that occurs as part of the song-game.

Musical song-games are indicated for people who will benefit from some extra fun or energy, beyond what is normally included in a music therapy strategy, in order to become involved. They have many of the same benefits that other types of re-creative methods have. No contraindications are known. They are used at the augmentative or intensive level of practice. Goals may be for clients to indicate preferences; follow one- or two-step directions; increase attention span; decrease impulsive behaviors; increase interaction with others; increase expressive/receptive language; decrease auditory processing time; and increase eye contact.

Preparation. The client should be in a comfortable position and able to see the therapist; the therapist should also be able to see the client and to make physical contact. The room should have as few distractions as possible to ensure that the client can focus on the music and the therapist. In a group setting, there should be room for all group members to respond and for the therapist to move from person to person. As much as possible, group members should be able to see one another in addition to the therapist. A semicircle is usually the ideal arrangement; however, arranging for times may also be appropriate. There should be room for whatever movement is required as part of the game.

What to observe. The therapist should look for any response and build on it. For people at higher levels of functioning, work to increase or improve their responses to a higher level. With lower-level clients, therapists should look for changes in affect or facial expression that indicates interest and/or anticipation of what is to come. Those with physical limitations will need to have easy and obvious ways to indicate a desire to provide a response (e.g., Big Mack).

Procedures. There are many possible ways to conduct a session using song-games. A basic procedure is to be sure that all are in a position to see the therapist and participate, and then give them some instructions to get their attention and orient them as to what will occur. Then the therapist will sing the song that goes with the game and encourage all to participate. It is likely that participants will require additional help, verbal and physical, and it is ideal if others can assist. The intent of the session is for a successful and enjoyable experience for the participants.

Some song-games include:

- Pulling. The therapist holds the client's hands while they are facing one another. The therapist controls the movement/pulling. *Verse 1:* Pulling, pulling, back and forth, pulling, pulling, back and forth. *Verse 2:* Faster, faster, back and forth, faster, faster, back and forth. *Verse 3:* Slowly, slowly, back and forth, slowly, slowly, back and forth. *Verse 4:* Repeat verse 1. *Tune:* Sol mi sol mi fa fa re. Fa re fa re sol sol do.
- Stevenson (2003) describ*es the us*e of a gamelike song, "The game 'I'm going to... (pause) get you!' *is played,* accompanied by moving toward the child to 'catch' him. The *child in tu*rn smiles, cowers or holds his hands in front of himself. He might also vocalize back 'aaahhh,' pretending to be afraid" (p. 84).
- Musical Rope Game, Rope Bells, and Bubbles from *Everyone Can Move* (Farnan & Johnson, 1988a) and Drop the Ball in the Basket from *Music Is For Everyone* (Farnan & Johnson, 1988b) are musical/movement song-games.

Adaptations. Other hide-and-seek or surprise songs can be adapted. Crowe (1999) described a musical hide-and-seek game where the therapist played her violin in different parts of the room and the client would try to locate her.

Guidelines for Compositional Music Therapy

In compositional music therapy, the therapist helps the client to write songs, lyrics, or instrumental pieces, or to create any kind of musical product, such as music videos or audiotape programs (Bruscia, 1998). Usually, the therapist simplifies the process by engaging the client in the easier aspects of composing (e.g., generating a melody or writing the lyrics of a song), and by taking responsibility for more technical aspects (e.g., harmonization, notation).

Compositional music therapy has been discussed very little in the music therapy literature for people with severe and multiple disabilities. This is probably because these clients are often not able to respond by composing due to their deficits in intellectual functioning. However, technology has made compositional music therapy within varied levels of structure possible (Magee & Burland, 2008a, 2008b; Magee et al., 2011; Martino & Bertolami, in press; Zigo, in press. Also see:

www.ablenetinc.com;
www.adaptivatin.com;
www.drakemusic.org;
www.helpkidzlearn.com.

GarageBand, for instance, makes composing possible for many people who could not previously consider it (Martino & Bertolami, in press), and many iPad applications can also facilitate composing. Some of the literature using composition with people with neurological and other problems requiring physical rehabilitation (Nagler & Lee, 1989) can be applied to those with ID.

Song (Vocal) Composition

Overview. Song or vocal composition occurs when the therapist and/or the client composes a song. It can be useful for those who would benefit from seeing a concrete product of their efforts, accomplishing a task, or having an opportunity to make choices. A certain level of cognition is required for the client to be aware of composing, although some of the procedures can be used even if the client is not aware of his or her role in the composition (the latter situation may still be helpful but might be labeled improvisation rather than composition).

This technique is used at the augmentative or intensive level of practice. The goals may be for the client to indicate preferences, respond to yes-no questions, follow one- or two-step directions; increase the frequency and variety of spontaneous vocalizations; increase attention span; decrease impulsive behaviors; increase expressive and receptive language; decrease auditory processing time; increase social interaction; be involved in reciprocal musical exchanges, including turn-taking, responding to musical suggestions, and initiating musical ideas; and make choices.

Preparation. The client should be in a comfortable position and able to see the therapist. The room should have as few distractions as possible to ensure that the client can focus on the music and the therapist. In a group setting, there should be room for all group members to respond and for the therapist to move from person to person. As much as possible, group members should be able to see one another in addition to the therapist; a semicircle is usually the ideal arrangement. A white board or something else on which to write words may be used. This could assist the therapist in keeping track of what is suggested and may be useful in that it is usual to write such things on a board. If the clients cannot read, the incorporation of pictures may be used in place of written text.

What to observe. Look for any type of response from the client, vocal/verbal or nonverbal, as these may indicate participation. The therapist's responses can help to develop even very small or tentative responses.

Procedures. The therapist and client(s) need to initially determine a topic for the composition. This will often be very concrete, perhaps something that occurs in the client's daily life or is a part of the immediate environment. The client should be given as much choice in the matter as possible. The topic should be relevant to the client's life and interests. Choosing the topic should not take so much time that there is not sufficient time for the composition. A large amount of structure will probably be useful in the composition, with the therapist making many of the decisions and allowing the client to focus on only what he or she can successfully contribute. This may mean that the therapist takes initiative in selecting the topic, many of the words, the musical style, and so forth. The therapist should be aware of the style of music from the client's culture and incorporate it when appropriate. The composition may extend over more than one session, but it is recommended that enough be accomplished in a single session that the client feels satisfied and experiences a sense of accomplishment.

Fill-in-the-blank methods, also called *song parodies,* may be employed. In this method, some words are left out of a familiar song, with new words filled in by the client. A song in which a client can respond, recommended earlier in the chapter, can be conceived of as a type of composition (perhaps a song parody), with the client participating in the composition by inserting his or her response. Many participants will probably make their contributions through voice-activated devices or language boards, thus incorporating technology.

Adaptations. Purely instrumental compositions may be appropriate for those who would benefit from seeing a concrete product of their efforts, accomplishing a task, or having an opportunity to make choices. Giving the client(s) choices of instruments to include or type of composition may be helpful. A large amount of structure will probably be useful in the composition, with the therapist making many of the decisions and allowing the client to focus on only what he or she can successfully contribute.

Composing can follow many formats, with the client possibly contributing melodic or rhythmic aspects, or selecting instruments to play or accentuate parts. It will be useful to write down or record digitally the results of the decisions so that the composition can be played and revised later. The composition may extend over more than one session, but it is recommended that enough be accomplished in a single session that the client feels satisfied and experiences a sense of accomplishment.

Some clients may recommend an instrument to play in the composition that is activated through technology. The spaces in songs that have been spoken of as being useful to leave so that people can respond could be conceived of as a type of composition, with the client participating in the composition by inserting his or her response.

Working with Caregivers

Since many with ID require enormous amounts of assistance and attention, the job of the caregiver is difficult and stressful. Caregivers usually spend many more hours with the person than do music therapists, and they are likely to be aware of things about the client that the music therapist does not know.

The music therapist may help parents or other caregivers find more pleasure in being with the client. Knoll (2012) suggests that music therapy can play an important role in helping the parent or other caregiver to find enjoyment in spending time with the client. Music can provide opportunities for them to share a pleasurable activity, potentially leading to a more positive relationship. Oldfield (2006) included as a goal that the music therapist could provide ideas for the mother on how to use music with the child.

Coleman (2002) provides some suggestions for working collaboratively with parents, staff, and administrators. These included using "active listening" approaches (i.e., empathizing with another person's perspective), identifying how music therapy aligns with the client's school/facility approaches, providing educational materials about music therapy, working cooperatively, and putting forth maximum-quality work (p. 209).

Research Evidence

Research was found using improvisational, re-creative, and receptive music therapy methods with people with ID. Although some of the research is useful in providing information on the methods, no randomized control trials evaluating music therapy with those with severe and multiple disabilities were found. No research was found on compositional music therapy methods.

Stephenson (2006), an Australian special education academic, was quite critical of music therapy and the lack of an evidence base for its practice. Subsequently, she and music therapist Katrina McFerran collaborated in discussions (McFerran & Stephenson, 2006) and research projects (McFerran & Stephenson, 2010). Their collaboration has led to a better understanding of the issues and some information on researching the effects of music therapy with people with severe disabilities, with the latter presented later in this section under Re-creative Music Therapy.

The Drake Music Project (www.drakemusic.org) uses electronic and computer technologies to enable people with profound disabilities to explore, compose, and perform music. Evaluation of the project (Watts & Ridley, 2006, 2007) addresses aspects of making music (improvisation, re-creation, composition) by people with various types of disabilities. Although the website description of the project includes music therapists among those who help to make music accessible, the evaluators make a clear distinction between what they are evaluating and music therapy.

Improvisational Music Therapy

Meadows (1995, 1996) provided insights into the experience of a child with severe and multiple disabilities in music therapy. He viewed a videotape of a session with a child, Becky, noting the child's actions, his actions, and his thoughts. After that, he interviewed Becky's teacher, who had also viewed the video. His observations and interpretations included not knowing whether Becky was aware of the music room or of what was to happen when they entered the room. After he started playing, specifically brushing the wind chimes, he felt that she knew and understood where she was. She knew to stretch back to brush the chimes with her head. He says, "Becky enjoyed brushing the chimes with her head. This was a purposeful action, and she may have even experimented with the way they touched her forehead. ... She appeared to react, and may have even interacted with me, and the music I created for her. Rather than being a series of isolated incidents, these actions and interactions appeared ongoing and related" (Meadows, 1995, pp. 6, 7).

Hooper (2002) examined his use of music to develop peer interaction by describing the responses of two people and comparing their responses with and without music. Although he did not find, in this instance, that music was as effective as the nonmusic condition, his description can lead to a better understanding of what was involved in his work. Hooper (1993) also presents a case study in which he took data throughout. He sang to the woman and played a tambourine, seeing gradually more responses. This case was used as an example of improvisation at different levels in the Guidelines for Improvisational Music Therapy section.

Oldfield and Adams (1990, 1995) randomly assigned 12 clients to two conditions, music therapy and play. All had profound learning difficulties, nine also had severe physical disabilities, and all had severe problems with communication and social interaction. Four of the clients, two from each condition, were selected for intensive study. Clients in both conditions received weekly half-hour music therapy or play sessions for six months, with the treatments reversed after six months. The music therapy sessions were very structured, with "much of every session [being] spent responding to, and improvising upon, the singing or playing of individual clients" (1990, p. 168). The play was similar to the type of activities usually done with these clients. Sessions were evaluated using time sampling of videotape recordings to observe the four specified clients, in each case recording behaviors that were targeted as goals for the person being observed. Three of the four people who were observed obtained higher scores in music therapy for some of their objectives.

Perry (2003) studied the development of intentional communication with children with ID. She conducted a qualitative research study in which she related improvisational music therapy to communication development in 10 school-age children, none of whom used any form of symbolic communication consistently. The purpose of the study was "to describe the patterns in the communication of children with varying levels of preintentional and early intentional communication and how the consequences of disability affected children's communication" (p. 231). All sessions included the use of improvisation, and composed songs and songs that emerged from the improvisation were also used. Instruments and vocalization were also part of the sessions. She presented children's communication levels and described their communications.

Rainey-Perry and Ri (2005) presented their work, as a music therapist and speech language therapist, with a group of older students who were in the transition between preintentional and early formal means of communication. Their aims were to initiate communication, indicate preferences, increase social communication, and establish the prerequisite skills for intentional communication. They described strategies, including the music therapist responding to the use of gaze as communication, for example, by offering a student the guitar when he looked at it, or stopping the music when the student looked away. The music therapist incorporated vocal responses, which occurred during both improvisation and songs, into her singing and playing.

Van Colle (2003) studied children with cerebral palsy and ID with two major aims: (a) to investigate the hypothesis that the role of the music therapist is like that of Winnicott's *good-enough mother,* and (b) to generate some broad guidelines for music therapy. She addressed three questions: (1) Did the children take a greater part in music therapy sessions over a period of time? (2) When did the major child-therapist interactions occur? (3) When the music therapist focused on an individual child, how could it be known that the child was aware of this attention? The sessions took place with two groups of four children each over a period of one academic year. The results of qualitative and quantitative analyses indicated that the children responded to music therapy and had some expectation of how the music worked. For example, some beat on the downbeat, vocalized in the therapist's tonality, and followed V7-I shifts. One child sang four notes of a scale. The author summarized by saying, "There was every indication that children with severe and multiple disabilities possessed and used a musical understanding which enabled them to connect and relate to the therapist" (p. ii).

Re-creative Music Therapy

Hooper (2002) worked with two women, one with multiple disabilities including severe ID and the other with severe ID, to develop peer interaction. Ten weekly sessions were held, with the first five being music therapy (music activities structured to encourage interaction and cooperation) and the next five being control sessions (ball and target games structured to encourage interaction and cooperation). He found that both techniques facilitated prompted interaction and increased the level of unprompted interaction in comparison with the baseline measure, and that there was also an absence of negative interactions.

Ghetti (2002) compared three musical treatment conditions to each other and to a repeated-measures baseline for each subject to see which condition led to the most time in combined alert and responsive behavior states of six children with profound disabilities. The conditions were: (a) a passive rhythmic stimulation condition, in which the therapist played steady rhythms on a bass drum; (b) contingent-continuation song singing, in which the therapist sang to and with each subject, accompanied by guitar; and (c) multisensory rhythm instrument–playing, in which auditory, visual, tactile, and kinesthetic stimulation from playing musical instruments was utilized. No differences in behavior states were found among the three conditions.

McFerran and Stephenson (2010) studied four students with severe disabilities, hypothesizing that the students would communicate more during music therapy interventions utilizing singing and recorded music than when they were interacting with the same therapist during other activities without music or singing. They presented data and results on only one of the students. Although they found a small advantage in the sessions that included music, there were problems with the reliability of the data. Much of their focus in presenting and telling about the research was on examining what should be changed to make future studies more useful.

Receptive Music Therapy

Wigram (1996) compared the effects of vibroacoustic therapy (VAS) with several other conditions and included studies of adults with severe and multiple disabilities as well as some non-clinical populations. In addition to the dissertation, he describes all of the research in Wigram (2005). In two of the studies, he evaluated the effects of VAS and other treatments with people with severe and multiple disabilities. Wigram (1996) says: "A study on 10 multiply handicapped adults with high muscle tone and spasm compared the effect of eight trials of VA therapy with a similar number of trials of relaxing music. A significantly greater range of movement was recorded after VA therapy than relaxing music. No significant difference was found in changes in blood pressure or heart rate" (p. 2). This or similar research was also reported in Wigram (1997b) and Wigram, McNaught, Cain, and Weekes (1997). Research using a similar design and showing success in reducing self-injurious behaviors was reported in Wigram (1993).

The results of the other portion of Wigram's (1996) dissertation research were described by him as: "Comparing the effect of VA therapy with music and movement-based physiotherapy (MMBP) and relaxing music alone on 27 subjects with high muscle tone and spasticity revealed no significant difference in range of movement between VA therapy and MMBP, but a significant difference comparing the combined results of MMBP and VA therapy with relaxing music alone. Additional trials found significant differences between VA therapy and music alone" (p. 2). This research was reported in Wigram (1997a).

In a recent 3-month randomized control trial of 89 children with spastic cerebral palsy and multiple disabilities (Katusic, Alimovic, & Mejaski-Bosnjak, in press), children received either regular physiotherapy (PT) or vibration therapy twice a week in addition to their PT program. Significant differences were found in spasticity level and gross motor function in the group that received the vibration therapy.

Many studies have investigated music as reinforcement, primarily in the 1970s and 1980s. Standley (1996) performed a meta-analysis of the effects of music as reinforcement for education and therapy objectives and found the greatest effect sizes (ES = 3.16) for subjects with mental disabilities (including all levels of IDs and also, in some studies, multiple disabilities).

Five studies investigated the effects of reinforcement controlled through automated devices. Hill, Brantner, and Spreat (1989) used contingent music to help a young woman with blindness and profound ID to remain in her seat. The music was very effective, with rock and jazz being considerably more successful than classical music. Ball, McCrady, and Hart (1975) used a transistor radio activated by a mercury switch to reinforce the head posture of two children with intellectual disabilities and severe cerebral palsy. Under the contingent music condition, dropping the head forward automatically terminated the music. A comparison of baseline and treatment phases showed that head orientation was strongly controlled by contingent music. Ball (1971) worked to control a stereotypical behavior (called a *blindism*) in a child with profound intellectual disabilities, using a mercury switch attached to the child's hair ribbon to activate a transistor radio when she held her head in a normal position and automatically terminate the music when she dropped her chin to her chest. Wolfe (1980) investigated the effect of interrupted music/silence and interrupted music/tone on the head posturing of 12 people with cerebral palsy and other disabilities, ranging in age from 3 to 37 years. Head control improved during the treatment conditions for four subjects, while one subject seemed to respond only to the music/tone condition, and the remaining subjects showed minimal improvement.

McClure, Moss, McPeters, and Kirkpatrick (1986) used an automated training device to decrease hand mouthing in a 9-year-old child with severe and profound multiple disabilities. Bilateral hand-switch placement of music and vibration resulted in substantial and sustained reduction of the incompatible behavior of hand mouthing. "When the subject depressed the switches and experienced the treatment contingency, he would smile, laugh, and bang his hand against the switches several times before continuing to keep the switches depressed. This response suggested the enjoyable nature of the treatment procedure and is one, if not the only, occurrence in which the subject was able to control his environment voluntarily" (p. 221).

Several studies reported mixed results on the reinforcing value of music. Greenwald (1978) did not find any substantial differences in the effectiveness of distorted music vs. interrupted music in decreasing self-stimulatory behaviors in adolescents with profound intellectual disabilities, including multiple disabilities. Saperston, Chan, Morphew, and Carsrud (1980) compared music listening and juice as reinforcement for learning in adults with profound intellectual and multiple disabilities and found that music was at least as useful as juice in increasing responses. Walmsley, Crichton, and Droog (1981) tested a music/biofeedback mechanism that was developed to help head position on five people with severe intellectual disabilities and cerebral palsy and found that head control improved for three, deteriorated for one, and remained the same for one. Ford (1999) studied the effect of a passive music activity, an active music activity, and a nonmusic activity on self-injurious behaviors in a woman with severe developmental disabilities and found positive effects of music in some areas.

Grove, Dalke, Fredericks, and Crowley (1975) found that social approval and music were effective in teaching children, ages 10 to 16, with multiple disabilities to hold their heads in an extended position. Removal of this contingency resulted in an abrupt reversal to pretreatment levels.

One study used contingent musical participation in addition to listening, comparing the two conditions. Holloway (1980) compared the effects of contingent music listening and contingent rhythm instrument-playing in increasing pre-academic and motor skills, with five of their participants having severe and multiple disabilities. Both types of music reinforcement had a positive effect, although no significant differences were discerned between them.

Several studies looked at aspects of conditioning music as a reinforcer. Dewson and Whiteley (1987) and Dorow (1975) found that music, a secondary reinforcer, could be conditioned as a positive reinforcer. In a study intended to provide information on how music could be most effective as a reinforcer, Dorow and Horton (1982) found that auditory stimuli were most effective at increasing activity when placed near to the heads of people with severe and multiple disabilities. Remington, Foxen, and Hogg (1977) made auditory stimulation contingent on a visually directed level-pulling response, first evaluating the feasibility of establishing an effective reinforcer from a range of possible reinforcing stimuli and, second, comparing the effectiveness of that reinforcer with a second auditory stimulus. The information gained concerning the effectiveness of auditory reinforcers has implications for behavior modification programs with these children.

Caron, Donnell, and Friedman (1996) played relaxation music for six adults with severe and profound multiple disabilities in an attempt to decrease bruxism (teeth grinding). They played New Age music for 20 minutes over five consecutive days. Data were collected through 10-second-interval recording of the presence or absence of bruxing behavior before, during, and after treatment. Four out of the six subjects demonstrated a decrease in bruxing behavior during treatment.

Wigram (1981) conducted an observational research study in which he observed the responses of a group of 12 children with severe and multiple disabilities, ages 9 to 19, to different pieces and types of music, looking at responses to solo or choral, vocal or instrumental, solo or orchestral, rhythmic or nonrhythmic, melodic or unmelodic, and contrasting styles of music. He was interested in the following questions: "(a) When is a patient listening or just hearing? (b) How long can one hold attention and with what type of music? (c) Does the volume of the music feature as important in determining perceptual ability and length of attention? (d) In general, do patients with certain handicaps listen better than patients with different handicaps? (e) Does memory play a part in developing an ability to listen in the severely and profoundly handicapped? (f) What are the worst and best effects to observe in noting the response to a piece of recorded music?" (p. 18).

Wigram (1981) found that several variables regarding the music, the environment, the staff, and the clients influenced the responses. Among his findings were that they had progressed in their attention since the earlier observation. He found some differences in responses depending upon whether music was played in the morning or afternoon (with these responses varying according to clients' level of functioning and the type of movement involved in their sessions); more attention at higher than at lower volumes; preference for vocal pieces, particularly when they were at the lower volume; preference for strong rhythmic pieces; and pieces played several times. Although Wigram's results do not necessarily apply beyond the children from whom he gathered the data, there is no doubt some similarity between these children's responses and those of others, and his model can be used for others who want to understand the listening preferences of their clients.

Summary and Conclusions

There is a great deal of literature that applies to people with severe and multiple disabilities. Some of this literature speaks of those with *severe or profound* intellectual disabilities (ID), often, of course, using terminology that was used when the articles were written but is no longer in use. When it was not clear, the literature was read to determine whether it actually applied to those with severe and multiple disabilities, and the best determination possible was made. Those with severe and profound levels of ID are very likely to have concomitant disabilities, so some of the literature was assumed to apply to those with severe and multiple disabilities even when this was not specified in the description.

Although much of what is written does not include detail on what is actually *done* with the clients—in other words, how the methods are used—this chapter has developed what can actually be done in working with those with severe and multiple disabilities. It is hoped that the descriptions and procedures that are spelled out will be helpful to those who work with or would like to work with people with severe and multiple disabilities. It is also suggested that future writing be more explicit about what is done in music therapy sessions.

Some useful descriptive and qualitative research studies on music therapy with those with severe and multiple disabilities was found and shared. No randomized control trials or other strong experimental research designs were included. This is a serious omission for music therapy and should be addressed.

Music therapy with individuals with severe and multiple disabilities is complex and rewarding. This chapter has documented current practice, with recommendations for continued growth of this area.

References

Ball, T. S. (1971). Comments: Blindism. In T. S. Ball (Ed.), *A guide for the instruction and training of the profoundly retarded and severely multi-handicapped child* (pp. 106–108). Santa Cruz, CA: Santa Cruz County Office of Education.

Ball, T. S., McCrady, R. E., & Hart, A. D. (1975). Automated reinforcement of head posture in two cerebral palsied retarded children. *Perceptual and Motor Skills, 40,* 619–622.

Baxter, H. T., Berghofer, J. A., MacEwan, L., Nelson, J., Peters, K., & Roberts, P. (2007). *The individualized music therapy assessment profile, IMTAP.* London: Jessica Kingsley Publishers.

Betz, S., & Held, J. (2012). *Betz Held strengths inventory for children with disabilities.* Walnut Creek, CA: Walnut Creek Music Therapy.

Bitcon, C. H. (1976). *Alike and different: The clinical and educational uses of Orff-Schulwerk.* Santa Ana, CA: Rosha Press.

Bitcon, C. H. (2000). *Alike and different: The clinical and educational uses of Orff-Schulwerk* (2nd ed.). Gilsum, NH: Barcelona Publishers.

Brunk, B., & Coleman, K. (2000). Development of a special education music therapy assessment process. *Music Therapy Perspectives, 18,* 59–68.

Bruscia, K. (1998). *Defining music therapy* (2nd ed.). Gilsum, NH: Barcelona Publishers.

Caron, J. R., Donnell, N. E., & Friedman, M. (1996). The reduction of bruxism using passive music listening with person having developmental disabilities. *Canadian Journal of Music Therapy, 4*(1), 58–73.

Cassidy, J. W. (1992). Communication disorders: Effects on children's ability to label musical characteristics. *Journal of Music Therapy, 29*(2), 113–124.

Charness, N., Clifton, J., & MacDonald, L. (1988). Case study of a musical "mono-savant": A cognitive-psychological focus. In L. K. Older & D. Fein (Eds.), *The exceptional brain: Neuropsychology of talent and special abilities* (pp. 277–294). New York, NY: Guilford Press.

Chase, K. M. (2004). Music therapy assessment for children with developmental disabilities: A survey study. *Journal of Music Therapy, 41,* 28–54.

Clark, C., & Chadwick, D. (1980). *Clinically adapted instruments for the multiply handicapped.* St. Louis, MO: MMB Music.

Coleman, K. A. (2002). Music therapy for learners with severe disabilities in a public school setting. In B. L. Wilson (Ed.), *Models of music therapy interventions in school settings* (2nd ed.). (pp. 197–210). Silver Spring, MD: American Music Therapy Association.

Coleman, K. A., & Brunk, B. K. (2003). *SEMTAP: Special education music therapy assessment process handbook* (2nd ed.). Grapevine, TX: Prelude Music Therapy.

Crowe, B. (1999). The special place of music for a multiply disabled girl. In J. Hibben (Ed.), *Inside music therapy* (pp. 199–202). Gilsum, NH: Barcelona Publishers.

Darrow, A-. A. (1984). A comparison of rhythmic responsiveness in normal and hearing-impaired children and an investigation of the relationship of rhythmic responsiveness to the suprasegmental aspects of speech perception. *Journal of Music Therapy, 21*(2), 48–66.

Dewson, M. R. J., & Whiteley, J. H. (1987). Sensory reinforcement of head-turning with nonambulatory, profoundly mentally retarded persons. *Research in Developmental Disabilities, 8,* 413–426.

DiGiammarino, M. (1990). Functional music skills of persons with mental retardation, *Journal of Music Therapy, 27*(4), 209–220.

Dorow, L. G. (1975). Conditioning music and approval as new reinforcers for imitative behavior with the severely retarded. *Journal of Music Therapy, 12*(1), 30–40.

Dorow, L. G., & Horton, J. J. (1982). Effect of the proximity of auditory stimuli and sung versus spoken stimuli on activity levels of severely/profoundly mentally retarded females. *Journal of Music Therapy, 19,* 114–124.

Education encyclopedia. (n.d.). http://education.stateuniversity.com/pages/2415/Severe-Multiple-Disabilities-Education-individuals-With.html">Severe and Education of individuals With Multiple Disabilities—Definition and Types of Severe and Multiple Disabilities.

Ellis, P. (1995). Incidental music: A case study in the development of a sound therapy. *British Journal of Music Education, 12*(1), 59–70.

Ellis, P. (1997). The music of sound: A new approach for children with severe and profound and multiple learning difficulties. *British Journal of Music Education, 14*(2), 173–186.

Farnan, L. (2002). Music therapy for learners with profound disabilities in a residential setting. In B. L. Wilson (Ed.), *Models of music therapy interventions in school settings* (2nd ed.). (pp. 165–182). Silver Spring, MD: American Music Therapy Association.

Farnan, L. (2003). Music therapy at Central Wisconsin Center for the Developmentally Disabled. *Voices: A World Forum for Music Therapy, 3*(2). Retrieved from https://normt.uib.no/index.php/voices/article/viewArticle/127/103

Farnan, L. (2010). *Music therapy and occupational therapy sensory stimulation and integration outline: "Sit and spin."* Unpublished document. Madison, WI: Central Wisconsin Center.

Farnan, L., & Johnson, F. (1988a). *Everyone can move.* Milwaukee, WI: Jenson Publications.

Farnan, L., & Johnson, F. (1988b). *Music is for everyone.* Milwaukee, WI: Jenson Publications.

Flowers, P. J., & Wang, C. (2002). Matching verbal description to music excerpt: The use of language by blind and sighted children. *Journal of Research in Music Education, 50*(3), 202–214.

Galerstein, N., Martin, K., & Powe, D. L. (1998). *Age appropriate activities for adults with profound mental retardation.* St. Louis, MO: MMB Music.

Ghetti, C. M. (2002). Comparison of the effectiveness of three music therapy conditions to modulate behavior states in students with profound disabilities: A pilot study. *Music Therapy Perspectives, 20,* 20–30.

Goodman, K. D. (2007). *Music therapy groupwork with special needs children: The evolving process.* Springfield, IL: Charles C. Thomas.

Greenwald, M. A. (1978). The effectiveness of distorted music versus interrupted music to decrease self-stimulatory behaviors in profoundly retarded adolescents. *Journal of Music Therapy, 15*(2), 58–66.

Grove, D. N., Dalke, B. A., Fredericks, H. D., & Crowley, R. F. (1975). Establishing appropriate head positioning with mentally and physically handicapped children. *Behavioral Engineering, 3*(2), 53–59.

Hill, J., Brantner, J., & Spreat, S. (1989). The effect of contingent music on the in-seat behavior of a blind young woman with profound mental retardation. *Education and Treatment of Children, 12*(2), 165–173.

Holloway, M. S. (1980). A comparison of passive and active music reinforcement to increase pre-academic and motor skills in severely retarded children and adolescents. *Journal of Music Therapy, 17*(2), 58–69.

Hooper, J. (1993). Developing interaction through shared musical experiences: A strategy to enhance and validate the descriptive approach. In M. Heal & T. Wigram (Eds.), *Music therapy in health and education* (pp. 208–213). London, England: Jessica Kingsley.

Hooper, J. (2002). Using music to develop peer interaction: An examination of the response of two subjects with a learning disability. *British Journal of Learning Disabilities, 30,* 166–170.

Hooper, J., Wigram, T., Carson, D., & Lindsay, B. (2008). A review of the music and intellectual disability literature (1943–2006): Part two—Experimental writing. *Music Therapy Perspectives, 26*(1), 80–96.

Johnson, F. L. (2002). Models of service delivery and their relation to the IEP. In B. L. Wilson (Ed.), *Models of music therapy interventions in school settings* (2nd ed.). (pp. 83–107). Silver Spring, MD: American Music Therapy Association.

Katusic, A., Alimovic, S., & Mejaski-Bosnjak, V. (in press). The effect of vibration therapy on spasticity and motor function in children with cerebral palsy: A randomized controlled trial. *NeuroRehabilitation.* DOI:10.3233/NRE-130817

Knoll, C. (2012). *Severe disabilities toolbox: Accessible music for people with limited skills.* Stephenville, TX: MusicWorks Publications.

Krout, R. (1987). Music therapy with multi-handicapped students: Individualizing treatment within a group setting. *Journal of Music Therapy, 24,* 2–13.

Levin, H., & Levin, G. (1998). Learning through music. Gilsum, NH: Barcelona Publishers.

Levin, H., & Levin, G. (2005). Let's make music. Gilsum, NH: Barcelona Publishers.

Madsen, C. K. (1981). Music therapy: A behavioral guide for the mentally retarded. Lawrence, KS: National Association for Music Therapy.

Madsen, C. K., & Madsen, C. H. (1998). *Teaching/discipline: A positive approach for educational development* (4th ed.). Raleigh, NC: Contemporary Publishing.

Magee, W. L., Bertolami, M., Kubicek, L., LaJoie, M., Martino, L., Sankowski, A., Townsend, J., Whitehead-Pleaux, A. M., & Zigo, J. B. (2011). Using music technology in music therapy with populations across the life span in medical and educational programs. *Music and Medicine, 3*(3), 146–153.

Magee, W. L., & Burland, K. (2008a). An exploratory study of the use of electronic music technologies in clinical music therapy. *Nordic Journal of Music Therapy, 17*(2), 124–141.

Magee, W. L., & Burland, K. (2008b). Using electronic music technologies in music therapy: Opportunities, limitations and clinical indicators. *British Journal of Music Therapy, 22*(1), 3–15.

Martino, L., & Bertolami, M. (in press). Using music technology with young people with visual impairments/blindness and multiple impairments. In W. L. Magee (Ed.), *Music technology in therapeutic and health settings.* Philadelphia, PA: Jessica Kingsley.

therapeutic and health settings. Philadelphia, PA: Jessica Kingsley.

McClure, J. T., Moss, R. A., McPeters, J. W., & Kirkpatrick, M. A. (1986). Reduction of hand mouthing by a boy with profound mental retardation. *Mental Retardation, 24,* 219–222.

McFerran, K., & Stephenson, J. (2006). Music therapy in special education: Do we need more evidence? *British Journal of Music Therapy, 20*(2), 121–128.

McFerran, K., & Stephenson, J. (2010). Facing the challenge: A music therapy investigation in the evidence-based framework. In V. Karkou & V. Karkou (Eds.), *Arts therapies in schools: Research and practice* (pp. 259–270). Philadelphia, PA: Jessica Kingsley.

Meadows, A. (1995). *How do I understand a child's experience in music therapy?* Unpublished paper. Philadelphia, PA: Temple University.

Meadows, A. (1996). What mechanisms can we use to understand our own and the client's experience in improvisational music therapy with working with children who are profoundly disabled? In H. Smeijsters & F. Mecklenbeck (Eds.), *Book of abstracts: Sound and psyche* (p. 39). Hamburg, Germany: Trialog.

Meadows, A. (1997). Music therapy for children with severe and profound multiple disabilities: A review of literature. *Australian Journal of Music Therapy, 7,* 3–17.

Meadows, A. (2002). Approaches to music and movement for children with severe and profound multiple disabilities. *Australian Journal of Music Therapy, 13,* 17–27.

Michel, D. E., & Rohrbacher, M. J. (1982). *The music therapy assessment profile for severely/profoundly handicapped persons, Research draft III (0–27 months level).* Unpublished manuscript. Denton, TX: Texas Woman's University.

Miller, L. (1987). Sensitivity to tonal structure in a developmentally disabled musical savant. *American Journal of Mental Deficiency, 91,* 467–471.

Miller, L. K. (1999). The savant syndrome: Intellectual impairment and exceptional skill. *Psychological Bulletin, 125*(1), 31–46.

Møller, A. S. (1996). Music as a means of contact and communication with the physically and mentally handicapped. In I. N. Pedersen & L. O. Bonde (Eds.), *Music therapy within multi-disciplinary teams* (pp. 147–153). Aalborg, Denmark: Aalborg University Press.

Møller, A. S. (n.d.) *The 5 levels of contact.* http://viss.skanderborg.dk/Default.aspx?ID=36598

NAfME. (n.d.). *National Standards for Music Education.* Retrieved from http://musiced.nafme.org/resources/national-standards-for-music-education/

Nagler, J. C., & Lee, M. H. M. (1989). Music therapy using computer music technology. In M. H. M. Lee (Ed.), *Rehabilitation, music and human well-being* (pp. 226–241). St. Louis, MO: MMB Music.

Nordoff, P., & Robbins, C. (1977). *Creative music therapy.* New York, NY: John Day.

Nordoff, P., & Robbins, C. (2007). *Creative music therapy: A guide to fostering clinical musicianship* (2nd ed., revised and expanded). Gilsum, NH: Barcelona Publishers.

Nowikas, S. (1999). Discovering meaning in Kelly's nonverbal expressions. In J. Hibben (Ed.), *Inside music therapy: Client experiences* (pp. 209–230). Gilsum, NH: Barcelona Publishers.

Ockelford, A., Welch, G., Jewell-Gore, L., Cheng, E., Vogiatzoglou, A., & Himonides, E. (2011). *Sounds of Intent, Phase 2:* Gauging the musical development of children with complex needs. *European Journal of Special Needs Education, 26*(2), 177–199. DOI: 10.1080/08856257.2011.563606

Oldfield, A. (2006). *Interactive music therapy: A positive approach.* Philadelphia, PA: Jessica Kingsley.

Oldfield, A., & Adams, M. (1990). The effects of music therapy on a group of profoundly mentally handicapped adults. *Journal of Mental Deficiency Research, 34,* 107–125.

Oldfield, A., & Adams, M. (1995). The effects of music therapy on a group of adults with profound learning difficulties. In A. Gilroy & C. Lee (Eds.), *Art and music: Therapy and research* (pp. 164–182). London: Routledge.

Orff, G. (1974). *The Orff music therapy: Active furthering of the development of the child.* London, England: Schott & Co.

Owens, W. A., & Grimm, W. (1941). A note regarding exceptional musical ability in a low-grade imbecile. *Journal of Educational Psychology, 32,* 636–637.

Perry, M. R. (2003). Relating improvisational music therapy with severely and multiply disabled children to communication development. *Journal of Music Therapy, 40*(3), 227–246.

Pfeifer, S. M. (1982). *Music therapy for handicapped children: Multi-handicapped.* Washington, DC: National Association for Music Therapy.

Pfeifer, S. M. (1989). A step in the right direction: Suggested strategies for implementing music therapy with the handicapped child. *Music Therapy Perspectives, 6*(1), 57–60.

Rafieyan, R. (2003). Meeting Rich: Individual music therapy with a man who has severe disabilities. In S. Hadley (Ed.), *Psychodynamic music therapy: Case studies* (pp. 339–355). Gilsum, NH: Barcelona Publishers.

Rainey-Perry, M. R., & Ri, C. J. (July 2005). *Developing intentional communication: A combined music and speech therapy approach.* Paper presented at 11th World Congress of Music Therapy, Brisbane, Australia.

Remington, R. E., Foxen, T., & Hogg, J. (1977). Auditory reinforcement in profoundly retarded multiply-handicapped children. *American Journal of Mental Deficiency, 82*(2), 299–304.

Ritchie, F. (1993). Opening doors: The effects of music therapy with people who have severe learning difficulties and display challenging behaviour. In M. Heal & T. Wigram (Eds.), *Music therapy in health and education* (pp. 91–102). Philadelphia, PA: Jessica Kingsley.

Ritholz, M. S., & Robbins, C. (1999). *Themes for therapy.* Bryn Mawr, PA: Theodore Presser.

Ritholz, M. S., & Robbins, C. (2003). *More themes for therapy.* Bryn Mawr, PA: Theodore Presser.

[Robbins: Nordoff-Robbins]. (1995). *Greetings and goodbyes.* Bryn Mawr, PA: Theodore Presser.

Robbins, C., & Nordoff, P. (1962). *The first book of children's play-songs.* Bryn Mawr, PA: Theodore Presser.

Robbins, C., & Nordoff, P. (1968). *The second book of children's play-songs.* Bryn Mawr, PA: Theodore Presser.

Robbins, C., & Nordoff, P. (1980a). *The third book of children's play-songs.* Bryn Mawr, PA: Theodore Presser.

Robbins, C., & Nordoff, P. (1980b). *The fifth book of children's play-songs.* Bryn Mawr, PA: Theodore Presser.

Robbins, C., & Robbins, C. (1991). Self-communications in Creative Music Therapy. In K. E. Bruscia (Ed.), *Case studies in music therapy* (pp. 55–72). Gilsum, NH: Barcelona Publishers.

Roberts, D. (1986, September). *A review of two case studies using music therapy with multihandicapped children.* Paper presented at the Twelfth National Conference of the Australian Music Therapy Association, Inc., Sydney, Australia.

Salas, J., & Gonzalez, D. (1991). Like singing with a bird: Improvisational music therapy with a blind four-year-old. In K. E. Bruscia (Ed.), *Case studies in music therapy* (pp. 17–27). Gilsum, NH: Barcelona Publishers.

Saperston, B. M., Chan, R., Morphew, C., & Carsrud, K. B. (1980). Music listening versus juice as a reinforcement for learning in profoundly mentally retarded individuals. *Journal of Music Therapy, 17,* 174–183.

Sekeles, C. (1996). *Music: Motion and emotion: The developmental-interactive model in music therapy.* Gilsum, NH: Barcelona Publishers.

Shoemark, H. (1991). The use of piano improvisation in developing interaction and participation in a blind boy with behavioral disturbances. In K. E. Bruscia (Ed.), *Case studies in music therapy* (pp. 29–38). Gilsum, NH: Barcelona Publishers.

Skille, O. (1989). Vibroacoustic therapy. *Music Therapy, 8*(1), 61–77.

Standley, J. M. (1996). A meta-analysis on the effects of music as reinforcement for education/therapy objectives. *Journal of Research in Music Education, 44,* 105–133.

Stephenson, J. (2006). Music therapy and the education of students with severe disabilities. *Education and Training in Developmental Disabilities, 41*(3), 290–299.

Stevenson, K. (2003). Music therapy assisted communication with children with severe disabilities. *New Zealand Journal of Music Therapy, 1,* 82–92.

Stordahl, J. (2002). Song recognition and appraisal: A comparison of children who use cochlear implants and normally hearing children. *Journal of Music Therapy, 39*(1), 2–19.

Thaut, M. H. (2005). *Rhythm, music, and the brain: Scientific foundations and clinical applications.* New York, NY: Routledge.

Van Colle, S. J. (2003). *Music therapy process with young people who have severe and multiple disabilities.* Unpublished Ph.D. thesis. Reading, UK: University of Reading.

Vogiatzoglou, A., Ockelford, A., Welch, G., & Himonides, E. (2011). Sounds of Intent: Interactive software to assess the musical development of children and young people with complex needs. *Music and Medicine, 3*(3), 189–195. DOI: 10.1177/1943862111403628

Voigt, M. (1999). Orff music therapy with multi-handicapped children. In T. Wigram & J. DeBacker (Eds.), *Clinical applications of music therapy in developmental disability, paediatrics and neurology* (pp. 166–182). Philadelphia, PA: Jessica Kingsley.

Walmsley, R. P., Crichton, L., & Droog, D. (1981). Music as a feedback mechanism for teaching head control to severely handicapped children: A pilot study. *Developmental Medicine & Child Neurology, 23*(6), 739–746.

Watson, T. (2002). Music therapy with adults with learning disabilities. In L. Bunt & S. Hoskyns (Eds.), *The handbook of music therapy* (pp. 97–114). New York, NY: Brunner-Routledge.

Watson, T. (2007). Working with people with profound and multiple learning disabilities in music therapy. In T. Watson (Ed.), *Music therapy with adults with learning disabilities* (pp. 98–111). Philadelphia, PA: Jessica Kingsley.

Watts, M., & Ridley, B. (2006). Never mind the bollocks: Here's the Drake Music Project: A capability perspective of dis/ability and musical identities. *Taboo: The Journal of Culture and Education, 10*(2), 99–107.

Watts, M., & Ridley, B. (2007). Evaluating musical dis/abilities: Operationalizing the capability approach. *International Journal of Research & Method in Education, 30*(2), 149–162.

Wheeler, B. L. (1999a). Experiencing pleasure in working with severely disabled children. *Journal of Music Therapy, 36,* 56–80.

Wheeler, B. L. (1999b). Lisa: The experience of a child with multiple disabilities. In J. Hibben (Ed.), *Inside music therapy: Client experiences* (pp. 237–246). Gilsum, NH: Barcelona Publishers.

Wigram, A. L. (1981). The value of recorded music for the severely handicapped. In *1981 International Year of Disabled People. The role of music therapy.* London: British Society for Music Therapy.

Wigram, A. L. (1996). *The effects of vibroacoustic therapy on clinical and non-clinical populations.* Unpublished dissertation. St. George's Hospital Medical School, London University, London.

Wigram, T. (1993). The feeling of sound: The effect of music and low frequency sound in reducing anxiety and challenging behaviour in clients with learning difficulties. In H. Payne (Ed.), *Handbook of inquiry in the arts therapies: One river, many currents* (pp. 177–196). Philadelphia, PA: Jessica Kingsley.

Wigram, T. (1997a). The effect of vibroacoustic therapy compared with music and movement based physiotherapy on multiply handicapped patients with high muscle tone and spasticity. In T. Wigram & C. Dileo (Eds.), *Music vibration and health* (pp. 69–85). Cherry Hill, NJ: Jeffrey Books.

Wigram, T. (1997b). The effect of VA therapy on multiply handicapped adults with high muscle tone and spasticity. In T. Wigram & C. Dileo (Eds.), *Music vibration and health* (pp. 57–68). Cherry Hill, NJ: Jeffrey Books.

Wigram, T. (2005). Music and sound vibration: Testing hypotheses as a series of case studies. In D. Aldridge (Ed.), *Case study designs in music therapy* (pp. 163–189). Philadelphia, PA: Jessica Kingsley.

Wigram, T., McNaught, J., Cain, J., & Weekes, L. (1997). Vibroacoustic therapy with adult patients with profound learning disabilities. In T. Wigram & C. Dileo (Eds.), *Music vibration and health* (pp. 157–167). Cherry Hill, NJ: Jeffrey Books.

Witt, A. E., & Steele, A. L. (1984). Music therapy for infant and parent: A case example. *Music Therapy Perspectives, 1*(4), 17–19.

Wolfe, D. E. (1980). The effect of automated interrupted music on head posturing of cerebral palsied individuals. *Journal of Music Therapy, 17*(4), 184–206.

Zenatti, A. (1975). Melodic memory tests: A comparison of normal children and mental defectives. *Journal of Research in Music Education, 23*(1), 41–52.

Zigo, J. (in press). Access to music making through switch and voice output technology for young people with multiple and complex needs in a school setting. In W. L. Magee (Ed.), *Music technology in therapeutic and health settings*. Philadelphia, PA: Jessica Kingsley.

NOTES

1. The author is grateful to many colleagues who provided information and gave input on aspects of this chapter. She would particularly like to thank music therapy colleagues Kathleen Coleman, Laurie Farnan, and Nina Galerstein, who gave feedback based on extensive experience with the type of clientele discussed in the chapter.

A

B

C

P

R

S

Guidelines for Music Therapy Practice
A Four Volume Series

GUIDELINES FOR MUSIC THERAPY PRACTICE IN DEVELOPMENTAL HEALTH
Edited by Michelle R. Hintz

GUIDELINES FOR MUSIC THERAPY PRACTICE IN MENTAL HEALTH
Edited by Lillian Eyre

21) Persons with Alzheimer's and Other Dementias: *Laurel Young*
22) Professional Burnout: *Darlene M. Brooks*
23) Stress Reduction and Wellness: *Seung-A Kim*
24) Musicians: *Gro Trondalen*
25) Spiritual Practices: *Annie Heiderscheit*

GUIDELINES FOR MUSIC THERAPY PRACTICE IN PEDIATRIC CARE
Edited by Joke Bradt

1) Introduction: *Joke Bradt*
2) Pain Management with Children: *Joke Bradt*
3) Premature Infants: *Monika Nöcker-Ribaupierre*
4) Full-Term Hospitalized Newborns: *Helen Shoemark*
5) Pediatric Intensive Care: *Claire Ghetti*
6) Surgical and Procedural Support for Children: *John Mondanaro*
7) Burn Care for Children: *Annette Whitehead-Pleaux*
8) Children with Cancer: *Beth Dun*
9) Palliative and End-of-Life Care for Children: *Kathryn Lindenfelser*
10) Brain Injuries and Rehabilitation in Children: *Jeanette Kennelly*
11) Respiratory Care for Children: *Joanne Loewy*
12) Medically Fragile Children in Low Awareness States: *Jennifer Townsend*
13) Children in General Inpatient Care: *Christine Neugebauer*

GUIDELINES FOR MUSIC THERAPY PRACTICE IN ADULT MEDICAL CARE
Edited by Joy Allen

1) Introduction: *Joy Allen*
2) Surgical and Procedural support: *Annie Heiderscheit*
3) Pain Management with Adults: *Joy Allen*
4) Adults in Critical Care: *Jeanette Tamplin*
5) Adults in Cardiac Care: *Christine Pollard Leist*
6) Adults with Stroke: *Simon Gilbertson*
7) Adults with Traumatic Brain Injury: *Victoria Policastro Vega*
8) Adults with Neurogenic Communication Disorders: *Nicki Cohen*
9) Adults with Neurogenerative Diseases: *Wendy Magee*
10) Adults with HIV/AIDS: *Douglas Keith*
11) Adults with Cancer: *Joy Allen*
12) Adults in Palliative/Hospice Care: *Amy Clement-Cortes*
13) Caring for Caregivers: *Barbara Daveson*

THE BARCELONA COLLECTION OF PRINT AND E-BOOKS 2013

ANALYTIC MUSIC THERAPY

- Essays on Analytical Music Therapy (Priestley)
- Music Therapy in Action (2nd Edition) (Priestley)
- The Dynamics of Music Psychotherapy (Bruscia)
- Group Analytic Music Therapy (Ahonen-Eerikäinen)

CASE STUDIES

- Case Examples of Guided Imagery and Music (Bruscia)
- Case Examples of Improvisational Music Therapy (Bruscia)
- Case Examples of Music Therapy for___ (Bruscia):
    - Alzheimer's Disease
    - Autism and Rett Syndrome
    - Children and Adolescents with Emotional or Behavioral Problems
    - Developmental Problems in Learning and Communication
    - End of Life
    - Event Trauma
    - Medical Conditions
    - Mood Disorders
    - Multiple Disabilities
    - Musicians
    - Personality Disorders
    - Schizophrenia and other Psychoses
    - Self-Development
    - Substance Use Disorders
    - Survivors of Abuse
- Case Examples of the Use of Songs in Psychotherapy (Bruscia)
- Studies in Music Therapy (Bruscia)
- Inside Music Therapy: Client Experiences (Hibben)
- Psychodynamic Music Therapy: Case Studies (Hadley)

CHILDREN WITH SPECIAL NEEDS

- Alike and Different: The Clinical and Educational Uses of Orff-Schulwerk – Second Edition (Bitcon)
- The Miracle of Music Therapy (Boxill)
- Music for Fun, Music for Learning (Birkenshaw-Fleming)
- Music: Motion and Emotion: The Developmental-Integrative Model in Music Therapy (Sekeles)
- Music, Therapy, and Early Childhood (Schwartz)
- Music Therapy in Special Education (Nordoff & Robbins)

- Therapy in Music for Handicapped Children (Nordoff & Robbins)

COMMUNITY MUSIC THERAPY

- Elaborations Toward a Notion of Community Music Therapy (Stige)
- Culture-Centered Music Therapy (Stige)

INFANCY AND EARLY CHILDHOOD

- Music, Therapy, and Early Childhood (Schwartz)
- Music Therapy for Premature and Newborn Infants (Nöcker-Ribaupierre)

END OF LIFE

- Music Therapy: Death and Grief (Sekeles)

FEMINISM

- Feminist Perspectives in Music Therapy (Hadley)

FIELDWORK AND INTERNSHIP TRAINING

- Clinical Training Guide for the Student Music Therapist (Wheeler, Shultis & Polen)
- Music Therapy: A Fieldwork Primer (Borczon)
- Music Therapy Supervision (Forinash)

GROUP WORK

- Music Therapy: Group Vignettes (Borczon)
- Music Therapy Improvisation for Groups: Essential Leadership Competencies (Gardstrom)

GUIDED IMAGERY AND MUSIC (BONNY METHOD)

- Guided Imagery and Music: The Bonny Method and Beyond (Bruscia & Grocke)
- Music and Consciousness: The Evolution of Guided Imagery and Music (Bonny)
- Music and Your Mind: Listening with a New Consciousness (Bonny & Savary)
- Music for the Imagination (Bruscia)

GUITAR

- Guitar Skills for Music Therapists and Music Educators (Meyer, De Villers, Ebnet)
- Use of the Guitar in Music Therapy (Oden)

IMPROVISATIONAL MUSIC THERAPY

- The Architecture of Aesthetic Music Therapy (Lee)
- Essays on Analytical Music Therapy (Priestley)
- Creative Music Therapy: A Guide to Fostering Clinical Musicianship – Second Edition with Four CDs (Nordoff & Robbins)
- Group Analytic Music Therapy (Ahonen-Eerikäinen)
- Healing Heritage: Paul Nordoff Exploring the Tonal Language of Music (Robbins & Robbins)
- Improvising in Styles: A Workbook for Music Therapists, Educators, and Musicians (Lee & Houde)
- Music as Therapy: A Dialogal Perspective (Garred)
- Music-Centered Music Therapy (Aigen)
- Music Therapy: Improvisation, Communication, and Culture (Ruud)
- Music Therapy Improvisation for Groups: Essential Leadership Competencies (Gardstrom)
- Paths of Development in Nordoff-Robbins Music Therapy (Aigen)

- Playin' in the Band: A Qualitative study of Popular Music Styles as Clinical Improvisation (Aigen)
- Sounding the Self: Analogy in Improvisational Music Therapy (Smeijsters)

MUSIC FOR CHILDREN TO SING AND PLAY

- Distant Bells (Levin & Levin)
- Learning Songs (Levin & Levin)
- Learning Through Music (Levin & Levin)
- Learning Through Songs (Levin & Levin)
- Let's Make Music (Levin & Levin)
- Music for Fun, Music for Learning (Birkenshaw-Fleming)
- Snow White: A Guide to Child-Centered Musical Theatre (Lauri, Groeschel, Robbins, Ritholz & Turry)
- Symphonics R Us (Levin & Levin)

NORDOFF-ROBBINS MUSIC THERAPY (CREATIVE MUSIC THERAPY)

- The Architecture of Aesthetic Music Therapy (Lee)
- Being in Music: Foundations of Nordoff-Robbins Music Therapy (Aigen)
- Conversations on Nordoff-Robbins Music Therapy (Verney & Ansdell)
- Creative Music Therapy: A Guide to Fostering Clinical Musicianship – Second Edition with Four CDs (Nordoff & Robbins)
- Healing Heritage: Paul Nordoff Exploring the Tonal Language of Music (Robbins & Robbins)
- Here We Are in Music: One Year with an Adolescent Creative Music Therapy Group (Aigen)
- A Journey into Creative Music Therapy (Robbins)
- Music Therapy in Special Education (Nordoff & Robbins)
- Paths of Development in Nordoff-Robbins Music Therapy (Aigen)
- Playin' in the Band: A Qualitative study of Popular Music Styles as Clinical Improvisation (Aigen)
- Therapy in Music for Handicapped Children (Nordoff & Robbins)

MUSIC THERAPY PRACTICE

- Guidelines for Music Therapy Practice in Mental Health (Eyre)
- Guidelines for Music Therapy Practice in Developmental Health (Hintz)
- Guidelines for Music Therapy Practice in Pediatric Care (Bradt)
- Guidelines for Music Therapy Practice in Adult Medical Care (Allen)

MUSIC PSYCHOTHERAPY

- The Dynamics of Music Psychotherapy (Bruscia)
- Essays on Analytical Music Therapy (Priestley)
- Emotional Processes in Music Therapy (Pellitteri)
- Group Analytic Music Therapy (Ahonen-Eerikäinen)
- Guided Imagery and Music: The Bonny Method and Beyond (Bruscia & Grocke)
- Music and Consciousness: The Evolution of Guided Imagery and Music (Bonny)
- Music and Your Mind: Listening with a New Consciousness (Bonny & Savary)

- Music Therapy: Group Vignettes (Borczon)
- Psychodynamic Music Therapy: Case Studies (Hadley)

ORFF-SCHULWERK
- Alike and Different: The Clinical and Educational Uses of Orff-Schulwerk – Second Edition (Bitcon)

PIANO
- Functional Piano for Music Therapists and Music Educators (Massicot)
- Improvising in Styles: A Workbook for Music Therapists, Educators, and Musicians (Lee & Houde)

PROFOUND MENTAL RETARDATION
- Age-Appropriate Activities for Adults with Profound Mental Retardation – Second Edition (Galerstein, Martin & Powe)

PSYCHODRAMA
- Acting Your Inner Music (Moreno)

PSYCHIATRY – MENTAL HEALTH
- Music Therapy in the Treatment of Adults with Mental Disorders: Theoretical Bases and Clinical Interventions (Unkefer & Thaut)
- Psychiatric Music Therapy in the Community: The Legacy of Florence Tyson (McGuire)
- Psychodynamic Music Therapy: Case Studies (Hadley)
- Resource-Oriented Music Therapy in Mental Health Care (Rolvsjord)

RACE
- Experience Race as a Music Therapist: Personal Narratives (Hadley)

RESEARCH
- A Guide to Writing and Presenting in Music Therapy (Aigen)
- Multiple Perspectives: A Guide to Qualitative Research in Music Therapy (Smeijsters)
- Music Therapy Research: Quantitative and Qualitative Perspectives – First Edition (1995) (Wheeler)
- Music Therapy Research – Second Edition (2005) (Wheeler)
- Playin' in the Band: A Qualitative study of Popular Music Styles as Clinical Improvisation (Aigen)
- Qualitative Inquiries in Music Therapy: A Monograph Series (Free Downloads Available Here)
- Qualitative Music Therapy Research: Beginning Dialogues (Langenberg, Frömmer & Aigen)

SUPERVISION
- Music Therapy Supervision (Forinash)

THEORY
- Culture-Centered Music Therapy (Stige)
- Defining Music Therapy – Second Edition (Bruscia)
- Emotional Processes in Music Therapy (Pellitteri)
- Music and Life in the Field of Play: An Anthology (Kenny)

- Music as Therapy: A Dialogal Perspective (Garred)
- Music-Centered Music Therapy (Aigen)
- Music Therapy and its Relationship to Current Treatment Theories (Ruud)
- Music Therapy: A Perspective from the Humanities (Ruud)
- Music Therapy: Improvisation, Communication, and Culture (Ruud)
- Music—The Therapeutic Edge: Readings from William W. Sears (Sears)
- The Music Within You (Katsh & Fishman)
- Readings on Music Therapy Theory (Bruscia)
- Resource-Oriented Music Therapy in Mental Health Care (Rolvsjord)
- The Rhythmic Language of Health and Disease (Rider)
- Sounding the Self: Analogy in Improvisational Music Therapy (Smeijsters)

VOICE

- Authentic Voices, Authentic Singing (Uhlig)
- Psychiatric Music Therapy in the Community: The Legacy of Florence Tyson (McGuire)